THE LAW OF PATENTS

AUSTRALIA
The Law Book Company Ltd.
Sydney : Melbourne : Brisbane

CANADA AND U.SA.
The Carswell Company Ltd.
Agincourt, Ontario

INDIA
N. M. Tripathi Private Ltd.
Bombay

ISRAEL
Steimatzky's Agency Ltd.
Jerusalem : Tel Aviv : Haifa

MALAYSIA : SINGAPORE : BRUNEI
Malayan Law Journal (Pte) Ltd.
Singapore

NEW ZEALAND
Sweet & Maxwell (N.Z.) Ltd.
Wellington

PAKISTAN
Pakistan Law House
Karachi

DEREK R. CHANDLER   1971

TERRELL

ON THE

LAW OF PATENTS

TWELFTH EDITION

BY

DOUGLAS FALCONER, M.B.E., B.SC.
One of Her Majesty's Counsel

WILLIAM ALDOUS, M.A.
of the Inner Temple, Barrister-at-Law

DAVID YOUNG, M.A.
of Lincoln's Inn, Barrister-at-Law

LONDON
SWEET & MAXWELL
1971

First edition.	By Thomas Terrell	1884
Second edition.	By Thomas Terrell	1889
Third edition.	By W. P. Rylands	1895
Fourth edition.	By Courtney Terrell	1906
Fifth edition.	By Courtney Terrell	1909
Sixth edition.	By Courtney Terrell and A. D. Jaffé ...	1921
Seventh edition.	By Courtney Terrell and D. H. Corsellis ...	1927
Eighth edition.	By J. R. Jones	1934
Ninth edition.	By K. E. Shelley, K.C.	1951
Tenth edition.	By K. E. Shelley, Q.C.	1961
Eleventh edition.	By Guy Aldous, Q.C., Douglas Falconer and William Aldous	1965
Twelfth edition.	By Douglas Falconer, Q.C., William Aldous and David Young	1971

Published in 1971 by
Sweet and Maxwell Limited
of 11 New Fetter Lane, London
and printed in Great Britain
by The Eastern Press Limited
of London and Reading

SBN   421   14650   8

©

Sweet & Maxwell Limited
1971

PREFACE

DURING the preparation of this new edition of *Terrell* the Report of the Banks Committee, which had been appointed to examine the British patent system and patent law, was published. Many of the recommendations in the Report are far-reaching and, no doubt, in due course the Report will lead to amending legislation. However, as was pointed out in the Preface to the last edition of this work, the book is intended for practitioners in the law, both specialist and general, and its aim has always been to set out reliably and accurately what is the current English law of patents. Accordingly we have not commented on the Report's recommendations in this edition. It will be for a future edition of *Terrell* to deal with any changes in our patent system and law that may be effected by any amending legislation resulting from the Report.

It has always been a feature of this work that in its presentation of the patent law the more important principles have been expressed in words quoted from the leading judgments. In preparing this new edition we have maintained this feature in the hope and belief that it is a valuable one.

Terrell was first published as long ago as 1884 and has already passed through eleven editions. In preparing this, the twelfth, edition we have endeavoured, as best we can, to ensure that the work shall continue to be one that may be relied upon by all practitioners in the law.

D. F.
W. A.
September 1971.   D. Y.

TABLE OF CONTENTS

TABLE OF CONTENTS

APPENDIX

Part 1

Part 2

TABLE OF CONTENTS

TABLE OF ABBREVIATIONS

A.C.	Law Reports, Appeal Cases 1891–
Ad. & E.	Adolphus and Ellis's Reports, K.B.
All E.R.	All England Reports.
App.Cas.	Law Reports. Appeal Cases, 1875–1890.
B. & S.	Best and Smith's Reports, Q.B.
Barn. & Ald.	Barnewall and Alderson's Reports, K.B.
Barn. & Cress.	Barnewall and Cresswell's Reports, K.B.
Beav.	Beavan's Reports, Rolls Court.
Bing.(N.S.)	Bingham's New Cases, C.P.
Bittl.Chamb.Rep.	Bittlestone's Chambers Reports.
Bl.Comm.	Blackstone's Commentaries.
Bos. & Pul.	Bosanquet and Puller's Reports, C.P.
C.B.	Common Bench Reports, or Manning, Granger and Scott's Reports.
C.B.(N.S.)	Common Bench Reports, New Series.
C.P.D.	Law Reports, Common Pleas Division.
C.S.	Cases in Court of Session (Scotland).
Cal.Close Rolls	Calendar of Close Rolls.
Cal.Pat.Rolls	Calendar of Patent Rolls.
Car. & Kir.	Carrington and Kirwan's Reports, N.P.
Car. & P.	Carrington and Payne's Reports, N.P.
Ch.	Law Reports, Chancery Division, 1891–
Ch.D.	Law Reports, Chancery Division, 1875–1890.
Co.Inst.	Coke's Institutes.
Co.Litt.	Coke on Littleton (1 Inst.).
Co.Rep.	Coke's Reports.
Com.Dig.	Comyn's Digest.
Coop.t.Cott.	Cooper *temp.* Cottenham.
Dav.P.C.	Davies' Patent Cases.
De G.F. & J.	De Gex, Fisher and Jones's Reports, Chancery.
De G. & J.	De Gex and Jones's Reports, Chancery.
De G.J. & S.	De Gex, Jones and Smith's Reports, Chancery.
De G.M. & G.	De Gex, Macnaghten and Gordon's Reports, Chancery.
De G. & Sm.	De Gex and Smale's Reports, Chancery.
Drew. & Sm.	Drewry and Smale's Reports, Chancery.
El. & Bl.	Ellis and Blackburn's Reports, Q.B.
Ex.D.	Law Reports, Exchequer Division.
Fed.Rep.	Federal Reporter (U.S.A.).
F.S.R.	Fleet Street Reports.
Giff.	Giffard's Reports, Chancery.
Godb.	Godbolt's Reports, K.B.
Good.P.C.	Goodeve's Patent Cases.
Griff.L.O.C.	Griffin's Law Officer's Cases.
Griff.P.C.	Griffin's Patent Cases.
H. & C.	Hurlstone and Coltman's Reports, Ex.
H. & N.	Hurlstone and Norman's Reports, Ex.
H.Bl.	Henry Blackstone's Reports, C.P.
H.L.C.	House of Lords Cases (Clark).
Hem. & M.	Hemming and Miller, Chancery.
Hindmarch	Hindmarch, Law of Patents.
Holt N.P.	Holt's Nisi Prius Reports.

xi

I.H.	Cases in the Court of Session (Scotland) Inner House.
Ir.Ch.	Cases in the Chancery Division (Ireland).
John. & H.	Johnson and Hemming's Reports, Chancery.
Jur.	The Jurist Reports.
Jur.(N.S.)	Jurist, New Series.
Kay & J.	Kay and Johnson's Reports, Chancery.
K.B.	Law Reports, King's Bench Division, 1901–
L.J.	Law Journal Reports.
L.Q.R.	Law Quarterly Review.
L.R.C.P.	Common Pleas Cases.
„ Ch.App.	Chancery Appeal Cases.
„ Eq.	Equity Cases.
„ Ex.	Exchequer Cases.
„ H.L.	English and Irish Appeal Cases, House of Lords.
„ P.C.	Privy Council Appeal Cases.
„ Q.B.	Queen's Bench Cases.
L.T.	Law Times Reports.
L.T.(N.S.)	Law Times Reports, New Series.
Lon.Journ.	London Journal.
Macr.P.C.	Macrory's Patent Cases.
Man. & G.	Manning and Granger's Reports, C.P.
Mee. & W.	Meeson and Welsby's Reports, Ex.
Moore K.B.	Sir F. Moore's Reports, King's Bench.
Moo.P.C.	Moore's Privy Council Cases.
Moo.P.C.(N.S.)	Moore's Privy Council Cases, New Series.
New Rep.	New Reports, 1862–1865.
Noy	Noy's Reports, K.B.
O.H.	Cases in the Court of Session (Scotland) Outer House.
P.	Law Reports, Probate Division, 1891–
P.D.	Law Reports, Probate Division.
Q.B.	Law Reports, Queen's Bench Division, 1891–
Q.B.D.	Law Reports, Queen's Bench Division, 1875–1890.
R.P.C.	Reports of Patent Cases.
R.P.C.(C.A.)	Reports of Patent Cases, decided in the Court of Appeal.
R.P.C.(H.L.)	Reports of Patent Cases, decided in the House of Lords.
R.P.C.(P.C.)	Reports of Patent Cases, decided in the Judicial Committee of the Privy Council.
R.S.C.	Rules of the Supreme Court.
Rot.Parl.	Rotuli Parliamentorum.
Rymer	Rymer's " Foedera."
S.C.	Court of Session Cases (Scotland).
S.R. & O.	Statutory Rules and Orders.
Salk.	Salkeld's Reports, K.B.
Skin.	Skinner's Reports, K.B.
Stark.N.P.	Starkie's Reports, N.P.
T.C.	Tax Cases.
T.C.A.	Tax Case Appeals (Leaflets).
T.L.R.	Times Law Reports.
T.R.	Term Reports.
Ves.	Vesey's Sen., Reports, Chancery.
Ves. & Bea.	Vesey and Beames's Reports, Chancery.
W.N.	Weekly Notes (Law Reports).
W.P.C.	Webster's Patent Cases.
W.R.	Weekly Reporter.

TABLE OF CASES

[All references are to paragraph numbers]

TABLE OF CASES

xvi

xxxiii

1

TABLE OF STATUTES

[All references are to paragraph numbers]

lv

1971 Courts Act

TABLE OF RULES AND ORDERS

[All references are to paragraph numbers]

[References in **bold** type denote where the text of the Rule or Order appears in full]

RULES OF THE SUPREME COURT

CHAPTER 1

LETTERS PATENT

1. INTRODUCTION AND HISTORY

1 Definition

"Letters Patent," that is, open letters, *literae patentes,* are so called "because they are not sealed up, but exposed to view, with the Great Seal pendant at the bottom, and are usually addressed by the Sovereign to all the subjects of the Realm." [1] They are the common form of making grants of dignities, appointments to certain offices of state and grants of privilege of various kinds, including monopoly rights in inventions. They derive their authority from the fact that they are issued under the Great Seal, "for all the King's subjects are bound to take notice of the King's Great Seal." [2]

2 The Seal of the Patent Office

In the case of letters patent for inventions the seal of the Patent Office has, since 1883,[3] been substituted for the Great Seal, and by section 21 (1) of the Patents Act, 1949, "A patent sealed with the seal of the Patent Office shall have the same effect as if it were sealed with the Great Seal of the United Kingdom, and shall have effect throughout the United Kingdom [4] and the Isle of Man." And by section 64 of the Patents and Designs Act, 1907 (which section remains unrepealed), "Impressions of the seal of the Patent Office shall be judicially noticed and admitted in evidence."

Letters patent for an invention may, therefore, be regarded as an "open document," sealed with the seal of the Patent Office, and containing a grant by the Crown of monopoly privileges in respect of an invention.

The following short outline of the history of the growth of the law and practice may perhaps be of service as an introduction to modern practice and legislation.

3 Early industrial grants

It has been recognised from the earliest times that the regulation of trade lay within the prerogative of the Crown. The charters and

---

[1] 2Bl.Comm., c. 21, s. 2.
[2] *East India Co.* v. *Sandys,* Skin. 224.
[3] 46 & 47 Vict. c. 57, s. 12. Certain other letters patent are also no longer issued under the Great Seal: see 40 & 41 Vict. c. 41, ss. 4 and 5.
[4] This includes Northern Ireland, but not the Republic of Ireland (see S.R. & O. 1923 No. 405), or the Channel Islands.

[1]

patents granted to the trade guilds and corporations are well known. Grants of special privileges were, however, also made to individuals from time to time. Thus between 1331 and 1452 various letters of protection were issued to foreign weavers and other craftsmen.[5] In 1347 we find a complaint in Parliament that an alien merchant had a monopoly of exporting Cornish tin [6]; while in 1376 John Peeche, Alderman of Walbrook Ward, was impeached in respect of a patent giving him the right to sell sweet wines in the City of London contrary to an ordinance of Parliament.[7]

The origin of the present patent system is to be found, however, in the " Monopoly System " inaugurated by Cecil in the reign of Queen Elizabeth I. While originally designed to encourage the setting up of new industries,[8] it is notorious that it became in fact a method of farming out the powers of the Crown in many respects. In the last parliament of the reign two Bills were introduced with the object of reforming the system, but were not proceeded with [9] as the Crown promised to recall some of the patents and that none " should be put in execution but such as should first have a trial according to law."

4   *The Case of Monopolies*

The only patent which was in fact tried in the courts was Darcy's Patent for the monopoly of importing, manufacturing and selling playing cards, which was the subject of the famous *Case of Monopolies*.[10] This patent was held invalid as being a monopoly illegal at common law, and also as being a licence for importation of playing cards contrary to certain statutes. The judgment [11] deals in some detail with the characteristics of illegal monopolies, and the conclusions to be drawn from it are that a monopoly was illegal at common law (1) if it prevented a craftsman from carrying on his ordinary trade,[12] or (2) if it tended to raise the price of a commodity and lower its quality, or (3) if the Crown was deceived in its grant, intending the grant to be for the public good, whereas it was in fact

---

5 See, *e.g.*, *Cal.Pat. Rolls* (1330–34) 161; (1967–70) 105; Rymer, x, 761; xi, 317.
6 Tydman of Lynnburgh, who had liberty to export tin without paying the customary tax : see *Rot.Parl.* ii, 168; *Cal. Close Rolls* (1346–49) 328.
7 The facts are obscure : see *Rot.Parl.* ii, 328; *Cal.Pat. Rolls* (1374–77) 448, 457; *Cal. Fine Rolls*, viii, 225, 227.
8 For the provisions of the early patents see Hulme, 12 L.Q.R. 145.
9 There is no record of their provisions.
10 Otherwise *Darcy* v. *Allein*, 1 W.P.C. 1; Noy 173; Moore K.B. 671; 11 Co.Rep. 84b. See the composite report in J. W. Gordon, K.C., *Monopolies by Patent*, London, 1897. There had been a previous action on the patent before the Privy Council : see Hulme, 16 L.Q.R. 51.
11 It only appears in Co.Rep. at p. 86.
12 Citing *Davenant* v. *Hurdis* (*Merchant Taylor's Case*) (1599) Moore K.B. 576.

not so.[13]   No mention was made of patents for new trades and inventions, but they were expressly admitted to be valid by the defendant's counsel during the course of the case.[14]

5   *The Book of Bounty*

In 1610 the proclamation usually known as "The Book of Bounty" was issued. This set forth "monopolies" as the first of the "special things for which We . . . command no suitor presume to move Us." Projects for new inventions were, however, excepted from this prohibition, provided they were not contrary to law or hurtful to the state and trade, or generally inconvenient.

The first judicial pronouncement on the legality of patents for inventions occurs, however, in 1614, when the following statement is to be found in the report of the *Clothworkers of Ipswich Case* [15]:

> "But if a man hath brought in a new invention and a new trade within the kingdom in peril of his life and consumption of his estate or stock, etc., or if a man hath made a new discovery of anything, in such cases the King of his grace and favour in recompense of his costs and travail may grant by charter unto him that he shall only use such a trade or trafique for a certain time, because at first people of the kingdom are ignorant, and have not the knowledge and skill to use it. But when the patent is expired the King cannot make a new grant thereof."

6   Statute of Monopolies, section 6

The abuses of the monopoly system finally became so scandalous that the agents most concerned in enforcing certain patents were impeached. Some twenty patents were thereupon revoked by proclamation, and others left for trial in the courts. At the same time a joint committee of both Houses of Parliament agreed a Bill which was finally passed on May 25, 1624.

This Act is the Statute of Monopolies. It recited the publication and effect of the Book of Bounty and declared all monopolies, dispensations, and grants to compound penalties void. All such grants were to be tried at common law; and by section 6 the foundations of modern patent law were laid down in the following terms:

> "Provided also (and be it declared and enacted) [16] that any declaration before mentioned shall not extend to any letters

---

[13] Citing *Earl of Kent's Case*, 21 Edw. 3, 47. The grant was also said to be *primae impressionis.*

[14] See the report in Gordon, *op. cit.* p. 205 at 219; Noy at 182.

[15] Godbolt 252.

[16] Words in brackets repealed by the S.L.R. Act 1888, s. 1, Sched., Part I.

patent and grants of privilege for the term of fourteen [*now sixteen* [17]] years or under, hereafter to be made, of the sole working or making of any manner of new manufactures within this realm, to the true and first inventor and inventors of such manufactures which others at the time of making such letters patent and grants shall not use, so as also they be not contrary to the law or mischievous to the state, by raising prices of commodities at home, or hurt of trade, or generally inconvenient."

7   The statute was intended to be declaratory of the common law.[18] For various reasons, but probably mainly on account of the exception in favour of corporations made by section 9, the Act had little practical effect for many years, and the Age of Monopolies did not finally come to an end until the outbreak of the Great Rebellion. Patents for inventions continued to be granted under the Commonwealth; and the law and practice remained almost unchanged until long after the Restoration.

In the early days of the patent system the greater part of all patent litigation had been conducted before the Privy Council.[19] All patents contained a proviso for revocation by that body, and questions of validity were normally tried before it. After the Restoration the Privy Council continued for some time to exercise this jurisdiction, but from about 1753 onwards patent litigation (with the exception of petitions for extension [20]) has been conducted in the Court of Chancery and Queen's Bench.

Prior to 1795 there were practically no reported cases on the construction of the Statute of Monopolies.[21] The statute was in fact virtually in the position of a new Act; and the development of modern patent law can be said to date, for practical purposes, from this period.

8 **Patents Act 1949**

Important changes in the procedure for obtaining the grant (including provisional protection) were introduced by the Act of 1852, and by the Acts of 1883 to 1888 [22] the system as we know it today came into being.

At the present time the law and practice is regulated by the

---

[17] s. 22.
[18] See Co.Inst. III, c. 85; *Feather* v. *R.*, 6 B. & S. 257 at p. 285; *Australian Gold, etc., Co.* v. *Lake View, etc., Ltd.*, 18 R.P.C. 105 at p. 114.
[19] For an account of the practice at this date, see Hulme, 33 L.Q.R. 65.
[20] Introduced by 5 & 6 Will. 4, c. 83.
[21] See Eyre L.C.J. in *Boulton* v. *Bull*, 2 H.Bl. 463.
[22] 46 & 47 Vict. c. 57; 48 & 49 Vict. c. 63; 49 & 50 Vict. c. 37; 51 & 52 Vict. c. 50.

Patents Act 1949 as amended by the Patents Act 1957, the Defence Contracts Act 1958 and the Patents and Designs (Renewals, Extension and Fees) Act 1961, by the Patents Rules 1968 [23] as amended by the Patents (Amendment) Rules 1969–1971,[24] by the Patents Appeal Tribunal Rules 1950 and 1959 [25] as amended by the Patents Appeal Tribunal (Amendment) Rules 1956–1970 [26] and by the Rules of the Supreme Court (Order 103).

There are also provisions relating to patents in other statutes [27] and the law is also governed by certain enactments of earlier date in so far as they remain unrepealed.[28]

9 Definition of invention

" Invention " is now defined [29] as meaning any manner of new manufacture the subject of letters patent and grant of privilege within section six of the Statute of Monopolies [30] and any new method or process of testing applicable to the improvement or control of manufacture, and includes an alleged invention.

The primary requirements of a valid patent may be summarised as follows:

The applicant, or one applicant, must be the true and first inventor or his personal representative or be an assignee deriving title from the true and first inventor. He must make a proper disclosure of his invention, and must clearly specify the limits of the monopoly claimed. The invention must be a " manufacture," or a method of controlling manufacture, new, useful, and not obvious to those skilled in the art to which it relates. Further, it must not be for an illegal purpose, and no valid patent must have already been granted for it. The patentee must also not abuse his monopoly rights after the patent has been sealed.

The grounds upon which a patent may be revoked are set out in section 32 of the Act of 1949 and are dealt with in detail hereafter.

---

[23] S.I. 1968 No. 1389.
[24] S.I. 1969 No. 482; S.I. 1969 No. 1706; S.I. 1970 No. 955; S.I. 1971 No. 263.
[25] S.I. 1950 No. 392; S.I. 1959 No. 278.
[26] S.I. 1956 No. 470; S.I. 1961 No. 1016; S.I. 1969 No. 500; S.I. 1970 No. 1074.
[27] Enemy Property Act 1953, s. 8; Atomic Energy Authority Act 1954, s. 6 (4), Sched. III; Northern Ireland Act 1962, ss. 7, 30; Monopolies and Mergers Act 1965, s. 1 (1), Sched. I; Criminal Justice Act 1967, s. 92 (1), Sched. III; Industrial Expansion Act 1968, s. 18, Sched. IV; Health Services and Public Health Act 1968, s. 59 (1); Administration of Justice Act 1969, ss. 24, 35.
[28] Statute of Monopolies 1623, s. 6; Patents and Designs Act 1907, ss. 47, 62–64; Patents Limits of Time Act 1939; Patents and Designs Act 1946; Atomic Energy Act 1946, s. 12; Crown Proceedings Act 1947, ss. 3, 21; Civil Aviation Act 1949, s. 53.
[29] s. 101.
[30] See § 6, *ante,* and 3 Co.Inst. 181; 1 W.P.C. 31n.

10   Effect of invalidity in part

If one of the claims of a patent is invalid the whole grant is void at common law,[31] and, prior to the Act of 1919, the patentee was in such cases unable to obtain any relief in respect of any other claim which was valid. The Act of 1919, however, introduced a new section into the Act of 1907, which enabled a patentee to obtain relief if some only of the claims were invalid. Section 62 now regulates cases of this kind.

11   2. FORM OF THE LETTERS PATENT

A patent is to be in such form as is authorised by the Rules.[32] The forms now in use are set out in the Fourth Schedule to the Patents Rules, 1968,[33] and letters patent, as issued at the present time, consist of six material parts:

1st. The address.
2nd. The recitals.
3rd. The grant.
4th. The prohibition.
5th. The provisos.
6th. The construction of the grant.

12   The address

The address is a public address from the Sovereign to " all to whom these presents shall come." Hindmarch gives the reason for this as being, that it contains bargains made between the public and patentee.[34]

13   The recitals

The recitals are two in number. The first recites the applicant's name and address, the title of his invention and the request for the grant.

14   The second recital gives the common law motive for the grant, which is the encouragement of inventions for the public good. There will be something analogous to a false suggestion if the subject-matter of the patent be immoral or illegal, and the patent will be void at common law. It is unlikely, however, that a grant would be made which could be avoided on this ground, as the Comptroller would refuse to grant a patent for an invention of which the use would, in his opinion, be contrary to law or morality.[35]

---

[31] See *Brunton* v. *Hawkes*, 4 Barn. & Ald. 541; *Morgan* v. *Seaward*, 1 W.P.C. 170; *Patterson* v. *Gas Light & Coke Co.*, 2 Ch.D. 812 at p. 833.
[32] s. 21 (3).
[33] See Appendix.
[34] Hindmarch, p. 40.   [35] s. 10 (1) (*b*).

The requirements as to novelty, utility, not being obvious, and adequate disclosure of the invention in the specifications are all based on the " suggestions " contained in these recitals.

15   The grant

" Know ye, therefore, that We of our especial grace, certain knowledge, and mere motion do by these presents, for Us, etc., give and grant unto the person(s) above named and any successor(s), executor(s), administrator(s) and assign(s) (each and any of whom are hereinafter referred to as the patentee) our especial licence, full power, sole privilege, and authority, that the patentee or any agent or licensee of the patentee and no others, may subject to the conditions and provisions prescribed by any statute or order for the time being in force at all times hereafter during the term of years herein mentioned, make, use, exercise and vend the said invention within our United Kingdom of Great Britain and Northern Ireland, and the Isle of Man, and that the patentee shall have and enjoy the whole profit and advantage from time to time accruing by reason of the said invention, during the term of sixteen years from the date hereunder written of these presents."

The prerogative of the Crown in relation to the granting or withholding of letters patent is expressly saved by the Act.[36]   It is exercised on behalf of the Crown by the Comptroller and by the Appeal Tribunal,[37] who may refuse the grant of a patent if there is a " lawful ground of objection " [38] apart from any specific powers of refusal conferred by the Act.[39]

16   *Nature of patent right*

It is the granting portion of the letters patent which creates the property in the monopoly rights, a species of property which is purely artificial in its nature.

A trade mark is also an exclusive right, but it differs from a patent, its object being to indicate a connection in the course of trade between the article and the registered proprietor of the trade mark.   It prevents persons from using the mark who are not (expressly or impliedly) entitled to use it, but places no restriction on dealing with identical goods.   A patent, however, prevents the public from making or using the patented article or process itself, but (notwithstanding the peculiar formal wording of the grant) does

---

[36] s. 102 (1).
[37] See *post*, § § 121, 122.
[38] s. 6 (2). See *Sevag's Appn.*, 55 R.P.C. 193 at p. 195.
[39] *A. and H.'s Appn.*, 44 R.P.C. 298; *Rex Co. and Rex Research Corp.* v. *Muirhead and Comptroller-General*, 44 R.P.C. 38; *Riddlesbarger's Appn.*, 53 R.P.C. 57.

not confer upon the patentee a right to manufacture according to his invention. "That," said Lord Herschell, "is a right which he would equally effectively have if there were no letters patent at all—only in that case all the world would equally have the right. What the letters patent confer is the right to exclude others from ... using a particular invention." [40] Accordingly a patentee's right is a chose in action and entirely distinct from the right of property in a chattel. It is, therefore, incapable of seizure, so that it cannot be taken under a writ of *fi. fa.*[41]; a vesting order may, however, be made in respect of it.[42]

It was held in *Edwards & Co.* v. *Picard* [43] by the Court of Appeal (Vaughan Williams and Buckley L.JJ., Moulton L.J. dissenting), that a receiver could not be appointed to receive any benefits that might accrue to the patentee in respect of his patents towards satisfaction of a judgment.

17 *No property in mere secret*

There is no property of the nature of an exclusive right save that of a patent, registered design, copyright, or trade mark. There is no exclusive right in a secret. The original possessor of a secret of manufacture cannot by any process of law prevent a person from acquiring the knowledge of his secret, or, having acquired it, from making such use of it, by publication or otherwise, as he may think proper,[44] unless such acts amount to a breach of contract, express or implied,[45] or a breach of confidence.[46]

18 *"The patentee"*

It will be observed that the word "patentee" is used in the modern grant referring to the applicant(s) and any successor(s), executor(s), administrator(s) and assign(s). Under the statute "patentee" means the person or persons for the time being entered

[40] *Steers* v. *Rogers,* 10 R.P.C. 245 at p. 251.
[41] *British Mutoscope and Biograph Co. Ltd.* v. *Homer,* 18 R.P.C. 177; *Heath's Patent,* 29 R.P.C. 389; *Steers* v. *Rogers,* 10 R.P.C. 245.
[42] *e.g., Heath's Patent,* 29 R.P.C. 389. See also *post,* § 605.
[43] [1909] 2 K.B. 903.
[44] *Canham* v. *Jones,* 2 Ves. & Bea. 218; *James* v. *James,* L.R. 13 Eq. 421; *Massam* v. *J. W. Thorley's Cattle Food Co.,* 6 Ch.D. 574; and see *United Indigo, etc., Ltd.* v. *Robinson,* 49 R.P.C. 178.
[45] See *Amber Size and Chemical Co. Ltd.* v. *Menzel,* 30 R.P.C. 433, and *Alperton Rubber Co.* v. *Manning,* 33 T.L.R. 205; 116 L.T. 499; and see *Smith* v. *Dickenson,* 3 Bos. & Pul. 630.
[46] *Saltman Engineering Co.* v. *Campbell Engineering Co.,* 65 R.P.C. 203; *Mechanical and General Inventions Ltd.* v. *Austin* [1935] A.C. 346; *Nicrotherm Electric Co. Ltd. and Others* v. *Percy and Another* [1956] R.P.C. 272. *Cf., Mustad* v. *Dosen* [1963] R.P.C. 41 explained in *Cranleigh Precision Engineering Ltd.* v. *Bryant and another* [1966] R.P.C. 81 at p. 95.

on the register of patents as grantee or proprietor of the patent,[47] and this may include assignees, executors and administrators of the original grantee, together with receivers and trustees in bankruptcy.

19 The prohibition

The prohibition in the patent commands " all our subjects, . . . that they do not at any time during the continuance of the said term either directly or indirectly make use of or put in practice the said invention, nor in anywise imitate the same, without the written consent, licence or agreement of the patentee on pain of incurring such penalties as may be justly inflicted on such offenders for their contempt of this our Royal command, and of being answerable to the patentee according to the law for damages thereby occasioned."

The above form of wording is similar to that usually adopted prior to the Act of 1883, which probably accounts for the retention of the word " penalties." [48]

The wording of the prohibition differs from that of the granting portion of the patent; the prohibition is, however, in aid of the grant, and not in derogation of it.[49]

20 The provisos

" Provided always that these letters patent shall be revocable on any of the grounds from time to time by law prescribed as grounds for revoking letters patent granted by Us and the same may be revoked and made void accordingly.[50]   Provided also that nothing herein contained shall prevent the granting of licences in such manner and for such considerations as they may by law be granted."

21 The construction

" And lastly, we do by these presents for us, our heirs and successors, grant unto the patentee that these our letters patent shall be construed in the most beneficial sense for the advantage of the patentee."   The meaning of these words is obscure, but they are not inserted in the patent for the purpose of ousting the common rule of construction of grants of the Crown, *viz.* that such grants shall be read most strongly against the grantee.   It would appear that they are a survival of the form used at the date when a patent was granted on an application which specified the " title " of the invention only, and have no significance today.[51]   In any case, this " beneficial

---

[47] s. 101.
[48] *Caldwell* v. *Van Vlissingen*, 21 L.J.Ch. 97.
[49] *Ibid.*
[50] See s. 32.
[51] See *Feather* v. *R.*, 6 B. & S. 257 at p. 287.

construction" applies only to the letters patent and not to the specification.[52]

22   Form of patent of addition

The form of a "Patent of Addition," [53] originally created by the Act of 1907, resembles that of an ordinary patent in all material particulars save that the term is limited to expire at the same date as that of the original patent.[54]

[The next paragraph is 31]

[52] *Electric and Musical Industries* v. *Lissen,* 56 R.P.C. 23 at p. 46. See *post,* § 181.
[53] See Patents Rules 1968, *post,* § 1396.
[54] s. 26 (5) and see *post,* §§ 133–141.

## CHAPTER 2

THE NATURE OF PATENTABLE INVENTIONS

31 Definition of invention

The Statute of Monopolies declared all grants of monopoly rights to be void at common law, but excepted letters patent and grants of privilege in respect of any " manner of new manufactures." [1] Under the present Act an invention, to be patentable, must either be a " manner of new manufacture the subject of letters patent and grant of privilege within section 6 of the Statute of Monopolies," or be a new method or process of testing applicable to the improvement or control of manufacture.[2] Although the definition of " invention " in the Act also includes an alleged invention,[2] these latter words are directed only to the question of novelty and not to whether there is disclosed a manner of manufacture.[3]

32 Manner of new manufacture

The requirement that the subject-matter of a patent must be " a manner of new manufacture " involves two separate considerations, *viz.*, Is it a manner of manufacture? Is it new? The first of these considerations is dealt with in this chapter and the second, that of novelty, is dealt with in a subsequent chapter.

33 In order to ascertain what is a " manner of manufacture " it is necessary to consider what has been decided by the courts. As was pointed out in a recent Australian case, *N.R.D.C.'s Application*,[4] by the High Court of Australia (Dixon C.J., Kitto and Windeyer JJ.), in a judgment referred to with approval in the judgment of the Divisional Court in *R.* v. *Patents Appeal Tribunal* (*ex p. Swift & Co.*) [5]: " It is a mistake, and a mistake likely to lead to an incorrect conclusion, to treat the question whether a given process or product is within the definition as if that question could be restated in the form : ' Is this a manner (or kind) of manufacture? ' It is a mistake which tends to limit one's thinking by reference to the idea of making tangible goods by hand or by machine, because ' manufacture,' as a word of everyday speech, generally conveys that idea. The right question is : ' Is this a proper subject of letters patent according to the prin-

---

[1] See *ante*, § 6.
[2] s. 101 (1).
[3] *R.* v. *Comptroller-General, ex p. Muntz*, 39 **R.P.C.** 335.
[4] [1961] R.P.C. 134.
[5] [1962] R.P.C. 37.

ciples which have been developed for the application of section 6
of the Statute of Monopolies? ' "

34 Processes

It is evident that if the construction of the words "new manufactures" were limited to the production of new articles, to the
exclusion of the process of manufacturing old articles by cheaper,
better and improved methods, the inducement which the common
law intended to give to inventors would be curtailed to very narrow
limits. Passages in the judgments in some of the early cases seem
to throw doubt on the validity of patents for processes,[6] but we find
that the courts gradually extended the meaning of the word "manufacture" to include improvements in manufacture and changes in
method which though small in themselves have great economic
importance.

35   In 1819 Abbott C.J. said [7] : "Now the word 'manufactures' . . .
may perhaps extend also to a new process to be carried on by known
implements, or elements, acting upon known substances, and ultimately producing some other known substance, but producing it in a
cheaper or more expeditious manner, or of a better or more useful
kind. But no merely philosophical or abstract principle can answer
to the word 'manufactures.' Something of a corporeal and substantial nature, something that can be made by man from the matters
subjected to his art and skill, or at the least of some new mode of
employing practically his art and skill, is requisite to satisfy this
word."

In 1841, in *Gibson and Campbell* v. *Brand*,[8] Tindal C.J. said:
"The patent is taken out 'for a new or improved process for the
manufacture of silk, and silk in combination with certain other fibrous
substances,' taken out therefore strictly for a process . . . undoubtedly
there is a very strong reason to suppose if the specification is carefully and properly prepared, so as to point out with great distinctness
and minuteness what the process is, that such a patent may be good
in law." [9]

36 Test to be applied

There have been many instances in which the Patent Office have
received applications for patents for ingenious ideas, but have refused
these on the ground that they could not be classed as "manufac-

---

[6] *e.g. Hornblower* v. *Boulton,* 8 T.R. 95.
[7] *R.* v. *Wheeler,* 2 Barn. & Ald. 345 at p. 349; see also *Ralston* v. *Smith*
(1865) 11 H.L.C. 223.
[8] 1 W.P.C. 627 at p. 633.
[9] And see *Boulton* v. *Bull,* 2 H.Bl. 463 at p. 468; *Crane* v. *Price,* 1 W.P.C.
393 at p. 409.

tures." It is possible that some of the applications that have been
refused in the past might now be considered as allowable under the
law as now clarified.

37　　In *G.E.C.'s Application*,[10] which was for a method of extinguishing
incendiary bombs, Morton J. put forward the " vendible product
test " : " In my view a method or process is a manner of manufacture
if it (a) results in the production of some vendible product, or
(b) improves or restores to its former condition a vendible product,
or (c) has the effect of preserving from deterioration some vendible
product to which it is applied. In saying this I am not attempting
to cover every case which may arise by a hard and fast rule." The
application was refused. But this test should not be regarded, as
Morton J. himself made clear, as a " hard and fast " rule and this
has been emphasised in a number of subsequent cases. It has also
been decided that, if this test is to be applied, then the word
" product " must be given a wide meaning.

38　　In *Cementation Co., Ltd.'s Application*,[11] which was for a method
of preventing and extinguishing underground fires by drilling holes
and injecting material to form fire-resistant barriers and further
material which, upon heating, liberated carbon dioxide, Evershed J.
said:

　　" According to the *Oxford Dictionary*, the word ' manufacture ' is defined as (a) the action or process of making by hand,
(b) the making of articles or material (now on a large scale) by
physical labour and mechanical power, and (c) a branch of
productive industry . . . having regard to the definitions in the
Oxford Dictionary and particularly to the reference in the second
of them to ' material ' and having regard also to the absence of
any narrow principle of construction in the authorities cited, it is
in my judgment impossible to say that beyond reasonable doubt
the processes here in question fall outside the ambit of the
Acts. . . .

　　" In my judgment Morton J., in the *G.E.C.* case, was primarily
directing his attention to the question whether and to what
extent a manner of manufacture extended to processes not
resulting in the creation of some new articles or material which
did not previously exist. The emphasis, therefore, is upon the
three activities of (a) production, (b) improvement or restoration,
and (c) prevention from deterioration. In using the noun
' product ' to denote the subject-matter of each of the three kinds

[10] 60 R.P.C. 1.
[11] 62 R.P.C. 151.

of activity the learned judge was, in my opinion, using a convenient and compendious term to indicate the article or material
resulting from the activity, and was not intending to limit by
reference to what may be the common acceptation today of the
word ' product ' that which results from a ' manufacture.' In any
case a further reference to the *Oxford Dictionary* discloses that
the second and third meanings of the word ' product ' are (a)
anything produced by nature or a natural process also collectively
—produce; fruit; and (b) that which is produced by any action,
operation, or work; a production; the result.

"In my judgment, therefore, if the word ' product ' is given
the full significance which I venture to think Morton J. himself
intended that it should bear, it cannot be asserted that the
material or formation which results from the application of either
of the applicants' processes is beyond reasonable doubt not a
' product ' within the terms of Morton J.'s rule; so that I reach
the same conclusion as that already stated by an application
of the terms of that rule."

The application was allowed.

39　　In *Rantzen's Application*,[12] which was for a method of signalling
involving the production of a complex electrical oscillation, Evershed
J. said:

"I find it difficult to apply to electricity the characteristics
of ' vendible product ' if by that phrase is meant something
which can be passed from one man to another upon a transaction
of purchase or sale. But ought the phrase to be so confined? . . .
I inquired during the course of the argument what was the
origin of and sanction for the formula ' vendible product.' I
am inclined to think that it took its origin from the need to
exclude from the scope of the Patents Acts processes the result
of which, however useful, could not be contemplated as falling
within their ambit, for example, methods or processes of treating
diseases of the human body. And it is no doubt true that a
manner of manufacture in its ordinary sense imports the idea
of making something; and by ' something ' is commonly understood something tangible and material. In the great majority
of cases at any rate, the use of the phrase ' vendible products '
in reference to the result of the process of manufacture aptly
assists in the true interpretation of the word ' manufacture ' by
laying proper emphasis upon the trading or industrial character
of the processes which are intended to be comprehended by the

[12] 64 R.P.C. 63.

Acts. Nevertheless, the phrase does not occur in the Acts themselves . . . the problem always remains one of the application to the facts of the particular case of the statutory phrase 'manner of new manufacture.' I conclude, therefore, that it would not be right, nor, as I think, in accordance with Morton J.'s intention to give to the term 'vendible product' a narrow or rigid construction by placing undue emphasis on the material requirements of what may otherwise fairly be regarded as the outcome of a process of manufacture; and such a view accords, as I think, with the language of Parker J. in the case of *Alsop's Patent* [13] to which Morton J. referred in the *G.E.C.* case." [14]

The application was allowed.

40 In *Reitzman* v. *Grahame-Chapman and Derustit Ltd.*[15] Jenkins L.J. remarked that: " Any criticism to which it (the Morton 'rule') may be open is certainly not on the score of its being too wide. . . ."

In *Elton and Leda Chemicals Ltd.'s Application*,[16] which was for a method of fog dispersal, and was allowed, Lloyd-Jacob J. said [17]: " Although an inventor may use no newly devised mechanism, nor produce a new substance, nonetheless, he may, by providing some new and useful effect, appropriate for himself a patent monopoly in such improved result by covering the mode or manner by means of which his result is secured. Seeing that the promise which he offers is some new and useful effect, there must of necessity be some product whereby the validity of his promise can be tested."

41 Referring to this passage, the High Court of Australia in *N.R.D.C.'s Application* said [18]:

" . . . the tenor of the passage seems to be that what is meant by a ' product ' in relation to a process is only something in which the new and useful effect may be observed. Sufficient authority has been cited to show that the ' something ' need not be a ' thing ' in the sense of an article; it may be any physical phenomenon in which the effect, be it creation or merely alteration, may be observed: a building (for example), a tract or stratum of land, an explosion, an electrical oscillation. It is, we think, only by understanding the word ' product ' as covering every end produced, and treating the word ' vendible ' as pointing only to the requirement of utility in practical affairs, that the

[13] 24 R.P.C. 733 at p. 752.
[14] 60 R.P.C. 1.
[15] 68 R.P.C. 25 at p. 32.
[16] [1957] R.P.C. 267.
[17] [1957] R.P.C. 267 at p. 268.
[18] [1961] R.P.C. 134 at p. 145.

language of Morton J.'s 'rule' may be accepted as wide enough
to convey the broad idea which the long line of decisions on
the subject has shown to be comprehended by the Statute."

42 Biochemical processes

A biochemical process has been held to be good subject-matter
for a patent. In *Commercial Solvents Corporation* v. *Synthetic
Products Co. Ltd.*[19] the patent was for a process for the production
of acetone and the like from grain by bacterial fermentation. No
attack was in fact made upon the patent on the ground that it was
not a " manufacture " within the meaning of the Statute of Monopolies, but Romer J. said [20]: " The problem that Dr. Weizman successfully solved was that of selecting some particular bacillus . . . that
would produce butyl alcohol and acetone in commercial quantities
better than any other known bacillus . . . he found such a bacillus
and his invention consists in the employment of that bacillus to
produce large yields of acetone and butyl alcohol under aerobic or
anaerobic conditions. In such an invention there is, in my opinion,
patentable subject-matter."

43 Agricultural cultivation

Methods of agricultural cultivation have been, in general, refused
patent protection.[21] An exception was a method of mushroom culture,
where the methods specified in the patent differed entirely from the
conditions appertaining under natural conditions.[22] But it is possible
that in future some patent applications for the production of agricultural products may be accepted in view of the case of *Swift's
Application (R. v. Patents Appeal Tribunal)*,[23] in which the invention
was a method of improving the tenderness of meat by injecting
enzyme solution into the live animal shortly before slaughter and the
Patents Appeal Tribunal had upheld the decision of the Comptroller
refusing to allow the application to proceed on the ground that the
subject-matter of the application was not a manner of new manufacture. On an application for an order of certiorari the Divisional
Court of the Queen's Bench quashed the decision of the Tribunal,

---

[19] 43 R.P.C. 185.
[20] 43 R.P.C. 185 at p. 225.
[21] *Hamilton-Adams' Appn.*, 35 R.P.C. 90; *Rau G.m.b.H.'s Appn.*, 52 R.P.C.
362; *Standard Oil Development Co.'s Appn.*, 68 R.P.C. 114; *Lenard's Appn.*,
71 R.P.C. 190; *N.V. Philips Gloeilampenfabriken's Appn.*, 71 R.P.C. 192;
Dow Chemical Co.'s Appn. [1956] R.P.C. 247; *Virginia-Carolina Chemical
Corporation's Appn.* [1958] R.P.C. 38; *American Chemical Paint Co.'s
Appn.* [1958] R.P.C. 47; *Canterbury Agricultural College's Appn.* [1958]
R.P.C. 85; *Goldhaft's Appn.* [1957] R.P.C. 276.
[22] *Szuecs's Appn.* [1956] R.P.C. 25.
[23] [1962] R.P.C. 37.

referring with approval to the judgment of the High Court of Australia in *N.R.D.C.'s Application*.[18]

44 Medical and Biological processes

A method of medical treatment of the human body is not a manner of manufacture, *e.g.* a method for treating disease of the human body,[24] or a method for birth control by oral administration of drugs,[25] or a method for inducing reduced awareness and loss of pain sensibility by sound recording.[26] But in *Puharich and Lawrence's Application*[27] it was held that a claim to a system for aiding hearing cannot be equated with a method of treatment and an application for a patent for such a system was allowed to proceed even though it involved a dental operation to effect insertion in a tooth of a radio receiver as part of such system. A method of treating disease in animals may, it seems, be a method of manufacture.[28] In *G.E.C.'s Application*,[29] an application for a method of producing mutant strains in micro-organisms by electrical treatment was refused; but it may be doubted whether this case was rightly decided in view of the subsequent decision in *Swift's Application*.[28]

45 Novel methods of operating known apparatus

Although patents have been granted for particular novel methods of operating internal combustion engines,[30] in *Rolls-Royce Ltd.'s Application*,[31] in which the application was for a novel method of operating a known type of jet aircraft using known controls, the application was refused on the ground that such a method was a flight plan and as such was not a manner of manufacture, the Patents Appeal Tribunal citing *D.A. & K.'s Application*[32] as authority for the proposition that a scheme or plan is not a manner of manufacture.

In the first of *Slee & Harris's Applications*[33] claims to a method of operating a computer in a particular way were refused as not for a manner of manufacture, being for a method of operating a known machine producing, as the end product, merely data, *i.e.* intellectual information, but a claim to the computer set in such a condition as to solve a particular problem was held not to be objectionable on this

24 *C. & W.'s Appn.*, 31 R.P.C. 235.
25 *London Rubber Industries Ltd.'s Patent* [1968] R.P.C. 31.
26 *Neva Corporation's Appn.* [1968] R.P.C. 481.
27 [1965] R.P.C. 395.
28 *U.S. Rubber Co.'s Appn.* [1964] R.P.C. 104.
29 [1961] R.P.C. 21.
30 See, *e.g.* Patent Specifications 196, 237 and 499, 974; and see also *Otto* v. *Linford*, 46 L.T.(N.S.) 35.
31 [1963] R.P.C. 251.
32 43 R.P.C. 154.
33 *Slee and Harris's Appns.* [1966] R.P.C. 194.

ground. However, in *Badger's Application* [34] a claim to a process for conditioning the operation of a computer and an associated plotter of known types and operating them so as to produce a layout for a system was allowed, presumably because the end product was a drawing. The distinction seems a fine one.

46   Other cases

Applications in respect of inventions relating to printed sheets and the like are refused if the arrangement of printed words or pictorial matter is directed to a purely visual or intellectual purpose, but are allowable if the printed or pictorial content is so arranged as to effect some mechanical operation.[35] Cases which have been refused include a system of printed envelopes,[36] new systems of indexing,[37] a printed explanation of the music on the back of a gramophone record,[38] a scheme for colouring camouflage,[39] a new system of musical notation,[40] architects' plans,[41] a navigational chart to enable the ascertainment of the position of an aircraft in flight [42] and others.[43] Cases which have been allowed include a newspaper page,[44] a device to enable a ship to navigate a channel,[45] a printed ticket designed to serve a mechanical purpose,[46] a printed sheet for teaching pronunciation and which could be used in a speaking machine [47] and time recording cards.[48] This principle has been extended to other articles, *e.g.*, cinematograph films and gramophone records.[49]

In the second of *Slee & Harris's Applications* [50] the claims were directed to programming means controlling a computer so as to perform a particular process, which programming means might be a

---

[34] [1970] R.P.C. 36.
[35] *Virginia-Carolina Chemical Corp.'s Appn. and other Appns.* [1958] R.P.C. 35 at p. 36.
[36] *Johnson's Appn.*, 19 R.P.C. 56.
[37] *Ward's Appn.*, 29 R.P.C. 79; *R's Appns.*, 40 R.P.C. 465.
[38] *S.'s Appn.*, 40 R.P.C. 461.
[39] *T.'s Appn.*, 37 R.P.C. 109.
[40] *M.'s Appn.*, 41 R.P.C. 159; *C.'s Appn.*, 37 R.P.C. 247.
[41] *E. S. P.'s Appn.*, 62 R.P.C. 87.
[42] *Kelvin and Hughes Ltd.'s Appn.*, 71 R.P.C. 103.
[43] *W. R.'s Appn.*, 41 R.P.C. 216; *D. A. & K.'s Appn.*, 43 R.P.C. 154; *R. P. C.'s Appn.*, 41 R.P.C. 156; *P.'s Appn.*, 41 R.P.C. 201; *A. E. W.'s Appn.*, 41 R.P.C. 529; *Johnson's Appn.*, 47 R.P.C. 361; *Littlewood's Appn.*, 71 R.P.C. 185.
[44] *Cooper's Appn.*, 19 R.P.C. 53.
[45] *Loth's Appn.*, 41 R.P.C. 273.
[46] *Fishburn's Appn.*, 57 R.P.C. 245.
[47] *Pitman's Appn.* [1969] R.P.C. 646.
[48] *Alderton and Barry's Appn.*, 59 R.P.C. 56.
[49] See, *e.g.*, *F.'s Appn.*, 72 R.P.C. 127; *American Optical Co.'s Appn.* [1958] R.P.C. 40; *C. M.'s Appn.*, 61 R.P.C. 63; *Huber's Appn.* [1956] R.P.C. 50.
[50] [1966] R.P.C. 194.

punched tape or a punched card. The application was allowed to proceed, the Hearing Officer considering that, although the programming means could be regarded as no more than a printed sheet, it was seriously arguable that the programming means was an integer which physically co-operated with the computer to control the latter to operate in a particular way. A similar type of claim was allowed by the Patents Appeal Tribunal in Gever's Application.[51]

47   Other ingenious subject-matters for which patents have been refused include a method of marking buoys as an aid to navigation,[52] a method of defence and attack against submarines,[53] methods of navigation,[54] pest destruction by fumigation,[55] a method of producing light [56] and a ship's propeller wherein the only novelty in the claim was the mental process by which the propeller blade thicknesses at different radial positions was determined,[57] but an application in respect of a method of fog dispersal was allowed.[58]

A method of collating statistical data using known means operating in its normal manner is not a manner of manufacture [59] nor is a mere scheme or plan.[60]

48 A discovery not a " manufacture "

A mere discovery is not proper subject-matter for a patent. In *Reynolds* v. *Herbert Smith & Co. Ltd.*[61] Buckley J. explained the distinction between a discovery and an invention in the following terms: " Discovery adds to the amount of human knowledge, but it does so only . . . by disclosing something. . . . Invention also adds to human knowledge, but not merely by disclosing something. Invention necessarily involves also the suggestion of an act to be done, and it must be an act which results in a new product, or a new result, or a new process, or a new combination for producing an old product or an old result." [62]

---

[51] [1970] R.P.C. 91 at p. 98.   [52] *W.'s Appn.*, 31 R.P.C. 141.
[53] *F.'s Appn.*, 37 R.P.C. 112.
[54] *A. L.'s Appn.*, 41 R.P.C. 615; *W. L.'s Appn.*, 41 R.P.C. 617.
[55] *Bovingdon's Appn.*, 64 R.P.C. 20.
[56] *Philips Electrical Industries Ltd.'s Appn.* [1959] R.P.C. 341.
[57] *Lips' Appn.* [1959] R.P.C. 35.
[58] *Elton & Leda Chemicals Ltd.'s Appn.* [1957] R.P.C. 267.
[59] *Stahl and Larsson Appn.* [1965] R.P.C. 596.
[60] *D. A. & K.'s Appn.*, 43 R.P.C. 154; *Hiller's Appn.* [1969] R.P.C. 267.
[61] 20 R.P.C. 123 at p. 126.
[62] And see *Lane-Fox* v. *Kensington & Knightsbridge Electric Lighting Co.*, 9 R.P.C. 413 at p. 416; *Chamberlain and Hookham Ltd.* v. *Mayor, etc., of Bradford*, 20 R.P.C. 673 at p. 687 (H.L.); *British Thomson-Houston Co. Ltd.* v. *Charlesworth Peebles & Co.*, 42 R.P.C. 180 at p. 209 (H.L.); *Heap* v. *Bradford Dyers' Association Ltd.*, 46 R.P.C. 254 at p. 264; *Reitzman* v. *Grahame-Chapman and Derustit Ltd.*, 67 R.P.C. 178; *Magnatex Ltd.* v. *Unicorn Products Ltd.*, 68 R.P.C. 117 at p. 122.

49   *A bare principle not a " manufacture "*

Nor can a claim be made for the monopoly of a natural principle, since that would be to claim the laws of nature, which have always existed.   Man merely discovers the principle; but if, in addition to discovering it, he can describe a method of utilising that principle so as to make it applicable to the production of a new manufacture, he can obtain a patent for the method, and to this extent will be protected in the application of the principle itself.

50   *Alleged claims to abstract principle*

Hope L.J.C., in directing the jury in the case of *Househill Co.* v. *Neilson*,[63] said: " I state to you the law to be that you may obtain a patent for a mode of carrying a principle into effect; and if you suggest and discover, not only the principle, but suggest and invent how it may be applied to a practical result by mechanical contrivance and apparatus, and show that you are aware that no particular sort or modification, or form of the apparatus, is essential, in order to obtain benefit from the principle, then you may take your patent for the mode of carrying it into effect, and are not under the necessity of describing and confining yourself to one form of apparatus."

51   In *Otto* v. *Linford*,[64] claim 1 of the plaintiff's specification ran as follows: " Admitting to the cylinder a mixture of combustible gas or vapour with air, separate from a charge of air or incombustible gas, so that the development of heat and the expansion or increase of pressure produced by the combustion *are rendered gradual* substantially as and for the purposes set forth."

Jessel M.R. in the Court of Appeal said[65]: " It is said that what is claimed is a principle . . . or, as it is sometimes termed, the ' idea ' of putting a cushion of air between the explosive mixture and the piston of the gas motor engine, so as to regulate, detain, or make gradual, what would otherwise be a sudden explosion.   Of course, that could not be patented.   I do not read the patent so; I read the patent as being to the effect that the patentee tells us that there is the idea which he wishes to carry out; but he also describes other kinds of machines which will carry it out; and he claims to carry it out substantially by one or other of these machines.   That is the subject of a patent." [66]

52   New substances

A patent may contain a claim for a new substance but the claim is to be construed as not extending to that substance when found in

---

[63] (1843) 1 W.P.C. 673 at p. 685.   [64] 46 L.T.(N.S.) 35.
[65] 46 L.T.(N.S.) 35 at p. 39.
[66] See also *Neilson* v. *Harford* (1841) 1 W.P.C. 295; *British Thomson-Houston Co. Ltd.* v. *Corona Lamp Works Ltd.*, 39 R.P.C. 49 at p. 70.

nature.[67] This provision of the 1949 Act would appear to resolve doubts which have been expressed whether a new " material," produced by no new means or process is patentable.[68]

53 Food or medicine

No patent claim may be made for a substance capable of being used as a food or medicine which is a mixture of known ingredients possessing only the aggregate of the known properties of the ingredients, or for a process producing such a substance by mere admixture.[69]

The words " food " and " intended for food or medicine " (which, it is submitted, are narrower than the words of the present Act, " capable of being used as food or medicine ") have been construed by the Law Officer as covering any substance which is either itself a food or may " be used in the preparation or production of an article, so as to make it ready for consumption " [70]; and the word " medicine " has been held to include substances which may be applied externally.[71]

Under the former law substances prepared or produced by chemical processes or intended for food or medicine could not be patented in themselves, but only when prepared or produced by the methods or processes of manufacture described in the specification or their obvious chemical equivalents. The removal of this restriction by the 1949 Act constitutes an important change in the law.

54 Method of testing

A further important enlargement of the field of patentable invention made by the 1949 Act is the inclusion of " any new method or process of testing applicable to the improvement or control of manufacture." [72] Applications have frequently been refused in the past for methods of testing in the course of manufacture, notwithstanding their ingenuity, on the ground that these did not constitute a " manner of manufacture." [73] This anomaly is now removed. But " a new apparatus for taking readings hitherto obtainable by other means " does not constitute a new method or process of testing

---

[67] s. 4 (7).

[68] See *Acetylene Illuminating Co. Ltd.* v. *United Alkali Co. Ltd.,* 22 R.P.C. 145 at p. 153; *British Thomson-Houston Co. Ltd.* v. *British Insulated and Helsby Cables Ltd.,* 42 R.P.C. 180 at p. 207; *Sharpe and Dohme Inc.* v. *Boots Pure Drugs Co. Ltd.,* 45 R.P.C. 153 at p. 174.

[69] s. 10 (1) (c). See *Arnold and I.C.I. Ltd.'s Appn.,* 59 R.P.C. 76.

[70] *W. K.-J. and W. Ltd.'s Appns.,* 39 R.P.C. 263; *E. M.'s Appn.,* 41 R.P.C. 590.

[71] *M.'s Appn.,* 39 R.P.C. 261.

[72] s. 101 (1).

[73] See, for example, *Hartridge's Appn.,* 62 R.P.C. 149.

merely because the results when obtained can be applied in known manner to secure valuable data.[74]

55 Power of Comptroller

The Comptroller may refuse an application for a patent if the invention claimed is contrary to well-established natural laws (*e.g.* for a mechanical perpetual motion machine) or if its use would be contrary to law and morality.[75] An application may also be refused where the grant would be refused under the Royal Prerogative and applications for contraceptive devices have been refused under this power.[76]

It is within the province of the Comptroller to decide whether the subject of an application is a " manner of manufacture," [77] so that it is unlikely that any invention which did not satisfy this requirement (or the alternative requirement introduced by the 1949 Act that the invention is a method of testing applicable to manufacture) would ever become the subject of a granted patent. There is in fact no reported case in which a patent has been held invalid merely on the ground that the invention claimed was not a manner of manufacture.

56   If there is any reasonable doubt whether the subject-matter of an application is a manner of manufacture, the application should be allowed to proceed.[78]

[The next paragraph is 71]

---

[74] *British Petroleum Co. Ltd.'s Appn.* [1958] R.P.C. 253.
[75] s. 10 (1). See *Pessers and Moody* v. *Haydon & Co.*, 26 R.P.C. 58; *Comptroller's Ruling C.*, 40 R.P.C., Appendix.
[76] s. 102 (1). See *A. & H.'s Appn.*, 44 R.P.C. 298; *Riddlesbargher's Appn.*, 53 R.P.C. 57.
[77] *R.* v. *Comptroller-General, ex p. Muntz*, 39 R.P.C. 335.
[78] *Swift's Appn.* (*R.* v. *P.A.T.*) [1962] R.P.C. 37; *London Rubber Industries Ltd.'s Patent* [1968] R.P.C. 31 at p. 35.

CHAPTER 3

THE APPLICANT AND APPLICATION

1. THE APPLICANT

71 Who may apply

A patent may be applied for by any person who claims to be the
" true and first inventor " or by the assignee of such person in respect
of the right to apply.[1] This right may be freely assigned to any
other person (and presumably again assigned as often as may be
desired) without any special formality. The inventor or his assignee
may apply alone or jointly with any other person or persons,[1] but
the person for the time being possessed of the right to apply must
always be one of the applicants. The personal representative of a
deceased inventor or assignee may apply or may assign the right to
apply.[2]

72 *Convention application*

A patent may also be applied for by a person who has made an
application for patent protection for the same invention,[3] in a " convention " country, or by the assignee of that person, provided that
the application is made within twelve months from the date of the
application in the convention country.[4] A convention country is one
declared as such by an Order in Council.[5] In the case of a convention application it is open to the foreign applicant and his assignee
to decide which of them shall be the applicant in this country.[6]

73 *Persons under incapacity and aliens*

It will be observed that there is no limitation whatever preventing
a person under an incapacity, either by reason of infancy or otherwise, from obtaining a patent, and even under the old law there does
not appear ever to have been a question as to whether an infant or
a married woman might become a grantee of letters patent.

It was always competent for an alien to obtain a patent [7]; but War
Emergency legislation has prevented letters patent being obtained by

---

[1] s. 1 (1).
[2] ss. 1 (3), 101 (1).
[3] See *post*, § 171, and *Schwarzkopf's Appn.* [1965] R.P.C. 387.
[4] s. 1 (2), and see *post*, § 108. See also s. 69.
[5] s. 68. See *post*, § 1572 and *Kromschröder's Patent* [1960] R.P.C. 75.
[6] *Wohl's Appn.*, 42 R.P.C. 45.
[7] *Wirth's Patent*, 12 Ch.D. 303; *Chappell v. Purday*, 14 M. & W. 303 at
p. 318; and *Carez's Appn.*, 6 R.P.C. 552.

an alien enemy or for an invention made in enemy territory during the period of hostilities.[8]

74 *Official committees*

In *Patterson* v. *Gas Light and Coke Co.*,[9] James L.J. in the Court of Appeal said: " . . . we deem it right to say that we think it at the least very questionable whether it can be competent for a member of an official commission or committee to take out a patent for the subject-matter of their official investigation. . . . The consideration for every patent is the communication of useful information to the public. What consideration is there where the information was already the property of the state?" In accordance with modern practice, however, patents are granted to servants of the Government, whether permanent or temporary, and by them under their agreements for service assigned to one of the Secretaries of State.

75 *Corporation*

Under section 1 of the Act it is clear that a patent may be applied for by a corporation as assignee, either alone or jointly with the true and first inventor or any other person; under the old law a corporation could not apply in the ordinary way open to an individual, whether as " inventor " or " importer," apparently because a corporation could not be said to invent in the modern sense of the word.[10] A corporation could, however, under the old law make an application without joining the " true and first inventor " where such application was made on a " communication from abroad," or under the International Convention.[11]

A foreign unincorporated trading body has been allowed to apply in this country for a patent under a convention application.[11a]

True and First Inventor

76 By section 6 of the Statute of Monopolies [12] one of the conditions of validity was that the patent should have been granted to the " true and first inventor." A patent may now be granted to an assignee but the identity of the true and first inventor is still important, as, except in the case of convention applications, the chain of title of the right to apply for a patent must be derived from him, he must be named in the application and a declaration that he assents to the application must be furnished.[13]

---

[8] 1946 Act, s. 4, *post*, § 1476. And see *Du Pont's Patent* [1961] R.P.C. 336.
[9] 2 Ch.D. 812 at p. 832.
[10] See Hindmarch, p. 34; *Carez's Appn.*, 6 R.P.C. 552; *Société Anonyme du Générateur du Temple's Appn.*, 13 R.P.C. 54.
[11] *Ibid. Post*, § 1531 *et seq.*
[11a] *Schwarzkopf's Appn.* [1965] R.P.C. 387.
[12] *Ante*, § 6.   [13] s. 2 (2) (3).

77   Patents granted to importers

In the early days of the patent system the word " inventor " had not acquired the usual meaning which it has now, and seems to have been used to designate a first introducer rather than a first deviser. *Hastings' Patent* of 1567 [14] for the making of frisadoes appears to have been granted in consideration of his having imported the skill of manufacturing them from abroad.   In *Matthey's Case* [14] the patent for knives with bone hafts and plates of latten was granted, " because, as the patent suggested, he brought the first use thereof from beyond the seas."   Again in *Clothworkers of Ipswich* [15] in 1614, both devisers and importers were clearly regarded as proper grantees of monopoly patents.

There is no doubt, therefore, that the words " true and first inventor " in the Statute of Monopolies were intended to include both:

(1) true and first inventors (in the modern popular sense), and
(2) true and first importers into the realm.

And in the first reported decision after the Statute of Monopolies, *Edgeberry* v. *Stephens*,[16] it is said, " for the statute speaks of new manufactures within this realm, so that if it be new here it is within the statute, for the Act intended to encourage new devices useful to the Kingdom, and whether learned by travel or by study it is the same thing." [17]

78   The effect of the earlier decisions was summed up by Jessel M.R. in *Plimpton* v. *Malcolmson* [18]: " What is the meaning of a first and true inventor?   To ascertain its meaning you must have recourse, no doubt, to various decisions given on the statute. . . .   As I understand shortly after the passing of the statute, the question arose whether a man could be called a first and true inventor who, in the popular sense, had never invented anything, but who having learned abroad (that is out of the realm, in a foreign country, because it has been decided that Scotland is within the realm for this purpose) that somebody else had invented something, quietly copied the invention, and brought it over to this country, and then took out a patent. As I said before, in the popular sense he had invented nothing.   But it was decided, and now, therefore, is the legal sense and meaning of the statute, that he was a first and true inventor within the statute. . . ." [19]

[14] Noy 183; J. W. Gordon, K.C., *Monopolies by Patent*, at p. 220, and see 1 W.P.C. at p. 6.
[15] Godb. 252.
[16] 1 W.P.C. 35; 2 Salk. 447.
[17] And see Eyre C.J. in *Boulton* v. *Bull* (1785) 2 H.Bl. 463 at p. 491.
[18] 3 Ch.D. 531 at p. 555.
[19] And see Jessel M.R. in *Marsden* v. *Saville Street Foundry and Engineering Co.*, 3 Ex.D. 203.

79 Inventors distinguished into classes

Long before the Act of 1852,[20] it had been the practice for the applicant to state in his declaration by virtue of which qualification he prayed for a patent.[21] The Patents Rules [22] have continued the old practice, and the present form of application,[23] which is a comprehensive form to be used in all cases other than convention applications, requires the applicant to state upon what ground he bases his claim to be entitled to apply and whether the invention was communicated to the applicant and, if so, the name, address and nationality of the communicator. There is no rule, however, to prevent a person, arriving in this country in possession of an invention which he has learned abroad, from describing himself merely as " the true and first inventor thereof."

In *Avery's Patent*,[24] Stirling J. said: " There is no decision that a patent, taken out as for an original invention, when in fact the invention patented was communicated from abroad, is void, though there is in the case of *Milligan* v. *Marsh* [25] what appears to be a dictum of Sir Page Wood V.-C. to that effect; nor is there any decision that where an invention is partly original and partly communicated from abroad, the part communicated from abroad ought to be distinguished in the specification; but in the case of *Renard* v. *Levinstein*,[26] Knight Bruce L.J. expressed great doubt upon the point. . . . That being so notwithstanding that the invention was founded on a communication received from abroad, it appears to me that it well might be held that the statutory declaration made by the applicant was true in point of law."

80   And Lindley L.J., in the case of *Moser* v. *Marsden*,[27] said: " Then it was suggested that as the English patentee had himself improved Grosselin's invention, the specification ought to have shown this on its face; and that as the whole invention was not communicated to the plaintiff by Grosselin, as stated by the plaintiff, the patent is bad. This point has been raised before, but as yet it has not found favour in any court. Nor ought it; there is no substance in it. The patentee is the true and first inventor within the meaning of the patent laws, whether he invents himself or whether he simply imports a foreign invention. I cannot see how he is anything but a true and first

---

[20] 15 & 16 Vict. c. 83.
[21] See Hindmarch, pp. 509, 510.
[22] *Post*, § 1349 *et seq.*
[23] Patents Form No. 1, *post*, § 1505.
[24] 36 Ch.D. 307 at p. 316.
[25] 2 Jur.(N.S.) 1083.
[26] 10 L.T.(N.S.) 177.
[27] 10 R.P.C. 350 at p. 359.

inventor if he does both; that is, if he both imports a foreign invention and improves it himself."

81 *Communication made abroad*

It was held in *Wirth's Patent* [28] that a patent may be granted to a foreign subject resident abroad for an invention communicated to him by another foreign subject also resident abroad. And in *Von Krogh's Application* [29] a Norwegian subject resident abroad who was the assignee of another Norwegian subject (also resident abroad) was permitted to apply in his own name as " true and first inventor."

The question whether the applicant is the true and first inventor must be clearly distinguished from the question of the beneficial ownership of the patent. The applicant may be merely the clerk or agent to whom the communication is made by the foreign inventor, so that he may hold the patent as trustee. In law he is, nevertheless, the true and first inventor whether his allegation of communication be true or not,[30] and save in so far as his relations with his employers are concerned he is in the legal position of a patentee.

82 If the invention originated in a foreign country and has been communicated from abroad the Comptroller will not enter into any inquiry as to whether it was obtained honestly or otherwise.[31] But where an invention originated in this country and was communicated here to a company, which had branches both here and abroad, and substantially the same invention was subsequently communicated to the applicant by the company's foreign branch, the onus was on the applicant to establish that the invention, the subject of the application, had been independently made.[32] Where all the information relating to the invention was derived by the applicant from a foreign communication in response to a letter written by the applicant in this country, the grant of a patent was refused.[33]

83 *Communication in this country*

A communication of an invention made in this country by one British subject to another does not make the person to whom the communication is made the true and first inventor within the meaning of the Statute of Monopolies.[34] In certain circumstances it might be necessary, however, to send over from abroad some person who

---

[28] 12 Ch.D. 303.
[29] 49 R.P.C. 417.
[30] *Beard* v. *Egerton*, 3 C.B. 97 at p. 129; *Nickels* v. *Ross*, 8 C.B. 679 at p. 723; *Steedman* v. *Marsh*, 2 Jur.(N.S.) 391; *Avery's Patent*, 36 Ch.D. 307.
[31] *McNeil's Appn.*, 24 R.P.C. 680; *Comptroller's Ruling* A, 29 R.P.C. (i).
[32] *Dicker's Patent*, 51 R.P.C. 392.
[33] *H.'s Appn.* [1956] R.P.C. 197.
[34] *Marsden* v. *Saville Street Foundry and Engineering Co.*, 3 Ex.D. 203, *per* Jessel M.R. at p. 206.

understood the invention, in order that the applicant might be able to understand and properly describe it in the specification. It is submitted that this would not prevent the communication from being a genuine " communication from abroad." [35]

84   " True inventor " and " novelty " distinguished

It must also be remembered that the question " Is the patentee the true and first inventor? " is entirely separate and distinct from the question " Is the invention itself new? " In the former case we are dealing with the history of an idea in the mind of a particular man; in the latter with the history of a manufacture.

The difference was pointed out by Tindal C.J. in *Gibson and Campbell* v. *Brand* [36]: " The defendant next says that these letters patent have not been granted to the true and first inventors, which you are aware is a condition required by the statute. Now a man may publish to the world that which is perfectly new in all its use, and has not before been enjoyed, and yet he may not be the first and true inventor; he may have borrowed it from some other person, he may have taken it from a book, he may have learnt it from a specification; and then the legislature never intended that a person who had taken all his knowledge from the act of another, from the labours and assiduity or ingenuity of another, should be the man who was to receive the benefit of another's skill. There is some distinction, although perhaps not a very broad one, between the plea which alleges the plaintiffs were not the first and true inventors and that on which I conceive the principal question between the parties will turn . . . whether the subject-matter of this patent was known in England at the time the letters patent were granted." [37]

85   In *Tennant's* case [38] a material part of the invention claimed was found to have been suggested to the patentee by a chemist at Glasgow. Lord Ellenborough held that the patent was invalid, *inter alia*, because the grantee was not the inventor. It will be observed in this case, that although it is possible that the patentee was the first person to use the particular method for making bleaching liquor, nevertheless, he was held not to be the inventor because the particular method of producing this bleaching liquor was thought out by someone else and communicated to him.

86   In *Cornish* v. *Keene*,[39] Tindal C.J. said: " Sometimes it is a material question to determine whether the party who got the patent

[35] Discussed but not decided in *Pilkington* v. *Yeakley Vacuum Hammer Co.*, 18 R.P.C. 459, and see (on same patent) *Jameson's Patent*, 19 R.P.C. 246.
[36] 1 W.P.C. 627 at p. 628.
[37] And see *Househill Co.* v. *Neilson*, 1 W.P.C. 673 at p. 689.
[38] 1 W.P.C. 125n.   [39] 1 W.P.C. 501 at p. 507.

was the real and original inventor or not; because these patents are granted as a reward, not only for the benefit conferred upon the public by the discovery, but also to the ingenuity of the first inventor; and although it is proved that it is a new discovery, so far as the world is concerned, yet if anybody is able to show that although that [*i.e.*, publication to the world] was new—that the party who got the patent was not the man whose ingenuity first discovered it, that he borrowed it from A or B, or had taken it from a book that was printed in England, and which was open to all the world—then, although the public had the benefit of it, it would be an important question whether he was the first and original inventor of it." There is no doubt that, in the circumstances stated by the Chief Justice, the person obtaining the patent would not be the true and first inventor.

The principle laid down in the cases cited above has invariably been followed.

87   A may have invented something; he may have made a few experiments with the invention, and then abandoned it (without publication). B may subsequently have invented the same thing, altogether independently of A. If B applies for letters patent he is at law the first inventor; but if it be shown that the process of invention was not carried on in B's mind at all, but that A communicated his ideas to B, although with the full intention of abandoning them, B will not be the first inventor.

In *Dollond's* case,[40] the patent had been granted for improvements in the manufacture of object-glasses for telescopes. Dr. H. had made and used similar object-glasses for his own purposes, but he had in no way published his invention. Dollond, without any communication from Dr. H. had reinvented these object-glasses; held that Dollond's patent was good.

88   In *Lewis* v. *Marling*,[41] Bayley J. said: " If I discover a thing for myself, it is no objection to my claim to a patent that another also has made the discovery, provided I first introduce it into public use." The suggestion in that case was that the patentee had acquired his invention by seeing a model of a similar machine which had been brought from America. It was disproved that he had seen the model, and consequently he was held to be first and true inventor.[42]

89 **Right of true and first inventor assignable**

In applying the cases cited above, regard must be had to the substantial change in the law made by the Patents Act 1949 in that

---

[40] 1 W.P.C. 43.
[41] 1 W.P.C. 493 at p. 496.
[42] And see *Permutit Co.* v. *Borrowman*, 43 R.P.C. 356 at p. 359.

the right of the true and first inventor to apply for a patent is now assignable. No formalities as to assignment are specified by the Act and although an assignment in writing is obviously to be preferred in order to avoid difficulties of proof, presumably an assignment may be effected orally. It is submitted that an assignment may even be implied from the conduct of the parties concerned. But where the applicant is an assignee of the true and first inventor, the latter's assent in writing to the making of the application is necessary.[43] This can be furnished at any time within a period of three months from the date of the application.[44] Presumably the assignment, whether oral or in writing, could be enforced in the same manner as any other contract and would be held to be of the kind that is specifically enforceable. For this purpose a mandatory order that the inventor do sign the declaration of assent to the making of the application would be necessary. Any person may claim to be mentioned in any application for a patent as the, or an, inventor, but such claim must be made within two months (subject to an extension to three months) of the date of publication of the application.[45]

90   Wrong applicant by mistake

In *Carter's Application* [46] the application was, through a mistake, made by a person who described himself as the true and first inventor but in fact was not so, merely having a financial interest in the invention. It was held that the application was void and that the application form could not be amended by substituting the name of the real inventor and joining him as co-applicant.

91   Master and servant

Master the inventor

The extent to which science has developed in modern times, and the immense labour and time required to work out the details of construction of a complicated machine, frequently make it impossible for one man to perfect his invention by himself. Inventors sometimes suggest the main idea to subordinates, and leave the practical working out of the details to the latter. This task often requires great skill. But this skill, while exercised in the employment of the master and under his general directions, does not necessarily entitle the servant or workman to claim an interest in the invention. Exactly to what extent the man who conceives an idea is entitled to include within his patent specification improvements suggested by the person he

[43] Patents Forms Nos. 1 and 4.
[44] r. 9 (2).
[45] s. 16.
[46] 49 R.P.C. 403.

employs to work out that idea is difficult to define, and must depend
upon the facts of each case; but the guiding principle is involved
in the question: " Is it the idea itself, or is it merely the method of
carrying the idea into effect, that constitutes the pith of the
invention? "

92   In *Allen* v. *Rawson*,[47] Erle J. directed the jury thus: " I take the
law to be that, if a person has discovered an improved principle, and
employs engineers, agents, or other persons to assist him in carrying
out that principle, and they in the course of experiments arising from
that employment make valuable discoveries accessory to the main
principle, and tending to carry that out in a better manner, such
improvements are the property of the inventor of the original
improved principle, and may be embodied in his patent; and if so
embodied the patent is not avoided by evidence that the servant or
agent made the suggestion of the subordinate improvement of the
primary and improved principle." This was confirmed by Tindal
C.J., who said [48]: " . . . when we see that the principle and object
of the invention are complete without it, I think it is too much that a
suggestion of a workman, employed in the course of the experiments,
of something calculated more easily to carry into effect the concep-
tions of the inventor, should render the whole patent void." This
case was followed by Buckley J. in *W. R. Smith's Patent*.[49]

93 *Servant the inventor*

However, where the servant has himself made the invention, he
will be the first and true inventor irrespective of whether he is bound
under an express or implied contract to give to the master the benefit
of any inventions which he (the servant) may make while in the
master's employ. In the latter class of cases there is usually no
doubt that the servant is the inventor and the only question for
decision is as to the right of the master to have the patent assigned
to or held in trust for him by the servant.

In *Minter* v. *Wells and Hart*,[50] Alderson B. said: " The patentee
claims under the patent, stating, in his petition to the Crown, that he
is the true inventor of the machine in question; and if it could be
shown that he was not the true inventor, but that someone else had
invented it, the Crown is deceived in that suggestion, which was the
foundation on which it granted the patent; and then the law is, that
the patent obtained under such circumstances would be void. . . .
If Sutton [a workman in the plaintiff's employ] suggested the prin-

[47] 1 C.B. 551 at p. 569.
[48] 1 C.B. at p. 574.
[49] 22 R.P.C. 57. And see *David and Woodley's Appn.*, Griff.P.C. 26.
[50] 1 W.P.C. 127 at p. 129.

ciple to Minter then he, Sutton, would be the inventor; if, on the other hand, Minter suggested the principle to Sutton, and Sutton was assisting him, then Minter would be the first and true inventor, and Sutton would be a machine, so to speak, which Minter uses for the purpose of enabling him to carry his original conception into effect."

94   In *Marshall and Naylor's Patent* [51] the servant had been requested to make the invention, and had in fact done so; but the patent was applied for by two directors of the company employing him. The patent was declared invalid.

In *Mellor* v. *Wm. Beardmore & Co. Ltd.*[52] in the Court of Session, Lord Ormidale said: " As I understand the law of the matter, the mere existence of a contract of service in no way disqualifies a servant from taking out a patent in his own name and entirely for his own benefit—and that notwithstanding that he has used his employer's time and materials to aid him in completing his invention—unless he has become bound by some agreement, either express or implied, to communicate the benefits of his invention to those in whose employment he is." [53]

95   Master entitled to servant's inventions

General principle

In every such case the answer to the question to be decided depends on what is the true construction of the contract between master and servant having regard to its subject-matter and the surrounding circumstances. The contract may be oral or in writing, express or implied, but no equitable principle or obligation is to be considered that does not arise out of the contractual relationship itself.[54]

But where it is within the duty of the employee to make the invention in question, the invention will be the property of the employer, unless there is some contractual term to the contrary. As

---

[51] 17 R.P.C. 553.
[52] 44 R.P.C. 175.
[53] See also *Heald's Appns.*, 8 R.P.C. 429.
[54] *Vokes Ltd.* v. *Heather*, 62 R.P.C. 135; *British Celanese Ltd.* v. *Moncrieff*, 65 R.P.C. 165; *Richmond & Co. Ltd.* v. *Wrightson*, 22 R.P.C. 25; *Edisonia Ltd.* v. *Forse*, 25 R.P.C. 546; *British Reinforced Concrete Engineering Co. Ltd.* v. *Lind*, 34 R.P.C. 101; *Hop Extract Co. Ltd.* v. *Horst*, 36 R.P.C. 177; *Mellor* v. *Wm. Beardmore & Co. Ltd.*, 44 R.P.C. 175(I.H.); *Reid and Sigrist Ltd.* v. *Moss and Mechanism Ltd.*, 49 R.P.C. 461; *Triplex Safety Glass Co. Ltd.* v. *Scorah*, 55 R.P.C. 21; *Barnet Instruments Ltd.* v. *Overton*, 66 R.P.C. 315; *Loewy Engineering Co. Ltd.'s Appn.*, 69 R.P.C. 3; *Riber* v. *Marsden Smith*, 69 R.P.C. 230; *Charles Sely Ltd.'s Appn.*, 71 R.P.C. 158; *Fine Industrial Commodities Ltd.* v. *Powling*, 71 R.P.C. 253; *Patchett* v. *Sterling Engineering Co. Ltd.* (1953) 70 R.P.C. 269; *British Syphon Co. Ltd.* v. *Homewood* [1956] R.P.C. 27, 225; *Anemostat (Scotland) Ltd.* v. *Michaelis* [1957] R.P.C. 167.

was stated by Viscount Simonds in *Patchett* v. *Sterling Engineering Co. Ltd.*[55]: " It is true enough that the rule that inventions made by an employee belong to the employer is sometimes spoken of as an implied term of the contract of service. In a sense it no doubt is an implied term in that it is not written out in the contract of service, but it is a term which, given the conditions which are here present, namely, inventions made by the employee in the course of his employment, which it was part of his duty to make, the law imports into the contract. It appears to me that it is only an implied term in the same sense that it is an implied term, though not written at large, in the contract of service of any workman that what he produces by the strength of his arm or the skill of his hand or the exercise of his inventive faculty shall become the property of the employer. . . . If it is patentable it is for the employer to say whether it shall be patented and he can require the employee to do what is necessary to that end. And if it is patented in the joint names, the employee holds his interest as trustee for the employer. If this is, as I think it clearly is, the law, it can only be excluded by an express agreement that it shall be varied and some other legal relationship created."

96 *Where relations confidential*

It may be that the relations between master and servant are of such a close and confidential character that it would be contrary to the resulting implied contractual relationship to allow the servant to retain the benefit of a patent granted to him.

97 In *Worthington Pumping Engine Co.* v. *Moore*[56] the plaintiffs employed the defendant as their agent and manager in England, and communications constantly passed between them as to improvements and alterations in the machines sold to suit the English market. The defendant was employed at a high rate of remuneration and a commission. There was no express stipulation as to inventions or original suggestions which might be made by the defendant. The defendant took out three patents for inventions which he employed in the business of the plaintiffs. He was subsequently dismissed and sought to restrain the plaintiffs from using the patented inventions. The action was for a declaration that the defendant should be declared a trustee of the patents on behalf of the plaintiffs. Byrne J. said[57]: " I desire to say that I recognise and quite appreciate the principle of those cases which have established that the mere existence of a contract of service does not *per se* disqualify a servant from taking

[55] 72 R.P.C. 50 at p. 56.
[56] 20 R.P.C. 41.
[57] 20 R.P.C. 41 at p. 48.

out a patent for an invention made by him during his term of service, even though the invention may relate to subject-matter germane to and useful to his employers in their business, and that, even though the servant may have made use of his employers' time and servants and materials in bringing his invention to completion, and may have allowed his employers to use the invention while in their employment; but, on the other hand, without repeating what has been so fully and admirably expressed by the Court of Appeal in the two cases of *Lamb* v. *Evans*[58] and *Robb* v. *Green*,[59] it is clear that all the circumstances must be considered in each case. I consider that, bearing in mind the principles laid down in the authorities to which I have referred, it is impossible to say in the present case that the defendant has established the right he claims, having regard to the obligations to be implied arising from his contract of service, and . . . I should be wrong in holding that he is entitled to continue to hold his patents as against the plaintiff."

98   When a workman is employed to solve a particular problem it is practically impossible for him successfully to contend that the solution and any patent in respect of it belongs to him and not to his employers. In *Adamson* v. *Kenworthy*,[60] Farwell J. said, in a passage often subsequently quoted with approval[61]: " I desire to guard myself against suggesting that every invention which is made by a person, even though he is a draughtsman in an office in an engineering firm, necessarily belongs to the firm. . . . I can well conceive that such a person might make an invention in respect of something which is outside his work altogether, having nothing to do with the work upon which his employers are engaged, in which case such an invention would be the draughtsman's own property. But, in my judgment, if a draughtsman is instructed by his employer to prepare a design for the purpose of solving a particular difficulty or problem, it is his business and his duty to do the best he can to produce the best design, using all the abilities which he may have, and if he does produce a design which solves the problem, as a result of the instructions that he has been given by his employer, then prima facie at any rate the design and the invention are the property of the employer and not of the employee."

99 *Enforcement of servant's obligations*

In order to enforce a servant's contractual obligations relating to any invention made by him a mandatory injunction may be granted,[62]

---

[58] [1893] 1 Ch. 218.   [59] [1895] 2 Q.B. 315.
[60] 49 R.P.C. 57.
[61] 49 R.P.C. 57 at p. 68.
[62] *Amplaudio Ltd.* v. *Snell*, 55 R.P.C. 237.

or the master may be permitted to apply for a patent in the servant's name.[63] Proceedings to determine the rights as between master and servant may be instituted before the Comptroller.[64]

Similarly, on the basis of express or implied contract, a servant may be sued for damages and an injunction to restrain him from publishing or making any use of secrets learned while in the service of the employer.[65]

Where an employee resisted a claim for assignment to the employer of an application for a patent on the ground that the employer had used the invention prior to the date of application for the patent, this plea was ordered to be struck out.[66]

100 *Apportionment of invention*

A serious objection to the old law was that an invention made by a servant and any patent granted in respect of it belonged wholly either to the master or to the servant and there were many instances where natural justice seemed to demand some apportionment of the rights between them. For example, if a works manager in charge of a process requiring to be operated under closely controlled conditions of temperature and humidity of his own initiative invented a new type of air-conditioning plant applicable not only to that factory but to any factory, restaurant or cinema, it would be manifestly unjust if his employers not only had free use of the invention for their own purposes, but could also collect royalties from all other users of the patented apparatus in fields wholly unrelated to their business, while the inventor got nothing. On the other hand the invention clearly would not belong exclusively to the servant, having regard to the principles laid down in, *e.g. Worthington Pumping Engine Co.* v. *Moore.*[67]

101   This difficulty has been sought to be removed by the present Act,[68] which empowers the Comptroller on application being made to him, or the High Court in proceedings before it between employer and employee, to apportion between the parties the benefit of the invention and of any patent unless satisfied that one of them is entitled to the whole. But these provisions of the Act may be

[63] *Forte* v. *Martinez,* 64 R.P.C. 26.
[64] s. 56 (1). *Loewy Engineering Co. Ltd.'s Appn.,* 69 R.P.C. 3; *Charles Sely Ltd.'s Appn.,* 71 R.P.C. 158.
[65] *Amber Size and Chemical Co. Ltd.* v. *Menzel,* 30 R.P.C. 433; *Alperton Rubber Co.* v. *Manning,* 116 L.T. 499; *Rex Co. and Rex Research Corp.* v. *Muirhead and Comptroller-General,* 44 R.P.C. 38; and see *United Indigo, etc., Ltd.* v. *Robinson,* 49 R.P.C. 178; *British Industrial Plastics Ltd.* v. *Ferguson and Doherty,* 58 R.P.C. 1.
[66] *Barrington Products (Leicester) Ltd.* v. *King* [1958] R.P.C. 212.
[67] 20 R.P.C. 41.
[68] s. 56 (2).

narrower in their effect than was as first assumed.[69] The procedure for making an application to the Comptroller for this purpose is simple,[70] but the Comptroller may decline to deal with the dispute if it appears to him that questions arise which would more properly be determined by the court.[71] It is submitted that if there were serious controversy as to the facts, other than matters of a technical character, or a difficult question of construction of the terms of a service agreement, it would be right for the Comptroller not to deal with the case but to leave the parties to take appropriate proceedings in the High Court, which could be initiated by either party. Both parties would no doubt ask for an order that the benefit of the invention and patent be apportioned in the manner specified in their pleadings.

A decision of the Comptroller has the same effect between the parties as a decision of the court.[72] An appeal lies from the Comptroller's decision to the Appeal Tribunal.[73]

102   Publication in fraud

An invention claimed in a complete specification is not anticipated by publication before the priority date of the claim [74] if the patentee or applicant proves (i) that the matter published was obtained from him or (where he is not himself the true and first inventor) from any person from whom he derives title; (ii) that the publication was made without his consent or the consent of any such person; and (iii) that where the patentee, or applicant, or any person from whom title is derived, learned of the publication before the date of the application, the application was made as soon as reasonably practicable thereafter.[75] These provisions apply equally to an application made originally in this country and to a convention application. But in order to obtain this protection (iv) the invention must not have been commercially worked before the priority date [76] in the United Kingdom, otherwise than for the purpose of reasonable trial,[77] either by, or with the consent of, the patentee or applicant or any person from whom he derives title.[77] Furthermore, an invention claimed in a complete specification is not anticipated by reason only of a prior

---

[69] See *Patchett* v. *Sterling Engineering Co. Ltd.*, 72 R.P.C. 50; Sir Kenneth Swan, Q.C., " Patent rights in an employee's invention," 75 L.Q.R. 77.
[70] See Patents Rules 1968, r. 118.
[71] Proviso to s. 56 (1).
[72] s. 56 (3).
[73] s. 56 (4). See *post*, § 457. As regards proceedings in Scotland, see s. 86.
[74] s. 5, and see *post*, § 165.
[75] s. 50 (2).
[76] See *post*, § 274 *et seq.*
[77] Proviso to s. 50 (2).

application for a patent for the same invention made in contravention of the rights of the subsequent applicant, or by any user or publication of the invention by such prior applicant, or by any other person in consequence of any disclosure of the invention by that prior applicant, made subsequent to the date of filing of the prior (wrongful) application and without the consent of the subsequent (rightful) applicant.[78]

103　　It will be observed that the protection given by the Act to the rightful patentee or applicant is concerned with two different cases, *viz.* (a) prior wrongful publication, irrespective of any application for a patent, and (b) prior wrongful patenting.

As necessary ancillary protection in case (b), it is provided that the claim shall not be anticipated by any publication made subsequent to the prior wrongful application, for after an application has been filed it is quite usual for the applicant freely to disclose the invention, as he is fully entitled so to do without any loss of rights. Furthermore, an application for a patent by the rightful applicant can be ante-dated to the date of the wrongful application.[79] So far as case (b) is concerned, the protection given to the rightful applicant is adequate, for provided he is the true and first inventor, or derives a valid title from him, any other application must be " in contravention of (his) rights " and it is only *his* consent that can defeat the protection afforded against any prior publication made subsequent to the wrongful prior application.

104　　But the protection given in respect of case (a), if the provisions of the Act are to be literally construed, would seem in one respect to be inadequate. Under the old law relief in respect of the " obtaining " (*i.e.* stealing) of an invention could be claimed only by the true and first inventor,[80] and this was logical enough as the true and first inventor was a necessary party to the application for a patent. But now that the right to apply can be freely assigned, the person who requires protection is the applicant, who may have acquired that right by payment of a substantial lump sum to the inventor. The latter may have made a prior disclosure of the invention in confidence to some other person, *e.g.* a previous prospective purchaser. The requirement that the patentee or applicant must prove (i) that the matter published was obtained from some person from whom he derives title, obviously does not detract from the protection. Nor, it is submitted does requirement (ii) that the publication was made without the consent of any such person, or requirement (iv) that there

---

[78] s. 50 (3). See *Dickinson's Appn.*, 44 R.P.C. 79.
[79] s. 53.
[80] Patents and Designs Act 1907, ss. 15 and 41.

has been no commercial working, for it must be an implied term of any assignment of the right to apply for a patent that the assignor has not already done or suffered anything, and will thereafter do nothing, to defeat that right. But as to requirement (iii),[81] suppose that the inventor, after having sold the invention, including the right to apply for a patent, learns that the person to whom he previously disclosed it is now using it on a commercial scale without obtaining, or even asking for, the consent of anyone. Since the inventor can get no benefit from passing on this information he may say and do nothing, and if his assignee, in ignorance of this user, delays making the application, e.g. because he is experimenting with the invention in order to perfect its use for some special purpose, the assignee's patent rights will, on a literal interpretation, be lost altogether, for the application will not have been made " as soon as reasonably practicable " after a " person from whom he derives title (i.e. the inventor) learned of the publication."

105   It is no answer to this difficulty to say that there is no hardship because a person in possession of an invention, if he desires patent protection for it, should in any event apply without delay. As the times for filing a detailed description (the complete specification) and putting the application in order for acceptance [82] are strictly limited, it is undesirable to make an application until the invention has been developed at any rate well beyond the stage of being merely a somewhat vague idea. On the other hand it would obviously have been wrong for the legislature to have permitted a person who had the right to apply for a patent to stand by while another person to whom the invention had been disclosed spent substantial sums in good faith in setting up a plant to operate the invention (e.g. in the belief that no question of confidence was involved) and thereafter to take out a patent to prevent that operation. It is submitted that the true construction of section 50 (2) (b) [83] avoids both these injustices and that the subsection means that protection against prior publication is lost if a person who for the time being is entitled to apply for a patent learns of the publication and yet no application is made as soon as reasonably practicable thereafter. The words " where . . . any person from whom he (the patentee or applicant) derives title learned of the publication . . ." should accordingly be construed as though they were " where any person from whom he derives title learned, *while possessed of such title*, of the publication. . . ."

[81] *Ante,* § 102.
[82] See *post,* § 123.
[83] *Post,* § 1188.

106 False claim to be inventor

An action against a defendant who has falsely represented that he is the true and first inventor would appear to be in the nature of an action for slander of title, and the plaintiff, in order to succeed, would have to prove malice and also special damage.[84] It is doubtful whether relief in the nature of a declaration that the plaintiff is the true inventor can be granted; in any case, such a declaration would not be made by the court in the absence of the Attorney-General, as it is a declaration affecting the rights of the Crown.[85]

2. PROCEDURE ON APPLICATION

107 The practice is regulated by the Patents Rules 1968, which came into force in November 1968 [86] as amended.

The Rules provide forms applicable to most circumstances. The Comptroller has power to modify these forms to meet particular cases [87] ; but he can only do so in order to use them for purposes similar to those for which they were primarily intended.[88]

Form 1 is a comprehensive form to be used in all cases except convention applications. Parts of the form inappropriate to a particular application should be deleted. Convention applications must be made on Form 1 Con [89] which is a comprehensive form for all convention applications, and parts inappropriate to any particular case should be deleted. Applications for the grant of a patent of addition [90] in lieu of an existing independent patent are made on Form 1 Add.

108 Convention application

The election to take the benefit of the procedure under the International Convention [91] must be taken before the expiry of the twelve months from the date of the first foreign application, and the applicant must specify that date which must be ascertained by reference to the law of the foreign country in question [92] and state that no application

---

[84] See *Killen* v. *MacMillan*, 48 R.P.C. 380; 49 R.P.C. 258; *cf. Wilde* v. *Thompson*, 20 R.P.C. 775 (C.A.).
[85] *Killen* v. *MacMillan*, 49 R.P.C. 258 at p. 261.
[86] S.I. 1968 No. 1389. See *post*, § 1349.
[87] r. 4.
[88] *Salles' Appn.*, 45 R.P.C. 61.
[89] See *Acetylene Illuminating Co.* v. *United Alkali Co.*, 19 R.P.C. 213; 20 R.P.C. 161.
[90] See *post*, § 132.
[91] See *post*, § 111 and *Gerhard Dirk's Appn.* [1960] R.P.C. 1.
[92] *Whitin Machine Works' Appn.*, 54 R.P.C. 278; *Monsanto Chemical Co.'s Appn.* [1964] R.P.C. 6.

for protection in respect of the invention has been made in a convention country before that date by the applicant or any person from whom he derives title.[93] The ultimate fate of the foreign application itself is irrelevant.[94] The claims of a convention application are a disclosure in the foreign application.[95]

109 Provisional or complete specification

Every non-convention application must be accompanied by either a provisional specification or a complete specification.[96] Every convention application must be accompanied by a complete specification.[96] A document consisting merely of a cross-reference to the convention document and claiming what is described and claimed therein is not a complete specification.[97] If the application is accompanied by a provisional specification a complete specification must be filed within twelve months (with a permissible extension of a further three months); otherwise the application is deemed to be abandoned.[98]

110 *Postdating*

Providing that the complete specification has been duly filed within fifteen months from the date of filing of the application,[99] an application can be made within such fifteen-month period [1] that the application for a patent be postdated up to six months (in the case of a convention application the period must also not exceed twelve months from the date of the foreign application) at the request of the applicant [2] who thereby gets more time for filing a complete specification or putting his application in order, but at the risk of having his patent wholly or partially invalidated by some disclosure or application made meanwhile. If the application or specification is amended the Comptroller may require postdating to the date of the amendment.[3] A complete specification accompanying an application may subsequently at the request of the applicant be treated as a provisional,[4] but in that case a new complete specification must be

---

[93] s. 2 (4). See *Kromschroeder's Patent* [1960] R.P.C. 75.
[94] *Comptroller's Ruling (A)*, 29 R.P.C. (i); *Electric and Musical Industries Ltd.*
v. *Lissen Ltd.*, 56 R.P.C. at p. 48.
[95] s. 5 (4), and see *post*, § 171 *et seq.* and § 437.
[96] s. 3 (1), *V.'s Appn.*, 56 R.P.C. 160. For the nature of a provisional specification, see *post*, § 163, and of a complete specification, *post*, § 177.
[97] *Ternescal Metallurgical Corpn.'s Appn.* [1964] R.P.C. 1.
[98] s. 3 (2).
[99] 1907 Act, s. 5; 1949 Act, Sched. III, para 3.
[1] *Parker's Appn.* [1962] R.P.C. 126.   [2] s. 6 (3).
[3] s. 6 (4). *Marrick Manufacturing Co. Ltd.'s Appn.* [1967] R.P.C. 606.
[4] s. 3 (4).

filed at latest within fifteen months of the application, which otherwise is deemed to be abandoned. It follows that the request to treat the original complete specification as a provisional must be made within that period.

111 *Convention documents*

In addition to the complete specification filed with every convention application there must be filed with the application, or within three months thereafter, a copy of the specification and drawings or documents filed in respect of the relevant application for protection in the convention country (or of each such application if the application in this country is based on more than one such foreign application), duly certified by the official chief or head of the Patent Office of the convention country, or otherwise verified to the satisfaction of the Comptroller.[5] In the case of a document in a foreign language, a translation verified by a statutory declaration is required.[5] Failure to comply substantially with the rules entails loss of the foreign date.[6]

112 *Cognate inventions*

Where two or more applications accompanied by provisional specifications have been filed in respect of inventions which are " cognate " or of which one is a " modification " of another, a single complete specification may be filed, or, if more than one complete specification has been filed, one only may, with the leave of the Comptroller, be proceeded with covering the subject-matter of all the provisional specifications.[7] Similarly, if applications for protection have been made in one or more convention countries in respect of two or more inventions similarly related, a single convention application may be filed within twelve months of the earliest of the foreign applications in respect of all those inventions.[8] If, however, separate convention applications are originally filed, they cannot, after the period of twelve months, be cognated by amendment.[9]   In either case if the Comptroller is of opinion that the inventions are not " cognate " or " modifications " one of another he may require either that all matter in excess of a single invention be deleted, or that the complete specification be divided into such number of complete specifications as may be necessary so that the application proceeds as a number of separate applications for single inventions.

---

[5] r. 15, Patents Rules 1968.
[6] *Salles' Appn.*, 45 R.P.C. 61.   *Sylvania Electric Products Inc.'s Appn.* [1970] R.P.C. 221.
[7] s. 3 (3).
[8] s. 2 (5).
[9] *Radio Corporation of America's Appn.*, 56 R.P.C. 157.

In the case of a convention application the separate convention applications may be treated as all having been filed on the original date of application.[10] Under the previous law it was a necessary condition for " cognating " that the same person should be the foreign applicant in each case [11] but the language of the present Act is wide enough to permit a single convention application even where the foreign applicants are different.[8]

Under the previous law a single complete specification could be filed in respect of such parts of two or more foreign applications as constituted a single invention.[12] The language of the present Act is less explicit but, it is submitted, the law in effect remains the same.

113 *Complete specification for single invention*

The claims of a complete specification must relate only to a " single " invention.[13] If objection is taken by the Comptroller to the complete specification on the ground that it claims more than one invention, so that the applicant is forced to amend by excising all but one, he may, nevertheless, secure protection for all the inventions by making a fresh application or applications in respect of the excised inventions and these applications may be ante-dated to a date not earlier than the date of the original application if the applicant so requests.[14] The words " not earlier than " set a limit to the relevant date; but will be read subject to the provisions of section 6 (3).[15] However the filing of a divisional application cannot be made after acceptance.[16]

These provisions apply both to non-convention and convention applications.

114 *What is a single invention*

Two or more inventions which are " cognate " or of which " one is a modification of another " may be properly regarded as a " single " invention. No definition can be given as to what constitutes a single invention. But it is submitted that if a novel general principle is disclosed, any machine or process which embodies that general principle can be regarded as an embodiment of a single invention, notwithstanding that there may also be disclosed additional optional details or non-fundamental variants which are claimed in subsidiary claims. But the mere fact that all the new disclosures relate to the

---

10 rr. 14 and 16, Patents Rules 1968.
11 *Standard Telephones and Cables Co.'s Appn.*, 52 R.P.C. 415.
12 1907 Act, s. 91 (2) as amended by Patents, etc., International Conventions Act 1938.
13 s. 4 (4) and *Mobil Oil Corporation's Appn.* [1969] R.P.C. 586.
14 s. 6 (5) and r. 13, Patents Rules 1968.
15 *Shotz's Appn.* [1968] R.P.C. 210.
16 *Mobil Oil Corporation's Appn., supra.*

same machine or process, which is not itself the invention claimed in that specification, does not make all such disclosures one invention.[17] Claims to intermediate and final chemical products do not necessarily relate to a single invention.[18] A patent, once granted, cannot afterwards be impugned on the ground that it was granted for more than one invention.[19]

115 Applicant may act by agent

The applicant must himself sign the application and certain other documents,[20] but for many matters he may employ an agent. Such an agent need not be a " patent agent,"[21] but he must be an agent duly authorised to the satisfaction of the Comptroller, who may refuse to recognise certain persons, for reasons related to their conduct or status, as agents.[22] A patent agent must be registered.[23]

116 Substitution and disputes

If the Comptroller is satisfied that by virtue of an assignment or agreement, or by operation of law, a claimant would be entitled to an interest in a patent when granted, he may direct that the application shall proceed in such names as the case may require.[24] If any dispute arises between joint applicants the Comptroller, after giving all parties an opportunity of being heard, may give such directions as he thinks fit.[25]

A notice, application or other document may be sent to the Patent Office by post,[26] and is deemed to have been given, made or filed at the time when the letter containing the same would be delivered in the ordinary course of post.[27]

117 Reference to examiner

When the complete specification has been filed the application and the complete specification (and the provisional specification if there be one) are referred to an examiner of the Patent Office.[28] If the examiner reports that the application or any specification does not

---

[17] *J.'s Appn.*, 42 R.P.C. 1; *Z.'s Appn.*, 27 R.P.C. 285. See also *Jones' Patent*, Griff.P.C. 285; *Robinson's Patent*, Griff.P.C. 267.
[18] *Celanese Corporation of America's Appn.*, 69 R.P.C. 227.
[19] s. 21 (4).
[20] r. 8, Patents Rules 1968.
[21] *Graham* v. *Fanta*, 9 R.P.C. 164, s. 101 (1).
[22] s. 89; r. 8 (3).
[23] s. 88. *Thompson* v. *Benton*, 49 R.P.C. 33, 400; *Thompson* v. *Brown*, 50 R.P.C. 389.
[24] s. 17 (1).
[25] s. 17 (5).
[26] s. 97.
[27] r. 6, Patents Rules 1968.
[28] s. 6 (1).

comply with the requirements of the Act, or of the Rules, or that there is some lawful ground of objection to the grant of a patent, the Comptroller may refuse to proceed with the application or may require it, or any specification, to be amended before proceeding.[29] The examiner investigates the novelty of the invention claimed[30] and whether it has been previously claimed.[31] The examiner's report is not binding on the Comptroller but is only to assist him.[32]

118 *Reports of examiners*

The examiner's investigations and reports under sections 7 and 8 are not open to public inspection or published, except pursuant to an order of the court in legal proceedings.[32] But after the complete specification has been published the result of any search made under these sections may be disclosed to any person who applies in the prescribed manner.[33] There is no power to amend an examiner's report, even though certain specifications may have been cited by mistake.[34] The examination and investigations required by the Act are not in any way a guarantee of validity and no liability can be incurred by the Department of Trade and Industry or any of its officers in connection with any such examination or investigation or any report or other proceedings consequent thereon.[35]

119 Powers of Comptroller

If the Comptroller is not satisfied as to novelty, he may refuse to accept the complete specification unless it is amended to his satisfaction.[36] If the Comptroller is of opinion that the invention is the subject of a prior claim of another specification which was not published at the relevant date,[37] he may direct a reference to that other specification, irrespective of its alleged invalidity, unless the applicant's specification is amended to his satisfaction,[38] but the

---

[29] s. 6 (2). See *Rex Co. and Another* v. *Muirhead and Comptroller-General*, 44 R.P.C. 38; *Sevag's Appn.*, 55 R.P.C. 193 at p. 195.

[30] s. 7.

[31] s. 8. See *Dreyfus's Appn.*, 44 R.P.C. 291; *Mathieson Alkali Works' Appn.*, 58 R.P.C. 118; *Clinical Products Ltd.'s Patent* [1963] R.P.C. 271; *Willey's Carbide Tool Co.'s Appn.* [1969] R.P.C. 33.

[32] *C.'s Appn.*, 7 R.P.C. 250.

[33] s. 79 (2); r. 32.

[34] *T.'s Appn.*, 42 R.P.C. 505.

[35] s. 11 (3).

[36] s. 7 (3).

[37] See *post*, § 165.

[38] s. 8 (2) (3). *Bowen's Appn.*, 72 R.P.C. 327; and see *General Electric Co. Ltd.'s Patent* [1959] R.P.C. 109 and *I.C.I. Ltd.'s Appn.* [1959] R.P.C. 103 and 115 for a review of the practice.

reference is not inserted unless and until the earlier patent is granted.[39]

120   The procedure prescribed is eminently fair to the applicant.[41] If the examiner reports that either of the above objections exists, the applicant is informed and given an opportunity of amending his specification. If he fails to submit satisfactory amendments a hearing is appointed [42] which the applicant may attend or not as he chooses, and thereafter the Comptroller prescribes such amendments as will remove the objection, if such are possible, and if these are not accepted the application may in the former case be refused and in the latter have a specific reference inserted to the earlier patent. In the case of prior claiming the complete specification may be accepted before the objection is removed and further time given to the applicant to deal with it. The Comptroller has similar powers of refusal in case of anticipation [43] and of inserting a specific reference after acceptance of the complete specification, and in the latter case even after grant.[44]

121   If it appears to the Comptroller that the use of the invention will be likely to infringe another patent he may at any time direct a specific reference to that other patent to be inserted in the complete specification as a warning to the public unless the applicant shows that there are reasonable grounds for contesting the validity of that other patent.[45] If that other patent is revoked or lapses, the reference may be deleted.[46]

In *Minister of Supply's Appn.*[47] it was held that reasonable grounds for contesting the validity of a patent were such that had " sufficient substance to call for argument and response." However, as stated by Whitford J., " this test must be applied with caution, because it cannot be enough for an applicant merely to produce an argument which gets an opponent to his feet. If having heard both sides the Tribunal considering the matter is able to form a clear view that the attack has little or no substance, then a specific reference should be ordered." [48]

[39] s. 8 (4).
[41] rr. 27–31.
[42] s. 81.
[43] s. 15.
[44] s. 11.
[45] s. 9 (1). *Studdert's Appn.*, 69 R.P.C. 338; *Ministry of Supply's Appn.*, 70 R.P.C. 219.
[46] s. 9 (2); r. 35.
[47] 72 R.P.C. 329 at p. 332.
[48] *Eastman Kodak Co.'s Appn.* [1970] F.S.R. 393 at p. 399.

The Comptroller may refuse the application if the invention claimed is contrary to well-established natural laws (*e.g.* for a mechanical perpetual motion machine) or if its use would be contrary to law or morality,[49] or be such, as, *e.g.* contraceptives, that the grant would be refused under the Royal Prerogative.[50]   And a mere mixture of ingredients for use as food or medicine cannot be patented.[49]   If an invention is capable of being used in an illegal manner, the Comptroller may require such use to be disclaimed.[51]

122 Appeal

An appeal from the Comptroller's decision in all these matters lies to the Appeal Tribunal,[52] including a decision based on some ground of objection not expressly mentioned in the parts of the Act discussed above.[53]

123 Time for putting application in order

Unless the applicant has complied with all the requirements imposed on him by the Act, including putting his complete specification into order for acceptance, within two years and six months from the date of filing of the complete specification (with a permissible extension of a further three months) the application becomes void, unless an appeal has been lodged in respect of it, or unless the time for appealing has not expired.[54]

124 *How time reckoned*

The months allowed are calendar months,[55] and are reckoned exclusive of the day of the application.[56]   In the event of the last day for doing any act falling on an " excluded " day, *i.e.* one on which the office is not open for purposes of the transaction by the public of business under the Act, *e.g.* a Saturday, such act may be done on

---

[49] s. 10 (1).   See *Pessers and Moody* v. *Haydon & Co.*, 26 R.P.C. 58; *Comptroller's Ruling C*, 40 R.P.C. Appendix.

[50] *A. & H.'s Appn.*, 44 R.P.C. 298; *Riddlesbarger's Appn.*, 53 R.P.C. 57 and see s. 102 (1).

[51] s. 10 (2).   See *Carpmael's Appn.*, 45 R.P.C. 411.

[52] s. 85, and see *post,* § 457.

[53] *Arnold and I.C.I. Ltd.'s Appn.*, 59 R.P.C. 76.

[54] s. 12; Patents Act 1957, s. 1; Patents Rules 1968, r. 37 (1).   See *Pensalt Chemicals Corp.'s Appn.* [1968] R.P.C. 27 and *Eickmann's Appn.* [1968] R.P.C. 112.

[55] 52 & 53 Vict. c. 63, s. 3.

[56] *Russell* v. *Ledsam*, 14 M. & W. 574 at p. 582; *Williams* v. *Nash*, 28 Beav. 93.

the next non-excluded day.[57] Postdating will not increase the time for putting the application in order.[58]

125 Amendment prior to acceptance

It is submitted that the Comptroller has power to allow amendment to a complete specification without postdating provided that new matter is not introduced. This includes widening the scope of the claims. However the claims as sought to be amended must be fairly based on the specification as filed. This power to amend is in the discretion of the Comptroller and will not be readily reversed on appeal.[59]

126 Acceptance

The application may be accepted by the Comptroller as soon as it is in order, and if not accepted within the time allowed for putting it in order shall be accepted as soon as may be thereafter.[60] The applicant may request postponement of acceptance up to twelve months from the date of filing of the complete specification without a fee, or up to fifteen months with a fee.[61] This is sometimes advantageous if foreign applications are being filed, based on the British application, or if it is desired to postpone publication of the complete specification for some commercial reason. On acceptance the Comptroller must give notice to the applicant and advertise, in the *Official Journal* (*Patents*), the fact of acceptance and the date on which the application and the specification or specifications will be open to public inspection.[62] Until that date neither the application nor any specification filed in pursuance of it is published by the Comptroller or is open to public inspection.[63]

127 Abandoned applications

In the event of an application being abandoned or becoming void, the application, specifications, drawings, specimens and samples which were left in connection with the application are not published, nor are they at any time open to public inspection,[65] except by order of the court.[66]

---

[57] s. 98 and rr. 147, 148.
[58] Patents Rules 1968, r. 37.
[59] *Shionogi & Co. Ltd.'s Appn.* [1967] R.P.C. 623.
[60] s. 13 (1).
[61] Proviso to s. 13 (1).
[62] s. 13 (2).
[63] s. 79 (1).
[65] s. 79.
[66] See, *e.g., Pneumatic Tyre Co.* v. *English Cycle, etc., Co. Ltd.*, 14 R.P.C. 851.

128   Grant and sealing of patent

If there is no opposition,[67] or the opposition is determined in favour of the grant being made, the patent is granted to the applicant or joint applicants and sealed with the seal of the Patent Office on payment of the prescribed fee.[68] If one of the joint applicants has died, the grant may be made to the survivor, if the personal representative of the deceased consents.[69]

129   A request for the patent to be sealed must be made not later than four months after the date of publication of the complete specification.[70] Special provisions, however, exist for sealing in the following cases [71] : (i) If any proceeding in relation to the application is pending [72] in any court or before the Comptroller or the Appeal Tribunal an extension of two months from the final determination of the proceedings is allowed. (ii) If the applicant or one of the applicants dies within the time within which sealing ought otherwise to be effected, the sealing may take place at any time within twelve months of the death, or at such later time as the Comptroller directs. (iii) Where hardship would be caused to an applicant in connection with a foreign application if the sealing took place at the prescribed time, the Comptroller may, upon payment of the prescribed fee, extend the time for sealing to the extent necessary to avoid hardship in the circumstances. (iv) If for any reason the patent cannot be sealed within the time allowed, an extension of three months may be obtained on payment of the prescribed fee. Once the seal has been affixed, it cannot be withdrawn.[73] If the failure to make a request within the time allowed by the Act [74] was unintentional, the Comptroller may nevertheless, within six months of the expiration of that time, order the patent to be sealed, subject to prior advertisement, the giving of opportunity for opposition and the protection of any persons who have begun to use the invention.[75]

130   *Dead grantee*

If a grantee has died or ceased to exist before the patent was sealed, the patent may be amended by substituting the name of the person to whom the patent should have been granted.[76]

---

[67] See *post*, Chap. 7.
[68] s. 19.
[69] s. 17 (4).
[70] s. 19 (2).
[71] s. 19 (2) (3) (4) and rr. 59, 60, 61.
[72] s. 19 (5).
[73] *Comptroller's Ruling (A)*, 59 R.P.C. 183.
[74] s. 19.
[75] s. 28.
[76] s. 20.

131 *Date and term*

A patent is dated with the date of filing of the complete specification and, subject to payment of renewal fees, lasts for sixteen years from that date.[77] This date is not the relevant date for purposes of considering novelty or prior claiming, for which the " priority date " is the only material date.[78]

132 *Duplicates*

The Comptroller may at any time seal a duplicate patent if the original one is lost or destroyed, or its non-production is satisfactorily accounted for.[80]

133 **Patents of Addition**

A new kind of patent, *viz.* a " Patent of Addition," was introduced by the Act of 1907 and its value was greatly enhanced by the present Act. If the applicant applies for, or has applied for, or has been granted, a patent for a main invention, he may apply for a patent of addition in respect of an improvement in or modification of the main invention.[81] Similarly, where a person has a patent for a main invention and also an independent patent for an improvement in or modification of the main invention, he may apply to the Comptroller to revoke the second patent and to grant to him a patent of addition for the same subject-matter and bearing the same date as the revoked independent patent.[82]

The term of a patent of addition is the same as that of the patent for the main invention. No renewal fees are payable in respect of a patent of addition.

134 *Requirements for patent of addition*

It is always desirable that the main patent should be the widest in scope, for in most, if not all, cases any additional detail could be regarded as an " improvement in or modification of " an invention covering broadly a general principle of construction or operation, but the converse would not necessarily be true. Furthermore, other patents of addition based on the same wide patent as the main patent could subsequently be obtained for different detail improvements: provided that they relate to improvements in or modifications of the main invention.[83] This might not be possible if the " patent for

---

[77] s. 22.
[78] See *post*, § 165.
[80] s. 80.
[81] s. 26 (1).
[82] s. 26 (2).
[83] *Elliott Brothers London's Appn.* [1967] R.P.C. 1.

the main invention " was itself limited to details. It not infrequently happens that the broadest aspect of an invention is not thought of until after an application limited to a more detailed embodiment has been made, so that the application for the wider embodiment is subsequent in date. This of itself is no bar to the patent granted on the subsequent application being a main patent and the first application being granted as a patent of addition thereto, but a patent cannot be granted as a patent of addition unless the date of filing of the complete specification is the same as, or later than, the date of filing of the complete specification in respect of the main invention.[84] This requirement is necessarily applicable both to the case where the application has not yet been granted and also where an independent patent is sought to be converted into a patent of addition, for otherwise the term of a patent of addition might be longer than that provided by the Act, viz. sixteen years from the date of filing of the complete specification.[85] In order to effect a conversion it is necessary only to file Form 1 Add.[86] There are no provisions requiring the filing of any further specifications, although some amendment of the complete specification, pursuant to section 29, may be desirable to make the patent suitable for conversion. It follows that in the case of a conversion the date of filing of the complete specification of the original independent patent or application is the relevant date, which must be not earlier than the date of filing of the complete specification in respect of the main invention. After a complete specification has been accepted, nothing can be done to change this date. If, however, the matter is still in the pre-acceptance stage, postdating of the date of filing of the complete specification is possible,[87] notwithstanding that the complete specification may in fact have been already prematurely filed. If there has been no publication of the invention, the original independent application can be abandoned and a fresh application made, enabling the complete specification to be filed at an appropriate later date. If publication has already taken place, so that the application must not be postdated to a date later than such publication, then if the complete specification accompanied the application and not more than fifteen months have elapsed it can be treated as a provisional[88] and an effective complete specification filed at an appropriate later date.[89] If the complete specification was filed pursuant to an application accompanied by

[84] s. 26 (3).
[85] s. 22.
[86] r. 9 (4).
[87] s. 6 (3).
[88] s. 3 (4).
[89] s. 3 (2).

a provisional specification, the latter may be cancelled and the application postdated to the date of filing of the complete specification [90] and then the complete specification may be treated as a provisional [88] and the effective complete specification filed subsequently.

135   It is also provided that the patent of addition shall not be sealed before the sealing of the patent for the main invention.[91] This is obviously necessary, for there must be some independent main patent in respect of which renewal fees are payable. If the application has not yet been sealed, the request for sealing of the patent of addition can (and must) be postponed for the same period as any postponement of the request for sealing of the patent for the main invention.[92] If the patent to be converted into a patent of addition is originally granted and sealed as an independent patent, it does not matter whether the patent for the main invention has already been sealed or not, for no conversion can take place until after the main patent has been granted and sealed, and, when it is, the method of conversion is to revoke the grant of the independent patent for the improvement or modification and thereafter grant a fresh patent (as a patent of addition),[93] which latter has then to be independently sealed so that the sealing must necessarily take place after the sealing of the main patent.

136   *Advantages of patent of addition*

It may be thought that this discussion as to ensuring that a single main patent is the earliest and that all others are patents of addition thereto is out of proportion to the value of a patent of addition when granted, but it is submitted that the change in the status of a patent of addition made by the present Act is perhaps the most beneficial feature it contains from the point of view of the patentee. There is no disadvantage affecting a patent of addition except that it expires at the same date as the main patent.[94] If the main patent is revoked the patent of addition can be converted (or reconverted) into an independent patent,[95] subject to renewal fees being thereafter payable in respect of it as though it had been originally granted as an independent patent.[96] Under the Act of 1907 the only advantage of a patent of addition was that no separate renewal fees were payable in respect of it. This advantage has been retained,[96] but the 1949 Act added the provision that the grant of a patent of addition shall

[90] s. 3 (5).
[91] s. 26 (4).
[92] s. 26 (4).
[93] s. 26 (2).
[94] s. 26 (5).
[95] s. 26 (5), proviso (b).
[96] s. 26 (6).

not be refused and a patent granted as a patent of addition shall not be revoked on the ground only that the invention claimed does not involve any inventive step having regard to the publication or use either of the main invention described in the complete specification relating thereto, or of any improvement in or modification of the main invention described in the complete specification of any previous patent of addition.[97]

137   One of the difficulties that has always confronted a prospective patentee is how to draft his main claim so as on the one hand to limit its scope to avoid the possibility that it will be held invalid because it includes obvious variants of prior disclosures, and on the other hand to frame it widely enough to prevent evasion by alternatives not within its language. Another difficulty, particularly in chemical cases, is how much detailed direction to give as to how to carry the invention into effect. The information must be accurate, or the patent will be invalid for insufficiency,[98] and if a number of alternatives are included, the cost of experimental verification may be prohibitive, while if some alternative is omitted it may turn out to be the really important one. In many cases it is impossible to draft the description and claims of a complete specification satisfactorily until the invention has been put into commercial use, and actual experience shows what features of the invention are essential and what details are unnecessary. But by the time this can be ascertained the complete specification has probably been accepted, or at any rate filed, and the invention has been widely published. It has frequently happened either that an unnecessary limitation has been put into the claims [99] or that some minor detail, which ultimately proves to be essential to success and the necessity for which is quite obvious when the invention is operated on a commercial scale, has been inadvertently omitted from the description in the complete specification. No effective amendment is possible if the application has already been accepted.[1] Even where this has not yet taken place, the introduction of any new matter by amendment may result in the application being postdated to the date of the amendment,[2] which date may be after the public use of the invention, so that the claim would be invalid because of prior user.

The provisions as to patents of addition give a solution of this difficulty. As soon as the defects of the original claim or description are appreciated, whether by the actual operation of the invention or

[97] s. 26 (7).
[98] See *post*, Chap. 5.
[99] See, for example, *Non-Drip Measure Co.* v. *Strangers*, 60 R.P.C. 135.
[1] See *post*, § § 475, 476.
[2] s. 6 (4).

otherwise, an application for a patent of addition can be filed, the complete specification having a narrower or wider claim than that of the main patent, as may be required, and containing any additional information that may be necessary. Such a patent cannot be refused, and is not invalidated, because of any prior publication or use of the main invention described in the complete specification relating thereto. The patent of addition must, of course, be applied for before the necessary modification or improvement is itself published or put into actual commercial use.

138 *Patent of addition must be for novel matter*

The claims of a patent of addition must be for novel matter not disclosed in the specification relating to the main invention.[3] The Comptroller has a discretion to allow or to refuse the conversion of an independent patent into a patent of addition.[4] The fact that the main patent is the subject of litigation in the High Court is not necessarily a bar to the grant of a patent of addition.[4] Where a patent is applied for as a patent of addition, its suitability as such should be determined at the time when the specification is otherwise in order for acceptance.[5]

139 *What is publication of main invention*

The question arises as to what amounts to " publication or use of the main invention described in the complete specification relating thereto." [6] Clearly this includes publication and use by the patentee and all persons deriving title from him. It is submitted that it also includes any publication or use of the invention by a person who acquired his knowledge of the invention directly or indirectly from the publication or use by the patentee or his licensees. But if there is an independent prior disclosure by a stranger of anticipating matter, it might be available as a ground of attack upon the validity of the patent of addition, notwithstanding that it may be included (as a result of simultaneous independent inventing) in the complete specification of the patent for the main invention. However, in *Monsanto Co. (Sayer's) Appn.*,[7] the Patents Appeal Tribunal expressed a contrary view.

140 *Possible conversion of invalid into valid patent*

If the application originally asks that a patent for an improvement or modification shall be granted as a patent of addition, but it subse-

---

[3] *P. and S.'s Appn.*, 69 R.P.C. 249; *Georgia Kaolin Co.'s Appn.* [1956] R.P.C. 121; *Welwyn Electrical Laboratories Ltd's Appn.* [1957] R.P.C. 143.
[4] s. 26 (2); *Van der Lely's Appn.* [1958] R.P.C. 383.
[5] *P. and S.'s Appn.*, 69 R.P.C. 249.
[6] s. 26 (7).
[7] [1969] R.P.C. 75.

quently appears that no patent can be granted for the main invention, *e.g.* because it has been anticipated, it is submitted that the request for the grant to be in the form of a patent of addition can be withdrawn and the patent granted as an independent patent. But in that case any prior publication or use of the main invention could be used to invalidate the patent. But an actual patent of addition is not invalidated by any publication or use of the main invention, notwithstanding that the patent for the latter may be revoked and the patent of addition made into an independent patent, for the protection is afforded to " a patent *granted* as a patent of addition," [8] and such a patent can, by order of the court or Comptroller, " *become* an independent patent," so that it does not lose its identity. It follows that if an independent patent for an improvement of another patent owned by the same patentee is invalid for the sole reason that it does not disclose any inventive step over the prior disclosure of that earlier patent, such an invalid independent patent can be revoked at the request of the patentee, and there may be substituted for it a patent of addition. This is unaffected by such prior disclosure and is therefore valid. Revocation of the earlier patent may result in the patent of addition becoming an independent patent. But it remains unaffected by the prior disclosure and continues to be valid.

141 Where the specification filed on an application for a patent of addition referred to two earlier patents as well as to the principal patent, and the improvement related to the processes of all three patents, a patent of addition was refused.[10] Where, however, a patent of addition had been granted, a second patent of addition was granted in respect of an improvement upon the original invention as improved by the subject-matter of the first patent of addition.[11]

142 Secret patents

Where application is made for a patent in respect of an invention of a class that has been notified to the Comptroller by the Secretary of State as relevant for defence purposes, the Comptroller may give directions for keeping secret any information concerning the invention.[12] The application may proceed up to acceptance of the complete specification but the acceptance is not advertised or the patent granted.[12] The position must be reviewed within the first nine months from the application and thereafter at least once a year.[13] If secrecy is waived the Comptroller may extend the time for doing anything

---

[8] s. 26 (7).
[10] *H. S. J.'s Appn.*, 31 R.P.C. 47.
[11] *McFeely's Appn.*, 29 R.P.C. 386.
[12] s. 18 (1) as amended by S.I. 1971 No. 719.   [13] s. 18 (2).

required in connection with the application.[13]   If any use of a secret invention is made by a government department after acceptance of the complete specification, or if the applicant suffers hardship by reason of the secrecy, compensation may be claimed.[14]   No renewal fees are payable during the period of secrecy.[15]

143   Restriction on application for foreign patents

No resident of the United Kingdom may apply for a foreign patent (except by written authority of the Comptroller) unless he has applied at least six weeks earlier for a patent for the same invention in the United Kingdom and no directions as to secrecy have been given, or are subsisting, in relation to that application.[16] Restrictions are also imposed by the Atomic Energy Act 1946 on application for patents relating to the production or use of atomic energy.[17]

Failure to comply with the above provisions is a criminal offence punishable by fine and imprisonment.[18]

3. RIGHTS ON APPLICATION AND PUBLICATION OF COMPLETE
SPECIFICATION

144   Provisional protection

After a provisional specification has been filed, or a complete specification which is subsequently treated as a provisional,[21] the use or publication of any matter described in any such specification cannot result in the refusal, revocation or invalidity of the patent.[22] Similarly, in the case of a convention application (which is necessarily accompanied by a complete specification [23]) the use or publication of any matter disclosed in the foreign application cannot have any such result.   In both cases the " priority date," *i.e.* the relevant date for the purpose of considering anticipation, may be the date of filing the provisional specification or the foreign application.[24] Accordingly, in general, the applicant, after complying with the minimum of formalities, has a limited period within which he can freely disclose his invention, *e.g.* for the purpose of obtaining financial assistance,

---

[14] s. 18 (3).
[15] s. 18 (4).
[16] s. 18 (5).
[17] *Post*, § 1730 *et seq.*   [18] s. 18 (6).
[21] s. 3 (4).   [22] s. 52 (1).
[23] s. 3 (1).   [24] s. 5, and see *post*, § 165.

without deleteriously affecting the monopoly rights he will ultimately get after complying with the much more stringent requirements that are necessary in order to get his application accepted and his patent granted.

145 Rights on publication of complete specification

After the date of publication of the complete specification [25] the applicant has the same privileges and rights as if a patent had been sealed on that date except that he cannot institute proceedings for infringement until the patent has in fact been sealed,[26] and no proceedings can be taken in respect of an infringement committed before the date of publication of the complete specification.[27]

4. LAPSED PATENTS

146 Lapsed patents

A patent which has been unintentionally allowed to lapse may be restored within three years under certain conditions specified in the Act and Rules.[28]

5. MARKING

147 Marking article " patented "

If any person falsely represents that any article sold by him is a patented article, he is liable on summary conviction to a fine not exceeding fifty pounds. To sell an article having stamped, engraved, or impressed thereon or otherwise applied thereto the word " patent," or " patented," or any other word expressing or implying that the article is patented is deemed to represent that the article is a patented article.[29]

Application for provisional protection does not entitle the applicant to sell his article marked " patent," [30] although he may properly use the words " patent applied for."

[25] s. 13 (2) (3).
[26] s. 13 (4).
[27] s. 22 (1).
[28] s. 27 and Patents Rules 1968, rr. 78 to 83. See *Brown's Patent*, 53 R.P.C. 394; *Shepherd's Patent*, 64 R.P.C. 1; *A/B Astra* v. *Pharmaceutical Manufacturing Co.* [1957] R.P.C. 16; *Salopian Engineers Ltd.'s Appn.* [1957] R.P.C. 351; *Spheric Structures Inc.'s Patent* [1958] R.P.C. 283; *Processed Surfaces Inc.'s Patent* [1958] R.P.C. 480; *Witton Engineering Co. Ltd.'s Patent* [1959] R.P.C. 53.
[29] s. 91, Criminal Justice Act 1967, s. 92 (1).
[30] See *R.* v. *Wallis*, 3 R.P.C. 1, and *R.* v. *Crampton*, 3 R.P.C. 367.

In order to constitute a defence to a prosecution under the section, the claims of the patent relied upon must, on a proper construction, cover the article which has been sold as " patented." [31]

It is no offence, however, to describe an article as " patented " after the complete specification has been published but before the patent is sealed.[32]

The fact that the article has at one time been the subject of a patent will not entitle the patentee to mark it as " patented " if the patent has expired, as the word implies that there is an existing patent.[33]

148   Marking article " licensed "

In a case where a licence had been revoked and the former licensees were sued for infringement, the words " manufactured under licence from the P. C. Co." were, upon a motion for an interlocutory injunction, ordered to be removed.[34]   But where " made under Ormond patent " appeared on the goods, the patentee failed in an action for passing off.[35]   Improper marking does not constitute a defence to an action for breach of contract not to sell the articles in question below a fixed price,[36] but as to the enforceability of such a contract having regard to the Resale Prices Act 1964, see *post*, § 648 *et seq.*

[The next paragraph is 161]

---

[31] *Esco Ltd.* v. *Rolo Ltd.*, 40 R.P.C. 471.
[32] *R.* v. *Townsend*, 13 R.P.C. 265.
[33] See *Cheavin* v. *Walker*, 5 Ch.D. 850; see also *Gridley* v. *Swinbourne*, 52 J.P. 791; 5 T.L.R. 71; *Cochrane* v. *Macnish* [1896] A.C. 225; *Marshall* v. *Ross*, L.R. 8 Eq. 651.
[34] *Post Card Automatic Supply Co.* v. *Samuel*, 6 R.P.C. 560; see *Austin Baldwin, etc.* v. *Greenwood, etc.*, 42 R.P.C. 454; *British and International Proprietaries Ltd.* v. *Selcol Products Ltd.* [1957] R.P.C. 3.
[35] *Ormond Engineering Co.* v. *Knopf*, 49 R.P.C. 634.
[36] *Ultra Electric Ltd.* v. *John Barnes & Co. Ltd.*, 54 R.P.C. 281.

CHAPTER 4

THE SPECIFICATION

1. HISTORY

161 History of the specification

In the early days of the patent system the working of the invention was part of the consideration for the grant; and in many cases provisions were inserted in the patent requiring the instruction of apprentices.[1] In the case of one invention only was the grantee required to publish a description of his invention [2]; and there is some reason for supposing that this was done at the instance of the patentee himself.[3]

The requirement of a specification appears to have been introduced originally merely as a means of ascertaining the ambit of the monopoly claimed, and not with a view to ensuring that the public were placed in possession of the invention, though this naturally followed. The original practice was merely to state the subject-matter of the invention in very general terms in the patent itself.[4] It was thus open to the patentee to allege that anything which fell within this general description was an infringement of the patent. The difficulties caused by this practice were met to a limited extent by introducing into the recitals technical details of the invention.[5] In 1711, however, we find it stated in Naismith's Patent No. 387 that the patentee " has proposed to ascertain " the details of his invention " in writing under his hand and seal to be enrolled in our Court of Chancery " within six months after the date of the patent. And after 1716 a proviso requiring this to be done was inserted in every patent.

162 The title

Until 1852 patents were granted in all cases upon applications which specified the " title " only of the invention, and no obligation to file a specification arose until the patent was sealed. The period of six months allowed for furnishing the description was to ensure

---

[1] See Hulme, 12, 13 L.Q.R.; Co.Inst. 3.
[2] *Sturtevant and Rovinson's Patents* (1611–12); see Supplement to Patent Office Series of Specifications.
[3] See Hulme, 16 L.Q.R.
[4] *e.g.* 1 W.P.C. 9; Gordon 240 (Gilbert's " Water Plough " Patent).
[5] *e.g.* Pownall's Patent No. 391 (1712).

that the inventor should not be forestalled before he could complete the invention and bring it to a practical form. It was, however, necessary that the specification should not be inconsistent with or wider than the " title " (which still continued to form the basis of the grant), and patents were frequently held invalid on the ground of variance between the title and the specification as constituting a " fraud on the Crown." [6] The 1852 Act effected a change in the procedure on application, and an inventor had thereafter to file either a " provisional " or a " complete " specification at the time he made his application. This practice has continued ever since.

It is now provided that every non-convention application shall be accompanied by either a complete specification or a provisional specification, and every convention application must be accompanied by a complete specification. [7]

2. PROVISIONAL SPECIFICATION

163 Nature of provisional specification

The Act itself gives very little in the way of express directions as to what the provisional specification shall contain. It must " describe the invention " and must " begin with a title indicating the subject to which the invention relates." [8]

But the function of the title today is altogether different from that which it formerly fulfilled. It is chiefly for the purpose of identifying the invention for reference and indexing, and its accuracy is a matter for the examiners at the Patent Office.

All that the provisional specification needs to contain is a description of the general nature of the invention, its field of applicability and the anticipated result,[9] and, provided that the nature of the invention is fairly disclosed, the inventor need not describe in the provisional specification any particular method of carrying it out [10]; nor need he state its advantages.[11] The Comptroller has power, however, to require drawings to be furnished with the provisional specification if he is of opinion they are necessary.[12]

---

[6] See *Brunton* v. *Hawkes*, 4 Barn. & Ald. 541; see also *Cochrane* v. *Smethurst*, Dav.P.C. 354; *R.* v. *Else*, 1 W.P.C. 76; *Bloxam* v. *Elsee*, 6 Barn. & Cress. 169; *Croll* v. *Edge*, 9 C.B. 479.

[7] s. 3 (1).

[8] s. 4 (1).

[9] *Per* Lloyd-Jacob J. in *I.C.I.'s Appn.* [1969] R.P.C. 574 at p. 583.

[10] *Woodward* v. *Sansum & Co.*, 4 R.P.C. 166 at p. 174.

[11] See *e.g. Pneumatic Tyre Co.* v. *East London Rubber Co.*, 14 R.P.C. 77 at p. 99.

[12] s. 4 (2).

164　Object of provisional specification

The primary object of the legislature in providing for the filing of a provisional specification is to enable the inventor to improve and perfect the invention during the period of " provisional protection." [13]

In *Newall* v. *Elliott* [14] Byles J. said: " The office of the provisional specification is only to describe generally and fairly the nature of the invention, and not to enter into all the minute details as to the manner in which the invention is to be carried out."

In *Stoner* v. *Todd* [15] Jessel M.R. said: " A provisional specification was never intended to be more than a mode of protecting an inventor until the time of filing a final specification; it was not intended to contain a complete description of the thing so as to enable any workman of ordinary skill to make it, but only to disclose the invention, fairly no doubt, but in its rough state," and, as explained by Lloyd-Jacob J., sitting as the Patents Appeal Tribunal, in *Glaxo Group Ltd.'s Appn.*,[16] " The interval of time between the filing of the two specifications [*i.e.* the provisional and the complete] is intended to provide an opportunity for the development and precise expression of the invention foreshadowed in the provisional. . . ."

165　Effect of provisional specification on " priority date "

While practically anything will serve as a provisional specification to enable an application to be filed, its precise content has now become a matter of very great importance for the purpose of ascertaining the " priority date " of every claim of the patent ultimately granted.[17]　No publication, use, or claiming in another patent, which occurs after the priority date of a claim, can affect its validity.　In the case of an application accompanied by a provisional specification, the priority date of a claim will be the date of the application if (but only if) the claim is " fairly based on the matter disclosed in that specification," [18] otherwise the priority date is the date of filing of the complete specification.[19]　After the date of application it is very probable that the invention will be published by the acts of the inventor or applicant himself, when attempting to exploit or finance the invention, in the belief that he now has provisional protection. If the claims ultimately granted are not fairly based on the disclosure in the provisional specification he will thereby have lost all chance of securing an effective monopoly.

[13] See *ante*, § 144.
[14] 4 C.B.(N.S.) 269 at p 293.
[15] 4 Ch.D. 58.
[16] *Glaxo Group Ltd.'s Appn.* [1968] R.P.C. 473 at p. 480.
[17] s. 5 (1) (2).
[18] s. 5 (2).
[19] s. 5 (6).

166 *Interpretation of " fairly based "*

The words " fairly based " have never previously been used in any Patents Act, but have now been considered by Lloyd-Jacob J. sitting as the Patents Appeal Tribunal (see *post*, § 168). It may be relevant to remember, however, that under the 1907 Act the words used in reference to disconformity between the inventions described in the provisional and complete specifications were " not substantially the same," [20] " other than that described in the provisional," [21] " is not the same," [22] and "further or different." [23] The transitional provisions of the present Act provide [24] that the provisions as to the priority date shall apply to pre-Act applications and that in a pre-Act case a claim " shall be deemed to be fairly based on the matter disclosed in the provisional specification unless the claim is for a further or different invention to that contained in the provisional specification." [25] On general principles of construction it is submitted that the legislature cannot have intended to reduce the existing rights of an applicant, there being no clear words in the present Act that compel such a result. Accordingly, it would seem that a claim is " fairly based " on the disclosure in the provisional specification unless it is for an invention which is " different " from everything there disclosed, for that one word really covers all the above-quoted phrases. It should, however, be interpreted in its ordinary sense and not in the highly specialised sense it acquired as a result of judicial decisions relating to the permissibility of amendment of the complete specification, after acceptance, under the old law, which forbade any amendment which resulted in making the invention claimed " substantially larger or substantially different from " the invention previously claimed.[26] Such decisions are now no longer applicable, as the right of the patentee to amend his complete specification has been enlarged.[27]

167 *What is a " different " invention*

In *Pneumatic Tyre Co. Ltd.* v. *Leicester Pneumatic Tyre and Automatic Valve Co.*[28] Lord Macnaghten said, in a passage which, it is submitted, is still good law: " It is the duty and the office of the provisional specification to declare the nature of the invention; but

[20] 1907 Act, s. 6 (3).
[21] 1907 Act, s. 11 (1) (*d*).
[22] 1907 Act, s. 25 (2) (*e*).
[23] 1907 Act, s. 42.
[24] Sched. III (2).
[25] Sched. III (2), proviso.
[26] 1907 Act, ss. 21, 22.
[27] See *post*, § 473.
[28] 16 R.P.C. 531 at p. 541.

when you come to the complete specification you have to declare particularly the nature of the invention and explain how it is to be carried out; and if in the interval between the provisional specification and the complete specification—an interval which is given to the applicant in order that he may perfect his invention—he discovers any better mode without altering the nature of his invention, of carrying it into effect, he is bound to disclose it in the complete specification." This last statement now has statutory recognition, for the Act requires that the complete specification must disclose the best method of performing the invention which was known to the applicant and for which he was entitled to claim protection,[29] *i.e.* the best method devised or adapted by him up to the date when the complete specification was filed.[30] And while it has for many years been the practice to draft the main claim (usually the first claim) as the widest claim and to have a number of subsidiary claims consisting of the main claim with the addition of one or more optional features, it has never been suggested that such claims constitute different inventions.

168 Rules to determine whether " fairly based "

In *Mond Nickel Co.'s Application* [31] Lloyd-Jacob J., sitting as the Patents Appeal Tribunal, said: " It seems to me that there is a threefold investigation which is called for. First, one has to inquire whether the alleged invention as claimed can be said to have been broadly described in the provisional specification, and only if an affirmative answer is given to that question does one proceed to the second question, which is: Is there anything in the provisional specification which is inconsistent with the alleged invention as claimed? If it is found, upon examination, that the invention as characterised in the claim includes something which is inconsistent with that which is described in the provisional specification, as at present advised I should think that it would be right to conclude that the claim could not have been fairly based upon the disclosure; but, assuming that those two burdens are satisfactorily surmounted, there is, I think, a third matter for inquiry: Does the claim include as a characteristic of the invention a feature as to which the provisional specification is wholly silent? "

169   In *Imperial Chemical Industries Ltd.'s Application* [32] Lloyd-Jacob J. said that in his above statement " the word ' broadly ' was used in respect of the description and carried the meaning of ' in a general sense,' such as would be exemplified by a statement in the provisional specification that reaction products were dissolved in hot water, where

[29] ss. 4 (3) (*a*), 32 (1) (*h*).
[30] *Cf.* 1907 Act, s. 25 (2) (*j*).
[31] [1956] R.P.C. 189 at p. 194.   [32] [1960] R.P.C. 223 at p. 228.

the complete specification introduced a specific temperature range. . . .
The function of the provisional specification is to provide a description of the alleged invention, and, if such description includes as
essential a requirement for its performance [three specified chemical
substances] as does this provisional specification, a claim which does
not require one such essential requirement to be adopted is neither
logically nor legitimately founded upon it." If this statement of the
law is applied generally and in all circumstances, it would seem to
follow that there must be in a provisional specification a description
in terms as wide or wider than the claim, if such is to be fairly
based on the provisional specification, and the fact that a provisional
specification does describe the invention in wide general terms will
not prevent a claim in the complete specification drafted in more
precise and restricted terms being fairly based on the disclosure in
that provisional specification.[33]

170   It will, therefore, be appreciated that it is highly desirable to draft
a provisional specification so that it includes a description of the
invention in the widest terms so that every feature of the invention
that may conceivably turn out to be new is described as inventive
and not merely as part of a combination which, however, if thought
to be inventive, should be separately described. But on no account
should the provisional specification contain any admission of prior
art. Such an admission will be deemed to have been made by the
applicant and if made erroneously may deprive him of his rights.[34]

The claims of a complete specification must be " fairly based on "
the matter disclosed in that specification,[35] but although the same
words " fairly based on " are used, their import in this connection is
quite different.[36]

171   Convention application priority date

All that has been said above in relation to the claim being fairly
based on a prior provisional specification is equally applicable to the
case where what purported to be a complete specification was filed
with the application and was subsequently treated as a provisional
specification.[37] In the case of convention applications the claim must
be fairly based on the matter disclosed in the application for protection in the foreign country in order to have the date of that foreign
application as the priority date.[38]

[33] British Drug Houses Ltd.'s Appn. [1964] R.P.C. 237; Glaxo Group Ltd.'s
    Appn. [1968] R.P.C. 473.
[34] Chapman and Cook v. Deltavis Ltd., 47 R.P.C. 163 at p. 173.
[35] s. 4 (4).   [36] See post, § 231.
[37] s. 3 (5).
[38] s. 5 (4), and see Hercules Inc.'s Appn. [1968] R.P.C. 203 and Westminster
    Banks Ltd.'s Patent [1967] R.P.C. 600 at p. 604.

172   Section 69 (2) [39] provides that " matter shall be deemed to have been disclosed in an application for protection in a convention country if it was claimed or disclosed (otherwise than by way of disclaimer or acknowledgment of prior art) in that application or in documents submitted by the applicant for protection in support of and at the same time as that application." In *E. I. du Pont de Nemours and Co.'s Application* [40] Lloyd-Jacob J., sitting as the Patents Appeal Tribunal, said: " It will be observed that this subsection specifically constitutes the claims a disclosure, but in doing so it expresses a distinction between matter claimed and matter disclosed. . . . It is not that the claims in a convention application are assimilated to the general disclosure in the body of the specification, but that they are deemed to constitute a disclosure of their own, so that, if another claim may be fairly based upon them, the applicant is entitled to priority therefor. This he secures in addition to his right to seek claims fairly based upon the disclosure in the body of the specification, for which he may claim the date to which his original application for patent protection entitles him."

If the complete specification is filed pursuant to two or more applications accompanied by provisional specifications or two or more convention applications, and a claim (being fairly based on the disclosure in more than one prior specification) might otherwise have more than one priority date, the earlier or earliest is the effective one.[41]

173 Reference to provisional specification

The provisional specification should be referred to for the purpose of establishing the priority date. It can also be referred to for any admissions that it may contain as to the prior art.[42]

174   Lord Esher stated in *Parkinson* v. *Simon*: " How are we to get at what is the real object of the plaintiffs' patent? I think it is true to say that you may look for that purpose at the provisional specification. For the object of the complete specification is to carry out in detail that which is more generally expressed in the provisional specification." [43] Although this statement may be open to criticism, it has been followed.[44] But if the provisional specification contains a description of the manner in which the invention may be carried

---

[39] *Post*, § 1208.

[40] 71 R.P.C. 263.

[41] s. 5 (5).

[42] *British Celanese Ltd.* v. *Courtaulds Ltd.*, 50 R.P.C. 259 at p. 270.

[43] *Parkinson* v. *Simon*, 11 R.P.C. 493 at p 503.

[44] *Chapman and Cook* v. *Deltavis Ltd.*, 47 R.P.C. 163 at p. 171; *British Celanese Ltd.* v. *Courtaulds Ltd.*, 50 R.P.C. 63 at p. 84.

into effect, it does not follow that, if the complete specification describes a better method, the earlier method is thereby disclaimed.[45]

175   " Disconformity " abolished

An allegation of " disconformity " between the invention claimed in the complete specification and that disclosed in the provisional can no longer be relied on as such, either against the grant of a patent or in support of a plea of invalidity. Under the present Act every claim has its own priority date. Where a claim includes a number of alternatives, there is no provision in the Act for attributing different priority dates to the different alternatives, and the claim as a whole will have the latest priority date to be attributable to any one of the alternatives.[46] However, in certain circumstances such a claim may be split so as to maintain the earliest priority date in respect of one claim.[47] If there was no disclosure of the invention the subject of the claim, by the applicant or a person from whom he derives title, in a provisional specification, or, in the case of a convention application, in the relevant foreign application, prior to the date when the claim itself was filed (it being part of the complete specification) the priority date of the claim will be the date of its filing.[48] In that case it can be attacked by reason of any disclosure occurring prior to that date irrespective of whether other claims have an earlier priority date or not. The substance of the law on this point, as it has existed since the 1907 Act,[49] has been altered little, if at all, by the present Act, but its form has been made more logical and it is now expressly provided that developments of or additions to the invention which was described in the provisional specification, or the relevant foreign application, which developments or additions are themselves patentable, may be included in the claims of the complete specification.[50] It is submitted that the numerous cases on disconformity decided before the 1907 Act came into force are now of no assistance, and even later cases are of little value having regard to the change in the law made by the 1949 Act.[51]

---

[45] *Sandow Ltd.* v. *Szalay,* 23 R.P.C. 6 at p. 14.
[46] *Thornhill's Appn.* [1962] R.P.C. 199.
[47] *Farbenfabriken Bayer A.G.'s Patent* [1966] R.P.C. 278; *Anderson's Appn.* [1966] F.S.R. 218; *Bristol Myers Co.'s Appn.* [1966] F.S.R. 223; *Wellcome Foundation Ltd.'s Appn.* [1968] R.P.C. 107.
[48] s. 5 (6).
[49] 1907 Act, s. 42.
[50] s. 4 (6).
[51] See for example, *Anderson's Patent,* 7 R.P.C. 323; *Birt's Appn.,* 9 R.P.C. 489; *Edward's Patent,* 11 R.P.C. 461; *Millar's Appn.,* 15 R.P.C. 718; *Hudson's Appn.,* 22 R.P.C. 218; *Ross's Appn.,* 30 R.P.C. 722; *Quain and Others' Appn.,* 40 R.P.C. 462; *Stromberg, etc., Co.'s Appn.,* 40 R.P.C. 405; *Zucker's Appn.,* 44 R.P.C. 257; *Andreas' Appn.,* 51 R.P.C. 188.

Although the complete specification of a convention application may now include claims to developments of or additions to the invention described in the relevant foreign application, the application will not be allowed to proceed as a convention application if such inclusion results in contravention of the proviso to section 1 (2) of the Act.[52]

176 *Drawings*

Both a provisional and a complete specification may, and, if the Comptroller so requires, must, contain drawings, and these are deemed to form part of the specification.[53] In practice a complete specification invariably contains drawings, except in the case of a chemical invention. It is rarely necessary for a provisional specification to have drawings, but it is useful to include them, as not only may the verbal description of the invention thereby be considerably shortened, but also one can be certain that no part of the inventive mechanism has been omitted, which may otherwise happen as the inventor may not appreciate what is the inventive step he has made over the prior art.

3. THE COMPLETE SPECIFICATION

177 Except in very unusual cases involving some degree of moral turpitude, the validity of a patent depends entirely on the content of the complete specification.[54] The drafting of this document is undoubtedly far the most important, and much the most difficult, task in patent practice. The positive requirements laid down by the Act are that the complete specification shall[55]:

(a) particularly describe the invention and the method by which it is to be performed;

(b) disclose the best method of performing the invention which is known to the applicant and for which he is entitled to claim protection;

(c) end with a claim or claims defining the scope of the invention claimed;

(d) have a claim or claims which

    (i) relate to a single invention

    (ii) are clear and succinct

    (iii) are fairly based on the matter disclosed in the complete specification.

[52] *Karlgaard's Appn.* [1966] R.P.C. 553.
[53] s. 4 (2).
[54] s. 32 (1).
[55] s. 4 (3), (4).

178   In addition to these positive requirements it is provided that the patent may be revoked for a number of reasons which relate to defects in the complete specification,[56] and these will be considered in the next chapter together with all the other grounds of invalidity of a patent.

General Principles of Construction

179 Origin of the claim

In *British United Shoe Machinery Co. Ltd.* v. *A. Fussell & Sons Ltd.*[57] Fletcher Moulton L.J. dealt with the history of distinct claims as part of specifications. After mentioning the proviso (formerly inserted in the patent itself), which required the patentee to state in writing the nature of his invention and the method of performing the same, he said: " These two things—the delimitation of the invention and full practical directions how to use it—are in their nature almost antagonistic. As it is the duty of the inventor to give the fullest practical information to the public, he is bound to put in, if, for instance, the invention is a process, quantities and times which are the best he knows. But it would be very cruel to hold him to the invention when carried out only with those best quantities and times, because a person could then take his invention in substance if he did not take it in quite the best way, and the value of the grant would be practically nothing. Hence inventors, in their own protection, took to introducing into their specifications language intended to distinguish between that which was there for the practical information of the public, and that which was there for delimitation of the invention. Out of that has arisen the practice, which originally was perfectly optional, of having a separate part of the specification primarily designed for delimitation. That is what we call the claim."

180 Construction is for court alone

The construction of the specification is for the court alone. Lindley L.J. in *Brooks* v. *Steele and Currie*,[58] said: " The judge may, and indeed generally must, be assisted by expert evidence to explain technical terms, to show the practical working of machinery described or drawn, and to point out what is old and what is new in the specification. Expert evidence is also admissible, and is often required to show the particulars in which an alleged invention has been used by an alleged infringer, and the real importance of whatever differences there may be between the plaintiff's invention and whatever is done by the defendant. But, after all, the nature of the

---

[56] s. 32.
[57] 25 R.P.C. 631 at p. 650.   [58] 14 R.P.C. 46 at p. 73.

invention for which a patent is granted must be ascertained from the specification, and has to be determined by the judge and not by a jury, nor by any expert or other witness. This is familiar law, although apparently often disregarded when witnesses are being examined." [59]

181   The actual form of the patent provides " that these our letters patent shall be construed in the most beneficial sense for the advantage of the patentee," but these words apply to the patent grant itself and have no relation to the words of the specification. In construing a specification there is no special rule of benevolent interpretation other than as applies to all documents. In *Needham and Kite* v. *Johnson & Co.*[60] Lindley L.J. said: " I do not like the expression ' benevolent interpretation.' I do not believe in it. The question is whether a given construction is the true construction; but, of course, if any patent is capable of more constructions than one, the general rule would be applied that you would put upon it that construction which makes it a valid patent rather than a construction which renders it invalid." [61]

In *British Thomson-Houston Co. Ltd.* v. *Corona Lamp Works Ltd.*[62] Lord Shaw said: " I think there is no rule, whether of benevolent or malevolent construction, which should apply to patent specifications. A specification must take its rank among all ordinary documents which are submitted to a reader for his guidance or instruction, and a reader ordinarily intelligent and versed in the subject-matter. Such a reader must be supposed to bring his stock of intelligence and knowledge to bear upon the document, not unduly to struggle with it, but anyhow to make the best of it; if, as the result, he understands what the invention is, can produce the object and achieve the manufacture by the help of the written and drawn pages, then the subject-matter of the invention cannot fail on the head of vagueness." [63]

[59] And see *Neilson* v. *Harford*, 1 W.P.C. 331 at p. 370; *Seed* v. *Higgins*, 30 L.J.Q.B. 314 at p. 317; *Hill* v. *Evans*, 31 L.J.Ch. 457 at p. 460; *Kaye* v. *Chubb & Sons Ltd.*, 4 R.P.C. 289 at p. 298; *Gadd & Mason* v. *Mayor, etc., of Manchester*, 9 R.P.C. 516 at p. 530; *British Dynamite Co.* v. *Krebs*, 13 R.P.C. 190 at p. 192; *Nestlé & Co. Ltd.* v. *Eugene Ltd.*, 38 R.P.C. 342 at p. 347; *Canadian General Electric Co. Ltd.* v. *Fada Radio Ltd.*, 47 R.P.C. 69 at p. 90.
[60] 1 R.P.C. 49 at p. 58.
[61] See also *Parkinson* v. *Simon*, 12 R.P.C. 403 at p. 411; *Submarine Signalling Co.* v. *Henry Hughes & Son Ltd.*, 49 R.P.C. 149 at p. 174; *Henriksen* v. *Tallon* [1965] R.P.C. 434 at p. 443.
[62] 39 R.P.C. 49 at p. 89.
[63] See also *Plimpton* v. *Spiller*, 6 Ch.D. 412 at p. 422; *Otto* v. *Linford*, 46 L.T.(N.S.) 35 at p. 39; *Cropper* v. *Smith & Hancock*, 1 R.P.C. 81 at pp. 88, 89; *Automatic Weighing Machine Co.* v. *Knight*, 6 R.P.C. 297 at p. 307; *Edison Bell Phonograph Co. Ltd.* v. *Smith*, 11 R.P.C. 389 at p. 400;

182   Construction of the claims

It is the normal principle of construction of a document that it should be construed as a whole so as to give a sensible consistent meaning to every part of it. The question as to the extent to which the body of the specification can be used to interpret the claims was canvassed in the House of Lords in *Electric and Musical Industries Ltd.* v. *Lissen Ltd.*,[64] a case in which there was a division of opinion. The statement as to the construction of the claims by Lord Russell is frequently cited, but in fact, as appears from Lord Macmillan's speech, there was no majority of the House in favour of his views. It can, however, be stated that it was accepted that " if the claims have a plain meaning in themselves, then advantage cannot be taken of the language used in the body of the specification to make them mean something different " [65] (*per* Lord Porter), but the case is not a conclusive authority for any wider principle as to the construction of a specification. The following extract [65] from the speech of Lord Russell is often cited, although perhaps without it always being fully appreciated that it was not as a whole accepted by a majority of the House of Lords, and has been frequently accepted as an accurate statement of the law: " The Court of Appeal have stated that in their opinion no special rules are applicable to the construction of a speci- fication, that it must be read as a whole and in the light of surround- ing circumstances; that it may be gathered from the specification that particular words bear an unusual meaning; and that, if possible, a specification should be construed so as not to lead to a foolish result or one which the patentee could not have contemplated. They further have pointed out that the claims have a particular function to dis- charge. With every word of this I agree; but I desire to add some- thing further in regard to the claim in a specification.

183   " The function of the claims is to define clearly and with precision the monopoly claimed, so that others may know the exact boundaries of the area within which they will be trespassers. Their primary object is to limit and not to extend the monopoly. What is not claimed is disclaimed. The claims must undoubtedly be read as part of the entire document, and not as a separate document; but the forbidden field must be found in the language of the claims and not elsewhere. It is not permissible, in my opinion, by reference to some language used in the earlier part of the specification, to change a claim which by its own language is a claim for one subject-matter

Benno Jaffé, etc., Fabrik v. *Richardson,* 11 R.P.C. 261 at p. 271; *Nobel's Explosives Co. Ltd.* v. *Anderson,* 11 R.P.C. 519 at p. 523; *Tolson* v. *Speight,* 13 R.P.C. 718 at p. 721; *E.M.I.* v. *Lissen,* 56 R.P.C. 23 at p. 46.
[64] 56 R.P.C. 23.
[65] 56 R.P.C. at p. 39.

into a claim for another and a different subject-matter, which is what you do when you alter the boundaries of the forbidden territory. A patentee who describes an invention in the body of a specification obtains no monopoly unless it is claimed in the claims. As Lord Cairns said, there is no such thing as infringement of the equity of a patent.[66]

" I would point out [67] that there is no question here of words in Claim 1 bearing any special or unusual meaning by reason either of a dictionary found elsewhere in the specification or of technical knowledge possessed by persons skilled in the art. The prima facie meaning of words used in a claim may not be their true meaning when read in the light of such a dictionary or of such technical knowledge; and in those circumstances a claim, when so construed, may bear a meaning different from that which it would have borne had no such assisting light been available. That is construing a document in accordance with the recognised canons of construction. But I know of no canon or principle which will justify one in departing from the unambiguous and grammatical meaning of a claim and narrowing or extending its scope by reading into it words which are not in it; or will justify one in using stray phrases in the body of a specification for the purpose of narrowing or widening the boundaries of the monopoly fixed by the plain words of a claim.

184   " A claim is a portion of the specification which fulfils a separate and distinct function. It, and it alone, defines the monopoly; and the patentee is under a statutory obligation to state in the claims clearly and distinctly what is the invention which he desires to protect. As Lord Chelmsford said in this House many years ago: ' The office of a claim is to define and limit with precision what it is which is claimed to have been invented and therefore patented.' [68] If the patentee has done this in a claim the language of which is plain and unambiguous, it is not open to your lordships to restrict or expand or qualify its scope by reference to the body of the specification. Lord Loreburn emphasised this when he said: ' The idea of allowing a patentee to use perfectly general language in the claim and subsequently to restrict or expand or qualify what is therein expressed by borrowing this or that gloss from other parts of the specification is wholly inadmissible.' [69] Sir Mark Romer expressed the same view in the following felicitous language: ' One may and one ought to refer to the body of the specification for the purpose of ascertaining

---

[66] *Dudgeon* v. *Thomson,* 3 App.Cas. 34.
[67] 56 R.P.C. at p. 41.
[68] *Harrison* v. *Anderston Foundry Co.,* 1 App.Cas. 574.
[69] *Ingersoll Sergeant Drill Co.* v. *Consolidated Pneumatic Tool Co.,* 25 R.P.C. 61 at p. 83.

the meaning of words and phrases used in the claims, or for the purpose of resolving difficulties of construction occasioned by the claims when read by themselves.   But where the construction of a claim when read by itself is plain, it is not, in my opinion, legitimate to diminish the ambit of the monopoly claimed merely because in the body of the specification the patentee has described his invention in more restricted terms than in the claim itself.' " [70]

185   But, as Lord Evershed M.R. stated in *Rosedale Associated Manufacturers Ltd.* v. *Carlton Tyre Saving Co. Ltd.*[71]: " It is no doubt true and has been well established (see, for example, the speech of Lord Russell of Killowen in the *E.M.I.* v. *Lissen* case) that you must construe the claims according to their terms upon ordinary principles, and that it is not legitimate to confine the scope of the claims by reference to some limitation which may be found in the body of the specification, but is not expressly or by proper inference reproduced in the claims themselves.   On the other hand, it is clearly no less legitimate and appropriate in approaching the construction of the claims to read the specification as a whole.   Thereby the necessary background is obtained and in some cases the meaning of the words used in the claims may be affected or defined by what is said in the body of the specification."   An example of how the body of the specification may affect the meaning of the claims is to be found in *British Thomson-Houston Co. Ltd., and Others* v. *Guildford Radio Stores* [72] where the body of the specification stated that " one feature of the invention consists in an effective means for smoothing out the rectified current supplied to the amplifying apparatus to such an extent that no disagreeable noise will be produced in the circuits by reason of the fact that an alternating source of supply is employed," and Claim 1 contained the words " the field-winding of the sound-reproducing device is employed to smooth out fluctuation in the rectified current."   It was argued that the claim was too wide in that it covered any degree of " smoothing," including cases which fell far short of the elimination of the objectionable noise, but Luxmoore J. held that the claim should be construed as limited to that degree of smoothing.

186 **Construction as date of publication**

A specification is to be construed with reference to the state of knowledge at the time it is published.[73]   Lord Esher M.R. in *Nobel's*

---

[70] *British Hartford-Fairmont Syndicate Ltd.* v. *Jackson Bros. (Knottingley) Ltd.,* 49 R.P.C. 495 at p. 556.   See also *Minerals Separation North American Corporation* v. *Noranda Mines Ltd.,* 69 R.P.C. 81.
[71] [1960] R.P.C. 59 at p. 69.   [72] 55 R.P.C. 71.
[73] *Badische Anilin und Soda Fabrik* v. *Levinstein,* 4 R.P.C. 449 at p. 463; *Lane-Fox* v. *Kensington and Knightsbridge Electric Lighting Co. Ltd.,* 9

Explosives Co. Ltd. v. *Anderson* [74] said: " Now what is the very first canon of construction of all written business documents? Why, that the court ought to construe them as if it had to construe them the day after they were published." [75]

187   Construction of amended specification

Where an amendment has been made after the date of publication of a complete specification, the amendment is for all purposes deemed to form part of the specification [76] and, therefore, the specification is to be read in the form in which it appears after amendment. In construing such a specification, however, reference may be made to the specification as originally published. [77]

188   Form of claim

As already stated (see § 177) the statute requires that a claim shall
(i) relate to a single invention;
(ii) be clear and succinct;
(iii) be fairly based on the matter disclosed in the complete specification.

Requirements (i) and (iii) are concerned with the content of the claim and are discussed elsewhere (as to (i) see §§ 113–114, *supra*, and as to (iii) see §§ 231–238, *post*). Requirement (ii) is the only statutory requirement as to the form of the claim.

It has long been the practice for claims to consist of a single statement which, when read with the preamble words " What I claim is," becomes a single sentence. In *Leonard's Appn.*[78] the applicants submitted claims each drafted in the form of a number of short sentences. The claims in that form were rejected by the Patent Office and the rejection was upheld by the Patents Appeal Tribunal (Lloyd Jacob J.) on the ground that the claims consisting as they did of disjunctive sentences would of necessity give rise to uncertainty as to the precise scope of the monopoly sought.

A claim may be limited by the result to be attained [79] provided

R.P.C. 413 at p. 417; *Presto Gear Case, etc., Co. Ltd.* v. *Orme, Evans & Co. Ltd.*, 18 R.P.C. 17 at p. 23; *Marconi's Wireless Telegraph Co. Ltd.* v. *Mullard Radio Valve Co. Ltd.*, 41 R.P.C. 323 at p. 334.

[74] 11 R.P.C. 519 at p. 523.
[75] And see *Ore Concentration Co. (1905) Ltd.* v. *Sulphide Corporation Ltd.*, 31 R.P.C. 206 at p. 224. See *American Cyanamid Co.* v. *Upjohn Co.* [1970] 1 W.L.R. 1507, *per* Lord Diplock.
[76] s. 31 (2).
[77] s. 31 (2), proviso. And see *Tecalemit Ltd.* v. *Ewarts Ltd.*, 44 R.P.C. 488 at p. 500; *Multiform Displays Ltd.* v. *Whitmarley Displays Ltd.* [1957] R.P.C. 260.
[78] [1966] R.P.C. 269.
[79] *No Fume Ltd.* v. *Frank Pritchard & Co. Ltd.* (1935) 52 R.P.C. 231.

that in, for instance, a claim for an article, the limitation is " sufficient to characterise the construction of the article claimed." [80]

189   " Substantially as described "

The claims at the end of a specification frequently end with the words " as herein described," or " substantially as herein described." The effect of these words on the ambit of the claim, both as regards novelty and infringement, is to be ascertained by reading the specification as a whole. It is an unprofitable exercise to attempt to reconcile the very large number of decisions that have been given as to the meaning of these words.[81]

The most recent judicial utterance on the subject has been made by Lord Morton in *Raleigh Cycle Co. Ltd.* v. *H. Miller & Co. Ltd.*,[82] in expressing the majority opinion of the House of Lords: " For many years it has been a common practice to insert as the last claim in a patent specification, a claim on the same lines as Claim 5 [83] in the present case. I think that the reason why such a claim has been inserted, in the present case and countless other cases, is as follows. The patentee fears that his earlier claims may be held invalid, because they cover too wide an area or fail sufficiently and clearly to ascertain the scope of the monopoly claimed. He reasons as follows: ' If I have made a patentable invention and have described the preferred embodiment of my invention clearly and accurately, and without any insufficiency in the directions given, I must surely be entitled to protection for that preferred embodiment,

---

[80] *Mullard Radio Valve Co. Ltd.* v. *British Belmont Radio Ltd.* 56 R.P.C. 1 at pp. 16 and 20.

[81] See, *e.g.*, *Curtis* v. *Platt*, 3 Ch.D. 135n.; *Westinghouse* v. *Lancashire and Yorkshire Ry.*, 1 R.P.C. 229 at p. 241; *Young and Neilson* v. *Rosenthal*, 1 R.P.C. 29 at p. 33; *Easterbrook* v. *Great Western Ry.*, 2 R.P.C. 201 at p. 208; *United Telephone Co.* v. *Bassano*, 3 R.P.C. 295 at p. 315; *Proctor* v. *Bennis*, 4 R.P.C. 333; *Lyon* v. *Goddard*, 11 R.P.C. 354 at p. 362; *Cassel Gold Extracting Co. Ltd.* v. *Cyanide Gold Recovery Syndicate*, 12 R.P.C. 232 at p. 257; *Parkinson* v. *Simon*, 12 R.P.C. 403 at p. 408; *North British Rubber Co.* v. *Gormully*, 14 R.P.C. 283; *Brooks* v. *Lamplugh*, 15 R.P.C. 33 at p. 49; *Welsbach Incandescent Gas Light Co. Ltd.* v. *New Incandescent, etc., Co. Ltd.*, 17 R.P.C. 237 at p. 250; *Ackroyd & Best Ltd.* v. *Thomas and Williams*, 21 R.P.C. 737 at pp. 749, 750; *Holmes* v. *Associated Newspapers Ltd.*, 27 R.P.C. 136; *Bonnard* v. *London General Omnibus Co. Ltd.*, 38 R.P.C. 1 at p. 9; *Thomas* v. *South Wales, etc., Co. Ltd.*, 42 R.P.C. 22; *Tecalemit Ltd.* v. *Ewarts Ltd.*, 44 R.P.C. 488; *Wright and Eagle Range Co. Ltd.* v. *General Gas Appliances Ltd.*, 46 R.P.C. 169; *Rose Street Foundry Ltd.* v. *India Rubber, etc., Ltd.*, 46 R.P.C. 294 at p. 311; *Wanganui* v. *Maunder and Beavan*, 47 R.P.C. 395; *Walsh* v. *Albert Baker & Co. Ltd.*, 47 R.P.C. 458; *Cincinnati Grinders Inc.* v. *B.S.A. Tools Ltd.*, 48 R.P.C. 33 at pp. 69, 82; *de Havilland's Appn.*, 49 R.P.C. 438; *Crabtree & Sons Ltd.* v. *Hoe & Co. Ltd.*, 53 R.P.C. 443.

[82] 65 R.P.C. 141 at p. 157.

[83] See *infra*.

and that protection may fairly extend to cover anything which is substantially the same as the preferred embodiment.'

190   " This reasoning seems sound to me, and I cannot doubt that if Claim 5 had read ' an electric generator for lighting a pedal cycle, constructed and arranged substantially as described herein and shown in the accompanying drawings,' it would have been a valid claim. . . . So far as I can see, there is no insufficiency or ambiguity in their description of the preferred embodiment of that invention, or in the accompanying drawings. In these circumstances, the patentees must surely be entitled to obtain at least this measure of protection . . . [It is objected that] Claim 5 is not a narrow claim, but a very wide one, at least as wide as Claim 1. It claims the invention ' as described ' and the drawings are referred to in the claim merely as an illustration of one form which the invention may take. This argument is based upon certain decided cases and in particular upon *Tucker* v. *Wandsworth Electrical Manufacturing Co. Ltd.*[84]

" Before turning to the authorities, I would point out that this is a strange construction to place upon the last of five claims in a specification. Is it really to be supposed that in his last claim the patentee merely intends to echo his first claim, adding a reference to the drawings which seems, on this footing, to be needless and possibly confusing? It is surely more likely that the last claim, referring to the drawings, is intended to be a narrow claim, incorporating the drawings as part of the description, and directed to saving the patent from revocation, if all wider claims are held to be bad.

191   " In *Hale* v. *Coombes*[85] Claim 1 was as follows: ' A projectile of the type herein referred to provided with a device which (etc., etc.) . . . substantially as described.' Claim 6 was as follows: ' Projectiles of the type herein referred to . . . constructed and arranged and adapted to operate substantially as hereinbefore described with reference to and shown respectively in Figs. 1 to 4 inclusive, in Figs. 5 and 6, in Figs. 7 and 8 and in Figs. 9 and 10 of the drawings.' The majority of this House held that Claim 6 was a good claim. Lord Sumner, after expressing the view that the words ' substantially as described ' in Claim 1 did not serve to restrict that claim within patentable limits, expressed himself[86] as follows: ' Claim 6, however, stands on a somewhat different footing, for, after the words " constructed and arranged and adapted to operate substantially as hereinbefore described " the inventor continues " with reference to and as shown respectively in " certain annexed figures. I think that

[84] 42 R.P.C. 531.
[85] 42 R.P.C. 328.
[86] 42 R.P.C. 328 at p. 346.

this addition bringing in the figures, which are clear in themselves, does limit Claim 6 to a contrivance which follows the figures and does not go beyond them. It virtually directs that the drawings are to be read into and as part of this claim, an unusual but permissible form to adopt (*Hattersley* v. *Hodgson* [87]). Thus Claim 6 does not merely stand or fall with the construction of Claim 1. . . .'

192   " In the case of *Hattersley* v. *Hodgson* . . . the relevant claims contain the words ' substantially as herein shown and described ' and Lord Macnaghten said [88]: ' I think the dobby which they claim is shown and described in the specification into which the patentees direct you to read the accompanying drawings,' and Lord Lindley observed: ' If his language can fairly be construed so as to render his patent valid, it is to be so construed,' an observation which may usefully be applied to the present case. In *Eyres Ltd.* v. *Grundy Ltd.*[89] a claim in the words ' a manhole or gully cover or grid constructed substantially as shown and described with reference to Figs. 1 to 4 or Figs. 5 and 6 ' was construed, and as I venture to think rightly construed, as being a narrow claim limited by the reference to the drawings, and as saving the patent from complete invalidity.

" Three cases were cited to us in which claims, somewhat similar in their working to Claim 5, were given a wide construction . . . *Turner* v. *Bowman*,[90] *Benton & Stone Ltd.* v. *Denston & Son* [91] and *Tucker* v. *Wandsworth Electrical Manufacturing Co. Ltd.*[92] I need say little about the first two of these cases, which preceded the decision of this House in *Hale* v. *Coombes.*[93] In each of them the patent in question was held to be valid and to have been infringed, but I cannot agree with all the observations made by Astbury J. in reference to the claims.

193   " In *Tucker's* case the only claims were in the following terms: ' (1) An electric switch adapted to co-operate by a quick make and break action (etc., etc.). . . . (2) An electric switch, substantially as herein set forth and illustrated.' Tomlin J. (as he then was) had held that Claim 1 was invalid but that Claim 2 was valid because it was limited to the specific switch, known as a ' tumbler ' switch, which was depicted in the drawings. The defendants appealed and the Court of Appeal held that Claim 2 was a wide claim, that it was

[87] 23 R.P.C. 192.
[88] 23 R.P.C. 192 at p. 201.
[89] 56 R.P.C. 253.
[90] 42 R.P.C. 29.
[91] 42 R.P.C. 284.
[92] 42 R P.C. 531.
[93] 42 R.P.C. 328.

open to the same objections as Claim 1 and that the patent was invalid . . . it seems to me that the Court of Appeal decided wrongly and Tomlin J. decided rightly. . . .

"It was suggested in argument that the word 'substantially' in Claim 5 might introduce uncertainty as to the scope of the monopoly. I cannot accept this suggestion. The word merely indicates that the patentees are not limiting their monopoly to an electric generator which corresponds in every detail with the generator shown in the drawings, but claim the right to object to the manufacture or sale of an electric generator which is in substance the same as the generator so shown. It may be said with some force that the rights of the patentees would have been the same if the word 'substantially' had been omitted from the claim. Even so, its presence cannot render the claim invalid. It may be a matter of some difficulty, in some cases, for the court to decide whether an alleged infringement [94] is or is not substantially the same as the electric generator shown in the drawings, but the court does not shrink from such a task."

The conclusion would appear to be that the words " substantially as described " are insufficient by themselves to limit a claim to the preferred embodiment described, but that if some reference to the drawings is also to be found in the limiting words, even though it is only by reason of the use of expressions such as " as shown " or " as illustrated," the claim is limited to something which is substantially that which is described and depicted in the accompanying figures.[95]

This view was taken by the House of Lords in the case of *Deere & Co.* v. *Harrison McGregor & Guest Ltd.*[96] when considering a claim to a device " constructed substantially as described and with reference to, or as illustrated by [certain drawings]." Lord Reid said,[97] referring to the *Raleigh* case, " That case appears to me to be ample authority for holding this patent valid, but it also shows that a claim of this kind cannot have a wide scope."

194　　It is desirable for the patentee to include a claim of this character, because it may result in his succeeding in an action and obtaining an injunction, where otherwise he would have failed altogether.[98] Moreover, such a claim is not limited to precisely what is illustrated in the drawings, but includes mechanism which, while differing in immaterial respects, adopts all the essentials of that illustrated, even though it may not fall within some of the other subsidiary claims.[99]

[94] See *post*, § 341 *et seq.*
[95] See *R. W. Crabtree & Sons Ltd.* v. *R. Hoe & Co. Ltd.*, 53 R.P.C. 443.
[96] [1965] R.P.C. 461.　　　　　　　　　　　　　　[97] At p. 476.
[98] *Raleigh* v. *Miller*, 65 R.P.C. 141; *Surface Silos Ltd.* v. *Beal* [1960] R.P.C. 154.
[99] *Raleigh* v. *Miller*, 65 R.P.C. 141 and case cited under note 96.

195 Duplication of claims

The court will if possible construe the claims so as to give a different meaning to different claims. In *Parkinson* v. *Simon* [1] Lord Esher M.R. said: " When you find a patent with several claims in it, you must, if you can, so construe those claims as to give an effective meaning to each of them. If there are several claims which are identical with each other, then some of them have no effect at all. It follows from the ordinary rules of construction that you must construe the different claims so as to make them effective if possible, to be different from each other in some respects, or else they are not effective." [2]

But if after properly construing the specification and claims, little or no difference can be found between two of the claims, " this circumstance affords no ground for departing from the reasonable and natural meaning of the language " [3]; and the fact that one claim is practically a repetition of another will not render the patent invalid.[4]

196 Effect of disclaimers

The inventor is to be presumed not to claim things which he must have known perfectly well were not new if a reasonable alternative construction is possible.[5]

The effect of a common form of specific reference was discussed in *Société, etc., Dewandre* v. *Citröen Cars Ltd.* [6] where one of the patents contained the following disclaimer: " I am aware of Patent 223214 [*i.e. Godeau*] and do not claim anything claimed therein." Romer L.J. said: " We are, therefore, invited by the patentee himself so to construe his claims as to exclude anything claimed by *Godeau*, and this we must do whether *Godeau's* claims be good or bad." [7]

[1] 11 R.P.C. 493 at p. 502.
[2] See also *Mergenthaler Linotype Co.* v. *Intertype Ltd.*, 43 R.P.C. 239 at p. 289; *Samuel Parkes & Co. Ltd.* v. *Cocker Bros. Ltd.*, 46 R.P.C. 241 at p. 247.
[3] *Per* Tomlin J. in *Brown* v. *Sperry Gyroscope Co. Ltd.*, 42 R.P.C. 111 at p. 136.
[4] *Per* Lindley L.J. in *Wenham Co. Ltd.* v. *Champion Gas Lamp Co.*, 9 R.P.C. 49 at p. 55; see also *New Vacuum, etc., Ltd.* v. *Steel & Wilson*, 32 R.P.C. 162 at p. 171; *Samuel Parkes & Co. Ltd.* v. *Cocker Bros. Ltd.*, 46 R.P.C. 241 at p. 247.
[5] *Haworth* v. *Hardcastle*, 1 W.P.C. 480 at p. 484; *Cropper* v. *Smith & Hancock*, 1 R.P.C. 81 at p. 85; *Lyon* v. *Goddard*, 10 R.P.C. 121 at p. 133; *Tubes Ltd.*, v. *Perfecta Seamless Steel Tube Co. Ltd.*, 20 R.P.C. 77 at p. 97.
[6] 47 R.P.C. 221 at p. 275.
[7] *Cf. Pugh* v. *Riley Cycle Co. Ltd.*, 30 R.P.C. 514 at p. 524.

It is to be observed that the effect of a specific reference (in the above form) may be to render the ambit of the claims vague or doubtful, and in such a case the patent would be bad for ambiguity.[8]

197   Previous constructions binding

When a specification has once received a judicial construction the court, in a subsequent action in respect of the same invention, will hold itself bound on that point by such previous decision,[9] but fresh evidence may be adduced in a subsequent action for the purpose of showing that that which before was not regarded as an anticipation is so in fact.[10]

[The next paragraph is 211]

----

[8] See *British Celanese Ltd.* v. *Courtaulds Ltd.*, 50 R.P.C. 259 at pp. 273, 284, and *post*, § 240 *et seq.*

[9] *Edison* v. *Holland*, 6 R.P.C. 243 at p. 276; *Automatic Weighing Machine Co.* v. *Combined Weighing Machine Co.*, 6 R.P.C. 367 at p. 370.

[10] *Shaw* v. *Day*, 11 R.P.C. 185 at p. 189; *Edison* v. *Holland*, 6 R.P.C. 243 at p. 277; *Flour Oxidizing Co. Ltd.* v. *Carr & Co. Ltd.*, 25 R.P.C. 428 at p. 448; *Higginson and Arundel* v. *Pyman*, 43 R.P.C. 291 at p. 300.

CHAPTER 5

GROUNDS OF REVOCATION

211 THE grounds upon which a patent can be revoked for invalidity are set out in section 32 (1) (*a*) to (*l*) of the 1949 Act and by section 32 (4) each of these grounds of invalidity can be relied upon as a defence to an action for infringement without the necessity of seeking revocation of the patent. The grounds of invalidity set out in the present Act follow to a large extent the grounds of invalidity introduced into the 1907 Act by section 3 of the 1932 Act as a codification of the grounds of invalidity previously established by the common law. The present grounds of invalidity are a complete code and whatever flexible powers the Court had under the common law have been absorbed into the Act.[1] It is, therefore, desirable that one should have regard to the language of the present Act in considering whether or not any particular ground of invalidity is made out, although, of course, the old authorities are binding where the law is unchanged. It is, therefore, proposed to deal with each of the grounds of invalidity specified by the present Act separately, commencing with those that relate to the invalidity being caused by the form of the specification. It will be appreciated that in fact there may be overlap between the various grounds of objection; for instance, a specification which describes and claims a mechanism, which will not attain the object stated, might be invalid for " insufficiency," " inutility " and " false suggestion."

1. INSUFFICIENCY

212 **Section 32 (1) (h):** " the complete specification does not sufficiently and fairly describe the invention and the method by which it is to be performed." [2]

The inventor is entitled to assume that the person to whom the specification is addressed will be in possession of the common knowledge in the art at the date of the specification. The language in which the invention is described and the extent to which details need be given will, therefore, depend upon such common knowledge and upon the class of person who will have to act upon the directions given in the specification.

---

[1] *American Cyanamid Co.* v. *Upjohn Co.* [1970] 1 W.L.R. 1507.
[2] See also s. 4 (3).

213   There may be an overlap between the objection of insufficiency under section 32 (1) *(h)* and that of insufficiently precise definition of the scope of the claims (s. 32 (1) *(i)*). In many cases these two objections can be kept separate, but in some cases this is impossible.[3]

It has been said that the directions should be sufficient to enable " a workman of competent skill in his art," or a " competent engineer " to carry the invention into effect.[4] It is clear, however, that the class of persons comprised in the words " skilled workmen " or " competent engineers " must depend upon the subject-matter with which the invention is concerned. For example, a workman, or even a foreman, in a chemical works might not possess the technical skill and knowledge to understand a new chemical process which the manager would have no difficulty in directing them to put in practice.

Thus, in *Incandescent Gas Light Co.* v. *De Mare Incandescent Gas Light System Ltd.*[5] Wills J. said: " The subject-matter of the specification is such that no one but a person possessing a very considerable amount of chemical knowledge could, at the date of the specification, be considered a competent workman."

The date at which the patent specification must be tested for sufficiency is the date of acceptance of the complete specification and this applies even if the specification is amended. If the specification is amended, it is the amended specification that must be considered.[6]

214   *More than one addressee*

The complexity of the problems arising in modern industries may necessitate more than one " addressee " of the specification. In *Osram Lamp Works Ltd.* v. *Pope's Electric Lamp Co.*[7] Lord Parker said: " A specification may be considered as addressed, at any rate primarily, to the persons who would in normal course have to act on the directions given for the performance. These persons may be assumed to possess not only a reasonable amount of common sense, but also a complete knowledge of the art or arts which have to be called into play in carrying the patentee's directions into effect. I say art or arts because in carrying out the directions given by the patentee it may well be necessary to call in aid more than one art. Some of the directions contained in a specification may have to be carried out by skilled mechanics, others by competent chemists. In such a case, the mechanic and chemist must be assumed to co-operate

---

[3] See *Summers* v. *Cold Metal Process*, 65 R.P.C. 75 at pp. 101 to 105.
[4] See *e.g. Morgan* v. *Seaward*, 1 W.P.C. 170 at p. 174; *Plimpton* v. *Malcolmson*, 3 Ch.D. 531.
[5] 13 R.P.C. 301 at p. 327.
[6] *Anxionnaz* v. *Rolls Royce Ltd.* [1967] R.P.C. 419 at pp. 471–472. See *American Cyanamid Co.* v. *Upjohn Co.* [1970] 1 W.L.R. 1507 at p. 1528, *per* Lord Diplock.   [7] 34 R.P.C. 369 at p. 391.

for the purpose in view, each making good any deficiency in the other's technical equipment. The specification cannot be considered insufficient merely because the mechanic without the aid of the chemist, or the chemist without the aid of the mechanic, would be unable to comprehend the meaning of, or to carry into effect, the direction given by the patentee."

215 *Degree of sufficiency required*

The general principles by which the " sufficiency " of the specification should be determined were stated by Lindley L.J. in *Edison and Swan Electric Co.* v. *Holland* [8] in the following way: " . . . in describing in what manner the invention is to be performed, the patentee does all that is necessary, if he makes it plain to persons having reasonable skill in doing such things as have to be done in order to work the patent, what they are to do in order to perform his invention. If . . . they are to do something the like of which has never been done before, he must tell them how to do it, if a reasonably competent workman would not himself see how to do it on reading the specification. . . ."

216 Generally speaking, therefore, the inventor is not required to give directions of a more minute nature than a person of ordinary skill and knowledge of the art might fairly be expected to need.[9] If, for example, the specification directs that a certain substance is to be used, it will be sufficient if the invention can be carried out with the substance sold commercially under that name even though the substance if chemically pure would be inoperative. Thus, in " Z " *Electric Lamp Co.* v. *Marples, Leach & Co.*[10] the specification prescribed the use of a substance known as " phospham " in the manufacture of incandescent electric lamps for a particular purpose. The defendants showed that " phospham " in the strictest chemical sense would not operate in the manner desired. The plaintiffs, on the other hand, showed that the substance as obtained from chemical manufacturers was not quite pure and that it would work satisfactorily. It was held that the addressee was the lamp manufacturer, and that he would in the ordinary course of business procure his " phospham " from the chemical manufacturer.

Again if it is necessary to use some old or well-known apparatus,

---

[8] 6 R.P.C. 243 at p. 289.
[9] See also *Boulton* v. *Bull*, 2 H.Bl. 463 at p. 478; *Morgan* v. *Seaward*, 1 W.P.C. 170 at p. 174; *Gaulard and Gibbs' Patent*, 6 R.P.C. 215 at p. 224; *Miller* v. *Clyde Bridge Steel Co.*, 8 R.P.C. 198 at p. 201; *Hopkinson* v. *St. James's and Pall Mall Lighting Co.*, 10 R.P.C. 46 at p. 61; *Kane & Pattison* v. *Boyle*, 18 R.P.C. 325 at p. 336.
[10] 27 R.P.C. 305 at p. 316; 737 at p. 744.

the specification need only refer to the apparatus by the name by which it is generally known. But should the success of the invention depend particularly on the manner in which a well-known apparatus is to be used, the directions must lay stress on this point, if it would not be obvious to the skilled man.

217   In *Badische Anilin und Soda Fabrik* v. *La Société, etc., du Rhône* [11] the specification directed (in an example) that two substances were to be heated together " in an autoclave." It was proved that in similar operations the trade frequently made use of autoclaves which were not made of iron, and that in many such operations enamelled autoclaves had advantages. The success of the plaintiff's process entirely depended, however, upon the use of an *iron* vessel, and the specification was declared insufficient.[12]

In the case of a chemical process, it is not permissible, by using general words such as " treating," " converting," or " replacing," to attempt to cover all possible methods, whether then known or subsequently to be discovered.[13]

218   *Limits of necessary experiments*

The directions given must be such as to enable the invention to be carried into effect without an excessive number of experiments.

In *Plimpton* v. *Malcolmson* [14] Jessel M.R. said " You must not give people mechanical problems and call them specifications." But the inventor cannot be expected to relieve the " competent workman " from all obligation to take trouble in carrying into effect the description in the specification. For example, in modern engineering practice no one would think of treating the drawings of a machine in a specification as working drawings: a certain amount of designing and calculation has to be carried out before a machine can be built, and the degree of knowledge requisite to perform such operations must be presumed in the person to whom the specification is addressed.

219   In *Edison and Swan Electric Light Co.* v. *Holland* [15] Cotton L.J. said: " The objection taken as a whole, was that the specification did not sufficiently show how the invention is to be carried into effect. It is necessary that this should be done so as to be intelligible, and to enable the thing to be made without further invention by . . . a person conversant in the subject. But in my opinion it is not

[11] 15 R.P.C. 359.

[12] See also *Wallace* v. *Tullis, Russell & Co. Ltd.*, 39 R.P.C. 3; *John Summers & Sons Ltd.* v. *The Cold Metal Process Co.*, 65 R.P.C. 75.

[13] *British Celanese Ltd.'s Appn.*, 51 R.P.C. 192.

[14] 3 Ch.D. 531 at p. 576.

[15] 6 R.P.C. 243 at p. 277.

necessary that such a person should be able to do the work without any trial or experiment, which, when it is new or especially delicate, may frequently be necessary, however clear the description may be."[16]

The degree of experiment which will be permissible is a question of fact in each case. In *Leonhardt* v. *Kallé* [17] the inventor had given six examples of the use of oxidisable substances in the process claimed, and one of the objections raised was that the specification showed no means for ascertaining what oxidisable substances were not suitable. Romer J. said: " Now, with reference to that, what has the patentee done, and what really could he do more? He has pointed out numerous oxidisable substances, and admittedly those oxidisable substances he mentioned are as good, if not better, and are more easily dealt with than the other oxidisable substances which are not specifically mentioned. Was it reasonable to suppose that the patentee ought to set himself down as a sort of dictionary to specify every known oxidisable substance, and to point out which of those could not give very useful results, or which might be disregarded? . . . I think, seeing what numerous examples are given, that it would be easy to a chemist . . . to ascertain in which one of the examples . . . the substance he is dealing with falls and apply that example."[18]

220 *No need to state advantages*

In general it is not necessary for the inventor to state the advantages of the invention. In *Badische Anilin und Soda Fabrik* v. *Levinstein* [19] the specification described four processes for the production of sulpho acids of oxynaphthaline applicable to dyeing and printing, and varying in colour from brown to red. All these processes were claimed, although only one of the shades was proved to have any practical value, and it was argued that the patent was bad on the ground that no description was given of the relative advantages of each particular shade of colour. It was held by the House of

---

[16] And see *Morgan* v. *Seaward*, 1 W.P.C. 170 at p. 176; *Otto* v. *Linford*, 46 L.T.(N.S.) 35 at p. 40; *British Dynamite Co.* v. *Krebs*, 13 R.P.C. 190 at p. 192; *Osram Lamp Works Ltd.* v. *Pope's Electric Lamp Co.*, 34 R.P.C. 369 at p. 391; *Watson, Laidlaw & Co.* v. *Pott & Others*, 27 R.P.C. 541 at p. 588; 28 R.P.C. 565 at p. 580; *Actiengesellschaft für Anilin, etc.* v. *Levinstein Ltd.*, 38 R.P.C. 277 at p. 291; *No-Fume Ltd.* v. *Frank Pitchford & Co. Ltd.*, 52 R.P.C. 231 at p. 243; *International de Lavaud Manufacturing Corporation Ltd.* v. *Clay Cross Co. Ltd.*, 58 R.P.C. 177; *John Summers & Sons Ltd.* v. *The Cold Metal Process Co.*, 65 R.P.C. 75.

[17] 12 R.P.C. 103 at p. 116.

[18] See also *Wegmann* v. *Corcoran*, 13 Ch.D. 65, and cases cited in note 16, *supra*.

[19] 4 R.P.C. 449.

Lords that to require such discrimination was to insist upon what was really impracticable; Lord Halsbury L.C. said: " Upon the principle contended for, each shade must not only be shown, but its excellence or popularity must be distinguished separately by the patentee. This, as it appears to me, reduces the obligation supposed to press upon the patentee to an absurdity." [20]

221　*Advantage whole essence of invention*

Where the attainment of a particular advantage constitutes the whole essence of the invention it may be necessary to state this advantage and to confine the claims to apparatus or processes that will achieve it in order properly to delimit the invention.[21]

222　*Drafting of a " selection " patent*

In the case of a " selection " patent,[22] *i.e.* one in which the inventive step resides in the discovery that one or more members of a previously known class have some special advantage for some particular purpose, the following requirements as to drafting have been laid down by Maugham J. in *I.G. Farbenindustrie A.G.'s Patents*[23]: " . . . it is necessary for the patentee to define in clear terms the nature of the characteristic which he alleges to be possessed by the selection for which he claims a monopoly. He has in truth disclosed no invention whatever if he merely says that the selected group possesses advantages. Apart altogether from the question of what is called sufficiency, he must disclose an invention; he fails to do this in the case of a selection for special characteristics, if he does not adequately define them."

223　*Alloys*

In *Mond Nickel Co. Ltd.'s Application*[24] the Appeal Tribunal said: " an applicant who claims an alloy must follow one of these courses: (1) he can claim an alloy by specifying all the ingredients of which it is composed, together with the range of proportions in which they are to be present, but he need not exclude impurities; (2) he can claim an alloy where it is to be used in connection with a well-known

---

[20] 4 R.P.C. 449 at p. 464. See also *Keith and Blackman Co. Ltd.* v. *Tilley, etc., Gas Syndicate*, 30 R.P.C. 537 at p. 546; *Roth* v. *Cracknell*, 38 R.P.C. 120 at p. 128.

[21] *Clay* v. *Allcock & Co. Ltd.*, 23 R.P.C. 745; *Clyde Nail Co. Ltd.* v. *Russell*, 33 R.P.C. 291 at p. 306; *Contraflo Condenser, etc., Co. Ltd.* v. *Hick, Hargreaves & Co. Ltd.*, 37 R.P.C. 89 at p. 103; *Thomas* v. *South Wales, etc., Engineering Co. Ltd.*, 42 R.P.C. 22 at p. 27; *I.G. Farbenindustrie A.G.'s Patents*, 47 R.P.C. 289 at p. 323.

[22] See *post*, § 329.

[23] 47 R.P.C. 289 at p. 323. See also *Esso Research and Eng. Co.'s Appn.* [1960] R.P.C. 35.

[24] 65 R.P.C. 123 at p. 125.

and understood commercial process, such as the manufacture of steel, by making it consist of the specific ingredients . . . stating the range of their respective proportions, together with the whole or any part of a class of incidental ingredients which are used in the particular trade at the date of the claim and which together with their respective ranges of proportions are well known in the particular trade; (3) he can claim an alloy where it is to be used in connection with a well-known and understood commercial process, such as the manufacture of steel, by making it consist of the specified ingredients together with one or more of a specified number of the incidental ingredients (using that phrase in the sense in which I have used it in the preceding paragraph) specifying the respective ranges of the proportions of such incidental ingredients.

" Further, in the case of a well-known and understood commercial process, in which all or any of a number of incidental ingredients (using the phrase as I have used it above) may be added at the option of the manufacturer, I am further of the opinion that, if he so desires, an applicant, instead of claiming an alloy, can claim a method of manufacture consisting, for instance, of the addition for a stated purpose (*e.g.* as an inoculant in the manufacture of cast iron) of specific ingredients, the range of the proportions of such respective ingredients being stated, and can state both in the body of the specification and in the claim that in carrying out his invention all or any of the incidental ingredients (using that phrase as I have used it above) may be added. In certain circumstances such a course may be found to be preferable to a claim for an alloy, and I see no objection to it in principle."

224 *Essential material*

" What the section requires is a sufficient description. This suggests in the context of a specification a number of words, illustrations, diagrams or symbols. It does not include an obligation to make available with the specification any particular substance." [25] Provided that all the materials and the process are sufficiently and fairly described then the requirements of the section are met.

225 *Effect of errors*

An error in a specification which may be said, in a sense, to be a technical error, will not render the patent invalid, although it be an error in description or drawing, provided it be such an error as the skilled addressee would at once observe and be in a position to

---

[25] *Per* Lord Guest in *American Cyanamid* v. *Upjohn Co.* [1970] 1 W.L.R. 1507 at p. 1520.

correct.[26]　If, however, experiments would be required to show that there was an error, the patent will be invalid.[27] It frequently occurs that the inventor states an erroneous theory as to the operation of the machine or process, the subject of the invention. This will not invalidate the patent [28] unless it amounts to a statement that would in practice be misleading, or amounts to a false suggestion.[29]

The question of the sufficiency of the specification is one of fact in each particular case and must be decided on the evidence.[30] The amount of detail which would be a sufficient description of one invention may be an insufficient description of another, and consequently a decision in one case cannot necessarily be applied by analogy to another.

2. NON-DISCLOSURE OF BEST METHOD KNOWN TO APPLICANT

226 Section 32 (1) (h): " the complete specification . . . does not disclose the best method of performing it (the invention) which was known to the applicant for the patent and for which he was entitled to claim protection."

The applicant must disclose the best method of performing the invention which was known to him and for which he was entitled to claim protection.[31]　Under the 1932 Act the patent was invalid if " the complete specification does not disclose the best method known to the applicant for the patent at the time when the complete specification was left at the Patent Office," [32] whether that method was a matter of public knowledge or not.[33] It is submitted that, by reason of the words, *supra*, in the present Act " and for which he was entitled to claim protection," the patentee is now relieved from this burden and need only disclose the best method known to him if it is something which could form the subject-matter of a patent application by him, *i.e.* something which is not publicly known and

---

[26] *No-Fume Ltd.* v. *Frank Pitchford & Co. Ltd.*, 52 R.P.C. 231 at p. 243.
[27] *Simpson* v. *Holliday*, L.R. 1 H.L. 315 at p. 321; *Otto* v. *Linford*, 46 L.T.(N.S.) 35 at p. 40; *Miller* v. *Scarle*, 10 R.P.C. 106 at p. 111; *British United Shoe Machinery Co.* v. *A. Fussell & Sons Ltd.*, 25 R.P.C. 368 at p. 385; *True and Variable Electric Lamp Syndicate* v. *Bryant Trading Syndicate*, 25 R.P.C. 461; *Knight* v. *Argylls Ltd.*, 30 R.P.C. 321 at p. 348.
[28] See *" Z " Electric Lamp Co.* v. *Marples, Leach & Co.*, 27 R.P.C. 737 at p. 746.
[29] As in *Monnet* v. *Beck*, 14 R.P.C. 777 at p. 847. *See* also *" Z " Electric Lamp Co.* v. *Marples, Leach & Co.*, 27 R.P.C. 737; *Le Rasoir Apollo's Patent*, 49 R.P.C. 1.
[30] *R.* v. *Arkwright*, 1 W.P.C. 64; *Hill* v. *Thompson & Forman*, 1 W.P.C. 235 at p. 237; *British Dynamite Co.* v. *Krebs*, 13 R.P.C. 190 at p. 192.
[31] s. 32 (1) (*h*).
[32] 1932 Act, s. 3, amending s. 25 (2) of 1907 Act.
[33] *Norton and Gregory* v. *Jacobs*, 54 R.P.C. 271 at p. 277.

constitutes a patentable advance on anything previously published. It is also submitted that the only knowledge that is material is that which was in the mind of the patentee at the priority date of the relevant claim, for just as no invention can now be given an earlier priority date than the date on which it was disclosed in a specification, so any method of operation of an inventive character subsequently devised by the applicant need not, and indeed should not, be included in the description of any invention the claim relating to which has an earlier priority date. It follows that previous decisions requiring the disclosure of any method of operation devised between the dates of filing the provisional and complete specifications are no longer good law.[34]

At common law a patent has always been held to be invalid if the inventor in his specification did not communicate all his knowledge regarding the invention, or if he misled the public.

227   *Invention communicated from abroad*

In *Wagmann* v. *Corcoran* [35] the patent had been granted on a communication from abroad. The rollers prescribed by the specification for use in the machine were obtained by the plaintiff from Italy, where the process of their manufacture was kept secret, but the specification did not mention this fact, and they could not be made from the description given. The specification was held to be insufficient and misleading. Fry J. held that " though the grantee of a patent for an invention communicated to him by a foreign resident abroad is only bound to tell the public all that he himself knows, yet if the original inventor has not told him enough to enable him so to describe the invention as that it can be constructed by the aid only of the specification, the patent will be invalid."[36]

The above case is distinguishable from the case of *Plimpton* v. *Malcolmson*,[37] where the question was whether the patentee, having disclosed a useful invention, was bound to disclose some fact more useful than the description actually given, which he himself did not know, but which was within the knowledge of the person communicating from abroad. It was properly held that he was not so bound, but it is obvious that he was bound to describe an invention in itself useful, and that he was bound to disclose all that he himself knew, and to give a sufficient description to work the invention.

[34] See *Crampton* v. *Patents Investments Ltd.*, 5 R.P.C. 382 at p. 397.
[35] 13 Ch.D. 65.
[36] As stated in the headnote, p. 66; see the judgment at p. 77 and 39 L.T.(N.S.) at p. 568. See also *Sturtz* v. *De la Rue*, 1 W.P.C. 83.
[37] 3 Ch.D. 531 at p. 582.

228   *Misleading description*

It has been held that if the patentee gives details in his specification which are not necessary to the invention, which of themselves do not constitute an invention, and which are merely put in for the purpose of misleading the public either as to the nature of the invention or as to how it is to be carried into effect, then the patent will be void.[38]

229   *Good faith of applicant*

The requirement that the best method known must be disclosed is not so much for perfection of detail as to ensure good faith on the part of the applicant. In *Tetley* v. *Easton*[39] Pollock C.B. said: " A man has no right to patent a principle and then give to the public the humblest instrument that can be made from his principle, and reserve to himself all the better part of it." And in *Heath* v. *Unwin*[40] Coleridge J. said: " If the inventor of an alleged discovery, knowing two equivalent agents for effecting the end, could, by the disclosure of one, preclude the public from the benefit of the other, he might, for his own profit, force upon the public an expensive and difficult process, keeping back the simple and cheap one, which would be directly contrary to the good faith required from every patentee in his communication with the public."[41]

230   In *British Dynamite Co.* v. *Krebs*[42] the inventor, Nobel, described a new explosive (dynamite) which, the specification stated, was to be made by causing nitro-glycerine (*per se* a dangerous liquid) to be absorbed by a porous unexplosive substance. He gave a list of such substances which were shown to be more or less useful. The resulting mass was safe and could be stored. He found subsequently that a well-known silicious earth (" kieselguhr ") possessed the requisites of porosity and power of absorption to a very high degree, and the dynamite actually manufactured was, in consequence, always produced by the aid of this material. Lord Hatherley, restoring the judgment of Fry J., said: " If it had been proved that the inventor, Nobel, knew the best material, which turned out to be a material called ' kieselguhr,' a silicious earth; if he had known of the existence of ' kieselguhr ' at the time, and that it would take up 75 per cent. of the nitro-glycerine, whereas some other materials specified by the patentee took up only 25 to 50 per cent., it would have been an

---

[38] See *Lewis* v. *Marling*, 1 W.P.C. 490 at p. 496.
[39] Macr.P.C. 48 at p. 76.
[40] 2 W.P.C. 236 at p. 243.
[41] And see *Wood* v. *Zimmer*, 1 W.P.C. 44n.; *Crossley* v. *Beverley*, 1 W.P.C. 112 at p. 117; *Morgan* v. *Seaward*, 1 W.P.C. 167 at p. 174; *Franc-Strohmenger & Cowan Inc.* v. *Peter Robinson Ltd.*, 47 R.P.C. 493 at p. 501.
[42] 13 R.P.C. 190 at p. 195.

objection to his patent to say that he, being in possession of the best mode of producing the most valuable dynamite, had not informed the public of that method."

In each of the cases quoted above it would seem that the information that was withheld, or assumed to have been withheld, amounted to a patentable invention and, therefore, the principle of those decisions is still applicable.

3. CLAIM NOT FAIRLY BASED

231   **Section 32 (1) (i):** ". . . any claim of the complete specification is not fairly based on the matter disclosed in the specification."

It was always a requirement at common law that the claim should not be more extensive than the invention.[43]

232   In *Mullard Radio Valve Co. Ltd.* v. *Philco Radio and Television Corporation*[44] the invention was concerned with obviating a defect which occurred in the use of a four-electrode thermionic valve when placed in the final amplifying stage and arranged so that the grid nearest the cathode was the " control " grid and the grid between the " control " grid and the anode was the " screening " grid; the invention consisted in inserting an additional " suppressor " grid between the " screening " grid and the anode, which " suppressor " grid was maintained at a relatively low potential. Whether a grid was the " control " grid or the " screening " grid or the " suppressor " grid depended not on its construction but on the external electric potentials applied to the electrodes. The claim in question was for " a discharge tube having at least three auxiliary electrodes between the cathode and the anode, characterised in that the auxiliary electrode nearest to the anode is directly connected to the cathode so as to be maintained continuously at the cathode potential." Lord Macmillan said[45]: " Is the patentee entitled to such a monopoly? He is entitled to say that a discharge tube so constructed is new, for discharge tubes with such a connection were not previously known or made; and he is entitled to say that such a discharge tube has patentable utility in the sense that it can be used and will work as a discharge tube. But is the claim justified by the inventive idea which the patentee has disclosed? . . . It was submitted that in a claim for an article it is sufficient to establish that the article is capable of being used to perform the invention, and that it is nothing

---

[43] *Hill* v. *Thompson and Forman*, 1 W.P.C. 235. And see *Gandy* v. *Reddaway*, 2 R.P.C. 49; *Dick* v. *Ellams*, 17 R.P.C. 196 at p. 200; *Woodrow* v. *Long Humphreys & Co. Ltd.*, 51 R.P.C. 25; *Gill's Appn.*, 54 R.P.C. 119.

[44] 53 R.P.C. 323.

[45] 53 R.P.C. 323 at p. 345.

to the purpose to show that it may also be used or abused in ways which do not perform the invention or which achieve some other and different results, unless, it can also be shown that the article claimed will not in certain circumstances work at all. But when an article is claimed its virtue must reside in itself. It must always be capable of giving the advantages which the patentee has told you may be expected from its use. A discharge tube having three or more electrodes of which the one nearest the anode is directly connected with the anode will not give the advantage which the patentee discovered and described unless the electrodes in its vicinity are used to perform particular functions in a particular order of arrangement. The article claimed is a discharge tube in which by virtue of its construction the grid nearest the anode will always be kept at the same potential as the cathode, and its construction will no doubt always ensure this. But the inventor's purpose was not to invent a discharge tube which should have this feature. If his problem had been to invent a tube in which the grid nearest the anode should always be at cathode potential, his problem could have been easily and obviously solved. Anyone could have told him that all he had to do was to establish a physical connection between the grid nearest to the anode and the cathode. His problem was to obviate disadvantages which arose when a screening grid was interposed between the control grid and the anode, a quite special and definite problem. I do not think that he is entitled to prevent anyone in future from making a valve in which the grid nearest to the anode is connected with the cathode merely because he has discovered that in a valve in which the other grids are utilised in a particular way this connection will give the special advantage which he discovered. It is because he has sought to do so that the claim is, in my opinion, too wide. The fact that an article of obvious construction is discovered to give a valuable and new benefit if employed in a particular way does not entitle the discoverer to prevent everyone else from making that article. A patentee is granted his monopoly in order to protect the invention which in his specification he has communicated to the public. He is not entitled to claim a monopoly more extensive than is necessary to protect that which he has himself said is his invention. . . . If an inventor claims an article as his invention but the article will only achieve his avowed object in a particular juxtaposition and his inventive idea consists in the discovery that in that particular juxtaposition it will give new and useful results, I do not think that he is entitled to claim the article at large apart from the juxtaposition which is essential to the achievement of those results. It was argued for the appellants that if an article is new, is useful and has subject-

[90]

matter, then it is necessarily patentable and entitled to protection. But a claim may be for an article which is new, which is useful and which has subject-matter, yet it may be too wide a claim because it extends beyond the subject-matter of the invention. The consideration which the patentee gives to the public disclosing his inventive idea entitles him in return to protection for an article which embodies his inventive idea but not for an article which, while capable of being used to carry his inventive idea into effect, is described in terms which cover things quite unrelated to his inventive idea, and which do not embody it at all."

233   This case has given rise to considerable discussion and it has even been suggested that in consequence of the passage referring to " juxtaposition " quoted above it has now become difficult to formulate a valid claim for an article *per se*. It is argued, for example, that a new and ingenious sparking plug cannot be claimed by itself, as it lies on sale in its carton on a shop counter, because it is of no value for the purpose for which it was invented until it has been suitably fixed in an internal combustion engine, and even then a motive fluid must be supplied to the engine and an electric current to the sparking plug. Accordingly, it has been questioned whether a claim to the sparking plug can be valid unless it be limited by reference to its use in an engine coupled with the provision of a suitable motive fluid and electric current. Obviously, only a user would infringe a claim so restricted, so that the manufacture and sale of the sparking plug could not be prevented and in practice the patentee's monopoly would be worthless. It is submitted that this view is based on an entire misconception of *Mullard* v. *Philco*, the reasoning in which can be simply expressed as follows. A claim for a combination of integers, even though some or all are oid, is permissible if a novel result is achieved by the combination.[46] But the claim must include (and, therefore, be limited by) all the necessary integers. In the case under discussion some of the necessary integers for the invention were the electric potentials to be applied to the electrodes. It was essential, therefore, that these electric potentials should be specified in the claim. As they were not, the claim was invalid. The actual article in question was held to be of an obvious and non-inventive character, the real invention requiring that it should be used in a particular way. The case has no application where the article itself requires an act of invention to produce it and is itself the subject-matter of the invention.

[46] See *post*, § 326.

Mullard v. *Philco* has been further explained in the course of the proceedings in which an unsuccessful attempt was made to amend the claim mentioned above.[47]

The Comptroller will not accept broad and indeterminate claims of a speculative character covering fields which the patentee has done nothing to explore.[48]

234 *Wide claims for new " principles "*

Where the patentee has disclosed a method of applying what is sometimes inaccurately referred to as " a new principle," *i.e.* a new general method of achieving some result, a wide claim is permissible. " Such a claim ought probably to be construed as a claim of monopoly for that arrangement carried out by any means substantially similar to those disclosed in the specification." [49]

235 *Claim for a " principle "*

In *Ridd Milking Machine Co. Ltd.* v. *Simplex Milking Machine Co. Ltd.*,[50] Lord Shaw said: " It might be possible in very many cases of a claim for apparatus—if the argument presented were sound— to evolve a claim for a principle from a description given of the results achieved, and to maintain accordingly that it was the principle of the invention in that sense which was the real subject of the claim. This is, in their Lordships' opinion, a method of construction of patent claims which is accompanied with serious danger . . . if any claim for a principle is made it must undoubtedly appear in the claim as that claim is stated, and must not be left to an inference resting on a general review of the specification, or a general search among the language employed therein for the meritorious element of principle or idea." [51]

In *Jupe* v. *Pratt*,[52] in the course of the argument, Alderson B.

[47] *Mullard Radio Valve Co. Ltd.* v. *British Belmont Radio Ltd. and Others*, 56 R.P.C. 1 at p. 10. See also *American Optical Co.'s Appn.* [1958] R.P.C. 40; *Mergenthaler Linotype Co.'s Appn.* [1958] R.P.C. 278.
[48] *Esau's Appn.*, 49 R.P.C. 85 at p. 87; *Shell Development Co.'s Appn.*, 64 R.P.C. 151; *Pottier's Appn.* [1967] R.P.C. 170.
[49] *Per* Wright J. in *Edison Bell Phonograph Co. Ltd.* v. *Smith*, 11 R.P.C. 148 at p. 163. And see *Automatic Weighing Machine Co.* v. *Knight*, 6 R.P.C. 297 at p. 304 (C.A.); *Ashworth* v. *English Card Clothing Co. Ltd.*, 20 R.P.C. 790.
[50] 33 R.P.C. 309 at p. 317.
[51] And see *Dudgeon* v. *Thomson*, 3 App.Cas. 34 at p. 44; *Incandescent Gas Light Co. Ltd.* v. *Sunlight Incandescent Gas Lamp Co. Ltd.*, 13 R.P.C. 333; *Presto Gear Case Co.* v. *Orme Evans & Co.*, 18 R.P.C. 17 at p. 23; *Ackroyd and Best Ltd.* v. *Thomas & Williams*, 21 R.P.C. 737 at p. 750; *Marconi's Wireless Telegraph Co.* v. *Mullard Radio Valve Co. Ltd.*, 41 R.P.C. 323 at p. 334; *British United Shoe Machinery Co. Ltd.* v. *Gimson Shoe Machinery Co. Ltd.* (*No. 2*), 46 R.P.C. 137 at p. 159.
[52] 1 W.P.C. 144 at p. 146.

said: " You cannot take out a patent for a principle. You may take out a patent for a principle coupled with the mode of carrying the principle into effect, provided you have not only discovered the principle but invented some mode of carrying it into effect. But then you must start with having invented some mode of carrying the principle into effect. If you have done that, then you are entitled to protect yourself from all the other modes of carrying the principle into effect, that being treated by the jury as a piracy of your original invention."

236 These words have been commented on in *R.C.A. Photophone Ltd.* v. *Gaumont British Picture Corporation Ltd.*[53] Lord Wright said [54]: " It is true that what is often, very inaptly, called a principle, by which is meant some general method of manufacture, may be validly claimed, so long as it is new, and the inventor describes one mode of carrying it into effect (*Jupe* v. *Pratt*); still, even in such a case, the precise ambit of the claim must depend on the language used." And Greene L.J. said [55] " . . . the words are not ' you are entitled to protection,' but ' you are entitled to protect yourself,' which appear to me clearly to mean that you are entitled to draft your claim in words wide enough to secure the protection desired." [56]

237 Nevertheless, a wide claim to a " principle " must not be so extensive as to amount to a claim to *any* method of solving a particular problem, and this is clearly illustrated by *British United Shoe Machinery Co. Ltd.* v. *Simon Collier Ltd.*,[57] where the patent was for a machine for performing some of the operations involved in bootmaking, more particularly trimming the edge of the sole. The position of the trimming knife at any moment was automatically governed by the position of a guide which bore upon another portion of the boot so that the width of the sole was varied in relation to that other portion. One of the patentee's claims was as follows: " In a sole trimming machine, a trimming knife, a guide, support therefor, and automatic means for automatically varying the relative positions of the knife and guide during the trimming operation for the purpose described." One method of effecting such automatic variation (by means of a cam) was described and made the subject of other claims.

---

[53] 53 R.P.C. 167.
[54] 53 R.P.C. 167 at p. 186.
[55] 53 R.P.C. 167 at p. 205.
[56] And see *Neilson* v. *Harford*, 1 W.P.C. 331 at p. 355; *Automatic Weighing Machine Co.* v. *Knight*, 6 R.P.C. 297 at p. 304; *Nobel's Explosives Co.* v. *Anderson*, 11 R.P.C. 519 at pp. 525, 527; *Ashworth* v. *English Card Clothing Co. Ltd.*, 20 R.P.C. 790 at p. 797; *British Vacuum Cleaner Co. Ltd.* v. *J. Robertshaw & Sons Ltd.*, 32 R.P.C. 424 at p. 435.
[57] 26 R.P.C. 21.

238   Parker J. said [58]: " If on the true construction of the specification, the claim is as wide as the defendants contend, the validity of the patent depends upon whether an inventor, who discloses one way of doing automatically for a particular purpose what, in existing machines, could be done for the same purpose, not indeed, automatically, but by the service or skill on the part of the workman, can obtain the grant of letters patent for all means of doing the same thing automatically for the same purpose. It appears from the judgment of Alderson B. in *Jupe* v. *Pratt* [59] . . . that though you cannot take out a patent for a principle, yet if the principle is new, and you show one mode of carrying it into effect, you may protect yourself against all other modes of carrying the principle into effect. If, however, the principle is not new, you can only protect yourself against those modes of carrying it into effect which are substantially the same as the mode you have yourself invented, the question being in each case what is the pith and marrow of the invention sought to be protected, and it being impossible to treat any principle already known as part of such pith and marrow. Thus, where the principle is old, a claim to all modes of carrying it into effect will avoid the patent as in *Patterson* v. *Gas Light and Coke Co.*[60] . . . In the present case, considering that in existing machines the relative position of knife and guide could be varied (though not automatically) . . . the problem was simply how to do automatically what could already be done by the skill of the workman. On the other hand, the principle which the inventor applies for the solution of the problem is the capacity of a cam to vary the relative position of two parts of a machine while the machine is running. Assuming this principle to be new, it might be possible for the inventor, having shown one method of applying it to the solution of the problem, to protect himself during the life of his patent from any other method of applying it for the same purpose, but I do not think that the novelty of the principle applied would enable him to make a valid claim for all means of solving the problem whether the same or a different principle were applied to its solution. If he could do so, it would seem to follow that the invention of one means to secure a particular end would entitle an inventor to protection against all means of attaining the same end. If, therefore, the claim be construed as including all automatic means of solving the problem (the

[58] 26 R.P.C. at p. 49.
[59] 1 W.P.C. 144 at p. 146. Approved, *Chamberlain & Hookham Ltd.* v. *Mayor, etc., of Bradford*, 20 R.P.C. 673 at p. 684; and see *British United Shoe Machinery Co.* v. *Standard Rotary Machine Co.*, 35 R.P.C. 33 at pp. 46 and 47.
[60] 2 Ch.D. 812.

" pith and marrow" is only relevant to a mode of putting a principle into effect and not to the principle

learned judge held that it had this meaning), I am of opinion it is too wide, and is not proper subject-matter for letters patent."[61]

239   *No need to " distinguish new from old "*

There is no need to discriminate in the claims themselves between the prior state of the art and the new features in fact introduced by the inventor. The reason for this was stated by Fletcher Moulton L.J. as follows [62]: " In the Act of 1883, for the first time, it was made a statutable duty to insert claims to define the invention, and that has been continued up to the present time; but the language of the statute follows that of the old proviso and leaves no doubt that the duty is only to define the invention for which the monopoly is claimed. The justice and sufficiency of that requirement are obvious. . . . A patentee often works solitarily. He has very little idea of what others are doing . . . and much of his work . . . has been to re-invent that which others, without his knowledge, have invented. The consequence is that the inventive act of the inventor can have no relevance or effect; . . . Then are we to say that he is to state what would have been the inventive act, supposing him to know the whole knowledge of the world? . . . Of course, if his ignorance has led him to claim something which is not novel he has to take the penalty. . . . But to say that he must also ascertain, under the penalty of his patent being bad, everything that preceded his invention, every approach from every side that persons have made to it, and must correctly indicate the little step which he has made in addition to these, . . . would be to require something of him which would be perfectly idle so far as regards utility to the public, and grossly unjust so far as the patentee is concerned. . . . A man must distinguish what is old from what is new *by* his claim; but he has not got to distinguish what is old from what is new *in* his claim. If the combination which he has claimed, and for which he asks a monopoly, is novel, that is sufficient. There is no obligation to go further and to state why it is novel, or what in it is novel."[63]

---

[61] And see *Submarine Signal Co.* v. *Hughes & Son Ltd.*, 49 R.P.C. 149 at p. 175; *Automatic Weighing Machine Co.* v. *Knight*, 6 R.P.C. 297 at p. 308; *R.C.A. Photophone Ltd.* v. *Gaumont British Picture Corporation Ltd.*, 53 R.P.C. 167 at p. 186.

[62] *British United Shoe Machinery Co. Ltd.* v. *A. Fussell & Sons Ltd.*, 25 R.P.C. 631 at p. 651.

[63] And see *Jackson* v. *Wolstenhulmes*, 1 R.P.C. 105 at p. 108; *Fellows* v. *T. W. Lench Ltd.*, 34 R.P.C. 45 at p. 55; *Marconi's Wireless Telegraph Co. Ltd.* v. *Mullard Radio Valve Co. Ltd.*, 41 R.P.C. 323 at p. 334; *Sonotone Corporation* v. *Multitone Electric Co. Ltd.*, 72 R.P.C. 131 at p. 140.

4. AMBIGUITY

240 **Section 32 (1) (i):** "the scope of any claim of the complete specification is not sufficiently and clearly defined."

This has been a requirement of patent law for many years.[64]

241 In defining the scope of the claims it is the duty of the patentee to mark out his territory clearly and without any ambiguity. In *Natural Colour Kinematograph Co. Ltd.* v. *Bioschemes Ltd. (Smith's Patent)*,[65] Lord Loreburn L.C. said: "This patent is bad for ambiguity in the specification. There seems to be some danger of the well-known rule of law against ambiguity being in practice invaded. Some of those who draft specifications and claims are apt to treat this industry as a trial of skill, in which the object is to make the claim very wide upon one interpretation of it, in order to prevent as many people as possible from competing with the patentee's business, and then to rely upon carefully prepared sentences in the specification which, it is hoped, will be just enough to limit the claim within safe dimensions if it is attacked in court. This leads to litigation as to the construction of specifications which could generally be avoided, if at the outset a sincere attempt were made to state exactly what was meant in plain language. The fear of a costly lawsuit is apt to deter any but wealthy competitors from contesting a patent. This is all wrong. It is an abuse which a court can prevent, whether a charge of ambiguity is or is not raised on the pleadings, because it affects the public by practically enlarging the monopoly, and does so by a kind of pressure which is very objectionable. It is the duty of a patentee to state clearly and distinctly, either in direct words or by clear and distinct reference, the nature and limits of what he claims. If he uses language which, when fairly read, is avoidably obscure or ambiguous, the patent is invalid, whether the defect be due to design, or to carelessness, or to want of skill. Where the invention is difficult to explain, due allowance will, of course, be made for any resulting difficulty in the language. But nothing can excuse the use of ambiguous language when simple language can easily be employed, and the only safe way is for the patentee to do his best to be clear and intelligible. It is necessary to emphasise this warning." [66]

242 In *British Ore Concentration Syndicate Ltd.* v. *Minerals Separation Ltd.*,[67] Lord Halsbury said: "The statute requires it [the

---

[64] *Philpott* v. *Hanbury*, 2 R.P.C. 33 at p. 38; *Edison and Swan Electric Co.* v. *Holland*, 6 R.P.C. 243 at p. 280.

[65] 32 R.P.C. 256 at p. 266.

[66] See also *Franc-Strohmenger and Cowan Inc.* v. *Peter Robinson Ltd.*, 47 R.P.C. 493 at p. 501.

[67] 27 R.P.C. 33 at p. 47.

specification] to be a distinct statement of what is the invention. . . .
If he [the applicant] designedly makes it ambiguous, in my judgment
the patent would undoubtedly be bad on that ground; but even if
negligently and unskilfully he fails to make distinct what his invention
is, I am of opinion that the condition is not fulfilled, and the
consequence would be that the patent would be bad." [68]

In examining a specification against which a plea of ambiguity
is raised it is necessary that the wording of the claim should be
interpreted according to the general principles of construction and
in the light of the common knowledge of the art. Thus when there
is a choice between two meanings, one should if possible reject that
meaning which leads to an absurd result and construe the claim
with the knowledge of the skilled addressee.[69] In *British Thomson-
Houston Co. Ltd.* v. *Corona Lamp Works Ltd.*,[70] the patent had
been granted in respect of gas-filled incandescent lamps, and the
inventor had discovered that new and valuable results were obtained
by making the filament of the lamp of " large " diameter. The
claim was as follows: " An incandescent electric lamp having a
filament of tungsten or other refractory metal of large diameter
or cross section or of concentrated (*i.e.* coiled) form and a gas
or vapour of low heat conductivity at relatively high pressure, the
combination being such that the filament may be raised to a much
higher temperature than is practicable in a vacuum lamp without
prohibitive vaporisation or deterioration or excessive shortening of
useful life, substantially as set forth." It was not denied that the
invention was valuable or that the directions in the body of the
specification were sufficient to enable the invention to be carried into
effect according to the examples given, but it was argued that the
word " large " was not sufficiently clear in its meaning to define the
ambit of the monopoly and that a manufacturer would have to
experiment with filaments of varying relative dimensions before he
could ascertain whether or not he was within the monopoly claimed—
the attainment of the stated advantages being the only criterion of
infringement. The House of Lords, however, held that there was no
valid objection to the claim; that the experiments necessary were
clearly within the competence of the manufacturers; that numerical

[68] And see *Linotype and Machinery Ltd.* v. *Hopkins*, 27 R.P.C. 109 at p. 112;
see also *e.g. Taylor's Patent*, 33 R.P.C. 138; *White* v. *Todd Oil Burners
Ltd.*, 46 R.P.C. 275; *Rose Street Foundry, etc., Co. Ltd.* v. *India Rubber
etc. and Telegraph Works Co. Ltd.*, 46 R.P.C. 294; *Cincinnati Grinders
Inc.* v. *B.S.A. Tools Ltd.*, 48 R.P.C. 33; *British Celanese Ltd.* v.
Courtaulds Ltd., 50 R.P.C. 259; *Minerals Separation North American
Corporation* v. *Noranda Mines Ltd.*, 69 R.P.C. 81.
[69] *Henriksen* v. *Tallon Ltd.* [1965] R.P.C. 434 at p. 443.
[70] 39 R.P.C. 49.

definition of the limits of " largeness " was unnecessary having regard to the common knowledge of the dimensions used in practice and under varying conditions, and that to require such a definition would be to open the door to evasion. And in the somewhat similar case of *Watson, Laidlaw & Co. Ltd.* v. *Potts, Cassels and Wiliamson* [71] Lord Shaw pointed out that it was important " not to permit a mathematical analysis to empty a description in plain language of its practical merit."

243   On the other hand, where a word or phrase of a somewhat vague character is used in the claim and is not defined in the body of the specification, it is a question of fact, to be determined on the evidence, whether the use of such word or phrase renders the claim invalid for ambiguity.[72] The fact that some part of a claim is capable of more than one construction does not necessarily mean that the claim is ambiguous.[69] It frequently happens that a patentee who is plaintiff in an action for infringement of the patent is forced to contend that some part of the claim has a meaning other than its ordinary or natural meaning in order to embrace the alleged infringement [73] or to save the claim from invalidity for some other reason, *e.g.* inutility,[74] with the consequence that the claim is ultimately held to be ambiguous. But a claim is not necessarily invalid for ambiguity merely because the patentee contends for a construction which the court is not prepared to adopt.[75]

A claim may be limited by the result to be attained and if so limited is not invalid for ambiguity,[76] provided that in, for instance, a claim for an article, the limitation is " sufficient to characterise the construction of the article claimed." [77]

244   The use of the word " substantially " in the claim, in phrases such as " substantially as described," or " substantially as described and shown in the drawings " does not render the claim invalid for ambiguity.[78] On the other hand, if the monopoly should be defined by reference to such general terms as " known methods " or " general methods," or equivalent phrases, this may lead to ambiguity.[79]

---

[71] 28 R.P.C. 565 at p. 581.
[72] *Unifloc Reagents Ltd.* v. *Newstead Colliery Ltd.*, 60 R.P.C. 165; *Martin* v. *Selsdon Fountain Pen Co. Ltd.*, 66 R.P.C. 193.
[73] *Pathé Cinema S.A.* v. *Coronel Camera Co.*, 57 R.P.C. 48.
[74] *Raleigh Cycle Co. Ltd.* v. *H. Miller & Co. Ltd.*, 65 R.P.C. 141; and see *E.M.I. Ltd.* v. *Lissen Ltd.*, 56 R.P.C. 23 at p. 40.
[75] *Slumberland Ltd.* v. *Burgess Bedding*, 68 R.P.C 87 at p. 98.
[76] *No-Fume Ltd.* v. *Frank Pitchford & Co. Ltd.*, 52 R.P.C. 231.
[77] *Mullard Radio Valve Co. Ltd.* v. *British Belmont Radio Ltd.*, 56 R.P.C. 1 at p. 16.
[78] *Raleigh Cycle Co. Ltd.* v. *H. Miller & Co. Ltd.*, 65 R.P.C. 141 at p. 159. And see *ante*, § 189.
[79] *British Celanese Ltd.'s Appn.*, 51 R.P.C. 192.

245 *Discrepancies in drawings*

The result of there being a discrepancy between the printed matter and the drawings depends upon whether the discrepancy produces ambiguity sufficient to mislead. If what is meant is clear to persons skilled in the art, then the specification is not ambiguous, and it is immaterial from which part of the specification they have drawn their information. If there is material ambiguity, the patent is invalid.[80]

5. INUTILITY

246 **Section 32 (1) (g):** " the invention, so far as claimed in any claim of the complete specification, is not useful."

Utility at common law

In *Elias* v. *Grovesend Tinplate Co.*,[81] Lindley L.J. said: " It is very singular that the Statute of James says nothing whatever about utility, but utility has been engrafted into it because of the words to which I have called attention; that is to say, it has been found mischievous to the State to grant patents which are not useful as well as new." [82]

247 **The test of utility**

Inutility, in the sense in which that word is used in modern patent law and practice, is concerned solely with the scope of the claim, and means that the claim covers a mechanism or a process which is useless for the purposes indicated by the patentee *i.e.* which does not produce the result or one of the results claimed in the specification. A patent would also be void for inutility if the invention was useless for any purpose whatsoever, but this is a circumstance which is unlikely to occur in practice.

In *Lane-Fox* v. *Kensington and Knightsbridge Electric Lighting Co. Ltd.*[83] the relevant claim was as follows: " The employment as described of secondary batteries as reservoirs of electricity in combination with a mode or system of distribution such as is hereinbefore explained." Lindley L.J. said [84]: " The utility of the alleged invention depends not on whether by following the directions in the complete specification all the results now necessary for commercial success can be obtained, but on whether by such directions the effects which the patentee professed to produce could be produced and on the practical utility of those effects . . . to judge of utility the directions in the

[80] See *e.g. Knight* v. *Argyll's Ltd.*, 30 R.P.C. 321 at p. 348.
[81] 7 R.P.C. 455 at p. 467.
[82] See also 3 Co.Inst. 181.
[83] [1892] 3 Ch. 424; 9 R.P.C. 413.
[84] [1892] 3 Ch. at p. 431; 9 R.P.C. at p. 417.

specification must be followed, and if the result is that the object sought to be obtained can be attained, and is practically useful at the time when the patent is granted, the test of utility is satisfied. . . . ' Useful for what?' is a question which must always be asked, and the answer must be useful for the purposes indicated by the patentee." [85]

248   In *Vidal Dyes Syndicate Ltd.* v. *Levinstein Ltd.*[86] Fletcher Moulton L.J. said: " By his specification, and the claim with which it concludes, the patentee delimits the area of his monopoly. If the validity of his patent is challenged, he has to show that all within that area is novel and useful. . . . It is a question involving the area of monopoly claimed, and if, on the proper construction of the specification, the court holds that the patentee has claimed a process which is so dangerous that an expert chemist would avoid it, or even a process which an expert chemist would take to be impossible, the consequence is . . . that his patent is invalid." [87]

249   In *Alsop's Patent*,[88] Parker J. said: " In considering the validity of a patent for a process it is, therefore, material to ascertain precisely what the patentee claims to be the result of the process for which the patent has been granted; the real consideration which he gives for the grant is the disclosure of a process which produces a result, and not the disclosure of a process which may or may not produce any result at all. If the patentee claims protection for a process for producing a result and that result cannot be produced by the process, in my opinion the consideration fails. Similarly, if the patentee claims a process producing two results combined and only one of these results is in fact produced by the process, there is a partial failure of consideration . . . and such partial failure of consideration is sufficient to avoid the patent. . . . Objections to patents on the grounds above referred to are sometimes treated as objections for want of utility, and when so treated the well known rule is that the utility of an invention depends upon whether, by following the directions of the patentee, the result which the patentee professed to produce can in fact be produced (see Lindley L.J. in *Lane-Fox* v. *Kensington, etc., Co., supra*). Want of utility in this sense must, however, in my opinion, be distinguished from want of utility in the sense of the invention being useless for any purpose whatsoever. In the case of an invention not serving any useful purpose at all, the

---

[85] See also *Mullard Radio Valve Co. Ltd.* v. *Philco Radio and Television Corporation*, 52 R.P.C. at p. 287.

[86] 29 R.P.C. 245 at pp. 268, 271.

[87] See also *Simpson* v. *Holliday*, L.R. 1 H.L. 315, quoted in *Vidal Dyes Syndicate Ltd.* v. *Levinstein Ltd.*, 29 R.P.C. at p. 271.

[88] 24 R.P.C. 733 at p. 752.

patent would no doubt be void, but not entirely for the same reason. It would probably be void at common law on the ground that the King's prerogative could not be properly exercised unless there were some consideration moving to the public, and the public could not be benefited by the disclosure of something absolutely useless. It would certainly be avoided as mischievous to the State and generally inconvenient within the Statute of Monopolies. But it may well be that an invention, which is void because it does not produce the result or one of the results claimed, may, nevertheless, be useful as producing other results."

In *Hatmaker* v. *Joseph Nathan & Co. Ltd.*,[89] Lord Birkenhead L.C. quoted with approval the above passage from Parker J.'s judgment, and said: "In other words, protection is purchased by the promise of results. It does not, and ought not to, survive the proved failure of the promise to produce the results." [90]

250　*Two classes of promise*

A distinction was, however, drawn by Parker J. in *Alsop's Patent*,[91] between two kinds of promise as follows: "There may be cases in which the result which the patentee claims to have produced can in fact be produced, but the patentee has gone on to detail the useful purposes to which such result can be applied, and that in fact the result produced cannot be applied to one or more of such purposes. In such a case I do not think the patent is necessarily void, provided there are purposes for which the result is useful. If it be avoided it can only be because it contains a misrepresentation so material that it can be said the Crown has been deceived. The importance of drawing a distinction between what the patentee claims to have effected by the invention for which he claims protection, and a statement of the additional purposes to which the invention can be applied is well illustrated by the case of *Lyon* v. *Goddard*." [92]　(In the latter case, the patentee claimed a disinfecting apparatus enabling the use of steam at high pressure in an inner chamber, but also pointed out that his apparatus could be used for disinfection by dry heat without steam, which second method did not differ from that of a previously known apparatus. The patent was held valid.)

251　In *Norton and Gregory Ltd.* v. *Jacobs* [93] Lord Greene M.R. said: " A claim made in language which upon its true construction would be wide enough to cover the use of reducing agents which are not

[89] 36 R.P.C. 231 at p. 237.
[90] See also *Raleigh Cycle Co. Ltd.* v. *H. Miller & Co. Ltd.*, 65 R.P.C. at p. 154.
[91] 24 R.P.C. 733 at p. 753.
[92] 11 R.P.C. 354.
[93] 54 R.P.C. 271 at pp. 275, 276.

effective to produce the desired result would be bad for inutility. . . . But it is said that the language of the claim must be construed so as to exclude any reducing agent which a chemist of ordinary skill would know, with or without experiment, to be unsuitable in view of the result to be achieved. We are unable to accept this argument. The fact that a skilled chemist desiring to use the invention would reject certain reducing agents as being unsuitable is one thing; it is quite a different thing to say that a claim must in point of construction be cut down so as to exclude those reducing agents because a skilled chemist would not use them. To adopt the latter proposition would be not to construe the specification but to amend it." [94]

252   It is immaterial to the question of inutility that no one expert in the art would be misled by the promise of the result, as was pointed out by Sir Raymond Evershed in *Sonotone Corporation* v. *Multitone Electric Co. Ltd.*[95]: " As regards inutility . . . the argument upon it turned largely upon the suggestion or promise implicit, as in our judgment it was, in page 2, lines 115 to 126, which relate most particularly to Claims 1 and 4. It is true, as the judge pointed out, that no one expert in the art might or would be misled by the promise. But in our judgment that fact does not of itself provide an answer to the objection, if the promise was made, as we hold, and is unfulfilled. . . . (See, for example, *Osram Lamp Works Ltd.* v. *Pope's Electric Lamp Co. Ltd.*,[96] *per* Lord Haldane.) This is not the kind of case in which, for the purposes at any rate of considering the validity of Claims 1 and 4, the promise made is fulfilled in fact though the reason assigned for the result is erroneous. (See, for example, " Z " *Electric Lamp Co. Ltd.* v. *Marples.*[97]) We, therefore, think, if it were necessary, that the objection of inutility would prevail to invalidate Claims 1 and 4 and consequentially Claims 2, 3 and 5 also. But, in our opinion, the objection ought not to prevail against Claim 6 (the claim to the drawings). The principle that the promise forms, or forms part of, the consideration for the monopoly does not appear to us, as we construe the specification, to be applicable to Claim 6. Alternatively, if the promise be properly related, as it were, to Claim 6, then, as we have already said, the promise seems to us to have been fulfilled though not for the reason exclusively assigned in the promise."

[94] See also *Raleigh Cycle Co. Ltd.* v. *Miller & Co. Ltd.*, 65 R.P.C. 141 at p. 155; *Minerals Separation North American Corporation* v. *Noranda Mines Ltd.*, 69 R.P.C. 81; *Henriksen* v. *Tallon Ltd.* [1965] R.P.C. 434.
[95] 72 R.P.C. at p. 146.
[96] 34 R.P.C. at p. 390.
[97] 27 R.P.C. at p. 737.

253 *Commercial success not necessary*

Utility in the patent law sense is in no way related to commercial success. In *Badische Anilin und Soda Fabrik* v. *Levinstein* [98] Lord Halsbury L.C. said: " The element of commercial pecuniary success has, as it appears to me, no relation to the question of utility in patent law generally, though, of course, where the question is of improvement by reason of cheaper production, such a consideration is of the very essence of the patent itself, and the thing claimed has not really been invented unless that condition is fulfilled."

254 *Subsequent improvement immaterial*

It is not an objection to the patent that the original form of the invention has been superseded by later improvements. In *Edison & Swan Electric Light Co.* v. *Holland* [99] Lindley L.J. said: " Edison's patent is said to be of no use, and the proof of this statement is said to be furnished by the fact that lamps are not made according to the patent, even by Edison himself. The utility of the patent must be judged by reference to the state of things at the date of the patent; if the invention was then useful, the fact that subsequent improvements have replaced the patented invention and rendered it obsolete and commercially of no value does not invalidate the patent." [1]

6. False Suggestion

255 **Section 32 (1) (j):** " the patent was obtained on a false suggestion or representation."

These words are wide enough to cover any false statement made by an applicant by which the Crown is deceived, but in a majority of cases such a false statement results also in some additional ground of invalidity which is separately defined. It is irrelevant whether or not there was deliberate falsehood by the patentee if the Crown was in fact misled, but " if false suggestion is alleged, it must be established on the basis of the documents in which the alleged false suggestion was made—the onus being, of course, on the objector." [2] The false statements could be made either in the application forms or in the complete specification. The patent is obtained upon the suggestions or representations set out in the recitals to the patent grant itself (see paras. 13–15, *supra*) and falsity in any of them will

[98] 4 R.P.C. 449 at p. 462.
[99] 6 R.P.C. 243 at p. 283.
[1] See also *Aktiengesellschaft für Autogene Aluminium Schweissung* v. *London Aluminium Co. Ltd.* (*No.* 2), 37 R.P.C. 153; 38 R.P.C. 163 (C.A.); 39 R.P.C. 296 (H.L.).
[2] *Kromschröder's Patent* [1960] R.P.C. 75 at p. 83. *Martin* v. *Scribal Pty. Ltd.* [1956] R.P.C. 215 at p. 224. See *Patent Concern N.V.* v. *Melotte Sales Co. Ltd.* [1968] R.P.C. 263.

be sufficient to invalidate the patent, if the false statement is of such materiality that the patent can be said to be " obtained " on it.[3]

7. Prior Grant

256   **Section 32 (1) (a):** " the invention, so far as claimed in any claim of the complete specification, was claimed in a valid claim of earlier priority date contained in the complete specification of another patent granted in the United Kingdom."

It has always been the law that a patent will be invalidated if the invention is shown to have been the subject of a valid prior grant.[4] Prior claiming is also a ground of opposition to the grant.[5]

257   The fact that there has been no prior publication is not material in this connection. It has been said that in order to render the second grant invalid, there must be proof " not only of similarity in essentials, but of identity." [6] If such be the law it would follow that the subsequent claim cannot be invalidated on the ground of prior claiming unless the two claims are for substantially the same invention, *i.e.* if one is larger or smaller in its scope than the other this ground of invalidity is inapplicable, even where the later claim is the larger.[7] But in view of the recent decisions, discussed in the next succeeding paragraph, it is not clear, however, whether such identity of invention in the two claims is necessary to render the later claim invalid.

258   Thus, in *Kromschröder's Patent (Revocation)*,[8] the Court of Appeal held that (a) Claim 1 of the patent in suit, 755462, claimed a gas meter of a certain construction, (b) this same gas meter was claimed under the description " through flow appliance " in Claim 1 of a prior patent specification 716771 in combination with certain " fittings for pipe lines," but that (c) as the monopolies claimed in the two claims were different in that in 755462 there was no limitation to the " fittings for pipe lines," there was no prior claiming. It will be observed that Claim 1 of the later patent 755462 could be said to be wider in scope than that of the earlier in that it contained no limitation to the " fittings for pipe lines " and that the decision of the Court of Appeal appears to have established that in such a case there is no need for the later claim to be so worded as to disclaim

---

[3] *Parry Husband's Appn.* [1965] R.P.C. 382; *Muccino's Appn.* [1968] R.P.C. 307.
[4] 1 W.P.C. 15, note (*h*).
[5] s. 14 (1) (*d*).
[6] *Per* Lord Guthrie in *Blackett* v. *Dickson and Mann Ltd.*, 26 R.P.C. 73 at p. 82. *Comptroller's Ruling*, 29 R.P.C. (D).
[7] *Comptroller's Ruling*, 39 R.P.C. (C); but *cf. Carpmael's Appn.*, 46 R.P.C. 321.
[8] [1960] R.P.C. 75.

the invention claimed in the earlier claim. The material passage of the judgment of the court is as follows:

" We will assume that the invention claimed in Claim 1 of Patent 755462 is included in Claim 1 of Patent 716771. But it is not, as an invention, itself the subject of a distinct claim in the latter patent. In our judgment, the language of paragraph (a) of section 32 (1) of the Act requires that it should be and the words ' claimed in a valid claim ' are not satisfied if the invention in question is only covered or comprehended by the claim as being a part or integer (however important) of some wider combination or ' arrangement ' which and which alone is the subject-matter of the claim. The words at the beginning of the paragraph—' the invention so far as claimed in any claim '—seem to us to postulate that the subject-matter contemplated must itself be that for which protection is claimed; and we think the same sense should be given to the later words—' claimed in a valid claim.' " [9]

259 Initially it appears to have been considered that the passage just quoted was authority for the view that identity of claim was required to establish the objection of prior claiming—see e.g. the decision of the Patents Appeal Tribunal in *Clinical Products Ltd.'s Patent.*[10] But in the subsequent cases of *Syntex S.A.'s Application* [11] and *Merck & Co. (Macek's) Patent* [12] (both cases concerned with prior claiming as a ground of opposition under section 14 (1) (c) of the Act) the Tribunal has held prior claiming to be established where the earlier claim was narrower in scope but for an invention falling within the monopoly claimed by the later (and wider) claim. In the latter case the Tribunal (Lloyd-Jacob J.), after referring to the judgment of the Court of Appeal in the *Kromschröder* case, said,[13]

" The 1949 Act introduced this phrase ' the invention so far as claimed in any claim ' not only in section 14 (1) (c) but elsewhere in the Act and in particular in section 14 (1) (b) (prior publication), section 14 (1) (d) (prior user) and section 14 (1) (e) (obviousness). . . . So far as concerns prior publication and prior user, if a claim to a manner of manufacture includes one embodiment of it which is not new, that claim has always been regarded as invalid whatever novel and ingenious embodiments the claim also covers (see *Molins* v. *Industrial Machinery Co. Ltd.*, 55 R.P.C. 31). So too with obviousness (*Woodrow* v. *Long Humphrey & Co.*, 51 R.P.C. 25); and unless and until the patentee has been able, by suitable amendment, to ex-

[9] [1960] R.P.C. 75 at p. 82.
[10] [1963] R.P.C. 271.
[11] [1966] R.P.C. 560.
[12] [1967] R.P.C. 157.
[13] *Ibid.* at pp. 162, 163.

clude from the claim the invalid portion of the monopoly, the taint
of invalidity attaches to it in its fullness and deprives it of monopoly
effect.

" There would appear to be no ground for construing the phrase
' the invention so far as claimed in any claim ' in different senses
in the sub-divisions of section 14 (1), so that, if the cited prior claim
on its fair construction can be seen to grant as a manner of manufacture that which the later claim on its fair construction would re-mono-
polise, the objection of prior claiming is established, and this despite
the inclusion in the later claim of variants of the manner of manufacture to which no objection can properly be raised."

260　　　　The Patents Appeal Tribunal is, of course, an inferior tribunal
and, if its decisions in the *Syntex* and *Merck* cases are not reconcilable
with the ratio of the decision in the *Kromschröder* case, they were
wrongly decided.　It is submitted that the Tribunal's decisions in the
Syntex and *Merck* cases can only be reconciled with the
Kromschröder case if the latter is regarded as having been decided
on the narrow ground that the claims in question were for different
inventions in that the earlier claim was for a combination of three
integers, namely, the gas meter, adaptor and connecting device,
whereas the later claim was for the gas meter *per se*.　It is to be
noted that in the case of *Traver Corporation's Application* [14] the
Patents Appeal Tribunal, following the *Kromschröder* case, held that
prior claiming was not established as the claims were differentiated in
that the later claim included a feature not specified in the earlier
claim.

The test for prior claiming enunciated in the *Merck* case has been
applied by the Patents Appeal Tribunal in subsequent cases.[15]　Thus
in *Wilkinson Sword Ltd.'s Application* [16] the applicants' claim was
held to be prior claimed although wider in scope than the cited prior
claim.　In *Ethyl Corporation's Application* [17] the Patents Appeal
Tribunal (Graham J.) held that when the earlier claim is broader than
the later claim and includes within it the area covered by the later
claim, the later claim is prior-claimed unless the later claim can be
justified on the basis of a selection patent (as to which see § 329 *post*).

261　　　　In considering prior claiming, confusion is sometimes created by
the consideration that manufacture according to the second claim may
constitute an infringement of the earlier claim, and manufacture
according to the earlier claim may equally be an infringement of the
later.　This, it is submitted, is wholly irrelevant in either case.

[14] [1964] R.P.C. 26; and see *Willey's Carbide Tool Co.'s Appn.* [1969] R.P.C.
33 but *cf. Pittsburgh Glass Co.'s Appn.* [1969] R.P.C. 628.
[15] See *e.g. Pittsburgh Plate Glass Co.'s Appn.* [1969] R.P.C. 628.
[16] [1970] R.P.C. 42.　　　　　　　　　　　　　　[17] [1970] R.P.C. 227.

262   There appears to be only one reported case where a patent has been clearly held by a court to be invalid on the ground of prior grant.[18] In order to be an effective prior grant the prior claim must be valid.[19]

263   Applications for patents have from time to time been refused on the ground of prior claiming where the invention claimed is in substance the same in both claims.[20] Where the later claim differed from the earlier only by the introduction of a feature that was a matter of common knowledge at the priority date of the earlier claim, the later claim was disallowed on opposition.[21] In *Commercial Solvent Corporation's Application*[22] Lloyd-Jacob J., sitting as the Patents Appeal Tribunal, said: "When the objection which is being considered is prior claiming, what the Patent Office and this Tribunal have to determine is whether such difference as appears between the two claims as a matter of language imports any real differentiation as a matter of inventive step,"[23] but it is submitted that this is no longer good law having regard to the *Kromschröder* decision, *supra*.

264   Where a chemical substance has been claimed in an earlier claim, an applicant who devises some new process of making the same chemical substance is not entitled to claim that substance *per se*, but he is not, of course, debarred from claiming the new process which he has devised, subject to a proper acknowledgment of the earlier patent.[24]

Where an application is divided into more than one application, no complete specification must include a claim for matter claimed in another, in the sense that no two claims must be coterminous.[25]

8. LACK OF NOVELTY

265 **Section 32 (1) (e):** "the invention, so far as claimed in any claim of the complete specification, is not new having regard to what was known or used before the priority date of the claim in the United Kingdom."

---

[18] *Rowland and Kennedy* v. *The Air Council*, 42 R.P.C. 433.
[19] See *Mica Insulator Co.* v. *Electrical Co.*, 15 R.P.C. 489; *Robertson* v. *Purdey*, 24 R.P.C. 273 at p. 297.
[20] *I.G. Farbenindustrie's Appn. for Revocation*, 51 R.P.C. 53; *Carpmael's Appn.*, 46 R.P.C. 321.
[21] *Babcock and Wilcox Ltd.'s Appn.*, 69 R.P.C. 224.
[22] 71 R.P.C. 143.
[23] See also *Imperial Chemical Industries Ltd.'s Appn.* [1957] R.P.C. 12; *Standard Telephones and Cables Ltd.'s Appn.* [1958] R.P.C. 108; *Kromschröder's Patent* [1960] R.P.C. 75.
[24] *Macfarlan (J. F.) and Co. Ltd.'s Appn.*, 71 R.P.C. 429.
[25] r. 13 (3); *Arrow Electric Switches Ltd.'s Appn.*, 61 R.P.C. 1.

266   Two quite separate questions have to be considered *viz.* (1) whether any particular document or act, having regard to its history and circumstances, is such as can be relied on against the validity of a claim having a later priority date [26] and, if the answer be Yes, (2) whether the contents of the document or the details of the act are such as to invalidate the claim on the ground of lack of novelty. Question (1) will be considered first.

Publication by Oral Disclosure

267   An invention can become " known " by a prior oral disclosure equally as by a prior published document or by a prior user. As Bowen L.J. said in *Humpherson* v. *Syer*: " I put aside questions of public use and treat this as a question of whether there has been a prior publication: that is, in other words, had this information been communicated to any member of the public who was free in law and equity to use it as he pleased. . . . If so, the information had been given to a member of the public and there was nothing further to serve as consideration for any patent." The disclosure in the above case was by the defendant and it was accepted, and it is submitted it is the law, that the mere knowledge by a third party unaccompanied by a disclosure free of conditions of secrecy does not make an invention " known." [27]

Publication by Documents

268   A claim is invalidated if the invention claimed in it was previously " known," [28] and, accordingly, the nature of the document which made it known is immaterial.

269 **What constitutes publication**
    In the case of a book or other document containing a description of the invention it is not necessary that it should have been sold in order to constitute a publication. Mere exhibition in a bookseller's window for sale, or sending it to a bookseller in this country to be sold, is sufficient publication.[29]

    It is the practice for the Patent Office library to receive copies of foreign specifications from abroad which are open to public inspection. A British patent may be invalidated by the fact that such a specification, or any other document containing a description of the invention claimed, was on view before the priority date of the British

---

[26] See *ante*, § 165.
[27] 4 R.P.C. 407 at p. 413; and see *Dollond's Case*, 1 W.P.C. 43.
[28] s. 32 (1) (*e*); see also *post*, § 286.
[29] *Lang* v. *Gisborne*, 31 Beav. 133 at p. 136; 31 L.J.Ch. 769.

application.[30] Prior publication in a foreign journal and in a foreign language (if commonly understood) will invalidate a British patent if it can be shown that a single copy was deposited in Great Britain in a public place, and was open to public inspection.[31]

270 Where a book, written in French, was in the British Museum in a room not ordinarily accessible to the public and only its title appeared in the catalogue in the public reading room, this was held not to be sufficient publication.[32] Whether or not the document is ordinarily accessible to the public appears to be the crucial test.[33] Where a German specification, six weeks earlier in date, was placed on the shelves of the Patent Office library in a place where members of the public in search of information of the kind in question would normally go, this was sufficient publication.[34] Where a document had been obtained from South Africa by an employee of a company, it was held that it had been published as the document had been communicated to a single member of the public without inhibiting fetter.[35]

A claim to a chemical substance cannot be sustained, notwithstanding that the substance may be put to novel use, when it has been disclosed in a prior publication.[36]

271 *Fifty-year-old specifications*

A claim in a complete specification is not invalidated by prior publication of the invention in a specification filed in pursuance of a United Kingdom application dated more than fifty years before the date of filing of such complete specification,[37] or in a specification describing the invention for the purposes of a foreign application made more than fifty years before that date.[38] Nor is it invalidated by publication in an official abridgment or extract of such a fifty-year-old specification.[39] A mere reference to an earlier specification by its number is not a fresh publication of the earlier specification; but republication may occur if there is a description and reference to the earlier specification.[40]

It is submitted, however, that a fifty-year-old specification could

---

[30] *Harris* v. *Rothwell*, 35 Ch.D. 416; 3 R.P.C. 383; 4 R.P.C. 225 (C.A.); *Pickard* v. *Prescott*, 9 R.P.C. 195.
[31] *V. D. Ltd.* v. *Boston Deep Sea Fishing Co. Ltd.*, 52 R.P.C. 303 at p. 328.
[32] *Otto* v. *Steel*, 31 Ch.D. 241; 3 R.P.C. 109.
[33] See also *Plimpton* v. *Malcolmson*, 3 Ch.D. 531; *Plimpton* v. *Spiller*, 6 Ch.D. 412.
[34] *Harris* v. *Rothwell*, 4 R.P.C. 225 at p. 232; 35 Ch.D. 416 at p. 431; and see *Humpherson* v. *Syer*, 4 R.P.C. 407 at p. 415.
[35] *Bristol-Myer's Co. Appn.* [1969] R.P.C. 146.
[36] *Gyogyszeripari Kutato Intezet's Appn.* [1958] R.P.C. 51.
[37] s. 50 (1) (*a*).
[38] s. 50 (1) (*b*).
[39] s. 50 (1) (*c*).
[40] *AMP Inc.* v. *Hellerman Ltd.* [1966] R.P.C. 159 at p. 183.

be used as evidence to support an allegation of prior user.[41] In the case of an abandoned application no specification relating to it is published,[42] yet the court has power to order the production of a specification filed on an abandoned application, not as an anticipation, but as evidence of collateral facts, and in the interests of justice.[43]

272 *Admission by patentee as to prior publication*

In *Chapman and Cook* v. *Deltavis Ltd.*[44] Clauson J. said: " . . . if a patentee, though entirely erroneously, does state by way of . . . recital in his specification that a particular form of thing is common . . . he will have, so to speak, recited himself out of court and I venture to doubt whether he could possibly maintain any claim to a monopoly in a thing which he has recognised to be something which existed." Such an admission may be binding on the patentee even though made only in the provisional specification.[45]

273 But this principle must not be taken too far, as was pointed out by the Court of Appeal in *Sonotone Corporation* v. *Multitone Electric Co. Ltd.*[46] where, after referring to the above observations of Clauson J., Sir Raymond Evershed M.R. stated:

" But the case supposed by Clauson J. was, in our judgment, wholly different from the present. It may well be that as between a patentee and the Crown, at any rate, a clear admission of the state of the prior art on the basis of which a particular monopoly had been claimed and granted could not subsequently be withdrawn or modified. But it does not seem to us necessarily to follow that in a case like the present where, we are assuming, an admission is made as regards some integers of a combination for which a monopoly is claimed, the patentee could not in an infringement action resile from his admission to the extent of attempting to show that some particular feature or integer or some particular combination which on this view he must be taken to have included in the known prior art was in fact not old or known at all."

Prior User

274 The prior user which will invalidate a patent under section 32 (1) (*e*) must be such as will make the invention " not new " and must, therefore, be " public use." As to the circumstances under which

---

[41] *AMP Inc.* v. *Hellerman Ltd.* [1966] R.P.C. 159 at p. 183.
[42] s. 79 (1).
[43] See *Pneumatic Tyre Co. Ltd.* v. *English Cycle Co.*, 14 R.P.C. 851.
[44] 47 R.P.C. 163 at p. 173.
[45] *British Celanese Ltd.* v. *Courtaulds Ltd.*, 50 R.P.C. 259 at p. 270.
[46] 72 R.P.C. at p. 140.

secret prior use will invalidate a patent under section 32 (1) (*l*), see *infra*.

In *Dollond's* case,[47] which is usually assumed to be a case of prior user, the objection to Dollond's patent was that he was not the inventor of the method of making new object-glasses, but that Dr. Hall had made the same discovery before him. It was held that, inasmuch as Dr. Hall had confined it to his closet, and the public were not acquainted with it, Dollond was to be considered the inventor. This appears to be a case where the prior user was both secret and experimental.

275   In *Carpenter* v. *Smith*[48] the patent sued on was for a lock. The defendant called a witness who proved that a similar lock had been used on a gate adjoining a public road for sixteen years prior to the patent. It was held that this invalidated the patent. Lord Abinger C.B. analysed the meaning of the words " public use." " Public use does not mean a use or exercise by the public, but a use or exercise in a public manner." In *Taylor's Patent*[49] the patent was for a fire-grate. It was revoked on the ground that a similar grate had been used in a private house in the ordinary way and under no conditions of secrecy.

276   In *Stead* v. *Anderson*[50] the alleged prior user consisted in the use on a private carriage-drive, the principal approach to a private house, of the kind of paving for which the patent was granted. Parke B. said: " If the mode of forming and laying blocks at Sir W. Worsley's had been precisely similar to the plaintiff's, that would have been sufficient user to destroy the plaintiff's patent, though put in practice in a spot to which the public had not free access." [51]

Even an admittedly experimental prior public working of the invention is sufficient to invalidate the patent (for the invention is thereby made known) unless such experimental working necessarily takes place in public, having regard to the nature of the invention.[52] It is submitted that " public working " in this connection means a user of the invention in such a manner that a skilled person present can see or deduce the details of the invention. In *Boyce* v. *Morris Motors Ltd.*,[53] where the alleged prior user related to a thermometer used on a motor-car during tests, Sargant L.J. said (distinguishing *Carpenter* v. *Smith*): " But here, the mere fact that these cars were

---

[47] 1766, unreported, but mentioned in 1 W.P.C. at p. 43.
[48] 1 W.P.C. 530; 9 M. & W. 300.
[49] 13 R.P.C. 482.
[50] 2 W.P.C. 151.
[51] And see *Humpherson* v. *Syer*, 4 R.P.C. 407 (C.A.).
[52] s. 51 (3). *Cave-Brown-Cave's Appn.* [1958] R.P.C. 429.
[53] 44 R.P.C. 105 at p. 149.

driven on the public highway did not give anybody the opportunity of stopping the car and asking to have a look into the top of the radiator to see what was there . . . there was no greater public user . . . than if the cars had been driven on a private testing ground. . . ."

277   A prior exhibition of a machine which is a failure will not affect the validity of a patent for a successful machine, even though there may be considerable similarity between the machines.[54]

278 *Three-mile limit for ships*
It was held in 1935 that in order to be available against validity an alleged prior user taking place in a ship must occur within the three-mile limit.[55]

279 *Means of knowledge by prior sale*
A single sale, not in confidence and before the priority date of the patent, of an article which discloses the invention on inspection, is sufficient to invalidate the patent.[56] The same rule applies to a patent for a process where examination of the articles produced by the process enable the nature of the process to be ascertained. Thus *Miller's Patent* [57] was granted for the manufacture of an alloy containing bismuth. The petitioners proved that there had been public sales of a similar alloy, called "Magnolia Metal," before the date of the patent, and that a skilful chemist could by analysis have detected its composition. Romer J., revoking the patent, said [58]: "The bismuth could have been detected, and I am satisfied that, if reasonable care and reasonable skill were used by analysts before the date of the patent, when this magnolia metal was sold, its constituents and the proper proportions of those constituents could have been ascertained, so that, the metal being sold, its constituents and their proportions could have been known, and it could have been made."

280   This judgment was approved and followed by the House of Lords in the case of *Stahlwerk Becker Aktiengesellschaft's Patent*,[59] where Lord Finlay L.C. said: "I think it would be very dangerous to introduce the doctrine which your lordships are now invited to introduce, either it must be actually shown that the knowledge had been acquired by some individual, or that there is a high probability

---

[54] *Murray* v. *Clayton*, 7 Ch.App. 570 at pp. 581–582.
[55] *V.D. Ltd.* v. *Boston, etc., Ltd.*, 52 R.P.C. 303 at p. 331.
[56] *Wood* v. *Zimmer*, Holt N.P. 58; 1 W.P.C. 44n.; *Honiball* v. *Bloomer*, 2 W.P.C. 199; *Lister* v. *Norton Bros. & Co.*, 3 R.P.C. 199 at p. 208; *Strachan and Henshaw Ltd.* v. *Pakcel*, 66 R.P.C. 49 at p. 68; *Wikmanshytte Bruks A.B.'s Appn.* [1961] R.P.C. 180.
[57] 15 R.P.C. 205.
[58] At p. 211.
[59] 36 R.P.C. 13.

that it had in fact been acquired. The law as to prior user seems to be this, that if the article has been manufactured and sold, that gives the means of knowledge to the purchaser, and that that is enough to establish prior user." [60]

281 *Offer to sell*

The fact that there was no demand for the article is irrelevant.[61] Deposit in a warehouse for the purposes of sale, but not amounting to a public exhibition as in a shop, has been held to be prior user.[62] An offer for sale in a foreign periodical which was circulated in this country has been held not to be an offer for sale made in this country.[63] It is suggested that an oral or written offer for sale unaccompanied by the goods themselves would not of itself constitute a prior user, but could provide evidence that a particular user was public and not secret.

282 *Samples*

The manufacture and distribution of samples for the purpose of testing the market may constitute a publication of the invention.[64] The gift of a sample of the invention to a government official as a private individual and not in his official capacity will invalidate a patent applied for subsequently.[65]

283 **Accidental prior user**

A mere accidental user is not of itself sufficient to invalidate a subsequent patent, particularly if what is done appears to point away from, rather than towards, the invention.[66]

In *Harwood* v. *Great Northern Ry.*[67] Blackburn J. said: " I cannot think that a man can use a manufacture . . . because accidentally and without in the least degree intending it, he does that thing which if it were habitually done on purpose and for the purpose of trade, would be a manufacture. I cannot think there is a use, either public or private . . . unless there be some knowledge and some

---

[60] And see *Hills* v. *London Gas Light Co.*, 5 H. & N. 312 at p. 336. And see also *Wikmanshytte Bruks A.B.'s Appn.* [1961] R.P.C. 180, where Mr. Vincent, Supt.Ex., held that a manufacture in London and sale f.o.b. London was not a prior user within s. 14 (1) (*d*); *Minnesota Mining & Manufacturing Co.'s Appn.* [1969] R.P.C. 95.

[61] *Losh* v. *Hague*, 1 W.P.C. 530 at p. 536.

[62] *Mullins* v. *Hart*, 3 Car. & Kir. 297.

[63] *Cincinnati Grinders (Inc.)* v. *B.S.A. Tools Ltd.*, 48 R.P.C. 33 at p. 51.

[64] *Hudson Scott & Sons Ltd.* v. *Barringer, etc., Ltd.*, 23 R.P.C. 79 at p. 87.

[65] *Fomento Industrial S.A.* v. *Mentmore Manufacturing Co. Ltd.* [1956] R.P.C. at p. 105.

[66] *Boyce* v. *Morris Motors Ltd.*, 44 R.P.C. 105 at p. 148.

[67] 29 L.J.Q.B. 193 at p. 202.

intention." The finding of the court was reversed in the House of Lords on another ground [68] and the point was not considered.

284 Experiments and trials

An experiment in the course of making the invention is not a prior publication by user.[69] The effect of experiments by way of reasonable trial of the invention made before the priority date of the claim is now clearly laid down in the Act,[70] and it is submitted that many of the dicta in cases dealing with this subject [71] prior to the 1949 Act are not now good law. The present law may be summarised as follows:

285   Any such trial which constitutes a disclosure in public of the invention or of information which renders the invention obvious will invalidate a patent of subsequent priority date unless:

    (1) (a) The invention is of such a nature that it is reasonably necessary for such trial to take place in public; and

        (b) (i) the trial is reasonable;

            (ii) takes place within one year before the priority date; and

            (iii) is by or with the consent of the patentee or applicant or a person from whom he derives title [72] ; or

    (2) the trial is secret.[73]

"Secret," it is submitted, means in this context something known only to a single operator or to persons all of whom have either imparted or received knowledge of the invention under a seal of confidence, express or implied.[74]

The mere fact that the user amounts to a "commercial working" of the invention does not necessarily make such user other than by way of "reasonable trial." [75] It must be a question of fact and degree in each case.

---

[68] 35 L.J.Q.B. 27; and see *post*, § 318.
[69] *Househill Co.* v. *Neilson*, 1 W.P.C. 673 at p. 708.
[70] ss. 32 (2), 50 (2), 51 (3).
[71] *Morgan* v. *Seaward*, 2 M. & W. 544 at p. 557; 1 W.P.C. 167 at p. 187; *Newall* v. *Elliott*, 4 C.B.(N.S.) 269 at p. 295; *Cornish* v. *Keene*, 1 W.P.C. 501 at p. 508; *Croysdale* v. *Fisher*, 1 R.P.C. 17 at p. 21; *Germ Milling Co.* v. *Robinson*, 3 R.P.C. 254, 399; *Morgan* v. *Windover*, 5 R.P.C. 295 at p. 302; *Elias* v. *Grovesend Tinplate Co.*, 7 R.P.C. 455 at p. 466; *Electrolytic Plating Apparatus Co.* v. *Holland*, 18 R.P.C. 521 at p. 526; *Robertson* v. *Purdey*, 24 R.P.C. 273.
[72] s. 51 (3).
[73] s. 32 (2).
[74] *Elias* v. *Grovesend Tinplate Co.*, 7 R.P.C. 455 at p. 466; *Hoe & Co.* v. *Foster and Sons*, 16 R.P.C. 33; *Poulton's Patent*, 23 R.P.C. 183, 506.
[75] See s. 50 (2), proviso. And see *Newall* v. *Elliott*, 4 C.B.(N.S.) at p. 295.

Protection Against Prior Publication

286   Under the Act an invention claimed in a complete specification is
deemed not to be " anticipated " if the invention was published
before the priority date of the claim in certain circumstances.[76]   It is
further provided that the Comptroller shall not refuse to accept a
complete specification or to grant a patent, and a patent shall not be
revoked or invalidated, by reason only of any circumstances which,
by virtue of these provisions of the Act, do not constitute an
anticipation of the invention.[77]   For example, in these cases a patent
cannot be invalidated on the ground that the invention has been
rendered obvious.   The cases are:

   (a)   Prior publication in a patent specification, or an abridgment
        of a patent specification, relating to a patent specification
        more than fifty years old.[78]

   (b)   If the matter published (i) was obtained from the applicant
        or from some person from whom he derives title,[79] (ii) was
        published without the consent of the person entitled, (iii) is
        the subject of a British or (in a convention case) of a foreign
        application made as soon as reasonably practicable after the
        applicant learned of the publication, and (iv) had not been
        commercially worked in the United Kingdom before the
        priority date of the claim (otherwise than for the purpose
        of reasonable trial) with the consent of the person entitled.[80]
        The word " obtained " includes matter obtained abroad.[81]

   (c)   If the publication took place pursuant to a patent application
        made in contravention of the rights of the person entitled, or
        by such wrongful applicant, or someone authorised by him,
        subsequent to such wrongful application.[82]   This provision
        will apply both where the wrongful application is fraudulently
        made and where it is made pursuant to a genuine
        misapprehension as to his rights by the applicant.   If the
        prior application is refused, or any patent granted is revoked,
        or the offending claims are excised by amendment, the
        subsequent rightful application can be ante-dated to the date
        of the earlier wrongful application for the purposes of the
        provisions of the Act relating to the priority date of the
        claims.[83]

---

[76] ss. 50, 51, 52.
[77] ss. 50 (4), 51 (4), 52 (1).
[78] s. 50 (1).   See *ante*, § 271.
[79] See *ante*, § 71.
[80] s. 50 (2).
[81] *Ethyl Corpn.'s Patent* [1966] R.P.C. 205.
[82] s. 50 (3).   [83] s. 53.

(d) If the publication took place because the invention was communicated to a government department or any person authorised by a government department, for investigation as to its merits.[84]

(e) If the publication took place for the purposes of an exhibition certified by the Department of Trade and Industry, or in a paper read by the inventor before a learned society,[85] provided that a patent is applied for in the United Kingdom[86] not later than six months after the opening of the exhibition, or the reading or publication of the paper.[87]

(f) Where a complete specification is filed pursuant to an application accompanied by a provisional specification, or pursuant to a convention application, no publication of any matter contained in such provisional specification or such convention application after the date of such provisional specification or convention application will invalidate the patent.[88]

Distinction Between Novelty and Obviousness

287 The law draws a distinction between " novelty " (the absence of novelty being commonly referred to as " anticipation ") and " obviousness " (commonly referred to in the older decided cases as " lack of subject-matter "). This latter phrase is nowhere used in the Act in this sense and is more appropriate to express the absence of any quality of a nature such as to make the invention inherently patentable than the absence of the quality of " inventiveness." For example, a new filing system or a new game of cards, however ingenious, is not patentable and could appropriately be described as lacking in subject-matter for invention.[89] Accordingly the expression " subject-matter " is never used in this book, except in quotations from judgments, in the sense of possessing the quality of inventiveness.

288 In *Gadd and Mason* v. *Mayor etc. of Manchester*[90] Lindley L.J. said: ". . . In considering subject-matter, novelty is assumed; the question is whether, assuming the invention to be new, it is one for which a patent can be granted. In considering novelty, the invention is assumed to be one for which a patent can be granted if new, and

---

[84] s. 51 (1).
[85] s. 51 (2).
[86] *Ethyl Corpn.'s Patent* [1963] R.P.C. 155.
[87] As regards pre-1949 Act patents, see Sched. III (9).
[88] s. 52, and see *ante,* § 165.
[89] See *ante,* Chap. 2.
[90] 9 R.P.C. 516 at p. 525.

the question is whether on that assumption it is new. Has it been disclosed before? If there is an earlier specification for the very same thing, the second invention is not new; but if the two things are different, the nature and extent of the difference have to be considered. The question becomes one of degree. But unless it can be said that the differences are practically immaterial, that there is no ingenuity in the second invention, no experiment necessary to show whether it can be successfully carried out or not, the second cannot be said to have been anticipated by the first. . . ."

289   The above statement of Lindley L.J. has been frequently cited for the purpose of contrasting " novelty " and " obviousness," but the distinction between these is better illustrated by *Molins* v. *Industrial Machinery Co. Ltd.*[91] The patentee had discovered that in a high-speed cigarette-making machine the filling of the cigarettes tended to become irregular, which defect was not apparent in earlier low-speed machines. The trouble was cured by imparting to the shower of tobacco falling upon the travelling band of paper in the machine a component of velocity in the direction of horizontal movement. Claim 1 of the patent was as follows: " A cigarette-making machine of the continuous rod type wherein the tobacco showered into the trough of the machine is given a movement in the direction of movement of the cigarette rod prior to the same engaging with the band or web of cigarette paper." An earlier specification of one *Bonsack* disclosed a machine which was not capable of being run at any speed at which this particular defect would manifest, but for some reason, which none of the experts were able to explain satisfactorily, *Bonsack* had provided an inclined shute for the tobacco which would necessarily impart a movement to it of the kind specified in the claim. Lord Greene M.R. said [92]: " I am satisfied that the discovery of the causes of the defect was by no means obvious and that an act of invention was necessary. The same remark applies to the realisation that the defect could be remedied by imparting to the falling tobacco a component of movement in the direction of the moving band. . . . (But) the claim includes every cigarette-making machine in which a component of movement in the direction of the travelling band or web is imparted to the shower of tobacco at whatever speed the machine runs or is capable of running. If the claim . . . covers a machine which is the subject-matter of an earlier patent, it is necessarily void. In the present case there is such an earlier patent and . . . the existence of that earlier patent is fatal to its validity. . . . But here an argument

[91] 55 R.P.C. 31.
[92] *Ibid.* at p. 38.

is put forward which I have some difficulty in following . . . *Bonsack's* specification does not explain for what purpose in the construction of his machine the trough is to be inclined. . . . It is said, as I follow the argument, that *Bonsack* cannot be an anticipation because it does not appear and ought not to be assumed that, in giving directions for the invention of his trough, he was envisaging the same problem as that with which the present inventor was concerned, and that if the problems were not the same, the validity of the present claim is not affected by the fact that this particular element is to be found inserted for no apparent purpose in *Bonsack's* machine. . . . (But) *Bonsack's* instruction is to make a machine of a particular kind. . . . The inclination which he gives to his trough is a physical part necessarily present in each machine made in accordance with his specification and is as much a part of the true nature of that machine as any other element in it " and the claim, as originally drafted, was held invalid for lack of novelty.

290　　An amendment was asked for and permitted by which the opening words of the claim were made to read: " A cigarette-making machine of the continuous rod type capable of moving at a speed of more than 900 cigarettes per minute. . . ." Lord Greene M.R. said [93]: " Now if the specification is amended in this way there can, in my opinion, be no suggestion that it is anticipated by *Bonsack*. A cigarette-making machine capable of running at a rate of 900 cigarettes a minute or more is a different machine from *Bonsack's* since *Bonsack's* machine could not run at anything approaching that speed."

291　　Therefore, anticipation is established if the claim, when properly construed, includes something which has previously been published.[94] If the prior disclosure does not fall within the words of the claim the latter is not invalid on the ground that the invention claimed is not new. The different question then has to be considered whether it was obvious and did not require any inventive step to reach the invention claimed from the general field of prior knowledge. In most cases this latter question is the one that gives rise to difficulty, for it is rare to find a prior disclosure that falls strictly within the wording of a claim since every claim has been the subject of careful investigation in the Patent Office before it has been allowed.

292　Test to be applied to prior document

　　The test whether the disclosure contained in a prior document is such as to invalidate a subsequent invention was stated by Lord

[93] 55 R.P.C. 31 at p. 43.
[94] See *Electric and Musical Industries Ltd.* v. *Lissen Ltd.*, 54 R.P.C. 307 at p. 324.

Westbury L.C. in *Hills* v. *Evans*[95] in the following terms: "The antecedent statement must, in order to invalidate the subsequent patent, be such that a person of ordinary knowledge of the subject would at once perceive and understand and be able practically to apply the discovery without the necessity of making further experiments . . . the information . . . given by the prior publication must, for the purposes of practical utility, be equal to that given by the subsequent patent."

293   As Lord Reid stated in *C. Van der Lely N.V.* v. *Bamfords Ltd.*[96]: "There are two branches of this statement. The first is that 'a person of ordinary knowledge of the subject would at once perceive and understand and be able practically to apply the discovery without the necessity of making further experiments ' . . . Lord Westbury must have meant experiments with a view to discovering something not disclosed. He cannot have meant to refer to the ordinary methods of trial and error which involve no inventive step and generally are necessary in applying any discovery to produce a practical result. . . . The other requirement is that ' the information given by the prior publication must for the purpose of practical utility be equal to that given by the subsequent patent.' There may be cases where the skilled man has to have the language of the publication translated for him or where he must get from a scientist the meaning of technical terms or ideas with which he is not familiar, but once he has got this he must be able to make the machine from what is disclosed by the prior publication."

294 *The " person of ordinary knowledge "*

The " person of ordinary knowledge " referred to by Lord Westbury is the typical addressee of the plaintiff's patent specification, the kind of person who would be expected to make a machine or carry out the process of the kind in question (see *per* Lord Reid in *C. Van der Lely N.V.* v. *Bamfords Ltd.*[97]). The dicta of Lord Watson in *King, Brown & Co.* v. *Anglo-American Brush Co.*[98] does not, it is submitted, mean in its context that the " persons of ordinary knowledge " are not the persons who would make the machine or carry out the process but are persons of superior knowledge such as " men of science and employers of labour," but, if it should have this meaning, then it is submitted that it is not good law. The correct statement of the law on this point is that set out in the last

---

[95] 31 L.J.Ch. 457 at p. 463. Also reported (1862) 4 De G. F. & J. 288, 45 E.R. 1193. See also *Armstrong Whitworth & Co. Ltd.* v. *Hardcastle*, 42 R.P.C. 543 at p. 555.
[96] [1963] R.P.C. 61 at p. 71.
[97] *Ibid.*
[98] 9 R.P.C. 313 at p. 320.

sentence of the above-quoted extract from Lord Reid's speech in *C. Van der Lely N.V.* v. *Bamfords Ltd.*[99]

295   In *Kaye* v. *Chubb & Sons Ltd.*[100] Lord Esher M.R. said: " I quite agree with what has been stated as to the law by Lord Westbury. If in the first patent which is thus alleged there is a general statement which gives no clear intimation either by its own construction or . . . by considering what would be the effect of it upon a hypothetical workman of ordinary skill . . . and if some other person coming with great skill and great care should, out of the general words, really produce something not inconsistent with them, but which is not disclosed by them, I quite agree that he can take out a patent, and he cannot be defeated, because that which is really his invention can be got within general words which describe nothing." [1] In *Gillette Safety Razor Co.* v. *Anglo-American Trading Co. Ltd.*[2] Lord Moulton said: " In ascertaining its effect the court must consider what it (the prior document) would convey to the public to whom it was addressed, *i.e.* to mechanicians. I recognise that it would be most unfair to subsequent patentees if we tested this by what it would convey or suggest to a mechanical genius; but, on the other hand, it would be equally unjust to the public to take it as though it were read only by mechanical idiots."

296   In *British Thomson-Houston Co. Ltd.* v. *Metropolitan-Vickers Ltd.*,[3] where the question was whether *Rosenberg's* invention (which was concerned with the bringing of synchronous electric machines into exact synchronism before establishing the electric connection) was anticipated by a prior specification of *Tesla*, Lord Dunedin said: " Would a man who was grappling with *Rosenberg's* problem . . . and had *Tesla's* specification in his hand have said: ' That gives me what I wish ' ? " These words have been frequently quoted and cited as providing a test by which inventiveness can be established. But, it is submitted, they are quite unhelpful for this purpose. In the first place the meaning of the words " what I wish " is not clear. They presumably do not mean " a solution of the problem " because one previously published solution cannot anticipate or render obvious an alternative solution which required a further act of invention to produce. It would seem that the words mean " the solution which the patentee subsequently disclosed and claimed." But in that case this is merely putting into different (and more obscure) words the very question that the test is supposed to give assistance in answering.

---

[99] See also *Ransberg Co.* v. *Aerostyle Ltd.* [1968] R.P.C. 287 at p. 299.
[100] 4 R.P.C. 289 at p. 298.
[1] Cited by Lord Upjohn in *Ransberg Co.* v. *Aerostyle Ltd., supra.*
[2] 30 R.P.C. 465 at p. 481.
[3] 45 R.P.C. 1.

British Thomson-Houston Co. Ltd. v. *Metropolitan-Vickers Ltd.*[3] has been lucidly explained by Lord Greene M.R. in *Molins* v. *Industrial Machinery Co. Ltd.*[4]

297 " Mosaic " of publications not legitimate

It is not legitimate to piece together a number of prior documents in order to produce an anticipation of the invention. In *Von Heyden* v. *Neustadt*[5] the defendants pleaded anticipation, and put in evidence a mass of paragraphs extracted from a large number of publications. James L.J. in his judgment, said: " We are of opinion that if it requires this mosaic of extracts, from annuals and treatises spread over a series of years, to prove the defendants' contention, that contention stands thereby self-condemned. . . . And even if it could be shown that a patentee made his discovery of a consecutive process by studying, collating and applying a number of facts discriminated in the pages of such works, his diligent study of such works would as much entitle him to the character of an inventor as the diligent study of the works of nature would do." [6]

And in *Lowndes' Patent*[7] Tomlin J. said: " It is not open to you to take a packet of prior documents and . . . by . . . putting a puzzle together produce what you say is a disclosure in the nature of a combination of the various elements which have been contained in the prior documents. I think it is necessary to point to a clear and specific disclosure of something which is said to be like the patentee's invention."

A series of papers which form a series of disclosures and refer to each other, so that " anyone reading one is referred by cross-references to the others," do not, however, form a mosaic.[8]

298 Construction of prior documents

The general rule for the construction of prior documents is the same as that for any other documents, *viz.* " that the document should be construed as if the court had to construe it at the date of publication, to the exclusion of information subsequently discovered." [9] In determining the meaning of the document regard

---

[4] 55 R.P.C. 31.
[5] 50 L.J.Ch. 126 at p. 128.
[6] And see *Rondo Co. Ltd.* v. *Gramophone Co. Ltd.*, 46 R.P.C. 378 at p. 391; *Pope Appliance Corpn.* v. *Spanish River, etc., Ltd.*, 46 R.P.C. 23; [1929] A.C. 269.
[7] 45 R.P.C. 48 at p. 57.
[8] *Sharpe & Dohme Inc.* v. *Boots Pure Drug Co. Ltd.*, 44 R.P.C. 367 at p. 402; 45 R.P.C. 153 at p. 180.
[9] *Ore Concentration Co. (1905) Ltd.* v. *Sulphide Corporation Ltd.*, 31 R.P.C. 206 at p. 224; *Nobel's Explosives Co. Ltd.* v. *Anderson*, 11 R.P.C. 519 at

may be had only to what is stated in the document itself, and parol evidence can be admitted merely " for the purpose of explaining words or symbols of art . . . and . . . of informing the court of relevant surrounding circumstances." [10]

299   But this does not apply to photographs, or presumably to drawings, as appears from the speech of Lord Reid in *C. Van der Lely N.V.* v. *Bamfords Ltd.*[11]: " There is no doubt that, where the matter alleged to amount to anticipation consists of a written description, the interpretation of that description is, like the interpretation of any document, a question for the court assisted where necessary by evidence regarding the meaning of technical language. It was argued that the same applies to a photograph. I do not think so. Lawyers are expected to be experts in the use of the English language, but we are not experts in the reading or interpretation of photographs. The question is what the eye of the man with appropriate engineering skill would see in the photograph, and that appears to me to be a matter of evidence. Where the evidence is contradictory the judge must decide. But the judge ought not in my opinion to attempt to read or construe the photograph himself; he looks at the photograph in determining which of the explanations given by the witnesses appears to be most worthy of acceptance."

The intention of the author of the document is not material.[12]

300 Common general knowledge

Prior knowledge sufficient to invalidate a patent need not be found in a particular document but may be common general knowledge, *i.e.*, such as every worker in the art may be expected to have as part of his technical equipment.[13] The relevant date at which the state of common general knowledge is to be considered is immediately before the priority date of the patent.[14] It follows that it is permissible to read a prior document in the light of common general knowledge as it exists at the date of the patent.[15] But such general knowledge must of course not be allowed to affect the construction to be placed on the prior document. Nor, it is submitted,

p. 523; see also *British Thomson-Houston Co. Ltd.* v. *Metropolitan-Vickers etc. Ltd.*, 45 R.P.C. 1 at p. 20.

[10] *Canadian General Electric Co. Ltd.* v. *Fada Radio Ltd.*, 47 R.P.C. 69 at p. 90.

[11] [1963] R.P.C. 61.

[12] *Ibid.*, and see *Kaye* v. *Chubb & Sons Ltd.*, 4 R.P.C. 289 at p. 298.

[13] *Automatic Coil Winder, etc., Co. Ltd.* v. *Taylor Electrical Instruments Ltd.*, 61 R.P.C. 41 at p. 43.

[14] See *B. T.-H. Co. Ltd.* v. *Stonebridge Electrical Co. Ltd.*, 33 R.P.C. 166 at p. 171.

[15] *Dewandre S.A.* v. *Citroen Cars Ltd.*, 47 R.P.C. 221 at p. 242; *Slumberland Ltd.* v. *Burgess Bedding*, 68 R.P.C. 87 at p. 99.

is it legitimate to invalidate a claim for a new combination or a new process by showing that some of the integers or steps are to be found in a prior disclosure while the remainder are matters of common knowledge, unless it can be proved that it would be obvious to combine all such features.

301　" Mere paper anticipation "

It has sometimes been said that if a prior disclosure is contained only in a document and there is no evidence that such disclosure has given rise to any practical result, this is " a mere paper anticipation " and must be appraised in some specially strict manner.[16] It is difficult to understand the relevance of this observation. If the document in fact discloses the invention and is to be found in a place (*e.g.* a public library) to which the public have access,[17] it is wholly immaterial that in fact no one has ever read it. From one point of view a well-known document which has not actually led to the invention should be regarded with much greater suspicion as an anticipation, for the failure of an obscure document to lead to a useful manufacture may be explained by the fact that no one having both the means and the inclination to put it into practice has ever seen it. It is submitted that any alleged prior disclosure in a document must be assessed on its own language, irrespective of how many or how few people may have seen it and how little action may have resulted from its publication.

302　Disclosure of machine processes

If a prior document discloses a machine which can operate only in a particular way, or if the document gives directions that the machine shall be operated in that way, a subsequent patent claiming a method or process consisting merely of that way of operation is invalid, notwithstanding that the actual machine disclosed in the prior document is impractical.[18] Similarly a claim for a chemical substance is invalid if that substance is disclosed in a prior published document even if the method of preparation disclosed in the prior document is erroneous.[19]

But the prior disclosure of a machine will not invalidate a claim for a process for which the machine is suitable unless the process as well as the machine is specifically disclosed. In *Flour Oxidizing Co.* v. *Carr & Co.*[20] Parker J. said: " When the question is solely one of

[16] See *Metropolitan-Vickers, etc. Ltd.* v. *B.T.-H. Co. Ltd.*, 43 R.P.C. 76 at p. 93.
[17] See *ante*, § 269.
[18] *Otto* v. *Linford*, 46 L.T.(N.S.) 35 at p. 44.
[19] *Smith Kline & French Laboratories' Appn.* [1960] R.P.C. 415.
[20] 25 R.P.C. 428 at p. 457.

prior publication it is not, in my opinion, enough to prove that an apparatus described in an earlier specification could have been used to produce this or that result.   It must also be shown that the specification contains clear and unmistakable direction so to use it."

The publication of a device provided with an adjustment is a complete publication of the device without the adjustment, because an ordinary mechanician would appreciate that the provision of the adjustment was optional.[21]

303   Inevitable result

It has been held by Graham J. in *General Tire & Rubber Co. v. Firestone Tyre & Rubber Co. Ltd.*[22] that if a prior document disclosing a process " gives instructions which, if followed, will inevitably produce a result which falls within the claim even if that result is not in fact described," that is sufficient to anticipate the claim.

304   Publication by drawing or photograph

A patent for a machine may be anticipated by a drawing or photograph of it unaccompanied by explanatory letterpress if published in a book or elsewhere so that it could become generally known, provided that any machinist would understand it, and could make the machine from the drawing without any further information, and without the exercise of ingenuity,[23] but making such inferences as the skilled addressee would make.[24]

9. OBVIOUSNESS

305   Section 32 (1) (f): " the invention, so far as claimed in any claim of the complete specification, is obvious and does not involve any inventive step having regard to what was known or used, before the priority date of the claim, in the United Kingdom."

306   In considering whether or not an invention is obvious, the way in which the inventor arrived at it is of no importance.[25]   Patents have been held valid for inventions that have been the result of the merest accident,[26] and for inventions imported from abroad.   But in considering whether any given invention can be considered obvious or

---

[21] *Gillette Safety Razor Co.* v. *Anglo-American Trading Co. Ltd.*, 30 R.P.C. 465 at p. 481.
[22] [1970] F.S.R. 268 at p. 296.
[23] *Herrburger, Schwander et Cie* v. *Squire*, 6 R.P.C. 194 at p. 198; *Electric Construction Co. Ltd.* v. *Imperial Tramways Co. Ltd.*, 17 R.P.C. 537 at p. 550; *C. Van der Lely N.V.* v. *Bamfords Ltd.* [1963] R.P.C. 61.
[24] *Lightning Fastener Co. Ltd.* v. *Colonial Fastener Co. Ltd.*, 51 R.P.C. 349 at p. 367; *Howaldt Ltd.* v. *Condrup Ltd.*, 54 R.P.C. 121 at p. 133.
[25] *Crane* v. *Price*, 1 W.P.C. 393 at p. 411.
[26] *Liardet* v. *Johnson*, 1 W.P.C. 53.

not having regard to prior knowledge or prior user it is necessary
to inquire whether in fact the new contrivance would be indicated
to the class of persons to whom the prior documents are addressed,
and who are concerned in the art with which the invention deals, by
an examination of the available prior knowledge.[27]

307   How obviousness to be judged

In *Allmanna Svenska Elektriska A/B* v. *The Burntisland Shipbuilding Co. Ltd.*[28] it was stated by the Court of Appeal: " The
matter of obviousness is to be judged by reference to the ' state of the
art ' in the light of all that was previously known by persons versed
in that art derived from experience of what was practically employed,
as well as from the contents of previous writings, specifications, text-
books and other documents. . . . When the relevant facts (as regards
the state of the art) are known, the question: Was the alleged
invention obvious? must in the end of all be as it were a kind of jury
question. The relevant question to be asked and answered is in form
and substance the question formulated by Sir Stafford Cripps and
cited by the Master of the Rolls in *Sharpe and Dohme Inc.* v. *Boots
Pure Drug Co. Ltd.*[29]: ' The real question is: Was it for all practical
purposes obvious to any skilled chemist in the state of chemical
knowledge existing at the date of the patent, which consists of the
chemical literature available . . . and his general chemical knowledge,
that he could manufacture valuable therapeutic agents by making the
higher alkyl resorcinols. . . .'

" It only remains to say that the question must be answered
objectively, for it is immaterial that. . . . the invention claimed was in
truth an invention of [the inventor] in the sense of being the result
of independent work and research on his part—without knowledge on
his part of many of the matters which must, on any view, be taken
into account by the court."

This statement of the law was approved by the House of Lords
in *Martin* v. *H. Millwood Ltd.*[30] Lord Morton said: " I entirely
agree with the reasoning of the Court of Appeal and would only add
that the court did not, of course, throw any doubt upon the principle
that there may be invention in a ' combination '; see, for instance,
British Celanese v. *Courtaulds Ltd.*, *per* Lord Tomlin." [31]

The Cripps form of question was adopted, in a modified form,
by the Court of Appeal in *Killick* v. *Pye*.[32]

[27] See *Martin* v. *H. Millwood Ltd.* [1956] R.P.C. 125 at p. 139.
[28] 69 R.P.C. 63 at p. 69.
[29] 45 R.P.C. 153 at p. 173.
[30] [1956] R.P.C. 125 at p. 139.
[31] 52 R.P.C. 171 at p. 193.
[32] [1958] R.P.C. 366 at p. 377.

308　　　But it is submitted that the " Cripps " form of question really does
no more than reduce the question " was the invention obvious? " into
the context of the particular case. It does not set any standard or test
by which obviousness is to be judged. However, the required
standard has been made clear in a number of cases. Thus in *Siddell*
v. *Vickers & Sons Ltd.*[33] Lord Herschell stated it as " so obvious that
it would at once occur to anyone acquainted with the subject, and
desirous of accomplishing the end." A much quoted test in similar
terms enunciated by Lopes L.J. in *Savage* v. *Harris & Sons*[34] was:
" The material question to be considered in a case like this is, whether
the alleged discovery lies so much out of the track of what was known
before as not naturally to suggest itself to a person thinking on the
subject; it must not be the obvious or natural suggestion of what was
previously known." It is submitted that in that test the " person
thinking on the subject " must be the notional skilled person in the
particular field.

In the recent case of *Technograph Printed Circuits Ltd.* v. *Mills &
Rockley (Electronics) Ltd.*,[35] it was alleged that the process of the
plaintiffs' patent was obvious in view of a prior published specification. Harman L.J.[36] said: " Counsel suggested that the proper
question to ask was not, could the one be derived from the other, but
would it be so derived? Would it in effect suggest itself? I think
this is the right test."

309　Quantum of Invention

In its judgment in the case of *Martin and Biro Swan Ltd.* v. *H.
Millwood Ltd.*[37] (subsequently affirmed by the House of Lords), the
Court of Appeal said " obviousness denies the presence of any inventive step whatever." [38] However, while some exercise of the inventive
faculty is required, the quantum of invention necessary to support a
patent is small. Thus Ormerod L.J., delivering the judgment of the
Court of Appeal in *Killick* v. *Pye*[32] stated: " It is well settled that the
validity of a patent, challenged on the ground of inventiveness, may be
established though the inventive step represent a very small
advance."

310　　　In considering whether the invention claimed is obvious, the
relevant comparison is not between the preferred embodiment of

[33] 15 App.Cas. 496; 7 R.P.C. 292 at p. 304.
[34] 13 R.P.C. 364 at p. 370.
[35] [1969] R.P.C. 395.
[36] *Ibid.* at p. 404.
[37] 71 R.P.C. 458.
[38] *Ibid.* at p. 466.

the invention claimed and the prior art. If any embodiment within the scope of the claim is obvious, then the claim is invalid.[39]

311 If the alleged invention is in fact obvious, it is not any the less so because it was not obvious to an expert called at the trial.[40]

312 *Simplicity no objection*

In *Siddell* v. *Vickers & Sons Ltd.*[33] Lord Herschell said: " If the apparatus be valuable by reason of its simplicity there is a danger of being misled by that very simplicity into the belief that no invention was needed to produce it. But experience has shown that not a few inventions . . . have been of so simple a character that once they have been made known it was difficult . . . not to believe that they must have been obvious to everybody." [41] There may be invention in what is merely simplification.[42] But matters of ordinary skilled designing or mere workship improvements cannot be considered as requiring the exercise of invention.[43]

313 *Commercial success*

In *Non-Drip Measure Co. Ltd.* v. *Strangers Ltd.*[44] Lord Russell said: " Whether there has or has not been an inventive step in constructing a device for giving effect to an idea which when given effect to seems a simple idea which ought to or might have occurred to anyone, is often a matter of dispute. More especially is this the case when many integers of the new device are already known. Nothing is easier than to say, after the event, that the thing was obvious and involved no invention. The words of Moulton L.J. in *British Westinghouse* v. *Braulik* [45] may well be called to mind in this connection: ' I confess ' (he said) ' that I view with suspicion arguments to the effect that a new combination, bringing with it new and important consequences in the shape of practical machines, is not an invention, because, when it has once been established, it is easy to show how it might be arrived at by starting from something known, and taking a series of apparently easy steps. This *ex post facto* analysis of inven-

---

[39] *Woodrow* v. *Long Humphreys & Co. Ltd.*, 51 R.P.C. 25; *Non-Drip Measure Co. Ltd.* v. *Strangers Ltd.*, 59 R.P.C. 1 at p. 23 (reversed in H.L. on other grounds).

[40] *John Wright and Eagle Range Ltd.* v. *General Gas Appliances Ltd.*, 46 R.P.C. 169 at p. 178; *Automatic Coil Winder etc. Co. Ltd.* v. *Taylor Electrical Instruments Ltd.*, 60 R.P.C. 111 at p. 119.

[41] See also *Thierry* v. *Riekman*, 14 R.P.C. 105.

[42] *Pope Appliance Corp.* v. *Spanish River etc. Mills Ltd.*, 46 R.P.C. 23 at p. 55 (P.C.).

[43] See *Safveans Aktie Bolag* v. *Ford Motor Co. (Eng.) Ltd.*, 44 R.P.C. 49 at p. 61; *Curtis & Son* v. *Heward & Co.*, 40 R.P.C. 53, 183; *Shaw* v. *Burnet & Co.*, 41 R.P.C. 432.

[44] 60 R.P.C. 135 at p. 142.

[45] 27 R.P.C. 209 at p. 230.

tion is unfair to the inventors and, in my opinion, it is not coun-
tenanced by English patent law. . . .' It is always pertinent to ask,
as to the article which is alleged to have been a mere workshop
improvement, and to have involved no inventive step, has it been a
commercial success? Has it supplied a want? Some language used
by Tomlin J. in *Samuel Parkes & Co. Ltd.* v. *Cocker Bros. Ltd.*[46]
may be cited as apposite: ' Nobody, however, has told me, and I
do not suppose that anybody ever will tell me, what is the precise
characteristic or quality the presence of which distinguishes invention
from workshop improvement. . . . The truth is that when once it
has been found . . . that the problem had awaited solution for many
years and that the device is in fact novel and superior to what had
gone before and has been widely used and used in preference to
alternative devices, it is, I think, practically impossible to say that
there is not present that scintilla of invention necessary to support
the patent.' ''[47]

314   While, as pointed out above, the practical utility and commercial
success of the invention may be a material factor in determining
whether the new result was obvious or not,[48] it is always necessary
to consider whether any commercial success is due to the patented
invention or to extraneous causes. In the latter event commercial
success is quite irrelevant when deciding whether the invention is
obvious.

     In *Longbottom* v. *Shaw*[49] Lord Herschell said: " Great reliance
is placed upon the fact that when this patent was taken out and
frames were made in accordance with it, there was a larger demand
for them. . . . I do not dispute that that is a matter to be taken
into consideration; but, again, it is obvious that it cannot be regarded
in any sense as conclusive. . . . If nothing be shown beyond the
fact that the new arrangement results in an improvement, and that
this improvement causes a demand for an apparatus made in accordance with the patent, I think that it is of very little importance."

315   And in *Wildey and White's Mfg. Co. Ltd.* v. *Freeman and Letrik
Ltd.*,[50] Maugham J. said: " In my opinion commercial success which
is shown to be due to the precise improvement the subject of the
specification ought to have considerable weight . . . and, *a fortiori*,
if it is shown that there is a long-felt want. . . . In the case,

---

[46] 46 R.P.C. 241 at p. 248.
[47] Cited with approval in *Technograph Printed Circuits Ltd.* v. *Mills &
Rockley (Electronics) Ltd.* [1969] R.P.C. 395 at p. 405.
[48] See *Hinks & Son* v. *Safety Lighting Co.,* 4 Ch.D. 607.
[49] 8 R.P.C. 333 at p. 336.
[50] 48 R.P.C. 405 at p. 414.

however, of such an article as we have here, a comb, . . . questions
of price, form, colour and design, quite apart from the question of
clever advertising, may well conduce to, or indeed, be completely
responsible for, the commercial success of the article." [51]

316 New use of old material or contrivance

In *Gadd and Mason* v. *Mayor etc. of Manchester* [52] the plaintiff's
invention was to keep gasometers vertical by means previously
described. Lindley L.J.,[53] after a review of the authorities, expressed
the law upon this subject by the two following propositions: " 1. A
patent for the mere new use of a known contrivance, without any
additional ingenuity in overcoming fresh difficulties, is bad, and
cannot be supported. If the new use involves no ingenuity, but is in
manner and purpose analogous to the old use, although not quite
the same, there is no invention: no manner of new manufacture
within the meaning of the statute of James. 2. On the other hand, a
patent for a new use of a known contrivance is good, and can be
supported if the new use involves practical difficulties which the
patentee has been the first to see and overcome by some ingenuity of
his own. An improved thing produced by a new and ingenious
application of a known contrivance to an old thing, is a manner of
new manufacture within the meaning of the statute. If, practically
speaking, there are no difficulties to be overcome in adapting an old
contrivance to a new purpose, there can be no ingenuity in overcoming them, there will be no invention, and the first rule will apply.
The same rule will, I apprehend, also apply to cases in which the
mode of overcoming the so-called difficulties is so obvious to everyone of ordinary intelligence and acquaintance with the subject-matter
of the patent, as to present no difficulty to any such person. Such
cases present no real difficulty to people conversant with the matter
in hand, and admit of no sufficient ingenuity to support a patent. If,
in these two classes of cases, patents could be supported, they would
be intolerable nuisances, and would seriously impede all improvements in the practical application of common knowledge. . . . But
unless an invention can be brought within one or other of the above

---

[51] And see *Gosnell* v. *Bishop*, 5 R.P.C. 151 at p. 158; *Haskell Golf Ball Co.
Ltd.* v. *Hutchinson (No. 2)*, 23 R.P.C. 301 at p. 313; *Thermos Ltd.* v.
Isola Ltd., 27 R.P.C. 388 at p. 398; *Erickson's Patent*, 40 R.P.C. 477 at p.
487; *B.T.-H.* v. *Charlesworth, Peebles & Co.*, 42 R.P.C. 180 at p. 195;
British United Shoe Machinery Co. Ltd. v. *E. A. Johnson & Co. Ltd.*,
42 R.P.C. 243 at p. 252; *Wright and Eagle Range Ltd.* v. *General Gas
Appliances Ltd.*, 46 R.P.C. 169 at p. 179; *Paper Sacks Proprietary Ltd.* v.
Cowper, 53 R.P.C. 31 at p. 54.
[52] 9 R.P.C. 516.
[53] *Ibid.* at p. 524.

classes, a patent for it cannot be held bad on the ground of want of subject-matter." [54] Although this judgment of Lindley L.J. must not be read as if it were a statute,[55] it has frequently been applied.[56]

317   Analogous user

In *Morgan & Co.* v. *Windover & Co.* the invention amounted to the use in the front part of a carriage of springs of a type formerly used in the rear part. The patent was held invalid in the House of Lords. Lord Herschell said: " . . . the mere adaptation to a new purpose of a known material or appliance, if that purpose be analogous to a purpose to which it has already been applied, and if the mode of application be also analogous so that no inventive faculty is required and no invention is displayed in the manner in which it is applied, is not the subject-matter for a patent . . . once it is admitted that all that can be claimed as new is the idea of putting it (the springs) in the front instead of at the back and that when once that idea was entertained, any workman told to do it would, without any instructions or any special mechanical skill, be able at once to do it, it seems to me that that really concludes the case. . . ." [57]

318   In *Harwood* v. *Great Northern Ry.*,[58] the patentee used a " fish plate " for joining together the ends of rails. The evidence showed that this particular form of joint had been applied in various mechanical contrivances, and notably in the joining together of pieces of timber used in bridge building, but not exactly the same kind of strains were involved. Lord Westbury L.C. said [59]: " Then the question is whether there can be any invention of the plaintiff in having taken that thing, which was a fish for a bridge, and having applied it as a fish for a railway. Upon that I think that the law is well and rightly settled, for there would be no end to the interferences with trades, and with the liberty of any mechanical

---

[54] See also *Hayward* v. *Hamilton,* Griff.P.C. 115; *Blakey & Co.* v. *Latham & Co.,* 6 R.P.C. 29, 184; *Morgan & Co.* v. *Windover & Co.,* 7 R.P.C. 131; *Lane-Fox* v. *Kensington & Knightbridge Electric Lighting Co. Ltd.,* 9 R.P.C. 413 at p. 416; *Savage* v. *Harris & Sons,* 13 R.P.C. 90, 364; *Brooks* v. *Lamplugh,* 15 R.P.C. 33; *British Liquid Air Co. Ltd.* v. *Brit. Oxygen Co. Ltd.,* 25 R.P.C. 218, 577 at p. 601; *British Vacuum Cleaner Co. Ltd.* v. *L. & S.W. Ry.,* 29 R.P.C. 309; *Merten's Patent,* 31 R.P.C. 373; *Bonnard* v. *London General Omnibus Co. Ltd.,* 38 R.P.C. 1; *Auster Ltd.* v. *Perfecta Motor Equipments Ltd.,* 41 R.P.C. 482.
[55] *Lister & Co. Ltd.'s Patent* [1966] R.P.C. 30.
[56] *e.g.* by the House of Lords in *Benmax* v. *Austin Motor Co. Ltd.,* 72 R.P.C. 39 at p. 44 and *Parks-Cramer Co.* v. *Thornton & Sons Ltd.* [1969] R.P.C. 112 at p. 128.
[57] 7 R.P.C. 131 at pp. 137, 138.
[58] 35 L.J.Q.B. 27.
[59] *Ibid.* at p. 38.

contrivance being adopted, if every slight difference in the application of a well-known thing were held to constitute a patent. . . . No sounder or more wholesome doctrine, I think, was ever established by the decisions which are referred to in the opinions of the four learned judges, who concur in the second opinion delivered to your lordships, namely, that you cannot have a patent for a well-known mechanical contrivance, merely because it is applied in a manner, or to a purpose which is analogous to the manner, or to the purpose in or to which it has been hitherto notoriously used." [60]

319　*Limits of doctrine of analogous user*

The decision in *Harwood* v. *Great Northern Ry.* was considered in *Pope Appliance Corporation* v. *Spanish River etc. Mills Ltd.*[61] and Lord Dunedin said: " Analogous user is what its name denotes, something which has to do with user. He [*i.e.* the trial judge] has applied the doctrine not to things used, but to things described. . . . The doctrine of analogous user only applies to cases as to things in actual use." Nevertheless, the question remains in every case whether the invention claimed is or is not obvious, having regard to what was previously known.[62] If the manufacture with which the claim is concerned is of a different kind from that of the prior disclosure this will, of course, be an important circumstance to be taken into account, but it does not necessarily follow that the invention claimed has sufficient of the inventive quality.

320　*Invention may lie in idea of new application*

However, if the idea of using the known contrivance for the new purpose was not an obvious idea, but involved some degree of ingenuity, the patent may well be valid notwithstanding that once the idea of the new application is conceived no further act of invention is required to put it into practice.[63] It has been said " a man who discovers that a known machine can produce effects which no one knew could be produced by it before may make a great and useful discovery, but if he does no more his discovery is not a patentable invention." [64] It is submitted that in its context this passage means

[60] And see *Blakey & Co.* v. *Latham & Co.*, 6 R.P.C. 184; *Singer* v. *Rudge Cycle Co.*, 11 R.P.C. 463; *Dredge* v. *Parnell*, 16 R.P.C. 625; *Acetylene Illuminating Co. Ltd.* v. *United Alkali Co.*, 22 R.P.C. 145 at p. 155; *British Oxygen Co.* v. *Maine Lighting Co.*, 41 R.P.C. 604; *Harris* v. *Brandreth*, 42 R.P.C. 471; *Magnatex Ltd.* v. *Unicorn Products Ltd.*, 68 R.P.C. 117; and *Benmax* v. *Austin Motor Co. Ltd.*, 72 R.P.C. 39.

[61] 46 R.P.C. 23 at p. 56.

[62] s. 32 (1) (*f*); and see *Allmana Svenska Elektriska* v. *Burntisland Shipbuilding Co. Ltd.*, 69 R.P.C. at pp. 69, 70.

[63] See *Muntz* v. *Foster*, 2 W.P.C. 93.

[64] *Lane-Fox* v. *Kensington etc. Co. Ltd.*, 9 R.P.C. 413 at p. 416.

(a) that a patent cannot be granted for a known machine or process merely because the applicant has discovered that such known machine or processes can be used for a novel purpose, and (b) that if the new " effects " are not a manner of manufacture (or, under the present law, a method of testing for purposes of manufacture) [65] no patent can be granted. It does *not* mean that a new process of manufacture is necessarily not patentable if it is to be effected by a machine or process known in itself.[66]

321   In *Hickton's Patent Syndicate* v. *Patents etc. Ltd.*,[67] the invention involved a conception by no means obvious. Once it had been conceived, however, it could not be denied that the application was obvious, and the trial judge had held the patent invalid on this ground. In the Court of Appeal Fletcher Moulton L.J. said [68]: " The learned judge says, ' an idea may be new and original and very meritorious, but unless there is some invention necessary for putting the idea into practice it is not patentable.' With the greatest respect for the learned judge, that, in my opinion, is quite contrary to the principles of patent law, and would deprive of their reward a very large number of meritorious inventions that have been made. I may say that this dictum is to the best of my knowledge supported by no case, and no case has been quoted to us which would justify it. . . . To say that the conception may be meritorious and may involve invention, and may be new and original, and simply because when you have once got the idea it is easy to carry it out, and that that deprives it of the title of being a new invention according to our patent law, is, I think, an extremely dangerous principle, and justified neither by reason, nor authority. . . . In my opinion, invention may lie in the idea, and it may lie in the way in which it is carried out, and it may be in the combination of the two; but if there is invention in the idea plus the way of carrying it out, then it is good subject-matter for letters patent." [69] By the last sentence, having regard to its context, the learned Lord Justice plainly means that if there is invention either in the idea itself, or in the means by which it is utilised, or in a combination of the two, then the patent cannot be invalid for lack of the inventive quality.

322   *Automaticity*

There cannot be invention in the mere idea of doing automatically

---

[65] See *ante*, § 54.
[66] See *Otto* v. *Linford*, 46 L.T.(N.S.) 35 at p. 39.
[67] 26 R.P.C. 339.
[68] At p. 347.
[69] And see *Benton & Stone Ltd.* v. *Thomas Denston & Son*, 42 R.P.C. 284 at p. 297; *Teste* v. *Coombes*, 41 R.P.C. 88 at p. 105; *Wright & Eagle Range Ltd.* v. *General Gas Appliances Ltd.*, 45 R.P.C. 346 at pp. 362, 363.

anything that was previously done manually.[70]   A claim which "is in effect a claim for the principle of automaticity . . . is not a claim that any patentee can make." [71]

323   Chemical cases

In the case of patents for chemical and metallurgical processes the principles applicable are precisely similar, and in the application of an old and well-known process to a new material the same question arises, that is to say, "was the new application obvious in view of the common knowledge?"   Some years ago a distinguished chemist stated, when giving evidence in such a case, that "there is no prevision in chemistry."   This phrase having been often repeated has given rise to the belief that the law applicable to chemical cases is peculiar.   This is not the case.   The unexpected nature of chemical reactions may make a chemist, who is aware that things may and do occur contrary to expectation, distrustful of his own belief in what to anticipate.[72]   The question of obviousness, however, has to be decided on the evidence in each particular case.

324

In *Osram Lamp Works Ltd.* v. *Pope's Electric Lamp Co.*,[73] Lord Parker said: "I agree that the invention consists merely in the application to tungsten and its compounds of a process (previously) invented and disclosed by Dr. Welsbach for making filaments of osmium or other metals of the platinum group.   This is good subject-matter, unless, having regard to what was generally known at the date of the patent sued upon, it was obvious without experiment or research that the process invented by Welsbach could be applied to tungsten and its compounds as well as to osmium or other metals of the platinum group.   I am not prepared to hold that this was obvious.   Indeed, all the facts appear to point to the contrary conclusion."   The patent was held valid.   On the other hand, in *British Thomson-Houston Co. Ltd.* v. *Duram Ltd.*[74] the patentees stated that they had discovered that tungsten became ductile if the coherent metal (rendered coherent by any suitable method) were heated, and claimed broadly, "The method of working tungsten which consists in subjecting the metal in a coherent form to the

---

[70] *British United Shoe Machinery Co. Ltd.* v. *Simon Collier Ltd.*, 26 R.P.C. 21 at pp. 48–50; *Submarine Signal Co.* v. *Henry Hughes & Son Ltd.*, 49 R.P.C. 149 at p. 175; *Parks-Cramer Co.* v. *Thornton & Sons Ltd.* [1969] R.P.C. 112 at p. 128.

[71] *Per* Romer L.J. in *Submarine Signal Co.* v. *Henry Hughes & Son Ltd.*, *loc. cit.*

[72] *Cf. Sharpe & Dohme Inc.* v. *Boots Pure Drug Co. Ltd.*, 45 R.P.C. 153 at p. 173.

[73] 34 R.P.C. 369 at p. 396.

[74] 35 R.P.C. 161.

action of heat while it is being operated on or manipulated." It was proved to be the common practice of metallurgists to work metals hot either to test their properties or in the course of industries, and that to apply such a process to tungsten was obvious. The patent was held invalid.[75]

325 Verification

If the alleged inventive step consists in fact merely in a verification of the published statements of other workers in the art, that will not be proper subject-matter for a patent. In *Sharpe & Dohme Inc.* v. *Boots Pure Drug Co. Ltd.*,[76] Astbury J., referring to certain of the documents cited, said: "If the statement is there, . . . it is a disclosure of a fact, and even if no chemist would have appreciated that it was right, if it turns out that it is right, you cannot take a patent out for verifying a prior statement." He held the patent to be invalid. The judgment was confirmed by the Court of Appeal.

In *Aktiengesellschaft für Aluminium Schweissung* v. *London Aluminium Co. Ltd.* (*No.* 2),[77] the patentee claimed a process for autogenously welding aluminium by the use of a very high temperature oxy-hydrogen blowpipe and a flux of a certain composition. It was proved that an identical flux was commonly known for soldering aluminium at a much lower temperature, but that no one would have suspected that this flux would have remained stable and unvolatilised at the higher temperature of the oxy-hydrogen blowpipe, although in fact its action as a flux to dissolve the oxide of aluminium was the same in both cases. It was held that in face of the unforeseen behaviour of the flux at the higher temperature there was invention in its use and a new process was made available to the public and that the patent was valid.

In the last-mentioned case, the basis of the invention was the discovery of a previously unknown characteristic of the flux. But there is no inventive step in merely appreciating that a known characteristic, previously regarded as a defect, could be an advantage. Thus in *Reymes-Cole* v. *Elite Hosiery Co. Ltd.*,[78] Diplock L.J. said: "It would seem an odd result of patent law if the plaintiff, by patenting as he has purported to do in the product claims of the specification stockings containing small tucks of this kind, could prevent manufacturers from continuing a process of manufacture which they had previously used in which such tucks were produced

---

[75] See also *Aero Carbon Light Co.* v. *Kidd,* 4 R.P.C. 535; *McLay* v. *Lawes & Co. Ltd.,* 22 R.P.C. 199; *Reitzman* v. *Grahame-Chapman,* 67 R.P.C. 178; *Magnatex Ltd.* v. *Unicorn Products Ltd.,* 68 R.P.C. 117.
[76] 44 R.P.C. 367 at p. 390.
[77] 39 R.P.C. 296.
[78] [1965] R.P.C. at p. 117.

accidentally, and from marketing the products of such process which contained an unintentional tuck. In my view, the law does not entail this consequence. The plaintiff may have been the first to recognise that a physical characteristic which was already well known, but regarded as an accidental imperfection in a stocking, was an advantage, but such recognition, without more, is not an invention, and does not involve any inventive step."

326 Combinations

In *British Celanese Ltd.* v. *Courtaulds Ltd.*[79] Lord Tomlin said: " It is accepted as sound law that a mere placing side by side of old integers so that each performs its own proper function independently of any of the others is not a patentable combination, but that where the old integers when placed together have some working interrelation producing a new or improved result then there is patentable subject-matter in the idea of the working interrelation brought about by the collocation of the integers."[80]

327 *The " Sausage Machine Case "*

The principle is illustrated by the well-known case of *Williams* v. *Nye*[81] (the " *Sausage Machine Case* "). The patent was for a machine for mincing meat and filling the minced meat into skins so as to make sausages. In fact it consisted of a well-known form of mincing machine which fed the meat to a well-known filling machine so as to combine in one apparatus two machines which had formerly been used separately. The mincing part performed no more than its already well-known functions, and the same remark is true of the filling part. The ultimate result was novel and useful, but there was no difficulty to be overcome and no invention.[82]

The principles to be applied in considering whether an invention consisting of a combination of old integers was obvious were stated in *Wood* v. *Gowshall Ltd.*[83] by Greene L.J. as follows: " The dissection of a combination into its constituent elements, and the examination of each element in order to see whether its use was obvious or not, is . . . a method which ought to be applied with great caution since it tends to obscure the fact that the invention claimed is the combination. Moreover, this method also tends to obscure the facts that the conception of the combination is what normally governs

[79] 52 R.P.C. 171 at p. 193.
[80] See also *Klaber's Patent*, 23 R.P.C. 461 at p. 469; *British United Shoe Machinery Co. Ltd.* v. *A. Fussell & Sons Ltd.*, 25 R.P.C. 631 at p. 657.
[81] 7 R.P.C. 62.
[82] See also *Wood* v. *Raphael*, 13 R.P.C. 730; 14 R.P.C. 496; *Layland* v. *Boldy & Sons Ltd.*, 30 R.P.C. 547.
[83] 54 R.P.C. 37 at p. 40.

and precedes the selection of the elements of which it is composed, and that the obviousness or otherwise of each act of selection must in general be examined in the light of this consideration. The real and ultimate question is: is the combination obvious or not? "

328 *Labour-saving machinery*

In certain classes of invention, such as automatic labour-saving machinery, a very small alteration in the selection and arrangement of the parts may produce an important result. In *British United Shoe Machinery Co. Ltd. v. A. Fussell & Sons Ltd.*[84] the patent was for a high-speed machine for screwing the soles of boots to the welts. Fletcher Moulton L.J. said [85] " Its merit is that it does this operation at a high speed, and with unvarying accuracy, so that you can work these machines so as to yield a huge output without making wasters. . . . When you come to a machine of this type, you have to alter very seriously the canons which influence you in deciding such questions as novelty. In the case of operations which have to be done under normal circumstances, in the absence of any special difficulties arising from speed, small and trivial alterations in the apparatus are viewed with suspicion, as possibly being idle variants; but when you come to machines which with this demand upon them still give uniform success, I think any tribunal will be very careful before it applies its ordinary ideas of what are mere idle and trivial changes to those alterations which have resulted in a success so triumphant. So that I approach the consideration of novelty in this case, *i.e.* of the importance of apparently slight variations in the combination, in a very humble spirit, willing to be taught by those who know the practical performance of the machine, and are able to judge of the means which render that practical performance so successful."

329 Selection

A selection from possible alternatives for the solution of a problem may afford subject-matter for a patent, but " a mere selection among possible alternatives is not subject-matter. A selection to be patentable must be a selection in order to secure some advantage or avoid some disadvantage. It must be an adaptation of means to ends impossible without exercise of the inventive faculty. It follows that in describing and ascertaining the nature of an invention consisting in the selection between possible alternatives, the advantages to be gained, or the disadvantages to be avoided ought to be referred to." [86]

---

[84] 25 R.P.C. 631.   [85] 25 R.P.C. 631 at p. 646.
[86] *Per* Lord Parker in *Clyde Nail Co.* v. *Russell*, 33 R.P.C. 291 at p. 306; and see *Thomas* v. *South Wales Colliery etc. Co. Ltd.*, 42 R.P.C. 22 at p. 27; *Safveans Aktie Bolag* v. *Ford Motor Co. (Eng.) Ltd.*, 44 R.P.C. 49 at p. 61.

The general principles governing the validity of such patents were discussed in *I.G. Farbenindustrie A.G.'s Patents* [87] by Maugham J., who pointed out that the following conditions must be fulfilled: (1) The selection must be based on securing some advantage (or avoiding some disadvantage) by the use of the selected members; (2) all the selected members must possess the required advantage; but a few exceptions here and there would not be sufficient to make the patent invalid; (3) the selection must be for " a quality of a special character " which is peculiar to the selected group, and this quality must not be one which would be obvious to an expert. Selection patents are usually concerned with chemical processes, but the question of obviousness is not essentially different from that which arises in other kinds of inventions. As Maugham J. pointed out: " If the selected compounds, being novel, possess a special property of an unexpected character . . . I cannot see that the inventive step essentially differs from the step in producing a new result by a new combination of well-known parts or indeed from using the common and well-known factors (cranks, rods, toothed wheels and so forth) employed in mechanics in the construction of a new machine." [88]

330 Evidence

In coming to a conclusion as to whether or not a claim contains a real inventive step over what was previously known or used, the court usually attaches considerable weight to the evidence of the inventor himself.[89] Evidence which shows that the invention was not obvious to the defendants at the priority date will be of considerable weight if the defendants were persons skilled in the art, *e.g.* (i) where the defendants at first contended that they had made the invention and offered to help the plaintiff to get a patent if they were granted a free licence,[90] or (ii) where the defendants introduced into a subsidiary claim of a patent specification of theirs the feature alleged to be obvious.[91] The evidence of a director of the defendant company that the invention was new to him has been held to be relevant on the issue of obviousness.[92] An *ad hoc* expert, however, may not give evidence that the invention is, or is not, obvious, that being a matter for the court itself to decide.[93] An expert may be asked, and may answer, the hypothetical question whether an examination of the

[87] 47 R.P.C. 289 at pp. 322, 323.
[88] 47 R.P.C. 289 at p. 321.
[89] *Lightning Fastener Co. Ltd. v. Colonial Fastener Co. Ltd.*, 51 R.P.C. 349 at p. 367; *Howaldt Ltd. v. Condrup Ltd.*, 54 R.P.C. 121 at p. 133.
[90] *Siddell v. Vickers*, 7 R.P.C. 293 at pp. 304, 305.
[91] *C. Van der Lely N.V. v. Bamfords Ltd.* [1961] R.P.C. 296 at p. 316.
[92] *McGlashan v. Gaskell & Chambers (Scotland) Ltd.*, 69 R.P.C. 43.
[93] *British Celanese Ltd. v. Courtaulds Ltd.*, 52 R.P.C. 171 at p. 196.

prior documents would have made the invention obvious to him, but such evidence carries little weight, for apart from its hypothetical nature the selection of prior documents has usually been deliberately made for the purposes of an action and the mind of an expert is not the proper criterion for judging whether there is an inventive step.[94]

10. APPLICANT NOT ENTITLED TO APPLY

331 **Section 32 (1) (b):** "the patent was granted on the application of a person not entitled under the provisions of this Act to apply therefor."

The question as to who is the person entitled under the provisions of the Patents Act to apply for a patent has been fully dealt with in Chapter 3. If the person who has applied is not the person entitled to apply, then the patent is invalid. This ground of invalidity can be raised by any person and is not limited to the person who should have been the proper applicant.[95]

11. PATENT OBTAINED IN CONTRAVENTION OF THE RIGHTS OF THE PETITIONER

332 **Section 32 (1) (c):** "the patent was obtained in contravention of the rights of the petitioner or any person under or through whom he claims."

There is an overlap between this and the preceding ground of revocation in that, where the applicant is not the "true and first inventor" but has "obtained" the invention in this country from the petitioner for revocation, then the patent would be invalid both under section 32 (1) (*b*) and under section 32 (1) (*c*). But it appears that under section 32 (1) (*c*) a petitioner can seek the revocation of a patent where the "obtaining" from him had taken place abroad and the patentee had applied, in contravention of the petitioner's rights (*e.g.* of confidence), for a patent in the U.K. In such a case the patentee could properly claim to be the "true and first inventor," being the "importer" of the invention, and, therefore, no case for revocation could be made under section 32 (1) (*b*), but, nevertheless, the patent could apparently be revoked under section 32 (1) (*c*) at the instance of the person from whom the invention had been obtained. There are, no doubt, other cases than the above where there will be no overlap, *e.g.* where a servant makes an invention and applies for a patent for it contrary to his conditions of employment. This ground of invalidity can only be alleged by the persons

[94] See *ante*, § § 294 and 295.
[95] *Cf.* s. 32 (1) (*c*) *infra*.

whose rights have been contravened by the obtaining of the grant of the patent.[96]

12. Invention not a Manufacture

333   **Section 32 (1) (d):** "the subject of any claim of the complete specification is not an invention within the meaning of this Act."

Having regard to the definition of "invention" in section 101 (1) of the Act and the inclusion of lack of novelty as a separate ground of revocation in section 32 (1) (e), it appears that this ground relates solely to whether the claim relates to a "manner of manufacture" or a "method or process of testing" as defined above. These requirements have been fully dealt with in Chapter 2, to which the reader is referred.

13. Use of Invention Illegal

334   **Section 32 (1) (k):** "the primary or intended use or exercise of the invention is contrary to law."

It will not be sufficient to establish invalidity on the above ground to prove that the invention could be used for purposes contrary to law (e.g. gaming).[97]   In order to establish this ground of revocation it must be proved that the "primary or intended" use is illegal. This ground of invalidity is to be found in section 6 of the Statute of Monopolies, but it does not appear that any patent has been held invalid upon this ground.

14. Prior Secret Use

335   **Section 32 (1) (l):** "the invention, so far as claimed in any claim of the complete specification, was secretly used in the United Kingdom, otherwise than as mentioned in subsection (2) of this section, before the priority date of that claim."

336   Not every case of secret prior user will invalidate the claim, because certain kinds are excluded by section 32 (2). Accordingly, if the secret prior user is only for the purpose of reasonable trial and experiment or is by or by authority of a government department to whom the applicant for a patent has disclosed the invention, or is by a third person to whom the applicant has disclosed the invention and takes place without the applicant's consent or acquiescence, then such secret prior user does not affect the validity of the claim.[98]

---

[96] See *Patent Concern N.V.* v. *Melotte Sales Co. Ltd.* [1968] R.P.C. 263.
[97] *Pessers & Moody* v. *Haydon & Co.*, 26 R.P.C. 58; *Walton* v. *Ahrens*, 56 R.P.C. 193 at p. 203.
[98] s. 32 (2).

Further, although a claim will be invalid for obviousness if it contains no inventive step over a public user, such is not the case with secret user, which cannot be relied upon in support of the plea of obviousness.[99]   There is often considerable difficulty in deciding whether or not a user was " for the purpose of reasonable trial or experiment only " (see under " Experiments and Trials " at § 284).

[The next paragraph is 341]

---

[99] s. 32 (1) (*e*), (*f*).

CHAPTER 6

INFRINGEMENT OF LETTERS PATENT

1. GENERAL

341 Royal Command in letters patent

The infringement of a patent is the doing, after the date of publication of the complete specification,[1] of that which the patent prohibits being done. The words of the Royal Command are as follows: " We do by these presents for Us, our heirs and successors, strictly command all our subjects whatsoever within our United Kingdom of Great Britain and Northern Ireland, and the Isle of Man, that they do not at any time during the continuance of the said term [sixteen years from the date hereunder written of these presents] either directly or indirectly make use of or put in practice the said invention, nor in anywise imitate the same, without the consent, licence or agreement of the said patentee in writing under this hand and seal, on pain of incurring such penalties as may be justly inflicted on such offenders for their contempt of this our Royal Command, and of being answerable to the patentee according to law for his damages thereby occasioned." [2]

342 No duty to warn infringers

There is no duty cast upon a patentee to inform persons that what they are doing amounts to an infringement of his patent; and if he knows of the infringement and omits to give a warning, he is not stopped from subsequently bringing an action.[3] If, however, the patentee were falsely to represent to a manufacturer that articles manufactured by him were not an infringement of the patent, and were thereby to induce him to spend money in further manufacture, or otherwise to place himself at a disadvantage, the conduct of the patentee would amount to acquiescence, and he could not succeed in an action for infringement.[4]

343 Declaration of non-infringement

Under the present Act [5] at any time after the date of publication of the complete specification any person may institute proceedings in

---

[1] s. 13.
[2] See Appendix and *ante*, § 19.
[3] *Proctor* v. *Bennis*, 4 R.P.C. 333.
[4] *Ibid*. at pp. 357, 358.   [5] s. 66.

the High Court against the applicant or patentee, as the case may be, or against an exclusive licensee, for a declaration that the use of any process, or the use or sale of any article, does not or would not constitute an infringement, if (a) the plaintiff has asked for a written acknowledgment of non-infringement and has furnished full particulars of the process or article and (b) such an acknowledgment has not been given. The costs of all parties must be paid by the plaintiff unless for special reasons the court orders otherwise.[6] Validity cannot be investigated in such proceedings.[7] It is submitted that a declaration of non-infringement would be binding against all successors in title of the defendant and that, therefore, this section provides a quick and comparatively inexpensive way of making sure whether or not any particular manufacture can be restrained by reason of the patent.

If the plaintiff's process or article, the subject of the proceedings, is held not to constitute an infringement of the defendant's patent, the declaration should be granted.[8]

344 " Infringement not novel "

If the defendant can prove that the act complained of is merely what was disclosed in a publication which can be relied on against the validity of the patent, without any substantial or patentable variation having been made, he must have a good defence. In *Gillette Safety Razor Co.* v. *Anglo-American Trading Co.*[9] Lord Moulton said: " I am of opinion that in this case the defendant's right to succeed can be established without an examination of the terms of the specification of the plaintiff's letters patent. I am aware that such a mode of deciding a patent case is unusual, but from the point of view of the public it is important that this method of viewing their rights should not be overlooked. In practical life it is often the only safeguard to the manufacturer. It is impossible for an ordinary member of the public to keep watch on all the numerous patents which are taken out and to ascertain the validity and scope of their claims. But he is entitled to feel secure if he knows that that which he is doing differs from that which has been done of old only in non-patentable variations such as the substitution of mechanical equivalents or changes of material, shape or size. The defence that ' the alleged infringement was not novel at the date of the plaintiff's letters patent,' is a good defence in law, and it would sometimes obviate the great length and

---

[6] s. 66 (2). See *Birmingham Sound Reproducers Ltd.* v. *Collaro Ltd.* [1956] R.P.C. 53 at p. 71; *Flexheat Ltd.* v. *Bolser* [1966] R.P.C. 374.

[7] s. 66 (3).

[8] *Rodi & Weinberger A.G.* v. *Henry Showell Ltd.* [1969] R.P.C. 367.

[9] 30 R.P.C. 465 at p. 480.

expense of patent cases if the defendant could and would put forth his case in this form, and thus spare himself the trouble of demonstrating on which horn of the well-known dilemma the plaintiff had impaled himself, invalidity or non-infringement." [10]

These dicta have, however, been considered and explained in *Page* v. *Brent Toy Products Ltd.*,[11] where the prior document in question was more than fifty years old and, therefore, could not be relied on as destroying novelty.[12] Evershed M.R. said [13]: "Lord Moulton was not stating that this plea, that the infringement was not novel, was a separate defence against a claim of infringement, but was confining himself to the case where the alternatives of invalidity or non-infringement were open to the defendant. He was stating ' This is a convenient brief form of raising, by way of pleading, the whole case. If the allegation is made good, then where the dilemma is present, the result must be that the plaintiff fails by being impaled on one horn or the other ' . . . in this case . . . there is no dilemma for the plaintiff; the plea of invalidity is not open to the defendants on this particular matter. And, in my judgment, the language of Lord Moulton does not entitle the defendants here to raise as a separate defence this form of words." Accordingly Lord Moulton's test is helpful in assisting a manufacturer to decide whether or not to proceed with some manufacture which may be an infringement of a patent, but it does not provide an additional defence to an action for infringement.

345　" Infringement " of invalid patent

It has been said that there cannot in any event be an infringement of an invalid patent,[14] but the word " infringement " is throughout used in the Act, and has been used in many judgments, as meaning " within the scope of the monopoly claimed."

346　Ignorance no excuse

It is equally an infringement whether the defendant acted in ignorance of the plaintiff's patent or not. In *Proctor* v. *Bennis* [15] Cotton L.J. said: " The right of the patentee does not depend on the defendant having notice that what he is doing is an infringement. If what he is doing is in fact an infringement, even although the

---

[10] See also *Proctor* v. *Bennis*, 4 R.P.C. 333 at p. 351; and *Cincinnati Grinders (Inc.)* v. *B.S.A. Tools Ltd.*, 48 R.P.C. 33 at p. 58.
[11] 67 R.P.C. 4.
[12] See *ante*, § 271.
[13] 67 R.P.C. at p. 13.
[14] See *Pittevil & Co.* v. *Brackelsberg Melting Processes Ltd.*, 49 R.P.C. 23 at p. 32.
[15] 4 R.P.C. 333 at p. 356.

defendant acts in the way which . . . was bona fide or honest, he will not be protected from an injunction by that. It does not depend on notice."

347   Innocent infringement

However, an infringer will not be liable in damages if he proves that at the date of infringement he was not aware, and had no reasonable ground for supposing, that the patent existed.[16] The marking of an article with the word " patent " or " patented " is not sufficient notice to make an infringer liable in damages unless the number of the patent accompanies such words.[16] But this special defence is not available to an infringer who has been informed of the existence of a patent application in respect of the article in question.[17]

348   Intention not relevant

In *Stead* v. *Anderson* [18] Wilde C.J. said: " We think it clear that the action is maintainable in respect of what the defendant does, not what he intends." [19]

If a person intending to infringe a patent does not in fact do so, he will not be taken to have infringed.[20]

Proof of an intention to infringe, apart from actual infringement, may justify an injunction to restrain infringement.[21]

349   Ascertainment whether there is " infringement "

In order to ascertain whether there has been infringement of a patent, one must (1) decide whether the acts alleged to have been done by the defendant are of such a nature that they are capable of constituting a breach of the Royal Command and have not been excused by some statutory provision, (2) construe the specification so as to ascertain what is the monopoly claimed and (3) decide whether the alleged infringer has in substance taken the invention for which a monopoly is claimed. Each of these questions will be considered in turn.

2. NATURE OF INFRINGING ACT

350   The Royal Command enjoins that no person shall "either directly or indirectly make use of or put in practice the said invention." This

---

[16] s. 59 (1), and see *Wilderman* v. *F. W. Berk & Co. Ltd.*, 42 R.P.C. 79 at p. 90; and see *post*, § 958.
[17] *Wilbec Plastics Ltd.* v. *Wilson Dawes Ltd.* [1966] R.P.C. 513.
[18] 2 W.P.C. 151 at p. 156.
[19] And see *Wright* v. *Hitchcock*, L.R. 5 Ex. 37 at p. 47; *Young* v. *Rosenthal*, 1 R.P.C. 29 at p. 39.
[20] *Newall* v. *Elliott*, 10 Jur.(N.S.) 954 at p. 958.
[21] See *post*, § 934 *et seq.*

prohibition is broken by making, using or selling the patented invention.

351   Patenting or granting of licence

Taking out a patent for a process or machine that infringes a prior patent does not amount to infringement,[22] nor does the granting of a licence to manufacture under a subsequent patent constitute infringement.[23]

352   Infringement by agents and servants

A person may infringe a patent by making the article himself, or by his agent, or by his servants. The agent and servants, it is true, will be considered as equally infringing the patent, and actions may be brought against them individually, but that in no way absolves the person who employs them for that purpose. In *Sykes* v. *Howarth* [24] the invention consisted in the application of cards or strips of leather covered with wire to rollers at " wide distances." A person who contracted to clothe rollers and supplied to a " nailer " cards of such width that when applied to the rollers they must of necessity leave wide spaces, and who himself paid the nailer, was held to have infringed the patent, though he alleged that his business was that of a card-maker only, and did not include the nailer's work. Fry J. said: " I have come to the conclusion that the nailer must be deemed to have been the agent, for the purpose of nailing on, of the defendant . . . there is a contract to clothe in the manner prescribed by the particulars given to the defendant, and that contract was carried into effect by a person paid by the defendant—the defendant himself receiving the total amount for which he contracted. The consequence is that in my judgment all the defences fail."

But actions against mere workmen who innocently help in an infringement, and are not the really guilty persons, will not be encouraged.[25]

353   *Company directors*

Directors of a limited liability company are only liable for infringements committed by the company if it be proved that the company acted as their agent, or that they expressly authorised the infringement.[26]

---

[22] *Tweedale* v. *Ashworth*, 7 R.P.C. 426 at p. 431.
[23] *Montgomerie* v. *Paterson*, 11 R.P.C. 221, 633.
[24] 12 Ch.D. 826 at p. 832.
[25] See *Savage* v. *Brindle*, 13 R.P.C. 266.
[26] *British Thomson-Houston Co. Ltd.* v. *Sterling Accessories Ltd.* [1924] 2 Ch. 33; 41 R.P.C. 311; see also *Cropper Minerva Machines Co. Ltd.* v. *Cropper, Charlton & Co. Ltd.*, 23 R.P.C. 388 at p. 392; *Pritchard and Constance (Wholesale) Ltd.* v. *Amata Ltd.*, 42 R.P.C. 63; *Reitzman* v.

354 Express instructions by patentee

Express instructions given by the patentee, or on his behalf, will negative infringement if they are specific directions to do that which is claimed in the specification, such directions amounting in effect to a licence.

In *Kelly* v. *Batchelar* [27] the plaintiff's patent was for a telescopic ladder, being two ladders joined together, the inner being raised or lowered by means of an endless cord. The plaintiff, for the purpose of adducing evidence of infringement, instructed an agent to order from the defendant an adjustable ladder with an endless cord. The defendant made a ladder to this order, but without a cord. The agent of the plaintiff said that it would not do, but must have a cord with pulleys, whereupon the defendant added the cord as instructed. In the action for infringement brought against the defendant, North J. held that the defendant acted upon the express instructions of the plaintiff's agent, who had power and authority to give such instructions, and, consequently, that making this ladder did not amount to an infringement of the plaintiff's patent.[28]

In *Dunlop Pneumatic Tyre Co.* v. *Neal* [29] the agent of the plaintiffs was sent to the defendant to ask him to repair an old tyre, the subject of the plaintiffs' patent, with a view to ascertaining whether the defendant was infringing the patent by purporting merely to repair tyres. The agent gave no express instructions as to what was to be done to the worn tyres beyond saying that they were to be repaired. It was held that what was done by the defendant amounted to infringement, and that in such a case he could not shelter himself behind the instructions of the plaintiff's agent.

355 Aiding and abetting infringement

There seems no reason why the general law should not apply to infringement of patent so that all persons will be liable for infringement if their acts are such as would make them joint tortfeasors under the general law. As Scrutton L.J. said in *The Koursk* [30]: " Certain classes of persons seem clearly to be joint tortfeasors: the agent who commits a tort in the course of his employment for his principal, and the principal; the servant who commits a tort in the course of his employment and his master; two persons who agree on common action, in the course of, and to further which, one of them

Grahame-Chapman and Derustit Ltd., 67 R.P.C. 178 at p. 185. See also
T. Oertli A.G. v. *E. J. Bowman Ltd.* [1956] R.P.C. 282.
[27] 10 R.P.C. 289.
[28] See also *Henser & Guignard* v. *Hardie,* 11 R.P.C. 421.
[29] 16 R.P.C. 247.
[30] [1924] P. 140 at p. 155.

commits a tort. These seem clearly joint tortfeasors; there is one tort committed by one of them on behalf of, or in concert with, another."

356   But, before a person can be said to be a joint tortfeasor, he must have acted in concert with another person in the commission of the tort. The mere sale in the ordinary way of business of goods, which the vendor is entitled to sell, is not tortious, even though the purchaser may subsequently use the goods wrongly. Thus the mere sale of articles which are not themselves protected by a patent, but which can be used for the purposes of infringement, will not amount to an infringement.

In *Townsend* v. *Haworth* [31] the invention was concerned with the use of certain known chemical compounds for preserving cloth from mildew. Jessel M.R. said: " No judge has ever said that the vendor of an ordinary ingredient does . . . a wrong if the purchaser . . . says, ' I want your compound because I want to preserve my cloth from mildew, and you and I know there is a patent, but still I wish to try the question with the patentee.' No one would doubt that that sale would be perfectly legal. . . ." And in *Sykes* v. *Howarth* [32] Fry J. said: " I entirely agree . . . that selling articles to persons to be used for the purpose of infringing a patent is not an infringement of the patent." [33]

357   In *Innes* v. *Short* [34] the plaintiff's patent was for the use of powdered zinc in boilers to prevent incrustation. The defendant sold bags of powdered zinc with directions for the use of the powder in boilers. Bingham J. granted an injunction to restrain the sale *in this manner*, and said: " There is no reason whatever why Mr. Short should not sell powdered zinc, and he will not be in the wrong, though he may know or expect that the people who buy it from him are going to use it in such a way as will amount to an infringement of Mr. Innes' patent rights. But he must not ask the people to use it in that way in order to induce them to buy his powdered zinc from him."

Parker J. in *Adhesive Dry Mounting Co.* v. *Trapp & Co.* [35] expressed the view that the above case was of doubtful authority, but it is submitted that it is justifiable upon the footing that Mr. Short was a joint infringer with the persons whom he procured to infringe the patent.

[31] 12 Ch.D. 831n.; 48 L.J.Ch. 770 at p. 771.
[32] 12 Ch.D. 826 at p. 833.
[33] See also *Dunlop Pneumatic Tyre Co. Ltd.* v. *David Moseley & Sons Ltd.*, 21 R.P.C. 274 at pp. 278–282; *White* v. *Todd Oil Burners Ltd.*, 46 R.P.C. 275 at p. 293.
[34] 15 R.P.C. 449.
[35] 27 R.P.C. 341 at p. 353.

358   Making and selling elements of combination

Similarly where the patent is for a combination there is no infringement in making or selling the separate elements of the combination, even though the manufacturer or vendor knows perfectly well that the separate elements are destined eventually to be combined so as to constitute an infringement.

In *Dunlop Pneumatic Tyre Co. Ltd. v. David Moseley & Sons Ltd.*[36] the patent was for a pneumatic tyre cover, held on to the rim of the wheel by wires passed through circumferential pockets in the edges of the cover. The defendants made and sold covers only, fitted with pockets, but without wires, and advertised them as " ready for wires." Vaughan Williams L.J. said [37]; " I wish to say that in my judgment this case would fail even though . . . these covers could not be used for any other purpose than fitting them into the plaintiffs' tyres under one or other of the patents."

But where the circumstances were such as to indicate very clearly that the person selling an element which did not infringe was practically in partnership with another person who completed the infringement, and the real object of his business was to aid in the infringement, an injunction was granted.[38]

359   *Selling constituent parts*

Making and selling all the constituent parts of a machine as a collection so that they could easily be put together might possibly amount to infringement.[39]   There may be a distinction between the case where the " collection " is made for the purpose of export, in which case no infringing machine would be made within the jurisdiction, and the case where the " collection " is sold for the purpose of assembling an infringing article within the jurisdiction so that the vendor of the " collection " is procuring an act of infringement of the patent. In the first case the court might hold that, although there was no textual infringement, there had been a taking of the substance of the invention. In the latter case the court might also hold that the vendor of the " collection " was liable as a joint-infringer with the persons who assembled the parts (see " Aiding and abetting infringement," *supra*).

---

[36] 21 R.P.C. 274.
[37] 21 R.P.C. at p. 280.
[38] *Incandescent Gas Light Co. Ltd. v. New Incandescent Mantle Co.*, 15 R.P.C. 81.
[39] See *United Telephone Co. v. Dale*, 25 Ch.D. 778 at p. 782; *Dunlop Pneumatic Tyre Co. Ltd. v. David Moseley & Sons Ltd.*, 21 R.P.C. 274 at p. 280; and *cf. Cincinnati Grinders (Inc.) v. B.S.A. Tools Ltd.*, 48 R.P.C. 33 at pp. 46–48, 58, 76.

360 *Where claim is for " method "*

It would appear that where the patent claims merely a " method " of doing something, or the " use " of apparatus, the manufacture or sale of a machine which can be used for the purposes of infringement is not an infringement [40] unless, possibly, the machine is so constructed that it cannot be used except in a manner which would constitute an infringement.[41]

361 *Where claim is for machine*

Where, however, the claim is " a machine claim and not a method claim," the manufacture or sale of a machine which contains an infringing device will be an infringement if such device is capable of being brought into use; and the fact that the machine can be, or is normally, used without bringing the device into operation is not material.[42]

362 Infringement by repairing

Difficult questions may arise where it is alleged that the patent has been infringed by what amounts to the manufacture of a new article under the guise of repairing an old article which has been made under the patent.   The tests by which such cases may be decided were stated by Kekewich J. in *Dunlop Pneumatic Tyre Co. Ltd. v. Holborn Tyre Co. Ltd.*[43]: " There are two tests which might equally well be applied to this question on the evidence. The first test would be this: In the alleged repair, has the workman so employed the patent as that in doing it he has taken an essential part of the patent and infringed it? . . .   But there is another test which, but for the existence of the patent, one would employ, and which I think is the real and most satisfactory test to employ now, and that is this: Is it substantially in common parlance, honestly, a new article, or is it an old article repaired? " [44]

In *United Telephone Co. v. Nelson* [45] it was held that the restoration of a broken instrument which had originally been licensed under the patent was an infringement; but the case is not fully reported.

[40] See *Townsend v. Haworth*, 48 L.J.Ch. 770; *Adhesive Dry Mounting Co. v. Trapp & Co.*, 27 R.P.C. 341.

[41] See *Cincinnati Grinders (Inc.) v. B.S.A. Tools Ltd.*, 48 R.P.C. 33, at pp. 48, 58; and *British United Shoe Machinery Co. Ltd. v. Gimson Shoe Machinery Co. Ltd.*, 45 R.P.C. 290 at p. 304.

[42] See *British United Shoe Machinery Co. Ltd. v. Gimson Shoe Machinery Co. Ltd.*, 45 R.P.C. 85 at p. 104; 45 R.P.C. 290 at pp. 301, 304, 308; see also *Robinson Ltd. v. Smith and Ritchie Ltd.*, 30 R.P.C. 63 at p. 73.

[43] 18 R.P.C. 222 at p. 226.

[44] See also *Dunlop Pneumatic Tyre Co. Ltd. v. Neal*, 16 R.P.C. 247; *Dunlop Pneumatic Tyre Co. Ltd. v. Excelsior Tyre etc. Co.*, 18 R.P.C. 209.

[45] [1887] W.N. 193.

It appears to be a question of fact whether an instrument is broken to such an extent as to destroy its identity so as to enable the patentee to say that the repair by its owner amounts in fact to the manufacture of a new article. In *Sirdar Rubber Co. Ltd.* v. *Wallington, Weston & Co.*,[46] Lord Halsbury said: " The principle is quite clear, although its application is sometimes difficult; you may prolong the life of a licensed article, but you must not make a new one under cover of repair."

363 Experiments

A " making use of or putting into practice " of the invention for the purposes of bona fide experiment does not constitute an infringement.

In *Frearson* v. *Loe* [47] Jessel M.R. said: " The other point raised was a curious one, and by no means free from difficulty, and what occurred with regard to that was this: that the defendant at various times made screw blanks . . . by various contrivances, by which no doubt screw blanks were made according to the plaintiff's patent of 1870, as well as that of 1875; they seem to have been an infringement of both. He said he did this merely by way of experiment, and no doubt if a man makes things merely by way of bona fide experiment, and not with the intention of selling and making use of the thing so made for the purpose of which a patent has been granted, but with a view of improving upon the invention, the subject of the patent, or with a view of seeing whether an improvement can be made or not, that is not an invasion of the exclusive rights granted by the patent. Patent rights were never granted to prevent persons of ingenuity exercising their talents in a fair way. But if there be neither using nor vending of the invention for profit, the mere making for the purpose of experiment and not for a fraudulent purpose ought not to be considered within the meaning of the prohibition, and if it were, it is certainly not the subject for an injunction." [48]

364 *Use to instruct pupils*

To purchase and use infringing articles for the purpose of instructing pupils and to enable them to pull them to pieces and put them together again is not mere experimental user, and amounts to an infringement.[49]

[46] 24 R.P.C. 539 at p. 543.
[47] 9 Ch.D. at p. 66.
[48] See also *Muntz* v. *Foster*, 2 W.P.C. 93 at p. 101; *Jones* v. *Pearce*, 1 W.P.C. 122 at p. 125; *Proctor* v. *Bayley & Son*, 6 R.P.C. 106, 538; *Pessers etc. Ltd.* v. *Newell & Co.*, 31 R.P.C. 51.
[49] *United Telephone Co.* v. *Sharples*, 2 R.P.C. 28.

365 Infringement by sale

In the case of a patent for a process or for a machine, the sale in this country of goods manufactured by that process or machine is an infringement. In *Townsend* v. *Haworth* [50] Jessel M.R. said: " What is every person prohibited from doing?   He is prohibited from making, using or vending the prohibited articles, and that, of course, includes in the case of machinery the product, if I may say so, of the machinery which is the subject of the patent.   It is what is produced by the patent." [51]

Such a sale is also an infringement even though the manufacture took place abroad.   In *Wright* v. *Hitchcock* [52] Kelly C.B. said: " If the law were otherwise, then when a man has patented an invention, another might, by merely crossing the Channel, and manufacturing abroad and selling in London . . . articles made by the patented process, wholly deprive the patentee of the benefit of his invention. It is, therefore, impossible to suppose that an exclusive right to vend is not given, and the defendants have, therefore, infringed the plaintiff's right. . . ." [53]

366 It is necessary, however, that the article should have been produced as a direct result of the use of a process or machine substantially the whole of which is the subject of a patent; if the patent covers only a minor improvement upon a machine, or a process, already known, the importation of the product will not be held to constitute infringement.   In *Wilderman* v. *F. W. Berk & Co. Ltd.*,[54] the patent related to an improvement in a part of an electrolytic machine for making caustic potash.   The defendants had imported caustic potash from abroad and the plaintiff proved that this had been made in Germany by means of an electrolytic cell fitted with the improvement which was the subject of his patent.   No evidence was adduced as to the materiality of the improvement in enabling the production of the caustic potash.   Tomlin J. said [55]: " It is urged on the plaintiff's behalf that once I am satisfied that there has been used in connection with the manufacture of an imported article, in however an unimportant or trifling respect, some apparatus or material in respect of which there is a subsisting patent, the importation of the article manufactured is necessarily an infringement.   I do not think that the cases to which I have been referred compel me to

---

[50] 12 Ch.D. 831.
[51] And see *United Horse Shoe and Nail Co. Ltd.* v. *Stewart & Co.*, 2 R.P.C. 122; *cf. Wilderman* v. *F. W. Berk & Co. Ltd.*, 42 R.P.C. 79.
[52] L.R. 5 Ex. 37 at p. 47.
[53] See also *Elmslie* v. *Boursier*, L.R. 9 Eq. 217; *Von Heyden* v. *Neustadt*, 14 Ch.D. 230; *Neilson* v. *Betts*, L.R. 5 H.L. 1 at p. 11.
[54] 42 R.P.C. 79.
[55] 42 R.P.C. at p. 88.

accept so wide a proposition, and I do not accept it. I cannot think, for example, that the employment of a patented cutting blowpipe or a patented hammer in the manufacture of some part of a locomotive would necessarily render the importation of the locomotive an infringement. In my judgment, each case must be determined on its own merits by reference to the nature of the invention, and the extent to which its employment played a part in the production of the article the importation of which is complained of. . . . I do not think that the plaintiff has proved, and I am not prepared to hold, that the device the subject-matter of the invention was of such a character, or was so used, in relation to the manufacture of the caustic potash in question, as to render the importation of such potash an infringement of the patent."

Where a patented process has been used in the course of manufacture of the article or substance which has been imported, the stage at which such process has been used is immaterial; and in *Saccharin Corporation Ltd.* v. *Anglo-Continental Chemical Works* [56] it was held that the importation was equally an infringement whether the process was used in the production of some intermediate substance or in effecting the final transformation into the substance imported.

367 Onus of proof

Where the defendant has used and sold articles alleged to have been made by a patented process, the onus of proving that they were in fact made by that process is on the plaintiff.

In *Cartsburn Sugar Refining Co.* v. *Sharp* [57] the alleged infringement consisted in the sale in England of cube sugar manufactured in America by a machine made in accordance with the specification of the complainers' (*i.e.* the plaintiffs') patent. Lord Kinnear, in his judgment, said [58]: " No witness has been examined of sufficient skill as a mechanic to give a detailed description of the machine in question. All that is proved is that it does not correspond in all respects, though in some respects it does correspond, to the description in Hersey's patent. It is said that as the manufacture complained of had taken place in America, it was incumbent on the respondents, upon the principle which received effect in the case of *Neilson* v. *Betts*,[59] to prove by negative evidence that it was not manufactured according to the specified process. I think no such onus lies upon the respondents in the present case, because there can be no question on

[56] 17 R.P.C. 307.
[57] 1 R.P.C. 181.
[58] 1 R.P.C. at p. 186.
[59] L.R. 5 H.L. 1.

the evidence that such articles as were sold by the respondents *may have been* produced by machinery which involved no infringement of the complainers' patent. That being so, it lay upon the complainers to prove their case, and as they took a commission to America for the purpose of proving it, there could have been no difficulty in their obtaining a sufficient description of the machine to which it is alleged they have traced the cubes of sugar sold by the respondents to enable them to establish the infringement, if infringement there was."

368 But where the articles were made abroad, and the plaintiffs in consequence could not be afforded full opportunity of inspecting the machinery by which they were made, it was held that it lay with the defendants to rebut a prima facie case made out by the plaintiffs.[60]

In the various *Saccharin* cases,[60] the plaintiffs were the owners of patents which covered all known processes of making saccharin. They were able to produce evidence to the effect that although it was conceivable that saccharin might be made in some other way, no other processes were then known to the scientific world. The defendants, who imported saccharin, could not give any satisfactory account of the way in which the imported substance was actually made. It was held that infringement had been established.

369 Contracts for delivery in United Kingdom and abroad

In *Gibson and Campbell* v. *Brand*[61] it was held that an order given by the defendant for the making of silk by a process which infringed the plaintiff's patent, which order was executed in England, was sufficient to satisfy the allegation that the defendant made, used, and put in practice the plaintiff's invention, though the silk was in fact made through the agency of others. Sir N. C. Tindal C.J. said: "This is quite sufficient to satisfy an allegation that he made those articles, for he that causes or procures to be made, may well be said to have made them himself."

In the case of goods manufactured abroad delivery must take place in this country to constitute an infringement. In *Badische Anilin und Soda Fabrik* v. *Johnson and the Basle Chemical Works*[62] a trader in England ordered goods from the defendant in Switzerland to be sent by post to England. The defendant addressed the goods

---

[60] *Saccharin Corporation* v. *Dawson*, 19 R.P.C. 169; *Saccharin Corporation* v. *Jackson*, 20 R.P.C. 611; *Saccharin Corporation* v. *Mack & Co.*, 23 R.P.C. 25; *Saccharin Corporation Ltd.* v. *National Saccharin Co. Ltd.*, 26 R.P.C. 654; and see *British Thomson-Houston Co.* v. *Charlesworth, Peebles & Co.* 40 R.P.C. 426 at p. 456.

[61] 1 W.P.C. 631.

[62] 14 R.P.C. 919.

to the trader in England and delivered them to the Swiss Post Office, by whom they were forwarded to England. The goods were manufactured according to an invention protected by the plaintiff's patent. It was held by the House of Lords that, since the contract of sale was completed by the delivery to the Post Office in Switzerland, and since the Post Office was the agent of the buyer and not of the vendor, the vendor had not made, used, exercised or vended the invention within the ambit of the patent, and that the patentee had no right of action against the vendor for an infringement of the patent.

370   In *Saccharin Corporation Ltd.* v. *Reitmeyer & Co.*[63] the facts were as follows: The defendant, while in England, contracted with persons in England for the delivery to them at a *foreign* port of goods manufactured on the Continent by a process similar to that protected by the plaintiff's English patent. Cozens-Hardy J. said: " Now it is plain that a patent is of local force . . . it is admitted that the defendant had not ' made ' or ' used ' and I think it is clear that he had not ' vended ' within the jurisdiction [see *Badische Anilin Co.* v. *Johnson and Basle Chemical Works, supra*]. It is said, however, that he has ' exercised ' the invention within the jurisdiction. It is remarkable that this word, which has been found in letters patent at least since 1621, so far as I am aware, has never been construed. I think, however, that it can only mean ' put in practice.' I do not think it can be taken to cover a transaction such as I have to deal with. The defendant, as a commission agent, contracted for delivery to the purchasers at a German port. He had no interest whatever in the case when delivered at the foreign port to the purchasers. He had no right to control its destination. I assume that he knew or suspected that the greater part of the stuff would find its way into this country, but I cannot regard that as material."

371   The House of Lords in *Badische Anilin und Soda Fabrik* v. *Hickson*[64] approved of the above decision. In this case it was argued on behalf of the plaintiff that as the vendor had set aside the goods in the foreign country, the property in them had passed, and there was a completed sale. Lord Loreburn said that although there was appropriation to the purchaser and a completed sale, the operation of completing the sale had not taken place in this country, and consequently there had been no infringement; he stated further that he agreed with Lord Davey, who said " the exclusive right of ' vending the invention ' must be construed consistently with the language of the Statute of Monopolies, and with regard to the general purpose of the patent to give the inventor the full benefit of his invention in this

[63] 17 R.P.C. 606.
[64] 23 R.P.C. 149.

country. . . . A contract to deliver the goods abroad does not in any way interfere with the patentee's rights to work and utilise his invention in this country. . . . Nor is it material to consider whether or when the property in the goods passed to the purchaser. It is lawful to be the owner of the goods if made and situate abroad, and neither the vendor nor the purchaser in my opinion thereby infringes the patent. The goods may or may not be afterwards brought into this country, and a different question will then arise, but that is no concern of the vendor after he has parted with them. I am of opinion that ' vending the invention ' in the common form of patent, is confined to selling goods made or brought into this country, and that the respondent in this case has not, directly or indirectly, made, used, or put in practice the appellant's invention within the meaning of the prohibition contained in the patent." Lord Atkinson's opinion is to the same effect.

372 Sending abroad

To export under a contract of sale, whether such contract was made here or abroad, is an infringement. In *British Motor Syndicate Ltd.* v. *John Taylor & Sons Ltd.*,[65] the defendants bought in England twenty-seven infringing articles; they sold seven of them and used another in England. The remaining nineteen were sent abroad to their French house in Paris, where they sold them to various foreign firms. The question was whether there had been an infringement in respect of these nineteen. Stirling J. decided that this was " making use of " the invention, and that the words " make use of " have a wider significance than the words " put in practice." The learned judge said: " In the present case the patented articles, when being transported from place to place in this country, were not serving the purpose for which they were patented, and in my opinion the defendants did not, during that transporting, exercise or put in practice the patented invention. What the defendants did was to carry these articles out of the Kingdom with a view to selling them; that is, with the object of turning them to profitable account." [66]

373 Purchase, transport and possession

Mere purchase, ownership, possession, or transport does not amount to infringement, unless it involves a user of the invention, although it may justify an injunction on the ground that it is strong evidence of a threat to use.[67]

---

[65] 17 R.P.C. 189, 723.
[66] See also *United Telephone Co.* v. *Sharples*, 2 R.P.C. 28.
[67] *Adair* v. *Young*, 12 Ch.D. 13; *Pessers etc., Ltd.* v. *Newell & Co.*, 31 R.P.C. 51 (disapproving *United Telephone Co.* v. *London and Globe etc. Co.*, 26 Ch.D. 766); *British Motor Syndicate* v. *John Taylor & Sons Ltd.*, 17 R.P.C.

374   In the case of *Neilson* v. *Betts* [68] the facts were as follows: Betts (the plaintiff) was the patentee of an invention for the manufacture of capsules for the purpose of covering bottles of liquid and protecting the contents from the action of the atmosphere. The patent did not extend to Scotland. Neilson and his co-appellants (the defendants) were persons who bottled beer in Glasgow for the Indian market. They bottled the beer and covered it with capsules, which were apparently made in Germany in accordance with Betts' specification. The beer was shipped by the appellants in vessels which called at Liverpool to complete their cargoes; on some occasions the beer was transhipped in England, but no cases of beer were opened, nor was any of the beer sold in this country. It was held by the House of Lords (affirming the judgments in the courts below) that as the object of Betts' invention was to make a capsule that would preserve beer, whilst the beer was in England it was being preserved by the use of Betts' invention, and consequently that there was an infringement of the patent.

Lord Chelmsford, in giving judgment in the court below, said [69]: " It is the employment of the machine or article for the purpose for which it was designed which constitutes its active use, and whether the capsules were intended for ornament, or for protection of the contents of the bottles upon which they were placed, the whole time they were in England they may be correctly said to be in active use for the very objects for which they were placed upon the bottles by the vendors. If the beer, after being purchased in Glasgow, had been sent to England, and had been afterwards sold here, there can be no doubt, I suppose, that this would have been an infringement, because it would have been a profitable user of the invention, and I cannot see how it can cease to be a user because England is not the final destination of the beer." [70]

In the case of *Adair* v. *Young* [71] certain pumps, which were an infringement of the plaintiff's patent, were fitted on board a British ship. There was no evidence of their having been used. It was held by the Court of Appeal that there had been no infringement, but as there was evidence of an intention to use the pumps, an injunction was granted against the use of the pumps.

723; *British United Shoe Machinery Co.* v. *Simon Collier Ltd.*, 26 R.P.C. 21, 534, at pp. 41, 538, and 27 R.P.C. 567; *Non-Drip Measure Co. Ltd.* v. *Strangers Ltd.*, 59 R.P.C. 1.
[68] L.R. 5 H.L. 1.
[69] L.R. 3 Ch.App. 429 at p. 439.
[70] See also *Nobel's Explosives Co.* v. *Jones, Scott & Co.*, 17 Ch.D. 721; *Universities of Oxford and Cambridge* v. *Richardson*, 6 Ves. 689; *Dunlop Pneumatic Tyre Co. Ltd.* v. *British and Colonial Motor Car Co. Ltd.*, 18 R.P.C. 313.   [71] 12 Ch.D. 13.

In the case of *Badische Anilin und Soda Fabrik* v. *Basle Chemical Works, Bindschedler* [72] a trader in England ordered goods from a manufacturer in Switzerland to be sent by post to England. The goods were manufactured in accordance with an English patent, but, since the contract of sale was completed by delivery to the Post Office in Switzerland and since the Post Office was the agent of the buyer and not of the defendant vendor, it was held that the defendant had not made, used, exercised or vended the invention within the ambit of the patent and there was no infringement.

375 Importation

Importation by way of trade of patented goods or goods made abroad by a patented process is an act of infringement. It was decided in *Pfizer Corporation* v. *Ministry of Health*, as stated by Lord Upjohn, " that where an importer imports into this country articles made abroad, but in accordance with a British patent, for the purpose of distributing and selling them in this country, he quite plainly is using and exercising the patent, and he thereby infringes the patent the moment he introduces them into this country." [73]

376 *Exposure for sale*

Possession accompanied by exposure for sale is an infringement, as it is a user of the invention for one of the purposes for which it was intended that the patentee alone should use it during the term of the patent.[74]

377 *Use on vessels and aircraft*

The use of an invention in or for the purposes of a vessel or aircraft registered in a convention country and coming temporarily into the United Kingdom, does not constitute an infringement.[75] Commercial aircraft registered in countries specified by Order in Council are protected from seizure or patent claims.[76]

A patent is not infringed by the use of the invention on board an English vessel abroad or outside the three-mile limit.[77]

378 *Agents for transhipment*

In the case of *Nobel's Explosives Co.* v. *Jones, Scott & Co.*[78] the Court of Appeal held that the defendants, who had merely acted

[72] [1898] A.C. 200.
[73] [1965] R.P.C. 261 and see also *Beecham Group Ltd.* v. *Bristol Laboratories Ltd.* [1967] R.P.C. 406.
[74] *British Motor Syndicate Ltd.* v. *John Taylor & Sons Ltd.*, 17 R.P.C. 723 at p. 729.
[75] s. 70.
[76] Civil Aviation Act 1949, s. 53.
[77] *Newall* v. *Elliott*, 10 Jur.(N.S.) 954; *V. D. Ltd.* v. *Boston Deep Sea Fishing Co. Ltd.*, 52 R.P.C. 303 at p. 331.   [78] 17 Ch.D. 721.

as Custom House agents for the transhipment of the patented article and never had any ownership in, or exercised any control over, the goods, had not infringed. This decision of the Court of Appeal was affirmed by the House of Lords.[79]

379 *Carriers*

An action may properly be brought against carriers of infringing articles for an injunction to restrain them from dealing with or disposing of such articles in any way.[80]

380 *Lending*

Lending is not selling and is not an infringement.[81]

381 **Effect of sale by patentee**

A patentee by himself or by his agent selling the patented article without limitation, sells with it the right of free disposition as to that article, and if he sells the article abroad, the purchaser may import and sell it in England. Lord Hatherley, in *Betts* v. *Willmott*,[82] said: " Unless it can be shown, not that there is some clear injunction to his agents, but that there is some clear communication to the party to whom the article is sold, I apprehend that inasmuch as he had the right of vending the goods in France, or Belgium or England, or in any other quarter of the globe, he transfers with the goods necessarily the licence to use them wherever the purchaser pleases. When a man has purchased an article he expects to have control of it, and there must be some clear and explicit agreement to the contrary to justify the vendor in saying that he has not given the purchaser his licence to sell the article, or to use it wherever he pleases as against himself."

382 Where, however, the owners of patents in Belgium and England for an invention for making glass lamp globes, by a deed executed in Belgium, granted a licence to the plaintiffs to manufacture under their invention in Belgium but not elsewhere, and the plaintiffs under this licence manufactured articles in Belgium and sold them in England, it was held by the Court of Appeal, affirming Pearson J., that the grant of the licence to use the patent in Belgium did not imply permission to sell the manufactured article in England in violation of the defendant's English patent.[83]

Similarly, if the patentee had assigned his patent rights in England,

[79] 8 App.Cas. 5.
[80] *Washburn and Moen Manufacturing Co.* v. *Cunard Steamship Co.*, 6 R.P.C. 398 at p. 403; see also *Upmann* v. *Elkan*, L.R. 7 Ch.App. 130.
[81] *United Telephone Co. Ltd.* v. *Henry & Co.*, 2 R.P.C. 11.
[82] L.R. 6 Ch.App. 239 at p. 245.
[83] *Société Anonyme des Manufactures de Glaces* v. *Tilghman's Patent Sand Blast Co.*, 25 Ch.D. 1; and see also *Beecham Group Ltd.* v. *International Products Ltd.* [1968] R.P.C. 129.

he could not manufacture in France and sell in England, and the sale by him of an article in France would carry with it no implied right to import into or sell in England. But if the rights under the patent are vested in one and the same person for both France and England, or if there are no monopoly rights in France, but only in England, the patentee could not make and sell in France and restrain the purchaser from selling or using the article in England, unless there was a special agreement for that purpose; and even then such agreement could not be held to attach to the article so as to prevent any person, in whose hands it might come without notice, from importing it.[84]

383 Limited licence

If a person acquires goods covered by a patent and at the time when he acquires those goods he has knowledge that a restrictive condition has been imposed in relation to them, any dealing with the goods in breach of such restrictive condition, constitutes an infringement.[85] The restrictive condition is not effective if such person has knowledge of it only after he has acquired the goods, even though he may receive such knowledge before reselling the goods.[86] But the Resale Prices Act 1964, s. 1, makes void conditions as to the minimum prices at which any goods shall be resold by dealers, unless the Restrictive Practices Court by order exempts such goods; see § 648 et seq.

384 Warranty under Sale of Goods Act

On the sale of an article there is an implied warranty (within section 12 of the Sale of Goods Act 1893) that the article sold is not an infringement of an existing patent.[87]

3. ASCERTAINMENT OF THE MONOPOLY CLAIMED

385 The principles applicable to the construction of the specification and its claims have been fully dealt with in Chapter 4, at § 179 et seq. It is only necessary to emphasise here that the specification and claims must be construed without reference to the alleged infringement and that what the court has to ascertain are the essential features or integers of the claim.[88]

---

[84] Betts v. Willmott, L.R. 6 Ch.App. 239.
[85] National Phonographic Co. of Australia Ltd. v. Menck, 28 R.P.C. 229; Columbia Graphophone Co. Ltd. v. Murray, 39 R.P.C. 239; Columbia Graphophone Co. Ltd. v. Thoms, 41 R.P.C. 294.
[86] Gillette Industries Ltd. v. Bernstein, 58 R.P.C. 271 at p. 282.
[87] Niblett v. Confectioners Materials Co. [1921] 3 K.B. 387 at pp. 394, 399, 403.
[88] Rodi & Weinberger A.G. v. Henry Showell Ltd. [1969] R.P.C. 367 at p. 391; Deere & Co. v. McGregor & Guest Ltd. [1965] R.P.C. 461 at p. 477.

4. WHAT AMOUNTS TO INFRINGEMENT

386 The general principle has been expressed as follows by Lord Upjohn in *Rodi & Weinberger A.G.* v. *Henry Showell Ltd.*[89]: " The essential integers [of the claims] having been ascertained, the infringing article must be considered. To constitute infringement the article must take each and every one of the essential integers of the claim."

If the alleged infringement possesses all the features or integers specified in the claim, there is infringement—" textual " or " literal " infringement. If there are differences so that there is not textual infringement, the alleged infringement may, nevertheless, infringe the claim if the differences are differences in inessentials. These inessential features or integers may be omitted altogether or be varied or be substituted by mechanical equivalents but, if, notwithstanding differences in inessentials, the alleged infringement possesses *all* the essential features or integers of the claim, it infringes—so-called infringement by taking the " substance " or " pith and marrow " of the claimed invention.

387 As Lord Reid stated in *C. Van der Lely N.V.* v. *Bamfords Ltd.*: " Copying an invention by taking its ' pith and marrow ' without textual infringement of the patent is an old and familiar abuse which the law has never been powerless to prevent. It may be that in doing so there is some illogicality, but our law has always preferred good sense to strict logic. The illogicality arises in this way. On the one hand the patentee is tied strictly to the invention which he claims and the mode of effecting an improvement which he says is his invention. Logically it would seem to follow that if another person is ingenious enough to effect that improvement by a slightly different method he will not infringe. But it has long been recognised that there ' may be an essence or substance of the invention underlying the mere accident of form; and that invention, like every other invention, may be pirated by a theft in a disguised or mutilated form, and it will be in every case a question of fact whether the alleged piracy is the same in substance and effect, or is a substantially new or different combination.' (*Per* James L.J. in *Clark* v. *Adie*.[90]) It was in *Clark* v. *Adie* [91] that Lord Cairns used the expression ' pith and marrow of the invention.' " [92]

388 But it is to be emphasised that if the alleged infringement does not possess one of the essential features or integers of the claim, there is no infringement, for the doctrine of " pith and marrow " has no

---

[89] [1969] R.P.C. 367 at p. 391.
[90] (1873) L.R. 10 Ch. 667.
[91] (1877) 2 App.Cas. 315 at p. 320.
[92] [1963] R.P.C. 61 at p. 75.

application where the alleged infringement differs from the claimed invention in an essential respect, that is to say, the doctrine applies only to inessentials. This has been made clear in a number of cases.

In *Marconi* v. *British Radio Telegraph and Telephone Co. Ltd.*,[93] Parker J. said: " It is a well-known rule of patent law that no one who borrows the substance of a patented invention can escape the consequences of infringement by making immaterial variations. From this point of view the question is whether the infringing apparatus is substantially the same as the apparatus said to have been infringed . . . where the patent is for a combination of parts or a process and the combination or process, besides being itself new, produces new and useful results, everyone who produces the same results by using the essential parts of the combination or process is an infringer, even though he has, in fact, altered the combination or process by omitting some unessential part or step and substituting another part or step, which is, in fact, equivalent to the part or step he has omitted . . . if that part of the combination, or that step in the process for which an equivalent has been substituted, be the essential feature or one of the essential features, then there is no room for the doctrine of equivalents."

In the recent *Rodi & Weinberger*[89] case Lord Upjohn said (*loc. cit.*:) " Non-essentials may be omitted or replaced by mechanical equivalents; there will still be infringement" and Lord Hodson said [94]: " This reference [in the judgment at first instance] to mechanical equivalence can only relate to inessentials, for it is only where there are differences in inessentials, while the alleged infringement possesses all the essential features or integers of the claim, that there will be infringement. ' Pith and marrow ' does not enlarge the scope of essentiality."

389　　It has sometimes been said that the principle of " substance " or " pith and marrow " ought to have no place under the modern system of drafting specifications with a multitude of claims. Undoubtedly, the doctrine was of much more importance in earlier days before the modern system of claims was developed, as cases such as *Clark* v. *Adie, Curtis* v. *Platt*[95] and *Proctor* v. *Bennis*[96] show. Thus Wills J. stated in *The Incandescent Gas Light Co. Ltd.* v. *The De Mare Incandescent Gas Light System Ltd.*[97]: " Infringement is a question of fact for the jury, if there be one; and the question is not whether the substantial part of the process said to be an infringement has

---

[93] 28 R.P.C. 181 at p. 217.
[94] [1969] R.P.C. 367 at p. 384.
[95] 3 Ch.D. 135n.
[96] 4 R.P.C. 333 at p. 355.
[97] 13 R.P.C. 301 at p. 330.

[161]

been taken from the specification, but the very different one, whether what is done or proposed to be done takes from the patentee the substance of his invention. A process might be wholly gathered from a specification and nowhere else, and yet be no infringement, if it did not take substantially the thing invented. What the thing invented is must be gathered from the specification alone, and the patentee cannot escape from the thing he has claimed as the standard, and the only standard, with which to compare the alleged infringement so as to see if it constitutes substantially the appropriation of the thing claimed. When, however, you come to make that comparison, how can you escape from considering the relative magnitude and value of the things taken and of those left or varied; it is seldom that the infringer does the thing, the whole thing, and nothing but the thing claimed by the specification. He always varies, adds, omits, and the only protection the patentee has in such a case lies, as has often been pointed out by every court, from the House of Lords downwards, in the good sense of the tribunal which has to decide whether the substance of the invention has been pirated."

But it is to be noted that in that case the only claim of the patent was as follows: " What I claim is: The manufacture substantially as herein described, of an illuminant appliance for gas and other burners, consisting of a cap or hood made of fabric impregnated with the substances mentioned and treated as set forth," a form of claim commonly employed in earlier days and which necessarily imposed on the court the burden of ascertaining the " substance " or " essence " of the invention from the description in the specification.

390   The doctrine of " substance " or " pith and marrow " is not dead, as was made clear by the Court of Appeal in *Birmingham Sound Reproducers Ltd.* v. *Collaro Ltd.*[98] and by the House of Lords in *Van der Lely N.V.* v. *Bamfords Ltd.*,[99] but it is submitted that in view of the detailed nature of modern claims there can be little scope for its application in practice nowadays. In the *Rodi*[1] case Lord Hodson said: " I am not suggesting that the doctrine of ' pith and marrow ' is dead. . . . The doctrine, as has often been pointed out, has lost much of its importance, at least since the passing of the Patents Act 1949. The modern form of claim covers all essential features, whereas in earlier days it was often necessary sometimes to search the specification for the ' pith and marrow ' of what was claimed."

391   Among the older cases there are many instances of infringement having been established by involving the doctrine of " substance " or

98 [1956] R.P.C. 232 at p. 244.
99 [1963] R.P.C. 61.   1 [1969] R.P.C. 367 at p. 384.

" pith and marrow," more particularly instances of the substitution of inessential features or integers by equivalents.

Russel v. *Cowley & Dixon* [2] may be cited as an early instance of an infringement by the use of a mechanical equivalent. In that case the invention claimed was the bringing to a welding heat of a long piece of iron of the proper quality, after having turned up its edges, and drawing it through a hole of the size of the intended tube, so as to compress together the edges and give it a complete circular form. The defendants turned up the skelp, and, after heating it in the furnace, passed it through two rollers with grooves: It was held as a fact that the two rollers with grooves were a mere mechanical equivalent for the hole through which the iron was passed according to the plaintiff's invention, and that the patent had been infringed.[3]

In *Benno Jaffé etc. Fabrik* v. *John Richardson & Co. Ltd.*[4] the patented invention was for a process of extracting lanolin and the claim specified, *inter alia*, treatment in a centrifugal depositing machine. The defendants' process took every step of the patented process except they substituted a depositing tank for the centrifugal machine. It was held that the essence of the invention was the stage in the process at which the treatment occurred whereas the particular method of treatment employed (the centrifugal machine) was not an essential and all the defendants had done was to substitute a " manu-facturing equivalent " for the centrifugal machine and that the patent had been infringed.

Marconi v. *British Radio Telegraph and Telephone Co. Ltd.*,[5] already referred to above (see § 388) was a case where the defendants substituted an electrical equivalent for what was held to be an inessential integer in the patented radio telegraphy system and were held to have infringed the patent.[6]

But, as might be expected from what has been stated above (in § 389), in more recent years most attempts to establish infringement

---

[2] 1 W.P.C. 459 at p. 462.
[3] *Benno Jaffé, etc., Fabrik* v. *John Richardson & Co. Ltd.*, 11 R.P.C. 261.
[4] 11 R.P.C. 261.
[5] 28 R.P.C. 181.
[6] And see also: *Proctor* v. *Bennis*, 4 R.P.C. 333; *Ehrlich* v. *Ihlee*, 5 R.P.C. 437 at p. 453; *Moore* v. *Thomson*, 7 R.P.C. 325; *Automatic Weighing Machine Co.* v. *National Exhibition Assoc. Ltd.*, 9 R.P.C. 41 at p. 44; *Incandescent Gas Light Co. Ltd.* v. *De Mare Incandescent Gas Light System Ltd.*, 13 R.P.C. 301 at p. 330; *Osram Lamp Works Ltd.* v. *"Z" Electric Lamp Co.*, 29 R.P.C. 401 at p. 424. *Cf. Curtis* v. *Platt*, 3 Ch.D. 135n.; *Gosnell* v. *Bishop*, 5 R.P.C. 151 at pp. 157, 158; *Tweedale* v. *Ashworth*, 9 R.P.C. 121 at p. 128; *Miller & Co.* v. *Clyde Bridge Steel Co. Ltd.*, 9 R.P.C. 470 at p. 478.

in reliance on the doctrine of " substance " have failed,[7] though not all.[8]

392   " Combination " does not protect integers individually

A patent for a combination is not infringed by taking separately the integers which are comprised in that combination. In *Clark* v. *Adie* [9] Lord Cairns said: " Suppose, my lords, that in a patent you have a patentee claiming protection for an invention consisting of parts which I will designate as A, B, C and D; he may at the same time claim that as to one of those parts, D, it is itself a new thing, and that as to another of those parts, C, it is itself a combination of things, which possibly were old in themselves, but which, put together and used as he puts them together and uses them, produce a result so new that he is entitled to protection for it as a new invention. In a patent of that kind the monopoly would or might be held to be granted, not only to the whole and complete thing described, but to those subordinate integers entering into the whole which I have described. But then, my lords, the invention must be described in that way; it must be made plain to ordinary apprehension, upon the ordinary rules of construction, that the patentee has had in his mind, and has intended to claim, protection for those subordinate integers; and moreover he is, as was said by the Lords Justices, at the peril of justifying those subordinate integers as themselves matters which ought properly to form the subject of a patent of invention." [10]

393   Selection and arrangement of parts

Where the claim is for a mechanical combination of selected parts arranged in a particular way so as to have a particular functional interaction, that particular selection, arrangement and interaction of parts constitutes the essence of the invention. In such a case those parts and the particular arrangement and functional

---

[7] See *e.g. Marconi Wireless Telegraphy Co.* v. *Mullard Radio Valve Co. Ltd.*, 41 R.P.C. 323; *Submarine Signal Co.* v. *Hughes & Son Ltd.*, 49 R.P.C. 149; *Marconi etc.* v. *Philips Lamps Ltd.*, 50 R.P.C. 287; *R.C.A. Photophone Ltd.* v. *Gaumont British Picture Corp. Ltd.*, 53 R.P.C. 167; *Slumberland Ltd.* v. *Burgess Bedding*, 68 R.P.C. 87; *Birmingham Sound Reproducers Ltd.* v. *Collaro Ltd.* [1956] R.P.C. 141; *Multiform Displays Ltd.* v. *Whitmarley Displays Ltd.* [1957] R.P.C. 260; *Haage* v. *Pegson Ltd.*, 53 R.P.C. 58; *Van der Lely N.V.* v. *Bamfords Ltd.* [1963] R.P.C. 61; *Rodi & Weinberger A.G.* v. *Henry Showell Ltd.* [1969] R.P.C. 367.

[8] *Pope Appliance Corp.* v. *Spanish River Pulp etc. Ltd.*, 46 R.P.C. 23 at p. 58; *Rheostatic Co. Ltd.* v. *Robert MacLaren & Co. Ltd.*, 53 R.P.C. 109; *Raleigh Cycle Co. Ltd.* v. *H. Miller & Son Ltd.*, 65 R.P.C. 141 at p. 160; *Beecham Group Ltd.* v. *Bristol Laboratories Ltd.* [1967] R.P.C. 406.

[9] 2 App.Cas. 315 at p. 321.

[10] And see *British United Shoe Machinery Co. Ltd.* v. *Fussell & Sons Ltd.*, 25 R.P.C. 631 at pp. 654, 655.

interaction will all be essential features of the claimed combination and for infringement one must find those selected parts arranged and interacting in that way. In *Rodi and Wienberger A.G.* v. *Henry Showell Ltd.*[11] Lord Upjohn said: " Furthermore, where the invention, as in this case, resides in a new combination of known integers but also merely in a new arrangement and interaction of ordinary working parts it is not sufficient to show that the same result is reached; the working parts must act on one another in the way claimed in the claim of this patent. This is well illustrated by *Birmingham Sound Reproducers Ltd.* v. *Collaro Ltd.*, where Lord Evershed M.R. delivering the judgment of the court said [11a]: " Thus the essence of the invention resides wholly in the selection and arrangement of the parts and the manner in which they interact when arranged in accordance with the invention. It is therefore essential to the invention that it should consist of the particular parts described in the claim arranged and acting upon each other in the way described in the claim.

The question therefore appears to be whether the allegedly infringing apparatus consists of substantially the same parts acting upon each other in substantially the same way as the apparatus claimed as constituting the invention. It is not enough to find that the parts comprised in the respondents' apparatus individually or collectively perform substantially similar functions to those performed individually or collectively by the parts comprised in the apparatus claimed as the appellants' invention, or that the respondents' apparatus produces the same result as the appellants' apparatus. It must be shown that the respondents' selection and arrangement of parts is substantially the same as the appellants' selection and arrangement of parts, for it is in such selection and arrangement that the appellants' invention resides."

394 Subsidiary claims

Where the specification contains a number of claims, the subsidiary claims are often drafted so as to add one integer to the combinations claimed in previous claims. In these circumstances the court is likely to hold that the added integer is the only inventive idea of that subsidiary claim and that the doctrines of " pith and marrow " or substance cannot be applied to that subsidiary claim so as to extend its scope to combinations not having that integer.

395   As Viscount Radcliffe stated in *C. Van der Lely N.V.* v. *Bamfords Ltd.*[12]: " When . . . this ' pith and marrow ' principle is invoked . . . one must be very careful to see that the inventor has

[11] [1969] R.P.C. 367 at p. 391.   [11a] (1956) R.P.C. 232 at p. 245.
[12] [1963] R.P.C. 61 at p. 78.

not by the actual form of his claim left open to the world the appropriation of just that property that he says has been filched from him . . . I cannot, for my part, see what inventive idea is claimed by Claim 11, regarded as a separate claim, except the idea of dismounting the hindmost wheels and bringing them forwards to a position adjacent to and parallel with the foremost wheels. Without that, Claim 11 adds nothing material to what is contained in Claim 10; and Claim 10, it is agreed, fails, because it is only a statement of general principle and is too wide and vague for enforceability. I cannot, therefore, embark upon an inquiry whether the dismountability of the hindmost wheels is an essential or unessential element of the invention claimed, because it seems to me that the patentee himself has told us by the way that he has drawn up Claim 11 that this dismountability of the hindmost wheels is the very element of his idea that makes it an invention. . . . The case has not revealed why they (the patentees) decided to concentrate on this aspect. . . . But . . . I think that, as the Court of Appeal thought, ' why they so confined the claim is not for us to speculate.' The fact is that they did; and it is not open to them to complain if others are found to have occupied the ground that they so deliberately refrained from enclosing."

396   In *Submarine Signal Co.* v. *Henry Hughes & Son Ltd.*[13] the patent related to measurement by the use of sound waves. There were twelve claims, and it was argued, *inter alia*, that in the case of the eleventh claim the defendants had merely substituted a mechanical equivalent for the first integer (an " electric oscillator ") mentioned in that claim. The Court of Appeal held that the doctrine of mechanical equivalents was not applicable to the claim in question, and that there had been no infringement. Romer L.J.[14] expressed the view that where the claims of a specification were very numerous, there was little scope for the doctrine of mechanical equivalents, and said: " If . . . a patentee in his claims were first of all to describe his invention by reference to seven integers and then in the next claim were to repeat the statement of his invention by reference to those seven integers but adding an eighth, it would be impossible to say that the eighth integer was not of the essence of the invention claimed in the second claim." The learned Lord Justice then pointed out that all the preceding claims referred to a " sound emitter," but that this expression had been changed in the eleventh claim to " electric oscillator," and said: " Now the patentee must have intended something by that change, and I think it useless for him to say in court

[13] 49 R.P.C. 149.
[14] *Ibid.* at p. 175.

that . . . an electric oscillator is not of the essence of the invention that he claims in Claim 11. That being so, the doctrine of mechanical equivalents appears to me to have no application to the present case. . . ."

397 *Substantially*

If a claim alleged to be infringed contains the word " substantially " or the phrase " substantially as described " it is for the court to decide whether infringement has taken place, though it may be a difficult question.[15]

398 *New substance*

Where a complete specification claims a new substance, the claim is to be construed as not extending to that substance when found in nature.[16]

[The next paragraph is 411]

---

[15] *Raleigh Cycle Co. Ltd.* v. *H. Miller & Son Ltd.*, 65 R.P.C. 141 at p. 160; and see *Deere & Co.* v. *Harrison, McGregor & Guest Ltd.* [1965] R.P.C. 461.

[16] s. 4 (7).

CHAPTER 7

OPPOSITION TO THE GRANT AND REVOCATION BY THE COMPTROLLER

1. GROUNDS OF OPPOSITION

411 Grounds of opposition

The grounds upon which the grant of a patent may be opposed have varied at different dates, and the alterations in the law made by the various Patent Acts have, therefore, to be borne in mind in considering the decided cases.

412 *Grounds under the Acts of 1883–1932*

Prior to the Act of 1883 any ground on which the validity of the grant could be attacked was also available for the purpose of opposition (*e.g.* prior user [1] or prior publication [2]). It was necessary, however, that the ground of opposition should be proved beyond any doubt,[3] as it was considered that, if any doubt existed, the patent should be sealed in order that the inventor should have the benefit of a trial in the courts.

The Act of 1883 reduced the grounds of opposition to three in number, namely, obtaining, prior patenting, and identity with a prior concurrent application.

The Act of 1888 abolished the last ground above mentioned and substituted that of disconformity introducing the subject-matter of the opponent's application.

The Act of 1907 altered the grounds of opposition to the following four: obtaining, prior claim within fifty years, insufficient or unfair description, and disconformity introducing the subject-matter of the opponent's application.

The Act of 1919 replaced the second of the above grounds by prior publication in a specification within fifty years, or in a document at any time, and prior (concurrent) claim, and added the ground of disconformity with a basic foreign application introducing the subject-matter of the opponent's application.

The Act of 1928 amended the grounds of opposition by making the date which the patent would bear if granted the relevant date in all cases of prior publication, prior (concurrent) claim, and

[1] *Re Samuda,* Hindmarch 534.
[2] *Adamson's Patent,* 25 L.J.Ch. 456.
[3] See *Tolhausen's Patent,* 14 W.R. 551; *Vincent's Patent,* L.R. 2 Ch.App. 341.

disconformity introducing the subject-matter of the opponent's application.

The grounds of opposition available under the 1907–1932 Acts may be summarised as follows:

(a) obtaining; (b) prior publication (i) in a (British or foreign) specification within fifty years, or (ii) in a document (except an official abridgment) at any time; (c) prior (concurrent) claim; (d) insufficient or unfair description; (e) disconformity introducing the subject-matter (i) of the opponent's application, or (ii) of an intervening publication; (f) disconformity with a basic foreign application introducing the subject-matter (i) of the opponent's application, or (ii) of an intervening publication.

413 *Present grounds of opposition*

Under the present Act [4] the previous grounds of opposition based on disconformity have disappeared owing to the provisions now subsisting as to the priority date of each claim,[5] but additional grounds have been added. Opposition may now be based on (a) obtaining; (b) prior publication (i) in a (British or foreign) specification within fifty years of the date of filing of the complete specification, or (ii) in any other document (except an official abridgment of a specification more than fifty years old); (c) prior (concurrent) claim; (d) prior user (other than secret use); (e) obviousness; (f) not within the definition of an invention; (g) insufficient or unfair description; (h) in the case of a convention application, application not made within twelve months of first foreign application. No other ground may be relied on.[6]

Of these grounds, (d) prior user, and (e) obviousness, are new; (f) is new in terms, but this ground was, as a matter of practice, held to be available under the previous Acts.[7]

414 *Time for opposition*

Notice of opposition must be given to the Comptroller within three months from the date of the publication of the complete specification.[4] No extension of this period can now be obtained.

415 **The opponent (locus standi to oppose)**

Under the Act of 1852 only those persons were at liberty to oppose who " had an interest in opposing the grant of the letters patent." This limitation was omitted in the Act of 1883 and subsequent Acts, although the law officer on an appeal was required to

---

[4] s. 14.
[5] See *ante*, § 165.
[6] *Usines Decoufle's Appn.* [1964] R.P.C. 85.
[7] See *R. v. Comptroller-General, ex p. Muntz*, 39 R.P.C. 335.

form an opinion as to whether an opponent was entitled to be heard. It was recognised, however, that if no restrictions were imposed necessitating some bona fide interest on the part of the opponent, the way would be opened to harassing and vexatious oppositions by persons who were not really concerned as to the grant or amendment of the patent.[8] The present Act expressly provides that the opponent must be " interested " and no doubt this word will be construed so as to require the opponent to have at least that amount of interest which would be necessary to exclude those persons who would not be affected by the grant or amendment of the patent but, as it is in the public interest that patents should not be wrongly granted, it is submitted that any real and substantial interest should be sufficient.

416   In *Merron's Application*[9] the Assistant Comptroller said: " There are three clear grounds upon which an opponent can establish *locus*; first, the possession of patents relating to the same matter as the application opposed; second, a manufacturing interest; and third, a trading interest. . . . The Solicitor-General, however, in *Clavel's Application*,[10] although he did not accept a proposition put before him that ' every opposition which is not frivolous, vexatious, or blackmailing ought to be admitted ' did imply that there might be grounds other than the (above) . . . sufficient to establish a sufficient *locus*. In these circumstances the (Patent) Office has regarded an organisation, which is a body representative of a number of individuals each of whom has a sufficient manufacturing or trading interest for the purpose of opposition proceedings, as having an interest adequate to allow them to stand as opponents. . . . The question arises whether the rule I have stated above should cover an organisation which includes among its members one company which of itself has a satisfactory *locus*. I think not. If this be the actual position then the constituent member company should have come forward as the opponent and should not have attempted to act through the organisation." [11] In *Badische Anilin A.G.'s Application* [12] the Hearing Officer decided that there was a fourth ground upon which an opponent could establish *locus, viz.*, a real definite and substantial financial interest.

8 See *R.* v. *Comptroller-General, ex p. Tomlinson*, 16 R.P.C. 233 at p. 244.
9 61 R.P.C. 91, at p. 92.
10 45 R.P.C. 222.
11 See also *Lancaster's Patent*, Griff.P.C. 293; *Stewart's Appn.*, 13 R.P.C. 627; *Meyer's Appn.*, 16 R.P.C. 526; 28 R.P.C., *Comptroller's Ruling B*; *Trigg's Appn.*, 62 R.P.C. 18; *Henri Baigent Ltd.'s Appn.*, 71 R.P.C. 441.
12 [1963] R.P.C. 19; and see *Continental Oil Co.'s Appn.* [1963] R.P.C. 32.

417   It will be sufficient if the opponent has a recognised interest at the date when the opposition is heard [13] provided that he was genuinely concerned with the invention at the time when the opposition was filed.[14]

The rights or interests of the opponent have also been held to be prejudiced where there is a disparaging reference in the applicant's specification to the opponent's apparatus or invention,[15] or where an opponent's trade mark is used in the applicant's specification as a descriptive term, and without pointing out that it is a " trade mark." [16] But an opponent who is estopped from disputing the validity by reason of his being an assignee, has no *locus*.[17]

418 *Future intention insufficient*

Mere possession of an article that might infringe, coupled with an intention to use it in the future, will not give the opponent a *locus standi*. In *New Things Ltd.'s Application*,[18] Sir S. O. Buckmaster S.-G. said: " I am not prepared to limit the interest which an opponent must show . . . to what is called a manufacturing interest. I think that is a mistake. A trading interest would also be sufficient, but the interest must be a real, definite, and substantial interest, and must not arise from something that the opponent proposes to do. So far as the present interest of the present opponent is concerned it is nothing but the possession and use . . . of this particular screen. The rest of his interest arises from something which he intends to do in the future, and which he may or may not accomplish; it appears to me that that intention gives him no more right to oppose than a man saying that he intended in the future to make a patented article would give him the right to be heard."

419 *Right to oppose not assignable*

A different opponent cannot be substituted by amendment after the expiry of the opposition period even if he acquires an interest from the original opponent.[19]

A person who is a mere agent for marketing goods in this country, and has no property in such goods, is not entitled to oppose, as the " interest " is, in such a case, " the interest of the principals from whom he gets the goods and not his interest." [20]

---

[13] 29 R.P.C., *Comptroller's Rulings B and C.*
[14] *Siemens-Schuckertwerke A.G.'s Appn.*, 55 R.P.C. 153 at p. 155.
[15] *Wadham's Appn.*, 27 R.P.C. 172; see also *Hetherington's Appn.*, 7 R.P.C. 419.
[16] 31 R.P.C., *Comptroller's Ruling A.*
[17] *Wantoch and Wray's Patent* [1968] R.P.C. 394.
[18] 31 R.P.C. 45.
[19] *Bamford's Appn.* [1959] R.P.C. 66.
[20] *Wheeler's Appn.*, 42 R.P.C. 509.

It is submitted than an opponent who establishes an interest entitling him to oppose may do so on any of the statutory grounds,[21] and that what appears to be a contrary decision [22] is wrong.

The question of *locus standi* is most conveniently dealt with when all the facts are before the tribunal, and it will not usually be decided as a preliminary point.[23]

Where it was decided that the opponent had no *locus standi*, the law officer refused to allow the notice of opposition to be amended by striking out the name of the opponent and substituting that of another person who would have been entitled to oppose.[24]

420   Collusive opposition

In a case where an opposition had been entered, and it was shown that the opposition was collusive and had been entered for the purpose of obtaining an extension of time for sealing, the law officer refused to allow a patent to be sealed.[25]   In *Kempton and Mollan's Application* [26] the opposition was successful before the Comptroller, and a patent was refused.   The applicant appealed, and, prior to the hearing of the appeal, came to an arrangement with the opponent to the effect that the opposition should be withdrawn.   Sir E. Carson S.-G. decided that the appeal could not be allowed by consent, since the Comptroller, in refusing the seal, was acting in a public capacity, and that the case must be decided on its merits alone.[27]

The grounds of opposition will now be considered in detail.

421   (a) " Obtaining "

That the applicant, or the person described in the application as the first and true inventor, obtained the invention or any part thereof from the opponent or from a person of whom the opponent is the personal representative.

422   *Patent stopped in clear cases only*

An opposition upon this ground usually involves the credibility of witnesses, and will not be decided against the applicant unless there is very little doubt on the facts, since the opponent always has an opportunity of having the question tried by the court on a petition to revoke the patent under section 32.[28]

---

[21] See *Stewart's Appn.*, 13 R.P.C. 627; 29 R.P.C., *Comptroller's Ruling C*; *cf. Morgan's Patent*, 5 R.P.C. 186.
[22] *J. & J.'s Appn.*, 19 R.P.C. 555.
[23] *Clavel's Appn.*, 45 R.P.C. 222.
[24] See *Heath and Frost's Patent*, Griff.P.C. 288 at p. 290.
[25] *A. B.'s Appn.*, 19 R.P.C. 403, 556.   [26] 22 R.P.C. 573.
[27] And see *Thomas and Prevost's Appn.*, 15 R.P.C. 257.
[28] See *Edmunds' Patent*, Griff.P.C. 281.

In *Stuart's Application*,[29] Sir E. Clarke S.-G. said: "I think that the law officer is only entitled to stop the issue of a patent, having examined all the evidence given on one side or the other, if he is so clearly of opinion that the opponent has made out his case that he would, if a jury were to find in favour of the applicant, refuse to accept it and overrule the decision on the ground that it was perverse and contrary to the obvious weight and effect of the evidence."[30]

423   But where the matter alleged to have been obtained was not to be found in the applicant's provisional specification but was to be found in his complete specification and was proved to have been communicated to the applicants before the complete specification was filed, it was held that the onus was on the applicants to show that they themselves had made the invention before the date of such communication.[31]

If the applicant is alleged to have "obtained" the invention by inspecting the opponent's machine, the Comptroller is not entitled to consider what inferences the applicant might naturally draw from what he saw unless such inferences are in accordance with the facts and were such as would inevitably be drawn by persons skilled in the art.[32]

It is material to consider whether the part of the invention alleged to have been obtained is a matter of common knowledge or has been published in such a way as to deprive the opponent of any rights in it, because, if this were the case, the opponent could not obtain any relief on the ground of obtaining. The Comptroller might, however, require a disclaimer of the part of the invention which was not novel.[33]

424   *Opposition by personal representative*

In *Edmunds' Patent*[34] the Comptroller was of opinion that the words "legal representative," which were then the relevant words, referred to the executor or administrator of a deceased person and did not include a person holding a power of attorney.[35] Presumably the words "personal representatives" would be similarly interpreted.

The words "obtained the invention" refer to the identity of the invention and do not necessarily imply that the person from whom it is obtained is the true and first inventor, or that he has taken out

---

[29] 9 R.P.C. 452.
[30] And see *Ross's Appn.*, 30 R.P.C. 722; *Chambers' Appn.*, 32 R.P.C. 416.
[31] *Perrett's Appn.*, 49 R.P.C. 406; see also *Dicker's Patent*, 51 R.P.C. 392.
[32] *Maley and Taunton's Appn.*, 49 R.P.C. 47.
[33] *Ashton and Knowles' Appn.*, 27 R.P.C. 181.
[34] Griff.P.C. 281.
[35] See also *Spiel's Patent*, 5 R.P.C. 281.

or even intended to take out a patent at all.[36] It has been held that a limited liability company (which would itself be incapable of making an invention) can oppose upon this ground without joining the true and first inventor, who may well have assigned his rights to it.[37]

An opponent who alleges that part of what is described in the applicant's specification was " obtained " from him is entitled to oppose on this ground, even though such part is not included in the applicant's claim.[38]

It is not necessary for an opponent under this section to prove that the applicant has acted fraudulently, although it is often part of his case.[39]

425 *Direct relationship necessary*

The opponent must show clearly that the invention in question was obtained from him, either directly or through his agent; or he must bring the applicant by evidence of notice or otherwise into some known legal relationship with himself. It will not be sufficient to show that the invention has been handed on from A to B through numerous intermediate parties, and that B has received it in entire innocence of the fact that it owed its origin to A. There must be some connection, known and recognised by the law, between A and B, and not merely a casual connection in which no proof of knowledge or notice is brought against B and no agency is proved. The Comptroller in deciding a case of alleged obtaining is not deciding the question of the true and first inventor, but whether A obtained the invention from B.[40]

In *Cotton's Application* [41] one of three co-applicants admitted obtaining the invention from the opponents. The latter did not appear at the hearing and the opposition was dismissed. It was held, however, that the applicant who made the admission could not be joined in the grant which was made to the other co-applicants.

Where the law officer was of opinion that both the applicant and the opponent had contributed materially to the inventions, terms were imposed giving both parties an interest in the patent.[42]

---

[36] *Thwaite's Appn.*, 9 R.P.C. 515.
[37] 40 R.P.C., *Comptroller's Ruling B.*
[38] See *Hetherington's Appn.*, 7 R.P.C. 419.
[39] *Griffin's Appn.*, 6 R.P.C. 296; 27 R.P.C., *Comptroller's Ruling A*; *Perrett's Appn.*, 49 R.P.C. 406.
[40] 27 R.P.C., *Comptroller's Ruling A.*
[41] 49 R.P.C. 411.
[42] See *Russell's Patent*, 2 De G.M. & J. 130; *Luke's Patent*, Griff.P.C. 294; *Eadie's Patent*, Griff.P.C. 279; *Evans and Otway's Patent*, Griff.P.C. 279; *Garthwaite's Patent*, Griff.P.C. 284; *Ashton and Knowles' Appn.*, 27 R.P.C. 181.

If a part of the subject-matter of an application has been obtained from the opponent, the Comptroller may require the specification to be amended by the exclusion of such part of the invention. In this case the opponent may then apply for and be granted a patent in respect of the part so excluded, having the same priority date as the original application.[43]

Where an application is withdrawn during an opposition and the Comptroller is satisfied that obtaining has taken place, an order should be made refusing the grant of a patent on the application so as to allow the opponent to apply for a patent.[44]

426 *No inquiry into obtaining abroad*

In the case of inventions imported from abroad no inquiry will be made into what happened outside the United Kingdom; the importer is the true and first inventor, and the means by which he may have obtained the invention abroad, even if fraudulent, are of no importance, since the merit of the invention consists in its introduction into this country.[45] Whether the importer will be compelled to hold his patent, when granted, in trust for the person from whom the invention was obtained abroad is a question of property which does not concern the Comptroller.[46]

The above rule applies even when the opponent has made a convention application [47] in respect of the same invention, which will have a priority date earlier that that of the applicant's application [48]; in such a case, however, the opponent would usually have good grounds for opposing the application on the ground of prior claiming.

The rule also applies where the applicant claims the priority date of a basic foreign application, and it is alleged that his foreign application was made in fraud of the rights of the opponent.[49] In such a case opposition proceedings in the foreign country might result in the foreign application being cancelled, but the rights of the applicant in this country would probably not be affected, and he could still claim the foreign date.[50]

---

[43] s. 53.

[44] *Page's Appn.* [1970] R.P.C. 1.

[45] *McNeil and the Pearson Fire Alarm Co.'s Appn.*, 24 R.P.C. 680; *Edmunds' Patent*, Griff.P.C. 281; *Higgins' Patent*, 9 R.P.C. 74. *Du Pont de Nemours & Co.'s Appn.* [1965] R.P.C. 582.

[46] *Ibid.*

[47] See *ante*, § 108.

[48] *Meurs-Gerkin's Appn.*, 27 R.P.C. 565.

[49] *Curwen's Appn.*, 30 R.P.C. 128; and see Comptroller's decision in this case, reported as 29 R.P.C., *Comptroller's Ruling A.* See also *Halsey's Appn.*, 31 R.P.C. 101.

[50] *Ibid.*

427 *Protection given by section 53*

Where fraud has been committed in this country, true and first inventors who have been the victims of fraudulent applications are protected by the provisions of section 53, under which they can secure the priority date that they would have had if their legitimate application had been filed on the date on which the fraudulent application was filed.

428 **(b) Prior publication**

That the invention claimed has been published [51] in the United Kingdom before the priority date of the claim in a patent specification or other document not being a patent specification (or an official abridgment thereof) filed pursuant to an application made either in the United Kingdom or abroad more than fifty years before the date of filing of the applicant's complete specification.[52]

In the case of each claim its relevant priority date will have to be considered [53] and certain prior publications may be available against some of the claims but not against others.[54]

429 *Distinction between availability and publication abolished*

Under the former law, if disclosure in a prior document, other than a patent specification, was relied on, it had to be shown by the opponent that the invention " had been made available to the public by publication " in that document.[55] The subtle distinction between the meaning of this phrase and " published " gave rise to several decisions but was abolished by the 1949 Act which in this connection uses the one word " published " throughout. A disclosure of a document in confidence, *e.g.* to a prospective customer, does not constitute " publication." [56]

430 *" Document "*

The word " document " refers to " something in the nature of a description of the invention and not to an example or model of the invention itself "; and a cardboard carton which had printed on it instructions for folding for use in a window display was held not to be a " document." [57]

---

[51] See *ante,* § 268. And see *Dalrymple's Appn.* [1957] R.P.C. 449.
[52] s. 14 (1) (*b*).
[53] See *ante,* § 165. And see *Shevlin's Patent,* 56 R.P.C. 285; *Brush Development Co.'s Appn.,* 72 R.P.C. 31.
[54] *Cf. Bruce's Appn.,* 39 R.P.C. 341.
[55] Act of 1907, s. 11 (1) (*b*). And see *Weir's Appn.,* 43 R.P.C. 39; *Mooney's Appn.,* 44 R.P.C. 294; and *Dalrymple's Appn.* [1957] R.P.C. 449.
[56] *Gallay Ltd.'s Appn.* [1959] R.P.C. 141.
[57] *Wood etc. Ltd.'s Appn.,* 43 R.P.C. 377; see also *Alderton and Barry's Appn.,* 59 R.P.C. 56.

431 *Anticipation*

The ordinary principles governing anticipation by documents[58] apply to opposition proceedings. The opponent must, therefore, show that there is a disclosure of the invention claimed in one of the prior documents[59]; and it is not permissible to make a " mosaic " of prior publications in order to produce an anticipation.[60]

If the applicant makes out a prima facie case that the matter contained in the prior publication was obtained from him and he has applied for a patent as soon as reasonably practicable after learning of such publication and has, therefore, fulfilled the conditions laid down in section 50 (2),[61] it will in general be right to allow the application to proceed to grant notwithstanding such prior publication.[62]

432 **(c) Prior (concurrent) claim**

That the invention claimed is the subject of a claim of earlier priority date contained in a complete specification published after the priority date of the applicant's claim.[63] The law as to what constitutes a prior grant has been laid down by the Court of Appeal in *Kromschröder's Patent*[64]; that case and subsequent decisions of the Patents Appeal Tribunal on prior claiming arising under section 14 (1) *(c)* are discussed earlier in §§ 258, 259 to which the reader is referred.

Similar considerations apply in this case, as in the case of the search under section 8. Although section 14 (1) *(c)* does not require that the earlier claim should be a valid claim to be an effective prior claim for this ground of objection, it appears that the validity of the prior claim may be considered. However, grant should be refused only in cases where there is no room for doubt as to the invalidity of the prior claim. Where validity of the cited prior grant is shown to be open to reasonable attack, the applicant should be given an opportunity to amend.[65] If the applicant offers by way of amendment to insert a reference by number to the patent of earlier priority date.

---

[58] See *ante*, § 269 *et seq.*

[59] See *e.g. Lowndes' Patent*, 45 R.P.C. 48; *Thornborough and Wilks' Patent*, 13 R.P.C. 115.

[60] See *e.g. Ammonia's Appn.*, 49 R.P.C. 409; *cf. Ross's Patent*, 8 R.P.C. 477. And see *ante*, § 297.

[61] See *ante*, § 102.

[62] *Monsanto Chemical Co.'s Appn.*, 59 R.P.C. 119.

[63] s. 14 (1) (c). See *ante*, § 256 *et seq.* See also *California Research Corporation's Appn.*, 69 R.P.C. 193.

[64] [1960] R.P.C. 75.

[65] *General Electric Co. Ltd.'s Patent* [1959] R.P.C. 103, 109; *Imperial Chemical Industries Ltd.'s Appn.* [1959] R.P.C. 109, 115; *Traver Corporation's Appn.* [1964] R.P.C. 26.

in general such an amendment should be accepted by the Comptroller.[65]   The respective priority date of each claim is obviously of the same importance as in the case of (b) above.

An application will not be refused on this ground if no patent has been granted on the earlier application.[66]   This will be so even if the earlier application, though at the moment void, might conceivably be revived and proceed to grant.[67]

433   (d) Prior user

That the invention claimed was used in the United Kingdom before the priority date of the claim.[68]

This ground of opposition was introduced for the first time by the 1949 Act.[69]   No account is to be taken of any secret use.[70]

To establish prior use it must be established that the use was considered by all parties to be public use.[71]

The standard of proof of prior use in cases before the Patent Office is high.   " Normally in the absence of cross-examination, this will involve corroboration of a mere statement as to recollection in a declaration, particularly where the time interval involved is considerable.   Such corroboration is often best found in documents contemporary with the fact to be proved. Each case, however, must be considered on its own facts. . . ." [72]

434   (e) Obviousness

That the invention claimed is obvious and clearly does not involve any inventive step having regard to prior publication [73] or prior user.[74]

" In determining an issue of obviousness, both the Superintending Examiner and the Patents Appeal Tribunal are entitled to and do make use of their own knowledge and experience of the relevant scientific and technical background to the subject-matter of the alleged invention." (*Per* Diplock L.J. in *Johns-Mansville Corp.'s Patent.*[75])

This ground of opposition was also introduced for the first time by the 1949 Act,[76] and as in the case of (d) above no account is to be

---

[66] s. 14 (3).
[67] *Du Pont de Nemours Co.'s Patent*, 61 R.P.C. 56; *Traver Corporation's Appn.* [1964] R.P.C. 26.
[68] See *ante*, § 274 *et seq.*
[69] s. 14 (1) (*d*). *Fernberg's Appn.* [1958] R.P.C. 133.
[70] s. 14 (3). *Gallay Ltd.'s Appn.* [1959] R.P.C. 141.
[71] *Price Bros. & Co. Ltd.'s Opposition* [1968] R.P.C. 324.
[72] *Seiller's Appn.* [1970] R.P.C. 103 at p. 106.
[73] See *ante*, § 268 *et seq.*
[74] See *ante*, § 274 *et seq.*
[75] [1967] R.P.C. 479 at p. 491.
[76] s. 14 (1) (*e*).

taken of any secret use. Having regard to the use of the word
" clearly," the legislature evidently intended that the benefit of any
doubt should be given to the applicant, but otherwise it would seem
the same principles are to be applied as in proceedings before the
court. The introduction of this new ground of opposition has
rendered inapplicable the very many decisions in which a distinction
was drawn between the circumstances in which the Comptroller might
refuse the grant on the ground that corresponded to the present (b)
above and those in which he had no such jurisdiction, because he
then had no power to investigate quantum of invention.

If on the face of the written evidence filed there appears to be a
bona fide conflict of fact or credible expert opinion upon a question
on the answer to which the decision as to obviousness depends, then
the patent should not be refused unless the Comptroller thinks fit to
order cross-examination of the witnesses and as a result the conflict
is clearly resolved in favour of the opponent.[77] It may be enough
that it is conclusively established that the person versed in the art
would assess the likelihood of success as sufficient to warrant actual
trial.[78]

Various tests of obviousness have been applied, *e.g.* " Would the
construction claimed in the applicant's specification be regarded by a
person skilled in the art as mere workshop modification? " [79]

435 (f) Not an invention as defined

That the subject of any claim is not an invention within the
meaning of the Act.[80]

This ground is now expressly included by the 1949 Act, but as a
matter of practice could previously be relied on, it being assumed
to be included within the following ground (g). It is submitted that
this ground must be deemed to include the right to refuse the grant
for the reasons enumerated in section 10, *viz,* that the invention
claimed is contrary to established natural laws, or contrary to law or
morality, or is a food or medicine consisting of a mere admixture of
known ingredients possessing only the aggregate of the known properties of those ingredients.[81]

---

[77] *General Electric Co.'s Patent Appn.* [1964] R.P.C. 413 at p. 453.
[78] *Johns-Manville Corpn.'s Patent* [1967] R.P.C. 479 at p. 494. And see *Dow
Corning Corpn.'s Appn.* [1969] R.P.C. 544.
[79] *Kiashek's Appn.,* 71 R.P.C. 339. See also *Bowaters Lloyd Pulp and Paper
Mills Ltd.'s Appn.* 71 R.P.C. 419; *Rusch's Appn.,* 72 R.P.C. 269; *Inventa
A.G.'s Appn.* [1956] R.P.C. 45; *Robert Burgess Junior's Appn.* [1956] R.P.C.
163; *Slegton's Appn.* [1957] R.P.C. 419; *Booker's Appn.* [1958] R.P.C. 195.
[80] See *ante,* § 31. And see *N.V. de Bataafsche Petroleum's Appn.,* 57 R.P.C.
341.
[81] See *ante,* § 53.

436   (g) Insufficient or unfair description

That the complete specification does not sufficiently or fairly describe the invention or the method by which it is to be performed.[82]

This ground may be relied upon in a proper case when matter not relevant to the invention which the applicant has really made is described in the body of the specification though not included in the claims [83] and where the specification omits essential matters. However, there is no general rule that chemical cases must contain examples.[84] The relevant date at which sufficiency is to be judged is, it is submitted, the date of publication of the complete specification.[85]

Thus where the applicant stated that his invention related to the treatment of a chemical substance named " Permutit," without pointing out that this word was the opponents' registered trade mark, the Comptroller held that this fact entitled them to oppose on this ground, because the inference to be drawn was that the word was descriptive of the chemical compound concerned, whereas the opponents had the right to retain the word as distinctive of their goods while varying the composition of the substance sold under it, and he ordered the specification to be amended.[86]

A statement derogatory to the invention which is the subject of the opponent's patent will also justify an opposition on this ground, and such statement will be deleted or amended.[87] The fact that the specification claims more than one invention may not render the description unfair or insufficient; [88] but the Comptroller has no discretion to grant a patent containing two inventions.

It seems that a specification is insufficient if it should contain a section 9 reference, but does not do so.[89]

If the Comptroller is not satisfied that the directions given in the specification are sufficient he may require a demonstration to be carried out; but this will only be done in very exceptional cases.[90] But this ground cannot be extended to include objections based on

---

[82] See *ante,* § 212; *Wadham's Appn.,* 27 R.P.C. 172; and *Dehn's Patent,* 49 R.P.C. 368.

[83] See *Wadham's Appn.,* 27 R.P.C. 172; *Francis' Appn.,* 27 R.P.C. 86; and see *Hetherington's Appn.,* 7 R.P.C. 419.

[84] *Mobil Oil Corpn.'s Appn.* [1970] F.S.R. 265.

[85] *American Cyanamid Co.* v. *Upjohn Co.* [1970] F.S.R. at p. 469.

[86] 31 R.P.C., *Comptroller's Ruling A.*

[87] *Wadham's Appn.,* 27 R.P.C. 172; *Ehrig and Keilhauer's Appn.,* 50 R.P.C. 176; see also *Guest and Barrow's Patent,* 5 R.P.C. 312; *Patchett's Appn. and opposition by Sterling Engineering Co. Ltd.* [1959] R.P.C. 57.

[88] *Illinois Tool Works' Appn.* [1966] R.P.C. 557. See *Mobil Oil Corpn.'s Appn.* [1969] R.P.C. 586.

[89] *Esso Engineering Co.'s Appn.* [1969] R.P.C. 174; and see *ante,* § 119 and *post,* § 445.

[90] 27 R.P.C., *Comptroller's Ruling D*; *Wylam's Appn.,* R.P.C. 421.

other statutory provisions of the Act not expressly stated as being permissible grounds of opposition.[91]

If there is any invention at all described in the applicant's specification, the remedy is not refusal, but a disentanglement of the true invention from confusing and irrelevant matter, and a proper delimitation of it.[92] If, however, the Comptroller is satisfied that the result claimed cannot be attained by following the directions given in the specification he will refuse the grant.[93]

In *Dann's Application* [94] Lloyd-Jacob J. held that it was necessary to differentiate between making materials available and identifying them. It was sufficient if the material was identified and became available before the date of the hearing. This decision has been affirmed by the House of Lords in *American Cyanamid Co.* v. *Upjohn Co.*[95]

437 (h) Convention application out of time

That in the case of a convention application, the application was not made within twelve months of the earliest foreign application by the applicant or a person from whom he derives title.[96]

This ground of opposition was introduced by the 1949 Act and where the necessary facts are proved in revocation proceedings it would seem that the patent must be revoked if the patent was obtained on a false representation.[97] However, prior to grant leave may be given to amend if there is no intention on behalf of the applicant to mislead.[98]

To establish this ground of opposition an opponent must allege in respect of a convention application that a period of more than twelve months has elapsed between the date of application in this country by an applicant, and the date when the applicant or the person through whom he derives the right to make that application has applied in his country of origin,[99] or, in the case of post-dating in the Convention country, the date on which the foreign application is deemed to have been filed.[1] Where there is more than one applicant,

[91] *Metz Laboratories Inc. Appn.*, 50 R.P.C. 355.
[92] *Schwarzkopf's Appn.*, 31 R.P.C. 437.
[93] See *Wylam's Appn.*, 49 R.P.C. 421.
[94] [1966] R.P.C. 532; see *Kyowa's Appn.* [1968] R.P.C. 101; [1969] R.P.C. 259.
[95] [1970] F.S.R. 443.
[96] s. 14 (1) (*h*).
[97] *Daimler-Benz A.G.'s Appn.*, 72 R.P.C. 235; *Gumbel's Patent* [1958] R.P.C. 1; but see *Union Carbide Corpn.'s Appn.* [1968] R.P.C. 44 and 371.
[98] *Parry-Husband's Appn.* [1965] R.P.C. 382; *Ajinomoto Co. Inc.'s Appn.* [1968] R.P.C. 384. See also *Harshaw Chemical Co.'s Patent* [1970] F.S.R. 101.
[99] *Minnesota Mining and Engineering Co.'s Appn.*, 69 R.P.C. 163.
[1] *Poly-Resin Products Ltd.'s Appn.* [1961] R.P.C. 228.

the word "applicant" means the applicants jointly or severally and similarly in regard to the word "person." [2]

Where there are two foreign applications by the same applicant relating to similar subject matter and the earlier application was made more than twelve months before the application in this country, the question may arise as to whether the applications in this country could have been based on the first foreign application. "The point for decision under section 14 (1) (h) can then be shortly stated as follows. Was the first application an application for protection for the invention the subject of the Letters Patent in Suit." [94] When considering this point "the whole of the disclosure in the first . . . application must be scrutinised for the ascertainment of the invention which it is sought to protect." [3]

2. Grant by the Comptroller

438 The general powers of the Comptroller to refuse the grant or to require amendment of the specification and the insertion of references are dealt with below.

It is the duty of the Comptroller to consider whether the opponent has made out his case upon grounds which may properly be relied upon; and the onus is upon the opponent. [4]

439 Duty as a public officer

The Comptroller (and the Appeal Tribunal) in his capacity of a public officer administering a prerogative of the Crown, is also under the duty of determining whether it is in the public interest that a specification should be amended, or whether the grant of the patent should be refused. [5] For this purpose he is entitled to avail himself of any information which may be before him, or which may be in the possession of the Patent Office, [6] and he may also consider matters not raised by notice of opposition. [7] The applicant will, however, be

---

[2] *Switzer's Patent* [1958] R.P.C. 415.

[3] *Kopat's Patent* [1965] R.P.C. 404; see *Westminster Bank Ltd.'s Patent* [1967] R.P.C. 600; *Alfa-Laval Aktiebolag's Appn.* [1968] R.P.C. 216; *Muccino's Appn.* [1968] R.P.C. 307.

[4] *Ross's Appn.*, 30 R.P.C. 722.

[5] *Wadham's Appn.*, 27 R.P.C. 172; 29 R.P.C., *Comptroller's Ruling E* ("*Wainwright's Case*"); *Johnson's Appn.*, 47 R.P.C. 519 at p. 525; see also *Kempton and Mollan's Appn.*, 22 R.P.C. 573; *Francis' Appn.*, 27 R.P.C. 86; cf. *Thomas and Prevost's Appn.*, 15 R.P.C. 257.

[6] *Hughes and Kennaugh's Appn.*, 27 R.P.C. 281; see also *Osterstrom and Wagner's Appn.*, 49 R.P.C. 565.

[7] *Daniel's Appn.*, 5 R.P.C. 413 at p. 414; *Hughes and Kennaugh's Appn.*, 27 R.P.C. 281; *Richards & Co.'s Appn.*, 41 R.P.C. 321; *Johnson's Appn.*, 47 R.P.C. 519.

granted an adjournment in cases of surprise,[8] and unreasonable conduct by the opponent may be penalised by the exercise of the Comptroller's discretion with regard to costs.[9]

It was previously held that the Comptroller might consider any publication which was brought to his notice before he had given his decision, even though the hearing had taken place.[10] This is now expressly provided in the 1949 Act.[11] Again, the Comptroller will not allow a specification to be framed in such a way that it will mislead the public as to the scope of the applicant's invention (or otherwise),[12] even though the opponent may have failed to establish his case and had costs awarded against him.[13]

Similarly, the Comptroller may order a specific reference to a specification other than one to which a reference has been requested by the opponent.[14]

Where there is a clear admission by the applicant that his invention has been published, the grant will be refused.[15] If, however, the facts be in dispute, the Comptroller will not investigate the matter[16]; nor will he decide technical or scientific questions as to which there is, on the evidence, a serious dispute.[17]

440 Power of amendment

Unless the application contains no novel feature (or, under the 1949 Act, no novel feature of an inventive character) it is the invariable practice of the Comptroller to give to the applicant an opportunity to limit his claims to what is novel and to make consequential alterations in the body of the specification.[18] The power of amendment, including amendment in opposition proceedings, is, however, limited by the provisions of section 31 (1),[19] *i.e.* the amendment must be by way of disclaimer, correction, or explanation. Further, unless the purpose of the amendment is to correct an obvious mistake, its effect must not be to introduce or claim anything not in

---

[8] *Hughes and Kennaugh's Appn.,* 27 R.P.C. 281.

[9] 27 R.P.C. *Comptroller's Ruling C.*

[10] *Osterstrom and Wagner's Appn.,* 49 R.P.C. 565.

[11] s. 15.

[12] *Lorrain's Patents,* 5 R.P.C. 142; *Newman's Patent,* 5 R.P.C. 271; see also *Hetherington's Appn.,* 7 R.P.C. 419.

[13] *Wadham's Appn.,* 27 R.P.C. 172.

[14] *George Richards & Co. Ltd.'s Appn.,* 41 R.P.C. 321.

[15] 29 R.P.C., *Comptroller's Ruling E* ("*Wainwrights Case*"); approved in *Barraclough's Appn.,* 37 R.P.C. 105, and *Alderton and Barry's Appn.,* 59 R.P.C. 56 at p. 63.

[16] *Ibid.*

[17] See *Pitt's Patent,* 5 R.P.C. 433; *Lake's Patent,* 6 R.P.C. 548; *Curtis and André's Appn.,* 9 R.P.C. 495.

[18] See *Eveno's Patent,* 49 R.P.C. 385 at p. 396.

[19] See *Johnson's Patent,* 55 R.P.C. 4 at p. 20.

substance disclosed in the specification before amendment, and every claim of the amended specification must fall wholly within the scope of a claim of the unamended specification.[20] Section 29 (6) enables an amendment to be made in opposition proceedings, or to meet any requirement or objection of the Comptroller, without the necessity of advertisement or other formalities. But it is the practice to order an applicant seeking amendments to give reasons for his application.[21] It is submitted, if the applicant wishes to make amendments which are not required to meet the opposition or some objection of the Comptroller, these must be the subject of a separate application under section 29 (1) to (5), and duly advertised.[22] Where, by an interim decision, leave was granted to submit amendments introducing a particular limitation into the claims, but the applicant submitted amendments of a quite different character, which were inconsistent with the interim decision, the application was refused.[23] Amendment is a discretionary remedy and it will not be assumed that a passage sought to be inserted into the specification was inadvertently omitted.[24]

441 Disclaimer

In order to make clear the precise scope of the invention claimed it is sometimes necessary to make an acknowledgment of the prior art in general terms (sometimes called a " general disclaimer "). If there is overlapping between the claims and those of a prior patent a specific disclaimer of the invention protected by such prior patent or a specific reference to it may be ordered. A general disclaimer is inserted for the purpose of preventing the applicant from alleging that his invention is wider than that which he is entitled to claim, both in his own interests, in order that his patent may not be invalid by reason of the claims being too wide, and also in the interests of the public, because the public are entitled to know what the patentee is entitled to claim, and to have a fair description of the existing state of knowledge.[25]

The object of a specific reference was stated by Luxmoore J. in *Daniel Adamson & Co. Ltd. and Kerfoot's Application*[26] in the following terms: " A specific reference is inserted in order to warn the public and to call attention to a relationship between the invention

---

[20] *Dubilier Condenser Co.* (1926) *Ltd.'s Appn.* [1956] R.P.C. 181.
[21] *Warnant's Appn.* [1956] R.P.C. 205.
[22] *Comptroller's Ruling A,* 56 R.P.C. Appendix.
[23] *Klangfilm A.G.'s Appn.* [1958] R.P.C. 237.
[24] *E. I. du Pont de Nemour's Appn.,* 69 R.P.C. 246.
[25] *Newman's Patent,* 5 R.P.C. 271; *Guest and Barrow's Patent,* 5 R.P.C. 312 at p. 315; *Lynde's Patent,* 5 R.P.C. 663; *Teague's Patent,* Griff.P.C. 298; see also *Anderton's Appn.,* Griff.L.O.C. 25.
[26] 50 R.P.C. 171 at p. 174.

described and claimed in the specification in which such reference appears and the invention described and claimed in the letters patent the subject of such specific reference."

442 Grounds for specific references

There appear to be two grounds for ordering a specific reference to an earlier patent, one somewhat vague and the other reasonably precise.[27]

443 *New departure*

The first ground was stated in *Baker's Application*[28] by Luxmoore J. as follows: " Does the invention covered by (the earlier patent) constitute a new departure in the particular art? If it does, the second question arises: Does the invention covered by (the application) follow the same lines? If this second question is also answered in the affirmative, the description of the new departure seems to be necessary, and, if the description is necessary so is the reference to (the earlier patent) as part of that description." [29]

The mere existence of a prior patent dealing with the same general subject as the applicant's specification is not necessarily a ground for the insertion of a specific reference. In *Wakfer & Peck's Application*[30] Sir Stanley Buckmaster S.-G. said: " The idea that any patent which protects what is called a principle is, therefore, a patent to which reference . . . must be made in the specification of any subsequent patent that affects similar matters is one to which I cannot accede . . . a specific reference should only be inserted when its absence would lead to confusion, to misunderstanding of the real nature of the invention, and to the risk that a person reading the specification might think that the discovery it described included or involved the discovery already protected by an undisclosed patent." [31]

444 This statement of the law was approved by Luxmoore J. (sitting as the Appeal Tribunal) in *Daniel Adamson & Co. Ltd. and Kerfoot's Application*[32] where a specific reference was refused on the ground that the applicants' invention did not embody that covered by the opponents' specification, and was in fact expressly distinguished in

[27] See *post,* § 445.
[28] 51 R.P.C. 145 at p. 146.
[29] See also *Hopkins' Patent,* 27 R.P.C. 72; *Société, etc., Rhone-Poulenc's Appn.,* 50 R.P.C. 230; *Richards & Co.'s Appn.,* 41 R.P.C. 321.
[30] 32 R.P.C. 199 at p. 202.
[31] And see *Best and Marshall's Patent,* 34 R.P.C. 205; *Sefton-Jones' Appn.,* 36 R.P.C. 23; see also *Hoskin's Patent,* Griff.P.C. 291; *Lynde's Patent,* 5 R.P.C. 663; *Wallace's Patent,* 6 R.P.C. 134; *Brownhill's Patent,* 6 R.P.C. 135; *Stell's Patent,* 8 R.P.C. 235; *Levinstein's Appn.,* 11 R.P.C. 348; *Brockie's Appn.,* 25 R.P.C. 813; *Woolldridge and Fox's Patent,* 37 R.P.C. 114.
[32] 50 R.P.C. 171.

the description from the known types of similar apparatus. In *British Celanese Ltd. and Others' Application*,[33] where the amendments proposed made the reference to the prior art accurate and free from ambiguity, the Appeal Tribunal also refused to order the insertion of a specific reference.[34]

In *Dewrance's Application*,[35] however, where certain limitations of the claims in the prior patent appeared to exclude the applicant's construction (as claimed), a specific reference was inserted by the Comptroller on the ground that the real substance of the invention described by the opponent had been incorporated in the applicant's design.

445 *Where invention within claim of earlier patent*

The second ground on which a specific reference may be ordered is that the use of the applicant's invention will necessarily fall within the claims of an earlier patent or a patent having the same priority date.[36] This ground is illustrated by the following cases.

In *Ucar's Patent*[37] Sargant J. said: "It seems to me that the question of warning the public that the patent before them is a patent which may not be available to be used at all, except with the consent of some other persons, is not the same as the question of warning them that there is a possibility that the patent in question may not be a patent which confers monopoly rights. It is a very different thing. Everyone dealing with the subject-matter of patents must know that the question of the monopoly rights of a patentee is always somewhat doubtful, and anyone attempting to take an assignment of the monopoly rights is in a different position from a person who is merely attempting to use the invention, and it is more necessary that a person should be warned that it is not safe to use the invention, than that a person should be warned that the monopoly rights are liable to some particular defect. I do not think, therefore, that specific references ought generally to be indulged in so much in the case merely of there being danger to the monopoly as in the case of there being danger with regard to the safe user of the patent."[38]

446 **Resistance of specific reference**

In *Brownback's Application*[39] the insertion of a specific reference was resisted notwithstanding that the application fell within the claims

[33] 50 R.P.C. 247.
[34] See also *Brockie's Appn.*, 25 R.P.C. 813; *Rinfrett's Appn.*, 36 R.P.C. 21; *Alltree's Appn.*, 41 R.P.C. 146; and *Lorrain's Patents*, 5 R.P.C. 142.
[35] 49 R.P.C. 424.
[36] *Ford Motor Co.'s Patent* [1970] R.P.C. 74.
[37] 39 R.P.C. 269 at p. 276.
[38] See also *Best and Marshall's Patent*, 34 R.P.C. 205.
[39] 59 R.P.C. 80.

of an earlier patent, on the ground that the earlier patent was invalid. Morton J. approved the following rules, laid down by the Superintending Examiner, that a specific reference should not be inserted (1) if the documents cited as prior art are such that, had they been before the Comptroller when the prior specification was under consideration, no patent would have been granted or a statutory reference [40] would have been inserted (implying the invalidity of one or more claims); (2) if the earlier patent in fact contains a statutory reference; (3) if the earlier specification, when construed as though containing all necessary references to the prior art,[41] clearly discloses no manner of new manufacture. Further, if the earlier patent is said to be invalid because of prior art which applies with equal force to the patent under consideration, then no reasonable grounds for contesting the validity of the earlier patent will be shown.[42]

These principles are in effect given statutory recognition by section 9 of the 1949 Act, which applies both during the examination stage of the application in opposition proceedings and in revocation proceedings under section 33. A decision as to infringement by a Scottish court will not bind the Comptroller.[43]

447   Prior user

The opponent's right to a specific reference was formerly not defeated by evidence of a prior user which would invalidate his own patent, inasmuch as the question of prior user was not regarded as suitable for trial before the Comptroller or the Law Officer.[44] But as the 1949 Act now includes prior user as a permissible ground of opposition, it is submitted that this is no longer the law and that the validity of the earlier patent to which a specific reference is sought, may now be attacked on the principles enunciated in *Brownback's Application, supra*. A possible lack of utility in the opponent's invention has been held not to affect the matter.[45] The applicant may adduce evidence to show that the earlier patent should be construed in a particular way in view of the prior art.[46]

448   Revocation of opponent's patent

Where the patent relied upon by the opponent is the subject of proceedings for revocation in the courts, the Comptroller will not postpone his decision as to the insertion of a specific reference until

---

[40] See *ante*, § 119.
[41] See *Compagnies Reunies des Glaces et Verres*, 48 R.P.C. at p. 188.
[42] *Hay's Appn.* [1970] R.P.C. 14.
[43] See *Young's Appn.*, 69 R.P.C. 56.
[44] *Barraclough's Appn.*, 37 R.P.C. 105.
[45] *Van Gelder's Patent*, 9 R.P.C. 325.
[46] *Thornborough and Wilks' Patent*, 13 R.P.C. 115 at p. 116.

such proceedings are concluded.[47] If, however, the result of the revocation proceedings were that the reference was thereafter misleading or irrelevant, it might, at the request of the applicant, subsequently be removed.[48]

Specific references to patents which have expired have in rare cases been inserted,[49] but this will not ordinarily be done,[50] nor will a reference be ordered to a patent which has been revoked [51]; and in the case of a specific reference being ordered to a prior " concurrent " application, the insertion of the reference is conditional upon a patent being granted on the earlier application.[52]

449 Form of reference

For many years a specific reference took the form of a statement that the grantee was aware of a particular patent, and did not claim what was therein claimed (or described).[53] A disclaimer, however, is to be regarded as an exception from the monopoly granted,[54] and the above form of reference was frequently open to the objection that it introduced ambiguity into the specification.[55] It is, therefore, now the practice to require a precise and accurate statement of what is disclaimed.[56]

In considering the form of disclaimer to be inserted in any given case it is to be remembered that although an applicant is entitled to refer by number to prior specifications in support of his statement of prior art, nevertheless, he is not entitled to put upon the public what he believes to be the true construction of such specifications, as the construction of written documents is a matter for the court.[57]

It is important from the point of view of the applicant, however, that the statement of what is disclaimed should be a fair and accurate one, as he is bound by any recitals of prior knowledge which appear in his own specification, even though such recitals be erroneous.[58]

A disclaimer in the terms of the claims of the specification referred to is in many cases a satisfactory form of reference.[59]

---

[47] *Hickman's Patent,* 49 R.P.C. 443; see also *Hoffman's Patent,* 7 R.P.C. 92.
[48] *Hickman's Patent, supra*; and see s. 9.
[49] See *Hall and Hall's Patent,* 5 R.P.C. 283.
[50] *Rinfrett's Appn.,* 36 R.P.C. 21.
[51] *British Celanese Ltd.'s Patents,* 49 R.P.C. 283.
[52] ss. 8 (3), 9, 14 (3); and see 27 R.P.C. 366, *Comptroller's Ruling G.*
[53] See *e.g. Lynde's Patent,* 5 R.P.C. 663.
[54] See *ante,* § 441.
[55] See *Société etc. Rhone-Poulenc's Appn.,* 50 R.P.C. 230; *British Celanese Ltd.* v. *Courtauld's Ltd.,* 50 R.P.C. 259 at p. 284.
[56] *Société etc. Rhone-Poulenc's Appn.,* 50 R.P.C. 230; see also *Baker's Appn.,* 51 R.P.C. 145.
[57] *Atherton's Patent,* 6 R.P.C. 547.
[58] *Chapman and Cook* v. *Deltavis Ltd.,* 47 R.P.C. 163 at p. 173.
[59] *Newton's Appn.,* 17 R.P.C. 123.

3. REVOCATION BY THE COMPTROLLER UNDER SECTION 33

450 *" Belated opposition "*

Within twelve months after sealing any person interested [60] who did not oppose the grant may apply to the Comptroller for revocation, but only on those grounds on which opposition could have been based.[61]   Other grounds of invalidity (*e.g.* ambiguity) cannot be relied upon.[62]   Revocation proceedings under section 33 can be based on the ground of prior claiming,[63] notwithstanding that the prior specification had not been published at the date of the notice of opposition [64] or did not exist at that date.[65]

If an action for infringement, or proceedings for the revocation, of the patent are pending in any court, the leave of the court is necessary before an application to the Comptroller for revocation can be made.[66]

451 *Remedies*

The Comptroller may order the patent to be revoked either unconditionally or unless suitable amendments are made, but no order for unconditional revocation is to be made unless the circumstances would have justified refusal of the grant.[67]

The powers and duties of the Comptroller are, therefore, the same as in opposition proceedings.   In order to obtain revocation the applicant " is under the . . . burden of making out his case in the clearest way." [68]

The Comptroller may only consider the grounds of revocation that are pleaded.[69]

An appeal from the Comptroller lies to the Appeal Tribunal.[70]

4. PRACTICE

452 The practice before the Comptroller is regulated in the case of oppositions by rules 39 to 48 of the Patents Rules 1968, and in the case of Applications for Revocation by rules 40 to 46 together with rules 96 and 97.

The Notice of Opposition (or Application for Revocation as the

---

[60] See *ante,* § 415 *et seq.*
[61] See *ante,* § 413.
[62] See *Dehn's Patent*, 49 R.P.C. 368 at p. 379.
[63] s. 14 (1) (c).
[64] *California Research Corpn.'s Appn.*, 69 R.P.C. 193.
[65] *E. I. du Pont de Nemours & Co.'s Patent* [1958] R.P.C. 247.
[66] s. 33 (1).
[67] s. 14 (3).
[68] *Per* Tomlin J. in *Lowndes' Patent*, 45 R.P.C. 48 at p. 57.
[69] *Polythane Fibres' Ltd.'s Appn.* [1968] R.P.C. 116.
[70] ss. 33 (4), 85 (1).

case may be) must state the grounds upon which the opponent relies. It must be accompanied by a Statement setting out fully the nature of the applicant's interest, the facts upon which he relies, and the relief sought, *i.e.* refusal of the grant, amendment, insertion of reference, etc. Further particulars of the Statement may be sought and ordered.[71] A copy of such Notice and Statement is sent by the Comptroller to the applicant (or patentee).

The fact that the opponent's Statement does not accompany the Notice of Opposition is not necessarily fatal as the Comptroller has a complete discretion to enlarge times.[72] The extent to which particulars of any allegation (*e.g.* prior user) must be given depends on the facts of each case. The practice is not so strict as in the High Court.[73]

453 If the applicant desires to contest the opposition he must within three months of the receipt of the Notice of Opposition and Statement file a Counter-statement setting out fully the grounds upon which the opposition is contested, and deliver a copy to the opponent. Within three months of receipt of such copy the opponent may file evidence by way of statutory declaration in support of his case, and must deliver to the applicant a copy thereof.

Within three months from the receipt of a copy of the opponent's evidence, the applicant may file evidence in answer, a copy of which must be sent to the opponent. The opponent may file further evidence within three months of the receipt of the applicant's evidence, a copy of which must be delivered to the applicant; such last-mentioned declarations must be confined to matters strictly in reply.

No further evidence may be left on either side except by leave of the Comptroller.[74] Two copies of any documents referred to, other than United Kingdom specifications, and two copies of attested translations of any documents in a foreign language must be supplied.

The issues must be adequately defined by the Statement and Counter-statement, and not left to be made clear by the declarations filed at a later stage. A Counter-statement which contains merely a bare denial of the opponent's allegations is not a sufficient compliance with the rules[75]: the Counter-statement must contain replies in a reasonable manner to each of the matters pleaded in the Statement

---

[71] *Morgan Refractories Ltd.'s Patent* [1968] R.P.C. 374.
[72] See *Morton and Others' Appn.*, 49 R.P.C. 404; see also r. 154, Patents Rules 1968.
[73] *James Gibbons Ltd.'s Patent (Revocation)* [1957] R.P.C. 155; *O'Shei's Appn.* [1958] R.P.C. 72; *Benz Ltd.'s Appn.* [1958] R.P.C. 78; *Cooper Mechanical Joints Ltd.'s Appn.* [1958] R.P.C. 459.
[74] *Bakelite Ltd.'s Appn.* [1958] R.P.C. 152; *Ford Motor Co. Ltd.'s Appn.* [1968] R.P.C. 221.
[75] See 46 R.P.C., *Comptroller's Ruling B*; 49 R.P.C., *Comptroller's Ruling A*.

by way of admission, denial or an offer to amend the complete specification and must set out any facts relied on.[76] If amendments are
offered in the Counter-statement and the opponents wish to rely upon
matters not pleaded, an application should be made to amend the
Statement.[77]

A party filing declarations which are unnecessary, or which raise
matters not relevant to the issues, may be penalised in costs.[78]

If either party wishes to refer at the hearing to a document which
has not previously been mentioned, he must give ten days' notice to
the other party and to the Comptroller.[79] This provision is not
intended, however, to allow important documents to be introduced at
the last moment, and an adjournment and amendment of the " pleadings " may be obtained if necessary.[80] But it is contrary to the public
interest that opposition proceedings should be unduly delayed and
the admission of evidence at a late stage raising new matter may
be refused.[81]

The Notice of Opposition may be amended so as to include all
documents to which it is desired to refer [82] and all grounds on which
it is proposed to rely,[83] but the addition of new grounds of opposition
may be refused if made at a very late stage or after unreasonable
delay.[84]

Where an agent, who has filed a Notice of Opposition in his own
name, but had signed it " agent to opponent," died before the date of
the hearing, the Notice of Opposition was amended by the insertion
of the name of the real opponent.[85]

454 Hearing

The parties, if they so wish, are entitled to a hearing, which will
be in public unless the Comptroller, after consultation with the
parties represented at the hearing, otherwise directs.[86] By rule 46
(1) of the Patents Rules 1958, fourteen days' notice of the date of
the hearing is given to the parties by the Comptroller; and each party
must notify the Comptroller whether or not he proposes to attend.

---

[76] *Marshall's Appn.* [1969] R.P.C. 83.
[77] *Horville Engineering Co. Ltd.'s Appn.* [1969] R.P.C. 266.
[78] *Brand's Appn.*, 12 R.P.C. 102. See also *Hedges' Appn.*, 12 R.P.C. 136.
[79] Patents Rules 1968, r. 45 (3).
[80] See 46 R.P.C., *Comptroller's Ruling B*.
[81] *The Permutit Co. Ltd.'s Appn.* [1964] R.P.C. 22.
[82] *Ibid.*; 27 R.P.C., *Comptroller's Ruling C*.
[83] *Linotype and Machinery Ltd.'s Appn.*, 54 R.P.C. 228; r. 152, Patents
     Rules 1968.
[84] *Phillips Petroleum Co.'s Appn.* [1964] R.P.C. 470.
[85] *Re Lake*, Griff.P.C. 35.
[86] ss. 14 (2), 33 (2).

If an opposition is withdrawn by agreement, neither party may thereafter give notice that he desires a hearing.[87]

Where the notice of the hearing miscarried, and the case was heard in the absence of the opponent, who desired to be heard, the Law Officer sent back the case for rehearing.[88]

If the applicant fails to deliver a Counter-statement but expressly leaves the issue to the decision of the Comptroller, the case will be decided "upon its merits and with due regard to the public interest." [89] Where in revocation proceedings pursuant to section 33 the patentees failed to file a Counter-statement notwithstanding repeated extensions of time it was held that the Comptroller had no duty to consider the merits of the case and the patent was revoked.[90] If a Counter-statement is filed, but the applicant does not appear at the hearing nor file evidence, then the inference may be drawn that the applicant sees no effective answer to the case made against his application.[91]

In *Hickman's Patent* [92] it was alleged that the decision in certain High Court proceedings (then pending) would affect the issues to be tried before the Comptroller. An adjournment of the hearing was, however, refused.[93]

The applicant for a patent (or the patentee as the case may be) has the right to begin in all cases except where the proceedings are based upon the ground of "obtaining." [94]

455 *Oral evidence*

The Comptroller has power to take oral evidence and to allow any witness to be cross-examined on his affidavit or declaration, but the parties have no right to insist upon this or themselves to require deponents or declarants to attend for cross-examination upon oath.[95]

The usual practice, if cross-examination is desired, is for the party desiring to cross-examine to inform the Comptroller, who will, if he thinks the request reasonable, usually inquire of the other party whether he will produce the witnesses for cross-examination without any order for their attendance. A party cannot prevent a witness from being cross-examined by withdrawing his declaration.[96] .

---

[87] *Cary and Gerrard and Wright's Appns.*, 42 R.P.C. 322.
[88] *Warman's Appn.*, Griff.L.O.C. 43.
[89] 44 R.P.C., *Comptroller's Ruling A*.
[90] *Fontaine Converting Works Inc.'s Patent* [1959] R.P.C. 72.
[91] *Eichengrun's Appn.*, 49 R.P.C. 435.
[92] 49 R.P.C. 443.
[93] *Cf. Hoffman's Patent*, 7 R.P.C. 92.
[94] 27 R.P.C., *Comptroller's Ruling F*.
[95] s. 83 (1).   *General Electric Co.'s Patent Appn.* [1964] R.P.C. 413 at p. 452.
[96] *Re Quartz Hill etc. Co.*, 21 Ch.D. 642.

The Comptroller has all the powers of an Official Referee of the Supreme Court as regards the attendance and examination of witnesses and the discovery and production of documents.[97] The attendance of witnesses may, therefore, be enforced by subpoena under Order 39, rule 4 of the Rules of the Supreme Court; and the effect is that the Comptroller has the same powers in respect of discovery and production of documents as a judge of the High Court. Privilege can be claimed for documents, if the conditions set out in Order 24, rule 5 are satisfied.[98]

456　Interim decision

The Appeal Tribunal has made suggestions as to the best way to proceed, following an interim decision of the Comptroller, if it is desired to challenge that decision or any part of it,[99] or to submit amendments to the Comptroller before challenging his decision on appeal.[1] However an appeal should be entered unless all parties agree that a reasonable chance exists of resolving the matters in issue.[2]

457　Appeals to Appeal Tribunal under section 14

An appeal lies to the Appeal Tribunal from any interlocutory [3] or final order made by the Comptroller in opposition proceedings under section 14 or revocation proceedings under section 33.[4] This tribunal was constituted by the 1932 Act, and consists of judges of the High Court (nominated by the Lord Chancellor); the proceedings, however, are not to be deemed High Court proceedings.[5] The nominated judges can sit *en banc.* The powers of the Appeal Tribunal are regulated by section 85 of the 1949 Act.[6] As regards right of audience the same practice as was subsisting prior to the coming into operation of the 1932 Act is to be observed.[7] Counsel, solicitors and patent agents are entitled to be heard as advocates. The Appeal Tribunal may, either of its own motion or on the application of any party, direct that the appeal be heard in public or, as the case may be, that the decision of the Tribunal on the appeal shall be given in public.[8]

The practice of the Appeal Tribunal is regulated by the Patents

---

[97] s. 83 (2); R.S.C., Ord. 36, r. 4.
[98] *Cooper Mechanical Joints Ltd.'s Appn.* [1958] R.P.C. 459.
[99] *L. Oertling Ltd.'s Appn.* [1959] R.P.C. 148.
[1] *E. I. Du Pont's Appn.* [1962] R.P.C. 228.
[2] *Du Pont de Nemours & Co.'s Appn.* [1969] R.P.C. 271.
[3] *Robertson's Appn.,* 47 R.P.C. 215.
[4] s. 85 (1).
[5] s. 85 (10).
[6] As amended by s. 26, Administration of Justice Act 1969.
[7] s. 85 (6).
[8] Patents Appeal Tribunal Rules 1959.

Appeal Tribunal Rules, 1950,[9] the Patents and Registered Designs Appeal Tribunal Fees Order 1970[10] the Patents Appeal Tribunal Rules 1959,[11] and the Patents Appeal Tribunal (Amendment) Rules 1956–1970.[12]

Notice of appeal must be given within fourteen days of the date of the decision appealed against in the case of a matter of procedure and within six weeks of the date of the decision in any other case.[13] The Comptroller may, however, extend the period, but if the specified period has expired and no extension has been granted, special leave to appeal must be obtained.[14] The Lord Chancellor may remit the whole (or part) of the fee payable if it appears that hardship will otherwise be caused.[15]

The notice of appeal must state the nature of the decision, and the parts appealed against.[16] A cross-appeal is necessary only if a respondent desires to contend that the actual decision of the hearing officer should be varied.[17] Thus if the Comptroller decides that a patent may be granted if the specification is amended, the applicant may appeal and contend that no amendment is necessary. If the opponent wishes to argue that even if the amendments are made no patent should be granted, a cross-appeal is necessary.[18] Where a respondent desires to contend on the appeal that the decision appealed against should be affirmed on grounds other than those set out in the decision, then he has to send, within seven days after receiving the notice of appeal or such further time as the Tribunal may direct to the appellant and to the Comptroller a notice specifying the grounds of his contention, and also has, within two days after doing so, to furnish the Registrar of the Tribunal with two copies of this notice.[19] Accurate estimates should be made as to the length of each hearing and a certificate stating the estimated length should be lodged fourteen days before the day fixed for the hearing.

458   A party may appeal on the question of costs alone; but the Comptroller's decision on costs will not be varied or reversed unless

---

[9] S.I. 1950 No. 392, *post*, § 1313 *et seq.*
[10] S.I. 1970 No. 529, *post*, § 1582 *et seq.*
[11] S.I. 1959 No. 278; *post*, § 1341 *et seq.*
[12] S.I. 1956 No. 470; S.I. 1961 No. 1016; S.I. 1969 No. 500; S.I. 1970 No. 1074; *post*, § 1313 *et seq.*
[13] Patents Appeal Tribunal Rules 1950, r. 1 (2), as amended by S.I. 1970 No. 1074.
[14] Patents Appeal Tribunal Rules 1950, r. 5, as amended by S.I. 1970 No. 1074.
[15] Patents Appeal Tribunal Fees Order 1970, r. 4.
[16] Patents Appeal Tribunal Rules 1950, r. 2.
[17] *Groombridge's Appn.*, 61 R.P.C. 53; and see *Bairstow's Patent*, 5 R.P.C. 286.
[18] *Ibid.*
[19] Patents Appeal Tribunal (Amendment) Rules 1961, r. 3 (1), as amended by S.I. 1969 No. 500.

it is shown that he took into account or failed to take into account relevant matters.[20]

459   The evidence at the hearing is the same as that used before the Comptroller, and no further evidence can be given except by leave,[21] which will not usually be given unless the Tribunal can be satisfied (1) that the new evidence was not in the possession of the party seeking to introduce it at the time of the original hearing and (2) that such party could not with the exercise of reasonable diligence have obtained such evidence for use at the original hearing.[22]   The attendance (for cross-examination) of witnesses who made declarations may be ordered,[23] and where such is ordered no limitation, save that of relevance, will be placed upon the scope of such oral evidence.[24] The appellant normally has the right to begin at the hearing, except that where there is an appeal and a cross-appeal the applicant for the patent normally begins.[25]

The Appeal Tribunal may obtain the assistance of an independent scientific adviser if it desires.[26]   The appeal is in the nature of a rehearing[27] but it has been the practice not to reverse the decision of the Comptroller on purely scientific or technical questions unless a plain or admitted mistake has been made.[28]   Now, however, that the Appeal Tribunal is constituted by a specialist patent judge, it is submitted that this practice ought not to be followed and that the appeal should be decided on the merits as though it were an original proceeding.

460   Mandamus, prohibition, certiorari   cf. Courts Act
Although under the old law writs of mandamus, prohibition and   1971
certiorari were consistently refused against the Comptroller and the Law Officer,[29] it is now clear that an order of mandamus or prohibition will lie against the Comptroller and an order of certiorari against the Patents Appeal Tribunal[30] for any unwarranted assumption of

---

[20] *Ford Motor Co. Ltd.'s Appn.* [1968] R.P.C. 400.
[21] Patents Appeal Tribunal Rules 1950, r. 7.
[22] *Toyo Tsushinki Kabushiki Kaisha's Appn.* [1962] R.P.C. 9 at p. 13.
[23] *Ibid.* rr. 9 and 10.
[24] *Bakelite Ltd.'s Appn.* [1958] R.P.C. 152 at p. 157.
[25] *Johnson & Johnson's Appn.* [1963] R.P.C. 40.
[26] Patent Appeal Tribunal Rules 1950, r. 11.
[27] *Zucker's Appn.*, 44 R.P.C. 257 at p. 262.
[28] See *Glossop's Patent*, Griff.P.C. 285; *Aire and Calder etc. Works and Walker's Appn.*, 5 R.P.C. 345; *Zucker's Appn.*, 44 R.P.C. 257 at p. 262.
[29] *Van Gelder's Patent*, 6 R.P.C. 22; *R. v. Comptroller-General, ex p. Muntz*, 39 R.P.C. 335; *Wingate's Appn.*, 48 R.P.C. 416; see also *R. v. Comptroller-General, ex p. Tomlinson*, 16 R.P.C. 233; [1899] 1 Q.B. 909.
[30] *R. v. Comptroller-General, ex p. Parke, Davis & Co.*, 70 R.P.C. 88; *Freeman and Heatrae Ltd.'s Appn.* [1959] R.P.C. 25; *R. v. Appeal Tribunal* [1956] R.P.C. 323; *Baldwin and Francis Ltd.'s Appn.* [1959] R.P.C. 221.

jurisdiction or for an error of law by the Tribunal which appears on the face of the "record." The "record" consists of the specification in suit, the decision of the Comptroller, the notice of the Appeal to the Tribunal and the decision of the Tribunal.[31] Leave has to be obtained from the Divisional Court to apply for the order of certiorari. Although the court has a discretion whether or not to make the order, it will normally do so if an error of law or an excess of jurisdiction can be established.[32] An error of construction of the specification would be an error of law upon which an order would be granted,[33] but if the error of law had no effect on the decision certiorari will be refused.[34]

461   Appeals to Court of Appeal

An appeal lies to the Court of Appeal from a decision of the Appeal Tribunal under section 33 ("belated opposition") where the effect of the decision is the revocation of the patent.[35] With the leave of the Appeal Tribunal an appeal lies to the Court of Appeal where a patent has been refused in opposition proceedings under section 14 on ground (d) (prior user) or ground (e) (obviousness).[36] In cases where leave must be sought from the Appeal Tribunal the application should be made within fourteen days of the date of the decision and if leave is granted the Appeal Tribunal will extend the time in which the Notice of Appeal should be served.[37] The Court of Appeal will not, in general, admit further evidence.[38]

462   Costs

The Comptroller and the Appeal Tribunal have power to award to any party such costs as they think reasonable and any such order may be made a rule of court[39] and thereby enforced.

463   *Security for costs*

The Comptroller and the Appeal Tribunal may also order security for costs against any opponent, or other person who invokes their litigious jurisdiction, if such person neither resides nor carries on business in the United Kingdom or Isle of Man.[40]

[31] *Baldwin and Francis Ltd.'s Appn.* [1959] R.P.C. 221.
[32] *Reg.* v. *P.A.T., ex p. Geigy* [1963] R.P.C. 341 at p. 366.
[33] *Reg.* v. *P.A.T., ex p. Geigy* [1963] R.P.C. 341.
[34] *Campex Research & Trading Corpn.'s Appn.* [1970] F.S.R. 35.
[35] s. 87 (1) (a).
[36] s. 87 (1) (c). See *Bowaters Lloyd Pulp and Paper Mills Ltd.'s Appn.,* 71 R.P.C. 419.
[37] *Practice Direction* [1969] R.P.C. 280.
[38] *Bataafsche Petroleum Maatschappij's Appn.* [1956] R.P.C. 254.
[39] ss. 82 (1), 85 (5).
[40] s. 82 (2).

If an opponent does not succeed in obtaining the full amount of relief asked for he will not necessarily be deprived of costs [41]; but if, after having been offered by the applicant substantially all that he ultimately is held entitled to, he persists in forcing the matter to a hearing he will get no costs.[42] Similarly, if the opposition is not contested by the applicant or, in the case of revocation proceedings, the patentee offers to surrender the patent,[43] the Comptroller in awarding costs will consider whether the proceedings might have been avoided if reasonable notice had been given to the applicant before the opposition or application for revocation was lodged.[44]

Where an adjournment is necessary by reason of the opponent introducing an important document into the case at a late stage a special award of costs may also be made.[45] If an opponent, though successful, overloads the case with unnecessary documents, no costs may be awarded.[46]

An appellant who abandons an appeal before the hearing will be ordered to pay the costs,[47] and if fresh evidence is called on the appeal and the appeal is allowed in consequence, the appellant may be refused costs.[48] A specific sum in respect of costs is usually named in the decision; but it has never been the practice to award an amount which will compensate the parties for the expense to which they may have been put.[49]

An application to make an order for costs a " rule of court " is made by Side Bar motion to the registrar in court.[50]

464   Transcript of proceedings and judgment

A transcript of the proceedings before the Appeal Tribunal can be obtained by any person who is a party to the proceedings, but may not be communicated to any other person without the leave of the Tribunal.[51] As regards transcripts of the judgment, in a case where only the applicant and the Patent Office are concerned, only the applicant can obtain a copy without the leave of the Tribunal. In

[41] 27 R.P.C., *Comptroller's Ruling H.*
[42] 27 R.P.C., *Comptroller's Ruling H.*
[43] See *infra.*
[44] rr. 47, 98, Patents Rules 1968.
[45] See 46 R.P.C., *Comptroller's Ruling B.*
[46] *Metallgesellschaft A.G.'s Appn.*, 51 R.P.C. 368.
[47] See *Knight's Appn.*, Griff.P.C. 35; *Metallgesellschaft A.G.'s Appn.*, 51 R.P.C. 368.
[48] See *Stubbs' Patent*, Griff.P.C. 298; *Chambers' Appn.*, 32 R.P.C. 416 at p. 420.
[49] See *Zucker's Appn.*, 44 R.P.C. 257 at p. 263; see also *Aire and Calder, etc., Works and Walker's Appn.*, 5 R.P.C. 345; *Stuart's Appn.*, 9 R.P.C. 452.
[50] *Practice Note* [1930] W.N. 9; *cf. Rawlinson's Appn.*, 45 R.P.C. 324 (Trade Mark).
[51] *G.E.C.'s Appn.*, 60 R.P.C. 1 at p. 7.

other cases, subject to any special direction which the Tribunal may give, any person can obtain a copy of the judgment.[52] In all cases copyright in the transcripts must be respected.

5. SURRENDER OF PATENT

465 A patentee may at any time by notice to the Comptroller offer to surrender his patent.[53] The object of this provision is to enable a patentee to avoid having proceedings for revocation brought against him and thereby being made liable for costs. The offer is advertised and any person interested (*e.g.* a licensee) may oppose.[54] An appeal to the Appeal Tribunal lies from the decision of the Comptroller.[55]

The practice is governed by rules 99 to 101 and 40 to 45 of the Patent Rules 1968. The notice is advertised in the *Official Journal* and any person desirous of opposing must give notice of opposition within one month of the advertisement. Such notice is accompanied by a statement (in duplicate) setting out the nature of the opponent's interest, the facts upon which he relies, and the relief he seeks.

[The next paragraph is 471.]

---

[52] *Practice Direction,* 58 R.P.C. Appendix.
[53] s. 34 (1).
[54] s. 34 (2).
[55] ss. 34 (5), 85 (1).

CHAPTER 8

AMENDMENT OF SPECIFICATIONS

471 The practice as to amendment of specifications as a result of the proceedings on application, or on account of opposition to the grant, or application for revocation by the Comptroller under section 33, has already been dealt with. In cases where the applicant or patentee desires to amend the specification after acceptance the relevant statutory provisions are contained in sections 29, 30 and 31 of the Act.

472 History of law

At the period when specifications were filed or enrolled in the Court of Chancery, the Master of the Rolls, as Keeper of the Records, had power at common law to correct errors in a specification, but this power was strictly limited to the correction of verbal or clerical errors arising from mistake or inadvertence.[1]

A patent may, however, be rendered invalid by reason of the patentee claiming something which is not new or not useful, or through some innocent misdescription or misrepresentation, and it has long been recognised that an opportunity to amend should be available to the patentee to cure such invalidity.[2] In some reported cases the language used in the judgments suggests that it is, or at any rate was under the old law, impermissible to amend an invalid claim,[3] but it is submitted that this was not the intention.[4]

473 *Statutory powers of amendment*

The common law power of amendment was too restricted to be of use in such cases, and by the Acts of 1835 and 1844 [5] the patentee was given power to file a disclaimer or a memorandum of alteration provided that by so doing he did not extend the ambit of his monopoly. Any such disclaimer or amendment, however, was made at the patentee's own peril, and, in a subsequent action involving the

---

[1] *Sharp's Patent*, 1 W.P.C. 641 at p. 649; *Gare's Patent*, 26 Ch.D. 105.
[2] See *May and Baker Ltd.* v. *Boots Pure Drug Co. Ltd.*, 67 R.P.C. 23 at p. 31.
[3] *e.g. National School of Salesmanship Ltd.* v. *Plomien Fuel Economiser Co. Ltd.*, 59 R.P.C. 149 at p. 152; *Re Airspeed Ltd., and Tiltman's Patent*, 57 R.P.C. 313 at p. 320.
[4] See *Raleigh Cycle Co. Ltd.* v. *H. Miller & Co. Ltd.*, 66 R.P.C. 253 at p. 262; *Molins* v. *Industrial Machinery Co. Ltd.*, 55 R.P.C. 31 at p. 42.
[5] 5 & 6 Will. 4, c. 83, and 7 & 8 Vict. c. 69.

validity of the patent, objection might be taken on the ground that it in fact extended the monopoly.

Section 18 of the 1883 Act permitted, in cases where there were no legal proceedings relating to the patent pending, amendments by disclaimer, correction or explanation. Where there were such legal proceedings pending the patentee had by section 19 to apply to the court for permission to apply to the Comptroller, only amendments by disclaimer being allowed in this case. Section 18 (9), also provided that the granting of leave to amend should be conclusive as to the permissibility of the amendment, save in cases of fraud, though this provision was not given its full effect until the decision of the House of Lords in *Moser* v. *Marsden*.[6]

The Act of 1907 by section 21 substantially re-enacted section 18 of the Act of 1883, and by section 22 (corresponding in other respects to section 19 of the Act of 1883) conferred upon the court itself power to allow amendments by way of disclaimer in any action for infringement or proceeding for revocation. This power was extended to cases of amendments by way of correction or explanation by the alteration effected in section 22 of the 1907 Act by the Act of 1919. This alteration must be borne in mind in considering the cases under section 22 which were decided prior to the 1919 Act.

474 *Powers of amendment*

The present Act substantially enlarged the right to amend as is pointed out below.

By section 76 of the Act the Comptroller has power to correct any clerical error in any patent, any application for a patent or any document filed in pursuance of such an application, or any error in the Register of Patents. It has been held that, where a clerical error in a foreign specification led to the same error in the corresponding British specification, this could not be corrected under section 76.[7] If, however, he is of opinion that the correction applied for would have a material effect on the meaning or scope of the document, and that it should not be made without notice to other persons, he may require notice of the application to be advertised. Any person may oppose, and if an opposition is entered the Comptroller shall give the parties an opportunity of being heard before making the correction. There is no provision in the Act for an appeal from the Comptroller's decision under this section. The procedure is regulated by rules 129 to 132 of the Patent Rules 1968.

It is to be observed that sections 29, 30 and 31 confer no power to amend an accepted provisional specification, and that except for

6 13 R.P.C. 24.
7 *Maere's Appn.* [1962] R.P.C. 182.

section 76, there are no express provisions for amendment of a provisional specification at the request of the applicant or patentee. It has been held, however, that an accepted provisional specification may be amended by excision.[8] An inaccurate title may also be rectified, but, except for clerical errors, no other forms of amendment are permissible.[9]

475 Present law

Under the present law an applicant for a patent or a patentee may at any time after acceptance of the complete specification apply to amend by way of disclaimer, correction or explanation. Unless the amendment is for the purpose of correcting an obvious mistake,[10] the following conditions must be fulfilled, *viz.*,

 (a) the amended specification must not claim or describe matter not in substance disclosed in the specification before the amendment; and

 (b) everything covered by an amended claim must have fallen within the scope of at least one claim prior to the amendment.[11]

These conditions have been substituted by the 1949 Act for those formerly subsisting under the previous Acts, *viz.*, that the amended specification should not claim an invention " substantially larger than or substantially different from " the invention previously claimed.[12] The provision as to the amendment being not " substantially larger " than the invention previously claimed has been re-enacted, although in different words.[13] The former provision as to the amended claim being not " substantially different " from that previously claimed has been repealed to the great advantage of patentees. These words have in the past been interpreted in a manner which has in many cases rendered the ostensible right of a patentee to amend largely illusory.[14] All the very many reported cases on the topic of " substantially different " are not now applicable.

476 It is submitted that the effect of the present Act is that the Comptroller or the court has jurisdiction to make any amendment in the body of the specification which does not involve the introduction of new matter and that any amendment can be made to claims,

---

[8] *Dart's Patent*, Griff.P.C. 307; *Brackett and McLay's Appn.*, 47 R.P.C. 335.
[9] *Brackett and McLay's Appn.*, 47 R.P.C. 335.
[10] See *Standard Telephones and Cables Ltd.'s Appn.*, 72 R.P.C. 19; *Tee-Pak Inc.'s Appn.* [1958] R.P.C. 396; *Alliance Flooring Co. Ltd.* v. *Winsorflor Ltd.* [1961] R.P.C. 95.
[11] s. 31 (1).
[12] ss. 21 and 22 of the 1907 Act.
[13] See *Westinghouse Electric Co. Ltd.'s Patent*, 56 R.P.C. 76 at p. 85.
[14] See *May & Baker Ltd.* v. *Boots Pure Drug Co. Ltd.*, 67 R.P.C. 23.

including the introduction of one or more new claims, provided that the claims as amended are fairly based [15] on the complete specification as accepted and that the amendments do " not make anything an infringement which is not an infringement already." [16]

477 Disclaimer: correction or explanation

Any cutting down of the scope of the claims is a " disclaimer " [17]; but the cutting down of the scope of the monopoly in one respect does not provide a justification for its extension in other respects.[18]

As Lord Denning stated in *AMP Inc.* v. *Hellerman Ltd.*[19]: " A disclaimer takes place whenever the patentee reduces the ambit of his monopoly, for he thereby renounces his previous claim in its fullest scope. This renunciation need not, however, be done in express terms. It is sufficient if it is done impliedly . . . once you add another essential feature to a combination, you produce a sub-combination: and amendment so as to limit the scope of the specification to a sub-combination which was within the original claim is disclaimer." The added feature need not be derived from features claimed as being inventive in the original specification.

It has been held that a passage in a specification which is " a definite affirmation of utility " of the invention claimed cannot be removed on the basis that it is a disclaimer.[20]

478

" Correction " is to be interpreted as " a putting right of some mistake that had been made in the preparation of the specification. . . . There are, therefore, two requirements to be met: (1) A mistake must be shown to have been made; (2) The proposed amendment must provide the proper substitute for the mistake so as to insure correctness. So far as the first of these is concerned, a mistake may be so obvious on the face of the document that no evidence would be required to establish its existence. But . . . unless and until the court is satisfied by perusal of the documents or by evidence that a mistake has occurred, the right to amend on this ground has not arisen." [21] But the draughtsman who fails to include a claim, which he was entitled to include, does not make a " mistake "

---

[15] See *ante*, § 231.
[16] *The Distillers Co. Ltd.'s Appn.*, 70 R.P.C. 221 at p. 223, *per* Lloyd-Jacob J.
[17] See *May and Baker Ltd.* v. *Boots Pure Drug Co. Ltd.*, 67 R.P.C. 23 at p. 40; *Antiference Ltd.* v. *Telerections Installations (Bristol) Ltd.* [1957] R.P.C. 31; *Schwank's Patent* [1958] R.P.C. 53; *Baker Perkins Ltd.'s Appn.* [1958] R.P.C. 267.
[18] *Sinkler's Appn.* [1967] R.P.C. 155.
[19] [1962] R.P.C. 55 at p. 71.
[20] *Antiference Ltd.* v. *Telerection Installations (Bristol) Ltd.* [1957] R.P.C. 31.
[21] *Distiller Co. Ltd.'s Appn.*, 70 R.P.C. 221 at p. 223, *per* Lloyd Jacob J.

in the above sense, unless he intended to include it and omitted it in error.[22] " Correction " includes correction of a misdescription.[23]

As regards " explanation," in *Beck and Justice's Patent*,[24] Sir R. Webster A.-G. said: " My idea of the function of an explanation . . . is to explain more clearly what is necessary to understand the meaning of the patentee at the time he patented the invention."

In *Johnson's Application*,[25] Sir S. T. Evans S.-G. said: " If a man uses a word in an ordinary sense—using it fairly—and if he finds that by some people . . . that word is taken to mean something that he did not intend it to mean, I think . . . that it is one of the cases intended to be covered by the first subsection under the word ' explanation.' "

479 Obvious mistake

To be " obvious " a mistake must be plainly evident from an examination of the documents in the case.[26] Evidence may be necessary to establish whether the mistake would have been so evident to a skilled reader.[27]

480 Vagueness or ambiguity

Where an amendment is of a vague nature and would create uncertainty as to what the new claim really means it will be refused.[28] If the original claim is ambiguous and susceptible of two interpretations, no amendment will be permitted which gives the patentee the benefit of the wider interpretation [29] as this may result in enlarging the scope of the monopoly.

481 Drawings

Drawings may be added or altered where necessary to define the amendment made,[30] and in *Morgan's Patent* [31] the Law Officer allowed a description to be added of something which was clearly shown in the original drawing and was within the ambit of the original claim.

---

[22] *Ibid.* and see *Tee-Pak Inc.'s Appn.* [1958] R.P.C. 396.
[23] And see *National Research Development Corpn.'s Appn.* [1957] R.P.C. 344.
[24] Griff.L.O.C. 10.
[25] 26 R.P.C. 780 at p. 783. See also *Merck & Co. Inc.'s Appn.*, 69 R.P.C. 285.
[26] *Tee-Pak Inc.'s Appn.* [1958] R.P.C. 396; *Standard Telephones and Cables Ltd.'s Appn.*, 72 R.P.C. 19; *Alliance Flooring Co. Ltd. v. Winsorflor Ltd.* [1961] R.P.C. 95; *Union Carbide Corpn.'s Appn.* [1969] R.P.C. 530; *Chevron Research Co.'s Patent* [1970] F.S.R. 357.
[27] *Wilson's Patent* [1968] R.P.C. 197.
[28] *Parkinson's Patent*, 13 R.P.C. 509 at p. 514.
[29] *Chain Bar Mill Co. Ltd.'s Appn.*, 58 R.P.C. 200 at p. 205.
[30] *Lang's Patent*, 7 R.P.C. 469.
[31] Griff.P.C. 17.

482   Reasons for amendment

When applying to the Comptroller to amend the complete specification under section 29, the applicant or patentee must give full particulars of the reasons for any amendment [32] and where no reason was shown, in the case of a specification which on the face of it was sufficient without amendment, the application was refused [33]; amendment, however, will not be refused merely on the ground that the reasons given for it are not conclusively sufficient. [34]

There is no express statutory requirement that reasons for making the application to amend shall be given when the application is made to the court under section 30, but reasons may be ordered to be given as one of the conditions of allowing the application to proceed. [35] If the reasons are not given with sufficient particularity, further and better reasons may be ordered. [36] Amendments inconsistent with the reasons may be refused. [37] But if a reason is prima facie sufficient, it is not the practice to probe too deeply into the question of reasons. [38]

483   Amendment of invalid patent

Where a court has held that a patent is invalid, and the proposed amendment does not remove the defect upon which the court based its decision, the amendment is not allowed. [39] The Comptroller may refuse an amendment if what remains is so small or so obviously a matter of common knowledge as not to warrant the grant of a patent. [40] It has been said that an opponent is not entitled to raise questions as to want of novelty or invention in the patent as it would stand if amended, [41] but it is submitted that this decision is wrong and that no amendment should be permitted which leaves the patent clearly invalid, whether for lack of invention, ambiguity, or other reason. In *Parry-Husband's Application* [42] it was held that leave to amend could be refused if it was shown that a patent was obtained upon a false suggestion.

[32] s. 29 (2).
[33] *Nordenfelt's Patent*, Griff.L.O.C. 18.
[34] *Ashworth's Patent*, Griff.L.O.C. 6; see also *Re Lake*, Griff.P.C. 16.
[35] See *National School of Salesmanship Ltd.* v. *Plomien Fuel Economiser Co. Ltd.*, 59 R.P.C. 95 at p. 103.
[36] *Strachan and Henshaw Ltd.* v. *Pakcel Ltd.*, 66 R.P.C. 49 at p. 61.
[37] *National School of Salesmanship Ltd.* v. *Plomien Fuel Economiser Co. Ltd.*, 59 R.P.C. 95 at p. 107.
[38] *Howlett's Appn.*, 58 R.P.C. 238 at p. 241.
[39] *Armstrong's Patent*, 13 R.P.C. 501 at p. 508; 14 R.P.C. 747; *Hennebique's Patent*, 28 R.P.C. 41; *Unifloc Reagents Ltd.* v. *Newstead Colliery Ltd.*, 60 R.P.C. 165 at p. 178; *Parks-Cramer Co.* v. *G. W. Thornton & Sons Ltd.* [1966] R.P.C. 99 at p. 134.
[40] 28 R.P.C. *Comptroller's Ruling A*; see also *Heath and Frost's Patent*, Griff.P.C. 310.
[41] *Kirk's Appn.*, 49 R.P.C. 412; *James Gibbons Ltd.'s Appn.* [1957] R.P.C. 158.
[42] [1965] R.P.C. 382.

484   Further amendments

The fact that an amendment has already been made is not of itself an objection to a subsequent application for a further amendment.[43]

485   Discretionary powers

The allowance or refusal of an amendment, which complies with the statutory requirements, or the imposition of conditions thereon, is within the discretion of the tribunal hearing the application and if the original claim was " covetous " amendment may be refused.[44] Where such a discretion has been exercised by a judge, the Court of Appeal will not interfere unless the discretion has been wrongly exercised.[45] But if the judge has attached insufficient weight to any relevant considerations, or has erred in principle or come to a conclusion unsupported by the evidence, then an appellate court will exercise its own discretion which may be in the contrary sense.[46]

It was held that prohibition will not lie to the Law Officer in the exercise of his discretion under section 21 of the 1907 Act.[47] *Semble,* it will not lie to the Appeal Tribunal in this respect.

486   Conduct of the patentee

The conduct of the person applying for leave to amend may be taken into account.[48] Thus, if the patentee has had a previous opportunity during opposition proceedings to make the necessary amendments, but has insisted on retaining his specification in its original form, leave to amend may be refused in subsequent proceedings in which the validity of the patent is attacked.[49] Further, if the evidence establishes that the patentees were aware of the deficiencies for a long time before applying to amend, that may result in leave to amend being refused.[50] But this would not apply to the deletion of invalid claims, where there are one or more valid

---

[43] *Chatwood's Patent Safe and Lock Co.* v. *Mercantile Bank of Lancashire Ltd.,* 17 R.P.C. 23.

[44] *Mullard Radio Valve Co. Ltd.* v. *British Belmont Radio Ltd.,* 56 R.P.C. 1 at p. 21; *Howlett's Appn.,* 58 R.P.C. 238 at p. 243; *Du Pont de Nemours Co.'s Appn.,* 69 R.P.C. 246.

[45] *Allen* v. *Doulton,* 4 R.P.C. 377 at p. 383; *Lang* v. *Whitecross Wire and Iron Co. Ltd.,* 6 R.P.C. 570; *Armstrong's Patent,* 14 R.P.C. 747 at p. 754 (C.A.); *Ludington Cigarette Machine Co.* v. *Baron Cigarette Machine Co.,* 17 R.P.C. 745 (H.L.); *British Thomson-Houston Co.'s Patent,* 36 R.P.C. 251.

[46] *Raleigh Cycle Co. Ltd.* v. *H. Miller & Co. Ltd.,* 67 R.P.C. 226; *Van der Lely (C.) N.V.* v. *Bamfords Ltd.* [1964] R.P.C. 54.

[47] *Van Gelder's Patent,* 6 R.P.C. 22. See *ante,* § 460.

[48] *Allison's Patent,* 15 R.P.C. 408.

[49] Per Maugham J., *I.G. Farbenindustrie A.G.'s Patents,* 47 R.P.C. 289 at p. 325.

[50] *Chrome-Alloying Co. Ltd.* v. *Metal Diffusions Ltd.* [1962] R.P.C. 33 at p. 35.

claims which have been infringed [51] and probably the court would not regard mere delay as a ground for refusing the deletion of any invalid claim.

Where the patentees persisted up to the House of Lords in seeking to make their claim cover as wide a field as possible and issued advertisements as to a decision of the court which were held to be misleading, permission to amend was refused.[52] However, a distinction is to be drawn between amendments whose purpose is to validate invalid claims and amendments whose purpose is to delete invalid claims so that the specification will thereafter only contain valid claims. Thus, where the patentee seeks to maintain invalid claims up to the House of Lords, knowing the grounds upon which they were ultimately held invalid, then, in the absence of exceptional circumstances, he will not be allowed to amend the invalid claims so as to validate them, but the invalid claims will be deleted with consequential amendments so as to maintain that part of the monopoly which was originally valid.[53]

487   Where the court decides that a patent is revocable on the ground of fraud it will not entertain an application for permission to amend the specification so as to disclaim those parts which have been fraudulently claimed, but will revoke the patent as a whole.[54] There is no burden on an applicant in amendment proceedings affirmatively to establish either good faith, or reasonable skill and knowledge, in the original drafting of the complete specification, as an essential pre-requisite for the grant of leave to amend.[55]

Where the Comptroller refuses leave to amend and his decision is not appealed against, a subsequent application in respect of the same amendments will not be considered unless satisfactory reasons are adduced for the former decision not having been appealed against.[56]

488 Imposition of conditions—

(a) *Under section 29*

Although the Comptroller has power to impose conditions when granting leave to amend the specification, it is not usual for him so to do.[57] The ordinary practice is for the Comptroller not to impose

---

[51] *Van der Lely (C.) N.V.* v. *Bamfords Ltd.* [1964] R.P.C. 54.
[52] *British Thomson-Houston Co.'s Patent,* 36 R.P.C. 251; and see *Klaber's Patent,* 22 R.P.C. 405 at p. 416 (C.A.).
[53] *Raleigh Cycle Co. Ltd.* v. *H. Miller & Co. Ltd.,* 67 R.P.C. 226; *Van der Lely (C.) N.V.* v. *Bamfords Ltd.* [1964] R.P.C. 54.
[54] *Ralston's Patent,* 26 R.P.C. 313.
[55] *Schwank's Patent* [1958] R.P.C. 53.
[56] *Arnold's Patent,* Griff.L.O.C. 5.
[57] *Ashworth's Patent,* Griff.P.C. 6; *Pietschmann's Patent,* Griff.P.C. 314; *Hearson's Patent,* 1 R.P.C. 213; *Andrew* v. *Crossley,* 9 R.P.C. 165 at p. 168.

any condition as to the bringing of actions in respect of acts done prior to the decision allowing the amendment, but to leave infringers to such protection as regards damages as is conferred by section 59 (3).[58] But in *Dorr Co. Inc.'s Application* [59] a term was imposed prohibiting the patentees from bringing any action in respect of machines manufactured by the opponents if such manufacture had been commenced prior to the date of the application for leave to amend the specification.

489   (b) *Under section 30*

Where application is made under section 30 the conditions which may be imposed are entirely within the discretion of the court, and a variety of orders have been made according to the circumstances of the particular case.[60]

Thus, where an injunction had been granted in an action for infringement, and the defendants subsequently petitioned for revocation and the patentees applied in the revocation proceedings for leave to amend, the injunction was dissolved as one of the terms of leave being given,[61] inasmuch as it would be highly inconvenient to try what might be a new issue on a motion to commit for breach of an injunction obtained before amendment.[62]

In the absence of special circumstances, however, no order will be made precluding the patentee from maintaining actions in respect of matters prior to the date at which leave to amend is given.[63]

The order usually made if leave to proceed with the application is granted [64] follows that settled in *Rheinische Gummi und Celluloid Fabrik* v. *British Xylonite Co. Ltd.*[65] It includes conditions that the patentee will not (pending the application) proceed with any pending actions for infringement, or threaten other actions, and will abide by any terms subsequently imposed as to costs, etc. If, ultimately, the amendments are allowed the usual form of order provides for the

---

[58] *Davies and Davies' Patent*, 28 R.P.C. 50; *Ainsworth's Patent*, 13 R.P.C. 76; *Pitt's Patent*, 18 R.P.C. 478; *cf. Cheesbrough's Patent*, Griff.P.C. 303.

[59] 59 R.P.C. 113 at p. 118.

[60] See *e.g.* Bray v. *Gardner*, 4 R.P.C. 40; *Deeley* v. *Perkes*, 13 R.P.C. 581; *Ludington Cigarette Machine Co.* v. *Baron Cigarette Machine Co.*, 17 R.P.C. 214, 745; *Geipel's Patent*, 20 R.P.C. 545; 21 R.P.C. 379; *Gillette Safety Razor Co.* v. *Luna Safety Razor Co. Ltd.*, 27 R.P.C. 527; *White's Patent* [1958] R.P.C. 287.

[61] *Kenrick and Jefferson's Patent*, 29 R.P.C. 25.

[62] See *Dudgeon* v. *Thomson*, 3 App.Cas. 34.

[63] *Gillette Safety Razor Co.* v. *Luna Safety Razor Co. Ltd.*, 27 R.P.C. 527 at p. 537.

[64] See *post*, § 496.

[65] 29 R.P.C. 672 at p. 673. See Appendix *post*, § 2009; see also *Hollandsche (N.V.) Glas-en Metaalbank* v. *Rockware Glass Syndicate Ltd.*, 48 R.P.C. 181 at p. 182.

payment by the patentee of the costs occasioned by the application in the action, and any other pending actions.[66]

490 Practice under section 29

The application to amend is advertised by the Comptroller and any person may oppose within one month (with the possibility of an extension of time up to a further three months) from the date of the advertisement.[67]   Under the former law an opponent had to establish his *locus standi*, but this is not required by the present Act.[68]   An appeal from the Comptroller lies to the Appeal Tribunal.[69]

Reasons for amendment must be given under section 29 (2) which places on the applicant an obligation of revealing fully why he wishes to alter his specification, and an application will be refused for failure to disclose these reasons.[70]   It is not the practice to require the reasons for amendment to be inserted in the statutory advertisements.

Where an error in the advertisement was corrected in a subsequent advertisement, the time for entering opposition was held to run from the date of the second advertisement.[71]

Where the amendments proposed (and allowed) on appeal differed from those proposed before the Comptroller, the matter was referred back to the Comptroller to determine whether re-advertisement was necessary, in which case any opponent would have been " at liberty to argue the matter afresh." [72]

491 *Evidence*

The Comptroller normally decides the question upon evidence by statutory declaration, but where necessary takes evidence *viva voce* in the same manner as he may upon an opposition.[73] The Comptroller also has power to order discovery, but will not usually do so as the patentee is under a duty to make full and frank disclosure.[74]

492 *Method of imposition of conditions*

The specification is considered to be amended from the moment that leave to amend is given, and the conditions imposed, if any, agreed to [75]; no written undertaking by the applicant is necessary,

[66] See cases in note 8 on p. 212.
[67] Patents Rules 1968, rr. 90 to 95.
[68] s. 29 (4).
[69] s. 29 (5).
[70] *Clevite Corpn.'s Patent* [1966] R.P.C. 199.
[71] *Hughes & Co.'s Appn.*, 48 R.P.C. 125.
[72] *Union Switch and Signal Co.'s Appn.*, 31 R.P.C. 289 at p. 293.
[73] s. 83.
[74] *Temmler-Werke's Patent* [1966] R.P.C. 187.
[75] *Andrew* v. *Crossley*, 9 R.P.C. 165.

although it is the practice in the Patent Office to require some such undertaking as conclusive evidence of the applicant's agreement,[76] since the written assent precludes the patentee from alleging that he did not accept the condition.[77]

493   *Costs*

Both the Comptroller and, on appeal, the Appeal Tribunal have power to award costs.[78]

In *Ashworth's Patent*,[79] the Law Officer refused to grant costs to the applicant although successful, on the ground that the specification was so loosely framed that it was natural that rival traders should oppose an application for leave to amend.

In *Lake's Patent*,[80] which was an unopposed application for leave to amend, the applicants appealed to the Law Officer, who allowed the appeal and said, " I may say that I think it would be better, as a matter of practice, that in the absence of very special circumstances the Comptroller-General should neither give nor receive costs." In modern practice before the Appeal Tribunal the Comptroller neither pays nor receives costs.

In *Morgan's Patent*,[81] which was a successful appeal to the Law Officer from the decision of the Comptroller-General, application was made for the return of the stamp on the notice of appeal. The application was refused.

494   **When legal proceedings are pending**

The Comptroller cannot entertain an application to amend the specification while any action for infringement or any proceeding for revocation is pending before the court,[82] although he may correct clerical errors in a specification at any time under section 76.

In *Cropper* v. *Smith and Hancock*,[83] the Comptroller, having declined leave to amend a specification under the corresponding provisions of the Act of 1883, on the ground that an appeal was pending to the House of Lords from a decision of the Court of Appeal, declaring the patent in question invalid, and that such appeal was " an action for infringement or other legal proceeding," an application to amend was made to the court. Chitty J. refused the application, holding that the words in question referred to an

---

[76] *Ibid.*
[77] *Ibid.*
[78] ss. 82 (1), 85 (5).
[79] Griff.P.C. 6.
[80] Griff.P.C. 16.
[81] Griff.P.C. 17.
[82] s. 29 (1).
[83] 28 Ch.D. 148; 1 R.P.C. 254.

action or proceeding before judgment, and consequently that the appeal to the House of Lords did not deprive the Comptroller of the power of amending the specification.[84]

It is submitted, however, that both the Court of Appeal and the House of Lords have inherent power to discharge the order of the trial judge and to remit the cause to the Chancery Division for amendment proceedings to be instituted under section 30, notwithstanding that no application to amend was made in the court of first instance. But obviously such power would only be exercised in most exceptional cases.[85] Where any claim is held valid and infringed an opportunity to amend under section 30 arises by virtue of the provisions of section 62.[86]

495 In *Brooks & Co. Ltd.* v. *Lycett's Saddle and Motor Accessories Co. Ltd.*,[87] notice of trial in an action for infringement had been given. An order was obtained for the action to stand over generally, with liberty to either party to restore, for a settlement to be arrived at. The negotiations proved abortive, but nothing more was done for two years, when the plaintiffs applied to the Comptroller for leave to amend their specification under section 18 of the Act of 1883, which leave was granted. The defendants afterwards applied to restore the infringement action to the list. On the trial of the action it was contended that this amendment was invalid, as the action had been " pending " at the time. Farwell J. decided that this was so, and allowed the action to stand over with leave to the defendants to apply to the court under section 19 of that Act.

Where the application for leave to amend had been made under section 18 of the 1883 Act, it was decided that the subsequent institution of legal proceedings did not suspend the application pending before the Comptroller,[88] and the amended specification is to be used in the trial of the action even when the action is brought in consequence of an action to restrain threats made on the strength of the unamended specification.[89] If all proceedings between the parties are disposed of by agreement, the jurisdiction under section 30 to allow amendment no longer exists.[90] Sections 29 and 30 create complementary and mutually exclusive jurisdictions.[90]

---

[84] And see *Lawrence* v. *Perry*, 2 R.P.C. 179 at p. 187; *Raleigh Cycle Co. Ltd.* v. *H. Miller & Co. Ltd.*, 66 R.P.C. 253 at p. 258; *Deshaw Reclamation Process Ltd.'s Appn.*, 69 R.P.C. 214.

[85] See *Raleigh Cycle Co. Ltd.* v. *H. Miller & Co. Ltd.*, 63 R.P.C. 113 at p. 138.

[86] See *post*, § 504.

[87] 21 R.P.C. 651.

[88] *Woolfe* v. *Automatic Picture Gallery Ltd.*, 20 R.P.C. 177 (C.A.).

[89] *Stepney Spare Motor Wheel Ltd.* v. *Hall*, 28 R.P.C. 381.

[90] *Lever Brothers and Unilever Ltd.'s Patent*, 72 R.P.C. 198.

Where notice of an intention to present a petition for revocation was given to the proposed respondents, who thereupon made an application to amend to the Comptroller, before the fiat of the Attorney-General (which was then necessary before the petition could be presented) had been obtained, it was held that there were no " proceedings pending "; and the petition was ordered to stand over on an undertaking being given to proceed with due diligence with the application to amend.[91]

496   Practice under section 30

The practice on application to the court under section 30 is regulated by Order 103, rule 17 of the Rules of the Supreme Court. The applicant must give notice to the Comptroller of his intention to apply, accompanied by a suitable draft advertisement, which the Comptroller must insert in the Official Journal (Patents).[92] The advertisement must include identification of the pending proceedings in which leave to amend is proposed to be applied for and the title of the invention.[93] The applicant then proceeds by motion in the pending proceedings, twenty-one days after the advertisement has appeared.[94] The Notice of Motion should ask for directions to be given for the hearing and determination thereof.[95] The Notice of Motion must be served with a copy of the specification as sought to be amended attached thereto as soon as may be after twenty-one days of the appearance of the advertisement.[96] On hearing the motion the court decides whether the application is to be allowed to proceed, and if so, upon what terms.[97] If leave to proceed is granted, directions are given as to the hearing of the motion and the evidence. Affidavit evidence may be ordered, and the motion in such cases is set down in the non-witness list and heard prior to the action (or petition). If *viva voce* evidence is necessary the motion is set down in the witness list. If there is likely to be considerable duplication of evidence on the motion and in the action (or petition), the motion is usually ordered to be heard concurrently with the proceedings in which it is made. Which course is to be adopted is entirely in the discretion of the judge before whom the motion comes, and the Court of Appeal will not review it.[98] The order usually

---

[91] *Re Western Electric Co. Ltd.'s Patent*, 50 R.P.C. 59.
[92] See form in Appendix.
[93] *Practice Direction* of Lloyd-Jacob J., Dec. 9, 1957; [1958] R.P.C. at p. 147; *Practice Direction* of Lloyd-Jacob J., June 30, 1965; [1965] R.P.C. 481.
[94] R.S.C., Ord. 103, r. 17 (2), *post*, § 1604.
[95] *Thermos Ltd.* v. *Vacco Ltd.* [1966] R.P.C. 23.
[96] *Phillips Petroleum Co.'s Patent* [1966] R.P.C. 243.
[97] Ord. 103, r. 17 (3).
[98] See *British Celanese Ltd.* v. *Courtaulds Ltd.*, 49 R.P.C. 345.

made at this stage follows the form settled in *Rheinische Gummi und Celluloid Fabrik* v. *British Xylonite Co. Ltd.*[99] In the past the advisability of hearing the motion to amend concurrently with the action has been doubted, because the question whether the amended claim was " substantially different "[1] was one that was quite independent of the issues in the action itself and the latter had, therefore, to be argued upon both hypotheses, with consequent increase in time and expense. Now that the inherent permissibility of the proposed amendments has been made a much simpler question,[2] it is thought that in most, if not all, cases the motion to amend will be directed to come on with the action or petition for revocation.[3]

497 *Discretion of court*

The court has an inherent discretion whether or not to allow the proceedings for amendment to proceed and as to any terms that should be imposed.[4] But in exercising that discretion a court must act judicially and, if it errs in principle or comes to a conclusion unsupported by the evidence or fails to give due weight to all relevant considerations, then an appellate court will exercise its own discretion.[5]

498 *Opposition*

Any person desiring to oppose the amendment must give notice within fourteen days of the publication of the advertisement, and having done so is entitled to be heard upon the motion [6] and to be served with the necessary papers.[7]

If the proposed amendments are allowed, leave is usually granted to continue the action (or petition) on the specification as amended, and to make the amendments necessary in the pleadings for that purpose. The form of order usually made follows that settled in *Lilley* v. *Artistic Novelties.*[8]

---

[99] 29 R.P.C. 672 at p. 683; and see *Hollandsche (N.V.) Glas-en Metaalbank* v. *Rockware Glass Syndicate Ltd.,* 48 R.P.C. 181; *British Celanese Ltd.* v. *Courtaulds Ltd.,* 49 R.P.C. 345.

[1] See *ante,* § 475.

[2] See *ante,* § 476.

[3] See *Nier's Patent,* 55 R.P.C. 1; *Radio* v. *Radio Heaters Ltd.,* 71 R.P.C. 194; and see obs. of Lord Radcliffe in *Amp. Inc.* v. *Hellerman* [1962] R.P.C. 55 at p. 69.

[4] See *Strachan and Henshaw Ltd.* v. *Pakcel Ltd.,* 66 R.P.C. 49 at p. 58; as to costs, see *Leopold Rado* v. *John Tye & Sons,* 72 R.P.C. 64.

[5] *Raleigh Cycle Co. Ltd.* v. *H. Miller & Co. Ltd.,* 67 R.P.C. 226; *Van der Lely (C.) N.V.* v. *Bamfords Ltd.* [1964] R.P.C. 54.

[6] R.S.C., Ord. 103, r. 17 (1).

[7] *Ibid.* r. 17 (2).

[8] 30 R.P.C. 18 at p. 20. See *post,* § 2010, see also *Hollandsche (N.V.) Glas-en Metaalbank* v. *Rockware Glass Syndicate Ltd.,* 48 R.P.C. 425; *Haslam*

499 Effect of amendment

Where leave is given to amend under either section 29 or section 30, two important consequences follow, *viz.* that the right of the patentee to make the amendment cannot be impeached, and that his right to the recovery of damages is limited in certain respects.

500 Leave to amend conclusive

Leave to amend granted by the Comptroller, the court, or the Appeal Tribunal is conclusive except in the case of fraud.[9] Furthermore, the amendment, for all purposes, is deemed to form part of the specification,[10] so that the amended specification stands in the place of the specification as originally published. The latter may, however, be referred to for the purpose of construing the amended specification.[11]

In *Moser* v. *Marsden*,[12] Lord Watson said: " In my opinion, the very object (of the corresponding provision) of the Act of 1883 was to make an amended claim, when admitted by the proper authorities, a complete substitute, to all effects and purposes, for the claim originally lodged by the patentee. The validity of the amended claim must, therefore, be determined in the same way, and on the same footing, as if it had formed part of the original specification; and the claim as it stood before amendment cannot be competently referred to, except as an aid in the construction of its language after amendment."

Until the decision of the House of Lords in the above case there had been considerable doubt as to the effect of this enactment, and numerous cases had been decided upon the question of whether, when a specification had been amended so as to include in the amended portion something that was itself invalid, the amendment only, or the whole patent, would be invalid.[13] These cases are no longer of importance.

501 Printing

Amended specifications were formerly printed with the deleted portions shown crossed through and the new wording in italics, but

---

Foundry and Engineering Co. v. *Goodfellow*, 37 Ch.D. 118 at p. 123, and *Gillette Safety Razor Co.* v. *Luna Safety Razor Co. Ltd.*, 27 R.P.C. 527.

[9] s. 31 (2). See *Trubenising Ltd.* v. *Steel and Glover Ltd.*, 62 R.P.C. 1 at p. 13.

[10] *Ibid.*

[11] *Ibid.* and see *Multiform Displays Ltd.* v. *Whitmarley Displays Ltd.* [1957] R.P.C. 260 at p. 262.

[12] 13 R.P.C. 24 at p. 31.

[13] See *Van Gelder's Patent*, 6 R.P.C. 22; *Gaulard and Gibbs' Patent*, 7 R.P.C. 367.

this is no longer done. A statement that the specification has been amended appears on the first page.

The reasons for an amendment form no part of the amendment itself [14] and evidence of proceedings on amendment is not admissible upon the question of the true construction of the amended specification.[15]

502   Damages

Where a specification is amended, no damages are awarded prior to the date of the decision allowing the amendment unless the court is satisfied that the specification as originally published was framed in good faith and with reasonable skill and knowledge.[16] It was held by Lloyd-Jacob J. in *Ronson Products Ltd.* v. *Lewis & Co.*, that: " where the drafting of the specification departs in a material respect from the intention of the applicant for protection, and this despite the transmission by the applicant to his patent agent of all relevant information, an acknowledgment of such agent, that the way he expressed himself in the passage in question was wrong in view of the information he had received, must establish the absence of reasonable skill and knowledge." [17]

503   Onus of proof

The onus of proof that the original claim was framed in good faith and with reasonable skill and knowledge lies on the patentee,[18] but it has been said by Greene M.R. that: " good faith and reasonable skill and knowledge would be assumed in the patentee's favour in the absence of internal or external evidence to the contrary." [19]

In *Kane and Pattison* v. *Boyle*,[20] Byrne J. said: " I think that what the patentee has to establish is that in his original specification he meant and intended to claim that which he had invented, and no more. . . . If the inventor has knowingly sought to include a field of subject-matter beyond that which he knows he has invented, I

---

[14] *Cannington* v. *Nuttall*, L.R. 5 H.L. 205 at pp. 227, 228.

[15] *Bowden Brake Co.* v. *Bowden Wire Ltd.*, 30 R.P.C. 561 at p. 571.

[16] s. 59 (3).

[17] [1963] R.P.C. 103 at p. 138.

[18] See *British United Shoe Machinery Co. Ltd.* v. *A. Fussell & Sons Ltd.*, 25 R.P.C. 368; *British United Shoe Machinery Co. Ltd.* v. *Gimson Shoe Machinery Co. Ltd.* (*No. 2*), 46 R.P.C. 137 at p. 164. Relief was granted in the following cases: *Hopkinson* v. *St. James and Pall Mall Electric Light Co. Ltd.*, 10 R.P.C. 46; *J. B. Brooks & Co. Ltd.* v. *E. Lycett Ltd.*, 20 R.P.C. 390; *J. B. Brooks & Co. Ltd.* v. *Rendall, Underwood & Co. Ltd.*, 24 R.P.C. 17.

[19] *Molins & Molins Machine Co. Ltd.* v. *Industrial Machinery Co. Ltd.*, 55 R.P.C. 31 at p. 33.

[20] 18 R.P.C. 325 at p. 338.

think he cannot be regarded as having framed his claim in good faith within the meaning of this particular section. . . ."

The fact that the original claim was not "framed in good faith and with reasonable skill and knowledge" does not, however, affect the validity of the patent, after it has been so amended as to render it unobjectionable in other respects.[21]

504   Amendment of partially valid patent

Under section 62 of the Act relief can be granted in an action in respect of any claim which is valid and infringed.[22] As a condition of granting relief the court may direct that the specification shall be amended upon an application made under section 30 [23] and such an application may be made whether or not all other issues in the proceedings have been determined.[24] In the absence of exceptional circumstances a patentee will not be allowed to amend invalid claims after he has sought to maintain their validity up to the House of Lords, but that circumstance will not affect the court in granting relief in respect of the claims held valid and infringed and ordering the invalid claims from being deleted with consequential amendments.[25]

505   There is, however, a distinction between an amendment " designed to assist in the enforcement of a valid claim and one designed to validate an invalid one. Where a claim has been found to be valid, the patentee has made good his claim to monopoly rights to that extent. But where a claim has been found to be invalid, the patentee has failed and it may well be said that no good reason exists why he should be accorded a second chance " (*per* Willmer L.J. in *Van der Lely (C.) N.V.* v. *Bamfords Ltd.*).[26] Accordingly, where section 62 applies, the court will normally be inclined to permit amendment, at least to the extent of deleting the invalid claims with the necessary consequential amendments, unless the patentee's conduct has been such that he ought to be " driven from the judgment seat." In *Van der Lely (C.) N.V.* v. *Bamfords Ltd.*, Pearson L.J. said: " The court has to consider and decide whether any, and if so what, amendments should be allowed; and, therefore, if it be shown that the applicant's behaviour in relation to the patent has been so bad that he ought to be driven from the judgment seat, the court can refuse

---

[21] See *British United Shoe Machinery Co. Ltd.* v. *A. Fussell & Sons Ltd.*, 25 R.P.C. 631 at p. 660.

[22] See *post*, § 969 *et seq.*

[23] See *ante*, § 496.

[24] s. 62 (3).

[25] *Raleigh Cycle Co. Ltd.* v. *H. Miller & Co. Ltd.*, 67 R.P.C. 226 at p. 236.

[26] [1964] R.P.C. 54 at p. 76.

to allow any amendment at all to be made. On the other hand, the court should have regard to the direction given (usually by the same court) under section 62 and would naturally be inclined to allow the amendments necessary for correction of the specification by striking out the invalid claims and making the consequential amendments in the body of the specification and in the valid claims . . . I think the court should prima facie be disposed to allow such amendments, because if they are not made, the invalid claims will remain in the patent as a potential ' nuisance to industry ' as it has been called." [27] There have been cases where the Court of Appeal has itself ordered the amendment to be made, but where there is any difficulty an appellate court would presumably order the application to be made in the High Court, possibly accompanied by an indication of the general kind of amendment that the appellate court would regard as satisfactory. It is to be noted that the court may allow the specification of a patent held invalid to be amended, instead of revoking the patent, even where no question of relief arises.[28]

[The next paragraph is 511]

[27] [1964] R.P.C. 54 at pp. 73, 74.
[28] s. 30 (1).

CHAPTER 9

EXTENSION OF THE TERM OF A PATENT

511 History

The term of a patent was limited by the Statute of Monopolies to fourteen years. In some cases, however, the patentee, through no fault of his own, failed during this period to reap a reward in any degree commensurate with the benefit he had conferred upon the public by disclosure of his invention. In such cases his only remedy was to apply for a private Act of Parliament extending the term of his patent.[1]

In the year 1835, however, by the Patent Act[2] (re-enacted in amended form by section 25 of the Act of 1883), the Crown was enabled to prolong the term of a patent for seven, or in exceptional cases, for fourteen, years upon the advice of the Judicial Committee of the Privy Council, which was given jurisdiction to hear petitions for such extension. By section 18 of the Act of 1907 this jurisdiction was transferred to the High Court. The considerations which were to guide the tribunal in arriving at a decision were, however, substantially unaltered.[3] The decisions of the Privy Council are, therefore, still applicable to petitions to the court.

The Act of 1919 reduced the maximum periods of extension to five and ten years respectively, and introduced a simplified form of procedure (by originating summons) for cases where the patentee relied solely upon loss due to hostilities between His Majesty and a foreign state.

512 Present law

The Act of 1949 provides that a patentee may apply for extension on the grounds of (a) inadequate remuneration[4] and (b) loss by reason of hostilities.[5] Furthermore, a licensee who is entitled to make, use, exercise and vend the invention to the exclusion of all other persons, except such persons as may be authorised by him, may also apply for an extension in respect of war loss, if he has

---

[1] See e.g. Watt's Act (15 Geo. 3, c. 61) and others reported at 1 W.P.C. p. 40n.
[2] 5 & 6 Will. 4, c. 83.
[3] See Fleming's Patent, 36 R.P.C. 55 at p. 70.
[4] s. 23.
[5] s. 24.

suffered such loss as licensee.[6]   (It is to be noted that an " exclusive licensee " as defined by the Act [7] is not necessarily so entitled, for there may be more than one "exclusive licensee," whereas only a sole licensee has the right to apply for extension.)

513   Procedure

An application for extension on the ground of inadequate remuneration must be made by petition presented to the High Court. An application for extension on the ground of war loss may be presented to the court or to the Comptroller and if made to the court may be by petition or originating summons; if it is made by petition both grounds for extension may be included therein.[8]   An applicant applying to the court in Scotland and relying on loss due to hostilities *must* apply by petition.[9]

1. APPLICATION ON GROUND OF INADEQUATE REMUNERATION

514   Proof

The principal matters which have to be proved by the petitioner were summarised in *Fleming's Patent* by Sargant J. in the following way: " There are . . . three main questions with which I have to deal.   (1) Is the invention one of more than ordinary utility?   (2) Has it been adequately remunerated?   (3) Is any absence of remuneration due to no fault of the patentee?" [10]

The court has to consider " the nature and merits of the invention in relation to the public, the profits made by the patentee as such, and all the circumstances of the case." [11]

The onus of proof is in all cases upon the petitioner, who must prove all the facts necessary to bring him within the section,[12] and this is the case even though no opposition be offered by the Crown.[13]

515   Degree of merit required

The merit which has to be shown is that of great practical utility, rather than that of exceptional ingenuity,[14] and is to be judged by

---

[6] s. 25.

[7] s. 101 (1).

[8] *Poulsen's Patent (No. 2)*, 38 R.P.C. 105 at p. 109; *Hunt's Patents*, 39 R.P.C. 131 at p. 139; *Morf's Patent*, 46 R.P.C. 335; *Carpenter's Patent*, 69 R.P.C. 179.

[9] See *Murray's Patent*, 49 R.P.C. 445, and s. 103 (4).

[10] 36 R.P.C. 55 at p. 70.

[11] s. 23 (5).

[12] *Fleming's Patent*, 36 R.P.C. 55 at p. 70; *Western Electric Co.'s Patent* [1965] R.P.C. 335.

[13] *Darby's Patent*, 8 R.P.C. 380 at p. 383.

[14] *Saxby's Patent*, L.R. 3 P.C. 292 at p. 294; *Maschinenfabrik Augsburg-Nürnberg A.G.'s Patent*, 47 R.P.C. 193 at p. 211.

the benefit which the invention has conferred or is likely to confer upon the public. The merit must be greater than that which would be required to support the grant of letters patent. In *Trantom's Patent* [15] Sargant J. said: " There is no doubt whatever that, before the court can exercise its jurisdiction in favour of a petitioner, it must be satisfied that there has been some merit considerably greater than is sufficient to support the grant of the patent itself,[16] and having regard to the nature and merits of the invention in relation to the public, I think the court has to find, as a condition precedent to exercising its jurisdiction in favour of the patentee, that there has been some considerable benefit given to the public by the inventor in respect of that invention. The patent must be one of more than ordinary merit or utility, and, of the two, it appears to me, having regard to the words, ' in relation to the public,' that the utility is an even more important factor than the inventiveness or skill shown in making the invention." [17]

The words " in relation to the public " mean " in relation to the British public." [18]

516   Novelty and obviousness as affecting merit

Questions of novelty and obviousness are material as affecting the value to the public of the disclosure made by the patentee. They are not, however, directly in issue.

In *Johnson's Patent* [19] Parker J. said: " The consideration which supports the grant of the monopoly granted by letters patent being in fact the disclosure of something of value to the public, it is only where this value largely exceeds the benefit derived by the patentee from his invention that the patentee can be said to have been inadequately remunerated; but, even where this inadequacy exists, there may be other circumstances sufficient to induce the court to refrain from exercising its power. The first question, therefore, which arises on a petition for extension is the nature of the disclosure contained in the specification. For, without deciding first on the nature of the disclosure made, it would be impossible to form an opinion on its value to the public. For the purpose of determining the nature of the disclosure made and its value to the public, questions of novelty and subject-matter, though not directly in issue, are necessarily of considerable materiality, for without considering what

[15] 34 R.P.C. 28 at p. 37.
[16] And see *Stoney's Patent*, 5 R.P.C. 518 at p. 520.
[17] And see *Fleming and Gale's Patents*, 36 R.P.C. 266; *Maschinenfabrik Augsburg-Nürnberg A.G.'s Patents*, 47 R.P.C. 193; *Greenwood and Hanson's Patent*, 59 R.P.C. 65 at p. 70.
[18] *Neufeldt and Kuhnke G.m.b.H.'s Patents*, 47 R.P.C. 553 at p. 565.
[19] [1909] 1 Ch. 114 at p. 118; 25 R.P.C. 709 at p. 723.

was already known at the date of the letters patent, it is impossible to arrive at any adequate conception of the nature of the disclosure made by the patentee, and in the same way, the value of this disclosure to the public cannot be altogether independent of the extent of inventive ingenuity required to arrive at the thing disclosed. While, therefore, it would be wrong to allow detailed scientific evidence such as is usual in actions for infringement or petitions for revocation, evidence as to novelty or subject-matter cannot be altogether excluded. It is the duty of the petitioner at the outset to bring to the notice of the court all that may in any way affect the judgment of the court in these matters.[20] The length to which the petitioner's witnesses should be cross-examined, and the extent to which an objector should be allowed to bring evidence impeaching the validity of a patent on the ground of want of novelty or subject-matter, must be left to the determination of the judge who hears the petition, having regard to the nature of the individual case. As a general rule, if, after hearing the evidence of the petitioner's witnesses, there be in the opinion of the court a prima facie case for upholding the validity of the patent in respect of novelty and subject-matter, the court need not, in my opinion, investigate the matter further. It is always open to an objector to challenge the validity of a patent in proceedings more appropriate for that purpose. The court on a petition for prolongation ought, in my opinion, to pay especial attention to the fact that the thing disclosed may be minute compared with the sum total of what was known before, and yet may be the *sine qua non* of the successful application of existing knowledge, and thus fall within the category of great inventions." [21]

517   Refusal if patent is obviously invalid

The validity of the patent may be considered amongst " all the circumstances of the case," and if the patent is clearly invalid, no extension will be granted. In *Worrall's Patent* [22] the specification contained a large number of claims, and the objection that three claims were clearly invalid was raised by the Crown. Sargant J., after holding that one of the claims was invalid, said [23]: " It is perfectly well established that the court has no jurisdiction to extend the term of letters patent which on the face of them are obviously bad. It is quite true that on applications for extensions the court

---

[20] And see *Livet's Patent*, 9 R.P.C. 327.
[21] And see *Stewart's Patent*, 3 R.P.C. 7; *Hood and Salamon's Patent*, 41 R.P.C. 592; *Maschinenfabrik Augsburg-Nürnberg A.G.'s Patents*, 47 R.P.C. 193; *Wilson's Patent*, 53 R.P.C. 1; *Ferguson's Patent*, 59 R.P.C. 171.
[22] 35 R.P.C. 226.
[23] 35 R.P.C. 226 at p. 228.

does not look as narrowly at the validity of letters patent as it does in a patent action, but . . . if on the face of a specification it is perfectly clear that the patent is bad, . . . no extension can be granted . . . there are three claims which are on the face of them hopelessly bad . . . our law is that if any one claim in a specification is obviously bad that vitiates and makes void the whole of the letters patent . . . and . . . I have no option but to dismiss the petition." [24] It is submitted that these words still contain a correct statement of the existing law, notwithstanding that in an action for infringement relief may be granted in respect of a valid claim which is infringed, regardless of any invalid claim,[25] and that in proceedings for revocation the court may allow the complete specification to be amended instead of revoking the patent.[26] But if the patent has been in fact amended so as to make it wholly valid, there would then seem to be no objection on this ground to an extension, and where the invalidity only became apparent in the Court of Appeal after an extension had been granted by the Comptroller but was under appeal, and it appeared that the Court of Appeal would have given leave to amend but for that pending appeal, the extension was confirmed by the Appeal Tribunal.[27]

518   Merit as affected by simplicity, improvements and non-user

The merit of the invention in relation to the public may be enhanced rather than diminished by its apparent simplicity.[28]

The fact that an invention has been considerably improved upon since it was patented does not of itself create any presumption against its merits.[29]

But where subsequent improvements have shut out the use of the invention, it would be difficult to establish the unusual merit which has to be proved.[30]

The extent to which the invention has been used is also material upon the question of merit. In *Neufeldt and Kuhnke G.m.b.H.'s Patents* [31] Luxmoore J. said: " The best test of utility must almost of necessity, I think, be the extent of the user after the stage of commercial manufacture is claimed to have been reached."

Non-user of the invention for the whole, or a great part, of the

[24] And see *Saxby's Patent*, L.R. 3 P.C. 292; *Lane-Fox's Patent*, 9 R.P.C. 411; *Fleming's Patent*, 36 R.P.C. 55.
[25] s. 62 (1).
[26] s. 30 (1).
[27] *Leggatt's Appn.*, 68 R.P.C. 156.
[28] *Muntz's Patent*, 2 W.P.C. 113 at p. 119; *Stoney's Patent*, 5 R.P.C. 518 at p. 522.
[29] *Galloway's Patent*, 1 W.P.C. 724 at p. 727; *Southby's Patent*, 8 R.P.C. 433. See also *Meyer's Patent*, 50 R.P.C. 341.
[30] *Nussey and Leachman's Patent*, 7 R.P.C. 22.
[31] 47 R.P.C. 553 at p. 565.

life of the patent thus creates a presumption against the merit of the invention, and this presumption can only be rebutted by strong evidence.[32]

519   The type of evidence required in explanation of non-user was indicated by Sargant J. in *Runcorn White Lead Co. Ltd.'s Patent* [33]: " Finally the petitioners' explanation of the non-success of the process seems to me to be weakened by the very variety of the reasons they put forward. In general, such an explanation to be satisfactory must rest on some broad ground such as a state monopoly, a very limited class of users, great expense in introduction, special experimental difficulties, and the like."

Thus in *Semet and Solvay's Patent* [34] it had been found impossible to obtain any practical introduction of the invention, partly by reason of expense, and partly owing to the prejudices of manufacturers. An extension was, however, granted, and Lord Watson said: " In some cases the fact that losses have been sustained during the currency of the patent might go far to show that the patented invention was not of public utility; but their lordships are satisfied that there is no room for such an inference in the present case. The invention appears to be one which, from its very nature, cannot reasonably be expected to come at once, or within a short period, into general use. Its adoption necessitates the destruction of existing, and the erection of new, apparatus, and will, therefore, in all probability, be gradual, as the old-fashioned apparatus wears out." [35]

520   Profits of " the patentee as such "

In considering any application for extension by the patentee (*i.e.* the registered proprietor [36]) the court is to have regard to " the profits made by the patentee as such." [37]

521   *Application by assignee*

The principle upon which extensions were granted by the Privy Council was that the inventor should be compensated for inadequacy of remuneration in comparison with the merit of his invention, and applications by assignees were not regarded with favour. On the other hand, an inventor who has made a loss is handicapped in his

---

[32] And see *Allan's Patent*, L.R. 1 P.C. 507; *Hughes' Patent*, 4 App.Cas. 174; *Fairey's Patent*, 54 R.P.C. 297; *Löffler's Patents*, 59 R.P.C. 49 at p. 56.

[33] 33 R.P.C. 201 at p. 214.

[34] 12 R.P.C. 10.

[35] And see *Herbert's Patent*, L.R. 1 P.C. 399; *Roper's Patent*, 4 R.P.C. 201; *Southby's Patent*, 8 R.P.C. 433; *Currie and Timmis' Patent*, 15 R.P.C. 63; *Ferranti's Patent*, 35 R.P.C. 149; *Hunt's Patents*, 39 R.P.C. 131; *Smith's Patents*, 39 R.P.C. 313; *MacLaurin's Patent*, 47 R.P.C. 14.

[36] s. 101 (1).

[37] s. 23 (5).

efforts to dispose of his invention unless his assignee will be in a position to apply for an extension. The former practice has, therefore, been relaxed, and extensions are now granted in proper cases where the patent has been assigned.[38]

In *McCulloch's Patent*[39] Lord Salvesen said: " I can draw no distinction between a patentee, who is the inventor. and an assignee to whom he has conveyed his rights on equitable terms, and who has incurred the greater part of the expense . . . more especially when the executors of the . . . patentee are concurring petitioners and will share in the benefits of any extension." [40]

522   *Application by importer*

It was at one time stated that the merit of an importer was less than that of an inventor, but that view has been abandoned and importers are " entitled to be put on somewhat, if not entirely, the same footing as inventors." [41]

The remuneration which has to be considered by the court is the total remuneration that has been earned by the invention. The meaning of the words " the patentee as such " in this connection was considered by Sargant J. in *Summers Brown's Patent*,[42] who said: " Over and over again applications have been made . . . by assignees of patents coming with the concurrence of the original patentee, and the phrase ' the patentee ' . . . has invariably been construed as meaning the successive patentees throughout the term of the patent, that is to say, the remuneration which has to be taken into account is not the remuneration merely of the patentee at the date of the application by petition, but it is the remuneration which has been earned by that person and by his predecessors in title." [43]

523   Where, therefore, the earlier owners of the patent have been adequately remunerated, an assignee who purchases the patent shortly before expiry will not be able to obtain an extension in the event of making a loss during the period of his ownership. In *Hopkinson's Patent*[44] the petitioners were the inventor and a company which had purchased the patent from an assignee of the inventor. Lord Hobhouse, after dealing with the authorities, said[45]: " It cannot be seriously contended that an assignee, who may have purchased a patent at a late period of its life, can, if he has lost money, come here alleging that he is by statute a patentee who has been inade-

---

[38] *See Maschinenfabrik Augsburg-Nürnberg A.G.'s Patents*, 47 R.P.C. 193 at p. 212.   [39] 25 R.P.C. 684 at p. 692.
[40] And see *Ritchie's Patent*, 31 R.P.C. 1; *Dickson's Patent*, 42 R.P.C. 463.
[41] *Berry's Patent*, 7 Moo.P.C. 187.   [42] 39 R.P.C. 367 at p. 370.
[43] And see *Western Electric Co. Ltd.'s Patent*, 48 R.P.C. 155 at p. 161; *Poulsen's Patent (No. 2)*, 38 R.P.C. 105; *Tribe's Patent*, 53 R.P.C. 131.
[44] 14 R.P.C. 5.   [45] At p. 10.

quately remunerated. . . . Their lordships consider that they would be departing both from authority and from sound principle if they were to hold that this company occupies the position of an inventor who has been inadequately remunerated. The company entered on a purely commercial speculation which, unluckily for them, has up to the present time proved unremunerative. They purchased it, or at least the beneficial interest, out and out, from a prior assignee of the inventor, who has, in one way or another, been well paid, and has now no claim or interest to ask for an extension." And an extension was refused.[46]

524 Accounts showing remuneration

Accounts showing the expenditure and receipts relating to the patent in question have to accompany the petition. These must be as clear and precise as possible. In *Saxby's Patent* [47] Lord Cairns stated the requirements in the following way: " Now it is the duty of every patentee who comes for the prolongation of his patent to take upon himself the onus of satisfying this Committee, in a manner which admits of no controversy, of what has been the amount of remuneration which, in every point of view, the invention has brought to him, in order that their lordships may be able to come to a conclusion whether that remuneration may fairly be considered a sufficient reward for his invention or not. It is not for this Committee to send back the accounts for further particulars, nor to dissect the accounts for the purpose of surmising what might be the real outcome if they were differently cast: it is for the applicant to bring his accounts before the Committee in a shape which will leave no doubt as to what the remuneration has been that he has received."

In *Hughes' Patent* [48] the petitioner had kept no books, but shortly before the presentation of the petition he had marked upon certain cheques drawn upon his private account approximately the amounts expended by him in working the patent. Upon these materials the accounts accompanying the petition were made up by the accountant, there being no vouchers or other corroboration. Prolongation was refused.[49] The requirements at the present time are as stringent as they were under the Privy Council practice.[50]

---

[46] And see *Bower-Barff's Patent*, 12 R.P.C. 383; *Tribe's Patent*, 53 R.P.C. 131; *Evans' Patent*, 54 R.P.C. 259.

[47] L.R. 3 P.C. 292; see *Phillips Electrical Ltd.'s Patent* [1970] F.S.R. 347 and *G.K.N. Somerset Wire Ltd.'s Patent* [1970] F.S.R. 335.

[48] 15 R.P.C. 370.

[49] And see *Henderson's Patent*, 18 R.P.C. 449; *Wüterich's Patent*, 20 R.P.C. 285.

[50] *Hunt's Patents*, 39 R.P.C. 131 at p. 138; and see *Lawrence and Kennedy's Patent*, 27 R.P.C. 252; *Neufeldt and Kuhnke G.m.b.H.'s Patents*, 47 R.P.C. 553; *Heron's Patent*, 57 R.P.C. 29.

While the absence of books or of proper accounts is usually fatal,[51] exceptions are sometimes made where a strong prima facie case has been made out. Thus, for instance, where the books of the petitioner relating to profits arising from his patent were lost during his bankruptcy, the account of profit and loss was taken upon his own evidence.[52] And where the estate of a deceased patentee was of little value, and no accounts had ever been kept, the petitioner, who was the administratrix and widow of the patentee, was examined to prove an allegation in the petition to the effect that there had been a considerable loss.[53] Where the invention was of exceptional merit, and it was clear that there had been a very heavy loss, it was held that extreme accuracy in the accounts was unnecessary.[54]

Where there are several patents in respect of the same general subject-matter in the hands of the petitioner, and licences are granted under them all jointly, it may be practically impossible to apportion receipts accurately as between the separate patents. In such a case the court has regard to the difficulties involved, and, if satisfied broadly as to the receipts, may not insist on the presentation of more exact accounts.[55]

525   Adjournment to amplify accounts

Should the accounts filed in the first instance be unsatisfactory, an adjournment of the hearing will sometimes be granted to allow the petitioner to amend,[56] but good reason must be disclosed, as otherwise the petition will be dismissed.[57]

526   What profits must be disclosed

The profits of persons interested in the patent either, for instance, as partners[58] or as part assignees or free licensees[59] must be shown, but not necessarily those made by licensees who pay royalties.[60] The profits from corresponding foreign patents, whether held by the

---

[51] *Yates and Kellett's Patent*, 12 App.Cas. 147; 4 R.P.C. 150; see *Ambler's Patent* [1965] R.P.C. 17; *Lawrence's Patent*, 9 R.P.C. 85; *Schidrowitz's Patent*, 55 R.P.C. 46.

[52] *Hutchison's Patent*, 14 Moo.P.C. 364.

[53] *Heath's Patent*, 8 Moo.P.C. 217; 2 W.P.C. 247.

[54] *Darby's Patent*, 8 R.P.C. 380; and see *Perry and Brown's Patents*, 48 R.P.C. 200; *Meyer's Patent*, 50 R.P.C. 341.

[55] *Dickson's Patent*, 42 R.P.C. 463.

[56] *Johnson and Atkinson's Patents*, L.R. 5 P.C. 87; *Meyer's Patent*, 50 R.P.C. 341.

[57] *Newton's Patent*, 9 App.Cas. 592; 1 R.P.C. 177; *Yates and Kellett's Patent*, 12 App.Cas. 147; 4 R.P.C. 150.

[58] *Pieper's Patent*, 12 R.P.C. 292.

[59] *Thomas' Patents*, 9 R.P.C. 367 at p. 373.

[60] *Ibid.*; *cf. Shone's Patent*, 9 R.P.C. 438.

petitioners or third parties, must also be shown [61]; and so must the proceeds of the sale by the inventor of his shares in a company formed to exploit the invention.[62]

527   Deductions allowed

In estimating profits deductions will be allowed in respect of expenses reasonably incurred. For example, deductions have been allowed in respect of expenses of experiments in perfecting the invention,[63] cost of taking out and maintaining the patent,[64] cost of properly conducted litigation necessary to maintain the patent and restrain infringements,[65] expenses in bringing the invention into general use,[66] personal expenses of patentee and reasonable payment in respect of time actually devoted by him or by his employees to bringing the invention into practical operation and to public notice,[67] and reasonable depreciation on buildings and plant.[68]

528   Future and foreign profits

In computing the patentee's profits, allowance must be made for those which will probably accrue before expiry of the patent,[69] but as petitions are usually only dealt with shortly before such expiry, the likelihood of substantial future profits before expiry is not great.

Profits on corresponding foreign patents are taken into account as being part of the " circumstances of the case," [70] whether such patents are in the hands of the petitioners or of third parties,[71] thereby continuing the settled practice of the Privy Council.[72]

529   Patentee's distinguished from manufacturer's profits

It is necessary to distinguish between profits or losses which the petitioner would in any case have made in his capacity of a manufacturer and such profits or losses as he makes by reason of his patent.[73] But in some cases the very fact of the ownership of a

---

[61] *Newton's Patent,* 1 R.P.C. 177; *Peach's Patent,* 19 R.P.C. 65; *Maschinenfabrik Augsburg-Nürnberg A.G.'s Patents,* 47 R.P.C. 193.
[62] *Poulsen's Patent,* 30 R.P.C. 597.
[63] *Davies' Patent,* 11 R.P.C. 27.
[64] *Roberts' Patent,* 1 W.P.C. 573.
[65] *Kay's Patent,* 1 W.P.C. 568.
[66] *Galloway's Patent,* 1 W.P.C. 724.
[67] *Furness' Patent,* 2 R.P.C. 175; *Michell's Patent,* 36 R.P.C. 223.
[68] *Trantom's Patent,* 34 R.P.C. 28 at p. 40.
[69] *Johnson's Patent,* 25 R.P.C. 709 at p. 727; *Fleming's Patent,* 36 R.P.C. 55.
[70] s. 23 (5).
[71] *Peach's Patent,* 19 R.P.C. 65; *Newton's Patent,* 1 R.P.C. 177; *Maschinenfabrik Augsburg-Nürnberg A.G.'s Patents,* 47 R.P.C. 193 at p. 214.
[72] *Johnson's Patent,* L.R. 4 P.C. 75; *Newton's Patent,* 1 R.P.C. 177; *Johnson's Patent,* 25 R.P.C. 709; *Maschinenfabrik Augsburg-Nürnberg A.G.'s Patents,* 47 R.P.C. 193.
[73] *Galloway's Patent,* 1 W.P.C. 724 at p. 729; *Thornycroft's Patent,* 16 R.P.C. 202.

patent will be sufficient to increase greatly the number of orders the patentee will receive as a manufacturer, and this will be taken into account in considering the remuneration. In *Saxby's Patent* [74] Lord Cairns said: " It has been decided more than once by this Committee that where the patentee is also the manufacturer the profits which he makes as manufacturer, although they may not be in a strict point of view profits of the patent, must undoubtedly be taken into consideration upon a question of this kind. It is obvious that in different manufactures there will be different degrees of connection between the business of the applicant as a manufacturer and his business or his position as the owner of a patent. There may be patents of some kind which have little or no connection with the business of a manufacturer, and there may be patents of a different kind, where there is an intimate connection with the business of the manufacturer, so that the possession of the patent virtually secures to the patentee his power of commanding orders as a manufacturer." [75]

530 *Remuneration as director and shareholder*

It would seem that remuneration received by the patentee as salary and fees for acting as managing director and director and dividends on shares ought not to be included as being part of the remuneration derived by him from the patent.[76]

The sufficiency of the patentee's remuneration is considered with regard to the importance of the invention and the benefit the public have derived from it. Thus what would be ample remuneration in respect of one invention might be entirely inadequate for another. At one time an extension was refused if the patentee had received £20,000 or more. This rule, however, is no longer applicable.[77]

531 **Default of patentee**

The inadequacy of the patentee's remuneration must not be due to his own default; thus, in *Pieper's Patent* [78] prolongation was refused upon the ground, amongst others, that no steps were taken to push the invention for two-and-a-half years after the date of the patent. Lord Watson said [79]: " Looking at the progressive amounts obtained from year to year under the English patent, it is by no means clear that if due activity had been shown in making the

---

[74] L.R. 3 P.C. 292 at p. 295.
[75] And see *Willans and Robinson's Patent*, 13 R.P.C. 550; *Fleming's Patent*, 36 R.P.C. 55; *cf. United Velvet Cutters Association Ltd.'s Appn.*, 37 R.P.C. 261; *Evans' Patent*, 54 R.P.C. 259.
[76] *Wilson's Patent*, 53 R.P.C. 1.
[77] See *Michell's Patent*, 36 R.P.C. 223 at p. 228; *Hunt's Patents*, 39 R.P.C. 131 at p. 139; *Perry and Brown's Patent*, 48 R.P.C. 200 at p. 212.
[78] 12 R.P.C. 292.
[79] 12 R.P.C. 292 at p. 295.

invention known to persons who were likely to use it in this country, there might not have been, during the last year or two's currency, a sum which, added to those which have actually been obtained, might have amounted to adequate remuneration."

In *Johnson's Patent* [80] Parker J. said: "I do not consider that the reasons given by the petitioner for not bringing his invention prominently before British manufacturers are at all satisfactory. His attitude of mind appears to have been that, if he could not persuade his own firm to give his invention a trial, he certainly would be unable to persuade anyone else, either in America or in England. This may have been quite true with regard to the invention in question, but it is, in my opinion, incumbent on a patentee who invokes the discretionary power conferred by [the Act] to prove that he has done all a patentee could do to launch his invention on the British market. If an invention be of that large value to the public which alone will justify the term of the patent being extended—and there is certainly a chance, and I should say a reasonable chance, of someone being found in this country enterprising enough to give it a trial—the least that can be required of the patentee is to show that he has made an effort to find such a person. The petitioner has been able to convince himself of the value of his process, and I cannot ignore the possibility that with reasonable effort he might have convinced others." [81]

If the patentee is in default in respect of a particular period, then he cannot obtain an extension based upon inadequate remuneration during that period. Nevertheless an extension may be obtained in respect of inadequate remuneration during the rest of the life of the patent.[82]

532 *Patent owned by government department*

A government department which becomes the patentee by assignment and chooses to keep the patent secret, even though this be necessary in the public interest, is not entitled to an extension.[83] On the other hand a service inventor who has assigned his patent to the Crown, but has subsequently had it re-assigned to him, with permission to exploit it commercially, may obtain an extension if, having regard to the merit of the invention, he has been inadequately remunerated.[84]

---

[80] 25 R.P.C. 709 at p. 727.
[81] See also *Poulsen's Patent*, 30 R.P.C. 597 at p. 607; *Hele-Shaw and Beacham's Patent*, 59 R.P.C. 29.
[82] *Fagioli's Patent* [1968] R.P.C. 79.
[83] *Moore and Gallop's Patent*, 65 R.P.C. 220.
[84] *Meredith and Cooke's Patents*, 59 R.P.C. 156.

533 *Manufacture exclusively abroad*

Failure to push the invention may be explained, but strong evidence is necessary for the purpose.[85] This is especially so where manufacture has taken place exclusively abroad.[86]

In *Société Chimique des Usines du Rhone's Patent*[87] Sargant J. said: " I may say that, with regard to an extension of the term of a patent under the ordinary jurisdiction my inclination would be very strong against granting any such extension, whatever the circumstances of the case, where it was the fact that the patented article had been manufactured exclusively abroad. I do not say that there are no cases in which such an extension might be granted, but, as a matter of fact, I have been referred to one only, where such an extension has been granted, and that a very peculiar case, *Hughes' Patent*,[88] and it is obvious that, if one of the objects of the grant of a patent is, as is expressly stated in the Act of 1919, to secure that new inventions should, so far as possible, be worked on a commercial scale in the United Kingdom without undue delay, it is a circumstance almost if not quite fatal to an extension in the ordinary sense of the term of a patent that it has never been worked in this Kingdom." [89]

If manufacture has once been commenced in this country the fact that there has been a considerable period of non-working subsequently is not necessarily a bar to extension.[90]

534 **Lapse of foreign patents**

The effect of a prolongation upon the public is always considered amongst " all the circumstances of the case." For example, where the foreign patents corresponding to a patent in respect of which a petition is presented have expired or are subject to a free licence and in consequence the manufacture may be carried on abroad free from royalties or restrictions, the possibility of prejudicial competition from abroad is an element unfavourable to the grant of an extension. Whether this disadvantage ought to outweigh such rights as a patentee may have to obtain an extension is a question of degree.[91]

In *Pieper's Patent*[92] Lord Watson said: " The patent sought to be prolonged is one of four, three of which were issued in continental countries; one of them expired four years ago, and the last of them

---

[85] *Roper's Patent*, 4 R.P.C. 201; *Henderson's Patent*, 18 R.P.C. 449 at pp. 453, 454.
[86] *General Tire and Rubber Co.'s Patent* [1968] R.P.C. 137.
[87] 39 R.P.C. 27 at p. 32.
[88] 4 App.Cas. 174.
[89] And see *Johnson's Patent*, L.R. 4 P.C. 75 at p. 80; *Poulsen's Patent*, 30 R.P.C. 597; *Neufeldt and Kuhnke G.m.b.H.'s Patents*, 47 R.P.C. 553.
[90] *Faries' Patent*, 43 R.P.C. 349 at p. 351.
[91] *Semet and Solvay's Patent*, 12 R.P.C. 10.
[92] 12 R.P.C. 292 at p. 294.

expired two years ago, since which date the patent in question has still been current, and Her Majesty's subjects exposed to some degree of prejudice, which was not occasioned to the inhabitants of any other country. Their Lordships are not prepared to say that, in these circumstances, there can be no renewal of the patent, but they are certainly prepared to go this length, that the circumstance of its being the last patent, the sole survivor, in these circumstances, is a great obstacle to granting a renewal of it. It would require very strong circumstances to warrant a renewal of the patent; and in this case their Lordships have not been able to find any circumstances which would warrant them in doing so." [93]

535 Existence of exclusive licence

The existence of an exclusive licence as a rule is not a point in favour of prolongation of a patent, but if there is no reason to suppose the public has suffered by reason of such an agreement, prolongation will not be refused upon that ground.[94] It may, however, be a condition that such licence be terminated in so far as it is exclusive.[95]

536 *Uberrima fides*

The utmost good faith is necessary in bringing before the court *all* facts relating to the remuneration of the patentee, or which may otherwise be relevant to " all the circumstances of the case." In *Ferranti's Patent*,[96] for example, it transpired at the hearing that the petitioner had long ago parted with a substantial interest in his invention, and this fact was not disclosed in the petition. Prolongation was refused without any further investigation.[97] In *Meyer's Patent*,[98] however, the applicants were allowed to amend their petition, and also to make a further disclosure of correspondence and documents, it being held that there was no want of bona fides on their part in the first instance.

537 Period of extension

The relation between the degree of merit of the invention and the remuneration received by the patentee together with the circumstances which in the future are likely to tend to a proper remuneration

---

[93] And see *Neufeldt and Kuhnke G.m.b.H.'s Patents*, 47 R.P.C. 553; *Heron's Patent*, 57 R.P.C. 29 at p. 48.
[94] *Darby's Patent*, 8 R.P.C. 380.
[95] *Shone's Patent*, 9 R.P.C. 438; and see *post*, § 543.
[96] 18 R.P.C. 518.
[97] See also *Standfield's Patent*, 15 R.P.C. 17; *Poulsen's Patent*, 30 R.P.C. 597; *Neufeldt and Kuhnke G.m.b.H.'s Patents*, 47 R.P.C. 553 at p. 568; *Schidrowitz's Patent*, 55 R.P.C. 46.
[98] 50 R.P.C. 341.

of the patentee are taken into consideration in determining for what period the patent shall be prolonged. Prolongation is limited to five years or, in an exceptional case, ten years.[99]

In *Stoney's Patent*[1] the patent was for improvements in sluice- or flood-gates, and Sir William Grove said[2]: "As to the duration of the term of prolongation the matter no doubt is a difficult one . . . it must depend very much upon the view which each mind takes of the particular invention to be dealt with, and, moreover, it must also depend not only upon the want of remuneration in the past, but upon the probability of remuneration in the future, and how soon that remuneration is likely to be attained. Now, in the case of a common application . . . relating to ordinary implements of daily use, when the patent once becomes known, and known to be useful, it will get rapidly into use, and if by some means it has been ignored by the public and the patentees come before the court for a prolongation of their patent, the mere advertisement, if I may so call it, of the petition for the prolongation of the patent would materially assist and start the invention, and that in the case of an invention of common and daily use would probably lead to its getting into rapid application, and to its becoming rapidly remunerative to the patentee. But this is not an invention of that description. It is from its nature an invention which cannot be very largely used, and which only applies to peculiar cases. . . . It can, therefore, only be profitably applied at all events in certain large undertakings, which must be few and far between. . . ." It was held to be an "exceptional case" and an extension of ten years was granted.

538 *"Exceptional case"*

The merit of the invention is one of the main elements to be considered in determining whether the case is an exceptional one, but the other "circumstances of the case" must also be considered. In *MacLaurin's Patent*[3] Lord Murray said: "I take an exceptional case to be one which is exceptional in its circumstances, and this includes 'all its circumstances' to which regard is paid . . . and not one of its circumstances alone."

And in *Perry and Brown's Patents*[4] Luxmoore J. said: "I think it is probably right to say that the exceptional cases may fall into three main classes: first of all, if the court is satisfied that the invention is of exceptional ingenuity and also satisfies the condition

[99] s. 23 (1).
[1] 5 R.P.C. 518.
[2] 5 R.P.C. 518 at p. 523.
[3] 47 R.P.C. 14 at p. 21.
[4] 48 R.P.C. 200 at p. 214.

that it is useful to the public. That, of course, is with regard to the
exceptional character of the invention itself. . . . The second head,
I think, is if the invention has sufficient merit to warrant an extension, and is also of exceptional benefit to the public. . . . The third
head is if, upon a review of the whole of the circumstances of the
case, it appears that the invention is inherently of such a character
that it must take longer than usual to get it on the market." [5] However these three classes are not definitive.[6] Where it is contended that
the invention is " exceptional," it is advisable for the patentee to
file evidence from an independent expert.[7]

539 *Extension of meritorious part*
       Where one part of the invention is sufficiently meritorious and
another part is not so, an extension of the term may be granted in
respect of the meritorious part only, incidental verbal alterations
being allowed in the extended claims so as to make them read
correctly, having regard to the omission of other claims.[8]

540 *Related patents*
       Where an extension is granted in respect of two patents, one of
which is later than and subsidiary to the other, the second patent is
usually extended until the date of expiry of the extended first patent.[9]

541 Imposition of conditions
       It has long been the practice in certain cases for the Privy Council,
and later for the court, to impose conditions upon which a patent
will be extended, and authority is given by the Act [10] for the court to
impose such restrictions, conditions and provisions as it thinks fit.

542 *Conditions in favour of inventor*
       Where the petitioner is an assignee, and offers to give to the
inventor some interest in the prolonged patent or some other
pecuniary benefit, the court may make the carrying out of such offer

---

[5] And see *Currie and Timmis' Patent*, 15 R.P.C. 63; *McCulloch's Patent*, 25
   R.P.C. 684; *Smith's Patents*, 39 R.P.C. 313; *Dickson's Patent*, 42 R.P.C. 463;
   Hilger (Adam) Ltd., Twyman and Green's Patents, 49 R.P.C. 245; *Moore's
   Patent*, 64 R.P.C. 5; *Pomieraniec's Patent*, 65 R.P.C. 33; *Whittle's Patent*,
   69 R.P.C. 121; *Garchey's Patents*, 71 R.P.C. 362. Where there is also a
   " war loss," see *Staatsmijnen in Limburg's Patent* [1962] R.P.C. at p. 131.
[6] *G.K.N. Somerset Wire Ltd.'s Patent* [1970] F.S.R. 335.
[7] *Elliott Brothers (London) Ltd.'s Patent* [1968] R.P.C. 186.
[8] *Lodge's Patent*, 28 R.P.C. 365; *Ferranti's Patent*, 35 R.P.C. 149; *Meyer's
   Patent*, 50 R.P.C. 341.
[9] *Church's Patent*, 3 R.P.C. 95; *Smith's Patents*, 39 R.P.C. 313 at p. 323;
   Stiff's Patents, 40 R.P.C. 459; *Schoop and Morf's Patents*, 43 R.P.C. 74.
   But see *Mikklesen's Patent*, 44 R.P.C. 12; *Western Electric Co. Ltd.'s
   Patent*, 49 R.P.C. 342.
[10] s. 23 (1).

a condition of the extension [11]; a similar condition has been imposed in an application based on war loss,[12] but it is doubtful whether the court will impose any such condition without such a previous offer by the petitioner.[13]

543 *Conditions in favour of public, or third parties*

Conditions are also sometimes imposed for the benefit of the public, ensuring that they shall be entitled to licences to use the invention upon reasonable terms. In *Lyon's Patent* [14] an exclusive licensee was required to renounce his exclusive licence,[15] and the extension was granted upon the condition that the petitioner should grant licences on the same terms to all persons who might desire to use the invention; and the royalty receivable was limited.[16] In other cases licences have been required to be granted, or articles supplied, upon terms to be fixed by arbitration.[17] Similar conditions have also been imposed in cases based on war loss.[18]

In *Church's Patents* [19] a condition was imposed that an unpaid mortgagee should be given the same security over the new patent that he had over the old.

It has also been made a condition that existing licences should be continued on the same terms,[20] and (in war loss extensions) that the applicants would use their best endeavours to procure the registration of existing and future licences.[21] Where the patent was indorsed " licences of right," the indorsement was ordered to remain but without prejudice to the right of the patentee to obtain cancellation thereof,[22] and an extension has been granted subject to the patent being so indorsed.[23] In *Howarth's Patent*,[24] where there was a verbal

---

[11] *Whitehouse's Patent,* 1 W.P.C. 473; *Ritchie's Patent,* 31 R.P.C. 1 at p. 8; *Goodwin and Smith's Patents,* 57 R.P.C. 1.

[12] *Hatfield and Reason Co.'s Patents,* 37 R.P.C. 273.

[13] *Ferranti's Patent,* 35 R.P.C. 149 at p. 160; *Dickson's Patent,* 42 R.P.C. 463 at p. 470; but see *Fleming and Gale's Patents,* 36 R.P.C. 266.

[14] 11 R.P.C. 537.

[15] See also *Shone's Patent,* 9 R.P.C. 438.

[16] See also *Hunt's Patents,* 39 R.P.C. 131; *Goodwin and Smith's Patents,* 57 R.P.C. 1.

[17] *Lodge's Patent,* 28 R.P.C. 365; *Dewar's Patent,* 35 R.P.C. 229; *Taylor's Patent,* 35 R.P.C. 247; *Michell's Patent,* 36 R.P.C. 223; *Fleming and Gale's Patents,* 36 R.P.C. 266.

[18] *Petersen's Patent,* 38 R.P.C. 267; *Hunt's Patents,* 39 R.P.C. 131; *Osborne and Nield's Patent,* 39 R.P.C. 143.

[19] 3 R.P.C. 95.

[20] *Hunt's Patents,* 39 R.P.C. 131 at p. 140.

[21] *Schoop and Morf's Patents,* 43 R.P.C. 74; *British Thomson-Houston Co. Ltd.'s Patent,* 46 R.P.C. 367; *Meyer's Patent,* 50 R.P.C. 341 at p. 355.

[22] *Sanders' Patent,* 48 R.P.C. 342.

[23] *Whitney and Others' Patents,* 60 R.P.C. 69.

[24] 39 R.P.C. 140.

licence, the applicant gave an undertaking to embody the agreement in a deed and register the same.

Where the applicant was not the beneficial owner, an extension has been granted subject to the patent being assigned and the assignment registered [25]; but this has not been followed.[26]

544 *Conditions where patent has expired*

Where an extension is granted but the patent has expired prior to the hearing of the application, conditions are imposed for the protection of persons who may have made use of the invention bona fide during the period between the date of expiry and the date of the order. The form of order normally made is that now known as the " New Gillette Order." [27]

545 More than one extension

Not more than one extension can be granted on the ground of insufficient remuneration to the patentee but one such extension can be granted in addition to one or more extensions on the ground of war loss.[28] The aggregate of war loss extensions must not exceed ten years [29] so that twenty years is the maximum possible extension.

546 Renewal fees

Renewal fees are not payable in respect of the extended term of a patent.

547 Practice

The practice upon petition for extension is regulated by Order 103, rr 3 to 8 [30] of the Rules of the Supreme Court.

548 Parties

The petition must be presented by " a patentee," that is to say, by the registered proprietor of the patent.[31] He is, therefore, a necessary party. Where, however, the patentee is an assignee, the practice is to join all previous patentees as co-petitioners. An exclusive licensee, though not " a patentee," should also be joined for the purpose of ensuring complete disclosure of all relevant facts and, if necessary, of releasing his exclusive rights under the licence.[32]

---

[25] *Panicali and Brenni's Patent*, 44 R.P.C. 509.
[26] *White and Gray's Patent*, 45 R.P.C. 119; *Smith (H. E.)'s Patent*, 46 R.P.C. 400 at p. 402.
[27] *Siemens Brothers & Co. Ltd.'s Patent*, 68 R.P.C. 61 at p. 63. See *post*, § 2023.
[28] s. 23 (6).
[29] s. 24 (7).
[30] *Post*, § 1590 *et seq.*
[31] ss. 23 (1), 101 (1).
[32] *Shone's Patent*, 9 R.P.C. 438.

If the registered proprietor is a bare trustee the beneficial owner should be joined.[33]

If the petitioner fails to provide evidence of his title to the invention an extension may be ordered subject to the petitioner proving his title to the satisfaction of the Comptroller.[34]

The court may dispense with the presence of former owners, particularly where the original inventor assigned the patent on grant in pursuance of a previous agreement.[35]

If any former owners refuse to join as co-petitioners it would appear necessary to make them respondents unless they are before the court as opponents.[36]   If they are joined as respondents then directions will be given on the appointed day for them to elect whether to withdraw from the proceeding or lodge and serve particulars of objections.[37]   The Comptroller must in any case be made a respondent.[38]

549   Petition

The petition should state the whole history of the patent and all facts which may be relevant for the consideration of the court.[39]

Two or more patents may be made the subject of the same petition,[40] provided that their respective dates of expiry will allow the petition to be presented within the specified time.

550   *Time of presenting the petition*

The petition must be presented not more than twelve months nor less than six months before expiry of the patent, but the court has discretion to allow it to be presented at any time before the date of expiry.[41]

Leave should be obtained to present the petition during the Long Vacation,[42] but every effort should be made to present the petition prior to the Long Vacation.[43]

Where it is necessary to apply after the specified date the petition should contain a statement that it is out of time and it should be

---

[33] *Bates' Patent*, 38 R.P.C. 385.
[34] *Fagioli's Patent* [1968] R.P.C. 79.
[35] *Dressler's Patent (No. 2)*, 46 R.P.C. 165; *Larsson's Patent*, 43 R.P.C. 179; *Smith's Patents*, 46 R.P.C. 166; *Clyde and Dobbie McInnes Ltd.'s Patent*, 46 R.P.C. 429.
[36] See *Beard and Scott's Patents*, 45 R.P.C. 31 (under subs. (6)).
[37] *Ajax Magnethermic Corpn.'s Patent* [1965] R.P.C. 480; and see [1966] R.P.C. 233 at p. 240.
[38] R.S.C., Ord. 103, r. 4 (1).
[39] *Singer-Cobble & Card's Patent* [1970] F.S.R. 188.
[40] *Church's Patent*, 3 R.P.C. 95.
[41] s. 23 (2).
[42] *Steffan's Patent*, 33 R.P.C. 324; *Wade's Patent* [1961] R.P.C. 26.
[43] *Philips Electrical Ltd.'s Patent* [1965] R.P.C. 96.

presented in the ordinary way. Affidavits stating the reason for the delay should be filed, and leave to present the petition out of time should be asked for when the application is made to fix the " appointed day " (see *infra*).[44] If on the " appointed day " the affidavit evidence is found to be insufficient, leave may be given to supplement this evidence.[45] If the delay is due to a deliberate election not to proceed at the proper time, the application will be refused,[46] but an explanation which shows that the delay was unintentional and inadvertent will normally be accepted.[47]

551　*Application*

The first step for a party intending to apply by petition is to give public notice of his intention by advertisement in certain specified classes of newspaper, which advertisements must contain certain specified information.[48] A copy of the advertisement must be sent to the Solicitor to the Department of Trade and Industry for publication in the *Official Journal* (Patents).[49]

The petition must be presented within one week of publication of the last advertisement, and a copy served on the Solicitor to the Department of Trade and Industry,[50] accompanied by an affidavit stating that all necessary advertisements have been published.[51] A petition that has not been duly advertised will not be considered by the court for any purpose.[52]

Application is made to the court on the day stated in the advertisements to fix the appointed day. Any opponent who has lodged a notice of opposition is entitled to be heard on this application.[53] Counsel on behalf of the Comptroller also appears. Any directions which may be necessary, such as leave to present the petition out of time, for example, should be applied for on this application.[54]

The petitioner must lodge at least three weeks before the appointed day two copies of the specification and two copies of the accounts. Two copies of the specification and of the accounts must also be served on the Solicitor to the Department of Trade and Industry, who has power to inspect his books.[55]

---

[44] *Ruth's Patent*, 48 R.P.C. 553.
[45] *Ambler's Patents* [1965] R.P.C. 17.
[46] *Petersen's Patent*, 38 R.P.C. 267.
[47] *Cossor A.C. Ltd.'s Appn.* [1960] R.P.C. 232.
[48] R.S.C., Ord. 103, r. 3. See *post*, § 1590 *et seq.*
[49] *Ibid.* r. 3 (2).
[50] *Ibid.* r. 4 (1).
[51] *Ibid.* r. 4 (5).
[52] *Victor Trief's Appn.*, 71 R.P.C. 99.
[53] Ord. 103, r. 5 (3).
[54] See *e.g. Maschinenfabrik Augsburg-Nürnberg A.G.'s Patents*, 47 R.P.C. 193.
[55] Ord. 103, r. 7 (1).

552 Opposition

Any person is entitled to oppose and a government department which opposes should be separately represented from the Comptroller where there may be differing views to be put forward by the Comptroller to the government department.[56]

An opponent must lodge his notice of opposition before the date mentioned in the original advertisements. He must also serve a copy of it upon the petitioner and the Solicitor to the Department of Trade and Industry.[57] Upon receiving the notice of opposition, the petitioner must serve a copy of the petition upon the opponent.[58]

Within three weeks of such service, the opponent must lodge two copies of his particulars of objections, and serve one copy upon the petitioner and three copies upon the Solicitor to the Department of Trade and Industry otherwise he is deemed to have abandoned the opposition.[59]

It would appear that the time for delivering particulars of objections runs during the Long Vacation.[60]

After the particulars of objections have been delivered an opponent becomes entitled to obtain copies of the accounts at his own expense,[61] and he must be served with notice of the appointed day.[62]

553 *Grounds of opposition*

An opposition may clearly be based on the grounds that the invention is not of sufficient merit to justify an extension, or that the patentee has in fact been adequately remunerated. Any matter which is relevant for the consideration of the court as one of " the circumstances of the case " is, however, available as a ground of opposition.

554 *Particulars of objections*

As to the form of the particulars of objections, the considerations that apply are those applicable to pleadings generally, that is to say, the information should be sufficient to inform the petitioner exactly what is alleged to prevent an extension being obtainable.[63] An opponent will be confined to the grounds stated in his particulars.[64]

The Comptroller need not give particulars of objections, nor particulars of any evidence he intends to adduce at the hearing of

---

[56] *Western Electric Co.'s Patent* [1965] R.P.C. 335 and see *Western Electric Co. Ltd.'s Patents*, 49 R.P.C. 342.
[57] Ord. 103, r. 5 (1).
[58] *Ibid.* r. 5 (2).
[59] *Ibid.* rr. 6 (1), 7 (2).
[60] See *Stearn's Patents*, 28 R.P.C. 663 at p. 664.
[61] Ord. 103, r. 7 (5).
[62] *Ibid.* r. 8 (1).
[63] *Johnson's Patent*, 25 R.P.C. 542 at p. 545.
[64] Ord. 103, r. 7 (4).

the petition.[65]   In practice, however, particulars are usually furnished as a matter of grace.[66]

The court has power to excuse compliance with the rules,[67] but not with statutory requirements.[68]   Thus the time for delivery of particulars of objections has been extended,[69] and so also has the time for lodging a notice of opposition,[70] but this will be done only for good reasons.[71]

555   Amendment

The court has jurisdiction under Order 20, rule 8, of the Rules of the Supreme Court to permit amendment of the petition and particulars of objections.[72]   An amendment may necessitate re-advertisement.

556   Setting down for hearing

The petition may not be entered for trial until the time for delivering the particulars of objections has expired and an affidavit has been lodged showing that the petition has been served on all opponents.[73]

557   *Adjournment*

If infringement proceedings are pending, the result of which may greatly affect the remuneration of the patentee and may determine other relevant questions, the application for extension may be adjourned.[74]

558   The hearing

Evidence at the hearing is normally given *viva voce*.   In *Schwerin's Patent*,[75] where the petitioners were a foreign company and an inventor resident abroad, prima facie proof of the devolution of interest and an abstract from the accounts were allowed to be given by sworn declaration.

Counsel appears at the hearing on behalf of the Comptroller.   His duty is as much to assist the court as to oppose, and, indeed, only to oppose when, in his judgment, an extension should not be granted.[76]

---

[65] *Ibid.* r. 15.
[66] *Hood and Salamon's Patent*, 41 R.P.C. 592 at p. 597; and see *Johnson's Patent*, 25 R.P.C. 709 at p. 728.
[67] R.S.C., Ord. 103, r. 14.
[68] *Frieze Greene's Patent*, 24 R.P.C. 464; *Stearn's Patents*, 28 R.P.C. 663.
[69] *Barton's Patents*, 29 R.P.C. 207; *Stearn's Patents*, 28 R.P.C. 663.
[70] *Maschinenfabrik Augsburg-Nürnberg A.G.'s Patents*, 47 R.P.C. 193.
[71] See *Hopkinson's Patent*, 13 R.P.C. 114.
[72] See *Meyer's Patent*, 50 R.P.C. 341.
[73] R.S.C., Ord. 103, r. 8.
[74] *G. M. Giannini & Co. Inc.'s Patent* [1956] R.P.C. 318.
[75] 31 R.P.C. 229.
[76] *Stoney's Patent*, 5 R.P.C. 518 at p. 522.

Where the opposition is withdrawn the court may require an explanation of the circumstances, and an affidavit that there is no collusion may also be required.[77]

559 Costs

The court may award costs to or against the opponents.[78] The principle on which they are awarded is the same whether the application is by petition or originating summons. It is as follows: The opponents will be awarded costs if the petition fails and the court has been materially assisted by the opposition.[79] In the same circumstances no costs will be given against them if an extension is granted.[80] If, however, the only effect of the opposition is to prolong the inquiry, no costs will be given the opponent even if the petition fails.[81] If there is no ground for the opposition costs may be awarded against the opponents.[82] Where there are several opponents only one set of costs will be given amongst them except under special circumstances.[83] The Comptroller may be awarded costs, including the costs of investigating the accounts.[84]

560 *Costs on withdrawal*

Where leave is granted to withdraw the petition only one set of costs is given amongst the opponents.[85] Where some of several co-petitioners withdrew by leave they were ordered to pay the costs of the opponents up to the date of their withdrawal, but without prejudice to any right of recovery from the other co-petitioners.[86] In inadequate remuneration cases it is not usual for costs to be awarded against an opponent who withdraws at an early stage.[87] However, in war loss cases opponents who withdrew after giving notice of opposition have been ordered to pay the costs in so far as they have been

---

[77] See *Meyer's Patent*, 50 R.P.C. 341 at p. 350; and *post*, § 578.

[78] R.S.C., Ord. 62, r. 6 (1) (*e*).

[79] See *Wield's Patent* (1871) L.R. 4 P.C. 89 at p. 92; *Maschinenfabrik Augsburg-Nürnberg A.G.'s Patents*, 47 R.P.C. 193.

[80] *Johnston's Patents*, 44 R.P.C. 254; *Dicker's Patent (No. 2)*, 44 R.P.C. 263; *British Thomson-Houston Co. Ltd.'s Patent*, 46 R.P.C. 367.

[81] *Muntz's Patent*, 2 W.P.C. 113 at p. 122.

[82] *Downton's Patent*, 1 W.P.C. 565 at p. 567.

[83] R.S.C., Ord. 62, r. 6 (1) (*e*). see *Western Electric Co.'s Patent* [1965] R.P.C. 335 at p. 346.

[84] See Administration of Justice (Miscellaneous Provisions) Act 1933, s. 7; *Tribe's Patent*, 53 R.P.C. 131; *Evans' Patent*, 54 R.P.C. 259; *Elkington's Patent*, 63 R.P.C. 50.

[85] *Imray's Patent*, 26 R.P.C. 11; *Stearn's Patents*, 28 R.P.C. 696; *Wade's Patent*, 46 R.P.C. 518.

[86] *Maschinenfabrik Augsburg-Nürnberg A.G.'s Patents*, 47 R.P.C. 193.

[87] *Western Electric Co.'s Patent* [1965] R.P.C. 335 at p. 346.

increased by the opposition.[88]   But where the opponents withdrew
by leave after an amendment of the petition, the petitioners were
ordered to pay the opponents' costs.[89]

2. APPLICATION ON GROUND OF WAR LOSS

561   The existence of hostilities between this country and foreign states
may cause a loss of remuneration to the patentee, as he may be
unable to exploit the invention owing to loss of markets, shortage of
material, or himself be engaged in war work.   The patentee may
apply at his option to the court or to the Comptroller for an extension
on these grounds.   If he applies to the court, he may go by petition
or by originating summons [90] and in the former case both inadequacy
of remuneration and war loss may be taken into account.   If the
Comptroller considers that an application made to him raises issues
more fitting to be decided by the court, he may refer the matter to
the court.[91]   There is no appeal from the decision of the court but
an appeal lies from the Comptroller to the Appeal Tribunal.[92]   In
practically every case an application for extension based on war loss
only is now made to the Comptroller.   Where a petition is based on
both grounds an extension may be granted on the ground of loss due
to hostilities alone.[93]

562   Alien enemies
This ground of extension is not applicable if the patentee is a
subject of an enemy state, or is a company the business of which is
managed, controlled by or carried on for the benefit of subjects of an
enemy state.[94]   In a case where the patents had been owned by alien
enemies on the outbreak of war, but their interest ceased after a
short period, it was held that this restriction did not apply.[95]   The
decree of an enemy government purporting to alter the nationality
of its nationals during hostilities will not be recognised.[96]

563   What must be proved
The matters to be proved by the applicant are: (1) That he has
suffered loss or damage; it is not sufficient merely to establish that

[88] See *Dressler's Patent*, 44 R.P.C. 203; *Martineau's Patent*, 44 R.P.C. 205;
British Thomson-Houston Co. Ltd.'s Patent, 46 R.P.C. 367.
[89] *Meyer's Patent*, 50 R.P.C. 341 at p. 350.
[90] s. 24 (4).   [91] s. 24 (2).
[92] s. 24 (9).
[93] *Petersen's Patent*, 38 R.P.C. 267; *Hunt's Patents*, 39 R.P.C. 131; *Morf's
Patent*, 46 R.P.C. 335.
[94] s. 24 (8).   And see *Ring Springs Patent*, 61 R.P.C. 73; *Giacchino's Patent*,
62 R.P.C. 143; *Mangold's Patent*, 68 R.P.C. 1.
[95] *Stirling's Patent*, 46 R.P.C. 133.
[96] *Lowenthal* v. *Att.-Gen.*, 65 R.P.C. 126.

there was a period when exploitation of the patent was impossible [97]; (2) That such loss was caused by hostilities between this country and a foreign state [98]; and (3) That he is not the subject of an enemy state.

"Foreign state" may include unrecognised states for this purpose.[98]

The onus of proof is on the applicant as to each of these matters.[99]

564 *Loss as patentee*

The loss must be suffered by "the patentee as such," or by a sole licensee.[1] The word "patentee" includes both the registered proprietor and any former owners, and the applicant may rely on loss suffered by an assignor.[2] Loss suffered during the period from the priority date of a foreign application to the date when application is made for the British patent under the International Convention can not be considered, because there can be no "patentee" before such application is made.[3] A licensee may be joined as a co-applicant.[4]

Persons receiving their remuneration in the form of dividends on shares,[5] or as commissions on sales,[6] have been held to suffer loss "as patentee."

565 *Loss as licensee*

A licensee must hold a formal executed licence, covering the period of the loss claimed, in order that he may institute proceedings for extension under section 25.[7] In an application for extension by a licensee, evidence from the patentee is necessary.[8]

566 *Nature of loss*

The fact that the loss has been suffered in common with other members of the community is immaterial,[9] and extensions have been

---

[97] *Marconi's Wireless Telegraph Co. Ltd.'s Patent* [1959] R.P.C. 267.

[98] *Al-Fin Corpn.'s Patent* [1970] R.P.C. 49.

[99] *Rushton's Patent*, 40 R.P.C. 30; *Wöhler's Patent*, 40 R.P.C. 49; *Evans' Patent*, 43 R.P.C. 345; *Stock's Patent*, 41 R.P.C. 647; *Johnson & Johnson (Gt. Britain) Ltd.'s Patent*, 71 R.P.C. 288; *National Broach and Machine Co.'s Appn.*, 71 R.P.C. 368; *Wade's Patent*, 72 R.P.C. 181.

[1] s. 25, and see *ante*, §§ 512, 520.

[2] *Summers Brown's Patent*, 39 R.P.C. 367; see also *Bennet's Patent*, 39 R.P.C. 447; *Mikklesen's Patent*, 44 R.P.C. 12; *Western Electric Co. Ltd.'s Patent*, 48 R.P.C. 155.

[3] *Ransburg & Ors' Patent* [1960] R.P.C. 242.

[4] *British Brass Fittings Ltd.'s Patent*, 60 R.P.C. 84.

[5] *Macgregor's Patent*, 40 R.P.C. 157; *Schutze's Patent*, 41 R.P.C. 343; *Chambers' Patent*, 44 R.P.C. 332.

[6] *Howarth's Patent*, 39 R.P.C. 140.

[7] *Courtauld's Ltd.'s Appn.* [1956] R.P.C. 208; *Kores Manufacturing Co. Ltd.'s Appn.* [1958] R.P.C. 448.

[8] *Pegson Ltd.'s Patent*, 71 R.P.C. 427.

[9] *United Velvet Cutters Association Ltd.'s Patent*, 37 R.P.C. 261.

granted where a loss was attributable *inter alia* to causes such as the following: lack of demand for the article in this country[10] or abroad,[11] difficulty in obtaining material and labour,[12] works being a controlled establishment[13] or engaged in manufacture of munitions,[14] absence of staff on war service,[15] Government restriction on manufacture,[16] and the like.[17] But loss due to inability to manufacture occasioned by the war, if stocks are available, and loss due to the threat of war cannot be considered.[18]

567   Measure of loss

The extension granted should be commensurate with the number of patented articles lost rather than related to the period of time apparently lost[19] though the latter may sometimes be the only reasonable basis.[20] Unless the Comptroller has not correctly appreciated the effect of the evidence, or has misdirected himself, the Patents Appeal Tribunal will not on appeal interfere with the Comptroller's estimation of the loss.[21]

If the loss has been suffered only in one field covered by the patent, an extension may be granted in respect of other fields, this result being secured by requiring the patent to be indorsed " licences of right "[22] and ordering that free licences shall be granted in the field wherein no loss has been suffered.[23]

The circumstances causing the loss or damage obviously may continue for some time after hostilities have ceased, and loss during such period may be relied upon.[24]

The effect of hostilities may, however, in some cases be to cause a loss of a purely temporary nature which will be recouped by

---

[10] *Crighton's Patent,* 39 R.P.C. 259.
[11] *Ewart & Son Ltd., and Ewart's Patent,* 40 R.P.C. 155.
[12] *Hatfield and Reason Manufacturing Co. Ltd.'s Patents,* 37 R.P.C. 273.
[13] *Jerram's Patent,* 40 R.P.C. 74.
[14] *Young's Patent,* 39 R.P.C. 364.
[15] *Metropolitan Co. and Greg's Patent,* 37 R.P.C. 266; *Claude's Patents,* 44 R.P.C. 17 at p. 18.
[16] *Bennet's Patent,* 39 R.P.C. 447; *Casmey's Patent,* 40 R.P.C. 99.
[17] And see *Wöhler's Patent,* 40 R.P.C. 49; *Brown and Brown's Patent,* 40 R.P.C. 95; *Matter's Patent,* 41 R.P.C. 341; *Wilderman's Patent,* 42 R.P.C. 42; *Sheffield and Twinderbarrow's Patent,* 43 R.P.C. 165; *Dicker's Patent,* 43 R.P.C. 167; *Bouyer's Patent,* 45 R.P.C. 268; *A. C. Neilsen Co.'s Patent,* 72 R.P.C. 251.
[18] *Allbook and Hashfield's Patent,* 61 R.P.C. 45.
[19] *Siemens Brothers & Co. Ltd.'s Patent,* 69 R.P.C. 96; *R. v. Appeal Tribunal, ex p. Champion Paper & Fibre Co.* [1956] R.P.C. 323.
[20] *Smyth Manufacturing Co.'s Patent,* 72 R.P.C. 112.
[21] *Chanoin's Patent,* 70 R.P.C. 181.
[22] See *post,* § 656 *et seq.*
[23] *Smith, Garnet and Randall's Patent,* 67 R.P.C. 170.
[24] *Sheffield and Twinderbarrow's Patent,* 43 R.P.C. 165.

abnormally large sales in the period immediately following the cessation of hostilities. In such cases the temporary loss cannot be relied upon.[25]

568 *Scope of claims*

In order to arrive at the correct measure of loss it may be necessary to put a provisional interpretation on the claims, which, however, would not be binding in any subsequent proceedings.[26] Any sums probably recoverable as damages, royalties or compensation in respect of Crown user must be taken into account when estimating the loss.[27]

569 **Accounts**

The accounts need not be as detailed as in the case of a petition, but they should be sufficient to show the contrast between the sales and receipts in normal times and those in the period affected by hostilities. The receipts for each year should be shown, and where the invention is in an article, the number of articles sold per annum should be given. Sales to the government must be taken into account, but where these yield a smaller profit or royalty than normal commercial sales they should be estimated at a lower rate.[28]

570 *Foreign patents and profits*

Though information as to corresponding foreign patents should be given, the lapse of such patents is not in practice considered.[29] But an extension may be reduced so that the British patents expire co-terminously with the foreign patents.[30]

Profits from foreign patents should be disclosed, but will not be taken into account unless due to the hostilities upon which the applicant relies.[31] Where a foreign applicant was prohibited by his municipal law from giving evidence to prove that increased profits during hostilities were not due to such hostilities an extension was refused.[32] Transfer of foreign markets by a parent company to the

---

[25] *Rushton's Patent*, 40 R.P.C. 30; *Western Electric Co. Ltd.'s Patent*, 49 R.P.C. 342; and see *Higginson and Arundel's Patent*, 44 R.P.C. 430 at p. 436; *cf. Bates' Patent*, 45 R.P.C. 270 at p. 274.

[26] *Weber's Patent*, 63 R.P.C. 154.

[27] *Harries' Patent*, 65 R.P.C. 132; *Martin and the Daimler Co. Ltd.'s Patent*, 65 R.P.C. 173; *Sarazin's Patent*, 64 R.P.C. 51.

[28] *Van Berkel's Patent*, 61 R.P.C. 85.

[29] *Haddan's Patents*, 41 R.P.C. 166; see also *Kay and Foxwell's Patent*, 42 R.P.C. 222.

[30] *Kettering and Chryst's Patent*, 42 R.P.C. 507.

[31] *Kay and Foxwell's Patent*, 42 R.P.C. 222; *Duffy and Firmosec's Patents*, 59 R.P.C. 124.

[32] *Von Kantzow's Patent*, 61 R.P.C. 109.

applicant, resulting in an increase of post-war export sales, need not be taken into account.[33]

571 *Manufacture exclusively abroad*

Where the patented article has been manufactured exclusively abroad and has been imported into this country through selling agents, this fact is not necessarily fatal in a war loss case.[34] But although an extension for war loss may be regarded as a substitutional term, its effect upon the public interest may be quite different from that of the original term and this must be taken into account.[35]

The provisions for extension on the ground of war loss are quite independent of those for extension on the ground of inadequate remuneration and it is submitted that the practice should be continued whereby in war loss cases no matters other than those set out above need be considered.

The utmost good faith must be shown in bringing all relevant facts to the notice of the court.[36]

The fact that the invention has not been worked at all in this country is not an objection to an extension where it is due to the existence of hostilities.[37]

Period

Where there has not been a " suspended demand " or other circumstances which adversely affect the applicant's case, the general practice is to grant an extension which shall be equal to the period of the useful life of the patent which has been affected by hostilities.[38]

572 **Conditions imposed**

An extension may be subjected to conditions such as the continuance of existing licences, and the registration of agreements and the like.[39] Where two patents are closely related as to subject-matter the latter may be made to expire with the earlier if both are extended.[40]

Any number of applications for extension on the ground of war loss may be made, provided the total extension does not exceed ten

---

[33] *Wayne Pump Co.'s Appn.*, 71 R.P.C. 268.

[34] *Société Chimique des Usines du Rhone's Patent*, 39 R.P.C. 27 at p. 32.

[35] *Von Kantzow's Patent (supra); Sandoz Ltd.'s Patent*, 71 R.P.C. 85.

[36] *Brown and Bostock's Patent*, 48 R.P.C. 215; *British Thomson-Houston Co. Ltd.'s Patents*, 49 R.P.C. 218; *Harries' Patents*, 68 R.P.C. 277; *Ever-Ready Co. (Gt. Britain) Ltd.'s Appn.* [1958] R.P.C. 431; *Gevaert Photo Producten N.V.'s Appn.* [1958] R.P.C. 443.

[37] *Dicker's Patent*, 43 R.P.C. 167; *Faries' Patent*, 43 R.P.C. 349.

[38] See *Société Chimique des Usines du Rhone's Patent*, 39 R.P.C. 27 at p. 33; *British Thomson-Houston Co. Ltd.'s Patent*, 46 R.P.C. 367; *Western Electric Co. Ltd.'s Patent*, 48 R.P.C. 218.

[39] See *ante*, § 543.   [40] See *ante*, § 540.

years.[41]   It is the usual practice to have regard only to such loss as has been proved prior to the date of the hearing and to leave any further loss to be dealt with by a subsequent application.

Where a patent has expired conditions are imposed protecting persons who have used the invention bona fide between the date of expiry and the date of the Order.[42]

573   Practice

The practice is regulated by Order 103, rules 9 to 15, of the Rules of the Supreme Court,[43] where the application is made to the court by originating summons, and by rules 70 to 77 of the Patents Rules 1968 [44] before the Comptroller.

The application must be made by the registered proprietor, and the loss suffered by former owners must be satisfactorily proved.

Two or more patents may be made the subject of one application,[45] so long as their respective expiry dates are sufficiently near to each other.

574   *Time*

The application must be made not more than twelve or less than six months before the expiration of the term of the patent, or at such later time as the court or Comptroller may allow.[46]   But no application may be made after expiry of the patent unless the court or Comptroller is satisfied that the applicant was unable to apply before expiry by reason of being on active service or by other circumstances due to hostilities.[47]   Leave may be granted to present a petition in the Long Vacation.[48]

575   *Successive applications*

In order to avoid the expense of a number of successive applications where the circumstances giving rise to war loss remain unchanged the court may postpone the hearing of a subsequent application.[49]

576   Order conclusive

The decision reached at the hearing of an application for extension on the ground of war loss is conclusive as to the basis on which it is

[41] s. 24 (7).
[42] *Barr's Patent*, 65 R.P.C. 327; *Morton's Patent*, 65 R.P.C. 357; *Siemens Brothers & Co. Ltd.'s Patent*, 68 R.P.C. at p. 63; and see *ante*, § 554.
[43] See *post*, § 1596 *et seq*.
[44] See *post*, § 1416 *et seq*.
[45] *Hatfield and Reason & Co.'s Patents*, 37 R.P.C. 273.
[46] s. 24 (3).   See *Löffler's Patent*, 56 R.P.C. 97; *Oxley Engineering Co. Ltd.'s Appn.*, 68 R.P.C. 153.
[47] s. 24 (3), proviso.
[48] *Philips Electrical's Patent* [1965] R.P.C. 96.
[49] *Molins' Patent*, 61 R.P.C. 69.

to be assessed and the extent of the loss during the period covered by it and cannot be reopened notwithstanding the possibility of a more accurate assessment having regard to subsequent events.[50]

However, in cases where the applicant is given an " interim " extension [51] a fresh opponent will not be prevented from raising an objection that may be relevant on an application for a further extension.[52]

577   Opposition

Any person is entitled to oppose, including a licensee.[53]   The procedure to be followed is set out in the relevant rules.[54]   In practice the only ground of opposition in a war loss case on which an opponent can hope to succeed is to establish that there has in fact been no loss due to hostilities.   Unless, therefore, an opponent can establish that the evidence filed on behalf of the applicant is incorrect, he is unlikely to succeed in his opposition.

The court has power to excuse compliance with the Rules [55] but not with statutory requirements.   Thus where a copy of an advertisement had been served on the Solicitor to the Department of Trade and Industry out of time the irregularity was excused.[56]

The production of documents may be obtained, but an opponent is not entitled to discovery of every document he may consider relevant.[57]   Evidence may be withheld from the opponents themselves and disclosed only to their legal advisers if this is desirable in the interests of justice.[58]

Evidence before the court is normally by affidavit only and before the Comptroller by statutory declaration.   Adjournments have sometimes been granted where the evidence is insufficient in order to enable it to be supplemented,[59] and usually an opportunity will be given of clearing up an ambiguity in an affidavit.[60]

---

[50] *Armstrong's Patent,* 66 R.P.C. 81; *Herbert Terry & Sons Ltd. and Carwardine's Appn.,* 71 R.P.C. 81; *Schramm's Patent,* 72 R.P.C. 114; *A.B.A. Specialities Co. Inc. Patent* [1957] R.P.C. 203.
[51] *Liebowitz's Appn.,* 72 R.P.C. 280.
[52] *Philips Electrical Ltd.'s Patent* [1970] F.S.R. 200.
[53] *Bristol Repetition Ltd.* v. *Fomento (Sterling Area) Ltd.* [1960] R.P.C. 163.
[54] See *post,* § 1418 *et seq.* and § 1599.
[55] Ord. 103, r. 14; as to the Comptroller, see Patents Rules 153 to 155.
[56] *Panicali and Brenni's Patent,* 44 R.P.C. 509; and see *Allen and Bennett Bros. Ltd.'s Patents,* 46 R.P.C. 397; *Champion Paper and Fibre Co. Ltd.'s Patent* [1958] R.P.C. 103; *cf. Houghton's Patent,* 43 R.P.C. 343.
[57] *British Thomson-Houston Co. Ltd.'s Patent,* 49 R.P.C. 218.
[58] *Kores Manufacturing Co. Ltd.'s Appn.* [1958] R.P.C. 448.
[59] *Wöhler's Patent,* 40 R.P.C. 49; *Evans' Patent,* 43 R.P.C. 345.
[60] *Armour Research's Patent* [1961] R.P.C. 65.

578   *Withdrawal of opposition*

If an opposition is withdrawn, the court in some cases may require an explanation of the circumstances.[61]

Where the opponent wrote a letter giving notice of withdrawal and did not appear at the hearing an affidavit exhibiting the notice was required.[62]   The fact that opposition was withdrawn will be stated in the order.[63]

579   **Costs**

The practice as to costs is regulated by R.S.C., Ord. 62, r. 6 (1) (*e*), and is similar to that on application by petition.[64]   If the application is made to the court and is unsuccessful the patentee will usually be ordered to pay the costs of the Comptroller[65] and may be ordered so to do even if an extension is granted.[66]   If an opponent withdraws before the hearing he will ordinarily be ordered to pay the applicant's costs in so far as they have been increased by the opposition.[67]   Costs may be awarded to an opponent even if the opposition is unsuccessful if the opposition is of assistance to the court.[68]

[The next paragraph is 599]

---

[61] *Argyll's Ltd., Perrot and Rubury's Patent*, 43 R.P.C. 161; and see *Western Electric Co. Ltd.'s Patents*, 45 R.P.C. 117.

[62] *Willmott's Patent*, 41 R.P.C. 646.

[63] *Willmott's Patent*, 41 R.P.C. 646; *Western Electric Co. Ltd.'s Patents*, 45 R.P.C. 117.   And see *ante*, § 558.

[64] See *ante*, §§ 559, 560.

[65] *Von Kantzow's Patent*, 61 R.P.C. 109; *Tootal, Broadhurst Lee Co.'s Patents*, 62 R.P.C. 23 at p. 41.

[66] *Martin and the Daimler Co. Ltd.'s Patent*, 65 R.P.C. 173.

[67] *Dressler's Patent*, 44 R.P.C. 203; *B.T.H. Co. Ltd.'s Patent*, 46 R.P.C. 367 at p. 378; *Tootal, Broadhurst Lee Co.'s Patents*, 62 R.P.C. 23 at p. 44.

[68] *Tootal, Broadhurst Lee Co.'s Patents*, *supra*, and 62 R.P.C. 160.

CHAPTER 10

DEVOLUTION, ASSIGNMENT, LICENCES OF RIGHT,
CO-OWNERSHIP AND REGISTRATION

1. DEVOLUTION

599 The patentee

Upon grant of letters patent the Comptroller causes the name, etc.,
of the applicant or applicants to be entered in the Register of Patents,
which is kept at the Patent Office, as grantee or grantees of the
patent.[1] Such person or persons thereby come within the definition
of the " patentee " contained in section 101 of the Act of 1949, that
is to say, " the person or persons for the time being entered on the
register of patents as grantee or proprietor of the patent," and " Subject to the provisions of this Act relating to co-ownership of patents,
and subject also to any rights vested in any other person of which
notice is entered in the register of patents . . . have power to assign,
grant licences under, or otherwise deal with the patent. . . . " [2]

600 Devolution and registration of proprietorship

The proprietorship of a patent may pass from the patentee by
operation of law (as on death or bankruptcy) or by assignment.
The new proprietor, in order to be able to exercise the rights of
the patentee, must, in accordance with section 74 (1), apply to the
Comptroller to register his title; and by section 74 (6) no document
or instrument in respect of which no entry has been made in the
register will be admitted in evidence in any court in proof of title to
the patent or to any interest therein unless the court otherwise directs.

601 Devolution on death or dissolution

The property in a patent passes, by operation of law, when the
patentee dies or becomes bankrupt, or, in the case of a company, is
dissolved. Upon the death of a patentee his interest in the property
passes to his executors or administrators, as the case may be, in the
like manner to the rest of his personal estate, that is to say, upon
trust to fulfil the provisions of the will, or, in case of intestacy, upon
trust for sale with power to postpone such sale.[3] If, however, the

[1] Patents Rules 1968, r. 123.
[2] s. 74 (4).
[3] See Administration of Estates Act 1925, s. 33 (1).

patentee dies intestate and without any next-of-kin the patent vests
in the Crown as *bona vacantia*.[4]

As to devolution on the death of a joint patentee, see *post*,
§ 665.

602   Any step which by the Patents Act is required to be taken by a
patentee may be taken by his executor or administrator; and an
application for a patent may also be made by (and the patent granted
to) the personal representative of any deceased person who, immediately before his death, was entitled to make such an application.[5]
The term " personal representative " no doubt means the executor or
administrator of the deceased, and not the holder of a power of
attorney.[6]

In the case of a joint application, where one of the applicants dies
before the patent is granted, the grant may be made to the surviving
applicant if the personal representative of the deceased consents.[7]

If a limited company is the owner of a patent (or a patent is held
in trust for it) and is dissolved without having assigned such patent,
the patent vests in the Crown as *bona vacantia*.[8] It has been held that
there is no merger in the Crown in these circumstances because the
monopoly right given by the patent " is not a right against the Crown
only; but is a right to prevent others from using the invention." [9]
Where, however, the company at the time of its dissolution held the
patent as a trustee for some other person, the patent does not vest in
the Crown as *bona vacantia*,[10] and the court may make a vesting
order vesting the rights in such person as the court may appoint.[11]

603   Charges on patents, or on licences under patents, by a limited
company will be void against the liquidator and the creditors unless
such charges are registered with the Registrar of Joint Stock Companies within twenty-one days of being created.[12] If the charge is
already in existence when the patent or licence is acquired by the
company, the company must furnish particulars to the Registrar of
Companies (for the purpose of registration) within twenty-one days of

---

[4] See Administration of Estates Act 1925, s. 46 (1) (vi).

[5] s. 1 (3). See *ante*, § 71.

[6] See *Edmunds' Patent*, Griff.P.C. 281; see also *Spiel's Patent*, 5 R.P.C. 281.

[7] s. 17 (4).

[8] See Companies Act 1948, s. 354.

[9] *Dutton's Patent*, 40 R.P.C. 84 at p. 86 (dissenting from *Re Taylor's
Agreement Trusts*, 21 R.P.C. 713); see also *Bates' Patent*, 38 R.P.C. 385,
and Law of Property Act 1925, s. 185.

[10] See Companies Act 1948, s. 354.

[11] See Trustee Act 1925, s. 51 (1) (ii); see also Law of Property Act 1925,
ss. 9, 181. For vesting orders made under Trustee Act 1893 see *e.g.*
Heath's Patent, 29 R.P.C., 389; *Dutton's Patent*, 40 R.P.C. 84.

[12] Companies Act 1948, s. 95 (1) and (2) (i).

acquiring the patent or licence concerned.[13]   As to the registration of mortgages etc. in the Register of Patents, see *post*, §§ 668 to 670.

604   Bankruptcy

Patents the property of a bankrupt patentee pass on his bankruptcy to his trustee in bankruptcy.   A secret process also has to be disclosed where it is part of the assets and goodwill of a business.[14] The trustee in bankruptcy is also entitled to call for after-acquired patents[15] and royalties,[16] but if he fails to call for such patents a bona fide sale for value will be valid against him.[17]   A patent held by a bankrupt patentee in trust for others does not pass upon his bankruptcy, even though the circumstances be such that he is the reputed owner.[18]

605   Writ of fieri facias

A patentee's right, being merely that of preventing others from working his invention, is a chose in action, and is incapable of seizure under a writ of *fieri facias*.[19]   A receiver will not be appointed in execution of a judgment, at any rate where it is not shown that the patentee is in receipt of profits by way of royalties or otherwise.[20] The extent to which a patentee's right can be said to have " no locality " is, however, doubtful.[21]

Articles manufactured in accordance with a patent can be seized and sold under a writ of *fieri facias*, but such seizure and sale do not give to the purchaser any rights beyond those which he would have acquired in the ordinary way; thus, if a person in possession of a patented chattel has only a limited and personal licence to use it, a purchaser, with notice of such licence, from a sheriff who has seized the article, does not acquire any licence to use it.[22]

---

[13] Companies Act 1948, s. 97 (1).

[14] See *Re Keene* [1922] 2 Ch. 475; *Cotton* v. *Gillard*, 44 L.J.Ch. 90.

[15] Bankruptcy Act 1914, s. 48 (5); *Hesse* v. *Stevenson*, 3 Bos. & Pul. 565 at p. 577; approved in *Re Roberts* [1900] 1 Q.B. 122.

[16] See *Re Graydon, ex p. Official Receiver* [1896] 1 Q.B. 417 at p. 419.

[17] Bankruptcy Act 1914, s. 47 (1); and see *Dyster* v. *Randall & Sons* [1926] Ch. 932.

[18] Bankruptcy Act 1914, s. 38.

[19] *British Mutoscope and Biograph Co.* v. *Homer,* 18 R.P.C. 177; and see *Edwards & Co.* v. *Picard* [1909] 2 K.B. 903 at p. 905.

[20] *Edwards & Co.* v. *Picard* [1909] 2 K.B. 903 (Moulton L.J. dissenting).

[21] See *English Scottish and Australian Bank Ltd.* v. *Inland Revenue Commissioners* [1932] A.C. 238, overruling *Smelting Co. of Australia Ltd.* v. *Commissioners of Inland Revenue* [1897] 1 Q.B. 175; and cases referred to in note 19, *supra.*

[22] *British Mutoscope and Biograph Co.* v. *Homer,* 18 R.P.C. 177.

2. ASSIGNMENTS AND LICENCES

606 At common law

It would appear that at common law a patentee could not assign his rights unless power to do so was given by the Crown.[23] The wording of the recitals in the letters patent, *viz.* ". . . . the said applicant (hereinafter together with his executors, administrators and assigns, or any of them, referred to as the patentee) . . . ," makes it clear, however, that the grantee is to have power to assign his rights. The right to grant licences is also recognised by the wording of the parts of the letters patent which contain " the grant " and in " the prohibition." [24]

607 By statute

By section 74 (4) of the Act the registered proprietor is given power to assign and grant licences; and by section 21 (1) an assignment for a part only of the United Kingdom may be made.[25]

The rights of co-owners to assign and grant licences are dealt with at § 664.

608 Difference between assignment and licence

There is a fundamental distinction between an assignment of a patent and a licence under a patent. By the former the assignee stands, when registered, in the shoes of the assignor, and is fully entitled to deal with the patent as he pleases, subject to the provisions of the Act as to the grant of compulsory licences.[26] A non-exclusive licensee, on the contrary, is merely permitted to do acts which would, but for the licence, be prohibited. Other contractual rights as between the parties may be created by the licence, as in the case of an exclusive licence, where the patentee contracts not to grant other licences, but the exclusive licensee (see below) now has a right in relation to the patent, which is more than contractual, and probably amounts to an interest.

609 *Exclusive licensee*

The Act of 1949 has given to an exclusive licensee an important new right, *viz.* to take proceedings in respect of infringement in his own name.[27] The patentee, if he does not join as a plaintiff, must be added as a defendant.[28] An " exclusive licensee " means a person who has been granted by the patentee some right in respect of the

---

[23] See *Duvergier* v. *Fellows,* 10 B. & C. 826 at p. 829.
[24] See Chap. 1.
[25] See *post,* § 661.
[26] See *post,* § 684 *et seq.*
[27] s. 63 (1).
[28] s. 63 (2).

patented invention to the exclusion of all other persons, including the patentee. There may, therefore, be several exclusive licensees, each having an exclusive licence in his own field and each may sue in respect of an infringement committed in contravention of his particular right.

610   *Form of assignment and licence*

An assignment must be by deed to convey the legal estate and thereby alter the proprietorship in a patent, as that which is created by deed can only be assigned by deed.[29]

It would appear from the words of the prohibition contained in the grant—" without the consent license or agreement of the said patentee in writing under his hand and seal "—that licences could only be given under seal; but in the second proviso occur the words " nothing herein contained shall prevent the granting of licences in such manner and for such consideration as they may by law be granted." Further, provided it be proved that there is an agreement that one party shall be permitted to do acts which would otherwise be infringements of the patent, such agreement, however made, will be enforceable, and neither party will be excused on the ground that it was not under seal [30]; and as this produces precisely the same legal consequences as the grant of a licence under seal, agreements not under seal are frequently made.

611   *Agreements to assign or grant licences*

Agreements, parol or otherwise, to assign or to grant licences are specifically enforceable in equity, and are governed by the ordinary rules relating to contract as to specific performance, consideration, etc. Such agreements must, however, be of the degree of definiteness required by law to constitute an enforceable contract; thus an agreement to grant a licence at will would not be enforceable, whereas an agreement to grant one for a definite period and on stated terms would be enforceable.[31]

Agreements to assign or to grant licences may be made prior to the grant of or even prior to application for the patent concerned.[32] Thus an agreement relating to a subsisting patent may contain provisions for the assignment of, or the grant of licences under, patents in respect of future improvements. An agreement to assign does not alter the proprietorship of a patent, but gives a right in equity to have the proprietorship altered in law.[33]

[29] Co.Litt. 9b, 172a; *Stewart* v. *Casey*, 9 R.P.C. 9 at pp. 11, 13.
[30] *Chanter* v. *Dewhurst*, 13 L.J.Ex. 198; *Crossley* v. *Dixon*, 10 H.L.C. 293; *Tweedale* v. *Howard & Bullough Ltd.*, 13 R.P.C. 522.
[31] See *e.g. Brake* v. *Radermacher*, 20 R.P.C. 631.
[32] See *e.g. Otto* v. *Singer*, 7 R.P.C. 7.
[33] *Stewart* v. *Casey*, 9 R.P.C. 9 at p. 14 (C.A.).

612   In the case of agreements to assign made prior to the grant of the patent, the Comptroller may, on application being made to him, direct the grant to be made to the assignee. Similarly (by a change in the law introduced by the Act of 1949) where some person other than the applicant or one of the applicants is entitled by virtue of an agreement or by operation of law to an assignment of the interest of the applicant or any of the applicants, or to an undivided share of the patent, the grant may be made accordingly.[34]

613 Notice

Agreements to assign are subject to the usual conditions of equitable assignments, and a person obtaining a legal assignment without notice of the equitable one can claim priority,[35] and can convey a good title, even though the subsequent purchaser from him may in fact have had notice.[36]

The ordinary rules as to " notice " apply to equities in respect of a patent in like manner as any other personal property.[37] Thus an assignee is bound by previous licences of which he had notice at the date of the assignment, but is apparently not affected by others, save, of course, in respect of articles sold in pursuance of the licence prior to the assignment.[38] In the same way a licensee who has notice of a prior agreement to assign may be restrained from infringing by the new proprietor, as soon as the latter's title has been perfected by a legal assignment and registration [39]; and, provided there was notice, the non-registration of the agreement until after the date of the licence does not afford the licensee any excuse.[40] In the above case it was held that the proviso to section 87 of the Act of 1883 (which corresponds to the above-mentioned proviso to section 74 (4) of the Act of 1949) was not limited to the case of equities appearing upon the register; there was, however, actual notice, and now that there is an obligation imposed (by section 74 of the Act) to register all assignments or licences, constructive notice of an agreement would be unlikely to be established in the absence of any indication upon the register.

The misdescription of the nature of a previous agreement, as where an assignment was described to a party as a licence, may

---

[34] s. 17 (1); Patents Rules, 1968, r. 56. See *ante,* § 116.
[35] *e.g.* as in *Wapshare Tube Co. Ltd.* v. *Hyde Imperial Rubber Co.,* 18 **R.P.C.** 374.
[36] *Actiengesellschaft für Cartonnagen Industrie* v. *Temler and Seeman,* 18 **R.P.C.** 6.
[37] s. 74 (4).
[38] See *Gillette Safety Razor Co. Ltd.* v. *A. W. Gamage Ltd.,* 25 **R.P.C.** 492.
[39] *New Ixion Tyre and Cycle Co.* v. *Spilsbury,* 15 **R.P.C.** 380, 567.
[40] *Ibid.*

not prevent such party's knowledge of its existence constituting constructive notice.[41]

In any event, early registration of licences or assignments or agreements confirming rights with regard to a patent is of great importance, the existence of such registration preventing the patentee from granting licences under or otherwise dealing with the patent save subject to such rights.[42]

614   Where an assignee of a patent covenants with the assignor for himself and his assigns that he will work the patent and pay certain royalties thereon to the assignor, a subsequent assignee with notice takes the patent subject to those covenants.[43]   In such a case there is no privity of contract between the assignor and the second assignee, but the rights of the assignor are analogous to a vendor's lien, and the second assignee cannot hold the rights which he has acquired without also fulfilling the obligations which may be said to attach to those rights, and consequently the terms of the original assignment become a matter of great importance.

In *Dansk Rekylriffel Syndikat Aktieselskab* v. *Snell*,[44] Neville J. said: " The obligation to fulfil the terms of the agreement, being with regard to the assignees not personal, but attached to the property which they acquired with notice of the terms upon which it was held by their assignor, disables them from holding the property without fulfilling the terms.   It appears to me that such an interest of the vendor, if not properly described as a vendor's lien, is closely analogous to it.[45]   The question involved is whether, upon the true construction of the original assignment, it was intended that the vendor should retain a charge upon the property, or that he should part with the property completely, looking solely to the personal liability of the purchaser to pay the consideration." [46]   In this case the existence of clauses in the original contract to the effect that the purchaser thereunder should keep the patent in force and should pay royalties, was held to indicate a reservation of interest in the vendor sufficient to bring the case within the above principle.

615 Assignor estopped from impeaching validity

When a patent has been assigned the new proprietor is entitled, in the absence of any provision in the assignment to the contrary,

---

[41] *Morey's Patent,* 25 Beav. 581.
[42] s. 74 (4).
[43] *Werderman* v. *Société Générale d'Electricité,* 19 Ch.D. 246 at pp. 251, 252.
[44] [1908] 2 Ch. 127 at p. 136.
[45] See also, *British Association of Glass Bottle Manufacturers* v. *Foster & Sons Ltd.,* 34 R.P.C. 217 at p. 224.
[46] See also *Bagot Pneumatic Tyre Co.* v. *Clipper Pneumatic Tyre Co.,* 19 R.P.C. 69 at p. 75; *Barker* v. *Stickney* [1919] 1 K.B. 121.

to prevent the assignor from manufacturing the patented article [47] ; and in any action brought for that purpose by the assignee (or by any person deriving title through him) the assignor is estopped by his deed of assignment from impeaching the validity of the patent.[48] Similarly, the assignor of a licence is estopped from alleging as against his assignees that the patent is invalid.[49] The estoppel in such cases is of a personal nature, and does not extend to the partner of an assignor even in an action in which both are joined as co-defendants.[50] Estoppel can " only operate in the same transaction as that in which it arises " [51]; it is limited to such implication of validity as may be contained in the deed to which the assignor has put his hand and seal, and does not exist, for instance, where there is an assignment by operation of law, as upon bankruptcy of the patentee.[52] The former patentee is not estopped as against the new owner of the patent either by matter of record contained in the letters patent itself, or by statements contained in a specification (which professes only fully to declare the nature of the invention and how it is to be carried into effect), or by representations contained in the application for letters patent unless it be shown that the other party relied upon such representations.[53] It is probable that there would be such estoppel against the patentee as between himself and the Crown.[54]

An assignor, where he is estopped from denying the validity of the patent, may, of course, contend for a construction of the specification which will exclude what he is in fact doing, and so long as it does not impugn the validity of the patent, may call evidence as to the state of the art in the light of which the specification must be construed.[55]

A person estopped from disputing the validity of a patent is, nevertheless, entitled to give evidence and assist in attacking its validity in proceedings to which he is not himself a party.[56]

---

[47] See e.g. Franklin Hocking & Co. Ltd. v. Franklin Hocking, 4 R.P.C. 255.
[48] Chambers v. Crichley, 33 Beav. 374.
[49] Gonville v. Hay, 21 R.P.C. 49.
[50] Heugh v. Chamberlain, 25 W.R. 742.
[51] Fuel Economy Co. Ltd. v. Murray, 47 R.P.C. 346 at p. 353; V. D. Ltd. v. Boston Deep Sea Fishing etc. Ltd., 52 R.P.C. 303 at p. 331; see also Compania Naviera Vasconzada v. Churchill & Sim [1906] 1 K.B. 237 at p. 251.
[52] Cropper v. Smith and Hancock, 1 R.P.C. 81.
[53] Ibid.
[54] Cropper v. Smith and Hancock, 1 R.P.C. 81 at p. 96.
[55] Franklin Hocking & Co. Ltd. v. Franklin Hocking, 4 R.P.C. 255, 434; 6 R.P.C. 69.
[56] London and Leicester Hosiery Co. v. Griswold, 3 R.P.C. 251.

616 Estoppel against licensee

It is frequently said that a licensee is estopped from denying the validity of the patent.[58] There is not, however, " an absolute estoppel in all cases and in all circumstances . . . but only an estoppel which is involved in and necessary to the exercise of the licence which the licensee has accepted." [59]

617   If the licence is limited in its scope, *e.g.*, in area, and the patentee brings an action against the licensee, not under the licence, but for infringement of the patent in respect of acts done outside the licensed area, then the licensee would not be estopped in the action for infringement from disputing the validity of the patent.[60] It appears that a licensee would never be estopped from alleging that the patent is invalid, if the action brought against him is for infringement of patent, but only when an action is brought against him under the licence to enforce its provisions. As Luxmoore J. said in *Fuel Economy Co. Ltd.* v. *Murray*[60]: " A licensee cannot challenge the validity of a patent in an action under the licence, the licence being admitted by the licensee, because the title is not in issue. But in an action for infringement a different set of circumstances arises altogether. It is not an action under the licence at all, and in such a case, so far as my judgment goes, no estoppel arises."

618   Further, where there is in an agreement for sale, or for a licence, a covenant that the patent is valid, the question of validity is open to the assignee or licensee, and may go to the root of the consideration.[61] The real question to be decided in such cases is: " Did the defendant buy a good and indefeasible patent right, or was the contract merely to place the defendant in the same situation as the plaintiff was with reference to the alleged patent? " [62] Where a patentee contracted to give to the defendant the *exclusive right to sell* certain things for which patents had been obtained, it was held that if one of the patents was invalid the consideration failed as the patentee could not confer the privileges which he agreed to confer.[63] Where there was an agreement for a licence subject to an inquiry into the validity of the patent, the intended licensee was held to be entitled to dispute the

---

[58] See *Crossley* v. *Dixon*, 10 H.L.C. 293 at p. 304; *Adie* v. *Clark*, 3 Ch.D. 134 at p. 144 (C.A.); 2 App.Cas. 423 at p. 425; *Cummings* v. *Stewart*, 30 R.P.C. 1 at p. 9.
[59] *Fuel Economy Co. Ltd.* v. *Murray*, 47 R.P.C. 346 at p. 358; see also *V. D. Ltd.* v. *Boston Deep Sea Fishing etc. Ltd.*, 52 R.P.C. 303 at p. 331.
[60] *Fuel Economy Co. Ltd.* v. *Murray*, 47 R.P.C. 346 at p. 353.
[61] *Nadel* v. *Martin*, 23 R.P.C. 41; *Henderson* v. *Shiels*, 24 R.P.C. 108.
[62] See *Hall* v. *Conder*, 26 L.J.C.P. 138 at p. 143. See also *Suhr* v. *Crofts (Engineers) Ltd.*, 49 R.P.C. 359.
[63] *Chanter* v. *Leese*, 5 Mee. & W. 698, as explained in *Hall* v. *Conder*, 26 L.J.C.P. 138 at p. 143.

validity of the patent in an action brought upon the agreement and for infringement of the patent.[64] The decision upon this point might have been otherwise if he had refrained from inquiring into the validity and had worked the patent for a long time and subsequently, when called upon to pay royalty, refused upon the ground of invalidity.[65] In a case, however, where there was a covenant that payments should cease if the patent became void by lack of novelty, it was held that this referred to the patent being held void in proceedings between the patentee and other parties, and that the licensee was not entitled to put the validity of the patent in issue in an action upon the licence.[66] The above principles apply equally where there is a licence not under seal,[67] and where the licence is a verbal one.[68]

619　　A licensee is entitled to contend that what he is doing is not within the terms of his licence, and where (as is ordinarily the case) such terms are defined by the claims of the specification, he is at liberty to adduce evidence of common knowledge in the light of which ambiguous claims will be construed. He is not, however, entitled, in an action brought under the licence, to prove facts which would be inconsistent with the validity of the patent,[69] though obviously he may plead that the patent has expired,[70] and also may dispute that the patent should be extended and the length of its extension.[71]

620　*Fraud*

A licensee is, of course, entitled to repudiate his licence on the ground of fraud or common mistake, and the invalidity of the patent, if known to the licensor at the time of granting the licence, may be an element constituting fraud [72]; if the licensee proposes to take this course he must plead fraud in distinct terms.[73]

---

[64] *Wilson* v. *Union Oil Mills Co. Ltd.*, 9 R.P.C. 57.
[65] *Ibid.*; see also *Suhr* v. *Crofts (Engineers) Ltd.*, 49 R.P.C. 359.
[66] *Mills* v. *Carson*, 10 R.P.C. 9.
[67] *Lawes* v. *Purser*, 6 El. & Bl. 930.
[68] *Crossley* v. *Dixon*, 10 H.L.C. 293.
[69] See *Clark* v. *Adie*, 2 App.Cas. 423 at pp. 426, 436; *Young and Beilby* v. *Hermand Oil Co. Ltd.*, 9 R.P.C. 373; *Jandus Arc Lamp etc. Co., Ltd.* v. *Johnson*, 17 R.P.C. 361 at p. 376; *Hay* v. *Gonville*, 26 R.P.C. 161 at p. 170; *Campbell* v. *G. Hopkins & Sons (Clerkenwell) Ltd.*, 50 R.P.C. 213 at p. 218.
[70] *Muirhead* v. *Commercial Cable Co.*, 11 R.P.C. 317 at p. 325. 12 R.P.C. 39 (C.A.).
[71] *Bristol Repetition Ltd.* v. *Fomento* [1960] R.P.C. 163.
[72] See *Lawes* v. *Purser*, 6 El. & Bl. 930 at p. 936.
[73] *McDougall Bros.* v. *Partington*, 7 R.P.C. 216; *Ashworth* v. *Law*, 7 R.P.C. 231 at p. 234.

621   No estoppel against licensee

Where the licence has been determined prior to the expiration of the patent and the patentee consequently sues the other party for infringement instead of for royalties under the licence, the defendant may contest the validity of the patent, and, it appears, is not under any estoppel merely because he once was a licensee.[74]

If the agreement to assign or grant a licence is purely executory, there is no estoppel.[75]

It would appear that the mere purchase of a patented article from the patentee or a licensee does not compel the purchaser to assume the position of a licensee in respect of the article and in consequence to be estopped from attacking the validity of the patent.[76]

622   Implication of terms

The ordinary rules of construction apply to assignments and licences, and their meaning may be determined by the court in the same way as in the case of other documents.[77] Terms will not be implied unless " on considering the terms of the contract in a reasonable and business manner, an implication necessarily arises that the parties must have intended that the suggested stipulation should exist." [78] Thus when a patent was assigned in consideration of royalties which were to continue payable while the patent was subsisting, and the assignee inadvertently allowed the patent to lapse by non-payment of a renewal fee, the court refused to imply into the contract a covenant that the assignee should keep the patent on foot.[79] The decision would probably be otherwise were the lapse of the patent due to a wilful act of the assignee.[80] Where a patentee covenanted with his licensee " by all means in his power to protect and defend the said letters patent from all infringements," it was held that he was thereby bound to maintain the patent in force by payment of the renewal fees.[81]

---

[74] *Crossley* v. *Dixon,* 10 H.L.C. 293; *Axmann* v. *Lund,* L.R. 18 Eq. 330 at pp. 337, 338. See also *Neilson* v. *Fothergill,* 1 W.P.C. 287; *Noton* v. *Brooks,* 7 H. & N. 499; *Ashworth* v. *Law,* 7 R.P.C. 231.

[75] See *Basset* v. *Graydon,* 14 R.P.C. 701 at p. 709; *Henderson* v. *Shiels,* 24 R.P.C. 108 at pp. 113, 115; *Suhr* v. *Crofts (Engineers) Ltd.,* 49 R.P.C. 359 at p. 365.

[76] See *Gillette Safety Razor Co.* v. *A. W. Gamage Ltd.,* 25 R.P.C. 492 at p. 500 *per* Warrington J.; 26 R.P.C. 745, *per* Parker J.

[77] See *E. I. du Pont de Nemours & Co.* v. *Imperial Chemical Industries Ltd.,* 67 R.P.C. 144.

[78] *Mills* v. *Carson,* 10 R.P.C. 9 at p. 15, quoting from *Hamlyn & Co.* v. *Wood & Co.* [1891] 2 Q.B. 488; see also *Campbell* v. *G. Hopkins & Sons (Clerkenwell) Ltd.,* 48 R.P.C. 38 at pp. 44, 45; *The Moorcock,* 14 P.D. 64 at p. 68.

[79] *Re Railway and Electric Appliances Co.,* 38 Ch.D. 597.   [80] *Ibid.*

[81] *Lines* v. *Usher,* 14 R.P.C. 206; see also *Cummings* v. *Stewart,* 30 R.P.C. 1.

623   In the absence of express warranty the maxim *caveat emptor* ordinarily applies to the assignments of patents and the grant of licences and there is no implied warranty that the patent is valid; the invalidity of the patent is no defence to an action brought by the assignor or patentee for the purchase price or for royalties.[82] There is not ordinarily any implied warranty in an assignment of a patent or a licence under a patent that the manufacture or sale of articles made under the patent will not infringe any other patents. Knowledge of and concealment of such a fact by the patentee might, however, amount to fraud on his part, and entitle the assignee or licensee to rescission of the contract.

There is not ordinarily any implied covenant that the licensee shall work the invention [83]; express provisions are, therefore, commonly inserted in licence agreements whereby the licensee undertakes to pay a minimum royalty whether he manufactures or not; and in the case of an exclusive licence, where there may be danger of what was formerly called "Abuse of Monopoly," [84] it is often thought desirable that the licensee should be bound actually to manufacture a certain number of articles each year.

624   *" Best endeavours "*

Some clauses of a commonly occurring kind have been interpreted, *e.g.* an audit clause [85] and an obligation by licensees to use " all diligence " and their " best endeavours " to promote the sale of the patented articles.[86] The last mentioned obligation is a particularly onerous one for a licensee.[86]

625   *" Beneficial owner "*

Where the assignor conveys as " beneficial owner " the covenants set out in the Second Schedule, Part I, of the Law of Property Act 1925 will be implied.[87]

626   Breach of licence

The general law relating to breach of contract is applicable to breaches of the terms contained in a licence.[88] It is, of course, open

---

[82] *Hall* v. *Conder* (1857) 26 L.J.C.P. 138; *Smith* v. *Buckingham,* 21 L.T. 819; *Liardet* v. *Hammond Electric Light & Power Co.,* 31 W.R. 710; *Bessimer* v. *Wright,* 31 L.T.(O.S.) 213.

[83] See *e.g. Re Railway and Electrical Appliances Co.,* 38 Ch.D. 597 at p. 608; *Cheetham* v. *Nuthall,* 10 R.P.C. 321 at p. 333.

[84] See Chap. 11.

[85] *Fomento (Sterling Area) Ltd.* v. *Selsdon Fountain Pen Co. Ltd.* [1958] R.P.C. 8.

[86] *Terrell* v. *Mabie Todd & Co. Ltd.,* 69 R.P.C. 234.

[87] Law of Property Act 1925, s. 76.

[88] See *National Carbonising Co. Ltd.* v. *British Coal Distillation Ltd.,* 54 R.P.C. 41.

to a licensee to contend that no royalties are payable on the articles he is producing as they do not fall within the scope of the claims of the patent,[89] unless he is estopped from so contending by his previous conduct.[90] Licences are frequently drafted so as to make royalties payable on all articles, whether they are covered by the claims or not.

627 *Conflict of laws*

Where there is an agreement between British nationals for the grant of a licence under British patents and an order of a foreign court purports to make such grant illegal, the matter must be resolved in accordance with the law relating to the comity of nations.[91]

628 **Revocability of licences**

The question of the rights of one or other party to terminate a licence has, where there has been no express provision in the agreement dealing with the matter, given rise to considerable difficulty, and it would seem that a certain amount of confusion has existed between equitable rights as arising from contract between licensor and licensee, and such purely legal rights as a licensor may in general possess to withdraw at his pleasure such permission as he may have given. The case of *Wood* v. *Leadbitter*,[92] which was heard at common law before the Judicature Act 1873, turned upon a technical point not of contract but of trespass upon land, and decided that a mere permission to go upon a person's land, unless accompanied by some transfer of interest or property, as where a right was conferred, for instance, to cut and remove the hay upon the land, was revocable at the pleasure of the owner of the land. An attempt was made in *Ward* v. *Livesey*[93] to apply this doctrine to a case of a licence under a patent, and it was held that the revocability of a licence depended on whether it was or was not " coupled with an interest." It appears, however, not to have been realised that, since the fusion of law and equity by the Judicature Act, the real point at issue is not any purely legal right that an owner may have of revoking his licence, but whether, upon the true construction of the *contract* between the parties, one or the other is debarred in equity from the exercise of such legal right.[94]

---

[89] *Dobson* v. *Adie Bros. Ltd.*, 52 R.P.C. 358; *Pytchley Autocar Co. Ltd.* v. *Vauxhall Motors Ltd.*, 58 R.P.C. 287.

[90] *Lyle-Meller* v. *A. Lewis & Co. (Westminster) Ltd.* [1956] R.P.C. 14.

[91] *British Nylon Spinners Ltd.* v. *Imperial Chemical Industries Ltd.*, 69 R.P.C. 288; 71 R.P.C. 327.

[92] 13 Mee. & W. 838.

[93] 5 R.P.C. 102.

[94] *Guyot* v. *Thomson*, 11 R.P.C. 541 at p. 552; and see *Kerrison* v. *Smith* [1897] 2 Q.B. 445; *Hurst* v. *Picture Theatres Ltd.* [1915] 1 K.B. 1; *British Actors Film Co. Ltd.* v. *Glover* [1918] 1 K.B. 299.

It may be that one or the other party is entitled to terminate at pleasure or upon the happening of certain events, and inferences have been drawn as to this from the nature of the obligations imposed upon one or other of the parties by the contract.[95] For instance, where a patentee by granting an exclusive licence debarred himself from working the invention and received a lump sum as part consideration for the grant of the licence, he was held not entitled to revoke it at his pleasure.[96] In an ordinary verbal licence, however, where nothing is said as to any precise duration of the term, the presumption is that the licence is terminable at the pleasure of either party.[97]

Where there are express provisions for termination upon certain specified events or by one of the parties to the contract, it will be inferred that there is no right of termination upon other events not so specified or by the other of the parties.[98] Thus, a breach of an independent covenant by the licensor to pay the renewal fees will not go to the root of the contract [99]; nor will the breach of a covenant to sue infringers,[1] or to give instruction as to the working of the invention.[2]

629 Termination if patent held invalid

Provisions are frequently inserted providing for the termination of the licence in the event of the patent being held to be invalid by a court of competent jurisdiction. In such a case, where the decision of the court of first instance is against the patent, but is reversed upon appeal and the patent is eventually upheld, the licence is still in force and the licensee liable for royalties thereunder.[3] The simplest course is to provide that the licence shall continue so long as the patent remains subsisting.

630 Statutory determination

At any time after the patent or all the patents included in a licence has or have ceased to be in force, and notwithstanding any provision in the licence or any contract to the contrary, either party may give three months' notice to determine the licence.[4] This right

---

[95] *Guyot* v. *Thomson, supra.*
[96] *Ibid.*
[97] *Crossley* v. *Dixon,* 10 H.L.C. 293; 32 L.J.Ch. 617; *Coppin* v. *Lloyd,* 15 R.P.C. 373.
[98] *Guyot* v. *Thomson,* 11 R.P.C. 541; *Cutlan* v. *Dawson,* 13 R.P.C. 710; 14 R.P.C. 249; *Patchett* v. *Sterling Engineering Co. Ltd.,* 70 R.P.C. 269.
[99] *Mills* v. *Carson,* 10 R.P.C. 9.
[1] *Huntoon Co.* v. *Kolynos (Inc.),* 47 R.P.C. 403 at pp. 416–429.
[2] *Campbell* v. *Jones,* 6 Term Rep. 570.
[3] *Cheetham* v. *Nuthall,* 10 R.P.C. 321.
[4] s. 58 (1).

becomes exercisable as soon as all the patents originally included in the licence have expired and it is irrelevant that patents have subsequently been granted for improvements, to the benefit of which the licensee is entitled by reason of the " improvements " clause in the licence.[5]

631 *Where no express power to determine*

In a case where the licence contained no provision as to the period for which it was to remain in force, it was held that the licence was determinable on reasonable notice.[6]

632 *Licences under several patents*

Where licences are granted under several patents or a group of patents, care is necessary to define the state of affairs which is to prevail when some but not all of the patents have expired. Such licences are often drafted in such a way that the licensee remains liable to pay royalties until the expiry of the last patent, even though he may be working only under the patents which have expired and not under the surviving ones at all.[7]

633 Notices

Where an assignment or licence was executed or came into operation after January 1, 1926, all notices required to be served thereunder must be in writing, and will be deemed to have been sufficiently served if they are left at, or sent by registered letter or by recorded delivery to, the last-known address of the party to be served.[8] In all such assignments and licences, the word " month " is to be deemed to mean " a calendar month " unless the context requires otherwise.[9]

634 Ambit of licences

The letters patent prohibit the making, using, exercising or vending of the invention. These terms have not the same meaning. A licence to " use and exercise " conveys the fullest rights, including that of importation.[10] A licence to " make " does not imply a licence to use or vend.[11] But a purchaser from a person who is

---

[5] *Advance Industries Ltd.* v. *Paul Frankfurther* [1958] R.P.C. 392.
[6] *Martin Baker Aircraft Co. Ltd.* v. *Canadian Flight Equipment Ltd.*, 72 R.P.C. 236.
[7] See *e.g. Siemens* v. *Taylor*, 9. R.P.C. 393.
[8] Law of Property Act 1925, s. 196 (1), (3), (4), (5).   Recorded Delivery Service Act 1962, ss. 1, 2.
[9] Law of Property Act 1925, s. 61.
[10] *Dunlop Pneumatic Tyre Co.* v. *North British Rubber Co.*, 21 R.P.C. 161 at pp. 181, 183.
[11] *Basset* v. *Graydon*, 14 R.P.C. 701 at pp. 708, 713; and see *Huntoon Co.* v. *Kolynos (Inc.)*, 47 R.P.C. 403 at p. 422.

licensed to " make and vend " has been held to be entitled to use and vend the article so purchased.[12]

635 *Assignment of licence and sub-licensing*

It seems that a mere licence under a patent is personal only, and does not authorise the licensee to grant sub-licences or to assign his licence.[13] But if there is anything which shows that there was an intention that the licence should not be limited exclusively to the individual the result may be otherwise.[14] Thus where a licence is expressed to be granted to a licensee and his assigns, or where provisions are made for the payment of royalties upon goods made by a sub-licensee, the licensee would clearly be entitled to assign or grant sub-licences as the case might be. In drafting a patent licence, therefore, care should be taken to make it clear by express language whether the licence is to be personal to the licensee or is to be assignable.

If a licensee is not entitled to assign, and the licensor knowingly accepts royalties from a purported assignee, the licensor is thereby estopped from disputing the assignment.[15]

Although a licensee under a personal licence is entitled to exercise his rights by his servants or agents, he is not entitled to exercise his rights in such a way that his " agents " are in substance " independent contractors." [16]

Where the benefit of a licence, in which the consideration is payable by way of a share of profits, is assigned by the licensor the assignee is entitled to an account from the licensee, provided that he puts himself into the position of the licensor by submitting to pay any moneys due from the licensor to the licensee,[17] but if the assignment be of a share only of the benefit of the licence he must join the other persons entitled, as the licensee is not bound to account separately to several parties.[18]

If the licensee has power to grant sub-licences, such sub-licences will determine upon the determination of his own licence unless it appears from the terms of his own licence that the contrary is intended.[19]

636 *Purchase of articles from patentee*

The owner of a United Kingdom patent who, by himself or his

---

[12] *Thomas* v. *Hunt,* 17 C.B.(N.S.) 183. See also *National Phonograph Co. of Australia* v. *Menck,* 28 R.P.C. 229.

[13] Hindmarch, 242; *Lawson* v. *Donald Macpherson & Co. Ltd.,* 14 R.P.C. 696.

[14] *Lawson* v. *Donald Macpherson & Co.,* 14 R.P.C. 696; and see also *National Carbonising Co. Ltd.* v. *British Coal Distillation Ltd.,* 54 R.P.C. 41.

[15] *Lawson* v. *Donald Macpherson & Co.,* loc. cit.

[16] *Howard and Bullough Ltd.* v. *Tweedales and Smalley,* 12 R.P.C. 519.

[17] *Bergmann* v. *Macmillan,* 17 Ch.D. 423.

[18] *Ibid.*

[19] See *Austin Baldwin & Co. Ltd.,* v. *Greenwood & Batley Ltd.,* 42 R.P.C. 454.

agent, sells the patented article abroad without reservation or condition, cannot restrain the importation of the article so sold in this country,[20] as the unconditional sale of an article implies the grant of authority to use and sell it co-extensive with the right of the vendor at the date of the sale.[21]   And a subsequent assignee of the patent is not entitled to restrain the further use or sale of goods sold under conditions such as to confer an absolute authority to use and sell so far as patent rights are concerned.[22]   But if a patentee assigned his patent and subsequently continued to make the goods abroad the assignee could, no doubt, restrain their importation or sale.[23]

637   *Licence under foreign patent*

A licence under a foreign patent to manufacture and sell thereunder granted by a patentee who also owns a British patent does not imply any licence to import articles so manufactured or sold in this country.[24]

638   **Covenants for improvements**

Covenants are frequently inserted in assignments and licences whereby the assignor or licensor undertakes to communicate to the other party any new discovery or invention which he may make or acquire connected with his invention and, if he obtains a patent for such new invention, to assign it to or to grant a licence to the other party.   In other cases the covenants are mutual, each party communicating improvements to the other.

Such covenants require care in wording in order to ensure that there is no danger of their being in restraint of trade, and in order to avoid unnecessary difficulties in deciding what is and what is not an " improvement."

639   *Patents subsequently acquired*

Agreements by the vendors of a patent to assign to the purchasers all patent rights that they may subsequently acquire of a like nature to the patent sold are not contrary to public policy.[25]   The danger to the purchasers of the destruction of the value of the rights which they have bought would otherwise be great, as inventors frequently continue to make inventions relating to the same art, and without such

---

20 *Betts* v. *Willmott,* L.R. 6 Ch.App. 239.
21 See *ibid.*; see also *Incandescent Gas Light Co. Ltd.* v. *Cantelo,* 12 R.P.C. 262 at p. 264; *National Phonograph Co. of Australia Ltd.* v. *Menck,* 28 R.P.C. 229.
22 *Ibid.*
23 See *Betts* v. *Willmott,* L.R. 6. Ch.App. 239 at p. 244.
24 *Société Anonyme des Manufactures de Glaces* v. *Tilghman's Patent Sand Blast Co.,* 25 Ch.D. 1 at p. 9; and see *Beecham Group Ltd.* v. *International Products Ltd.* [1968] R.P.C. 129.
25 *Printing and Numerical Registering Co.* v. *Sampson,* L.R. 19 Eq. 462.

protection the purchasers would be exposed to competition from the vendors with the benefit of their previous experience.[26] The validity of such contracts, as always where the question is one of restraint of trade, depends upon whether they extend further than is necessary to protect the reasonable rights of the parties in the circumstances of the case, and covenants by a vendor not to make or sell the invention at all, or the product obtained by the patented or any similar process which would be in competition with it, may be perfectly valid [27]; the period over which the disability imposed is to last and the area over which it is to extend are material factors to be considered in each case.

640 *Ambit of covenants for improvements*

It is difficult to foretell at the time of making a contract the precise nature of the " improvement " which it will be desired to cover. The ambit of the rights conferred depends entirely upon the construction of the contract.[28] Sometimes " improvements " are defined as being confined to articles or processes which would be an infringement of the patent in question; in other cases it may be desired to secure any further inventions relating to the particular art. The words " improvement upon," unless otherwise qualified, are ambiguous in that, for instance, in the case of a machine, they may relate to some alteration in its design which will enable it to perform its duty better or more cheaply, or they may relate to a different machine which performs the same duty in a different and better way; the former meaning is that usually adopted, and a separate and distinct invention, although relating to the same general subject-matter, cannot usually be described as an improvement.[29] Notwithstanding this ambiguity, it is usually best, when drafting a licence, merely to use the word " improvements," without attempting any more precise definition, as the parties are usually reluctant to agree to anything more detailed and even an elaborate and complicated clause often gives rise to disputes as to its true construction.

641   In *Linotype and Machinery Ltd.* v. *Hopkins*,[30] where the licensor covenanted to communicate " every improvement in or addition to

---

[26] *Ibid.*

[27] See *Nordenfelt* v. *Maxim Nordenfelt etc. Co. Ltd.* [1894] A.C. 535; *Mouchel* v. *Cubitt & Co.*, 24 R.P.C. 194.

[28] See *Valveless Gas Engine Syndicate Ltd.* v. *Day,* 16 R.P.C. 97; *Osram-Robertson Lamp Works Ltd.* v. *Public Trustee,* 37 R.P.C. 189; *Vislok Ltd.* v. *Peters,* 44 R.P.C. 235.

[29] *Davies* v. *Davies Patent Boiler Ltd.,* 25 R.P.C. 823; *Sadgrove* v. *Godfrey,* 37 R.P.C. 7 at pp. 20, 21; *Vislok Ltd.* v. *Peters,* 44 R.P.C. 235. See also *Davies* v. *Curtis & Harvey Ltd.,* 20 R.P.C. 561.

[30] 25 R.P.C. 349, 665; 27 R.P.C. 109.

the Hopkins machine or mode of applying the same or any discovery useful to the manufacture thereof," the Court of Appeal, having regard to these words, would not agree that any improvement of which the company was to have the benefit should necessarily be limited to something that was an infringement of the original patent assigned, and in the same case Lord Loreburn [31] said: "I think that any part does constitute an improvement, if it can be adapted to this machine, and it would make it cheaper and more effective or in any way easier or more useful or valuable, or in any other way make it a preferable article in commerce."

In *National Broach etc. Co.* v. *Churchill Gear Machines Ltd.*[32] the licensee covenanted to " communicate to [the licensor] all details of any improvements which may be developed during the subsistence " of the licence agreement and to apply for patents if so requested by the licensor. A question in the case was when the duty to communicate something which had been developed arose. The House of Lords held it was impossible to lay down any criterion and the court, looking at the matter through technical eyes, must answer the question in any particular case in all the circumstances of that case, but, if an idea has arisen which may lead to some patentable improvement, the obligation to communicate will arise at a very early stage as the licensor must have time to consider whether he wanted patents applied for.

642 Limited licences

Licences frequently contain clauses limiting the licensee's right so that he is not entitled to work the patent in any way he chooses. Care is necessary that such licences do not contravene section 57 of the Act, and that terms are not included which are void under the Resale Prices Act 1964 or contrary to the public interest having regard to the Restrictive Trade Practices Acts 1956 and 1968. But, subject to those exceptions which will be referred to subsequently in this Chapter, " a patentee has a right, not merely by sale without reserve to give an unlimited right to the purchaser to use, and thereby to make in effect a grant from which he cannot derogate, but may attach to it conditions, and if these conditions are broken, then there is no licence, because the licence is bound up with the observance of the conditions." [33]

---

[31] 27 R.P.C. at p. 113.
[32] [1967] R.P.C. 99 at pp. 110, 111.
[33] *Per* Kennedy J. in *Incandescent Gas Light Co. Ltd.* v. *Brogden,* 16 R.P.C. 179 at p. 183; and see *Incandescent Gas Light Co. Ltd.* v. *Cantelo,* 12 R.P.C. 262 at p. 264.

643 *Conditions void under section 57 of the Patents Act 1949*

A common type of limitation imposed before the Act of 1907 was that the patented article should not be used save in conjunction with some other article produced by the patentee, for example, that patented gas mantles should only be used in conjunction with the patentee's gas burners,[34] or that the patented machine alone should be used and that the user should purchase his raw materials from the patentee. Conditions of this kind can, however, no longer be imposed, as by section 57 (1) of the Act any condition in a contract for the sale or lease of a patented article, or in a licence to use or work a patented article or process, is void which purports (i) to restrict the right of the licensee to acquire where he pleases any article not protected by the patent, or (ii) to prohibit or restrict the licensee from using any article or process (whether patented or not) which does not belong to the licensor.[35]

644 *No bar to restrictions on sales by licensee*

It is to be observed that the prohibition imposed by section 57 does not apply to selling [36] and, therefore, the licensor may impose a condition that the licensee shall not sell any goods except such as are protected by the patent. Furthermore, it is expressly provided that a condition of a contract shall not be void by reason only that it prohibits any person from selling goods other than those supplied by a specified person.[37] Accordingly, a patentee can make it a condition of a grant of a selling agency that the agent shall not sell the goods of anyone else.

645 *Spare parts*

A licensor may reserve the right, in a contract for the use of a patented article, to supply such new parts as are required to keep it in repair.

646 *Condition not necessarily invalid*

Contracts of the kind referred to in subsection (1) of section 57 are not invariably to be deemed invalid. The section was designed for the protection of persons such as repairers in a small way of business who (apart from its provisions) would practically be compelled to enter into contracts of that kind in order to obtain a lease

---

[34] See *e.g. Incandescent Gas Light Co. Ltd.* v. *Cantelo*, 12 R.P.C. 262; *Incandescent Gas Light Co. Ltd.* v. *Brogden*, 16 R.P.C. 179.

[35] See *Sarason* v. *Frenay*, 31 R.P.C. 252, 330; *Huntoon Co.* v. *Kolynos (Inc.)*, 47 R.P.C. 403; *Tool Metal Manufacturing Co. Ltd.* v. *Tungsten Electric Co. Ltd.*, 72 R.P.C. 209 at p. 218; *Thomas Hunter Ltd.'s Patent* [1965] R.P.C. 416 (an Irish case).

[36] s. 57 (1).

[37] s. 57 (5).

of a necessary machine, and it was not the purpose of the section to interfere with contracts which had been voluntarily entered into by parties who had the opportunity clearly laid before them of purchasing or hiring upon different terms. Accordingly, subsection (3) provides that such a condition is not void provided (i) a contract on reasonable terms without the condition was offered at the time when the actual contract was made, and (ii) the condition can be determined on three months' notice in writing and subject to the payment of compensation.

The onus of proving that an alternative contract, on reasonable terms and without the restriction, was offered to the other party is upon the vendor, lessor or licensor.[38]

647 *Defence in infringement action*

Subsection (1) of section 57 is of a penal nature, and subsection (2) provides that in proceedings against any person for infringement of a patent it shall be a defence to prove that at the time of the infringement there was in force[39] a contract relating to that patent and containing a condition void under this section. The fact that the contract concerned was made with a third party and not with the defendant is not material.[40]

A plaintiff who has had to discontinue an action owing to the defendant pleading the existence of a contract containing unlawful conditions, may commence a fresh action against the same defendant for infringement of the same patent after the offending contract has been terminated,[41] but is not entitled to recover damages for infringements committed while the offending contract was in force.[42]

648 **Resale price maintenance conditions void under the Resale Prices Act**

Formerly it was not uncommon for patented goods to be supplied subject to a condition as to the minimum price at which they could be resold retail. However, the Resale Prices Act 1964 has now been enacted with a view to abolishing resale price maintenance of goods except where the Restrictive Practices Court have ordered such goods to be exempted from the provisions of the Act.

649   By section 1 (1) of this Act any term or condition of a contract for the sale of goods by a supplier to a dealer, or of any agreement between a supplier and a dealer relating to such a sale, shall be

---

[38] s. 57 (4).
[39] See *Trubenising Ltd.* v. *Steel and Glover Ltd.*, 62 R.P.C. 1 at p. 15.
[40] *Sarason* v. *Frenay*, 31 R.P.C. 252, 330 (C.A.).
[41] *Aktiengesellschaft für Autogene Aluminium Schweissung* v. *London Aluminium Co. Ltd.*, 36 R.P.C. 29.
[42] s. 57 (2) overruling *Aktiengesellschaft für Autogene Aluminium Schweissung* v. *London Aluminium Co. Ltd.* (No. 2), 40 R.P.C. 107.

void in so far as it purports to establish or provide for the establishment of minimum prices to be charged on the resale of the goods in the United Kingdom. (For the purposes of the Act a supplier is defined as " a person carrying on a business of selling goods other than a business in which goods are sold only by retail " and a dealer as " a person carrying on a business of selling goods, whether by wholesale or by retail." [43]) Furthermore, it is unlawful for a supplier of goods to include any such term or condition in any contract of sale or agreement relating to the sale of goods, or to require, as a condition of supplying goods to a dealer, the inclusion in any contract or any agreement of any such term or condition, or to notify to dealers, or publish in relation to goods, a minimum price for the goods on resale.[44]

650   Section 1 (2) expressly enacts that section 1 of the Act applies to patented articles (including articles made by a patented process) as it applies to other goods; and that notice of any term or condition which is void by virtue of the section, or which would be so void if included in a contract of sale or agreement relating to the sale of any such article, shall be of no effect for the purpose of limiting the right of a dealer to dispose of that article without infringement of the patent. However, the proviso to section 1 (2) provides that nothing in section 1 of the Act shall affect the validity, as between the parties and their successors, of any term or condition of a licence granted by the proprietor of a patent or by a licensee under any such licence, or of any assignment of a patent, so far as it regulates the price at which articles produced or processed by the licensee or assignee may be sold by him.

651   It is to be noted that the foregoing provisions of section 1 (1) of the Act have no application to any patented articles registered under the Act as an " exempt " class of goods, *i.e.* registered as exempt pursuant to an order of the Restrictive Practices Court under section 5 of the Act [45] or so registered temporarily pending the determination of a reference to the court in respect thereof.[46]

It is also to be noted that the presence in any contract of sale or other agreement of a term or condition void by virtue of the provisions of section 1 (1) of the Act does not affect the enforceability of the contract or agreement except in respect of the void term or condition.[47]

[43] s. 11 (1).
[44] s. 1 (1).
[45] s. 5 (1).
[46] s. 6 (3).
[47] s. 1 (3).

652   The effect of section 1 of the Resale Prices Act 1964 in relation to patented goods may be summarised as follows:

    (i) A patent licence, including a licence granted by a licensee (*i.e.* a sub-licence), may lawfully include a term or condition which regulates the price at which the licensee (or sub-licensee) may sell the patented articles made or processed by him under the licence and such a term is not void under the Act.

    (ii) Similarly, a patent assignment may lawfully include a term or condition regulating the price at which the assignee may sell the patented articles made or processed by him.

    (iii) Where patented articles, not being articles within any exempted class of goods registered under the Act, are supplied to a dealer for resale (whether for resale, wholesale or retail) no term or condition which fixes the minimum resale price, wholesale or retail, may be imposed by the supplier. Any such term purported to be imposed by a supplier in respect of any such articles will be void and may be ignored by any dealer who acquires the articles for resale, whether he acquires the articles direct from that supplier or after they have passed through the hands of another trader or other traders and even though he acquires them with notice of such purported term or condition.

653   Effect of the Restrictive Trade Practices Act

The Restrictive Trade Practices Act 1956 does not apply to patent licences or sub-licences or assignments of patents or the right to apply for patents, or to agreements to grant licences or sub-licences or to assign which contain restrictions only in respect of the use of the patented invention or articles made by the use of that invention (see section 8 (4)). But, if there are restrictions other than the above and such restrictions fall within section 6 (1) of the Act, then the agreement will have to be registered under the Act. Further the Restrictive Trade Practices Act 1968 provides in section 7 that agreements which are registrable and are not registered shall be void and that it shall be illegal to give effect to or enforce or purport to enforce such an agreement.

654   Purchaser without notice of limited licence

A purchaser of patented goods without notice of restrictions affecting such goods is free to use and sell them in any way he chooses.[48] But if at the time of his purchase he has notice of any restrictions affecting the patented goods (other than restrictions that are void under section 57 of the Patents Act or section 1 of the Resale Prices Act) and contravenes such restrictions he is liable to be sued for infringement by the patentee, as the restrictions are " not contractual but are incident to and a limitation of the grant of the licence to use, so that, if the conditions are broken, there is no grant at all." [49]

The question of the knowledge of the defendant is one of fact in each case, as to which the passing of some leaflet or label with the goods at the time of sale may or may not be sufficient evidence according to the nature of the goods and the general circumstances. It is not essential that the purchaser should have knowledge of the precise restrictions concerned so long as he has knowledge of their nature and existence and means of knowledge of their exact extent.[50] Registration of the limited licence at the Patent Office is not in itself equivalent to notice of the limitations to a purchaser of an article.[51]

655　　It is submitted that just as a patentee may impose restrictions on the otherwise unlimited licence implied by the sale of a patented article, so a licensee may similarly impose restrictions upon articles made and sold by him pursuant to his licence and provided these restrictions are not void and have been sufficiently brought to the notice of the purchaser any contravention of them constitutes an infringement in respect of which a patentee or an exclusive licensee [52] may take action. The contrary is suggested in one reported case,[53] but there the order of the court of first instance was discharged by

[48] See *Betts* v. *Willmott*, L.R. 6 Ch.App. 239 at p. 245; *Incandescent Gas Light Co. Ltd.* v. *Cantelo*, 12 R.P.C. 262; *Incandescent Gas Light Co. Ltd.* v. *Brogden*, 16 R.P.C. 179; *Scottish Vacuum Cleaner Co. Ltd.* v. *Provincial Cinematograph Theatres Ltd.*, 32 R.P.C. 353; *Hazeltine Corporation* v. *Lissen Ltd.*, 56 R.P.C. 62.

[49] *Per* Farwell J. in *British Mutoscope and Biograph Co. Ltd.* v. *Homer*, 18 R.P.C. 177 at p. 179; see also *National Phonograph Co. of Australia Ltd.* v. *Menck*, 28 R.P.C. 229 at p. 248; see also *Columbia Phonograph Co. General* v. *Regent Fittings Co.*, 30 R.P.C. 484; *Columbia Graphophone Co.* v. *Vanner*, 33 R.P.C. 104; *Columbia Graphophone Co. Ltd.* v. *Murray*, 39 R.P.C. 239; *Columbia Graphophone Co. Ltd.* v. *Thoms*, 41 R.P.C. 294; *Dunlop Rubber Co. Ltd.* v. *Longlife Battery Depot* [1958] R.P.C. 473; all cases decided prior to Resale Prices Act 1964 and relating to breaches of restrictions as to the resale prices of the articles.

[50] See *Columbia Graphophone Co. Ltd.* v. *Murray*, 39 R.P.C. 239; *cf. Badische Anilin und Soda Fabrik* v. *Isler*, 23 R.P.C. 633.

[51] *Heap* v. *Hartley*, 42 Ch.D. 461; 5 R.P.C. 603 at p. 608; 6 R.P.C. 495 (C.A.); *Scottish Vacuum Cleaner Co.* v. *Provincial Cinematograph Theatres Ltd.*, 32 R.P.C. 353 (O.H.).

[52] See *ante*, § 609.

[53] *Gillette Safety Razor Co. Ltd.* v. *A. W. Gamage Ltd.*, 25 R.P.C. 492.

the Court of Appeal [54] and in the subsequent proceedings the contention that the limitation of the licence was invalid appears to have been dropped.[55]

3. Licences of Right

656 By the provisions of section 35 of the Act a patentee may voluntarily throw his invention open to anyone who cares to ask for a licence on terms to be agreed with him, or in default of agreement, on terms to be settled by the Comptroller. In each case the terms will depend on the relevant facts of that case.[56] Or if a case of abuse of his monopoly is made out against him under section 37 (see Chapter 11) the Comptroller may, as one of the remedies applicable, make an order throwing the invention open in the same way. The patentee gains some advantages: he reduces the risk that he may be held at any time to have abused his monopoly; to some small extent he advertises his invention and gives manufacturers or financiers the knowledge that the invention may be used on reasonable terms, and by subsection (2) (*d*) his renewal fees are reduced to a half of what they would otherwise have been. The patentee must satisfy the Comptroller that he is not precluded by contract from granting licences under the patent.[57] Any person entered in the register as having an interest in the patent must be given an opportunity of being heard.[58]

657 Rights after endorsement

After the endorsement has been made any existing licensee may apply to the Comptroller to exchange his licence for one granted pursuant to the endorsement.[59] An infringer (other than by importation) may undertake to accept a licence to be settled by the Comptroller, in which case no injunction will be granted and the damages will be limited to double what the royalties would have been if the licence had been granted before the earliest infringement.[60]

658 Right to sue for infringement

A licensee under a patent endorsed " licences of right " may, apart from agreement to the contrary, call upon the patentee to take proceedings for infringement and if the patentee does not do so within two months the licensee may institute proceedings in his own

[54] 25 R.P.C. 782.
[55] 26 R.P.C. 745.
[56] See *Casson's Patent* [1970] F.S.R. 433.
[57] s. 35 (4).
[58] s. 35 (1).
[59] s. 35 (2) (*b*).
[60] s. 35 (2) (*c*).

name, joining the patentee as a defendant.[61]   The patentee is not liable for costs unless he enters an appearance and takes part in the proceedings.

659   Endorsement includes patents of addition

Any application for the endorsement of a patent of addition is to be treated as an application for the endorsement of the main patent also and any application for the endorsement of a patent is to be treated as an application in respect of all patents of addition also.[62] It follows that the status of any patent of addition must always be the same as that of the main patent.

660   Cancellation of endorsement

The patentee may apply at any time for cancellation of the endorsement " licences of right " and if the balance of renewal fees is paid as though there had been no endorsement and the Comptroller is satisfied that there is no existing licence, or that all licensees agree, the endorsement will be cancelled.[63]   In that case the rights and liabilities of the patentee are as if no endorsement had been made.[64] However, where a patentee sought to cancel an endorsement after an application for a licence had been made, the cancellation was allowed subject to the grant of the licence for which application had been made.[65]   The application for cancellation of the endorsement must be advertised and any person interested may give notice of opposition.[66]

Any person who claims that the patentee is precluded by a contract from granting licences, in which contract the claimant is interested, may apply within two months of the endorsement for its cancellation.[67]   The Comptroller must give notice of such an application to the patentee, who may oppose.[66]

An appeal from the Comptroller in all matters relating to licences of right lies to the Appeal Tribunal.[68]

4. CO-OWNERSHIP

661   Ownership of patent for limited area

By the proviso to section 21 (1) of the Act a patent may be assigned for any place in or part of the United Kingdom or Isle of Man as effectually as if it were granted so as to extend to that place

[61] s. 35 (3).
[62] s. 35 (5).
[63] s. 36 (1).
[64] s. 36 (4).
[65] *Casson's Patent* [1970] F.S.R. 433.
[66] s. 36 (5).   See *Serenyi's Patent,* 55 R.P.C. 228.
[67] s. 36 (2); Patent Rules 1968, r. 105.
[68] ss. 35 (7), 36 (8).

or part only. In such circumstances the assignee would be owner of his share of the patent in severality, and could sue or grant licences in respect of acts done or to be done in the area to which his portion of the patent extended and would not, apart from contract, be liable to account in any way to the owner of the rest of the patent.

662   Co-ownership

Co-ownership of a patent may arise by the patent being granted to joint applicants or by assignment. The title of a co-owner must be entered in the register.[69] Apart from an agreement to the contrary, joint grantees are each entitled to an equal undivided share in the patent[70] and every registered co-owner is entitled, by himself or his agents, to make, use, exercise and vend the patented invention for his own benefit without accounting to the other or others.[71] It is submitted that the word " agent " in this connection must be narrowly interpreted and does not include an independent contractor.[72]

663   *The right to sue*

One co-owner can sue for infringement without joining his fellow patentees, but the more usual course is to join them so as to avoid any difficulty or inconvenience which may arise from an attempt to assess the damages due in their absence.[73]

664   Licence and assignment

Apart from an agreement to the contrary no licence can be granted by one or more co-owners and no assignment can be made of the share of any co-owner without the consent of all persons who are registered as grantee or proprietor of the patent.[74] But the purchaser of an article sold by one co-owner becomes entitled to deal with it just as though it had been sold by a sole patentee.[75]

It is, nevertheless, submitted that there has been no alteration in the law in this respect and that, upon general principles, even before the Act of 1949 one co-owner could not, apart from express agreement, assign his undivided share without the knowledge and consent of all co-owners.

[69] s. 74 (1), (6).
[70] s. 54 (1). *Young* v. *Wilson*, 72 R.P.C. 351.
[71] s. 54 (2).
[72] See *Howard & Bullough Ltd.* v. *Tweedales and Smalley*, 12 R.P.C. 519.
[73] See *post*, § 796.
[74] s. 54 (3).
[75] s. 54 (4).

665   Devolution of title

The rules of law applicable to the devolution of personal property generally apply in relation to patents as they apply in relation to other choses in action.[77]   Accordingly, the undivided share of a co-owner of a patent devolves upon his personal representatives.

666   Power of Comptroller

Any co-owner may apply to the Comptroller for directions regarding the sale or lease of the patent or any interest therein, or the grant of licences.[78]   This provision is to prevent the proper exploitation of a patent being unreasonably prevented by one or more co-owners. The procedure is governed by rules 116 and 117 of the Patents Rules 1968.[79]   If a person ordered to execute any instrument or do any other act fails to do so within fourteen days of being requested to do so, the Comptroller may give directions empowering some other person to perform such act.[80]   All co-owners or any person in default must be given notice and an opportunity of being heard before the Comptroller makes any order.[81]   An appeal lies to the Appeal Tribunal and from the Appeal Tribunal to the Court of Appeal.[82]

667   Trustees and personal representatives

The provisions of the Act as to co-ownership do not affect the mutual rights or obligations of trustees or personal representatives, or their rights and obligations as such.[83]

5. REGISTRATION

668   Register of Patents

There is kept at the Patent Office a Register of Patents open to public inspection, in which are entered particulars of patents in force, assignments, licences and other matters affecting validity or proprietorship.[84]

Where a person becomes entitled to a patent, or a share or interest in a patent, he must apply to have his title registered.[85]

---

[77] s. 54 (5).
[78] s. 55 (1). *Florey & Others' Patent* [1962] R.P.C. 186.
[79] *Post*, §§ 1462, 1463.
[80] s. 55 (2). *Florey & Others' Patent* [1962] R.P.C. 186 at p. 194.
[81] s. 55 (3). *Florey & Others' Patent* [1962] R.P.C. 186.
[82] ss. 55 (4), 87 (1) (*b*). As regards proceedings in Scotland, see ss. 86, 87 (3).
[83] ss. 54 (5), 55 (5).
[84] s. 73.
[85] s. 74 (1), (2).

The practice is regulated by rules 123 to 128 of the Patents Rules 1968.

It is to be observed that registration is compulsory, and that non-registration of a relevant document may be fatal to the successful proof of title to, or an interest in, the patent concerned.[86]

Omission to register may, however, be rectified at any time [87] and the registration will then date back to the date of the agreement.[88] But until the register is rectified, it is in effect conclusive evidence of the right of the person registered as proprietor to sue for infringement.[89] The fee payable upon applications for registration made after the expiration of six months from the date of acquisition of interest is increased.

669   Nature of title registered

A person's interest or estate in a patent will only be registered as what it is; for instance, a person will not be registered as proprietor unless he has the legal estate in the patent.[90] A mortgagee will be registered as mortgagee and not as proprietor even though the mortgage be a legal one.[91] Provided, however, that documents are properly executed and are produced from the proper custody, the Comptroller will not go into the question of whether there was consideration or of the circumstances of their execution.[92]

670   Registrable documents

No notice of any trust is to be entered in the register,[93] but documents affecting the proprietorship of the patent, whether by creating trusts or otherwise, are not to be excluded.[94] Documents containing an agreement to be registrable must, however, be complete, and of such a nature that specific performance of the agreement could be enforced, as otherwise no legal or equitable interest in the patent or proprietorship thereof would pass.[95]

The Comptroller may refuse to enter upon the Register of Patents a document dated before the patent, upon the ground that it does not contain a sufficient proof of title, but it would appear that if the

---

[86] s. 74 (6).
[87] s. 75.
[88] See *Hassall* v. *Wright*, 40 L.J.Ch. 145 at p. 146.
[89] *Martin* v. *Scrib Ltd.*, 67 R.P.C. 127.
[90] 27 R.P.C., *Comptroller's Ruling E.*
[91] See *Van Gelder Apsimon & Co. Ltd.* v. *Sowerby Bridge Flour Society Ltd.*, 7 R.P.C. 208.
[92] 27 R.P.C., *Comptroller's Ruling E.*
[93] s. 73 (4).
[94] *Stewart* v. *Casey*, 9 R.P.C. 9.
[95] *Haslett* v. *Hutchinson*, 8 R.P.C. 457; *Fletcher's Patent*, 10 R.P.C. 252; *Morey's Patent*, 25 Beav. 581.

objection does not apply and if the subject-matter of the document is clearly identifiable with the patent concerned, the fact that it is dated prior to the date of the patent is not in itself a bar to registration.[96]

The Comptroller may refuse to register documents if he is not satisfied that they are properly stamped.[97]

671 Certificate of the Comptroller

A certificate by the Comptroller as to any entry which he is authorised to make or as to any other thing which he is authorised to do is prima facie evidence of the matters so certified.[98] Certified copies of any entry will be furnished by the Comptroller on payment of the prescribed fee, and will be admitted in proceedings in all courts without further proof or production of the originals.[99]

672 Information. Caveat

Any person interested in a particular patent may leave a request at the Patent Office to be informed of certain matters, for example, of any attempt to register an assignment or other document in connection with the patent in question.[1] Notice will then be given to the person who has left the request and registration will be suspended for a few days so as to enable the person interested to apply to the courts for leave to serve notice of motion to prevent registration if he so desires.

The matters in respect of which information may be obtained are set out in rule 135 of the Patents Rules 1968 [2] and include matters relating to the filing and acceptance of the complete specification, the sealing of the patent, the payment of renewal fees, the expiry of the patent and any matters in respect of which an entry must be made in the register.

673 Rectification of register by the court

The court may, on the application of any person aggrieved, rectify the register.[3]

The application is made by motion and is heard by the Patents Judge in the Chancery Division. The applicant must forthwith serve

[96] *Parnell's Patent*, 5 R.P.C. 126.
[97] See 54 & 55 Vict. c. 39, s. 17; *cf. Maynard* v. *Consolidated Kent Collieries*, 19 T.L.R. 448.
[98] s. 77.
[99] ss. 73 (2), 77 (2).
[1] s. 78.
[2] See *post*, § 1482.
[3] s. 75.

an office copy of the application on the Comptroller, who enters notice of the application on the register.[4]

Clerical errors in the register may be corrected by the Comptroller on application made to him in the prescribed manner.[5]

674 Falsifying entries

It is an offence to make a false entry in the register or a writing falsely purporting to be a copy of an entry, or to produce or tender in evidence any such writing knowing it to be false.[6]

675 False use of " Patent Office "

If any person uses on his place of business, or on any document issued by him, the words " Patent Office " or any other words suggesting that his place of business is, or is officially connected with, the Patent Office, he is liable on summary conviction to a fine not exceeding £20.[7]

[The next paragraph is 681]

---

[4] Patents Rules 1968, r. 149.
[5] s. 76; Patents Rules 1968, rr. 129–132.
[6] s. 90.
[7] s. 91 (2).

CHAPTER 11

COMPULSORY LICENCES (ABUSE OF MONOPOLY)

1. HISTORY

681 As has already been stated, the early industrial " monopoly " patents were granted with a view to establishing new industries in this country. By the Statute of Monopolies a patent was void if hurtful to trade or generally inconvenient. The common form of grant also provided for revocation by the Privy Council if the grant was prejudicial or inconvenient to the King's subjects.[1] Many patents were in fact revoked for non-working during the seventeeenth century[2]; but the courts later held that manufacture under the patent in this country was not essential,[3] and prior to the Act of 1883 there were no statutory provisions whereby a patentee could be forced to grant a licence if he abused his monopoly rights. By section 22 of that Act the Board of Trade was given power to order the grant of a compulsory licence where: (1) the patent was not being worked in the United Kingdom; or (2) the reasonable requirements of the public with respect to the invention were not satisfied; or (3) any person was prevented from working or using an invention of which he was possessed.

There are only a few cases reported, however, of applications under this Act.[4]

682 By the Act of 1902 the jurisdiction of the Board of Trade was transferred to the Judicial Committee of the Privy Council, who might not only order a compulsory licence, but also revoke the patent if the granting of licences would be an inadequate remedy. No applications under this procedure are reported.

By section 24 of the Act of 1907 the jurisdiction was transferred to the court which was given power to order the grant of compulsory licences or to revoke the patent in cases where the reasonable requirements of the public in respect of the patented invention had

---

[1] See Chap. 1, and *Hatschek's Patents*, 26 R.P.C. 228.
[2] See Hulme, E. W., 13 L.Q.R. 313; 33 *ibid.* 71.
[3] See *Badische Anilin und Soda Fabrik* v. *W. G. Thompson Ltd. and Others*, 21 R.P.C. 473.
[4] *Continental Gas Gluhlicht etc. Petition*, 15 R.P.C. 727; *Levenstein's Petition*, 15 R.P.C. 732; *Hulton and Bleakley's Petition*, 15 R.P.C. 749; *Bartlett's Patent*, 16 R.P.C. 641; and see J. W. Gordon, *Compulsory Licences* (London, 1899).

not been satisfied; and by section 27 of that Act the Comptroller was given power (subject to an appeal to the court) to revoke the patent in cases where manufacture was carried on wholly or mainly abroad.

The Act of 1919 repealed sections 24 and 27 of the 1907 Act and substituted a new section 27, whereby the Comptroller was given jurisdiction in all cases where abuse of monopoly rights was alleged, his decision being subject to an appeal to the court. That section was subsequently amended and extended by the Acts of 1928 and 1932.

683   1949 Act

The present Act further extended the grounds on which a compulsory licence may be obtained or the patent endorsed " licences of right," [5] or, in the last resort, the patent revoked. It has long been a popular misconception that patents are frequently applied for or purchased in order that the inventions covered thereby may be stifled for the benefit of rival commercial interests and in consequence of this belief importance has been attached to the somewhat elaborate provisions designed to prevent " abuse of monopoly." (These actual words are not used in the present Act.)   In fact, no reliable evidence of even a single instance of such a suppression of an invention has ever been forthcoming, in spite of efforts of a Royal Commission to unearth it, if it in fact existed.

2. GROUNDS FOR COMPULSORY LICENCE

684   The right to obtain a compulsory licence arises in two main cases:

  (i)   where there has been inadequate working or oppressive conduct by the patentee,[6] and

  (ii)   where the invention is concerned with food or medicine, or a surgical or curative device.[7]

An application under (i) for compulsory licence or to have the patent endorsed " licences of right," cannot be made until three years have elapsed from the date of sealing of the patent.[8]   The applicant must be a " person interested," [9] and he must make out a

---

[5] See *ante*, § 656 *et seq.*
[6] s. 37.
[7] s. 41.
[8] s. 37 (1).   See *Cathro's Appn.*, 51 R.P.C. 75 at p. 79.

prima facie case before the Comptroller will allow the application to proceed.[9]

685 Objects to be attained

By section 39, the Comptroller is to exercise his powers with a view to securing the following purposes:

(a) that inventions which can be worked on a commercial scale in the United Kingdom shall be worked there to the fullest practicable extent;

(b) that the inventor or other person entitled shall receive reasonable remuneration;

(c) that the interests of any person working or developing an invention in the United Kingdom shall not be prejudiced.

The Comptroller is also to take into account:

(a) the nature of the invention, how long the patent has been sealed and what user the patentee or any licensee has already made;

(b) the qualifications of a prospective licensee; and

(c) the risks the latter must undertake;

but the Comptroller need not take into account matters arising subsequent to the application for a compulsory licence.[10]

686 *Commercial scale*

The Act of 1919 contained a special definition of " working on a commercial scale," [13] but the present Act provides no definition of " commercial scale " and these words must, therefore, be given their natural and ordinary meaning, *i.e.* " in contradistinction to research work or work in the laboratory." [14]

687 Grounds

There are five classes of cases in which the act or default of the patentee can give rise to an application for a compulsory licence. These classes are not mutually exclusive; but unless the circumstances relied upon fall within one or other of the classes, no relief can be granted under the section.[15] The classes are:

---

[9] s. 43 (2). See *Co-operative Union Ltd.'s Appns.*, 50 R.P.C. 161 at p. 163; cf. *Hatschek's Patents*, 26 R.P.C. 228 at pp. 245–247.

[10] s. 39 (2).

[13] Act of 1919, s. 93.

[14] *McKechnie Bros. Ltd.'s Appn.*, 51 R.P.C. 461 at p. 468.

[15] See *Brownie Wireless Co. Ltd.'s Appns.*, 46 R.P.C. 457 at p. 471.

688 **(a) Non-working in the United Kingdom, section 37 (2) (a)**

"*That the patented invention, being capable of being commercially worked in the United Kingdom, is not being commercially worked therein or is not being so worked to the fullest extent that is reasonably practicable*";

The onus is upon the applicants to establish that the patented invention is not being worked to the fullest extent that is reasonably possible, *i.e.* at the rate of production which is practicable and necessary to meet the demand for the patented invention. In order to establish a case under this subsection it will normally be necessary for an applicant to bring evidence to show what the demand for the invention might reasonably be expected to be and how far short production in the United Kingdom fails to supply that demand.[16]

689 "*Patented invention*"

The meaning of the words " patented invention " requires some discussion in considering the obligation on the patentee to establish working on a commercial scale. In the case of an invention involving a small improvement in a complicated machine, a question arises as to the obligation on the patentee to manufacture. Again, if the patent is for the combination of old parts, there is the question whether the mere assembling in this country of parts made abroad is sufficient to comply with the section. In *Lakes' Patent*,[17] the Comptroller said:
" As a general rule a patentee ought not to be called upon to manufacture any mechanism or machine which he has not specifically described and claimed in his specification. . . . There may be, of course, cases in which it is impossible to sever the various elements claimed in combination, and in such cases different considerations may arise. If, however, the general principle stated is correct, the following general results would seem to follow, *viz.*: if the patentee has claimed a wholly new machine or mechanism, he must manufacture that in this country or run the risk of coming within the provisions of the section. . . . If he claims a new improvement in a well-known machine, he must manufacture the improvement, and not necessarily the whole machine; but if he claims the improvement in combination with a machine consisting of well-known parts it may be that he must besides manufacturing the improvement put together the whole machine in this country, or at any rate the combination he claims. If his invention merely consists in a new combination of old and well-known elements, it would seem sufficient for him prima facie to put together the whole machine in this country, and it is not necessary for him to manufacture the old and

---

[16] *Kamborian's Patent* [1961] R.P.C. 403 at p. 405.
[17] 26 R.P.C. 443 at p. 447.

well-known parts which are also possibly the subject-matter of prior patents; but different considerations may again arise where important alterations in the known parts are necessary for the new combination. Each case must, of course, be decided on its merits, and in each case it will have to be determined on a proper construction of the patentee's specification, what the patentee's invention really is, and what are its essential features." [18]

690   *Manufacture by infringers*

The words " patented invention " are comparable with the words " patented article or process " in section 27 of the 1907 Act. It was held under that section that the words were descriptive of the manufacture itself, and that manufacture by infringers might be relied upon by the patentee.[19] This would appear to be the case under the present law also.

691   *Relevant date*

In *McKechnie Bros. Ltd.'s Application* [20] Luxmoore J. said: " the actual facts existing at the date of hearing may be considered as well as those existing at the date of the filing of the application. . . . It is, of course, of first-class importance to consider the actual position at the date of the application; for if there is no actual working at that date, it may well be that the subsequent working has been arranged solely for the purpose of defeating the application and is not really bona fide." [21]

692   *Commercial working discontinued*

A patentee cannot resist an application for a compulsory licence merely on the ground that there has at one time been commercial working in this country if such working has been discontinued.[22]

Under the former section an applicant had to show that the patented invention was worked exclusively or mainly abroad, and the patentee had to furnish satisfactory reasons why manufacture to an adequate extent was not carried on in the United Kingdom. The cases decided under that section may be of some assistance in construing the words " fullest extent that is reasonably practicable " of the present section.

693   In *Hatschek's Patents* [23] Parker J. said: " I do not think that any reasons can be satisfactory which do not account for the inadequacy

---

[18] And see *Hill's Patent,* 32 R.P.C. 475; *Wardwell's Patent,* 30 R.P.C. 408; and *cf. Co-operative Union Ltd.'s Appns.,* 50 R.P.C. 161.
[19] See Parker J. in *Mercedes Daimler Co.'s Patents,* 27 R.P.C. 762 at p. 768.
[20] 51 R.P.C. 461 at p. 467.
[21] See also *Fabricmeter Co. Ltd.'s Appn.,* 53 R.P.C. 307.
[22] *Cathro's Appn.,* 51 R.P.C. 75 at p. 79.
[23] [1909] 2 Ch. 68; 26 R.P.C. 228 at p. 241.

of the extent to which the patented article is manufactured or the patented process is carried on in this country by causes operating irrespective of any abuse of the monopoly granted by the patent. The first thing, therefore, for the patentee to do is, by full disclosure of the manner in which he exercised his patent rights, to free himself from all suspicion of having done anything to hamper the industry of the United Kingdom." The learned judge then dealt with the case of a patentee who had favoured foreign manufacturers to the disadvantage of British ones. Under the present section, although the British and foreign manufacturers may have been treated on an equality by the patentee, he is, nevertheless, under the obligation to furnish an explanation of the circumstances which have prevented the establishment of commercial manufacture in this country. On this point the further observations of the learned judge [24] are applicable: "Certainly the fact that persons who were carrying on the industry in this country would make smaller profits than persons carrying it on abroad would, in my opinion, be no satisfactory reason at all. I can conceive cases in which a patentee . . . may find it impossible to work . . . in the United Kingdom because of the nature of the invention, or because of local conditions which prevail here but not in other countries, although these cases must, I think, be rare. . . . But it can never, in my opinion, be sufficient for a patentee, defending himself under the section, to prove that he cannot now start an industry with any chance of profit."

The last sentence of the learned judge needs further explanation; he went on to say that the reason for there being no chance of profit might be that the foreign manufacturers had become firmly established in consequence of the patentee having favoured foreign trade at the expense of home trade. It is suggested that, in the absence of circumstances of that kind, the fact that there was no hope of profit, or that a loss was to be expected, would constitute a defence to an application under the present section.[25]

694   *Absence of demand*

The proof of absence of any demand for the invention in this country is not of itself a sufficient defence. In *Boult's Patent* [26] the Comptroller said: "The consideration of the adequacy of manufacture in this country does no doubt depend to some extent upon the demand existing for the article here or in neutral markets, but it does not follow that, if there is no demand existing, there is no obligation

[24] 26 R.P.C. at p. 243.
[25] And see *Boult's Patent*, 26 R.P.C. 383 at p. 387; also *Kent's Patent*, 26 R.P.C. 666 at p. 670.
[26] 26 R.P.C. 383 at p. 387.

on a patentee to start an industry here. If he does in fact manufacture in foreign countries, and if there is in fact a demand for the article or process abroad, the absence of any demand here does not seem to be a valid excuse. The patentee must, in such cases, make an effort to create a demand here, and the establishment of an industry will in itself help to create in many cases a demand for the article or process in question."

Where, however, the type of engine to which the invention was applicable had been almost superseded, so that it would not have been commercially advisable to establish a manufacture of the patented mechanism in this country, and the patentee had merely charged royalties on imported French machines of a special kind, containing the patented mechanism, it was held that he had furnished a sufficiently satisfactory reason to comply with the requirements of the former law.[27]

But it is not " open to a patentee, who has already filled the bulk of a largely non-recurrent demand for a patented article in this country by importation from abroad and who then, under the stimulus of an application for a compulsory licence, has arranged for a manufacture to be started here, to say that such a manufacture must be considered to be ' adequate and reasonable under all the circumstances ' for the purpose in question merely because it is sufficient, or he considers it sufficient, to meet so much of the demand as has remained unsupplied from abroad." [28]

The Comptroller will not usually consider whether the demand would be increased if a lower price were charged; but if the price asked for articles made in this country is higher than that charged for the imported article, it becomes necessary to inquire whether the price is a bona fide one, or one merely adopted for the purpose of checking and diminishing the demand for the home-manufactured article.[29]

695 *Fear of infringement action*

In *Taylor's Patent* [30] the patentee showed that he dared not establish manufacture in this country for fear of an infringement action under a master patent owned by the applicants for revocation, who had in fact refused the offer of a licence under the patent in question. Parker J. refused to revoke the patent, and held that the patentee was not bound, as the applicants contended, to apply for a voluntary or a compulsory licence under the applicants' patent. Had the applicants been able to show, however, that they had been ready and

[27] *Osborn's Patent,* 26 R.P.C. 819.
[28] *Fabricmeter Co. Ltd.'s Appn.,* 53 R.P.C. 307 at p. 312.
[29] *Kent's Patent,* 26 R.P.C. 666 at p. 670.   [30] 29 R.P.C. 296.

willing to grant the patentee a licence on reasonable terms the decision might have been otherwise.

696   *Requisite skill exclusively foreign*

It will not avail the patentee to allege that the special skill and experience necessary to enable the invention to be carried into effect can only be found abroad,[31] although it may well be that an invention requiring special skill and the establishment of a factory with special tools may need a longer time to develop than one in which these features are not present. It is incumbent on the patentee to take steps to import the necessary tools and skilled labour to effect manufacture in this country.

In *Kent's Patent*[32] the Comptroller said: "I shall always decline to accept, as a rule, any argument based on the impossibility of securing an efficient manufacture of special machinery in this country,[33] but I think it is natural for a patentee who desires to put the best possible machine upon the market to be somewhat over-scrupulous at first in obtaining his materials, and supervising the construction of his machine."

697   *Circumstances beyond patentee's control*

Under the former law, if the patentee could be shown to have done his best to establish a manufacture in the United Kingdom, and to have failed for reasons beyond his control, he was not held to have abused his monopoly. In *Bremer's Patent*,[34] Parker J. said: "In my opinion, the company have throughout used, and still are using, their best endeavours to fulfil the obligation arising under the Act of 1907 by establishing in this country an industry in the article, the subject of their patent, and they have further proved, to my satisfaction, that their want of success up to the present time has been due to circumstances beyond their own control, and not to the manner in which they have exercised the rights conferred upon them by the patent in question. The Act of 1907 was never meant to penalise want of success when the patentee has done his best, and I cannot, therefore, come to the conclusion that the patent ought to be revoked." But having regard to the changed language of the present section[35] it is doubtful whether this decision would now be followed.

698   *Power to adjourn the application*

If the circumstances are such as to justify the Comptroller in

---

[31] *Johnson's Patent*, 26 R.P.C. 52.
[32] 26 R.P.C. 666 at p. 670.
[33] And see *Wardwell's Patent*, 30 R.P.C. 408; *A. Hamson & Son (London) Ltd.'s Appn.* [1958] R.P.C. 88.
[34] 26 R.P.C. 449 at p. 465.
[35] s. 37 (2) (*a*).

affording the patentee more time to establish manufacture in this country, he may adjourn the application.[36]

699   **(b) Unreasonable terms and importation, section 37 (2) (b)**

" *That a demand for the patented article in the United Kingdom is not being met on reasonable terms, or is being met to a substantial extent by importation* ";

The words " patented article " include articles made by a patented process.[37] It would appear that they would not be held to cover articles made by a patented machine if the machine alone could properly be said to be " the ' patented article ' under . . . [the] . . . patent." [38]

700   *Demand must be existing*

The demand must be an actual one and not merely one which the applicant for a licence hopes and expects to create if and when he obtains a licence.[39]

The matters which have to be taken into consideration in determining what constitute " reasonable terms " are similar to those which have to be considered under paragraph (d) in the case of licences, and are dealt with below.

In *Robin Electric Lamp Co. Ltd.'s Petition* [40] the patentees required an undertaking from their licensees not to sell articles (in which the patented invention was used) below a specified price. This resulted in the price of such articles being considerably higher in this country than abroad. The supply was adequate to meet the demands of the public, and there was no evidence that the price was " so high as to be a serious burden to the consumer or to be unreasonable "; and it was held that there had not been a default by the patentees.

701   **(c) Working prevented by importation, section 37 (2) (c)**

" *That the commercial working of the invention in the United Kingdom is being prevented or hindered by the importation of the patented article* ";

If the invention is actually being adequately worked in this country it is not necessarily a ground for granting a compulsory licence under this head that certain specialised applications of the invention are not being met by manufacture here.[41]

---

[36] s. 37 (3), proviso (*a*).
[37] s. 37 (5).
[38] See *Co-operative Union Ltd.'s Appns.*, 50 R.P.C. 161 at p. 163; and see § 689 *ante*.
[39] *Cathro's Appn.*, 51 R.P.C. 75 at p. 82.
[40] 32 R.P.C. 202.
[41] *Cathro's Appn.*, 51 R.P.C. 75 at p. 81.

702   (d) Refusal of reasonable terms, section 37 (2) (d)

"*That by reason of the refusal of the patentee to grant a licence or licences on reasonable terms—*

(*i*) *a market for the export of the patented article manufactured in the United Kingdom is not being supplied; or*

(*ii*) *the working or efficient working in the United Kingdom of any other patented invention which makes a substantial contribution to the art is prevented or hindered; or*

(*iii*) *the establishment or development of commercial or industrial activities in the United Kingdom is unfairly prejudiced*";

No order for endorsement of the patent " licences of right " is to be made on ground (i) above and any licence granted on that ground may restrict the countries in which the patented article may be sold or used by the licensee.[42]   And no order is to be made on ground (ii) above unless the applicant is willing to grant a reciprocal licence on reasonable terms.[43]

It has been held that before any application could be made under the former provisions corresponding to this paragraph there must have been either a complete refusal to grant a licence or the terms upon which it was offered must have been unreasonable.[44]

It is submitted that this general principle will continue to be followed, but the applicant is now in no way prejudiced by the fact that he has already accepted a licence or made any admission in relation thereto.[45]

703   "*Reasonable terms*"

As to what constitutes "reasonable terms," Luxmoore J. in *Brownie Wireless Co. Ltd.'s Applications* [46] said: "The answer to the question must in each case depend on a careful consideration of all the surrounding circumstances.   The nature of the invention . . . the terms of the licences (if any) already granted, the expenditure and liabilities of the patentee in respect of the patent, the requirements of the purchasing public, and so on."   It was argued that the royalty was out of proportion to the cost and selling price, and that a reduction would result in a greatly increased public demand.   The learned judge held there was no evidence to support the latter contention, and said [47]: "There is in fact no necessary relationship between cost price or selling price . . . and the royalty which a patentee is entitled to ask. . . .   The best test of whether a royalty is reasonable in amount or the reverse is: How much are manufacturers who are anxious to make and deal with the patented article

---

[42] s. 37 (3), proviso (*b*).   [43] s. 37 (3), proviso (*c*).
[44] *Loewe Radio Co. Ltd.'s Appns.*, 46 R.P.C. 479 at pp. 489, 490.
[45] s. 37 (4).   [46] 46 R.P.C. 457 at p. 473.   [47] 46 R.P.C. 457 at p. 475.

on commercial lines ready and willing to pay? . . ." He held on the evidence that the royalty was reasonable, that terms prohibiting export and providing for payment of royalty on non-patented articles were reasonable in the circumstances, and that in view of the nature of the invention it was reasonable to require licensees to take a licence under all patents belonging to a given group and to refuse to grant licences under individual patents.

704 "*Commercial or industrial activities*"

Under the corresponding provisions of the previous law it was held that the words "trade or industry of the United Kingdom" should be construed in a wide sense.[48] It is submitted that the words "commercial or industrial activities in the United Kingdom" are even wider than the former words. But the previous requirement under this ground that "it is in the public interest that a licence or licences should be granted"[49] has been abolished and this must be borne in mind when considering cases decided under the earlier Acts.

705 **(e) Unreasonable conditions, section 37 (2) (e)**

"*That by reason of conditions imposed by the patentee upon the grant of licences under the patent, or upon the purchase, hire or use of the patented article or process, the manufacture, use or sale of materials not protected by the patent,*[50] *or the establishment or development of commercial or industrial activities*[51] *in the United Kingdom is unfairly prejudiced*";

Where the patentees inserted in a limited licence conditions which prohibited the sale of the patented article to a specified class of retailers, it was held that such retailers were not "unfairly prejudiced" within the meaning of the provisions of the previous law.[52]

706 **Terms**

In each case the terms upon which a compulsory licence will be granted will depend on the particular facts of the case.

In *Farmers Marketing & Supply Ltd.'s Patent*[52a] a licence to manufacture abroad and import was refused. However a licence to import has been granted,[52b] but in that case a bar was placed on the licensee to prevent export.

---

[48] *Brownie Wireless Co. Ltd.'s Appns.*, 46 R.P.C. 457 at p. 478; and see *Robin Electric Lamp Co. Ltd.'s Petition*, 32 R.P.C. 202 at p. 213.
[49] Act of 1907, s. 27 (2) (*d*).
[50] See *ante*, § 642 *et seq.*, and *Colbourne Engineering Co. Ltd.'s Appn.*, 72 R.P.C. 169.   [51] See *supra*.
[52] *Co-operative Union Ltd.'s Appn.*, 50 R.P.C. 161 at pp. 164, 165.
[52a] [1966] R.P.C. 546.
[52b] *Hoffman-La Roche & Co. A.G.'s Patent* [1969] R.P.C. 504 and also [1970] F.S.R. 225.

707   Application by Crown

A government department may apply after the expiry of three years from the date of sealing of a patent on any one or more of the grounds set out above that the patent shall be endorsed " licences of right " or that a licence may be granted to some specified person.[53]

708   Report on Monopolies

Under the Monopolies and Restrictive Practices (Inquiry and Control) Act 1948,[54] the Monopolies and Restrictive Practices Commission may lay a report before Parliament alleging the existence of undesirable monopolistic practices with a view to a resolution being passed declaring that such conditions exist. In that event, if the goods in question include patented articles or articles made by a patented process, a competent authority under that Act may apply to the Comptroller for an order cancelling any restrictive conditions contained in an existing licence, or for the endorsement of the patent " licences of right," or both.[55]

709   Alternative remedies

Where the Comptroller is satisfied that one or more of the conditions set out above is satisfied, he may order the patent to be endorsed " licences of right " (thus enabling any person interested thereafter to obtain a licence on reasonable terms as of right) [56] or he may order the grant of a licence to the applicant.[57] If the Comptroller is satisfied that conditions imposed by the patentee on the grant of licences, or upon the purchase, hire or use of the patented article or process, unfairly prejudice the manufacture, sale or use of materials not protected by the patent, he may also order the grant of licences to customers of the applicant.[58] If the applicant is already a licensee, the Comptroller may amend the existing licence or order it to be cancelled and grant a new licence.[59] If the Comptroller orders the grant of a licence he may deprive the patentee of any right to make, use, exercise or vend the invention, or to grant licences, and may revoke all existing licences.[60] The Comptroller will not, however, grant a compulsory licence if it would be futile to do so, e.g. if manufacture under that licence would necessarily infringe another patent in respect of which no compulsory licence could be obtained.[61]

---

[53] s. 40 (1).
[54] 11 & 12 Geo. 6, c. 66. See also Monopolies and Mergers Act 1965, s. 1 (1), Sched. 1, Pt. III, para. 9 (3).
[55] s. 40 (3), (4).   [56] See *ante*, § 656 *et seq.*
[57] s. 37 (3). For examples of compulsory licences, see *McKechnie Bros. Ltd.'s Appn.*, 51 R.P.C. at pp. 454, 472; *Cathro's Appn.*, 51 R.P.C. 475 at p. 483.
[58] s. 38 (1).   [59] s. 38 (2).   [60] s. 38 (3).
[61] *Cathro's Appn.*, 51 R.P.C. 475 at p. 488.

710 Revocation

Where an order for the grant of a licence has been made, any person interested may apply after the expiration of two years from the date of that order for the revocation of the patent upon the same grounds. If the Comptroller is satisfied that such grounds exist *and* that neither the endorsement " licences of right " nor the grant of a compulsory licence will achieve the desired result, he may revoke the patent.[62] The order for revocation may either be unconditional, or only to take effect if the patentee fails to comply with conditions imposed in the order within a specified time, which may subsequently be extended if good cause is shown.[63]

711 Licences for production of food and medicine

Where a patent is in force in respect of a substance, or a process for producing a substance, which is capable of being used as, or for the production of, food or medicine, the Comptroller may, on the application of an interested party, order the grant of a licence.[64] A similar application may be made in respect of a patent for an invention capable of being used as or as part of a surgical or curative device.[65] Under such a licence the licensee has no rights except in relation to food, medicine, or surgical or curative devices.[66] " Curative devices " must have some remedial property or properties and are not preventive or protective devices.[67] It is to be noted that, notwithstanding the provisions of the International Convention [68] and section 45 (3), an application on this ground can be made at any time, whereas an application for a compulsory licence based on " abuse of monopoly " can be made only after the expiration of three years from the date of sealing.[69]

A compulsory licence under these provisions in respect of an invention relating to food or medicine or a surgical or curative device may be granted for importation of the substance or device,[70] but an application for such a licence may be refused as contrary to the public interest.[71]

---

[62] s. 42.
[63] s. 42 (2). And see *Warring and Kortenbach's Patent*, 26 R.P.C. 163; *Weber's Patent*, 26 R.P.C. 300; 27 R.P.C. 30; *Boult's Patent*, 26 R.P.C. 383; *Wardwell's Patent*, 30 R.P.C. 408; *Intertype's Appn.*, 43 R.P.C. 305.
[64] s. 41 (1). See *Glaxo Laboratories Ltd.'s Appn.*, 58 R.P.C. 12.
[65] s. 41 (1) (c).   [66] s. 41 (3).
[67] *Eastman Kodak Co.'s Patents* [1968] R.P.C. 390.
[68] See Art. 5 (A) (4), *post*, § 1864.
[69] *Parke, Davis & Co. v. Comptroller General of Patents etc.*, 71 R.P.C. 169.
[70] *Hoffman-La Roche & Co. A.G. & Geigy A.G. v. Inter-Continental Pharmaceuticals Ltd.* [1965] R.P.C. 226 at p. 231; *Hoffman-La Roche & Co. A.G.'s Patent* [1969] R.P.C. 304.
[71] *Farmers' Marketing & Supply Co. Ltd.'s Patent* [1966] R.P.C. 546.

3. Practice

712   The procedure to be followed is laid down in section 43 and is further provided for in rules 108 to 116 of the amended Patent Rules 1968. The application is made on Form 47 setting forth the facts and the relief asked for, and must be verified by declarations which must also support an allegation of interest. If the Comptroller is not satisfied that a bona fide interest is disclosed, and a prima face case for relief is made out, the application will be dismissed at this stage.[72] If, however, he is satisfied on these points, the applicant is directed to serve copies on the patentee and on all persons appearing, from the entries in the Register, to be interested. The application is also advertised in the *Official Journal*. The patentee, or any other person desiring to oppose the application, delivers a notice of opposition containing a statement, verified by declaration, setting out the grounds on which the application is opposed. The Comptroller normally decides the case after giving the applicant and the opponent an opportunity of being heard.[73]

Unless the terms of the licence are agreed, they are settled by the Comptroller. The Comptroller has no power to antedate the grant of a licence,[74] and the licence will run from the decision or order of the Comptroller which settles all the terms of the licence.[75]

713   Reference to Arbitrator

If the parties consent, or the proceedings require a prolonged examination of documents of any scientific or local investigation, the Comptroller may refer the whole proceedings, or any issue of fact, to an arbitrator.[76]

714   Appeal

An appeal from any order of the Comptroller and from any award of the arbitrator (unless otherwise agreed before the award is made) lies to the Appeal Tribunal.[77]

715   Infringement action pending

Even though a compulsory licence has been applied for an interlocutory injunction may be granted.[78] Further, an action for infringement will not, in general, be stayed pending the outcome of an application for a compulsory licence.[79]

[The next paragraph is 721]

---

[72] *Co-operative Union Ltd.'s Appns.*, 50 R.P.C. 161.   [73] s. 43 (5).
[74] *Hoffman-La Roche & Co. A.G.* v. *Inter-Continental Pharmaceuticals Ltd.* [1965] R.P.C. 226.
[75] *Geigy S.A.'s Patent* [1966] R.P.C. 250.   [76] s. 44 (3).
[77] s. 44 (1), (3); s. 85.   [78] See *post*, § 824.
[79] *Pfizer Corpn.* v. *D.D.S.A. Pharmaceuticals Ltd.* [1966] R.P.C. 44.

CHAPTER 12

PETITION FOR REVOCATION

721 Petition

Section 32 of the Act provides that revocation of a patent may be obtained by any person interested on petition to the court. The grounds available to a petitioner are also available as defences to an action for infringement,[1] and are dealt with in detail in Chapter 14.[2] It was formerly necessary for an intending petitioner to obtain the fiat of the Attorney-General before presenting his petition, except in certain special cases.[3] It is submitted that no preliminary formality is now necessary before the petition is presented, but that it may be resisted on the ground that the petitioner has no bona fide interest in revoking the patent *i.e.* no interest such as would give him a *locus standi* in opposition proceedings.[4]

722 *Counterclaim in action for infringement*

The defendant in an action for infringement may counterclaim for revocation without presenting a petition.[5] The practice in such cases is dealt with in Chapter 14. A counterclaim for revocation may be proceeded with even though the action by the plaintiff is stayed, discontinued or dismissed.[6] In some circumstances concurrent proceedings by petition for the revocation of a patent may be allowed to proceed.[7]

723 *No declaration of invalidity*

An action cannot be brought claiming a declaration that a patent is invalid,[8] the proper course being to petition for revocation. It is probable that a petition would lie for the revocation of a patent which had expired.[9]

---

[1] s. 32 (4).
[2] See *post*, § 791 *et seq.*
[3] Act of 1907, s. 25 (4).
[4] *Ante*, § 415 *et seq.* And see *White's Patent* [1957] R.P.C. 405.
[5] s. 61.
[6] See R.S.C., Ord. 15, r. 2.
[7] *Lever Bros. and Unilever Ltd.'s Patent*, 69 R.P.C. 117.
[8] *North-Eastern Marine Engineering Co.* v. *Leeds Forge Co.*, 23 R.P.C. 529; *Traction Corpn.* v. *Bennett*, 25 R.P.C. 819 at p. 822; *cf. Killen* v. *Mac-Millan*, 49 R.P.C. 258 at p. 260.
[9] *North-Eastern Marine Engineering Co.* v. *Leeds Forge Co.*, 23 R.P.C. 529, at p. 531. See also *John Summers & Sons Ltd.* v. *The Cold Metal Process Co. Ltd.*, 65 R.P.C. 75 at p. 91.

724   Parties

The person upon whom a petition should be served is the registered proprietor of the patent. It is customary also to serve any other persons who at the time the petition is presented appear upon the register as being beneficially interested in the patent.[10]

Where an assignment had been executed after the petition had been presented, the name of the assignee was ordered to be substituted for that of the original respondent to the petition.[11]

725   The Tribunal

Petitions for revocation in England come before the High Court and will ordinarily be heard by one of the special Patents Judges.[12] In Scotland proceedings for revocation are in the form of an action of reduction,[13] and are heard by the Court of Session.[14]

726   Practice before trial

The practice is regulated by Order 103, rules 2, 17 to 19 and 21 to 27 of the Rules of the Supreme Court, and is in most respects similar to or identical with the practice in actions for infringement.[15]

727   *Service of petition*

The proceedings are commenced by the presentation of a petition [16] to the court, and its service upon the respondent in the same way as a writ. Particulars of the objections to the validity of the patent on which the petitioner is going to rely must be served with the petition.[17] The practice as to these particulars is the same as in the case of an action for infringement in which the issue of invalidity is raised.[18]

728   *Service out of jurisdiction*

Where the patentee or other person interested in the patent is out of the jurisdiction, notice should be given to such person by registered letter that the petition has been presented, as the court will not decree the revocation of a patent without giving all interested parties an opportunity of being heard; but the mere fact that the patentee is out of the jurisdiction will not prevent the institution of proceedings

---

[10] See *Avery's Patent*, 36 Ch.D. 307; 4 R.P.C. 152, 322.
[11] *Haddan's Patent*, 2 R.P.C. 218.
[12] s. 84 (1).
[13] s. 103 (2).
[14] s. 103 (3).
[15] See Chap. 14.
[16] See Appendix *post*, § 2017.
[17] R.S.C., Ord. 103, r. 18.
[18] See Chap. 14; R.S.C., Ord. 103, rr. 21–24.

for revocation.[19] The usual order in such cases is that notice of the proceedings be sent to the patentee or other proposed respondent, and that unless he appear, the petition is not to come into the list for hearing except by leave of the judge.[20]

A respondent residing out of the jurisdiction will not be ordered to give security for costs.[21]

729 *Application for directions*

Order 103, rule 26, applies to petitions for revocation, and at any rate a contested petition cannot be heard until an application for directions under this rule has been disposed of.

730 *Discovery, interrogatories and inspection*

The directions which have to be obtained under this rule,[22] and the practice as to discovery of documents, interrogatories and inspection, are the same as in the case of an action for infringement.[23]

731　The trial

Right to begin

By Order 103, rule 18 (3), of the Rules of the Supreme Court, the respondent is entitled to begin and give evidence in support of the patent, and if the petitioner gives evidence impeaching the validity of the patent the respondent is entitled to reply.

732 *Onus of proof*

The evidence which will be required of the respondent in the first instance will be very slight, and will be similar to that which he would give as to the validity of the patent were he plaintiff in an action for infringement. The petitioner will then have to prove the case he alleges in his petition and particulars, and the respondent has the right of reply. It is presumably to preserve this right of reply that the respondent is put in a position similar to that of a plaintiff at the trial.

The nature of the evidence required, and the procedure generally, at the trial is similar to that at the trial of an action for infringement.[24] Petitions for revocation are tried upon *viva voce* evidence.[25]

---

[19] *Drummond's Patent*, 43 Ch.D. 80, 6 R.P.C. 576; *Kay's Patent*, 11 R.P.C. 279; *Goerz and Hoegh's Patent*, 12 R.P.C. 370; *Cerckel's Patent*, 15 R.P.C. 500.

[20] *King & Co.'s Trade Mark*, 9 R.P.C. 350; [1892] 2 Ch. 462; *Kay's Patent*, 11 R.P.C. 279.

[21] *Miller's Patent*, 11 R.P.C. 55.

[22] See *post*, §§ 916, 917.

[23] See Chap. 14; *Haddan's Patent*, 54 L.J.Ch. 126. See also *Sommerfeld's Patent* [1956] R.P.C. 77; *Compania Uruguaya de Fomento Industrial S.A.'s Petition* [1957] R.P.C. 283, 314.

[24] See Chap. 14.

[25] *Gaulard and Gibbs' Patent*, 34 Ch.D. 396.

733   *Res judicata*

Where a defendant in an action for infringement puts in issue the validity of the patent, but does not counterclaim for its revocation, the question arises whether the validity of the patent can be relitigated in subsequent proceedings for revocation. Under the previous law it was held that such former proceedings were no bar to a petitioner who had the Attorney-General's fiat to present the petition, on the ground that he was then acting as a member of the public and not as an individual.[26] Now that the necessity for the fiat has been abolished it is submitted that if the defendant failed to establish the invalidity of the patent in the action, he would thereafter be debarred from raising the same issue in a subsequent petition for revocation.[27]

734   *Amendment of specification*

Section 30 of the Act applies to petitions for revocation as well as to actions for infringement, and a patentee may be allowed, in certain circumstances, to amend his specification after revocation proceedings have been commenced. The practice in such applications is dealt with in Chapter 8.

735   *The remedy*

If in any proceedings for revocation the court decides that the patent is invalid, the court may allow the specification to be amended instead of revoking the patent.[28]

An order for revocation will only be made in open court, and will not be made in chambers even though the patentee consents.[29]

736   *Stay pending appeal*

It is usual to stay the order for revocation pending an appeal.[30] The form of order made in such cases follows that made in *Cincinnati Grinders (Inc.)* v. *B.S.A. Tools Ltd.*[31] An undertaking is, however, required that the patentees will not apply to the Comptroller to amend their specification pending the appeal.[32] An undertaking not to advertise or threaten has also been required.[33] Such orders are

---

[26] *Shoe Machinery Co. Ltd.* v. *Cutlan*, 12 R.P.C. 530; *Deeley's Patent*, 12 R.P.C. 192; *Lewis and Stirkler's Patent*, 14 R.P.C. 24; and see *Poulton's Patent*, 23 R.P.C. 506 but *cf. Shoe Machinery Co. Ltd.* v. *Cutlan (No. 2)*, 13 R.P.C. 141.

[27] See *Jameson's Patent*, 19 R.P.C. 246.

[28] s. 30 (1).

[29] *Clifton's Patent*, 21 R.P.C. 515.

[30] See *e.g. Klaber's Patent*, 22 R.P.C. 405; *Waterhouse's Patent*, 23 R.P.C. 470; *cf. Stahlwerk Becker A.G.'s Patent*, 35 R.P.C. 81.

[31] 48 R.P.C. 33 at p. 60.

[32] *Ibid.* and see also *Le Rasoir Apollo's Patent*, 49 R.P.C. 1 at p. 15.

[33] *Amalgamated Carburetters Ltd.* v. *Bowden Wire Ltd.*, 48 R.P.C. 105 at p. 122; see also *Klaber's Patent*, 22 R.P.C. 405 at p. 416.

otherwise to be presented at the Patent Office (together with Patents Form 69) forthwith by the person in whose favour they are made.[34]

737 *Certificates*

A successful petitioner should obtain a certificate that the various particulars of objections have been proved.[35]

If any claim whose validity is contested is found to be valid, the court may so certify, and in that case in any subsequent proceedings the party upholding the validity of the patent, if finally successful, may recover his costs as between solicitor and client.[36]

738 *Costs*

The principles governing the award of costs are the same as in the case of actions for infringement.[37]

An order for revocation will usually include an order for the respondent to pay the petitioner's costs, and this is so even though the order is made by consent, and no previous notice of the intention to present a petition has been given to the patentee (which would enable the latter to surrender his patent under section 34).[38]

739 Appeals

Appeals upon petitions for revocation are to the Court of Appeal and (with leave) to the House of Lords as in ordinary actions.

[The next paragraph is 755]

---

[34] Patents Rules 1968, r. 150.
[35] R.S.C., Ord. 62, Appendix 2, Part X, 4 (3), and see Chap. 14.
[36] s. 64.
[37] See Chap. 14.
[38] *Aylott's Patent*, 28 R.P.C. 227; *Merryweather's Patent*, 29 R.P.C. 64; *Berry's Patent*, 32 R.P.C. 350.

CHAPTER 13

ACTION TO RESTRAIN THREATS

755 History

Prior to the Act of 1883 the proprietor of a patent might issue threats of proceedings for infringement without rendering himself liable for any damage which he might occasion thereby, provided such threats were made bona fide. It was open to an injured person to apply for an injunction to restrain the patentee from continuing to threaten him, but he could be successful only by showing that the statements made were in fact untrue,[1] and that the defendant intended, even after they were found to be untrue, to repeat them.[2]

In the case of malicious threats an action for damages lay similar to that of slander of title, when the plaintiff had to show that the threat made by the defendant amounted to a " malicious attempt to injure the plaintiffs by asserting a claim of right against his own knowledge that it was without any foundation,"[3] and that actual damage had resulted from the threats.[4] Such an action could, and may still, be maintained quite independently of any provisions of the Patents Acts.[5]

756 *Statutes prior to the 1932 Act*

Section 32 of the 1883 Act and section 36 of the 1907–1928 Acts gave a statutory right of action, in certain limited cases,[6] to any person who was damaged by groundless threats of infringement proceedings, whether such threats were made bona fide or not.[7] These sections were aimed at " a patentee who causes damage by disseminating threats which he dare not or will not justify by an action, who is ' willing to wound, but yet afraid to strike '."[8] They only applied, however, in cases where threats were made by the

---

1 *Halsey* v. *Brotherhood*, 15 Ch.D. 514; 19 Ch.D. 386.
2 *Sugg* v. *Bray*, 2 R.P.C. 223 at p. 246.
3 *Per* Blackburn J. in *Wren* v. *Weild*, L.R. 4 Q.B. 730 at p. 737. See also *Halsey* v. *Brotherhood*, 19 Ch.D. 386 at p. 388.
4 See *e.g. Farr* v. *Weatherhead and Harding*, 49 R.P.C. 262 at p. 267.
5 See *Cars* v. *Bland Light Syndicate Ltd.*, 28 R.P.C. 33; *Mentmore Manufacturing Co. Ltd.* v. *Fomento (Sterling Area) Ltd.*, 72 R.P.C. 157.
6 See *e.g. Diamond Coal Cutter Co.* v. *Mining Appliances Co.*, 32 R.P.C. 569.
7 *Skinner & Co.* v. *Perry*, 10 R.P.C. 1 at p. 8 (C.A.).
8 *Day* v. *Foster*, 7 R.P.C. 54 at p. 60; see also *Skinner & Co.* v. *Perry*, 1 at p. 5 (C.A.).

patentee,[9] or some person claiming to have an interest in a patent,[10] and they did not apply if an action for infringement was " commenced and prosecuted with due diligence." It was also held that section 36 of the 1907–1928 Acts had no application where no patent had in fact been sealed.[11]

757 *The 1932 Act*

The Act of 1932 repealed section 36 of the 1907–1928 Acts and enacted a new section in its place which gave a remedy for groundless threats irrespective of whether the person making the threats did or did not have any interest in a patent. That section also revoked the previous statutory defence to an action for threats of commencing and prosecuting an action for infringement with due diligence.

758   Present Law

Section 65 of the Act of 1949 substantially re-enacts section 36 of the Act of 1932, but is more clearly drafted. Under the present law, if any person (whether or not he is interested in a patent or patent application) by circulars, advertisements, or otherwise, threatens any other person with proceedings for infringements of a patent, any person aggrieved (not merely the person threatened) may claim relief. Unless the defendant proves that the acts in respect of which the threats were made would constitute an infringement of a patent or of rights arising from the publication of a complete specification [12] in respect of a claim not shown by the plaintiff to be invalid, the plaintiff can obtain a declaration that the threats are unjustifiable, an injunction to restrain their continuance and damages. It is, however, expressly declared [13] that a mere notification of the existence of a patent does not constitute such a threat.

759 *Bona fides immaterial*

It is no defence to an action for threats under section 65 that the threats were made in good faith in the honest belief that the act complained of was an infringement of a valid claim.[14] The right at common law to take proceedings for malicious threats remains unaffected by the statutory provisions as to threats.

760 *Must be within jurisdiction*

The threat complained of must have been made within the jurisdiction in order to be actionable, for otherwise no tort will have been committed within the jurisdiction.[15]

---

[9] Prior to the 1919 Act.   [10] Under the 1907–1928 Acts.
[11] See *Ellis & Sons Ltd.* v. *Pogson*, 40 R.P.C. 62, 179.
[12] See *ante*, § 145.   [13] s. 65 (3). See note 29, *post*.
[14] See *Skinner & Co.* v. *Perry*, 10 R.P.C. 1 at p. 8.
[15] *Egg Fillers etc. Ltd.* v. *Holed-Tite Packing Corpn.*, 51 R.P.C. 9.

761 *Circulation by an agent*

It has been held that the circulation by an agent of threats made by his principal was not the making of a threat by the agent unless such a method was only a cloak to conceal the fact that the threats were really made by the agent himself.[16]

762 **Nature of threats**

The cause of action given by the subsection is not similar to libel, and there is no question of publication; the manner in which the threat is made is, therefore, not material. In *Skinner & Co.* v. *Perry* [17] the plaintiffs complained of two threats—one in the form of a letter to a third party, who had inquired of the defendants whether they thought that the plaintiffs' article of manufacture infringed the defendants' patent; the other contained in a letter from the defendants to the plaintiffs themselves in reply to similar inquiries. It was held that the words " or otherwise " in the section were not to be construed *ejusdem generis* with the preceding words " circulars, advertisements." In giving judgment for the plaintiffs, Bowen L.J. said [18]: " Using language in its ordinary sense, it is difficult to see that an intimation ceases to be a threat because it is addressed to a third person in answer to an inquiry, or because it is addressed to the person himself. We are not dealing with libel or questions of publication—we are dealing with threats. If I threaten a man that I will bring an action against him, I threaten him nonetheless because I address that intimation to himself, and I threaten him nonetheless because I address the intimation to a third person."

A letter by a solicitor before issuing a writ, or in proposing a compromise, is a threat within the meaning of the subsection if it conveys an intimation that proceedings will be taken to restrain infringement,[19] and even if made in answer to inquiries.[20] Verbal statements may amount to threats within the meaning of the sub-section,[21] and the fact that the interviews or letters are stated to be " without prejudice " will not affect the matter.[22] It has, however,

16 See *Ellam* v. *Martyn & Co.*, 16 R.P.C. 28.
17 10 R.P.C. 1.
18 10 R.P.C. 1 at p. 5.
19 See *e.g. Driffield Cake Co.* v. *Waterloo Mills Cake Co.*, 3 R.P.C. 46; *Combined Weighing etc. Machine Co.* v. *Automatic Weighing Machine Co.*, 6 R.P.C. 502; *Day* v. *Foster*, 7 R.P.C. 54 at p. 58; *Douglass* v. *Pintsch's Patent Lighting Co. Ltd.*, 13 R.P.C. 673; *H.V.E. (Electric) Ltd.* v. *Cufflin Holdings Ltd.* [1964] R.P.C. 149; and the cases referred to in note 21 *infra.*
20 *Skinner & Co.* v. *Perry*, 10 R.P.C. 1.
21 See *Kurtz* v. *Spence*, 5 R.P.C. 161; *Ellis & Sons Ltd.* v. *Pogson*, 40 R.P.C. 62; *Luna Advertising Co. Ltd.* v. *Burnham & Co.*, 45 R.P.C. 258; see also *Farr* v. *Weatherhead and Harding*, 49 R.P.C. 262.
22 See *Kurtz* v. *Spence*, 5 R.P.C. 161 at p. 173.

been held that if a solicitor says "I shall advise my clients to commence proceedings" this is not a threat within the section by the solicitor personally because clients do not always take their solicitor's advice.[23] This case may be explainable on the ground that the action was against the solicitor personally, and it is submitted that, if such a letter were written by a solicitor on behalf of a client, it would be a threat within the section by the client.[24]

763 *Background to be considered*

Regard must be had to the background in which the alleged threat is made.[25] The threat of an action for infringement may be made by implication. In *Luna Advertising Co. Ltd.* v. *Burnham & Co.*[26] a representative of the defendants called on a customer of the plaintiffs and stated that a sign exhibited outside the customer's premises was an infringement of his firm's patent, and requested that it should be removed. Clauson J. granted an interlocutory injunction, and said [27]: "I think that an interview of this kind, . . . between business men, although nobody speaks of solicitors and writs, has no real meaning except to convey . . . that the threatener has legal rights and means to enforce them . . . in the way in which they are naturally enforced, *i.e.* by legal proceedings." [28]

764 *Notification of patent*

A mere notification of the existence of a patent does not constitute a threat.[29] But if words are added to the effect that what is complained of constitutes an infringement of the patent, this will constitute a threat.[30]

765 *General warnings*

In order that a threat may be actionable under the Act it must be directed against any "other person." [31] It is submitted that this means that it must be possible to identify one or more of the persons said to be threatened with the same particularity as is necessary in

---

[23] *Earls Utilities* v. *Harrison*, 52 R.P.C. 77.

[24] See *H.V.E. Electric Ltd.* v. *Cufflin Holdings Ltd.* [1964] R.P.C. 149 at p. 156.

[25] *Surridge's Patents Ltd.* v. *Trico-Folberth Ltd.*, 53 R.P.C. 420 at pp. 423, 424.

[26] 45 R.P.C. 258.

[27] 45 R.P.C. 258 at p. 260.

[28] See also *Willis & Bates Ltd.* v. *Tilley Lamp Co.*, 61 R.P.C. 8.

[29] s. 65 (3). *Paul Trading Co. Ltd.* v. *J. Marksmith & Co. Ltd.*, 69 R.P.C. 301; *C. and P. Development Co. (London) Ltd.* v. *Sisabro Novelty Co. Ltd.*, 70 R.P.C. 277.

[30] *Finkelstein* v. *Billig*, 47 R.P.C. 516; *C. and P. Development Co. (London) Ltd.* v. *Sisabro Novelty Co. Ltd.*, 70 R.P.C. 277.

[31] s. 65 (1).

the case of an action for defamation where the words complained of refer to a class or group.[32]

In *Challender* v. *Royle*,[33] Bowen L.J. said: " Everybody, it seems to me, has still a right to issue a general warning to pirates not to pirate, and to infringers not to infringe, and to warn the public that the patent to which the patentee is entitled, and under which he claims, is one which he intends to enforce.

" But my language must not be misunderstood on this point. It does not follow that because a threat is so worded as in mere language apparently and grammatically to apply only to the future that, therefore, it may not be in any particular case in substance, and, in fact, applicable to what has been done. Supposing, for a moment, that a manufacturer is making and issuing machines which the patentee considers to be infringements of his patent; if with reference to that act done, or to those machines made, the patentee endeavours to guard himself against this section by merely issuing a threat in the air, it seems to me he would not escape if the true gist of what he has done is to apply that threat to a particular person and to a particular act." [34]

766   *Threats as to the future*

Threats that acts to be done in the future will constitute an infringement are actionable.[35]

767   *Threats when action pending*

A statement that an action for infringement has been commenced against a specified person, coupled with a general warning against dealing in infringing goods, may constitute a contempt of court if it suggests that the validity of the patent has been determined and that the defendant has in fact infringed,[36] or if it misrepresents what has in fact taken place in proceedings before the court.[37] The general principle is, however, that an application to commit for contempt of court should not be made " unless the thing done is of such a nature as to require the arbitrary and summary interference of the court in

---

[32] See *Knupffer* v. *London Express Newspaper Ltd.* [1944] A.C. 116.

[33] 4 R.P.C. 363 at p. 375.

[34] See also *Weldrics Ltd.* v. *Quasi-Arc Co. Ltd.*, 39 R.P.C. 323; *Cars* v. *Bland Light Syndicate Ltd.*, 28 R.P.C. 33; *Boneham and Hart* v. *Hirst Bros. & Co. Ltd.*, 34 R.P.C. 209; *Martin and Another* v. *Selsdon Fountain Pen Co. Ltd. and Another*, 66 R.P.C. 193 at p. 215.

[35] s. 65 (1) (2). And see *Johnson* v. *Edge*, 9 R.P.C. 142.

[36] See *Goulard & Gibbs* v. *Sir Coutts Lindsay & Co. Ltd., and Ferranti*, 4 R.P.C. 189 at p. 190; *St. Mungo Mfg. Co. Ltd.* v. *Hutchison, Main & Co. Ltd.*, 25 R.P.C. 356 at p. 360.

[37] See *Gillette Safety Razor Co.* v. *A. W. Gamage Ltd.*, 24 R.P.C. 1; *Mentmore Manufacturing Co. Ltd.* v. *Fomento (Sterling Area) Ltd.*, 72 R.P.C. 157.

order to enable justice to be duly and properly administered without any interruption or interference. . . ." [38] The courts have refused to consider as contempt of court advertisements which referred to certain specified goods as " infringing " goods, or goods " offered for sale in infringement " of the letters patent, apparently upon the ground that a patentee was entitled to say. " The patent is a good one; I am going to maintain that it is a good patent and that you are infringing it." [39]

It would appear, however, that an advertisement which stated that an action for infringement had been commenced against a specified person and that others dealing in similar goods would also be proceeded against would be a threat which could be restrained under the provisions of section 65 (1). It is submitted that the fact that an action is pending is not material.

768 Any person aggrieved may sue

The statutory right of action is not limited merely to the person to whom the threats are directly made; any person aggrieved,[40] such as a rival patentee, to whom damage is occasioned by the issue of the threats is entitled to relief. Thus in *Johnson* v. *Edge* [41] where circulars were issued to the trade intimating that the articles manufactured and sold by the plaintiff were infringements of the defendant's patent and that proceedings would be taken against any person dealing with such articles, and in consequence injury was done to the plaintiff's business, it was held that the plaintiff was a person aggrieved and could maintain an action, although no threats were made to him personally.[42] However, in *Reymes-Cole* v. *Elite Hosiery Co. Ltd.*,[43] the defendants were held not to be persons aggrieved as they had ceased production of the type of stocking prior to the threat being made.

---

[38] *Hunt* v. *Clarke*, 58 L.J.Q.B. 490 at p. 493; *Re New Gold Coast Exploration Co.* [1901] 1 Ch. 860.
[39] See *Haskell Golf Ball Co.* v. *Hutchison and Main*, 21 R.P.C. 497 at p. 500; see also *Fenner* v. *Wilson & Co. Ltd.*, 10 R.P.C. 283; *De Mare's Patent*, 16 R.P.C. 528; *Dunlop Pneumatic Type Co. Ltd.* v. *Clifton Rubber Co. Ltd.*, 19 R.P.C. 527; *British Vacuum Cleaner Co. Ltd.* v. *Suction Cleaners Ltd.*, 21 R.P.C. 300; *Mullard Radio Valve Co. Ltd.* v. *Rothermel Corpn. Ltd.*, 51 R.P.C. 1; *Selsdon Fountain Pen Co. Ltd.* v. *Miles Martin Pen Co. Ltd.*, 65 R.P.C. 365 at p. 367.
[40] s. 65 (1).
[41] 9 R.P.C. 142.
[42] And see *e.g. Challender* v. *Royle*, 4 R.P.C. 363 at p. 371; *Kensington and Knightsbridge Electric Lighting Co. Ltd.* v. *Lane Fox Electrical Co. Ltd.*, 8 R.P.C. 277; *Douglass* v. *Pintsch's Patent Lighting Co. Ltd.*, 13 R.P.C. 673; *Hoffnung* v. *Salsbury*, 16 R.P.C. 375; *Luna Advertising Co. Ltd.* v. *Burnham & Co.*, 45 R.P.C. 258; *Reymes-Cole* v. *Elite Hosiery Co. Ltd.* [1965] R.P.C. 102.
[43] [1965] R.P.C. 102 at p. 112.

769 *" Threatens any person "*

It is not necessary in order that the threat should be actionable that it should be communicated either directly or through an agent to the person threatened; the words " threatens any person " do not mean only " communicates a threat to any person " but include also the expression of a threat, by circulars, advertisements, or otherwise, in relation to any person.[44]

770 Where a patent has been sealed

If there is a patent in existence, the defendant may defend the action on the ground that the acts in respect of which the threats were made constitute an infringement of some claim. The onus then shifts to the plaintiff, who may rebut the allegation of infringement and attack the validity of that claim in the same way as in an action for infringement.[45] It is to be observed that the defendant need not be the registered proprietor of, or have any interest in, the patent.

If the specification has been amended after the threats and before the action, the issues of infringement and validity must presumably be tried with reference to the amended document, and not the specification as it stood at the date when the threats were made.[46]

771 Where no patent is sealed

It is also a defence that the acts in respect of which the proceedings were threatened constitute an infringement of rights arising from the publication (following acceptance) of the complete specification.[47] These rights are the same as those possessed by the proprietor of the patent after the patent is sealed, except that no action for infringement can be commenced until after the patent has been sealed.[48] As in the case of a granted patent, the plaintiff can attack the validity of the claims alleged to be infringed and presumably on the same grounds.[49] Under the former Acts the plaintiff could rebut a prima facie proof of infringement, where the patent had not been sealed, only by showing that the relevant claim was capable of being successfully opposed. As the permissible grounds of opposition were limited, this was a more difficult task, and the illogical result followed that it was much safer to threaten on a patent application before it had been sealed, provided it had been accepted. This anomaly has now been removed.

[44] *John Summers & Sons Ltd.* v. *The Cold Metal Process Co.*, 65 R.P.C. 75 at p. 96.
[45] s. 65 (2).
[46] See s. 31 (2), and *cf. Hall* v. *Stepney Spare Motor Wheel Ltd.*, 27 R.P.C. 233; 28 R.P.C. 381.
[47] s. 65 (2).
[48] s. 13 (4).
[49] s. 65 (2).

In this case also the defendant need not be an applicant for the patent or in any way interested in the application, or in the patent if granted.

Where a complete specification has been filed, but has not been published at the date when the threats are made, it is submitted that the defendant has no defence to the action. But an application to strike out a defence which alleged that there would be infringement, when the specification was published, was refused.[50] This is also the case where the threat is made on the basis of a provisional specification, or where no application for a patent is in fact pending. In all three cases any " person aggrieved " has a cause of action, whether or not the defendant has acted *mala fide*.

772 Counterclaim for infringement

Prior to the amendments made by the 1932 Act it was a defence if an action for infringement was begun and prosecuted with due diligence, either against the plaintiff or some other person, and if this was done the action for threats was thereupon stayed. It is no longer possible for a defendant to get rid of an action for threats in this way. But should he desire to sue the plaintiff for infringement it is now the usual practice to do so by way of counterclaim. The plaintiff may then deliver a counterclaim to the counterclaim claiming revocation of the patent.[51]

773 Right to begin

In *Lewis Falk Ltd.* v. *Jacobwitz* [52] Morton J. said: " It is for a plaintiff in a ' threats ' action first to prove the threat or threats and, once that has been done, the onus shifts to the defendant, and the burden is on him to prove that the acts, in respect of which proceedings are threatened, constitute, or if done would constitute, an infringement of a patent. . . . If the defendant succeeds in proving this, the burden then shifts again to the plaintiff to prove, if he can, that the patent . . . is invalid. In the present case one threat is admitted, and it is, therefore, for the defendant to open his case first." [53]

774 Interlocutory injunction

The general principles upon which such an injunction should be granted were considered in *Challender* v. *Royle* [54] which was decided

[50] *Lebel Products* v. *Steel (W.) & Co. Ltd.*, 72 R.P.C. 115.
[51] See *John Summers & Sons Ltd.* v. *The Cold Metal Process Co.*, 65 R.P.C. 75.
[52] 61 R.P.C. 116 at p. 118.
[53] See also *John Summers & Sons Ltd.* v. *The Cold Metal Process Co.*, 65 R.P.C. 75; *Pearson* v. *Holden*, 65 R.P.C. 424 at p. 428.
[54] 4 R.P.C. 363 at p. 372; 36 Ch.D. 425 at p. 436.

under the 1883 Act, and Cotton L.J. said: " It is very true that in all cases of interlocutory injunction the court does consider and ought to consider the balance of convenience and inconvenience in granting or refusing the injunction. But there is another and very material question to be considered—Has the plaintiff made out a prima facie case? That is to say, if the evidence remains as it is, is it probable that at the hearing of the action he will get a decree in his favour? Therefore, although I quite agree that the court ought not on an interlocutory injunction to attempt finally to decide the question whether the act complained of is an infringement, or (if the question of the validity of the patent is raised) whether the patent is a valid one or not, yet in my opinion it ought to be satisfied that on one or both of those two points the plaintiff in the action has made out a prima facie case, and unless the court is so satisfied it would be wrong to grant an injunction merely on the ground that it cannot do the defendant any harm."

In *Colley* v. *Hart*,[55] North J., in granting an interlocutory injunction to restrain threats, said: " . . . what turns the scale . . . in my opinion, is, that this is a case in which the defendant chose to make threats without bringing an action; and if his rights are being interfered with he has a remedy in the ordinary way of bringing his action; but if he does not choose to do so he must take the consequences. When there is a doubt whether the thing does infringe what he calls his rights or not, the fact that the defendant refrains from bringing an action to assert his rights is a fact I cannot leave out of consideration in forming an opinion as to whether he has such rights or not. . . ."

But, where the defendant had commenced proceedings for infringement of his patent but did not file evidence to establish that his threats were justifiable, an interlocutory injunction was granted.[56]

An interlocutory injunction has been refused: where an allegation of infringement made by the defendant was not answered [57]; where an action was already pending in which infringement and validity would be determined, and that action had been set down for trial [58]; where six weeks' delay occurred between knowledge of the alleged threats and the notice of motion.[59]

---

[55] 6 R.P.C. 17 at p. 20.

[56] *H.V.E. Electric Ltd.* v. *Cufflin Holdings Ltd.* [1964] R.P.C. 149.

[57] *Cabaret Electric Co. Ltd.* v. *Marconi's Wireless Telegraph Co. Ltd.*, 52 R.P.C. 104.

[58] *Sydney Marks and Another* v. *Scott's " Keepdrye " Dartboard Co.*, 57 R.P.C. 351; *Selsdon Fountain Pen Co. Ltd.* v. *Miles Martin Pen Co. Ltd.*, 65 R.P.C. 365.

[59] *Selsdon Fountain Pen Co. Ltd.* v. *British Joint Association etc.*, 67 R.P.C. 108.

775 *If mala fides is relied on*

If for any reason it is intended to rely upon mala fides on the part of the defendant, the fact should be brought out upon the affidavits on any motion which may be made for an interlocutory injunction and not concealed until the actual trial.[60]

776 Particulars

The defendant in an action under section 65 is entitled to particulars of the threats upon which the plaintiff relies,[61] and the plaintiff is entitled, if the defendant seeks to justify, to particulars of the acts which are said to constitute infringement of the patent [62]; and if the validity of the patent is put in question the general rules relating to particulars of objections will apply.[63]   Where there was a doubt upon which patents the defendants had based their threats, the court ordered that the defendants should deliver to the plaintiffs a list of such patents.[64]   And where the plaintiffs alleged that the threats were made by the defendants' agents, it was held that the defendants were entitled to particulars of the names of those agents.[65]

777 Declaration, injunction, damages

By the terms of section 65 (2), the plaintiff, if successful, is entitled to (1) a declaration that the threats are unjustifiable, (2) an injunction against the continuance of the threats, and (3) damages. A declaration will not, however, be made by consent or in default of defence.[66]   But the plaintiff will not be entitled to any relief, even if he proves that the threat made in respect of infringement of a number of patents could not be justified in respect of some of the patents, provided that the defendant can justify the threat in respect of one patent. In *Rosedale Associated Manufacturers Ltd.* v. *Carlton Tyre Saving Co. Ltd.*, Lord Evershed M.R. said [67]: " Prima facie the right to relief which section 65 (2) postulates depends upon the defendant in the action failing to prove that the acts in respect of which the threats were made did or would constitute an infringement of ' a patent.' Prima facie, therefore, the defendant's burden is discharged if he does prove infringement of ' a ' that is any patent."

---

[60] See *English and American Machinery Co. Ltd.* v. *Gare Machine Co. Ltd.*, 11 R.P.C. 627 at p. 631.

[61] *Law* v. *Ashworth*, 7 R.P.C. 86.

[62] *Reymes-Cole* v. *Elite Hosiery Co. Ltd.* [1961] R.P.C. 277.

[63] *Law* v. *Ashworth*, 7 R.P.C. 86; *Union Electrical Power etc. Co.* v. *Electrical Storage Co.*, 5 R.P.C. 329.

[64] *Union Electrical Power etc. Co.* v. *Electrical Storage Co.*, 38 Ch.D. 325; 5 R.P.C. 329.

[65] *Dowson-Taylor & Co. Ltd.* v. *The Drosophore Co. Ltd.*, 11 R.P.C. 653.

[66] *Corn Products Co. Ltd.* v. *N.V. Schoeton*, 56 R.P.C. 59; and *R. Demuth Ltd.* v. *Inter-Pan Ltd.* [1967] R.P.C. 75.

[67] [1960] R.P.C. 59 at p. 62.

The quantum of damage may be assessed by the judge at the trial,[68] but the ordinary form of order directs an inquiry.[69] The measure of damages is that ordinarily applicable in cases of tort, and damages can only be recovered if they are the natural and reasonable consequences of the threats [70] and must be due to the threats alone. In *Ungar* v. *Sugg* [71] Lord Esher M.R. said: " But then what is the liability? It must be for damage done by the threats—not damage done by anything else. They [*i.e.*, the defendants] are not liable for the damage which is the result of any rumour getting about in the trade which is not their act. They are liable for the damages caused by their own act—the threats which they have made, and which they have caused to be made known to the people to whom their circulars were given." The defendants will not be liable for damage caused by threats not authorised to be made by them (*ibid.*).

Damages suffered through the loss of a contract,[72] or the breaking off of negotiations for a contract,[73] are recoverable. Where the plaintiff was not inconvenienced by the threat, the court in its discretion may make no order in the action.[74]

778 Certificates of validity

Under the former law a so-called " certificate of validity " (*i.e.* that the validity of any claim had come into question) could only be given in an action for infringement of a patent.[75] In a threats action, therefore, unless the patentee counterclaimed for infringement, no such certificate could be granted. Under the 1949 Act a certificate may be granted if in any proceedings before the court the validity of a claim is contested,[76] and this might well arise in a threats action even where there was no counterclaim. If such a certificate is granted, in any subsequent proceedings for infringement or revocation, a patentee who obtains a final order or judgment in his favour becomes entitled to costs as between solicitor and client [77] unless the court otherwise directs. He is not, however, entitled to such increased allowance of costs in a subsequent threats action, as the latter cannot be said to be " proceedings for infringement."

[The next paragraph is 790]

[68] *e.g. Cars* v. *Bland Light Syndicate Ltd.*, 28 R.P.C. 33; *Horne* v. *Johnston Bros.*, 38 R.P.C. 366.
[69] *e.g. Hoffnung* v. *Salsbury*, 16 R.P.C. 375; *Pittevil & Co.* v. *Brackelsberg Melting Processes Ltd.*, 49 R.P.C. 73.
[70] See *Horne* v. *Johnston Bros.*, 38 R.P.C. 366 at p. 372.
[71] 9 R.P.C. 114 at p. 118.
[72] *Skinner & Co.* v. *Perry*, 11 R.P.C. 406; see also *Hoffnung* v. *Salsbury*, 16 R.P.C. 375. [73] *Solanite Signs Ltd.* v. *Wood*, 50 R.P.C. 315.
[74] *Tudor Accessories Ltd.* v. *J. N. Somers Ltd.* [1960] R.P.C. 215.
[75] Act of 1907, s. 35.
[76] s. 64. [77] s. 64 (2).

## CHAPTER 14

ACTION FOR INFRINGEMENT

790 AN action for infringement is the method by which a patentee can in the last resort enforce his patent privileges.

The courts are bound to take notice of the patent and to give legal effect to it to the extent of affording to the patentee a monopoly of the invention which he has claimed, subject, however, to the provisions of section 57 (2) of the Act, provided that it be not shown that the grant is invalid.

791 Expired patent

An action may be brought after the date of expiry of the patent [1] and damages recovered in respect of infringements committed before such date.

1. PARTIES

792 The plaintiff

The plaintiff will normally be the patentee, *i.e.* the person or persons for the time being entered on the register as grantee or proprietor of the patent,[2] for it is to him or them that the Crown has granted a monopoly.[3] Section 63 of the Act, however, enables an exclusive licensee [4] to sue for infringement in his own name. The patentee must, unless he consents to join as a plaintiff, be joined as a defendant, but he is not liable for any costs unless he enters an appearance and takes part in the proceedings.[6] In order to prove his title as an exclusive licensee, the latter must have registered his licence.[7]

The patentee may have become such either by registration as grantee upon grant of the patent,[8] or by subsequent registration as proprietor upon application made at the Patent Office after becoming

---

[1] See *e.g. Paterson Engineering Co. Ltd.* v. *Candy Filter Co. Ltd.*, 50 R.P.C. 1.
[2] s. 101 (1); and see *Martin and Another* v. *Scrib Ltd.*, 67 R.P.C. 127.
[3] See *ante*, § 18.
[4] See *ante*, § 609.
[6] s. 63 (2). See *British and International Proprietaries Ltd.* v. *Selcol Products Ltd.* [1957] R.P.C. 1.
[7] s. 74.
[8] See *ante*, § 128.

entitled to the patent by assignment, transmission, or other operation of law.[9]

793 *Licensees under sections 35 and 37*

In the cases of licences granted under a patent endorsed " licences of right "[10] (except where the licence is settled by agreement and expressly provides otherwise) or granted compulsorily by the Comptroller,[11] the licensee may call upon the patentee to take proceedings for infringement and if the patentee refuses or neglects to do so within two months may institute such proceedings in his own name, making the patentee a defendant.[12] As in the case of an action by an exclusive licensee, the patentee is not liable for any costs unless he enters an appearance and takes part in the proceedings.

794 *Assignee*

An assignment of a patent does not *per se* include an accrued right of action for infringements committed prior to the assignment.[13] Where the patent has been assigned after the commencement of the action the assignee may be added as a necessary party.[14]

795 *Proprietor of part of patent*

A proprietor of a separate and distinct part of a patent has been held entitled to sue for infringement of such part without joining the proprietors of the other parts of the patent.[15] Similarly, it is submitted, a proprietor of a portion of a patent in respect of a certain territory can bring an action for infringements committed within his territory as sole plaintiff.[16]

796 *Co-owners*

Where two or more persons are co-owners of a patent, it appears that one may sue for infringement without joining the others,[17] the principle being that the injury done constitutes a distinct and separate wrong to each of the owners.[18]

Difficulties may, however, arise upon the assessment of damages

---

[9] See Chap. 10.
[10] s. 35. See *ante*, § 656 *et seq.*
[11] See Chap. 11.
[12] ss. 35 (3), 38 (4).
[13] *Wilderman* v. *F. W. Berk & Co. Ltd.*, 42 R.P.C. 79 at p. 90; see also *United Horse Shoe and Nail Co. Ltd.* v. *Stewart & Co.*, 5 R.P.C. 260.
[14] See *Bates Valve Bag Co.* v. *B. Kershaw & Co. (1920) Ltd.*, 50 R.P.C. 43, and R.S.C., Ord. 15, rr. 6, 7, 8.
[15] *Dunnicliff* v. *Mallett*, 7 C.B.(N.S.) 209; 29 L.J.C.P. 70.
[16] See s. 21 (1).
[17] See *Sheehan* v. *Great Eastern Ry.*, 16 Ch.D. 59; *Turner* v. *Bowman*, 42 R.P.C. 29.
[18] *Ibid.* and *cf.* as to copyright, *Lauri* v. *Renad* [1892] 3 Ch. 402; and as to trade marks, *Dent* v. *Turpin*, 30 L.J.Ch. 495.

where one co-owner of a patent sues alone.[19] It appears probable that if he does so he will be entitled to recover damages in proportion to his interest in the patent,[20] but if the analogy of a case upon contract is to be applied to one founded upon tort, it seems that all other co-owners should be joined, if possible, in order that an account may be taken of the amount due to them all, without having recourse to a series of actions.[21]

797 *Alien enemies in time of war*

An alien enemy cannot institute or maintain an action in the courts as plaintiff,[22] nor as a co-plaintiff in a case of joint ownership of a patent,[23] unless he is merely a formal party.[24] He can, however, defend an action or appeal against a decision in a case in which he has been attacked [25]; and as a defence to proceedings for revocation he can apply to the court for leave to amend his specification.[26]

798 **The defendant**

Any person infringing a patent by himself or by his servants or agents, whether by manufacture, importation, sale, offer for sale or use is liable and may be made a defendant and sued for damages, and, if there be shown by act or word any threat or intent to continue to infringe, for an injunction, but no other person is liable.

799 *Assignee of infringer's business*

Thus an assignee of the business of a defendant, the assignment being subsequent to the issue of the writ, cannot be joined by the defendant as a co-defendant.[27]

800 *Manufacturers*

The manufacturer and patentee of a machine, the use of which is claimed to be an infringement of another patent, cannot compel the plaintiff to join him as a co-defendant with the person by whom the machine is used and against whom the action for infringement is brought.[28] He would probably, however, be so entitled if the action

---

[19] See *Whitehead and Poole Ltd.* v. *Farmer & Sons Ltd.*, 35 R.P.C. 241; *Turner* v. *Bowman*, 42 R.P.C. 29 at p. 41.

[20] See *Wilkinson* v. *Haygarth*, 12 Ad. & E. 837 at p. 850; *Powell* v. *Head*, 12 Ch.D. 686.

[21] See *Bergmann* v. *Macmillan*, 17 Ch.D. 423.

[22] *Porter* v. *Freudenberg* [1915] 1 K.B. 857.

[23] *Actiengesellschaft für Anilin Fabrikation* v. *Levinstein Ltd.*, 32 R.P.C. 140.

[24] *Mercedes Daimler Motor Co. Ltd.* v. *Maudslay Motor Co. Ltd.*, 32 R.P.C. 149.

[25] *Merten's Patent*, 32 R.P.C. 109.

[26] *Stahlwerk Becker A.G.'s Patent*, 34 R.P.C. 332.

[27] *Briggs* v. *Lardeur*, 2 R.P.C. 13.

[28] *Moser* v. *Marsden* [1892] 1 Ch. 487; 9 R.P.C. 214.

were brought against his agent in respect of goods which were his property.[29]

801 *Directors of company*

Directors of a limited company are only liable in respect of infringements committed by the company if it be proved that the company committed the infringements as their agent, or that they expressly authorised the acts of infringement.[30] In such a case particulars should be given of any facts on which the plaintiff intends to rely.[31]

The existence of the relationship of principal and agent is not to be inferred from the mere fact that the directors in question may be sole directors and sole shareholders of the company.[32] If, however, a company is formed for the express purpose of doing a wrongful act, or if, when formed, those in control expressly direct that a wrongful act be done, such individuals as well as the company are responsible.[33]

802 *Proper course where infringers numerous*

In the case of *Bovill* v. *Crane*[34] it was stated by Sir W. Page-Wood V.-C. that in cases where there were numerous infringers a patentee might well " select that which he thought the best in order to try the question fairly, and proceed in that case to obtain his interlocutory injunction. He might write at the same time to all the others who were *in simili casu*, and say to them: ' Are you willing to take this as a notice to you that the present case is to determine yours? Otherwise I shall proceed against you by way of interlocutory injunction; and if you will not object on the ground of delay, I do not mean to file bills against all of you at once. Am I to understand that you make no objection of that kind? If you do not object I shall file a bill against only one of you.' I do not think any court could complain of a patentee for taking the course I am suggesting," and stated further that such conduct would not in itself debar

---

[29] *Vavasseur* v. *Krupp*, 9 Ch.D. 351.
[30] *British Thomson-Houston Co. Ltd.* v. *Sterling Accessories Ltd.* [1924] 2 Ch. 33; 41 R.P.C. 311; see also *Cropper Minerva Machines Co. Ltd.* v. *Cropper, Charlton & Co. Ltd.*, 23 R.P.C. 388 at p. 392; *Pritchard and Constance (Wholesale) Ltd.* v. *Amata Ltd.*, 42 R.P.C. 63 (trade name); *Leggatt* v. *Hood*, 67 R.P.C. 134; *Oertli A.G.* v. *E. J. Bowman Ltd. and Others* [1956] R.P.C. 282; [1957] R.P.C. 388.
[31] *British Thomson-Houston Co. Ltd.* v. *Irradiant Lamp Works Ltd.*, 41 R.P.C. 338.
[32] *Rainham Chemical Works* v. *Belvedere Fish Guano Co.* [1921] 2 A.C. 465.
[33] *Ibid.* See also *Middlemas and Wood* v. *Moliver & Co. Ltd.*, 38 R.P.C. 97; *Performing Right Society Ltd.* v. *Ciryl Theatrical Syndicate Ltd.* [1924] 1 K.B. 1.
[34] L.R. 1 Eq. 388.

the patentee (owing to the delay) from obtaining interlocutory injunctions.[35]

The usual course is for the patentee to select the main sources of supply of infringing articles and to obtain a decision in an action against a representative infringer, and, if the decision of such action is in his favour, to proceed against the others. Where there were two actions on the same patent in which the issues and defences were substantially the same, the second action was stayed pending the trial of the first action, the defendant in the second action undertaking to submit to an order similar to any order which the plaintiff might obtain in the first action.[36]

803 *Carriers*

An action may properly be brought against innocent carriers who have infringed by importing articles to restrain them from dealing with or handing over such articles to other persons,[37] and on the discovery of the name of the consignee, such consignee should be joined as a co-defendant in the action.[38] The carriers will be absolved from all liability if they make full disclosure of the names of the consignors and consignees of the goods complained of.

804 **Third party procedure**

Where an indemnity was given to the defendants, after the commencement of the action, by a third party who had manufactured the infringing articles, it was held that the person giving such an indemnity should be joined as a party under Order 16, rules 1 and 2.[39] Such third party will only be bound by the decision of the court in so far as the decision falls within the terms of the order by which he was directed to appear, and if the plaintiffs neglect to amend by joining him as a defendant they will not be able to obtain an injunction against him as well as against the actual defendant.[40]

A defendant, however, is not entitled to compel the plaintiff to join as co-defendant a person who supplied the defendant with the

---

[35] See also *Foxwell* v. *Webster*, 3 New Rep. 103; *North British Rubber Co. Ltd.* v. *Gormully and Jeffery Manufacturing Co.*, 12 R.P.C. 17.

[36] *Multiple Utilities Co. Ltd.* v. *Souch*, 46 R.P.C. 402; *McCreath* v. *Mayor etc. of South Shields and Baker*, 49 R.P.C. 349; *Gillette Industries Ltd.* v. *Albert*, 57 R.P.C. 85; *White* v. *Glove (Industrial) Manufacturing Co. Ltd.* [1958] R.P.C. 142; *Reymes-Cole* v. *West Riding Hosiery Ltd.* [1961] R.P.C. 273.

[37] *Upmann* v. *Elkan*, L.R. 7 Ch.App. 130; *Washburn and Moen Manufacturing Co.* v. *Cunard Steamship Co.*, 6 R.P.C. 398.

[38] *Washburn and Moen Manufacturing Co.* v. *Cunard Steamship Co.*, 6 R.P.C. 398.

[39] *Edison and Swan Electric Light Co.* v. *Holland*, 33 Ch.D. 497; 3 R.P.C. 395 (under R.S.C., Ord. 16, rr. 1, 2).

[40] *Edison and Swan Electric Light Co.* v. *Holland*, 41 Ch.D. 28; 6 R.P.C. 243 at p. 286.

machine, the use of which is alleged to be an infringement, and who, the defendant alleges, is a licensee of the plaintiff; the question of infringement can be properly and conveniently tried without such joinder.[41] Unless the defendant can join such person as a third party under Order 16, his only course is to commence a separate action against him.

805 Change of parties by death, etc.

The procedure where a change of parties is necessitated by death, bankruptcy, etc. or one or other of them is regulated by Order 15 of the Rules of the Supreme Court.

2. THE TRIBUNAL

806 Patents Judges

Actions for infringement in England are ordinarily tried by the special Patents Judges who are attached to the Chancery Division of the High Court. By Order 103, rule 2, all patent proceedings must be initiated in that Division, and under the present practice are assigned to Group A. The Patents Judges have been selected by the Lord Chancellor[42] to hear applications for extensions of the term of a patent[43] and have also been appointed the Appeal Tribunal[44] to hear appeals from the Comptroller.

807 Reference to Comptroller

Under section 67 a dispute between a patentee or an exclusive licensee and any other person as to infringement of any claim, or as to the validity of any claim alleged to be infringed, may by agreement be referred to the Comptroller,[45] who may, however, decline to deal with it, if questions are involved which would more properly be determined by the court. Damages are limited (unless otherwise agreed) to £1,000. There is no appeal and a decision of the Comptroller is not binding on any party in subsequent proceedings, but no relief can thereafter be obtained in respect of any infringement dealt with before the Comptroller.

808 County courts

County courts have no jurisdiction where the validity of the patent is put in issue, as a patent confers a " franchise " within the meaning

---

[41] *Evans* v. *Central Electric Supply Co. Ltd.*, 40 R.P.C. 357.
[42] See s. 84 (1).
[43] ss. 23, 24.
[44] s. 85, as amended by s. 24 of the Administration of Justice Act 1969.
[45] See *Central Electricity Generating Board and another* v. *Chamberlain and Hookham Ltd.* [1958] R.P.C. 217.

of section 39 of the County Courts Act 1959.[46] It would appear also that the Patents Act of 1883 by the definition of the words " the Court " (repealed in section 101 (1) of the present Act) conferred a jurisdiction to try infringement actions, whether validity was involved or not, on the High Court to the exclusion of the county courts, and that such exclusion was not removed by section 56 of the County Courts Act 1888 (now section 39 of the County Courts Act 1959).[47] A plaintiff who commences an infringement action in the county court cannot remove it to the High Court by certiorari.[48] Actions for royalties under licences have, however, been tried in the county court.[49]

**809	Scotland, etc.**

Actions in respect of infringements committed in Scotland, Northern Ireland or the Isle of Man are heard in the respective courts of such parts of the realm, such courts having power also to consider questions of validity, and the Court of Session in Scotland having power to hear proceedings for revocation of a patent.

The application of the Act to Scotland is provided for by section 103; to Northern Ireland by section 104; and to the Isle of Man by section 105.

**810	Palatine court**

The Court of the County Palatine of Lancaster has exercised jurisdiction to hear actions for infringement and to decide the issue of validity.[50]

**811	Juries**

Patent actions are to be tried without a jury unless the court otherwise directs [51]; and such direction is only given in cases where fraud or libel of some kind is alleged.[52]

**812	Scientific advisers**

In an action for infringement or in any other proceedings under the Act an independent scientific adviser may be appointed to assist

[46] R. v. County Court Judge of Halifax [1891] 1 Q.B. 793; 8 R.P.C. 388 at p. 394.
[47] Ibid.
[48] Giusti Patents and Engineering Works Ltd. v. Maggs, 40 R.P.C. 199.
[49] See Cutlan v. Dawson, 13 R.P.C. 710; 14 R.P.C. 249.
[50] See e.g. J. D. Insulating and Refrigerating Co. Ltd. v. Thos. Anderson Ltd., 41 R.P.C. 1; Chain Bar Mill Co. v. William Wild Ltd., 56 R.P.C. 446; 57 R.P.C. 111.
[51] s. 24 (4).
[52] See Rhodes and Edmondson v. British Cotton and Wool Dyers' Association Ltd., 28 R.P.C. 67; and see the remarks of Lord Selborne L.C. in Patent Marine Inventions Co. v. Chadburn, L.R. 16 Eq. 447.

the court or to inquire and report upon any question of fact or opinion not involving questions of law or construction.[53] Experts have been called in where there is a conflict of evidence to make experiments and to report to the court.[54] The duty of an expert so appointed " is, instead of determining issues of fact, or of law, to find the materials upon which the court is to act." [55] It is the duty of the court to look at the expert's report and obtain from it (with or without cross-examination, as the case may be) whatever help it can, but the court is not bound to accept the report.[56] In a case in which an assessor was employed in the court of first instance his written statement was read to the Court of Appeal when the case came before it.[57]

3. PRACTICE BEFORE TRIAL

813 General

The practice of the High Court is regulated by Order 103, rules 19 to 26, of the Rules of the Supreme Court, which refer more especially to actions for infringement.

These rules do not apply to the Scottish courts, and as by section 103 (1) nothing in the Act is to affect the forms of process in Scotland, the practice there apart from such rules as may be made by the Scottish courts seems to remain what it was under the Act of 1883 so far as particulars and costs are concerned.[58]

814 The writ

Issue

Actions in the High Court in England are commenced by the issue of a writ from the Central Office or from a District Registry.[59]

815 *Indorsement*

In nearly all actions for infringement the writ is indorsed [60] with a claim for (1) an injunction; (2) damages; and (3) delivery up to the plaintiffs or destruction of all infringing articles in the possession of the defendants.[61]

---

[53] s. 84 (2); R.S.C., Ord. 103, r. 27, *post*, § 1614; and see *Marconi v. Helsby Wireless Telegraph Co. Ltd.*, 31 R.P.C. 121.
[54] See *Badische Anilin und Soda Fabrik v. Levinstein*, 24 Ch.D. 156; *Moore v. Bennett*, 1 R.P.C. 129; *North British Rubber Co. Ltd. v. Macintosh & Co. Ltd.*, 11 R.P.C. 477.
[55] *Per* Bramwell L.J. in *Mellin v. Monico*, 3 C.P.D. 142 at p. 149.
[56] *Non-Drip Measure Co. Ltd. v. Strangers Ltd.*, 59 R.P.C. 1 at p. 24.
[57] *Hattersley & Sons Ltd. v. Hodgson Ltd.*, 22 R.P.C. 229.
[58] And see *Mica Insulators Co. Ltd. v. Bruce, Peebles & Co. Ltd.*, 22 R.P.C. 527.   [59] R.S.C., Ord. 5.
[60] See R.S.C., Ord. 6.
[61] See Appendix *post*, § 1998.

816 *More than one cause of action*

Writs are frequently indorsed with claims in respect of infringements of more than one patent, and sometimes with claims with regard to analogous matters such as infringement of designs, trade marks, etc. The question of separate causes of action being dealt with in the same or in separate actions is regulated by Order 15 of the Rules of the Supreme Court.

Where the plaintiffs sued on twenty-three patents (all of which related to the process of making saccharin), the action was ordered to be limited to three patents to be selected by the plaintiffs.[62]

817 *Service*

Service of the writ is regulated by Orders 10, 11 and 65 of the Rules of the Supreme Court.

818 *Service out of jurisdiction*

The practice as to service out of the jurisdiction is regulated by Order 11, of the Rules of the Supreme Court. An application must be supported by an affidavit stating *inter alia* the ground upon which the application is made,[63] and it should also state facts which, if proved, would be a sufficient foundation for the cause of action alleged.[64]

Where leave is asked to serve a writ in Scotland or Northern Ireland and there is a concurrent remedy in such part of the United Kingdom the court, in coming to its decision, will have regard to the comparative cost and convenience of the action being proceeded with in England or in such other part of the United Kingdom.[65] Questions affecting such decision would be whether the defendant carried on a substantial business in England and whether an injunction in England would really be effective against him.[66]

Service out of the jurisdiction will be permitted upon any person who is a necessary and proper party to an action properly brought against some other person duly served within the jurisdiction,[67] as,

---

[62] *Saccharin Corpn. Ltd.* v. *Wild & Co.*, 20 R.P.C. 243; see also *Saccharin Corpn. Ltd.* v. *R. White & Sons Ltd.*, 20 R.P.C. 454 (C.A.); *cf. Saccharin Corpn. Ltd.* v. *Alliance Chemical Co. Ltd.*, 22 R.P.C. 175.

[63] R.S.C., Ord. 11, r. 4.

[64] *Badische Anilin und Soda Fabrik* v. *Chemische Fabrik Vormals Sandoz*, 20 R.P.C. 413; 21 R.P.C. 345, 533 at p. 539; see also *Badische Anilin und Soda Fabrik* v. *W. G. Thompson Ltd.*, 20 R.P.C. 422; *British Oxygen Co. Ltd.* v. *Gesellschaft für Industriegasverwertung M.B.H.*, 48 R.P.C. 130.

[65] R.S.C., Ord. 11, r. 4; and see *Kinahan* v. *Kinahan*, 45 Ch.D. 78; *Logan* v. *Bank of Scotland* [1906] 1 K.B. 141.

[66] See *Speckhart* v. *Campbell, Achnach & Co.*, Bitt. Cha. Cas. 196, 248; *Burland* v. *Broxburn Oil Co.*, 41 Ch.D. 542.

[67] R.S.C., Ord. 11, r. 1; and see *Massey* v. *Haynes & Co.*, 21 Q.B.D. 330.

for instance, upon the consignees of infringing goods in respect of which an action had been brought against the carriers thereof.[68]

819　Entry of appearance

The next step is ordinarily an entry of appearance by the defendant.[69]

820　Default of appearance and defence

The procedure in case of default of appearance by the defendant is regulated by R.S.C., Order 13. Where as is usually the case there is a claim for an injunction and there is default of appearance, upon the filing of an affidavit of service and of a statement of claim by the plaintiff the action proceeds in the ordinary way.[70] On motion for judgment in default of defence, the order for delivery up must identify the goods to be delivered up.[71]

821　Joinder of additional parties

The joinder of additional parties is regulated by Order 15, rules 6 and 8, of the Rules of the Supreme Court. The court has juris-diction to allow intervention by a third party if the proposed intervener can make out a prima facie case that his legal rights may be prejudicially affected by an order made in the action.[72]

822　Where one defendant only appears

A question has arisen as to what should be done if on an action against two defendants for the same infringement one of them fails to appear. If the cause of action was severable the plaintiff might move, under Order 19, r. 7, for judgment against the defendant who failed to deliver a defence.[73] The defendant who appeared might, however, succeed in establishing the invalidity of the patent, and the difficulty arises as to the position of the other defendant.

On the whole it may be said that an injunction is an equitable remedy, and that it would be contrary to principle for the same tribunal which had pronounced a patent to be invalid to restrain a member of the public from doing what could not be an infringe-ment. This might not, however, be the case where the reason for

---

[68] *Washburn and Moen Manufacturing Co.* v. *Cunard Steamship Co.*, 6 R.P.C. 398.

[69] R.S.C., Ord. 12.

[70] R.S.C., Ord. 13, r. 6.

[71] *Paton Culvert & Co. Ltd.* v. *Rosedale Associated Manufacturers Ltd.* [1966] R.P.C. 61.

[72] *Amon* v. *Raphael Tuck & Sons Ltd.* [1956] R.P.C. 29.

[73] See *Weinberg* v. *Balkan Sobranie Cigarettes Ltd.*, 40 R.P.C. 399 (trade mark).

the non-appearance of the one defendant proves to be that he is unable to contest the validity of the patent owing to his being a licensee, as, under these circumstances, the plaintiff's rights against him would really be contractual and such defendant might have disentitled himself from working the invention save on a royalty basis, apart from any question of validity of the patent.

In *Actiengesellschaft für Cartonnagen Industrie* v. *Remus and Burgon* [74] one defendant had put the validity of the patent in issue and Chitty J. refused leave to set down the action on motion for judgment against the other defendant who had not delivered a defence, but did not consent to judgment.

In *Savage Brothers Ltd.* v. *Brindle and another* [75] a motion for judgment against one defendant stood over until the trial; after the hearing he consented to an injunction, but the other defendant succeeded in upsetting the patent. Farwell J. granted the injunction asked for, but *quaere* whether this practice would be followed today.

823 Interlocutory injunctions

Where it appears to the court " just or convenient " the plaintiff can obtain an injunction to restrain the defendant from infringing pending the trial of the action.[76] Such application is made in the Chancery Division to the Patents Judge by motion normally after service of notice of motion upon the defendant, or in rare cases *ex parte*.

824 *Principles governing granting of interlocutory injunctions*

In *Challender* v. *Royle*,[77] which was an action for threats, Cotton L.J. dealt with the principles upon which interlocutory injunctions are granted, principles which are equally applicable to infringement actions; that is that the court has to be satisfied on all the evidence before it that there is a prima facie case that the patent is valid and infringed, and further, that the balance of convenience and inconvenience is in favour of the interlocutory injunction being granted.[78] Where there are reasonable grounds for disputing either validity or infringement, the court is unlikely to be able to come to any decision on an interlocutory application, but will probably conclude that it is unable to say that a prima facie case has been made out and will refuse the application.

---

[74] 12 R.P.C. 94.
[75] 17 R.P.C. 228 at p. 233.
[76] Judicature Act 1925, s. 45; R.S.C., Ord. 29.
[77] 36 Ch.D. 425 at p. 436; 4 R.P.C. 363 at p. 372.
[78] See *ante*, § 774; and *Plimpton* v. *Spiller*, 4 Ch.D. 286; *Bonnella* v. *Espir*, 43 R.P.C. 159; *Chelton (Poppits) Ltd.* v. *A. Goldston Ltd.* [1957] R.P.C. 416.

In *Zaidener* v. *Barrisdale Engineers Ltd.*,[79] Willmer L.J. said: " I take it to be well settled that an interlocutory injunction will not normally be granted where damages will provide an adequate remedy should the claim succeed. Furthermore, I have always understood the rule to be that the court will not grant an interlocutory injunction unless satisfied that there is a real probability of the plaintiff succeeding on the trial of the suit. I know of no reason why this rule should not be applied in an action where the validity of a patent is in question as in any other form of action."

In modern practice it is unlikely that an interlocutory injunction restraining the manufacture or sale of an article, or the use of a process, will be granted, unless the patent has already been litigated and held to be valid, or unless it has been generally acknowledged to be valid for a substantial time, *e.g.* by the absence of any challenge and the acceptance by competitors of licences under it.

An interlocutory injunction may be granted in the case of patents falling within section 41, if the defendant has applied for a compulsory licence under that section but he infringes that patent during the period when his application is still pending.[80] Further, an interlocutory injunction may be granted in respect of a valid claim even though other claims in the specification are not prima facie valid.[81]

825 *Ex parte injunctions*

An *ex parte* injunction may be granted after the issue of the writ and before service thereof, but only where it can be shown that great injury will accrue to the plaintiff by delay, that the patent is probably valid, that the plaintiff is the proper person to sue, that the defendant committed the act complained of, and that such an act is prima facie an infringement. Such *ex parte* injunctions will normally be granted for a few days only.[82]

826 *Interlocutory undertaking to deliver up*

Where in interlocutory proceedings the defendants gave an undertaking to deliver up confidential documents, an affidavit verifying compliance with the undertaking was ordered to be made.[83]

827 *Notice of motion*

Notice of motion may be served without leave with the writ, or at

[79] [1968] R.P.C. 488 at p. 495.
[80] *Hoffman-La Roche & Co. A.G.* v. *Inter-Continental Pharmaceuticals Ltd.* [1965] R.P.C. 226.
[81] *Hoffman-La Roche & Co. A.G.* v. *D.D.S.A. Pharmaceuticals Ltd.* [1965] R.P.C. 503.
[82] See *British Thomson-Houston Co. Ltd.* v. *Phillip Henry & Co. Ltd.*, 45 R.P.C. 218; see also *Gardner* v. *Broadbent*, 2 Jur.(N.S.) 1041; and Ord. 8, r. 2.
[83] *Kangol Industries Ltd.* v. *Alfred Bray & Sons Ltd.*, 70 R.P.C. 15.

any time before the time for entering an appearance has expired, or subsequently.[84]

828 *Practice*

Applications for interlocutory injunctions are heard and decided upon affidavit evidence in open court. Motions in actions and matters relating to patents are made to the special Patents Judges and not to the non-witness Judge of the group to which the proceeding is assigned.[85]

829 *Nature of affidavits*

The plaintiff's affidavits should clearly point out of what the alleged infringement consists, and depose to the novelty and utility of the invention. Affidavits on " information and belief " must state the sources of the information.[86] An injunction granted prior to statement of claim will be dissolved if the statement of claim when delivered is not consistent with the affidavits upon which the injunction was granted.[87]

830 *Prima facie evidence of validity*

The plaintiff must first establish such facts as will satisfy the court that there are strong prima facie reasons for acting on the supposition that the patent is valid. The most cogent evidence for this purpose is either that there has been a previous trial in which the patent has been held to be valid,[88] or that the patentee has worked and enjoyed the patent for many years without dispute [89]; or it may be that as between the parties the plaintiff is relieved from the onus of establishing validity, as where the defendant has admitted it [90] or is so placed in his relationship to the plaintiff as to be estopped from denying it.[91]

831 *Patent must have been used*

What amounts to long enjoyment is difficult to define, but decided cases would appear to suggest that undisturbed enjoyment for six years would be sufficient [92]; but the user of the invention during that

---

[84] R.S.C., Ord. 8, r. 4.
[85] *Practice Direction* [1961] R.P.C. 75.
[86] *Saccharin Corpn.* v. *Chemical and Drugs Co.*, 15 R.P.C. 53; *Badische Anilin und Soda Fabrik* v. *W. G. Thompson Ltd.*, 19 R.P.C. 502.
[87] *Stocking* v. *Llewellyn*, 3 L.T. 33.
[88] *Hayward* v. *Pavement Light Co.*, Griff.P.C. 124.
[89] *Dudgeon* v. *Thomson*, 30 L.T.(N.S.) 244; *Betts* v. *Menzies*, 3 Jur.(N.S.) 357 at p. 358; *Muntz* v. *Foster*, 2 W.P.C. 93 at p. 95; *Rothwell* v. *King*, 3 R.P.C. 379.
[90] *Dircks* v. *Mellor*, 26 Lon.Journ. 268.
[91] *Dudgeon* v. *Thomson*, 30 L.T.(N.S.) 244; *Clarke* v. *Fergusson*, 1 Griff. 184; 5 Jur.(N.S.) 1155.
[92] *Bickford* v. *Skewes*, 1 W.P.C. 211; *Rothwell* v. *King*, 3 R.P.C. 379.

[321]

time must be active. The mere possession of a patent for a long period does not of itself give rise to a presumption of its validity.[93]

832   *Seldom granted for new patent*

An interlocutory injunction is seldom granted in the case of a new patent [94] even though the defendant refuses to undertake to keep an account [95] if it is opposed on an arguable ground.

In *Clarke* v. *Nichols* [96] the patent was less than a year old. Notice of motion was served with the writ, but the defendant did not appear. The affidavit by the plaintiff stated that prior to the purchase of the patent he had caused a full investigation to be made into its validity by his patent agents, and that he was advised that it was valid, and to the best of his knowledge, information and belief, it was valid now. The injunction was granted.

833   *Not granted if validity is challenged*

An interlocutory injunction will not be granted, however, even in the case of an old patent if the defendant challenges the validity of the patent and shows that there is a question as to this which has to be tried.

In *Marshall and Lace Web Spring Co. Ltd.* v. *Crown Bedding Co. Ltd.*,[97] Romer J. said: " So far as I know . . . the only difference between a motion where the patent is old and a motion where the patent is new is this: in the latter case it is sufficient for the defendant's counsel . . . to state at the bar that he proposes to dispute the validity of the patent, and that the question . . . will have to be decided at the trial. Where the patent . . . is more than six years of age . . . it is not sufficient for the defendant to state at the bar that he proposes to dispute the validity of the patent; he must show by affidavit some ground for supposing that he has a chance of successfully disputing the patent at the trial." [98]

But under modern practice it is very doubtful whether a mere statement by the defendant's counsel that he proposes to dispute the validity of the patent is sufficient and it is probable that the court will require to be satisfied by argument or evidence that there are arguable grounds for disputing validity. As Lord Evershed M.R. said in *Newman* v. *British and International Proprietaries* [99]: " *Ex*

[93] *Plympton* v. *Malcolmson*, 44 L.J.Ch. 257; L.R. 20 Eq. 37.
[94] See *Smith* v. *Grigg Ltd.*, 41 R.P.C. 149 at p. 153; see also *Jackson* v. *Needle*, 1 R.P.C. 174; *Trautner* v. *Patmore*, 29 R.P.C. 60; *Zaidener* v. *Barrisdale Engineers Ltd.* [1968] R.P.C. 488.
[95] *Lister* v. *Norton Bros. & Co. Ltd.*, 1 R.P.C. 114; *Jackson* v. *Needle*, 1 R.P.C. 174; *British Tanning Co.* v. *Groth*, 7 R.P.C. 1.
[96] 12 R.P.C. 310.   [97] 46 R.P.C. 267 at p. 269.
[98] And see *Holophane Ltd.* v. *Berend & Co.*, 15 R.P.C. 18 at p. 19.
[99] [1962] R.P.C. 90 at 93.

facie, here is a grant made after a declaration that there was no lawful ground for objection. I should have thought there was an onus on the defendants to show some ground for challenging the validity. Of course, you may be able to say if you look at it [the patent specification] there is something on the face of the document which vitiates it."

834 *Patent previously held valid*

Where a patent has been held valid in previous litigation, and particularly if this has been carried to the House of Lords, an interlocutory injunction will ordinarily be granted if a prima facie case of infringement is established, notwithstanding that the defendant may urge additional grounds tending to invalidate the patent.[100]

835 *Delay will bar right*

An interlocutory injunction will not be granted in cases where the plaintiff is guilty of delay after learning of the infringement.

In *North British Rubber Co. v. Gormully and Jeffery Co.*,[1] Chitty J. said: " Now I am not aware, having regard to patents, that there is any substantial ground of distinction between an interlocutory injunction upon a patent right and upon any other. The principles appear to me to be substantially the same; and the general rule of the court is that a person who comes to ask for that remedy, which is granted with despatch and for the purposes of protecting rights until the trial, should come promptly." [2]

The amount of delay which will prevent the granting of an interlocutory injunction will, of course, vary with the nature of the patent and the circumstances of the trade.

The delay may, in some cases, be satisfactorily explained, as in a case where the plaintiffs' solicitors advised them not to commence an action until the defendants appeared to be in a condition of sufficient financial soundness to undertake manufacture of the infringing articles.[3]

Delay in proceeding against persons who are not parties to the application in question is no ground for refusing an injunction, if there has been no delay in proceeding against the defendant.[4]

[100] *Heine, Solly & Co. v. Norden*, 21 R.P.C. 513; *British Thomson-Houston Co. Ltd. v. B. T. T. Electric Lamp and Accessories Co.*, 39 R.P.C. 167; *Bloom v. Imperial Lighting Co.*, 52 R.P.C. 162.
[1] 12 R.P.C. 17 at p. 20.
[2] See also *Bovill v. Crate*, L.R. 1 Eq. 388; *Aluminium Co. v. Domeiere*, 15 R.P.C. 32; *Gillette Safety Razor Co. v. A. W. Gamage Ltd.*, 24 R.P.C. 1; *Versil Ltd. v. Cork Insulation and Asbestos Co. Ltd.* [1966] R.P.C. 76.
[3] *United Telephone Co. v. Equitable Telephone Association*, 5 R.P.C. 233.
[4] *Pneumatic Tyre Co. v. Warrilow*, 13 R.P.C. 284.

836 *Usual course on application*

Under the present practice, if the defendant disputes validity or infringement upon what appear prima facie to be reasonable grounds, and the patent has not previously been litigated or otherwise established, it is usual for the court to order the motion to stand until the trial of the action on the condition that the defendant undertakes to keep an account of all articles made and sold by him. Even if the defendant refuses to undertake to keep an account, the court must still decide whether a sufficiently strong case has been made out for interlocutory relief.[5] In considering what course should be adopted, the court will be influenced chiefly by the balance of convenience and the probability of injury to either side. The plaintiff will be required to give an undertaking to pay any damages occasioned by an interlocutory injunction if it should appear subsequently that the defendant was in the right.[6] Where an undertaking is given to the court in lieu of an interlocutory injunction a cross-undertaking in damages will be inserted in the order unless the contrary is agreed and expressed at the time.[7] And the discontinuance of the action will not prevent the cross-undertaking being enforced.[8] An undertaking in damages will not be required from the Crown or anyone suing on the Crown's behalf.[9]

For form of injunction, including an undertaking as to damages, see Appendix *post*, §§ 2000 and 2001.

837 *Treating motion as trial of action*

Where, as sometimes happens, during the proceedings for an interlocutory injunction, the parties come to terms, they can agree, subject to the consent of the court, to treat the hearing of the motion as the trial of the action and for an agreed form of judgment to be entered forthwith, the further expense of an action being thereby avoided.

838 *Plaintiff entitled to order in court*

Where the defendants offered to consent to judgment, the order to be made on a summons in Chambers, it was held that the plaintiffs were entitled to an order made in open court, and to the costs of the motion for judgment.[10]

839 **Nature of pleadings**

Pleadings generally are regulated by Order 18, rules 6 and 7, of

[5] See *British Tanning Co. Ltd.* v. *Groth,* 7 R.P.C. 1.
[6] See *Graham* v. *Campbell,* 7 Ch.D. 490 (undertaking enforced).
[7] *Practice Note* [1904] W.N. 203, 208.
[8] *Newcomen* v. *Coulson,* 7 Ch.D. 764; *Rothwell* v. *King,* 4 R.P.C. 76.
[9] *Secretary of State for War* v. *Cope,* 36 R.P.C. 273 (registered design).
[10] *Smith and Jones Ltd.* v. *Service, Reeve & Co.,* 31 R.P.C. 319.

the Rules of the Supreme Court, which requires all material facts to be pleaded and prohibits the pleading of evidence. The forms generally used are set out in the Appendix.

840   Statement of claim

The statement of claim may be served with the writ, or at any time within fourteen days after the defendant has entered an appearance.[11]   It should allege that the plaintiff is the registered proprietor of the letters patent sued on; and it is usual to allege that the patent is valid, though it is doubtful whether this is necessary, as " a patent is prima facie good as long as it stands." [12]   It is not necessary to set out facts material to the validity.[13]   If the specification has been amended such facts should be pleaded together with an averment that the specification and claims as originally filed were framed in good faith and with reasonable skill and knowledge.[14]

If a certificate that validity was contested has been granted in a previous action so as to entitle the plaintiff to solicitor and client costs under section 64 of the Act, the certificate and the claim to such costs should be pleaded.[15]

A plaintiff is entitled to amend his statement of claim without leave once at any time before the pleadings are closed by serving the amended pleading upon the defendant or his solicitor.[16]

841   Particulars of infringements

In an action for infringement the plaintiff must serve " particulars of infringements," [17]   i.e. particulars of the times, places, occasions, and manner in which the plaintiff says the defendant has infringed his letters patent. The defendant must have full, fair, and distinct notice of the case to be made against him.[18]

842   *Actionable infringement must be alleged*

The particulars of infringements must allege an actionable infringement, i.e. an act committed subsequent to the date of publication

---

[11] Ord. 18, r. 1.
[12] *Halsey* v. *Brotherhood*, 15 Ch.D. 514 at p. 521; see also *Amory* v. *Brown*, L.R. 8 Eq. 663 at p. 664.
[13] See *Amory* v. *Brown*, L.R. 8 Eq. 663; *Ward Bros.* v. *J. Hill & Son*, 18 R.P.C. 481, *per* Wills J. at p. 491, following *Young* v. *White*, 23 L.J.Ch. 190, and *Harris* v. *Rothwell*, 4 R.P.C. 225.
[14] See *Kane and Pattison* v. *Boyle*, 18 R.P.C. 325 at p. 337, and s. 62.
[15] *Pneumatic Tyre Co. Ltd.* v. *Chisholm*, 13 R.P.C. 488.
[16] See R.S.C., Ord. 20, r. 3 and Ord. 18.
[17] See Ord. 103, rr. 19, 22, 23, and Appendix. See also *Salopian Engineers Ltd.* v. *The Salop Trailer Co. Ltd.*, 71 R.P.C. 223.
[18] *Needham* v. *Oxley*, 1 Hem. & M. 248; *Mandleberg* v. *Morley*, 10 R.P.C. 256; *Batley* v. *Kynock (No. 2)*, L.R. 19 Eq. 229 at p. 231.

of the complete specification,[19] or else the statement of claim may be struck out.[20] But a mere threat to infringe, if made after that date, is sufficient.[21]

843 *Which claims infringed*

The plaintiff cannot be required to place a construction upon his patent in his particulars of infringements.[22] All he need do is to indicate which claims of his patent he relies upon and by what act he considers the defendant to have infringed, and if these two points be made clear without adducing specific instances, that will be sufficient.[23] There is no objection to a plaintiff stating that he relies on *all* the claims of his specification, and it is a matter of costs at the trial if this course has been taken unreasonably.[24]

844 *Type of infringement should be specified*

It is customary to state that the patent has been infringed and " in particular (*e.g.*) by the sale, on the —— day of ——, 19—, to one A B, of an article constructed according to the invention described and claimed in claim No. —." This is for the purpose of identifying the type of act complained of; a plaintiff does not thereby limit his rights to damages to the specified example only.

845 *Infringements after action brought*

When an action is brought in respect of a particular type of infringement, and to restrain the threatened infringement by continued manufacture of that type (the usual way in which an action is framed), the plaintiffs will not be allowed to give evidence of infringements of a different type, committed after action brought to justify the allegation of intention to infringe; the proper course is to apply to amend the particulars of infringements.[25]

846 *Degrees of particularity required against vendor*

Where an action is brought against a mere vendor of articles alleged to have been made by a process which infringes the plaintiff's patent, a greater degree of precision is required in the particulars of infringements than if the defendant had been the manufacturer himself.

[19] s. 13 (4).
[20] See *Schuster v. Hine, Parker & Co. Ltd.*, 52 R.P.C. 345.
[21] *Bloom v. Shulman*, 51 R.P.C. 308.
[22] *Wenham Co. Ltd. v. Champion Gas Co. Ltd.*, 8 R.P.C. 22.
[23] *Actiengesellschaft für Anilin Fabrikation v. Levinstein Ltd.*, 29 R.P.C. 677; but *cf. Marsden v. Albrecht*, 27 R.P.C. 785 (C.A.); *Actiengesellschaft für Autogene Aluminium Schweissung v. London Aluminium Co. Ltd.*, 36 R.P.C. 199.
[24] *Haslam & Co. v. Hall*, 4 R.P.C. 203 at p. 206.
[25] *Shoe Machinery Co. Ltd. v. Cutlan*, 12 R.P.C. 342 at p. 358; *Welsbach Incandescent Gas Light Co. Ltd. v. Dowle*, 16 R.P.C. 391.

In *Mandleberg* v. *Morley* [26] Stirling J. said: " Now if a manu-facturer is attacked for infringing a patent by a particular process he does not want to be told in the shape of particulars, or otherwise, what the process is he is using. He knows what the process he is using is. But it is a very different thing with respect to a vendor. The vendor does not know with certainty what process is being used by the person from whom he himself buys, and who manufactures the article."

In that case the particulars of infringements alleged that: " The plaintiffs complain that each of the said letters patent of the plaintiffs have been infringed by the sale and exposure for sale by the defendants of each of the said garments known as ' The Champion,' and ' The Distingué,' and by the sale and exposure for sale of other waterproof garments made by the manufacturers of ' The Champion,' ' The Distingué,' and ' The Tropical Odourless,' but not bearing their distinguishing names, but which unnamed garments are manufactured by similar processes to the three named garments." It was held that the reference to unnamed garments was not sufficiently specific, as it was not clear that the unnamed garments referred to were substantially the same as those which were specifically mentioned.

847 *Further and better particulars*

If the particulars served are too general, the defendant should apply for further and better particulars under Order 18, rule 12; but " It lies on the party who alleges that for the honest purpose of his litigation he wants further information or limitation, to satisfy the court that he is really placed in a difficulty by the particulars as they stand." [27] Further particulars of infringements have sometimes been postponed until after discovery on the ground that the defendant knew the breaches which he had committed better than the plaintiff.[28]

848 *Evidence admitted if within particulars*

If at the trial evidence is tendered which comes within the literal meaning of the particulars it will be admitted, notwithstanding that the particulars are too general, as the defendant should have objected to the particulars, and not have waited until the trial to make his objection.[29]

849 In *Sykes* v. *Howarth* [30] the plaintiff having delivered particulars of infringements specifying certain sales by the defendant of rollers,

[26] 10 R.P.C. 256 at p. 260.
[27] *Per* Wills J. in *Haslam & Co.* v. *Hall*, 4 R.P.C. 203 at 207; and see R.S.C., Ord. 18, r. 12.
[28] *Russell* v. *Hatfield*, Griff.P.C. 204; 2 R.P.C. 144. See also *Mullard Radio Valve Co. Ltd.* v. *Tungsram Electric Lamp Works (Great Britain) Ltd.*, 49 R.P.C. 299.
[29] See *post*, § 892.
[30] 12 Ch.D. 826 at p. 830.

and in particular to Shaw and Smith, the defendant in answer to inter-rogatories, admitted sales to Hirst. Fry J., in giving judgment, said: " In this case I think I must admit the evidence tendered in respect of Hirst's case. It is said that in respect of those cases which are not mentioned by name in the particulars of breaches, the plaintiff cannot give evidence. It may be that the particulars were not sufficient, or tended to embarrass. But the defendant did not apply for amended particulars, according to the case of *Hull* v. *Bollard*.[31] It apears to me I have to inquire what is the meaning of the particulars. I find the case of Hirst is within the literal meaning of the particulars. If I had found that the case of Hirst was likely to create surprise, or likely to introduce any point not raised by Smith's or Shaw's case, I should probably have given an opportunity to the defendant to bring fresh evidence. I have asked whether there is any witness not here whom the defendants would desire to bring in respect of Hirst's case, and have received no satisfactory answer on that point, and must assume that there is no such witness."

Conversely, where the particulars of infringements complained of infringement by user only, the court refused to enter into the question as to whether there had been infringement by manufacturing the articles complained of.[32]

Particulars of infringements may also be ordered in actions which, though not strictly actions for infringement, involve the question of infringement as an issue; this is done under the ordinary jurisdiction of the court.[33]

850   Defence

The defence must be served within fourteen days from the time limited for appearance, or from the service of the statement of claim (whichever is the later).[34]

The following defences [35] are available in an action for infringement:

(1) Denial that the plaintiff is the registered grantee or proprietor, or an exclusive licensee, as the case may be.

(2) Leave or licence of the patentee.

(3) Denial of infringement or, as a defence to a claim for an injunction, of any threat or intent to infringe.

(4) Allegation that all claims alleged to be infringed are invalid.

---

[31] 25 L.J.Ex. 304 at p. 306.
[32] *Henser and Guignard* v. *Hardie*, 11 R.P.C. 421 at p. 427.
[33] R.S.C., Ord. 18, r. 12; see *e.g. Wren* v. *Weild*, L.R. 4 Q.B. 213.
[34] R.S.C., Ord. 18, r. 2.
[35] For precedents, see Appendix.

(5) Allegation of existence of contract offending against section 57 of the Act.

(6) As defence to claim for damages, allegation of innocent infringement or other special circumstances specified in section 59 of the Act.

851 Counterclaim for revocation

Under section 61 of the Act a defendant may counterclaim for revocation of the patent; where he does so, the plaintiff should serve a defence to such counterclaim. If the plaintiff discontinues the action the defendant may still proceed upon his counterclaim,[36] and if no defence thereto has been served may move for judgment in default of service of defence.[37]

Dealing with the above pleas in defence:

852 Title to sue

(1) If and so long as the plaintiff is registered as the grantee or proprietor of, or as an exclusive licensee under, the patent, it is submitted that his title to sue is thereby established for the purposes of an action for infringement.[38] If the defendant wishes to dispute the plaintiff's title, he must move the court for an order that the register may be rectified under section 75 of the Act.

853 Leave or licence

(2) Where a defendant pleads leave or licence of the patentee he should particularise the circumstances, stating, if the licence be alleged to have been verbal, the time and place at which it was given and by whom, or if alleged to be in writing, identifying the document by date and otherwise. The onus of proof is upon the defendant,[39] and a defendant relying on the existence of a licence cannot attack the validity of the patent.[40]

854 Denial of infringement

(3) A mere denial of infringement, which need not be further particularised, puts the plaintiff to the proof (a) that the defendant has committed the acts complained of in the particulars of breaches; (b) that such acts are an infringement of the letters patent, and in proving infringement with regard to goods purchased by the defendant it is incumbent upon the patentee to give evidence that such goods

---

[36] R.S.C., Ord. 15, r. 2.

[37] *e.g. Coventry Radiator Co. Ltd.* v. *Coventry Motor Fittings Co. Ltd.,* 34 R.P.C. 239.

[38] ss. 73, 74, 101 (1); *Martin and another* v. *Scrib Ltd.,* 67 R.P.C. 127.

[39] *British Thomson-Houston Co. Ltd.* v. *British Insulated and Helsby Cables Ltd.,* 41 R.P.C. 345 at p. 375; see also *Whitehead and Poole* v. *Farmer & Sons Ltd.,* 35 R.P.C. 241.   [40] See Chap. 10.

were not produced by himself or his agents.[41]　Where a defendant admitted importing the substance alleged to infringe, but denied knowledge of the process by which it was made and denied infringement, particulars of the method by which the substance was made were not ordered.[42]

855　*Admission of certain infringements only*

Where a statement of defence admitted infringement in ten instances and no more, and the plaintiffs elected to move for judgment upon such admissions under Order 27, rule 3, it was held that they were entitled to an inquiry as to damages as to those ten instances only, and that all evidence as to any other instances of infringement alleged to have been committed by the defendant must be excluded.[43]

856　Invalidity

(4) The grounds upon which invalidity may be alleged are set out in section 32 (1) of the Act, and the particulars required in each case are dealt with below.

857　*Estoppel* (i) *by conduct*

It is not every defendant who is entitled to attack the validity of a patent.　The position in this respect of an assignor of, or a licensee under, a patent is dealt with in Chapter 10.[44]

858　(ii) *by record*

Where judgment has been given in an action, and the record shows that some question has been put in issue and decided,[45] whether such judgment be by consent or otherwise,[46] either party to the litigation is thenceforth estopped in subsequent proceedings between the same parties from alleging and proving facts inconsistent with the correctness of such decision.

Thus where judgment is given for a plaintiff in an action for infringement, the patent being held to be valid and to have been infringed, the defendant if sued again by the patentee will be estopped from denying that the acts previously complained of were an infringement or that the patent is valid,[47] even though he seek to attack its validity upon entirely new grounds.[48]　Conversely, if the

---

[41] *Betts* v. *Willmott*, L.R. 6 Ch.App. 239.
[42] *Parke, Davis & Co.* v. *Allen and Hanburys Ltd.*, 70 R.P.C. 123.
[43] *United Telephone Co.* v. *Donohoe*, 31 Ch.D. 399; 3 R.P.C. 45.
[44] See *ante*, § 615 *et seq.*
[45] See *Goucher* v. *Clayton*, 11 Jur.(N.S.) 107; 34 L.J.Ch. 239; see also *Murex Welding Processes Ltd.* v. *Weldrics (1922) Ltd.*, 50 R.P.C. 178 at p. 182.
[46] *Thomson* v. *Moore*, 6 R.P.C. 426; 7 R.P.C. 325; *Brown* v. *Hastie & Co. Ltd.*, 23 R.P.C. 361.
[47] *Thomson* v. *Moore*, 6 R.P.C. 426; 7 R.P.C. 325.
[48] *Shoe Machinery Co.* v. *Cutlan (No. 2)* [1896] 1 Ch. 667; 13 R.P.C. 141.

patent were held to be invalid the patentee could not, unless the ground of invalidity had been removed by amendment,[49] bring a fresh infringement action against the same defendant.[50]

As to the position where there has been an action for infringement and the defendant subsequently petitions for revocation of the patent, see paragraph 733, *ante,* and cases there noted.

There seems to be no reported case as to whether, where an issue has been decided in opposition proceedings (for instance, whether a claim is prior claimed by a claim in another specification of a granted patent) and the same issue is raised in a subsequent infringement action between the same parties, the issue is *res judicata.*[51] But it is submitted that the general principles of *res judicata* and issue estoppel should apply in such a case and the party seeking to relitigate the same issue already decided in the opposition proceedings would be estopped *per rem judicatum.*

859   *Estoppel personal only*

Estoppel is personal, and exists only against those whose conduct gave rise to it, and persons claiming through them, or, in the case of estoppel by record, only in proceedings between the same parties. Thus, it does not run against the partner of a person estopped [52] nor against a person who was not actually a party to the previous action [53] even though he may have supported one of such parties by financing his defence under a contract of indemnity.[54]   Where a question of infringement was submitted to an arbitrator, who found that the letters patent were not illegal or void, it was held in a subsequent action for infringement between the parties that such award did not estop the defendant from several pleas in which he alleged facts inconsistent with validity of the patent, it only being possible to gather by inference that the arbitrator must have considered such allegations in making his award.[55]   As to a point upon which a direct decision has been given in an arbitration, the award would, however, act subsequently as an estoppel between the parties.[56]

The discontinuance of an action by a plaintiff does not create any estoppel against him by record, and unless there be a term of the order allowing discontinuance that no fresh action shall be brought

[49] See *Deeley's Patent,* 11 R.P.C. 72.
[50] *Horrocks* v. *Stubbs,* 12 R.P.C. 540.
[51] But see *Atlas Chemical Industries Inc.'s Appn.* [1969] F.S.R. 25.
[52] *Heugh* v. *Chamberlain,* 25 W.R. 742; *Goucher* v. *Clayton,* 11 Jur.(N.S.) 107; 34 L.J.Ch. 239.
[53] *Ibid.; Otto* v. *Steel,* 3 R.P.C. 109.
[54] *Gammons* v. *Singer Manufacturing Co.,* 22 R.P.C. 452 at p. 459 (C.A.).
[55] *Newall* v. *Elliot,* 1 H. & C. 797; 32 L.J.Ex. 120.
[56] See Arbitration Act 1950.

on the same patent against the defendant, the plaintiff is entitled to commence a fresh action in respect of the same infringement.[57]

860　*Effect of decision between different parties*

Where there has been a previous decision upon the validity of a patent by a court of co-ordinate or superior jurisdiction, which by reason of having been given in proceedings between different parties does not operate as an estoppel, strong additional evidence will be required in order to reverse the previous finding, and the court will usually hold itself bound by previous decisions on the question of the construction of the specification.[58]

Where a party produces evidence at the trial of an action to prove a certain fact and at the trial of a subsequent action against a different party produces other witnesses whose evidence is inconsistent with such fact, although the original evidence does not create any estoppel and is not admissible as evidence in the subsequent action,[59] the court will scrutinise the new evidence with great care, the more especially if the witnesses called in the first action do not give evidence in the second action to explain that the previous evidence was the result of some mistake.[60]

861　**Contract with void conditions**

(5) By section 57 of the Act, if there has been inserted into any contract, in force at the time of the infringement and made by or with the consent of the plaintiff, certain conditions specified in that section, this constitutes a defence to the action.

The nature of the conditions made void by section 57 is dealt with in Chapter 10.[61]

Order 103, rule 19 (3), of the Rules of the Supreme Court, provides that a defendant relying on this defence must serve with his defence full particulars of the contract and the particular conditions thereon on which he relies, but provided that there appears to be some substance in the allegation and it is not put forward for the purpose

---

[57] See *e.g. Haskell Golf Ball Co. Ltd.* v. *Hutchinson* 22 R.P.C. 205; *Murex Welding Processes Ltd.* v. *Weldrics (1922) Ltd.*, 50 R.P.C. 178 at p. 183.

[58] *Otto* v. *Steel*, 3 R.P.C. 109 at p. 114; *Automatic Weighing Machine Co.* v. *Combined Weighing Machine Co.*, 6 R.P.C. 367; *Edison* v. *Holland*, 6 R.P.C. 243; *Flour Oxidising Co. Ltd.* v. *Carr & Co. Ltd.*, 25 R.P.C. 428 at p. 448; *Higginson and Arundel* v. *Pyman*, 43 R.P.C. 291 at p. 300.

[59] *British Thomson-Houston Co. Ltd.* v. *British Insulated and Helsby Cables Ltd.*, 41 R.P.C. 345 at pp. 353–357, 376–390.

[60] *Ibid.*, 41 R.P.C. 345 at p. 408; 42 R.P.C. 180 at pp. 199, 200.

[61] See *ante*, § 643 *et seq.*

of getting a "fishing" discovery, an application for further particulars may be ordered to stand over till after discovery.[62]

862   Ignorance of patent, defence as to damages

(6) Section 59 (1) provides that a patentee shall not be entitled to recover damages from a defendant who proves that he was not aware of the patent, and had no reasonable means of making himself aware of it.[63]

For the purposes of pleading it is submitted that the defendant should merely state that " at the date of the infringement alleged, he was not aware, nor had reasonable means of making himself aware, of the patent." The onus of proof is expressly laid upon the defendant.

863   *Failure to pay renewal fee*

Section 59 (2) provides that the court may refuse to award damages in respect of any infringement committed during any period in respect of which a renewal fee remained unpaid.

864   *Amendment of specification*

Subsection (3) provides that where the specification has been amended no damages shall be awarded before the date of amendment unless the court is satisfied that the specification as originally published was framed in good faith and with reasonable skill and knowledge.

865   *" Gillette " defence*

In *Gillette Safety Razor Co.* v. *Anglo-American Trading Co.*[64] Lord Moulton used words that have sometimes been interpreted as suggesting a further defence, *viz.* that the alleged infringement was not novel at the relevant date. These words have now been explained in *Page* v. *Brent Toy Products.*[65] It is submitted that particulars of objections drafted in this manner would not comply with the requirements of Order 103, rule 21,[66] and that, therefore, this plea can no longer be regarded as admissible for any purpose, notwithstanding that it forms a useful test by which to judge the chances of success in the action and a basis for argument on behalf of the defendant. Where, however, a defendant had assigned the patent to the plaintiff

---

[62] See *e.g. Sarason* v. *Frenay*, 31 R.P.C. 252; see also *Gerrard Industries Ltd.* v. *Box Wiring Co. Ltd.*, 50 R.P.C. 125; *Soapless Foam Ltd.* v. *The Physical Treatments Institute Ltd.*, 52 R.P.C. 256.

[63] See *post,* § 958.

[64] 30 R.P.C. 465 at p. 480.

[65] 67 R.P.C. 4 at p. 33. See *ante,* § 344.

[66] See *Hardaker* v. *Boucher & Co. Ltd.*, 51 R.P.C. 278. See also *V. D. Ltd.* v. *Boston Deep Sea Fishing Co. Ltd.*, 52 R.P.C. 1.

(and was, therefore, estopped from denying its validity) and, when sued for infringement by the assignee, contended that on the true construction of the claims he had not infringed, but that if the claims were read more widely they would be invalid for anticipation, the court refused to strike out this plea, although it appeared to be unnecessary.[67]

866   Default of defence

Where the defendant makes default in serving a defence, the plaintiff may, under Order 19, rule 7, of the Rules of the Supreme Court, set down the action on motion for judgment in default of defence, or where one of several defendants makes such default and the cause of action is severable, the plaintiff may proceed in the same way with regard to such individual.[68] The defence may be amended without leave once before the pleadings are closed but thereafter leave to amend is required.[69]

867   Particulars of objections

If the defendant disputes validity he must deliver with his defence, and if he counterclaims for revocation he must deliver with his counterclaim adequate particulars of all the objections to validity on which he relies.[70] The requirements of particulars of objections differ materially from those of particulars of breaches, since in the case of the latter the specification tells the defendant what the patentee claims and the defendant well knows what he himself is doing.[71] Particulars of objections must give to the plaintiff such information as will inform him as to the case he has to meet, and enable him to prepare for trial by investigation or research without danger of surprise.

Particulars of a similar nature have been ordered under Order 18, rule 12, in actions, other than those for infringement, where the validity of a patent comes in issue.[72]

868   Grounds of invalidity

The grounds of invalidity which may be relied on as a defence to an action for infringement, and also in a counterclaim for revocation, are set out in detail in section 32 (1) of the Act. Each ground relied upon must be separately specified. The grounds are as follows:

869   Prior grant

"*That the invention, so far as claimed in any claim of the complete specification, was claimed in a valid claim of earlier priority*

---

[67] *Hocking* v. *Hocking*, 3 R.P.C. 291.   [68] R.S.C., Ord. 19, r. 7.
[69] R.S.C., Ord. 20, rr. 3, 5.   [70] R.S.C., Ord. 103, rr. 21, 22, 23.
[71] See *Cheetham* v. *Oldham and Fogg*, 5 R.P.C. 624 at p. 626.   [72] See over.

date contained in the complete specification of another patent granted in the United Kingdom." [73]

This objection is distinct from that of want of novelty, and must be pleaded separately.[74] The particulars should state the number of the prior patent, the name of the grantee thereof, and identify the relevant claim or claims. A patentee, who does not admit the validity of an alleged prior grant, will be ordered to give particulars of his objections to its validity.[75]

870 Applicant not entitled to apply

" That the patent was granted on the application of a person not entitled under the provisions of this Act to apply therefor." [76]

The wording of this ground of objection has been enlarged in order to conform to the provisions of the Act whereby the patent may be applied for by the true and first inventor or by an assignee of the right to make the application. It is submitted that just as under the previous practice it was necessary to give particulars as to whom the defendant alleged to be the true and first inventor, so now particulars should be given sufficient to identify the person alleged to have had the right to apply,[77] but that where fraud is not alleged, no further particulars need be given.[78]

An allegation of fraudulent conduct is not essential under this ground of invalidity, as the basis of the allegation is the deceit of the Crown by the claim made (on application for the patent) that the applicant was entitled to apply. Fraud, however, is usually involved, and where this is so, the particulars required are further governed by Order 18, rule 12, of the Rules of the Supreme Court.

871 Patent obtained in fraud

" That the patent was obtained in contravention of the rights of the petitioner or any person under or through whom he claims." [79]

In this case, also, if there is an allegation of fraudulent conduct, the particulars necessary are governed by Order 18, rule 12, of the Rules of the Supreme Court.[80]

---

[72] See e.g. Hazlehurst v. Rylands, 9 R.P.C. 1. Cf. Suhr v. Crofts (Engineers) Ltd., 49 R.P.C. 359.
[73] See ante, § 256 et seq. and Electric & Musical Industries Ltd. v. Radio & Allied Industries Ltd. [1960] R.P.C. 115.
[74] See Blackett v. Dickson and Mann Ltd., 26 R.P.C. 73 at p. 82 (O.H.).
[75] Electric & Musical Industries Ltd. v. Radio & Allied Industries Ltd. [1960] R.P.C. 115.
[76] See ante, § 71.
[77] See Stroud v. Humber Ltd., 24 R.P.C. 141 at p. 151; Smith's Patent, 29 R.P.C. 339.
[78] See Sylow-Hansen v. June Hair etc. Ltd., 65 R.P.C. 421.
[79] See ante, §§ 102, 332.
[80] See Colthurst and Hyde Ltd. v. Stewart Engineering Co. Ltd., 67 R.P.C. 87.

If a patent is revoked on this ground, the Comptroller may direct that an application for a patent for the same invention by the rightful applicant shall be deemed to have the priority date of the revoked patent.[81]

Leave was given to amend the particulars of objections to raise new material where it was alleged to have been inserted into a complete specification before acceptance and this new matter originated from the defendants.[82]

872 Not within definition of invention

" *That the subject of any claim of the complete specification is not an invention within the meaning of this Act.*" [83]

The issue which is intended to be raised by this plea is that the invention is not a " manner of . . . manufacture the subject of letters patent and grant of privilege within section six of the Statute of Monopolies " or a " method or process of testing applicable to the improvement or control of manufacture." [84] Such objection need not be further particularised.[85] The definition of " invention " contains the word " new " and also " includes an alleged invention," [84] but it is submitted that these latter considerations are not adequately raised by this plea.[86] Thus whether the invention is " new " must be dealt with under the following paragraph.

873 Novelty

" *That the invention, so far as claimed in any claim of the complete specification, is not new having regard to what was known or used, before the priority date of the claim,[87] in the United Kingdom.*" [88]

Order 103, rule 21, requires detailed particulars to be given under this plea, stating the time and place of the previous publication or user alleged, and, in the case of the prior user, a sufficient identification of it, the names of those alleged to have made such prior user,[89] whether the same has continued down to the date of the patent, and, if not, the earliest and latest dates at which such prior user is alleged to have taken place.[90] In the case of machinery or apparatus the

---

[81] s. 53.
[82] *Sandoz Ltd.* v. *Rousel Laboratories Ltd.* [1966] R.P.C. 308.
[83] See *ante*, § 31 *et seq.*   [84] s. 101 (1).
[85] *Hardaker* v. *Boucher & Co. Ltd.*, 51 R.P.C. 278.
[86] See *General Electric Co. Ltd.* v. *Thorn Electrical Industries Ltd.*, 64 R.P.C. 22.   [87] See *ante*, § 165.
[88] See *ante*, § 265; and *Armstrong, Whitworth & Co. Ltd.* v. *Hardcastle*, 42 R.P.C. 543 at p. 555.
[89] See *Leggatt* v. *Hood*, 66 R.P.C. 293.
[90] See *British Thomson-Houston Co. Ltd.* v. *Crompton Parkinson Ltd.*, 52 R.P.C. 409.

particulars must further state whether it is in existence and where it can be inspected. If it is in existence, unless the party relying on it offers, or uses his best endeavours to obtain, inspection of it, evidence relating to it cannot be given; nor can evidence be given which is at variance with any statement contained in the particulars.

874 *Documentary publication*

Prior documents must be pleaded specifically, together with the time and place of their publication, the usual course with regard to patent specifications being to allege their publication by deposit upon or about some date upon the shelves of the National Library of Science and Invention, and with regard to books or newspapers to give similar details, so as to enable the plaintiff to find and identify them, and further to specify the pages or chapters relied upon.

Whether or not a defendant will be required to give particulars of the exact passages of the prior documents relied upon, or to point out specifically what part or parts of the plaintiff's specification he alleges to be affected thereby, will depend upon the circumstances of the case and the nature of the documents.[91] Where it appeared that the defendant had, figuratively speaking, " thrown at the head " of the plaintiff a large number of complicated specifications without any attempt at discrimination, further particulars were required.[92] If however, the defendant bona fide relies upon the whole of one or more documents, and the subject-matter is simple, his particulars of objections will not be interfered with.[93]

875 *Publication by prior user*

In the case of prior user the requirements as to particulars are particularly stringent with respect to user of machinery and apparatus, as the defendant is required to do his best to procure inspection thereof for the plaintiff. But this does not necessarily apply to an alleged prior user of a process. In *Minerals Separation Ltd.* v. *Ore Concentration (1905) Ltd.*,[94] where the patent was a patent solely for a process, it was held that the fact that machinery or apparatus may have been necessary in the carrying out of the alleged prior user did not entitle the plaintiff to particulars as to such apparatus or machinery, or to inspection thereof, and an order for the production of or information as to the existence of samples of the materials used

---

[91] *Heathfield* v. *Greenway,* 11 R.P.C. 17; *Marchant and Another* v. *J. A. Prestwich & Co. Ltd.,* 66 R.P.C. 117.

[92] *Holliday* v. *Heppenstall Bros.,* 6 R.P.C. 320; *Sidebottom* v. *Fielden,* 8 R.P.C. 266 at p. 270; *Heathfield* v. *Greenway,* 11 R.P.C. 17.

[93] *Siemens* v. *Karo, Barnett & Co.,* 8 R.P.C. 376; *Nettlefolds Ltd.* v. *Reynolds,* 8 R.P.C. 410; *Edison-Bell Consolidated Phonograph Co.* v. *Columbia Phonograph Co.,* 18 R.P.C. 4.

[94] [1909] 1 Ch. 744; 26 R.P.C. 413.

in or resulting from the process was refused. Cozens-Hardy M.R. said [95]: " It seems to me that we cannot impose upon the defendant in a patent action any greater liability than is justified by that rule (now rule 21) and it does not seem to me to be relevant to urge that something beyond and outside that rule will enable the plaintiffs better to prepare for trial and will minimise expense. . . . If the patent is one for machinery or apparatus, great detail is required by the rule . . . drawings have to be furnished and experiments have to be permitted, always qualifying that statement by the fact that it must be within the power of defendants to furnish the drawings and allow the experiment. But when the patent is for a process, and merely for a process, no such detailed particulars are required. All that the rule exacts is a description sufficient to identify such alleged prior user. . . . The patent relates to a process, and there is nothing either in the body of the specification or in the claim at the end which justifies us in exacting from the defendants any further particulars as to the nature of the apparatus used in working the particular process; nor do I think it is within our jurisdiction to require the defendants to say whether they have any samples of the ores so treated, or to require them to say whether they will allow the plaintiffs to have inspection of such samples and to make tests therefrom."

876　　　Where the apparatus alleged to constitute a prior user is in existence, the defendant is not required to supply any description further than is required merely to identify the prior user so as to enable the plaintiff, if inspection be obtainable, to inspect it, but where the apparatus is no longer in existence, the drawings or description must be sufficient to show what is going to be alleged at the trial to have been the nature of the article the user of which is relied on as a prior user,[96] and it is submitted that the same principle would apply as regards a process, that is to say, that, inspection not being required by the rule in such a case, the description of the prior user should identify it in the sense not only of when and where it took place, but also of, so far as it be relevant, *what* precisely it was that took place at the time and place alleged.[97]

The same reasoning applies where the patent is for a particular prescription of ingredients; in such circumstances particulars will only be ordered of the ingredients used in the alleged prior user.[98]

---

[95] 26 R.P.C. at p. 421.
[96] *Crosthwaite Fire Bar Syndicate Ltd.* v. *Senior*, 26 R.P.C. 260 at p. 263.
[97] See *e.g. Minerals Separation Ltd.* v. *Ore Concentration Co. (1905) Ltd.* [1909] 1 Ch. 744; 26 R.P.C. 413 at p. 423.
[98] *Stahlwerk Becker A.G.'s Patent*, 34 R.P.C. 332.

877   In *Avery* v. *Ashworth, Son & Co.*[99] the defendants in their particulars of objections stated that they would rely " either by way of anticipation or as showing the scope of the claims . . . upon matters known to the plaintiffs, in consequence of which the plaintiffs " at an earlier date had applied to amend their specification by disclaimer. The defendants were directed to deliver full particulars of the " matters " alleged. The further particulars delivered consisted of a statement that the defendants would rely upon all the matters contained in the particulars of objections which had been delivered in an action by the plaintiffs against other defendants upon another patent several years before. This, and the original paragraph, were ordered to be struck out.

Where the defendants pleaded a public use and sale of articles manufactured by certain specified machines, particulars were ordered of the names and addresses of persons to whom the articles were alleged to have been sold, and of the dates of such sales.[1]

878 *Secret use irrelevant*
Secret prior user cannot be relied on in support of this plea.[2]

879 Obviousness
"*That the invention, so far as claimed in any claim of the complete specification, is obvious and does not involve any inventive step having regard to what was known or used, before the priority date of the claim, in the United Kingdom.*"[3]

This ground of objection has been commonly, but most inappropriately, called " want of subject-matter." It must be specifically pleaded.[4]

880 *Prior knowledge*
The prior knowledge that can be relied upon in order to attack validity (sometimes called " public knowledge ") may be of two kinds, *viz.* (1) that contained in some particular document or documents or used by some particular individual or group, and (2) common general knowledge. In the case of the former, particulars of the publication of the document, or of the user, as the case may be, must be given, but provided that a document is proved to have been published,[5] it is irrelevant that no person is proved to have

---

[99] 32 R.P.C. 463, 560; 33 R.P.C. 235.
[1] See *British United Shoe Machinery Co. Ltd.* v. *Albert Pemberton & Co.,* 47 R.P.C. 134 at p. 141.
[2] s. 32 (2).
[3] See *ante*, § 305.
[4] *Holliday* v. *Heppenstall Bros.,* 6 R.P.C. 320 at p. 327; 41 Ch.D. 109; *Phillips* v. *Ivel Cycle Co. Ltd.,* 7 R.P.C. 77 at p. 82.
[5] See *ante*, § 268 *et seq.*

seen or read it, or to have any knowledge of its contents. Similar considerations apply to a prior user, provided it is not secret. In that case it cannot be relied on in support of this plea.[6] " Common general knowledge," or, as it is sometimes termed, " common knowledge " or " public general knowledge," means " the information which, at the date of the patent in question, is common knowledge in the art or science to which the alleged invention relates, so as to be known to duly qualified persons engaged in that art or science " [7]; in other words, it is part of the mental equipment necessary for competency in that art or science concerned.

881 *Common general knowledge*

Proof of common knowledge is given by witnesses competent to speak upon the matter, who, to supplement their own recollections, may refer to standard works upon the subject which were published at the time and which were known to them.[8] The publication at or before the relevant date of other documents such as patent specifications may be to some extent prima facie evidence tending to show that the statements contained in them were part of the common knowledge, but is far from complete proof, as the statements may well have been discredited or forgotten or merely ignored [9]; evidence may, however, be given to prove that such statements did become part of the common knowledge.[10]

In *British Celanese Ltd.* v. *Courtaulds Ltd.*[11] it was argued that evidence-in-chief could not prove common knowledge. Clauson J. said: " I have a man properly informed in the art who knows so and so. I can infer that everybody properly informed in the art will have some knowledge because they have exactly the same opportunity as he has. . . . I must be satisfied that he has not an excess of any peculiar or special sort of knowledge, but that what he is telling me is what he has acquired in his ordinary practice as a man engaged in the art."

882 *Particulars not ordinarily required*

If the defendant proposes to rely on common general knowledge he should state in general terms the nature of the prior knowledge relied on, but in a normal case detailed particulars will not be

[6] s. 32 (2).
[7] *British Thomson-Houston Co. Ltd.* v. *Stonebridge Electrical Co. Ltd.,* 33 R.P.C. 166 at p. 171. See *ante,* § 300.
[8] *Holliday* v. *Heppenstall Bros.,* 41 Ch.D. 109; 6 R.P.C. 320 at p. 326.
[9] *The Solvo Laundry Supply Co. Ltd.* v. *Mackie,* 10 R.P.C. 68; *Holliday* v. *Heppenstall,* 6 R.P.C. 320 at p. 327; *Metropolitan-Vickers etc. Co. Ltd.* v. *British Thomson-Houston Co. Ltd.,* 43 R.P.C. 76 at p. 93.
[10] *Sutcliffe* v. *Thomas Abbott,* 20 R.P.C. 50 at p. 55.
[11] 50 R.P.C. 63 at p. 90.

required.[12] But the defendant may not rely, in support of an objection of common knowledge, upon documents of limited publicity (such as patent specifications) unless they have been particularised in some way before the trial.[13]

883 *Appeal on question of obviousness*

The circumstances in which a finding of fact as to obviousness by the trial judge will be reversed on appeal were discussed in *Benmax* v. *Austin Motor Co. Ltd.* Lord Simonds said [14]: " Fifty years ago in *Montgomerie & Co. Ltd.* v. *Wallace James* [15] Lord Halsbury said: ' But where no question arises as to truthfulness, and where the question is as to the proper inferences to be drawn from truthful evidence, then the original tribunal is in no better position to decide than the judges of an Appellate Court.' And in *Mersey Docks and Harbour Board* v. *Proctor* [16] Lord Cave said: ' The procedure on an appeal from a judge sitting without a jury is not governed by the rules applicable to a motion for a new trial after a verdict of a jury. In such a case it is the duty of the Court of Appeal to make up its own mind, not disregarding the judgment appealed from and giving special weight to that judgment in cases where the credibility of witnesses comes into question, but with full liberty to draw its own inference from the facts proved or admitted, and to decide accordingly.' It appears to me that these statements are consonant with the Rules of Court which prescribe that ' An appeal to the Court of Appeal shall be by way of re-hearing ' and that ' the Court of Appeal shall have powers to draw inferences of fact and to give any judgment and make any order that ought to have been made.' This does not mean that an Appellate Court should lightly differ from the finding of a trial judge on a question of fact, and I would say that it would be difficult for it to do so where the finding turned solely on the credibility of a witness. But I cannot help thinking that some confusion may have arisen from failure to distinguish between the finding of a specific fact and a finding of fact which is really an inference from facts specifically found, or, as it has sometimes been said, between the perception and evaluation of facts. An example of

---

[12] *Holliday* v. *Heppenstall*, 6 R.P.C. 320; *McCreath* v. *Mayor etc. of South Shields and Baker*, 49 R.P.C. 349; *American Chain and Cable Co. Inc.* v. *Hall's Barton Ropery Co. Ltd.*, 55 R.P.C. 287 at p. 293; *Walton* v. *Hawtins Ltd.*, 65 R.P.C. 69.

[13] *British Thomson-Houston Co. Ltd.* v. *Stonebridge Electrical Co. Ltd.*, 33 R.P.C. 166 at p. 171; *English and American Machinery Co. Ltd.* v. *Union Boot and Shoe Machine Co. Ltd.*, 11 R.P.C. 367 at pp. 373, 374. And see *Killick* v. *Pye Ltd.* [1958] R.P.C. 366 at p. 376.

[14] 72 R.P.C. 39 at p. 42.

[15] [1904] A.C. 73.

[16] [1923] A.C. 253.

this distinction may be seen in any case in which a plaintiff alleges negligence on the part of the defendant. Here it must first be determined what the defendant in fact did and, secondly, whether what he did amounted in the circumstances (which must also so far as relevant be found as specific facts) to negligence. A jury finds that the defendant has been negligent and that is an end of the matter, unless its verdict can be upset according to well-established rules. A judge sitting without a jury would fall short of his duty if he did not first find the facts and then draw from them the inference of fact whether or not the defendant had been negligent. This is a simple illustration of a process in which it may often be difficult to say what is simple fact and what is inference from fact, or, to repeat what I have said, what is perception, what evaluation. Nor is it of any importance to do so except to explain why, as I think, different views have been expressed as to the duty of an Appellate Tribunal in relation to a finding by a trial judge. For I have found on the one hand universal reluctance to reject a finding of specific fact, particularly where the finding could be founded on the credibility or bearing of a witness, and on the other hand no less a willingness to form an independent opinion about the proper inference of fact, subject only to the weight which should as a matter of course be given to the opinion of the learned judge. But the statement of the proper function of the Appellate Court will be influenced by the extent to which the mind of the speaker is directed to the one or other of the two aspects of the problem. In a case like that under appeal where, so far as I can see, there can be no dispute about any relevant specific fact, much less any dispute arising out of the credibility of witnesses, but the sole question is whether the proper inference from those facts is that the patent in suit disclosed an inventive step, I do not hesitate to say that an Appellate Court should form an independent opinion, though it will naturally attach importance to the judgment of the trial judge."

884   Utility

" *That the invention, so far as claimed in any claim of the complete specification, is not useful.*" [17]

Where it is intended to rely on the fact that an example of the invention which is the subject of a claim of the patent in suit cannot be made to work, either at all or as described in the specification, particulars are required.[18]

885   Insufficiency

" *That the complete specification does not sufficiently and fairly*

[17] See *ante*, § 246.   [18] R.S.C., Ord. 103, r. 21 (3).

describe the invention and the method by which it is to be performed,
or does not disclose the best method of performing it which was
known to the applicant for the patent and for which he was entitled
to claim protection." [19]

The objection upon the first part of this ground should be
accompanied where possible by particulars of the alleged defects and
of the point at which a workman would meet with difficulty in
carrying out the directions given.[20]   Where, however, the objection
is not that one cannot carry out the directions given, but that if one
does carry them out the result described is not attained, further
particulars are not required.[21]

886 *Best method not disclosed*

In most cases it is unlikely that a defendant would be in a position
to rely upon the second part of this ground. It may happen, however,
during the course of the trial that evidence is given on behalf of the
plaintiff which will allow of this objection being taken. In such a
case an amendment of the pleadings would readily be granted [22]; but
the application for leave to amend should be made at as early a
stage as possible in order that the plaintiff may have an opportunity
of considering the objection and calling further evidence on the
point.[23]

Where this objection is pleaded it would appear necessary to give
particulars of what is alleged not to have been disclosed in order that
the plaintiff may be informed as to the case he has to meet. It is,
however, permissible to plead this ground without giving such particulars if the defendant is only pleading a dilemma arising on proof of
his particulars of insufficiency, *viz.,* that either the patentee did not
know how to carry out the invention or alternatively, if he did know,
he must have been aware of a method not described in his
specification.[24]

887 Ambiguity

" *That the scope of any claim of the complete specification is not*
sufficiently and clearly defined [25] *or that any claim of the complete*
specification is not fairly based on the matter disclosed in the
specification." [26]

[19] See *ante,* §§ 212, 226.
[20] *Crompton* v. *Anglo-American Brush Corporation Ltd.* (*No.* 2), 4 R.P.C.
197; *Heathfield* v. *Greenway,* 11 R.P.C. 17.
[21] See *e.g.* " *Z* " *Electric Lamp Manufacturing Co. Ltd.* v. *Marples, Leach*
& Co. Ltd., 26 R.P.C. 762 (C.A.).
[22] *Franc-Strohmenger & Cowan Inc.* v. *Peter Robinson Ltd.,* 47 R.P.C. 493
at p. 502.   [23] *Ibid.*
[24] *Anxionnaz* v. *Ministry of Aviation* [1966] R.P.C. 21.
[25] See *ante,* § 240.   [26] See *ante,* § 231.

In a case decided under section 29 of the Act of 1883 it was held that a plea that " The specification does not sufficiently define the extent or limits of the invention claimed " need not be further particularised,[27] and this is still the general practice.

In *Natural Colour Kinematograph Co. Ltd.* v. *Bioschemes Ltd.*,[28] Lord Loreburn said, in holding the patent bad for ambiguity, that a court might and should hold a patent to be invalid upon the ground of ambiguity, even though such a point had not been raised upon the pleadings.[29] The absence of the plea might, however, prejudicially affect the defendant as regards costs, and it is advisable to include it specifically in the particulars of objections if it is to be taken.[30] What may be regarded as an instance where the second half of this plea was applicable is to be found in *Mullard Radio Valve Co. Ltd.* v. *Philco Radio and Television Corporation Ltd.*[31] This contention, like ambiguity, can be raised even if not specifically pleaded.

888 False suggestion or representation

" *That the patent was obtained on a false suggestion or representation.*" [33]

In modern practice this plea is usually concerned with the allegation that some promise contained in the specification is not fulfilled even when the directions therein contained are properly followed, and in such cases the same matters may also constitute inutility. Obviously, particulars must be given sufficient to identify the false suggestion or representation alleged.[34] There are, however, other cases in which this plea would be appropriate. Thus where the patent sued on had been granted out of time under the provisions of the 1914 Patents, Designs and Trade Marks (Temporary Rules) Act, the defendants pleaded *inter alia* that such patents had been granted upon representations made on the application form, which were untrue. This being a plea of misrepresentation (and in fact of fraud on the Crown), appropriate particulars were ordered.[35]

889 Invention contrary to law

" *That the primary or intended use or exercise of the invention is contrary to law.*"

[27] *Minerals Separation Ltd.* v. *British Ore Concentration Ltd.*, 24 R.P.C. 790; *Marconi Wireless Telegraph Co. Ltd.* v. *Cramer & Co. Ltd.*, 49 R.P.C. 400.
[28] 32 R.P.C. 256 at p. 266.
[29] And see *Safveans Aktie Bolag* v. *Ford Motor Co. (Eng.) Ltd.*, 44 R.P.C. 49 at p. 56, and *Franc-Strohmenger & Cowan Inc.* v. *Peter Robinson Ltd.*, 47 R.P.C. 493 at p. 500.
[30] See *e.g. Heathfield* v. *Greenway*, 11 R.P.C. 17 at p. 20.
[31] 53 R.P.C. 323. See *ante*, § 232.
[33] See *ante*, § 255.
[34] And see *Godfrey L. Cabot Inc.* v. *Philblack Ltd.* [1961] R.P.C. 53.
[35] *e.g. Tecalemit Ltd.* v. *Ex-A-Gun Ltd.*, 44 R.P.C. 62.

This objection has only rarely been taken.[36] The only particulars which would seem to be necessary are in cases where it is contended that the use of the invention is contrary to the provisions of a particular statute.

890 Prior secret user

" *That the invention, so far as claimed in any claim of the complete specification, was secretly used in the United Kingdom, otherwise than as mentioned in subsection (2) of this section* [32], *before the priority date of that claim.*"

Section 32 (2) provides that no account shall be taken of any secret prior user which was:

(a) for the purpose of reasonable trial or experiment only;

(b) by or with the authority of a government department consequent upon a communication of the invention by the applicant or by a person from whom he derives title;

(c) by any other person, in consequence of such a communication, if made without consent.

Particulars must be given as in the case of a non-secret prior user.[37]

891 Extension granted null and void

In *Anxionnaz* v. *Rolls Royce Ltd.*[38] it was sought to plead that an extension which was obtained on the ground of fraud was null and void. Whether or not fraud vitiates an order for extension was not decided; but it is submitted an order obtained by fraud is void.

892 Admissibility of evidence having regard to particulars

Order 103, rule 24, provides that no evidence may be admitted in proof of any alleged infringement or objection that is not raised in the particulars, except by leave of the court, to be given on suitable terms.

The discretion of the court under this rule is separate and distinct from its discretion under Order 103, rule 22, as to amendment of particulars.[39] While the court would exercise its discretion so as to avoid an injustice, it would be unlikely to admit evidence, outside the particulars, relating to individual prior users or constructions. It might, however, admit evidence as to what was practically common knowledge.[40]

---

[36] See *Pessers and Moody* v. *Haydon & Co.*, 26 R.P.C. 58.
[37] See *ante*, § 274, and Ord. 103, r. 21. And see *Strachan and Henshaw Ltd.* v. *Pakcel Ltd.*, 66 R.P.C. 49 at p. 55.
[38] [1965] R.P.C. 122.
[39] See § 894 *et seq., post.*
[40] *Britain* v. *Hirsch*, 5 R.P.C. 226 at p. 231.

In *British United Shoe Machinery Co. Ltd.* v. *A. Fussell & Sons Ltd.*,[41] the specification had been amended, and the judge at the trial held that the original claims were not framed with reasonable skill and knowledge. The defendant, in the Court of Appeal, attempted to rely on this finding of fact as an additional ground of invalidity, but the court would not allow this course as the objection had not been pleaded, and they saw no grounds for going beyond the particulars of objections.

In *Cropper* v. *Smith and Hancock*[42] the defendants, who were partners, were sued in respect of a joint infringement. Owing to an unfounded fear that Hancock might be estopped from disputing the validity of the patent they severed their defences, and while Smith delivered particulars of objections to validity, Hancock did not do so. The patent was held to be invalid by the Court of Appeal, but owing to the lack of particulars judgment was given, nevertheless, against Hancock, restraining him from further infringement. The House of Lords, however, held that judgment should be given for Hancock as well as for Smith, and penalised the former merely by refusing him costs of the appeal. In the course of his judgment the Lord Chancellor (Earl of Selborne) said [43]: " If it so happened . . . that the defendants were persons whose cases were wholly distinct, who had nothing to do with each other, whose acts were acts for which each of them was severally and solely responsible, and in which the others of them had no interest, if that case arose, it might be that a court of justice, applying this section of the statute, might properly hold that one defendant who had not given full particulars should have no benefit from what had been done by another defendant, with whom he had no connection or concern, and whose case was entirely separate from his own. What the consequences of that might be it is not necessary at present to say. But where there is a case, as I said, not expressly noticed or provided for in terms by the section, of co-defendants who are sued as being jointly liable for their joint and common acts, whose cases on the face of the plaintiffs' pleadings and their own are not separate as to the substance, though they may sever in the conduct of their defences, then as to that case, if the substance of the statute and its substantial objects are complied with, I see no words in it which say that justice is not to be done in the case because one of the defendants has neglected or omitted or refused in point of form to put in the particulars which have been put in by the other, who is *in pari casu*."

Apart from the exercise of the discretion of the court, the same

41 25 R.P.C. 631 at pp. 659, 660.
42 10 App.Cas. 249; 2 R.P.C. 17.
43 10 App.Cas. at p. 254; 2 R.P.C. at p. 22.

practice is applicable to actions for infringement as to other actions, *viz.*, that evidence is admissible if the wording of the particulars of objections is sufficiently wide to cover it, even though such wording be vague and general in its terms. The party aggrieved should apply before the hearing for further and better particulars so as to be sure of not being taken by surprise.[44]

In *Sugg* v. *Silber*[45] Mellish L.J. said: " In my opinion there is a very large difference between a case where a judge has been applied to and has ordered further particulars in order to state an objection more specifically, and a case where at the trial the plaintiff asserts that the defendant ought to be prevented from availing himself of an objection. It is perfectly obvious that, if . . . the two questions are the same, and that wherever the court would order further particulars because the objection had not been particularly specified, it would also hold that the party was precluded from raising it at the trial, nobody would be foolish enough to apply to a judge for further particulars." [46]

893 Amendment of particulars

Order 103, rule 22, provides that particulars of infringement and particulars of objections may from time to time be amended by leave of the court upon such terms as may be just.

894 *Amendment of particulars of objections before trial*

Amendments of particulars of objections under this rule are usually permitted upon application made before trial, the terms imposed being such that the plaintiff shall not be prejudiced by the defectiveness of the particulars as originally delivered. The form of order which is almost invariably followed [47] is that made in the case of *Baird* v. *Moule's Patent Earth Closet Co.*, which is set out in the report of *Edison Telephone Co.* v. *India Rubber Co.*[48] and printed at § 2007, *post*. The effect of such order is to give to the plaintiff the option either of discontinuing the action or of proceeding therewith. If he discontinues he has to pay the costs up to and including the original particulars of objections, the defendant paying the costs subsequent to that time. If he proceeds with the action the defendants have to pay the costs of the application to amend,[49] and in other respects the action proceeds in the ordinary way.

---

[44] See R.S.C., Ord. 18, r. 12.
[45] (1877) 2 Q.B.D. 493 at p. 495.
[46] And see *Neilson* v. *Harford*, 1 W.P.C. 295 at p. 370; *Hull* v. *Bollard*, 25 L.J.Ex. 304.
[47] See *e.g. Ehrlich* v. *Ihlee*, 4 R.P.C. 115; *Wilson* v. *Wilson & Co. Ltd.*, 16 R.P.C. 315; *Lusty & Sons* v. *G. W. Scott & Sons Ltd.*, 48 R.P.C. 475.
[48] 17 Ch.D. 137 at p. 139n.
[49] And see *Bloxham* v. *Kee-Less Clock Co.*, 39 R.P.C. 195 at p. 211.

A similar form of order is made in the case of the particulars of objections in a counterclaim for revocation.[50]

Where the particulars of objections were permitted to be amended a second time, it was ordered that if the plaintiff discontinued, the defendant should pay the costs as from the date when the amended particulars of objections were delivered.[51]

Where the defendants applied for leave to amend upon the eve of the trial, such leave was granted, and, the plaintiffs deciding to proceed, it was ordered that the defendants should pay the costs occasioned by the amendment and, also, the costs unnecessarily caused to the plaintiffs by the amendment being made so late.[52]

895 *Amendment of particulars at the trial*

Where the application to amend is made at the trial such leave will only be granted if the new matter has only been recently discovered, and could not with reasonable diligence have been discovered before.[53] A general discussion of the principles applicable to amendment is to be found in the judgment of Bowen L.J. in *Cropper* v. *Smith and Hancock*.[54]

Where the defendant wishes to add further objections in consequence of evidence given by the plaintiff's witnesses during the trial, the application to amend should be made at the earliest opportunity, in order that the plaintiff may have an opportunity to consider the matter and call further evidence if necessary.[55]

In *Badische Anilin und Soda Fabrik* v. *La Société Chimique*[56] it became clear during the course of the trial that the specification of the patent sued upon was insufficient, and the defendants applied for leave to amend the particulars by inserting an objection on this ground. Leave was granted to amend, the plaintiffs having a fortnight to elect whether they would continue the action, the terms upon which such leave should be granted being left for argument until the plaintiffs had elected. On the hearing the plaintiffs elected to continue, and the patent was declared invalid as a result of the new objection, but all costs of and occasioned by the application to

---

[50] *See* v. *Scott-Paine*, 50 R.P.C. 56; *Strachan and Henshaw Ltd.* v. *Pakcel Ltd.*, 66 R.P.C. 49 at p. 56; *Betts* v. *Ideal Capsules Ltd.*, 68 R.P.C. 23.

[51] *Wilson* v. *Wilson & Co. Ltd.*, 16 R.P.C. 315; *Lever Brothers and Unilever Ltd.'s Patent*, 70 R.P.C. 275.

[52] *Parker* v. *Maignen's Filtre Rapide Co.*, 5 R.P.C. 207.

[53] *Moss* v. *Malings*, 33 Ch.D. 603; 3 R.P.C. 373 at p. 375; and see *British United Shoe Machinery Co. Ltd.* v. *A. Fussell & Sons Ltd.*, 25 R.P.C. 631 at pp. 659, 660.

[54] (1884) 26 Ch.D. 700 at p. 710; 1 R.P.C. 81 at p. 95.

[55] See *Franc-Strohmenger & Cowan Inc.* v. *Peter Robinson Ltd.*, 47 R.P.C. 493 at p. 502.

[56] 14 R.P.C. 875 at pp. 881, 892.

amend, and all costs thrown away by reason of the amendment being made so late, were given to the plaintiffs.[57]

In *Birtwhistle* v. *Sumner Engineering Co. Ltd.*[58] the defendants at the trial desired to give evidence as to the use of an article (pleaded as a " prior user ") by persons other than those mentioned in the particulars of objections. They were allowed to amend by adding the names of such persons upon the terms of the ordinary *Baird* v. *Moule* order.

The terms on which amendment will be allowed are a matter for the discretion of the court, and such terms will not, in general, be reviewed by the Court of Appeal.[59]

896 *Amendment in Court of Appeal*

In *Pirrie* v. *York Street Flax Spinning Co. Ltd.*[60] leave to amend particulars of objections was granted by the Court of Appeal in Ireland pending appeal.

In *Shoe Machinery Co. Ltd.* v. *Cutlan*[61] the Court of Appeal decided that they had jurisdiction to permit amendment of the particulars of objections although in that particular case they declined to do so, and the same rule has been held to apply to the Scottish Inner House.[62] The Court of Appeal is, however, very reluctant to permit such amendments.[63]

897 Reply

The plaintiff may deliver a reply setting out facts which may tend to negative some of the pleas raised by the particulars of objections, *e.g.* that the invention was obvious. Although evidence of such facts could be called at the trial without these being pleaded, to set them out in a reply may be advantageous from the point of view of obtaining a wider discovery.[64]

898 Discovery

Interrogatories

Order 26, rules 1 and 3, of the Rules of the Supreme Court, provide that either party to an action, with the leave of the court, or

---

[57] See also *Allen* v. *Horton,* 10 R.P.C. 412; *Westley, Richards & Co.* v. *Perkes,* 10 R.P.C. 181 at p. 186.

[58] 46 R.P.C. 59 at p. 67.

[59] *Wilson* v. *Wilson & Co. Ltd.,* 16 R.P.C. 315 (C.A.).

[60] 11 R.P.C. 429 at p. 431.

[61] [1896] 1 Ch. 108; 12 R.P.C. 530.

[62] *Watson, Laidlaw & Co. Ltd.* v. *Pott, Cassels and Williamson,* 26 R.P.C. 349 at p. 360.

[63] See *e.g. Alsop Flour Process Ltd.* v. *Flour Oxidising Co. Ltd.,* 24 R.P.C. 349 (C.A.); 25 R.P.C. 477 (H.L.).

[64] See *Laurence Scott and Electromotors Ltd.* v. *General Electric Co. Ltd.,* 55 R.P.C. 233.

a judge, may interrogate the other party. The particular interrogatories sought to be delivered have to be submitted to the court, which will take into account any offer made to deliver particulars, make admissions, or produce relevant documents, and only gives leave as to such interrogatories as are considered necessary for a fair trial or for saving costs.[65]

Interrogatories must be relevant to some issue, and, if not, will not be allowed, even though they consist of questions which might be put in cross-examination at the trial.[66] Where the party from whom information is required is a company or corporation, interrogatories may be delivered to the proper officer, *e.g.* the secretary of such company or corporation, who answers on its behalf.[67]

899 *Documents*

Order 24, rule 1, of the Rules of the Supreme Court, provides that after close of pleadings there shall be discovery of documents by both parties. Such discovery may be made by exchanging lists of documents or upon oath by affidavits.

Application may also be made by either party for discovery on oath of relevant [68] documents in the possession or power of the other party. The court thereupon will make such order as it may think fit, having regard to the necessity for such discovery for a fair trial or for saving costs.[69]

900   General principles as to discovery

Discovery, whether of documents or by interrogatories, is a powerful weapon, which by its nature is particularly liable to abuse when actions between traders are concerned, and its utilisation is watched by the court with care lest, on the one hand, facts material to the dispute before it be concealed, or, on the other, immaterial facts be elicited with some ulterior motive. Discovery, as was stated by Lord Watson in *Ind, Coope & Co.* v. *Emmerson*,[70] is a " matter of remedy and not matter of right."

Objection may be taken to interrogatories at the time when leave is sought to administer them or objection may be made to answering them, even though such leave to administer has been granted. Discovery of documents when ordered must be given completely as

---

[65] R.S.C., Ord. 26, r. 1.
[66] R.S.C., Ord. 26, rr. 1, 3.
[67] R.S.C., Ord. 26, r. 2.
[68] See *Martin* v. *Scrib Ltd.*, 66 R.P.C. 340; 67 R.P.C. 127; *Sonotone Corporation* v. *Multitone Electric Co. Ltd.*, 70 R.P.C. 83; *Martin* v. *H. Millwood Ltd.*, 71 R.P.C. 316.
[69] R.S.C., Ord. 24, rr. 3, 7, 8, 13, 14, 16.
[70] 12 App.Cas. 300 at p. 309; and see *Martin* v. *Scrib Ltd.*, 67 R.P.C. 127.

far as the mention of all relevant documents in the affidavit is concerned, privilege being claimed in respect of such documents so mentioned as the other party is not entitled to see.[71] The ordinary principles as to objections to answer interrogatories or to produce documents apply to patent cases.

901   Time for discovery

Since it is not possible to say precisely what the issues between the parties are before the defence is delivered, neither party, except under special circumstances, will be allowed to interrogate, or obtain discovery of documents,[72] until that stage of the action has been reached. But thereafter discovery will not be delayed merely because it is inconvenient to a party to give it immediately.[73]

Nor will interrogatories be allowed or discovery of documents ordered before trial as to facts which will only become relevant after trial as, for instance, with regard to the extent of the defendant's infringements—a fact which is not material until the inquiry as to damages.[74] The practice as to discovery upon such inquiry as to damages is dealt with below.[75] The fact, however, that the question of validity of a patent may have to be decided before the plaintiff can enforce his rights as regards infringement does not render inadmissible interrogatories as to the acts of infringement as defined in the particulars of infringements, because, as a matter of convenience, the issues of validity and infringement are always heard together or in immediate succession.[76]

902   Where issues not properly defined

The issues in patent cases to which both interrogatories and discovery of documents must be relevant are not the broad issues of validity and infringement, but those issues as narrowed down by the particulars of objections or infringements.

Thus, where the particulars of infringements alleged infringement of a process in general terms, and also specified a particular instance of infringement, it was held that the plaintiff was only entitled to interrogate as to the particular act complained of.[77]

---

71 *Carnegie Steel Co.* v. *Bell Bros. Ltd.*, 24 R.P.C. 82 at p. 93.
72 *Woolfe* v. *Automatic Picture Gallery Ltd.*, 19 R.P.C. 161.
73 *British United Shoe Machinery Co. Ltd.* v. *Holdfast Boots Ltd.*, 51 R.P.C. 489.
74 *De La Rue* v. *Dickenson*, 3 K. & J. 388; *Lea* v. *Saxby*, 32 L.T.(N.S.) 731; *Fennessy* v. *Clark*, 37 Ch.D. 184; but *cf.* R.S.C., Ord. 24, r. 4.
75 See *post*, § 963.
76 *Benno Jaffé und Darmstaedter Lanolin Fabrik* v. *John Richardson & Co. Ltd.*, 10 R.P.C. 136; *cf. Rawes* v. *Chance*, 7 R.P.C. 275.
77 *Actiengesellschaft etc. Aluminium Schweissung* v. *London Aluminium Co. Ltd. (No. 2)*, 36 R.P.C. 199; but see *Alliance Flooring Co. Ltd.* v. *Winsorflor Ltd.* [1961] R.P.C. 375.

Similarly, where the defendant alleged invalidity by reason of certain facts within the knowledge of the plaintiff, it was held that the issue was not the validity of the patent generally, but only as limited by the particulars of objections, and that a plaintiff should not be ordered to disclose every document which might suggest invalidity irrespective of whether it related to the particular grounds relied upon by the defendant.[78]

903　*Documents not to be construed*

Interrogatories the reply to which by either party would involve placing a construction upon the specification are not permissible.[79] Nor ordinarily will interrogatories be permitted, the determination of the relevance of which depends upon the construction of the specification.[80]

904　*Issue of infringement*

The plaintiff may interrogate the defendant or obtain discovery as to facts relevant to points in issue [81] with respect to the particular act instanced as an alleged infringement in the particulars of infringements, both as to whether the act was performed and as to the details which tend to show whether or not it was an infringement.

Thus, a plaintiff may administer interrogatories framed upon portions of his specification and ask the defendant whether he has used the processes described therein and forming part of his invention, taking them step by step,[82] but he may not go further and ask, " If you do not use that process, tell me what you do use " [83]; nor is he entitled to interrogate the defendant in further detail than is given in the specification with the object of meeting a possible objection to the sufficiency of the description in his specification.[84]

905　*Names of defendant's customers*

A defendant cannot conceal the name of his customer in the case of the specific article complained of, and as regards that article may

---

[78] *Avery Ltd.* v. *Ashworth, Son & Co. Ltd.*, 32 R.P.C. 463, 560; *cf. Edison and Swan United Electric Light Co.* v. *Holland*, 5 R.P.C. 213.

[79] *Wenham Co. Ltd.* v. *Champion Gas Lamp Co. Ltd.*, 8 R.P.C. 22; *Bibby & Baron Ltd.* v. *Duerden*, 27 R.P.C. 283 (C.A.).

[80] *Delta Metal Co. Ltd.* v. *Maxim Nordenfelt Guns and Ammunition Co. Ltd.*, 8 R.P.C. 169.

[81] See *Marriott* v. *Chamberlain*, 17 Q.B.D. 154 at p. 163; *Nash* v. *Layton* [1911] 2 Ch. 71.

[82] *Benno Jaffé und Darmstaedter Lanolin Fabrik* v. *John Richardson & Co. Ltd.*, 10 R.P.C. 136; and see *Sharpe & Dohme Inc.* v. *Boots Pure Drug Co. Ltd.*, 44 R.P.C. 69.

[83] *Actiengesellschaft für Anilin Fabrikation* v. *Levinstein Ltd.*, 30 R.P.C. 401 (C.A.); *Osram Lamp Works Ltd.* v. *Pope's Electric Lamp Co.*, 31 R.P.C. 313.

[84] *Actiengesellschaft für Anilin Fabrikation* v. *Levinstein Ltd.*, 30 R.P.C. 673.

be interrogated as to whether he has supplied it to anybody and to whom, unless, of course, he has already admitted the sale thereof in his defence.[85] A plaintiff is not, however, entitled to discover before trial the names of the defendant's customers generally, as this only becomes relevant if he establishes his case and obtains an inquiry into damages.

906　*Names of defendant's suppliers*

The names of the persons who supplied the defendant with goods alleged to infringe are not normally relevant to any issue between the parties; but where the defendants dealt in a chemical product, all known processes for the manufacture of which were alleged to be covered by patents owned by the plaintiffs, interrogatories as to the sources of the defendants' supply were permitted by the Court of Appeal on the ground that the answers would probably enable the plaintiffs to ascertain whether the substance had been manufactured by an infringing process or not.[86]

Such a probability has also been held to exist where the plaintiffs alleged that they had knowledge of the processes employed at certain works and that, if informed as to the source of the defendants' goods, they would be enabled, utilising such knowledge, to prove infringement.[87]

An allegation by the defendant that his process is a secret one would not seem to render necessary any departure from the above principles with regard to interrogatories,[88] though, of course, it may have a material effect upon an application for inspection of the process.[89]

907　**Discovery relating to issue of validity**

Interrogatories or discovery of documents relating to the issue of validity may be obtained by either party. In *Sharpe & Dohme Inc. v. Boots Pure Drug Co. Ltd.*[90] the plaintiffs were allowed to interrogate as to whether the substance of the chemical composition and constitution set forth in their specification was " a new substance at the date of the patent," and whether it was " a substance produced

---

[85] See *Lister v. Norton Bros. & Co. Ltd.*, 2 R.P.C. 68; see also *Stahlwerk Becker A.G.'s Patent*, 34 R.P.C. 344.

[86] *Saccharin Corporation v. Haines*, 15 R.P.C. 344; and see *Stahlwerk Becker A.G.'s Patent*, 34 R.P.C. 344.

[87] *Osram Lamp Works Ltd. v. Gabriel Lamp Co.*, 31 R.P.C. 230 (C.A.).

[88] See *Renard v. Levinstein*, 3 New Rep. 665; 10 L.T.(N.S.) 94. See also *Reddaway & Co. Ltd. v. Flynn*, 30 R.P.C. 16; *Helps v. Mayor etc. of Oldham*, 40 R.P.C. 68. *Cf. Sorbo etc. Products Ltd. v. Defries*, 47 R.P.C. 454 (secret process).

[89] See *post*, § 911.

[90] 44 R.P.C. 69.

by a chemical process." In *Haslam* v. *Hall* [91] the plaintiffs had, before becoming the owners, made preparations to dispute the validity of the patent. The defendants were given discovery of the documents in such proceedings except those which had come into existence for communication to the solicitors for the purposes of the litigation. [92]

908 Prior user

As regards prior user of machinery or apparatus the requirements with regard to particulars and inspection are so stringent that it is unlikely that further information could in most cases properly be obtained by interrogatories or discovery of documents. Where the prior user is of a process, the information afforded by the particulars may need supplementing. It was held, however, in *Delta Metal Co. Ltd.* v. *Maxim Nordenfelt Ltd.*, [93] where the plaintiff interrogated with respect to a prior user as to the precise process used, that an answer that the prior user was substantially the process as described in the plaintiff's specification was sufficient.

And in *Crossley* v. *Tomey*, [94] where the defendant was required to state whether he was not making articles in all respects identical with those of the plaintiff, and to set forth in what respects they differed, and by what process they were made, it was held that the defendant (who alleged prior user by himself and others) had sufficiently answered by stating that, save so far as the articles manufactured by him before the date of the patent were similar to those of the plaintiff, the articles he now made differed from those made by the plaintiff, but he could not show in what they differed without ocular demonstration.

The interrogatory or application for discovery will not be allowed if it would disclose the evidence by which the other party will support its own case. In *Brown's Patent* [95] Buckley L.J. said: " The broad statement is still true that a party can only interrogate to support his own case and not to ascertain the evidence of his opponent in order to destroy his opponent's case."

Thus in *Carnegie Steel Co.* v. *Bell Bros. Ltd.*, [96] the defendants objected to allow inspection of certain documents referred to in their affidavit of documents, which documents, they said, referred solely to certain prior users alleged in their particulars of objections. It was

---

[91] 5 R.P.C. 1 at p. 9.
[92] And see *Bown* v. *Sansom, Teale & Co.,* 5 R.P.C. 510; *Edison and Swan United Electric Light Co.* v. *Holland,* 5 R.P.C. 213; *Thomson* v. *Hughes,* 7 R.P.C. 187; *Avery Ltd.* v. *Ashworth, Son & Co. Ltd.,* 32 R.P.C. 463, 560.
[93] 8 R.P.C. 169.
[94] 2 Ch.D. 533.
[95] 24 R.P.C. 61 at p. 64.
[96] 24 R.P.C. 82.

held that the documents were privileged, and Buckley L.J. said[97]: " Particulars of prior user must be given; evidence of prior user need not be given; and it does not follow that every document relating to prior user is a particular of prior user; it may be something which may assist the defendant to prove the prior user, but that he is not bound to produce. I am not aware of any principle which in a patent action any more than any other action compels the defendant to produce documents of that description." [98]

909   Objection of lack of utility

In *Rylands* v. *Ashley's Patent Bottle Co.*,[99] where the defendant pleaded that the invention patented was not useful, the Court of Appeal allowed an interrogatory on behalf of the defendant asking whether it had not been found necessary to use some and what modifications in the process described in the specification; but Lindley L.J. said [1] that an answer which left out " the ' what ' " might be sufficient.

910   Claim of privilege

Communications between a litigant and his professional legal adviser are privileged, whether at the time they are made litigation be pending or anticipated or not; similarly communications from some other person to such adviser are also privileged, but only if made when litigation is pending or anticipated. Formerly, patent agents when performing their ordinary work were not considered as professional legal advisers and communications with them were not privileged.[2] However, the position of patent agents in this regard has been altered by section 15 of the Civil Evidence Act 1968 and now in proceedings before the Patent Office or the Appeal Tribunal legal privilege for communications applies as if the proceedings were before the court and the patent agent in question were the solicitor acting for the party. Documents prepared by a party's solicitors for the purpose of obtaining the fiat of the Attorney-General to enable the party to counterclaim for revocation (as was then necessary) were held to be privileged documents.[3]

911   Inspection

By Order 103, rule 26, before an action for infringement is set down for trial, an application under that rule must be made and

---

[97] 24 R.P.C. 82 at p. 92.
[98] See also *Stahlwerk Becker A.G.'s Patent*, 34 R.P.C. 332.
[99] 7 R.P.C. 175.
[1] 7 R.P.C. 175 at p. 182.
[2] *Moseley* v. *Victoria Rubber Co.*, 3 R.P.C. 351.
[3] *Vigneron-Dahl Ltd.* v. *Pettit and Pettit Ltd.*, 42 R.P.C. 431.

disposed of; under paragraph 2 (*f*) of the rule the court may give directions for the making of experiments, tests, inspections or reports.

The power to order an inspection has, however, always been assumed by the courts. In *Bovill* v. *Moore* [4] Lord Eldon said: " There is no use in this court directing an action to be brought, if it does not possess the power to have the action properly tried. The plaintiff has a patent for a machine used in making bobbin lace. The defendant is a manufacturer of that article; and, as the plaintiff alleges, he is making it with a machine constructed upon the principle of the machine protected by plaintiff's patent. Now the manufactory of the defendant is carried on in secret. The machine which the defendant uses to make bobbin lace, and which the plaintiff alleges to be a piracy of his invention, is in the defendant's own possession, and no one can have access to it without his permission. The evidence of the piracy, at present, is the bobbin lace made by the defendant. The witnesses say that this lace must have been manufactured by the plaintiff's machine, or by a machine similar to it in principle. This is obviously in a great measure conjecture. No court can be content with evidence of this description. There must be an order that plaintiff's witnesses shall be permitted before the trial of the action to inspect the defendant's machine and to see it work." [5]

The object which the court has in view in all cases where an inspection is permitted is to ensure that the true facts of the case shall be carefully sifted [6]; but at the same time care will be taken that the process of the law is not abused, and that an action for infringement shall not be made a means and lever for the discovery of other persons' secrets.

912 *Prima facie case of infringement necessary*

The court requires, before granting an order for inspection, to be satisfied that inspection is essential to enable the plaintiff to prove his case, and, in general, that a prima facie case of infringement has been made out.[7]

913 *May be limited to scientific witnesses*

When the interests of justice require, the inspection will be granted

---

[4] (1815) 2 Coop.t.Cott. 56n.
[5] See also *McDougall Bros.* v. *Partington* (*No.* 2), 7 R.P.C. 351 at p. 357.
[6] See *e.g. Osram Lamp Works Ltd.* v. *British Union Lamp Works Ltd.*, 31 R.P.C. 309.
[7] *Piggott* v. *Anglo-American Telegraph Co.*, 19 L.T.(N.S.) 46; *Batley* v. *Kynock*, L.R. 19 Eq. 90; *Germ Milling Co. Ltd.* v. *Robinson*, 1 R.P.C. 217; *Cheetham* v. *Oldham and Fogg*, 5 R.P.C. 617; *British Thomson-Houston Co. Ltd.* v. *Duram Ltd.* (*No.* 2), 37 R.P.C. 121; *American Chain and Cable Co. Inc.* v. *Hall's Barton Ropery Co. Ltd.* 55 R.P.C. 287. But see *British Xylonite Co. Ltd.* v. *Fibrenyle Ltd.* [1959] R.P.C. 252.

to scientific witnesses, who will be required to keep any secrets which they may have discovered and which do not affect the question of infringement.[8]

In *British Thomson-Houston Co. Ltd. v. Duram Ltd. (No. 2)*,[9] the plaintiffs filed an affidavit of an expert who deposed that he had examined the defendants' products and believed that they could only have been produced by the aid of the plaintiffs' patented process. Inspection of defendants' process was asked for and the defendants swore that their process was a valuable secret. Astbury J. gave leave to the plaintiffs to administer interrogatories, and to ask for samples,[10] and refused to entertain the application for inspection until it should be shown that the answers by the defendants would be insufficient to enable the plaintiffs to present their case.

In a case where the plaintiff's right to inspection depended upon a contract, the construction of which was disputed, and he was unable to show that inspection was necessary to prepare his case, it was held that no inspection should be granted, on the ground that the right depended upon the question to be determined at the trial.[11]

And where the defendant delivered to the plaintiff specimens of the alleged infringing articles, the latter was not allowed to see those articles in actual use on the defendant's premises.[12]

914 *Mutual inspection*

Where it is necessary, the court will order the defendant and the plaintiff to give mutual inspection, and to show both the patented machine and the alleged infringement at work, and to permit either party to take away any of the work or samples of the work which has been done in their presence.[13]

915 *Time for application*

The usual practice is to make the application on the hearing of the summons under Order 103, rule 26.[14] An order has been made before delivery of the statement of claim [15]; and also upon an application for

---

[8] See *e.g. Flower v. Lloyd* [1876] W.N. 169, 230; *Swain v. Edlin-Sinclair Tyre Co.*, 20 R.P.C. 435; *British Celanese Ltd. v. Courtaulds Ltd.*, 50 R.P.C. 63 at p. 80; *Coloured Asphalt Co. Ltd. v. British Asphalt and Bitumen Ltd.*, 53 R.P.C. 89. See also *British Syphon Co. Ltd. v. Homewood* [1956] R.P.C. 225. *British Xylonite Co. Ltd. v. Fibrenyle Ltd.* [1959] R.P.C. 252.

[9] 37 R.P.C. 121.

[10] See also *Patent Type Founding Co. v. Walter*, 8 W.R. 353.

[11] *McDougall Bros. v. Partington (No. 2)*, 7 R.P.C. 351, 472.

[12] *Sidebottom v. Fielden*, 8 R.P.C. 266.

[13] *Davenport v. Jepson*, 1 New Rep. 307; *Amies v. Kelsey*, 22 L.J.Q.B. 84; see also *Germ Milling Co. v. Robinson*, 1 R.P.C. 11.

[14] *Post*, § 1613.

[15] *Edler v. Victoria Press Manufacturing Co.*, 27 R.P.C. 114.

an interlocutory injunction as a condition of the refusal of such injunction.[16] Any evidence in support must be on affidavit.

916   Practice under Order 103, rule 26

No action can be set down for trial until a summons under Order 103, rule 26, has been disposed of. The plaintiff should issue such a summons as soon as he becomes entitled to give notice of trial and if he fails to do so within fourteen days the defendant may do so.[14] Each party may apply at the hearing of the summons for any directions which they desire and should notify the other party as to the directions for which it is proposed to ask.[17] The directions usually required are as to further particulars, inspection of apparatus or processes, number of scientific witnesses to be allowed, and as to evidence of experiments being limited to those performed in the presence of the scientific witnesses of both parties.[18] The rule as originally drafted contemplated the exchange of " statements " setting out the substantial issues between the parties, which statements, it was hoped, would result in a saving of expense at the trial. In several cases elaborate orders for this purpose were made[19] and it has been discussed whether the statements should necessarily be reciprocal.[20] But experience has shown that the effect of these statements is merely to increase the length of the trial[21] and it is unlikely they will be ordered in future. A dispute as to whether the defendants should identify the particular integers alleged to be disclosed by the prior documents relied on is appropriately dealt with under this procedure.[22] The usual form of order under this rule relating to the mutual disclosure of models, photographs, experiments, etc., has been approved by the court.[23]

If the plaintiff unduly delays his application under the above rule the defendant may apply under Order 25, rule 1 (4), to dismiss the action for want of prosecution.[24]

---

[16] *Webb* v. *Kynoch,* 15 R.P.C. 269 at p. 273.

[17] See *Solaflex Signs Amalgamated Ltd.* v. *Allan Manufacturing Co. Ltd.,* 48 R.P.C. 577.

[18] See *e.g. Junkers* v. *Ford Motor Car Co. Ltd. and Cooper,* 49 R.P.C. 345 at p. 348.

[19] See *e.g. Fraser* v. *Simpsons (Piccadilly) Ltd.,* 54 R.P.C. 199; *British Thomson-Houston Co. Ltd.* v. *Tungstalite Ltd.,* 55 R.P.C. 280; *Whatmough* v. *Morris Motors Ltd.,* 56 R.P.C. 69.

[20] *Kove's Patent,* 60 R.P.C. 152.

[21] See *Unifloc Reagents Ltd.* v. *Newstead Colliery Ltd.,* 60 R.P.C. 165 at p. 191.

[22] See *Marchant* v. *J. A. Prestwich & Co. Ltd.,* 66 R.P.C. 117.

[23] *Hewitt* v. *Gascoigne Crowther Ltd.* [1964] R.P.C. 370.

[24] *Baird Television Ltd.* v. *Gramophone Co. Ltd.,* 49 R.P.C. 227; *White* v. *Glove (Industrial) Manufacturing Co. Ltd.* [1958] R.P.C. 142.

917 *Step in the action*

The delivery of a statement pursuant to an order made under this rule is a sufficient proceeding in the action to disentitle the plaintiff to serve notice of discontinuance under Order 21, rule 2.[25]

4. The Trial

918 Date of trial

In the ordinary way the date of trial will not be altered because the validity of the patent is about to be considered in other proceedings,[26] but where there are several actions on the same patent and the issues and defences are similar, the practice is to stay them until the principal action has been heard.[27]

919 Right to begin

In actions for infringement the plaintiff has the right to begin and to reply, notwithstanding that the burden of proof may really be on the defendant, as in cases where the real question is one of invalidity owing to prior user or prior publication. This applies also to petitions for revocation, where the patentee has the right to begin.[28]

920 Trial of preliminary issue

Where more than one issue is raised, directions may be given for the trial of one of the issues as a preliminary point.[29] In general, however, this will only be done where it appears probable that the trial of such issue will decide the action.[30]

In *Sarason* v. *Frenay* [31] the defendant pleaded *inter alia* that the plaintiff had inserted into a contract a condition contravening the statutory provisions now re-enacted in section 57. This point was ordered to be tried as a preliminary issue, and, being decided in favour of the defendant, the action was dismissed. In *Hanks* v. *Coombes*,[32] where the trial of the issue of infringement would have involved heavy expense, and related to apparatus of a secret character, the issue of validity was ordered to be heard first.[33]

[25] *Barclay Davit Co. Ltd.* v. *Samuel Taylor*, 63 R.P.C. 27.
[26] See *Muntz* v. *Foster*, 2 W.P.C. 93n.
[27] See *ante*, § 816.   [28] R.S.C., Ord. 103, r. 18 (3).
[29] See R.S.C., Ord. 103, r. 26; see also Ord. 18, r. 11 and Ord. 33, r. 3; *Toogood & Jones Ltd.* v. *Soccerette Ltd.* [1959] R.P.C. 265.
[30] See Jessel M.R. in *Emma Silver Mining Co.* v. *Grant*, 11 Ch.D. 918 at p. 927; *Piercy* v. *Young*, 15 Ch.D. 475; see also *United Telephone Co.* v. *Mattishead*, 3 R.P.C. 213; *Kurtz* v. *Spence*, 5 R.P.C. 161; *Bescol (Electrics) Ltd.* v. *Merlin Mouldings Ltd.*, 69 R.P.C. 159; *A/B Astra* v. *Pharmaceutical Mfg. Co.*, 69 R.P.C. 312; [1956] R.P.C. 265.
[31] 31 R.P.C. 252, 330.   [32] 44 R.P.C. 305; 45 R.P.C. 237.
[33] And see *e.g. Woolfe* v. *Automatic Picture Gallery Ltd.*, 19 R.P.C. 425; *Stephenson, Blake & Co.* v. *Grant, Legros & Co. Ltd.*, 34 R.P.C. 192 (registered design); *Murex Welding Processes Ltd.* v. *Weldrics (1922) Ltd.*, 50 R.P.C. 178.

921 Trial in camera

Where the defendant alleged that his process was a secret, part of the hearing was conducted *in camera* and the shorthand notes were ordered to be impounded.[34]

922 Burden of proof of infringement

The burden of proving infringement (where it is denied) is on the plaintiff, and, if he is unable to prove it, there is no necessity for entering upon the question of validity, unless there is a counterclaim for revocation. It may, however, not be possible for the plaintiff to ascertain precisely what the defendant has done, especially where the defendant's manufacture is carried on abroad; and in such circumstances, if the plaintiff makes out a prima facie case which the defendant does not answer, it will probably be sufficient.[35] Where the infringement complained of is the sale or user merely of a patented article, and the plaintiff manufactures such articles himself, he must, in order to throw the onus on to the defendant, prove that the article was not made by himself or his agent.[36]

Where the defendant does not appear at the trial but has disputed the validity of the patent in his defence, it is usual for the plaintiff to give prima facie proof of validity, but it has been doubted whether such proof is strictly necessary.[37]

923 Sequence of issues

In determining the issues raised in a patent action the court must first construe the specification and claims of the patent.[38] Next it must be determined whether the claims, or some of them, are valid, having regard to the matters set out in the particulars of objections.[39] The court must then consider the evidence relating to and the admissions concerning the alleged infringing act and come to a conclusion whether it falls within the ambit of one or more valid claims.[40] Finally, the court must decide what relief shall be given.

924 Proof of title

The patentee must prove that he is the registered proprietor of the patent in suit. This, where not admitted, is proved by the production of a certified copy of or extract from the register, which is admissible as evidence by virtue of section 77 of the Act.

[34] *Badische Anilin und Soda Fabrik* v. *Levinstein*, 2 R.P.C. 73; 24 Ch.D. 156.
[35] *British Thomson-Houston Co. Ltd.* v. *Charlesworth, Peebles & Co.*, 40 R.P.C. 426 at p. 456.
[36] *Betts* v. *Willmott*, L.R. 6 Ch.App. 239.
[37] See *Weber* v. *Xetal Products Ltd.*, 50 R.P.C. 211.
[38] See *ante,* § 179 *et seq.*
[39] See *ante,* Chaps. 4 and 5.
[40] See *ante,* Chap. 6.

The plaintiff is never in practice required to prove the actual grant itself, or the specification, but this can, if required, be done by the production of the patent itself or a certified copy thereof, sealed with the seal of the Patent Office,[41] and of a certified copy of the specification.

If a defendant desires to prove the absence of an entry from the register he may do so by producing a certificate from the Comptroller in accordance with section 77 of the Act.

925 Issue of validity

The issue of validity is subdivided into the various objections pleaded in the particulars of objections. The plaintiff usually gives prima facie evidence in support of his patent in respect of the objections taken because it is forensically advantageous for him to do so, but it is submitted that there is no need for him to do more than to establish his title to a subsisting patent, for the grant of a monopoly by the Crown must be deemed prima facie to be valid. Having proved this much, the onus is thereby shifted on to the defendant. In the case, however, of an objection that the applicant for the patent was not a person entitled under the Act to apply,[42] it is submitted that the onus is upon the defendant from the start.[43] If the defendant succeeds in establishing a case against the plaintiff, the latter will be permitted, before the defendant's counsel sums up, to call rebutting evidence,[44] but the defendant will not be allowed, after his counsel has summed up, to adduce still further evidence to corroborate his own case.[45]

Where the objection is want of novelty by reason of publication in a written document, the actual publication of the document must, of course, be proved by the defendant, unless, as is usual, publication is admitted by the plaintiff. Similarly, the onus of proof of an alleged prior user is on the defendant and must be fully discharged.[46] Where publication was admitted by inadvertence, leave to withdraw the admission was granted on special terms as to costs.[47]

926 The construction of every document is for the court, following the ordinary rules of construction relating to written documents, guided by evidence as to the meaning of technical terms therein and as to

[41] s. 21 (1).
[42] s. 32 (1) (h).
[43] See *Young* v. *White*, 23 L.J.Ch. 190 at p. 196; *Ward Bros.* v. *J. Hill & Sons*, 18 R.P.C. 481 at p. 490.
[44] *Penn* v. *Jack and Others*, L.R. 2 Eq. 314.
[45] *Ibid.*
[46] See *Dick* v. *Tullis & Son*, 13 R.P.C. 149 at p. 162; *British United Shoe Machinery Co. Ltd.* v. *Albert Pemberton & Co.*, 47 R.P.C. 134 at p. 158.
[47] *Van der Lely N.V.* v. *Bamfords Ltd.* [1959] R.P.C. 99.

the common knowledge at the material date. But this does not apply to photographs or presumably to drawings of any kind; as Lord Reid said in *Van der Lely (C.) N.V.* v. *Bamfords Ltd.*[48]: " There is no doubt that, where the matter alleged to amount to anticipation consists of a written description, the interpretation of that description is, like the interpretation of any document, a question for the court assisted where necessary by evidence regarding the meaning of technical language. It was argued that the same applies to a photograph. I do not think so. Lawyers are expected to be experts in the use of the English language, but we are not experts in the reading or interpretation of photographs. The question is what the eye of the man with appropriate engineering skill and experience would see in the photograph, and that appears to me to be a matter for evidence. Where the evidence is contradictory the judge must decide. But the judge ought not, in my opinion, to attempt to read or construe the photograph himself; he looks at the photograph in determining which of the explanations given by the witnesses appears to be most worthy of acceptance." The decision as to the identity or otherwise of the process or apparatus disclosed by a prior document with that of the patent in suit is, however, one of fact, and where the identity is not obvious upon the face of the documents expert evidence is admissible to resolve the doubt,[49] but an expert must give his evidence upon some stated hypothesis as to the construction of the document, and must not purport to construe the document himself.[50] The disclosure which a document (whether it be an alleged anticipation or a specification the sufficiency of which is in dispute) would make to a competent technician is sometimes tested by handing it to a suitable person who is ignorant of the points in issue in the case, and seeing what he does in endeavouring to follow its instructions and what results he arrives at.[51]

927 *Expert evidence*

The evidence usually given as to validity apart from that as to specific facts, such as prior users or commercial success, is that of witnesses who have expert scientific knowledge and are well acquainted with the art to which the invention relates. Such evidence is admissible as to the intelligibility and sufficiency of the specification

---

[48] [1963] R.P.C. 61 at p. 71.
[49] *Betts* v. *Menzies*, 10 H.L.Cas. 117 at pp. 153, 154; *British Thomson-Houston Co. Ltd.* v. *British Insulated and Helsby Cables Ltd.*, 41 R.P.C. 345 at pp. 399, 400. And see *ante*, § 30.
[50] *British Celanese* v. *Courtaulds*, 52 R.P.C. 171 at p. 196.
[51] See *e.g. Actiengesellschaft für Autogene Aluminium Schweissung* v. *London Aluminium Co. (No. 2)*, 37 R.P.C. 153 at p. 164; 39 R.P.C. 296 at p. 309; *British Thomson-Houston Co. Ltd.* v. *British Insulated and Helsby Cables Ltd.*, 41 R.P.C. 345 at p. 407.

to a competent technician, as to the novelty and utility of the invention, as to the state of common knowledge in the art at material dates, and as to the meaning of technical terms. The principles as to the degrees of intelligibility, sufficiency, novelty and utility required are, of course, matters of law for the court, as also is the question of whether the alleged invention is inherently proper subject-matter for letters patent.

Experts cannot be asked to give their opinions directly upon the questions which are before the court for its decision, whether they be of law or fact; their evidence must be confined to the facts upon which such decision may be based. Thus, an expert cannot be asked whether or not there has been an infringement or whether or not an invention is obvious, but he may be asked as to the nature of the alleged infringing acts or as to the problem solved by the patentee and the nature of the difficulties involved in its solution.

928 The function of an expert was very clearly explained by Lindley L.J. in *Brooks* v. *Steele and Currie* [52]: " It is necessary to examine the patent, and to ascertain first what the patented invention really is; and, secondly, whether the defendants have used that invention. In this, as in all cases, the nature of the invention must be ascertained from the specification, the interpretation of which is for the judge, and not for any expert. The judge may, and, indeed, generally must, be assisted by expert evidence to explain technical terms, to show the practical working of machinery described or drawn, and to point out what is old and what is new in the specification. Expert evidence is also admissible and is often required to show the particulars in which an alleged invention has been used by an alleged infringer, and the real importance of whatever differences there may be between the plaintiff's invention and whatever is done by the defendant. But, after all, the nature of the invention for which a patent is granted must be ascertained from the specification, and has to be determined by the judge and not by a jury, nor by any expert or other witness. This is familiar law, although apparently often disregarded when witnesses are being examined." [53]

As to the function of an expert in proving " common knowledge," see the observations of Clauson J. in *British Celanese Ltd.* v. *Courtaulds Ltd.* [54] As to the function of an expert in proving what a photograph or drawing discloses, see § 927, *supra*.

---

[52] 14 R.P.C. 46 at p. 73.
[53] See also *Graphic Arts Co.* v. *Hunters Ltd.,* 27 R.P.C. 677 at p. 687; and *Joseph Crosfield Ltd.* v. *Techno-Chemical Laboratories Ltd.,* 30 R.P.C. 297 at p. 309; *British Celanese* v. *Courtaulds,* 52 R.P.C. 171 at p. 196.
[54] 50 R.P.C. 63 at p. 90, quoted *ante*, § 881.

929   A party is not bound in proceedings against one party by evidence given on its behalf by experts or others in previous proceedings against some other party, nor is such evidence admissible against it in the subsequent proceedings as an admission.[55] If, however, it be proved that such evidence was given, this fact may be very material as showing the previous conduct of the party or of the witnesses where such conduct throws light on any question in issue in the subsequent action.[56] Witnesses may, of course, always be cross-examined as to statements which they themselves have made in previous proceedings.[57] The plaintiff's witnesses can be cross-examined on documents contained in the Patent Office file of the application for the patent in suit, which file can be obtained by *subpoena duces tecum*.[58]

930   *Experiments*

It is now the invariable practice to limit the evidence relating to experiments that may be given, without special leave of the court, by the order made pursuant to the application under Order 103, rule 26.[59] It is usual to provide that each party shall demonstrate his experiments to the other party, or give such information as he has regarding experiments made by a third person,[60] as a condition precedent to evidence of such experiments being given. This is designed to prevent either side being taken by surprise, with the consequent necessity for an adjournment while counter-experiments are performed. Experiments as to matters which arise during the hearing of the action have, however, been allowed.[61] An analysis to establish infringement is not an " experiment " and evidence of it is therefore admissible, even if evidence of experiments not previously demonstrated may not be given.[62]

931   *Number of experts*

The number of experts (*i.e.* scientific witnesses entitled to give their opinion to the court) may be limited by the order made under Order 103, rule 26 [59] (two being the usual number), but the court would allow further experts to be called where their evidence is con-

---

[55] *British Thomson-Houston Co. Ltd.* v. *British Insulated and Helsby Cables Ltd.*, 41 R.P.C. 345; 42 R.P.C. 180. But see Civil Evidence Act 1968.

[56] *Ibid.*

[57] See *British Hartford-Fairmont Syndicate Ltd.* v. *Jackson Bros. (Knottingley) Ltd.*, 49 R.P.C. 495 at p. 532.

[58] *Cascelloid Ltd.* v. *Milex Star Eng. Co. Ltd.*, 70 R.P.C. 28 at p. 35.

[59] *Post*, § 1613.

[60] *Oak Manufacturing Co. Ltd.* v. *The Plessey Co. Ltd.*, 67 R.P.C. 71.

[61] See *British Celanese Ltd.* v. *Courtaulds Ltd.*, 50 R.P.C. 63 at p. 84.

[62] *International de Lavaud etc. Ltd.* v. *Stanton Ironworks Co. Ltd.*, 58 R.P.C. 177 at p. 198.

cerned with different aspects of the case.[63]　It is not however the present practice to make any such order in patent actions.

932　Amendment of specification

Under section 30 of the Act, the court has power in an action for infringement or petition for revocation to make an order allowing the patentee to amend his complete specification by way of disclaimer, correction or explanation.　The practice as to this is dealt with in Chapter 8.

5. THE REMEDY

933　The remedy sought or granted in an action for infringement may consist of an injunction, damages or, at the option of the plaintiff, an account of profits in lieu of damages,[64] and delivery up or destruction of all infringing articles in the possession or power of the defendant.

(a) Injunction

934　Injunction based on threat to infringe

The basis of an injunction is the threat, actual or implied, on the part of the defendant that he is about to do an act which is in violation of the plaintiff's right; so that not only must it be clear that the plaintiff has rights, but also that the defendant has done something which induces the court to believe that he is about to infringe those rights.

The fact that he has been guilty of an infringement of the patent rights will, in most circumstances, be sufficient evidence that he intends to continue his infringement, but, whether he has actually infringed the patent or not, it will be sufficient if he has threatened to infringe it.　Actual infringement is merely evidence upon which the court implies an intention to continue in the same course.

935　In *Frearson* v. *Loe*,[65] Jessel M.R. said: " I am not aware of any suit or action in the Court of Chancery which has been succcessful on the part of a patentee, without infringement having been proved; but in my opinion, on principle there is no reason why a patentee should not succeed in obtaining an injunction without proving actual infringement.　I think, for this reason, where the defendant alleges an intention to infringe, and claims the right to infringe, the mischief done by the threatened infringement of the patent is very great, and

---

[63] *Ibid.* and see *Medical Supply Association* v. *Charles F. Thackrey Ltd.*, 66 R.P.C. 120 at p. 126.

[64] s. 60.

[65] 9 Ch.D. 48 at p. 65.

I see no reason why a patentee should not be entitled to the same protection as every other person is entitled to claim from the court from threatened injury, where that threatened injury will be very serious. No part of the jurisdiction of the old Court of Chancery was considered more valuable than that exercise of jurisdiction which prevented material injury being inflicted, and no subject was more frequently the cause of bills for injunction than the class of cases which were brought to restrain threatened injury, as distinguished from injury which was already accomplished. It seems to me, when you consider the nature of a patent right, that where there is a deliberate intention expressed, and about to be carried into execution, to infringe certain letters patent under the claim of a right to use the invention patented, the plaintiff is entitled to come to this court to restrain that threatened injury. Of course, it must be plain that what is threatened to be done is an infringement."

In *Dowling* v. *Billington* [66] two acts which fell within the claims of the plaintiffs' patent were proved, the first of which took place prior to the acceptance of the complete specification by the Comptroller, while the second was committed a few days after the commencement of the action. Chatterton V.-C. held that neither of these acts constituted an actionable infringement; but inasmuch as the conduct of the defendant showed a deliberate intention to infringe, the plaintiffs were entitled to an injunction upon the principle laid down by Jessel M.R. in *Frearson* v. *Loe, supra*; and this judgment was upheld by the Court of Appeal.

936 *Evidence of acts after action brought*

Evidence of acts after action brought is inadmissible, except for the purpose of showing that the defendant has an intention of infringing in the future. In *Welsbach Incandescent Gas Light Co.* v. *Dowle* [67] the plaintiffs attempted to call evidence of acts done since the issue of the writ, not in order to establish threatened infringement, but to strengthen and explain evidence of actual infringement before the writ. Bruce J. refused to admit such evidence.

937 *Contrast of actual and threatened infringements*

If what has been done since action brought differs in any way from what was done before, and is relied on as evidence of the intention to infringe, the defendant must have clear notice of the nature of the infringement which he is alleged to be contemplating. In *Shoe Machinery Co. Ltd.* v. *Cutlan* [68] Romer J. said: " Two kinds of action may be brought by a plaintiff patentee. The one is based on

[66] 7 R.P.C. 191.
[67] 16 R.P.C. 391.
[68] 12 R.P.C. 342 at p. 357.

this—that the defendant has infringed before action brought, and in respect of this the plaintiff is entitled to claim damages, or an account, and an injunction to prevent similar infringements in the future. The other action is based on the fact, not that the defendant has infringed, but that he threatens and intends to infringe; and in this case the plaintiff may claim an injunction to restrain the threatened infringement. Of course, you may find both kinds of action combined in one, but they are distinct in themselves in several respects. In the first, the plaintiff has to give particulars of breaches. . . . In the other, of necessity, there can be no particulars of breaches; but to avoid unfairness to the defendant, care is always taken that he shall have fair notice as to the nature and particulars of the special infringement he is alleged to be contemplating; and then, no doubt, if after action he commits that special infringement, or substantially that infringement, evidence of it can be given, as it is evidence to show that the plaintiff was right in his allegation that, at the date of action brought, the defendant was threatening and intending to infringe. I may add that if an action, as originally brought by a plaintiff patentee, is of the first class only, but he finds that the defendant has, since action brought, infringed in a way substantially different from his former infringements, leave would be given by the court to the plaintiff in a proper case, and on proper terms, to amend his action, and to bring these subsequent infringements before the court to be dealt with once and for all with the prior infringements."

938 *Actual infringement evidence of intention*

The actual infringement of the patent is taken by the court to imply an intention to continue the infringement, notwithstanding any promises not to do so, unless it be clear that there is in fact no intention to continue infringing, and an injunction will be granted. Shadwell V.-C. in *Losh* v. *Hague* [69] said: " If a threat had been used, and the defendant revokes the threat, that I can understand as making the plaintiff satisfied; but if once the thing complained of has been done, I apprehend this court interferes, notwithstanding any promise the defendant may make not to do the same thing again." [70]

939 *Mere possession is not necessarily threat*

Possession of an infringing machine may give rise to a presumption of a threat to infringe, but the presumption may be rebutted by evidence of non-user and of the absence of any such intention and in that case no injunction will be granted. [71]

---

[69] 1 W.P.C. 200.
[70] See also *Geary* v. *Norton*, 1 De G. & Sm. 9.
[71] *British United Shoe Machinery Co. Ltd.* v. *Simon Collier Ltd.*, 27 R.P.C. 567. See *ante*, § 373.

In the case of *Adair* v. *Young* [72] the defendant was the captain of a ship which was fitted with certain pumps which were an infringement of the plaintiff's patent. No act of using the pumps was proved; but it was shown that the ship was not supplied with other pumps. It was held that the possession of the pumps under such circumstances, although not of itself amounting to an infringement, was evidence upon which the court would infer that the defendant intended to use the pumps should occasion require. And the court, Brett and Cotton L.JJ. (James L.J. dissenting), granted an injunction.

940   *Abandoned user*

In *Proctor* v. *Bayley & Son* [73] the infringement complained of took place six years before the trial of the action. It was proved that the user continued only for a few months, after which the machines were abandoned as unsatisfactory. It was held by the Court of Appeal, reversing the decision of Bristowe V.-C., that it was clear that the defendants had no intention whatever of continuing the wrongful act, and consequently that it was not a proper case in which an injunction should be granted. Cotton L.J. in his judgment said [74]: " There is no doubt that it was a good patent, and we must also take it that the defendants have infringed; but the point is this: Is there any ground here which would justify the court in exercising the extraordinary jurisdiction of the Court of Chancery in granting an injunction? That, I think, has been a good deal lost sight of in the argument. It is not because a man has done a wrong that an injunction will be granted against him. If a man has done a wrong which will not be continued, at common law damages may be obtained for the wrong done, which the common law says is sufficient indemnity for that wrong; but then the Court of Chancery says this, in the exercise of its extraordinary jurisdiction: We will not be satisfied with that; we will grant an injunction, because a wrongful act has been done, in order to prevent that wrongful act; and they grant an injunction where a wrongful act has been done, and the court is satisfied of the probability of the continuance of the wrongful act. . . . But here, although the defendants did infringe the plaintiff's patent, we must consider all the circumstances of the case in order to guide us in the consideration of this: Ought the court to draw the inference that there will be a continuance of the wrongful act so as to justify the court in granting the extraordinary interference and the protection which is exercised by the court of equity? " [75]

[72] 12 Ch.D. 13.
[73] 42 Ch.D. 390; 6 R.P.C. 538.
[74] 6 R.P.C. 538 at p. 541.
[75] See also *Hudson* v. *Chatteris Engineering Co.,* 15 R.P.C. 438; *Wilderman* v. *F. W. Berk & Co. Ltd.,* 42 R.P.C. 79 at p. 90; [1925] 1 Ch. 116.

941 Acquiescence and delay

Positive acquiescence will bar the right of the patentee to an injunction if it amounts to a representation to the defendant that he is free to do what would otherwise be an infringement.[76] Thus, if a defendant constructed machinery, for instance, in ignorance of the existence of the plaintiff's patent, and the plaintiff, aware of such ignorance, lay by in silence and later attempted to obtain an injunction, such relief would probably be refused.[77] Otherwise, however, laches, while a bar to the obtaining of an interlocutory order, would not bar the right to a perpetual injunction as " there must be more than mere delay to disentitle a man to his legal rights." [78]

942 Suspension of injunction

Where the immediate operation of an injunction would cause great public inconvenience, such operation may be suspended for a time to minimise such inconvenience. Thus in *Hopkinson* v. *St. James'* and *Pall Mall Electric Light Co. Ltd.*[79] the injunction was suspended for six months on account of the exceptional public inconvenience which would be caused by suddenly stopping the use of the three-wire electric lighting system, the defendants undertaking to keep an account in the meantime.

It has been said that the operation of an injunction will not usually be suspended pending an appeal.[80] A stay will, however, be ordered where such an injunction would cause extensive unemployment.[81] It will probably not be ordered where the defendant is merely a dealer or agent for sale and not a manufacturer.[82] But the question whether or not a stay should be ordered is a matter for the discretion of the court. In recent years there have been orders made by the High Court and the Court of Appeal that the injunction should be stayed for such time as to enable the defendants to give notice of, or present a petition of appeal, the stay to continue thereafter so long as the defendant prosecuted his appeal with due diligence, provided that the defendant undertook to keep an account.[83]

[76] *Proctor* v. *Bennis*, 4 R.P.C. 333 at p. 356; 36 Ch.D. 740.
[77] *Ibid.* See *Electrolux Ltd.* v. *Electrix Ltd.* 71 R.P.C. 23.
[78] *Van der Lely (C.) N.V.* v. *Bamfords* [1964] R.P.C. 54, *per* Harman L.J. at p. 81 citing *Fullwood* v. *Fullwood* (1878) 9 Ch.D. 176.
[79] 10 R.P.C. 46 at p. 62.
[80] *e.g. Samuel Parkes & Co. Ltd.* v. *Cocker Bros. Ltd.*, 46 R.P.C. 241.
[81] See *e.g. Leeds Forge Co. Ltd.* v. *Deighton's Patent Flue and Tube Co. Ltd.*, 18 R.P.C. 233 at p. 240; *British Thomson-Houston Co. Ltd.* v. *British Insulated and Helsby Cables Ltd.*, 41 R.P.C. 345 at p. 375; and see *Bonnard* v. *London General Omnibus Co. Ltd.*, 36 R.P.C. 307.
[82] *Lanston Monotype Corpn. Ltd.* v. *Martin J. Slattery*, 42 R.P.C. 366 at p. 396.
[83] *Martin* v. *Selsdon Fountain Pen Co. Ltd.*, 66 R.P.C. 193 at p. 216; *Martin* v. *H. Millwood Ltd.*, 71 R.P.C. 458 at p. 472; *Rosedale Associated Manu-*

943 Form of injunction

The ordinary form in which injunctions are now granted is " that the defendants, by themselves, their servants or agents be restrained from infringing the plaintiffs' Letters Patent No. ——." But however it is worded, an injunction not to infringe a patent cannot be effective after the patent has ceased to be in force.[84]

In *Saccharin Corporation* v. *Dawson* [85] and *Saccharin Corporation* v. *Jackson* [86] actions were brought upon several patents. It was impossible to say which patent had been infringed, but it was clear that one of them must have been. An injunction was granted in respect of all the patents for the life of the patent which would earliest expire.

944   In *Dunlop Pneumatic Tyre Co. Ltd.* v. *Clifton Rubber Co. Ltd.*,[87] where there was another action pending on the same patent against the defendants in which another type of infringement was alleged, the injunction was in general form but the plaintiffs undertook not to move to commit in respect of such other alleged infringement but to raise the issue in the other action.

Where an infringer was also a Crown contractor within the meaning of section 29 of the Act of 1907 (now replaced by section 46) the injunction was granted " without prejudice to the rights of the Crown under section 29." [88]

Before the introduction of the practice of ordering delivery up to the plaintiff or destruction of all infringing articles in the defendant's power or possession, it was customary, where necessary, to grant an injunction to restrain the defendant from using or selling, after expiry of the patent, infringing goods manufactured during the term of the patent,[89] but such an order would not now be necessary.

945 Enforcement of injunction

A person against whom an injunction has been granted or who has given an undertaking in court is liable to be committed, should he be guilty of a breach of such injunction or undertaking, and a person aiding and abetting such a person and with knowledge of the injunction is also guilty of contempt,[90] but an application for com-

facturers Ltd. v. *Carlton Tyre Saving Co. Ltd.* [1959] R.P.C. 189 at pp. 219, 220.
[84] *Daw* v. *Eley,* L.R. 3 Eq. 496 at p. 508.
[85] 19 R.P.C. 169.
[86] 20 R.P.C. 611.
[87] 20 R.P.C. 393.
[88] *Commercial Solvents Corpn.* v. *Synthetic Products Co. Ltd.,* 43 R.P.C. 185 at p. 238.
[89] See *Crossley* v. *Beverley,* 1 W.P.C. 112.
[90] *Incandescent Gas Light Co.* v. *Sluce,* 17 R.P.C. 173.

mittal, involving as it does the liberty of the subject, will require the strictest proof in its support.[91]

Where an injunction was granted against a limited liability company restraining it, its servants, agents and workmen from infringing a patent, and such injunction was broken by infringement, the injunction was enforced both against the company and its directors, though the enforcement was not pushed to the extent of an order for sequestration or committal.[92] It does not appear from the report precisely how the directors were concerned in the breach, but somewhat different considerations may be applicable in such a motion for contempt from those ordinarily applicable in the case of an action for infringement in which directors are made parties.[93]

Where an injunction is granted in the ordinary form and the patent is subsequently held in other proceedings to be invalid, it is suggested that the proper course is for the party against whom the injunction was made to apply for the injunction to be removed. Where the patent has actually been revoked such injunction ceases automatically and no such application is necessary.

946 *Subsequent amendment of specification*

In *Dudgeon* v. *Thomson* [94] the plaintiff had obtained an injunction. The specification was subsequently amended, and after this had been done he took proceedings to enforce the injunction. The House of Lords held that he should have brought a new action, since the new specification might be open to objection, and was not the same as the old specification.

(b) Damages

947 Damages or account of profits

A successful plaintiff is entitled to damages in respect of actual infringements of his patent, or, at his option, an account of profits. This latter remedy was abolished by the Act of 1919, but has been reintroduced by the present Act.[95] It is to be noted that the profits, or, it may be, losses, made by the infringer are not of any relevance in computing the damage caused to the patentee by his infringements.[96]

---

[91] *Dick* v. *Haslam*, 8 R.P.C. 196.

[92] *Spencer* v. *Ancoats Vale Rubber Co. Ltd.*, 6 R.P.C. 46; see also *Lancashire Explosives Co. Ltd.* v. *Roburite Explosives Co. Ltd.*, 13 R.P.C. 429 at p. 441; *Hattersley & Sons Ltd.* v. *Hodgson Ltd.*, 22 R.P.C. 229 at p. 239.

[93] See *ante*, § 353. See also *Multiform Displays Ltd.* v. *Whitmarley Displays Ltd.* [1956] R.P.C. 143 (reversed in the House of Lords on other grounds [1957] R.P.C. 260); [1957] R.P.C. 401.

[94] 3 App.Cas. 34.

[95] s. 60.

[96] *United Horse Shoe and Nail Co. Ltd.* v. *Stewart & Co.*, 13 App.Cas. 401; 5 R.P.C. 260 at p. 267.

The fact that contracts containing terms contrary to section 57 of the Act were in existence at the date of the infringements will prevent the plaintiff recovering damages for such infringements.[97]

948   Principle on which damages assessed

The principle to be applied in assessing damages is that the plaintiff should be restored by monetary compensation to the position which he would have occupied but for the wrongful acts of the defendant, provided always that such loss as he proves is "the natural and direct consequence of the defendant's acts." [98]

Patentees derive their remuneration in respect of their inventions either by utilising their monopoly rights to enable them to obtain increased profits as manufacturers, or by permitting others to use their inventions under licence in consideration of royalty payments. In the latter case the determination of the damages accruing from infringements is usually a relatively simple matter, it being generally assumed that the damage is equal to the amount which the infringer would have had to pay had he had a licence upon the terms normally granted by the patentee.[99] Where, however, the patentee makes his profits as manufacturer (whether or not he grants licences in addition) rather more difficult questions arise, such as whether the infringement has deprived him of manufacturer's profits equivalent to those which he would have made had he had the sale of the infringing goods, and what, if any, other damage may have been occasioned to him by their unauthorised sale. Other classes of damage which a manufacturer may well sustain by such illegal competition are loss of goodwill and business connection or losses due to the necessity to reduce the prices of his wares to meet such competition. The onus of proving damage is, of course, upon the plaintiff in each case, but the burden is greatly lightened by the readiness of the court to infer that the wrongful invasion of a patentee's monopoly will in the ordinary course of events cause damage to him, and, further, the court will not be deterred from awarding substantial sums in damages by reason of the difficulty or impossibility of proof of precise figures by means of which the amount of damage can be mathematically calculated.

---

[97] s. 57 (2), overruling *Actiengesellschaft für Autogene Aluminium Schweissung* v. *London Aluminium Co. Ltd. (No. 2)*, 40 R.P.C. 107.

[98] *Per* Lord Macnaghten, *United Horse Shoe and Nail Co. Ltd.* v. *Stewart & Co.*, 13 App.Cas. 401; 5 R.P.C. 260 at p. 268.

[99] See *e.g. Penn* v. *Jack*, L.R. 5 Eq. 81; *English and American Machinery Co.* v. *Union Boot and Shoe Machine Co.*, 13 R.P.C. 64; *Pneumatic Tyre Co. Ltd.* v. *Puncture Proof Pneumatic Tyre Co. Ltd.*, 16 R.P.C. 209; *British Motor Syndicate* v. *John Taylor & Sons Ltd.*, 17 R.P.C. 723; *British Thomson-Houston Co. Ltd.* v. *Naamlooze Vennootschap Pope's Metaaldraadlampenfabriek*, 40 R.P.C. 119 (C.S.) at p. 127.

949   In *Ungar* v. *Sugg*,[1] an action in respect of " threats," Wright J. said: " No one can doubt that in this case there was substantial damage, and the difficulty and impossibility of stating the precise ground for assessing it at any particular figure does not seem to be a sufficient reason for giving only a nominal sum." And Lord Esher M.R. in the Court of Appeal said [2]: " They were problematical damages, and had to be what is called guessed at: that is, not a mere guess, as if you were tossing up for the thing, but it must come to a mere question of what, in the mind of the person who has to estimate them, was a fair sum."

Where the patentee is a manufacturer and does not grant licences, the assessment of damages is especially difficult with regard to infringements which do not actually compete directly with the goods manufactured by him; for instance, where they are of a totally different quality or price or where it is established that, for some other reason, the order in any case would not have gone to him. In such cases the defendant is not excused from the payment of substantial damages, but is compelled to pay what would, upon a reasonable estimate, be the royalty which the patentee could have fairly obtained under the circumstances.

950   In *Watson, Laidlaw & Co. Ltd.* v. *Pott, Cassels and Williamson* [3] Lord Shaw said: " If with regard to the general trade which was done, or would have been done by the plaintiffs within their ordinary range of trade, damages be assessed, these ought, of course, to enter the account and to stand. But in addition there remains that class of business which the plaintiffs would not have done; and in such case it appears to me that the correct and full measure is only reached by adding that a patentee is also entitled, on the principle of price or hire, to a royalty for the unauthorised sale or use of every one of the infringing machines in a market which the infringer, if left to himself, might not have reached. Otherwise, that property which consists in the monopoly of the patented articles granted to the patentee has been invaded, and indeed abstracted, and the law when appealed to would be standing by and allowing the invader or abstractor to go free. In such cases a royalty is an excellent key to unlock the difficulty, and I am in entire accord with the principle laid down by Lord Moulton in *Meters Ltd.* v. *Metropolitan Gas Meters Ltd.*[4] Each of the infringements was an actionable wrong, and although it may have been committed in a range of business or

[1] 8 R.P.C. 385 at p. 388.
[2] 9 R.P.C. 114 at p. 117.
[3] 31 R.P.C. 104 at p. 120.
[4] 28 R.P.C. 157 at p. 163.

of territory which the patentee may not have reached, he is entitled to hire or royalty in respect of each unauthorised use of his property. Otherwise the remedy might fall unjustly short of the wrong." [5]

Where a manufacturer seeks to recover damages on account of reduction of his prices he must establish that the reduction was necessitated by the defendant's wrongful competition and was not the result of the ordinary exigencies of trade.[6]

951   In *American Braided Wire Co.* v. *Thomson* [7] the patent infringed was one for the manufacture of a particular form of bustle; no one else being able to put a similar bustle on the market without infringing that patent, the plaintiffs did not reduce their prices until compelled to do so by the defendants, and then only reduced them to the level quoted by the defendants. The official referee came to the conclusion that the plaintiffs would have made, but for the infringement, all the sales that they did make and also the sales made by the defendants, in each case at the plaintiffs' original prices, and awarded damages accordingly. This assessment of damages was upheld by the Court of Appeal.[8]

Price reductions may, to some extent, counterbalance the loss of profit which they cause to the patentee on each article by the increased demand for such articles which they create among the public and this may be taken into consideration.[9]

952   *Regard had to plaintiffs' establishment charges*

In *Leeds Forge Co. Ltd.* v. *Deighton's Patent Flue Co.*,[10] it was held that in arriving at the damages due to competition, regard should be had to the fact that had the plaintiffs received the orders which in fact went to the defendants, they would have been able to make a profit larger than the profit actually made by themselves on similar articles, or by the defendants on the articles actually made in infringement, since the proportion borne on account of establishment charges by each article made would have been materially reduced.

---

[5] And see *British United Shoe Machinery Co. Ltd.* v. *A. Fussell & Sons Ltd.*, 27 R.P.C. 205; *British Thomson-Houston Co. Ltd.* v. *Naamlooze Vennootschap Pope's Metaaldraadlampenfabriek*, 40 R.P.C. 119 (C.S.) at pp. 127, 128.

[6] *Alexander & Co.* v. *Henry & Co. and others*, 12 R.P.C. 360 at p. 367; *United Horse Shoe and Nail Co. Ltd.* v. *Stewart & Co.*, 13 App.Cas. 401; 5 R.P.C. 260.

[7] 7 R.P.C. 152.

[8] And see *Wellman and others* v. *Burstinghaus*, 28 R.P.C. 326.

[9] See *e.g. American Braided Wire Co.* v. *Thomson*, 44 Ch.D. 274; 7 R.P.C. 152.

[10] 25 R.P.C. 209.

953 *Importance of invention irrelevant*

The importance of the plaintiff's invention or of the portion of that invention which the defendant has taken, or the ease with which the defendant could have manufactured his goods without infringing the plaintiff's patent, are not in themselves material upon the assessment of the damages suffered by the plaintiff. The principle is that if the defendant's acts are wrongful, the degree of their wrongfulness does not matter, and the defendant must pay such damage as is, in fact, occasioned to the plaintiff by his acts.[11]

Where the infringement is a mere accessory of the article manufactured and sold by the defendant, the plaintiff is only entitled to recover damages in respect of that accessory alone.[12] But where it is an integral part of a machine as a whole, damages may be based on the fact that the plaintiff has lost an order for the whole machine, and the profits on the whole machine must be taken into account.[13]

Where a patentee sues a manufacturer of infringing articles and recovers damages for infringement the articles are thereafter free for use by the public if the damages have been assessed upon the basis of total loss of the profit which the patentee would have made had he supplied them himself.[14] Where, on the contrary, the patentee's custom was to hire out articles on an annual royalty basis, and he recovered an agreed sum by way of damages from the manufacturer of infringing articles, it was held that the articles were only " franked " thereby up to the date of sale by the manufacturer and that users were liable in respect of any use subsequent thereto.[14]

954 *Types of infringement not fully determined*

Where certain of the types of alleged infringement were not exemplified in the particulars of breaches and so were not the subject of any express findings, it was ordered that this question should be determined as a preliminary issue in the inquiry.[15]

955 Damages where exclusive licensee plaintiff

In awarding damages or granting any other relief to an exclusive licensee who sues as plaintiff, the court must take into consideration only the loss suffered or likely to be suffered by the actual exclusive licensee. If the latter claims an account of profits in lieu of damages,

---

[11] See *United Horse Shoe and Nail Co. Ltd. v. Stewart & Co.*, 13 App.Cas. 401; 3 R.P.C. 139 (C.S.) at p. 143; 5 R.P.C. 260 at p. 267.
[12] *Clement Talbot Ltd. v. Wilson and another*, 26 R.P.C. 467; see also *United Telephone Co. v. Walker and others*, 4 R.P.C. 63.
[13] *Meters Ltd. v. Metropolitan Gas Meters Ltd.*, 27 R.P.C. 721; 28 R.P.C. 157.
[14] *United Telephone Co. v. Walker and others*, 4 R.P.C. 63; see also *Penn v. Bibby*, L.R. 3 Eq. 308 at p. 311.
[15] *Cleveland Graphite Bronze Co. Ltd. v. Glacier Metal Co. Ltd.*, 68 R.P.C. 181.

the profits to be considered are those earned by means of the infringement so far as it constitutes an infringement of the rights of the exclusive licensee as such.[16]   Obviously no infringement committed before the date of the exclusive licence can be taken into account.

956 Date from which damages are recoverable

The date from which damages should be reckoned in cases where a patent has been amended or where some of the claims are held to be invalid is dealt with in Chapter 8.   In ordinary cases damages are recoverable (subject to the six years' limit of the Statute of Limitations) from the date of publication of the complete specification.[17]   The court may, if it thinks fit, refuse to award damages in respect of infringements committed during any period in which the patentee is in default of payment of renewal fees.[18]

957 Position of assignee

An assignment of a patent does not, *per se* transfer an accrued right of action for infringement[19] but such a right can be expressly assigned in the same manner as any other chose in action.[19]

958 Innocent infringers

Damages may not be awarded against a defendant who proves that at the date of the infringement he was not aware, and had no reasonable ground for supposing, that the patent existed.[20]   This special defence is not available to an infringer who has been informed of the existence of a patent application in respect of the article in question.[21]   It was decided by Lloyd-Jacob J. in *Benmax* v. *Austin Motor Co. Ltd.*[22] that the protection given by section 59 (1) of the Act " is absolute. . . . It is not in terms directed to the division of a continuing period of infringing use between a state of ignorance and a state of knowledge of the plaintiff's rights . . . a defendant who seeks to avail himself of the protection afforded by section 59 (1) must plead and prove a complete ignorance of the existence of the patent monopoly during the period in which the wrongful acts were being done." It is an open question whether, having regard to the scheme of the Act as a whole, the word " damages " should be construed as including an account of profits for this purpose so that an innocent infringer would not be pecuniarily liable at all.   The marking of an

16 s. 63.
17 s. 13 (4).
18 s. 59 (2).
19 *Wilderman* v. *F. W. Berk & Co. Ltd.*, 42 R.P.C. 79 at p. 90.
20 s. 59 (1); and see *ante*, § 347.
21 *Wilbec Plastics Ltd.* v. *Wilson Dawes Ltd.* [1966] R.P.C. 513.
22 70 R.P.C. 143 at p. 156.

article with the word " patent " or " patented," is not sufficient notice unless the number of the patent is also given.[20] This provision does not affect the plaintiff's right to an injunction.

### 959	Patents indorsed " licences of right "

If a patent is indorsed " licences of right," [23] in proceedings for infringement (otherwise than by way of importation) if the defendant undertakes to take a licence to be settled by the Comptroller no injunction will be made and the damages will not exceed double the amount payable by him as licensee if the licence had been granted before the earliest infringement.[24]

### 960	Form of order

Where damages are given, the usual form of order is to direct an inquiry as to damages, the costs thereof being reserved, with liberty to apply [25]; and where the action is in respect of certain claims of the patent only, the inquiry is limited as to infringement of the claims sued upon.[26]

### 961	*Stay of inquiry*

Where there is an appeal the inquiry as to damages may be stayed until the judgment in the Court of Appeal.[27]

### 962	*Where patent afterwards revoked*

Where an injunction was obtained in an action, and an inquiry as to damages ordered, and after judgment, but before the inquiry, the patent was revoked on the petition of the defendant in the action, who adducd further reasons for attacking its validity, it was held that this fact did not preclude the inquiry from being prosecuted and the damages recovered. Parker J. decided the case on the basis of an estoppel operating against the defendant. The Court of Appeal, in confirming the judgment, decided the case on the basis of *res judicata*.[28]

### 963	*Discovery on inquiry as to damages*

Where an inquiry as to damages is directed the same principles as to discovery of documents apply as in the case of any other issue

---

[23] See *ante*, § 656 *et seq.*
[24] s. 35 (2) (c).
[25] *British Thomson-Houston Co. Ltd.* v. *G. and R. Agency,* 42 R.P.C. 305.
[26] *e.g. Benjamin Electric Ltd. and Igranic Co. Ltd.* v. *Garnett Whiteley & Co. Ltd.,* 47 R.P.C. 44.
[27] *Samuel Parkes & Co. Ltd.* v. *Cocker Bros. Ltd.,* 46 R.P.C. 241; *Benjamin Electric Ltd. and Igranic Co. Ltd.* v. *Garnett Whiteley & Co. Ltd.,* 47 R.P.C. 44.
[28] *Poulton* v. *Adjustable Cover and Boiler Block Co.,* 25 R.P.C. 529, 661.

which has to be tried between the parties.[29] The defendant must give full discovery, and will be required to set out the names and addresses of the persons to whom machines, made in infringement of the patent, have been sold[30]; but not ordinarily the names of the agents concerned in the transaction.[31]

The plaintiff may also be ordered to give discovery of his business books if he alleges a falling off of profits[32]; and of documents relating to prime cost of machinery.[33]

964 *Costs of inquiry*

If the defendant, before the inquiry, should offer a sum in satisfaction, that fact should be recited in the order so that it may be considered upon the question of costs when that question comes to be decided.[34] The costs of the inquiry are usually given to the plaintiff if the damages found due exceed the sum offered by the defendant; but they are usually given to the defendant if the damages do not exceed the sum offered.[35]

965 **Order for delivery up or destruction**

Under the modern practice a successful plaintiff can obtain an order for the destruction or delivery up of infringing goods in the possession of the defendant, so as to ensure that such goods are not retained in order to be placed upon the market after the expiry of the patent.

966 *History of order*

In the early case of *Crossley* v. *Beverley*,[36] the possibility above referred to was dealt with by the grant of an injunction perpetually restraining the defendant from selling infringing goods made during the continuance of the patent. In *Betts* v. *De Vitre*[37] an inquiry was ordered as to what infringing goods the defendants had, and it was

---

[29] *British United Shoe Machinery Co. Ltd.* v. *Lambert Howarth & Sons Ltd.*, 46 R.P.C. 315 at p. 317.

[30] *Murray* v. *Clayton*, L.R. 15 Eq. 115; *American Braided Wire Co.* v. *Thompson & Co.* (*No.* 2), 5 R.P.C. 375; *Saccharin Corporation* v. *Chemicals & Drugs Co. Ltd.*, 17 R.P.C. 612.

[31] *Murray* v. *Clayton*, L.R. 15 Eq. 115.

[32] *Hamilton & Co.* v. *Neilson*, 26 R.P.C. 671.

[33] *British United Shoe Machinery Co. Ltd.* v. *Lambert Howarth & Sons Ltd.*, 46 R.P.C. 315 at p. 320.

[34] *Fettes* v. *Williams*, 25 R.P.C. 511; *British Vacuum Co.* v. *Exton Hotels Co. Ltd.*, 25 R.P.C. 617.

[35] *Clement Talbot Ltd.* v. *Wilson and Another*, 26 R.P.C. 467.

[36] 1 W.P.C. 112.

[37] 34 L.J.Ch. 289.

ordered that such goods should be destroyed in the plaintiff's presence.[38] In *Plimpton* v. *Malcolmson* [39] the defendant was ordered to deliver up or to destroy or render unfit for use infringing articles.

967 *Form of order*

The principle underlying the above cases (from which the practice of making the present form of order originated) seems to be the same in each case, *viz.* that the court should protect the patentee from any use after the expiry of his patent of infringing articles made during its currency, and also that such destruction or delivery up would render still more effective the injunction ordinarily granted by the court prohibiting their use during the term of the patent. To this end, though the normal form of the order is for actual destruction or delivery up of infringing articles, it is modified in suitable cases, as, for instance, where an infringing article can be rendered non-infringing by some alteration or by the removal of some part.[40] Nor will an order be made for the delivery up of an article which is not itself an infringement but may be used as part of an infringing apparatus.[41]

The defendant is not entitled to any compensation for loss caused to him by such destruction or delivery up, and cannot set off the value of goods delivered up against a claim for damages.[42] But there is no question of confiscation of infringing articles, in the sense that the defendant is deprived of his property in them, the only purpose of the order being the rendering of the goods non-infringing to the satisfaction of the patentee.[43] The ordinary order, therefore, gives the infringer the choice between destruction or delivery up, but in a case where the order was made only for delivery up without any objection being made at the time by the defendant, it was held, upon a subsequent motion to vary the minutes so as to give the defendant the option, that the original order, not having been objected to, must stand.[44]

In aid of the above-mentioned order the defendant will be ordered

---

[38] See also *Frearson* v. *Loe*, 9 Ch.D. 48 at p. 67.
[39] *Seton on Judgments* (7th ed.) p. 630.
[40] *Merganthaler Linotype Co.* v. *Intertype Ltd. and others*, 43 R.P.C. 381; see also *Siddell* v. *Vickers, Sons & Co. Ltd.*, 5 R.P.C. 81 at p. 101; *Howes and Burley* v. *Webber*, 12 R.P.C. 465; *Aktiengesellschaft für Autogene Aluminium Schweissung* v. *London Aluminium Co. Ltd. (No. 2)*, 37 R.P.C. 153 at p. 170; *British United Shoe Machinery Co. Ltd.* v. *Gimson Shoe Machinery Co. Ltd.*, 45 R.P.C. 85.
[41] *Electric and Musical Industries Ltd.* v. *Lissen Ltd.*, 54 R.P.C. 5 at p. 35.
[42] *United Telephone Co.* v. *Walker*, 4 R.P.C. 63 at p. 67.
[43] *Vavasseur* v. *Krupp*, 9 Ch.D. 351 at p. 360.
[44] *British Westinghouse Electric and Manufacturing Co. Ltd.* v. *Electrical Co. Ltd.*, 28 R.P.C. 517 at p. 531.

to make discovery upon oath as to any infringing goods in his possession or power.[45]

968 *Stay of order*

The order for delivery up may be stayed pending an appeal.[46]

969 **Relief for infringement of partially valid patent**

If in proceedings for infringement one or more claims are held to be invalid but some claim is valid and infringed the court may always grant an injunction.[47] Indeed, once infringement of a valid claim is proved, the patentee is prima facie entitled under section 62 of the Act to an injunction. As Pearson L.J. said in *Van der Lely (C.) N.V.* v. *Bamfords Ltd.*[48]: " Under these provisions . . . it is clear that the claims can be considered separately, and the invalidity of some only of the claims does not invalidate the whole patent, and does not prevent the giving of relief in respect of the claims which are valid. Indeed, I think that the section gives to the patentee a prima facie right to relief subject to the qualifications provided. Under subsection (1) he can apply for an injunction and the court has the usual discretion with regard to the granting of an injunction. If a breach of a legal right is established and there is no equitable bar to the granting of an injunction, and no bar has arisen under subsection (3) of the section, the court will (or at any rate normally would) grant an injunction. It is to be noted that an injunction can be granted without any amendment of the patent."

970 Where a valid claim has been infringed, the mere fact that there has been delay in seeking to amend is no ground for refusing an injunction. As Harman L.J. stated in *Van der Lely (C.) N.V.* v. *Bamfords Ltd.*[49]: " If the relief asked be by way of injunction, on the ordinary principles well known in the Court of Chancery, where a man's legal rights have been invaded, mere delay will not deprive him of relief; that is stated by Fry J. in the well-known decision *Fullwood* v. *Fullwood*[50] where he said that there must be more than mere delay to disentitle a man to his legal rights." The court may also grant relief by way of damages and costs (and, it is submitted, an account of profits[51]) if the plaintiff proves that any invalid claim

---

[45] See *e.g. British Thomson-Houston Co. Ltd.* v. *Irradiant Lamp Works Ltd.*, 40 R.P.C. 243.
[46] *e.g. British United Shoe Machinery Co. Ltd.* v. *Lambert Howarth & Sons Ltd.*, 44 R.P.C. 511; *Samuel Parkes & Co. Ltd.* v. *Cocker Bros. Ltd.*, 46 R.P.C. 241.
[47] s. 62.
[48] [1964] R.P.C. 54 at p. 73.
[49] [1964] R.P.C. 54 at p. 81.
[50] (1878) 9 Ch.D. 176.
[51] s. 60.

was framed in good faith and with reasonable skill and knowledge [52]; but the court has a discretion as to the costs and to the date from which damages should be reckoned. The court may, and no doubt normally will, direct that the specification shall be amended to its satisfaction upon an application made by the patentee under section 30,[53] whether or not all other issues have been determined.[54] Presumably the amendments will have to be such as will validate the patent. These provisions have been applied where the patent has expired but was subsequently extended.[55] Cases decided under the former law [56] are of doubtful authority and must in any case be read in relation to the language of the statutes in force at the time.

(c) Certificates

971	At the close of an action for infringement a litigant must apply to the court for certificates as to certain matters in which he has been successful. The plaintiff should apply for a certificate that his particulars of infringements have been proven or were reasonable and proper, and where the issue of validity is raised and the patent is upheld, the plaintiff should also obtain a certificate of contested validity entitling him to a special privilege in subsequent actions. Where the patent is held to be invalid the defendant must obtain a certificate that his particulars of objections have been proven or have been reasonable and proper.[57]

972 Certificate of contested validity

In order to prevent a patentee from being put repeatedly to the expense of defending successive attacks on the validity of his patent, it is enacted that a court may in any proceedings certify that validity of any claim [58] was contested in those proceedings and in that case, if in any subsequent proceedings for infringement or for revocation of the patent the patentee is successful, he is entitled to costs as between solicitor and client so far as that claim is concerned unless the court otherwise directs.[59]

Both as regards the grant of a certificate of contested validity and

[52] s. 62 (2).

[53] See *ante*, § 496; *Surface Silos Ltd.* v. *Beal* [1960] R.P.C. 154.

[54] s. 62 (3).

[55] *Leggatt* v. *Hood's Original Darts Accessories Ltd.,* 68 R.P.C. 3.

[56] See *e.g. Tucker* v. *Wandsworth,* 42 R.P.C. 480; *Eyres* v. *Grundy,* 56 R.P.C. 253; *Raleigh Cycle Co. Ltd.* v. *H. Miller & Co. Ltd.,* 67 R.P.C. 226.

[57] See *post,* § 976.

[58] See *Ludlow Jute Co. Ltd.* v. *James Low & Co. Ltd.,* 70 R.P.C. 69.

[59] s. 64. Under R.S.C., Ord. 62, the " solicitor and client " basis of taxation is now referred to as the " common fund " basis.

as regards the subsequent direction depriving a plaintiff of solicitor and client costs, the power conferred upon the court is purely discretionary, and is exercised upon the facts of the particular case before the court. It is difficult, therefore, to extract from the many reported decisions any guiding principles upon which such certificates or directions should be granted.

In general, however, a certificate will not be granted unless there has been a real contest as to validity,[60] although in exceptional circumstances the court may depart from this rule.[61]

Where the question of validity was disputed upon a certain construction of a specification only, and not generally, a certificate has been refused.[62]

When a certificate of validity has once been granted there is no need for another in a subsequent action upon the same patent.[63] In one case, however, a fresh certificate was granted where validity was attacked on new grounds.[64]

If the specification is amended after the granting of the certificate, so as to affect the claim or claims certified, the certificate will no longer hold good, and a new one must be applied for in any subsequent action.[65]

Certificates are granted in respect of any individual claims of a patent which come into question.[66]

973   Certificate in threats action

Under the previous law it was doubtful whether a certificate of contested validity could be granted in a threats action.[67] The words of the present Act [68] are plainly wide enough to enable this to be done.

The Vice-Chancellor of the Palatine Court has jurisdiction to grant

---

[60] *Gillette Industries Ltd., v. Bernstein,* 58 R.P.C. 271 at p. 285; *Martin v. C.B. Projection (Engineering) Ltd.,* 65 R.P.C. 361. See also *British Thomson-Houston Co. Ltd., v. Corona Lamp Works Ltd.,* 39 R.P.C. 49 at p. 93; *Auster Ltd. v. Perfecta Motor Equipments Ltd.,* 41 R.P.C. 482 at p. 498.

[61] *Gillette Industries Ltd. v. Bernstein,* 58 R.P.C. 271 at p. 285.

[62] *New Inverted Incandescent Gas Lamp Co. Ltd. v. Globe Light Ltd.,* 23 R.P.C. 157; and see *Morris and Bastert v. Young,* 12 R.P.C. 455 at pp. 464, 465.

[63] *Edison and Swan Electric Light Co. v. Holland,* 6 R.P.C. 243 at p. 287.

[64] See *Flour Oxidising Co. Ltd. v. J. and R. Hutchinson,* 26 R.P.C. 597 at p. 638.

[65] *Brooks & Co. Ltd. v. Rendall, Underwood & Co. Ltd.,* 24 R.P.C. 17 at p. 27.

[66] s. 64; and see *e.g. Marconi's Wireless Telegraph Co. Ltd. v. Mullard Radio Valve Co. Ltd.,* 40 R.P.C. 1 at p. 27; *British United Shoe Machinery Co. Ltd. v. Gimson Shoe Machinery Co. Ltd. (No. 2),* 46 R.P.C. 137.

[67] See *e.g. Crampton v. Patents Investments Co.,* 5 R.P.C. 382; *Pittevil & Co. v. Brackelsberg Melting Processes Ltd.,* 49 R.P.C. 73.

[68] s. 64.

a certificate by virtue of section 3 of the Chancery of Lancaster Act 1890. Such certificates can also be granted by the Court of Appeal when a decision by the court of first instance is reversed.[69]

Where a patent which has been held to be invalid in the lower courts is held valid by the House of Lords, the practice is for the House of Lords to remit the matter to the Chancery Division with a direction to grant a certificate of validity and, where necessary, such other certificates to which the patentee may be entitled.[70]

It has been held that a certificate that the validity of a claim came in question is not a judgment or order within section 19 of the Judicature Act 1873 (now section 21 (1) of the Judicature Act 1925); and no appeal, therefore, lies from the decision of the judge granting or withholding the certificate.[71]

974 The subsequent action

A certificate of contested validity granted in one action will not affect the costs in another, although decided at a later date, provided that the latter proceedings were instituted before the grant of the certificate in the earlier action.[72]

975 *Discretion as to costs*

The court in the subsequent action has an unlimited discretion, which it exercises in view of the facts of the particular case; thus, a direction depriving the plaintiffs of solicitor and client costs was made where the second action was vexatious [73] or where the issue of validity was not raised therein, and the defendants were innocent infringers [74] or had a plausible argument with respect to non-infringement.[75] The mere fact that validity is not disputed in the subsequent action is not, however, sufficient to cause such a direction to be made,[76] some special reason being required.[77]

Solicitor and client costs are refused in respect of the issue of validity where the plaintiff is successful upon that issue but fails

---

[69] See *Cole* v. *Saqui*, 40 Ch.D. 132; 6 R.P.C. 41 at p. 45.
[70] *British Thomson-Houston Co. Ltd.* v. *Corona Lamp Works Ltd.*, 39 R.P.C. 49 at p. 95.
[71] *Haslam & Co.* v. *Hall (No. 2)*, 5 R.P.C. 144.
[72] *Automatic Weighing Machine Co.* v. *International Hygienic Society*, 6 R.P.C. 475 at p. 480; *Saccharin Corpn. Ltd.* v. *Anglo-Continental Chemical Works Ltd.* [1901] 1 Ch. 414; 17 R.P.C. 307 at p. 320.
[73] *Proctor* v. *Sutton Lodge Chemical Co.*, 5 R.P.C. 184.
[74] *Boyd* v. *Tootal Broadhurst Lee Co. Ltd.*, 11 R.P.C. 175 at p. 185.
[75] *Saccharin Corpn. Ltd.* v. *Dawson*, 19 R.P.C. 169 at p. 173.
[76] *United Telephone Co. Ltd.* v. *Patterson*, 6 R.P.C. 140; *British Vacuum Cleaner Co.* v. *Exton Hotels Ltd.*, 25 R.P.C. 617 at p. 629.
[77] *Welsbach Incandescent Gas Light Co. Ltd.* v. *Daylight Incandescent Mantle Co. Ltd.*, 16 R.P.C. 344 at p. 353.

owing to non-infringement, as the party relying on the validity of the patent must obtain a final order or judgment in his favour.[78]

The court has on occasion refused to go behind the certificate of validity and inquire as to the circumstances in which it was granted [79]; but the modern tendency is to order only party and party costs in cases where the real substantial trial of validity has taken place in the subsequent action.[80]

In *Otto* v. *Steel* [81] solicitor and client costs were refused on the ground that the validity of the patent was attacked on new grounds,[82] but it is unlikely that that case will be followed at the present time, save in exceptional circumstances.

Solicitor and client costs have also been refused where the patent has been amended since the certificate of validity was granted.[83]

976 Certificates as to particulars of infringements and of objections

Order 62, Appendix 2, Part X, 4 (3) of the Rules of the Supreme Court,[84] provides that if an action, or petition or counterclaim for revocation, proceeds to trial, no costs shall be allowed in respect of any issues raised in the particulars of infringements or particulars of objections unless the court certifies that such issues or particulars have been proven or are reasonable and proper.[85] If the action does not proceed to trial, the costs of these matters are in the discretion of the Taxing Master. The time for obtaining such certificates is at the conclusion of the trial, and omission to apply then will subject the party to the costs of any later application to that end, though it will not preclude him from obtaining a certificate if he applies within a reasonable time.[86]

977 Infringements

Where the defendant does not appear at the trial the court will usually certify for the particulars of infringements on the ground that the defendant's non-appearance is evidence that they are reasonable.[87]

---

[78] s. 64 (2) and see *Higginson and Arundel* v. *Pyman*, 43 R.P.C. 113 at p. 136.
[79] *Fabriques de Produits Chimique etc.* v. *Lafitte*, 16 R.P.C. 61 at p. 68; *Peter Pilkington Ltd.* v. *B. and S. Massey*, 21 R.P.C. 421 at p. 438; *Badische Anilin und Soda Fabrik* v. *W. G. Thompson & Co. Ltd.*, 21 R.P.C. 473 at p. 480.
[80] *British Thomson-Houston Co. Ltd.* v. *Corona Lamp Works Ltd.*, 39 R.P.C. 49 at p. 93; *Auster Ltd.* v. *Perfecta Motor Equipments Ltd.*, 41 R.P.C. 482 at p. 498.   [81] 3 R.P.C. 109 at p. 120.
[82] See also *Flour Oxidising Co. Ltd.* v. *J. and R. Hutchinson*, 26 R.P.C. 597 at p. 638.
[83] *J. B. Brooks & Co. Ltd.* v. *Rendall, Underwood & Co. Ltd.*, 24 R.P.C. 17 at p 27.   [84] *Post*, § 1621.
[85] See *e.g. Reitzman* v. *Grahame-Chapman*, 67 R.P.C. 178 at p. 195.
[86] *Rowcliffe* v. *Morris*, 3 R.P.C. 145; *Duckett* v. *Sankey*, 16 R.P.C. 357.
[87] *Brooks* v. *Hall*, 21 R.P.C. 29; *Saccharin Corpn. Ltd.* v. *Skidmore*, 21 R.P.C. 31.

A certificate as to particulars of infringements having been " reasonable and proper," but not that they have been " proved," [88] may be obtained where a plaintiff is awarded the costs of the issue of infringement even though he may have failed in his action on account of invalidity of his patent.[89]

978 *Objections*

As to the particulars of objections, the practice is now well settled that when the action goes to trial, the court will not certify unless they have been proven or the defendants can actually show that they are reasonable and proper; and so, where the action came on for hearing, and the plaintiff's case broke down by reason of certain of the particulars being proven, the court would not go through the other particulars with a view to ascertaining whether they were reasonable and proper, and a certificate was granted only as to those upon which the action was decided [90]; but where a number of prior users were pleaded, some of which were put to the plaintiff's witnesses in cross-examination, a certificate was granted as to these latter, notwithstanding that it became unnecessary to prove them all.[91]   And when the defendant succeeds on the issue of infringement and the issue of validity is not considered, the particulars of objections will not be certified.[92]

979   Where the patent was held invalid for want of inventiveness, insufficiency and prior user, and the decision was upheld on appeal as to the first two grounds but not as to the last, the Court of Appeal refused to vary the certificate as to particulars of objections.[93]

In some cases it may be reasonable to put a number of specifications to a witness *en bloc*, and if thereupon he concedes the point, the certificate may allow each specification.[94]

Where one of the items in the particulars of objections is relied on as an anticipation, but fails in this capacity, the court may nevertheless, certify for it, if it has been useful in illustrating the state of the art or otherwise.[95]

---

[88] *United Telephone Co.* v. *Harrison, Cox-Walker & Co.*, 21 Ch.D. 720 at p. 747.
[89] *Kane* v. *Guest & Co.*, 16 R.P.C. 433 at p. 443.
[90] *Boyd* v. *Horrocks*, 6 R.P.C. 152 at p. 162; *Longbottom* v. *Shaw*, 6 R.P.C. 143, 510; *Bowen* v. *Pearson & Sons Ltd.*, 42 R.P.C. 101.
[91] *Franc-Strohmenger and Cowan Inc.* v. *Peter Robinson Ltd.*, 47 R.P.C. 493 at p. 515.
[92] *Peter Pilkington Ltd.* v. *Massey*, 21 R.P.C. 696 at p. 712.
[93] *Wright and Eagle Range Ltd.* v. *General Gas Appliances Ltd.*, 45 R.P.C. 346; 46 R.P.C. 169 at p. 183.
[94] *Cooper Patent Anchor Rail Joint Co. Ltd.* v. *London County Council*, 23 R.P.C. 289 at p. 297.
[95] *Castner-Kellner Alkali Co. Ltd.* v. *Commercial Development Co. Ltd.*, 16 R.P.C. 251 at p. 276; and see *Nettlefolds Ltd.* v. *Reynolds*, 9 R.P.C. 270

And it may occur that costs incurred by a defendant in respect of an investigation into prior knowledge may be allowed as part of the costs of his defence in limiting the plaintiff's claim, although no certificate as to the particulars of the objections may have been granted.[96]

The rule does not, of course, prevent a party *against* whom objections are particularised from recovering his costs if successful upon such objections.[97]

980   If when a case is called on for hearing the plaintiff abandons it, or does not appear, the case is deemed not to have proceeded to trial, and no certificate as to particulars of objections will be granted; the costs of the particulars of objections are then in the discretion of the Taxing Master.[98] Similarly, if several patents are sued on in the same action, but some of them are abandoned at the trial, a certificate for the particulars of objections will be refused in respect of such patents.[99]

Where a certificate has been granted in respect of a few only out of numerous objections it appears to have been the practice upon taxation for the total cost in respect of all the objections to be apportioned among the certified and uncertified ones more or less in proportion to the number contained in each category. This practice appears clearly to be wrong, it being more proper for the costs connected with the certified objections to be taxed upon the same footing as if they had been the only ones pleaded [1]; that is to say, an attempt should be made to ascertain the actual amount of costs incurred in respect of each.

(d) Costs

981 Apportionment of costs

Where both validity and infringement are in issue and the plaintiff fails upon one of these issues only, the costs are dealt with in the

---

at p. 290; *Cassel Gold Extracting Co. Ltd.* v. *Cyanide Gold Recovery Syndicate,* 12 R.P.C. 303; *Birch* v. *Harrap & Co.,* 13 R.P.C. 615 at p. 622.

[96] *Piggott & Co. Ltd.* v. *Corporation of Hanley,* 23 R.P.C. 639; *Marconi's Wireless Telegraph Co. Ltd.* v. *Mullard Radio Valve Co. Ltd.,* 40 R.P.C. 1 at p. 29.

[97] *Sunlight Incandescent Gas Lamp Co. Ltd.* v. *Incandescent Gas Light Co.* 14 R.P.C. 757 at pp. 775, 776.

[98] *British, Foreign and Colonial etc. Co. Ltd.* v. *Metropolitan Gas Meters Ltd.* [1912] 2 Ch. 82; 29 R.P.C. 303; *Babcock and Wilcox Ltd.* v. *Water Tube Boiler and Engineering Co.,* 27 R.P.C. 626; *McCreath* v. *Mayor etc. of South Shields and Baker,* 50 R.P.C. 119; see also R.S.C., Ord. 62, App. 2 Pt. X, 4 (3).

[99] *Textile Patents Ltd.* v. *Weinbrenner,* 42 R.P.C. 515; *Lamson Paragon Supply Co. Ltd.* v. *Carter-Davis Ltd.,* 48 R.P.C. 133.

[1] *Clorious* v. *Tonner,* 39 R.P.C. 242 at p. 252.

discretion of the court according to the circumstances of the particular case. The practice of the court has not been uniform. In some cases where the issues were sufficiently distinct and where the costs had been materially increased by the defendant fighting the issue in respect of which the plaintiff was successful, the costs of that issue were given to the plaintiff,[2] or were given to neither side.[3] In some cases where a patent is held to be invalid by reason of some only of the objections particularised against it and not of the others, the plaintiff has been granted the cost of the unsuccessful objections and the defendant that of the successful ones.[4] In several cases, however, where patents were held invalid, it was held that the defendant had acted reasonably in pleading non-infringement, even though, save in so far as it might always be said that there could be no infringement of an invalid patent, he did not succeed in establishing that plea, and costs of the issue of infringement were awarded to the defendant.[5]

982 But where a defendant has succeeded upon the issue of infringement but failed upon that of validity, the plaintiff is sometimes given the costs of the issue of validity. In *Badische Anilin und Soda Fabrik* v. *Levinstein*,[6] Bowen L.J. said: " I am of opinion in this case that the plaintiffs should have the costs occasioned by the issues raised by the particulars of breaches, and that in respect of all the other costs the costs in the action should follow the usual result and be awarded to the successful party. It seems to me that without laying down any hard-and-fast line, or trying to fetter our discretion at a future period, in any other case, we are acting on a sensible and sound principle, namely, the principle that the parties ought not, even if right in the action, to add to the expenses of an action by fighting issues in which they are in the wrong. It may be very reasonable with regard to their

[2] See *e.g. Badische Anilin und Soda Fabrik* v. *Levinstein*, 29 Ch.D. 366 at p. 418; 2 R.P.C. 73 at p. 118; *Haslam Co.* v. *Hall*, 5 R.P.C. 1 at p. 25; *Cassel Gold Extracting Co. Ltd.* v. *Cyanide Gold Recovery Syndicate*, 11 R.P.C. 638 at p. 652; *Metropolitan-Vickers Electrical Co. Ltd.* v. *British Thomson-Houston Co. Ltd.*, 42 R.P.C. 143 at p. 178; *Godfrey* v. *Hancock & Co. (Engineers) Ltd.*, 42 R.P.C. 407 at p. 431; *Higginson and Arundel* v. *Pyman*, 43 R.P.C. 113 at 134; *N.V. Hollandsche Glas-en Metaalbank* v. *Rockware Glass Syndicate Ltd.*, 49 R.P.C. 288 at p. 323.
[3] See *e.g. Needham and Kite* v. *Johnson & Co.*, 1 R.P.C. 49 at p. 59; *Peter Pilkington Ltd.* v. *Massey*, 21 R.P.C. 696 at p. 712; *Rondo Co. Ltd.* v. *Gramophone Co. Ltd.*, 46 R.P.C. 378 at p. 395.
[4] *Lister* v. *Norton Bros. & Co.*, 3 R.P.C. 199 at p. 211.
[5] See *e.g. Guilbert-Martin* v. *Kerr and Jubb*, 4 R.P.C. 18 at p. 23; *Kaye* v. *Chubb & Sons Ltd.*, 4 R.P.C. 289 at p. 300; *Blakey & Co.* v. *Latham & Co.*, 6 R.P.C. 29 at p. 38; 184 at p. 190; *Westley, Richards & Co.* v. *Perkes* 10 R.P.C. 181 at p. 194; *Haskell Golf Ball Co. Ltd.* v. *Hutchinson (No. 2)*, 23 R.P.C. 125; *Harris* v. *Brandreth*, 42 R.P.C. 471 at p. 479; *White* v. *Todd Oil Burners Ltd.*, 46 R.P.C. 275 at p. 293.
[6] 29 Ch.D. 366 at p. 418; 2 R.P.C. 73 at p. 118.

own interest, and may help them in the conduct of the action, that they should raise issues in which, in the end, they are defeated, but the defendant who does so does it in his own interest, and I think he ought to do it at his own expense. The order, therefore, I think, ought to be as I have stated." [7]

This practice was also followed where non-infringement was found and the patents were held valid, although on the construction of the specification argued by the plaintiffs they would have been invalid.[8] The same practice was followed in *Marconi's Wireless Telegraph Co. Ltd.* v. *Mullard Radio Valve Co. Ltd.*[9] the defendants being given amongst their costs upon the issue of infringement the cost of putting in evidence such of the matters referred to in their particulars of objections as were necessary for the purpose of explaining the scope and ambit of the plaintiff's patent.[10]

But in *Vaisey* v. *Toddlers Footwear (1954) Ltd.*,[11] where the defendants failed on the issue of validity but succeeded on the issue of infringement, a different course was adopted, the defendants being given the costs of the action less the costs incurred in respect of those particulars in the particulars of objections not certified as reasonable and proper. If some only of the claims pleaded as having been infringed are found to be infringed while others are not infringed the plaintiff will normally get the whole of the costs.[12]

983 Costs where patent partially valid

If the patentee obtains relief in respect of some claim which is held valid and infringed in a case where one or more other claims are invalid,[13] no costs will be awarded to him unless he proves that the invalid claims were framed in good faith and with reasonable skill and knowledge.[14]

Where actions are brought upon more than one patent and the

[7] See also *No-Fume Ltd.* v. *Frank Pitchford & Co. Ltd.*, 52 R.P.C. 231 at p. 253 but see *Vaisey* v. *Toddlers Footwear (1954) Ltd.* [1957] R.P.C. 90 at pp. 103–104.
[8] *N.V. Hollandsche Glas-en Metaalbank* v. *Rockware Glass Syndicate Ltd.*, 49 R.P.C. 288.
[9] 40 R.P.C. 1 at p. 29; 40 R.P.C. 159 at p. 178.
[10] See also *Brown* v. *Sperry Gyroscope Co. Ltd.*, 42 R.P.C. 111 at p. 141; *and Marconi Wireless Telegraph Co. Ltd.* v. *Philips Lamps Ltd.*, 50 R.P.C. 287 at p. 314.
[11] [1957] R.P.C. 90 at pp. 103–104.
[12] See *e.g. Auster Ltd.* v. *Perfecta Motor Equipments Ltd.*, 41 R.P.C. 482 at p. 498; *Mergenthaler Linotype Co.* v. *Intertype Ltd.*, 43 R.P.C. 239 at p. 270; but cf. *Mouchel* v. *Coignet*, 23 R.P.C. 649.
[13] s. 62 (1).
[14] s. 62 (2) and see *Hale* v. *Coombes*, 42 R.P.C. 328 at p. 350; *Ronson Products Ltd.* v. *Lewis & Co.* [1963] R.P.C. 103 at p. 138.

plaintiff is successful as to some but not all of the patents sued on, it is usual for the costs to be apportioned.[15]

Where apportionment would be very difficult and expensive the judge at the trial will, instead of making an order as to costs in the usual form, order that the entire taxed costs are to be divided between the parties in definite proportions,[16] or where it seems fair to him will award no costs at all.[17]

984 Costs of inspection and experiments

The costs of an inspection are in the discretion of the court [18]; but if the inspection was necessary and proper the costs thereof are recoverable even though it was made without an order of the court.[19] The costs of experiments may be disallowed if they are not properly conducted in accordance with the order of the court.[20]

985 Costs on higher scale

There is no provision in Order 62 of the Rules of the Supreme Court for the court certifying that costs should be on " the higher scale " or for " three counsel," but the Taxing Master would follow any such intimation by the court in exercising his discretion as to the fees allowable on taxation.

Costs on the higher scale are only certified in cases of exceptional difficulty,[21] and in recent years have seldom been certified except in chemical cases.[22]

---

[15] See e.g. Hocking v. Fraser, 3 R.P.C. 3; Brooks v. Lamplugh, 15 R.P.C. 33 at p. 52.

[16] See e.g. Incandescent Gas Light Co. Ltd. v. Sunlight Incandescent Gas Lamp Co. Ltd., 13 R.P.C. 333 at p. 345; Monnet v. Beck, 14 R.P.C. 777 at p. 850; Lektophone Corpn. v. S. G. Brown Ltd., 46 R.P.C. 203 at p. 235; Lister v. Thorp, Medley & Co., 47 R.P.C. 99 at p. 114; Marconi Wireless Telegraph Co. Ltd. v. Philips Lamps Ltd., 50 R.P.C. 287 at p. 313; Vaisey v. Toddlers Footwear (1954) Ltd. [1957] R.P.C. 90 at p. 103; Birmingham Sound Reproducers Ltd. v. Collaro Ltd. [1956] R.P.C. 53 at p. 71.

[17] Hale v. Coombes, 40 R.P.C. 283 at p. 319; Rondo Co. Ltd. v. Gramophone Co. Ltd., 46 R.P.C. 378 at p. 396.

[18] Mitchell v. Darley Main Colliery Co., (1883) 10 Q.B.D. 457.

[19] Ashworth v. English Card Clothing Co. Ltd., 21 R.P.C. 353.

[20] Reitzman v. Grahame-Chapman, 67 R.P.C. 178 at p. 195.

[21] See General Signal Co. v. Westinghouse, 56 R.P.C. 295 at p. 394.

[22] The following are the cases in which they have been allowed since 1907: Andrews' Patent, 24 R.P.C. 349; Max Müller's Patent, 24 R.P.C. 465; Alsop's Patent, 24 R.P.C. 733; Flour Oxidising Co. Ltd. v. Carr & Co. Ltd., 25 R.P.C. 428; British Liquid Air Co. Ltd. v. British Oxygen Co. Ltd., 25 R.P.C. 218, 577; Carnegie Steel Co. v. Bell Bros. Ltd., 26 R.P.C. 265; Vidal Dyes Syndicate Ltd. v. Levinstein Ltd., 28 R.P.C. 541; Joseph Crosfield & Sons Ltd. v. Techno-Chemical Laboratories Ltd., 30 R.P.C. 297; Commercial Solvents Corporation v. Synthetic Products Co. Ltd., 43 R.P.C. 185; I. G. Farbenindustrie A.G.'s Patents, 47 R.P.C. 289; May and Baker's Patent, 65 R.P.C. 255 at p. 304. Costs on the higher scale were refused in John Summers & Sons Ltd. v. The Cold Metal Process Co., 65 R.P.C. 75 at p. 122.

Costs on the higher scale have been refused although the costs of three counsel have been allowed.[23]

986   *Three counsel*

The principle upon which costs on the higher scale and the costs of briefing three counsel should be certified were discussed, and the authorities considered, by Buckley J. in *Dunlop Pneumatic Tyre Co.* v. *Wapshare Tube Co.*,[24] where both were certified.[25]

The question of allowing costs of three counsel is sometimes left to the Taxing Master with or without an intimation of the court's opinion upon the point.[26]

987   **Costs of shorthand notes**

The costs of transcripts of the shorthand notes are usually agreed between the parties before the trial commences, but in default of such an arrangement they will not be allowed unless they have been of material assistance to the court in shortening the amount of time the case has taken or otherwise.[27]

988   **Declaration as to non-infringement**

Where an action is commenced for a declaration to be made under section 66 of the Patents Act that a certain process or article does not infringe a claim of a patent, then the costs of all parties to the action will be ordered to be paid by the plaintiff unless for special reasons the court thinks fit to order otherwise.[28]

989   **Several defendants**

Where an action is brought against two defendants and the case against one of them is settled, and the action proceeds against the other and judgment is recovered, then unless a special order as to costs is made no deduction on taxation will be made from the general

---

[23] *Marconi* v. *British Radio Telegraph and Telephone Co. Ltd.*, 28 R.P.C. 181. See also *Commercial Solvents Corporation* v. *Synthetic Products Co. Ltd.*, 43 R.P.C. 185 at p. 238; *Société Anonyme Servo-Frein Dewandre* v. *Citroen Cars Ltd.*, 47 R.P.C. 221 at p. 261; *John Summers & Sons Ltd.* v. *The Cold Metal Process Co.*, 65 R.P.C. 75 at p. 122.

[24] 17 R.P.C. 433 at p. 459.

[25] See also *Bradford Dyers' Association Ltd.* v. *Bury*, 19 R.P.C. 125.

[26] *British Thomson-Houston Co. Ltd.* v. *British Insulated and Helsby Cables Ltd.*, 41 R.P.C. 345 at p. 375; *Commercial Solvents Corporation* v. *Synthetic Products Co. Ltd.*, 43 R.P.C. 185 at p. 238.

[27] See *e.g. Castner-Kellner Alkali Co.* v. *Commercial Development Co. Ltd.*, 16 R.P.C. 251 at p. 275; *Palmer Tyre Co. Ltd.* v. *Pneumatic Tyre Co. Ltd.*, 16 R.P.C. 451 at p. 496; *British Westinghouse Electric and Manufacturing Co. Ltd.* v. *Braulik*, 27 R.P.C. 209 at p. 233.

[28] s. 66 (2).

costs of the action to represent the amount incurred as against the defendant whose case was settled.[29]

990 Minutes

Judgment having been recovered, minutes of judgment should be prepared. Care should be exercised, when an inquiry is directed, that provision be made for the payment of costs to the plaintiff up to and including the hearing, otherwise the payment of all costs will be delayed until the final account has been taken.

991 Undertaking to return costs

A common course with regard to costs is for the solicitor to the successful party to give an undertaking to return the costs in the event of a successful appeal.[30] In *Ackroyd and Best Ltd.* v. *Thomas and Williams,*[31] where the solicitors declined to give the undertaking, Joyce J. stayed the payment of costs, but refused to stay the taxation.

992 No appeal as to costs

Section 31 (1) (*h*) of the Judicature (Consolidation) Act 1925 provides that there shall be no appeal as to costs save where the costs are a matter of right, and not discretionary.[32]

993 Action based on undertaking or contract

If a defendant has given an undertaking or entered into a contract not to infringe a patent (*e.g.* as part of the terms of settlement of a previous action or threatened action) such a bargain can be enforced, notwithstanding the invalidity of the patent.[33] Such an agreement or undertaking will normally be assumed to subsist for the life of the patent.[34]

994 Compromise of action affecting infant children

Where a patent action is continued by the personal representatives of a deceased patentee and the interests of infant children are involved, a compromise of the action must be sanctioned by the court.[35]

---

[29] *Kelly's Directories Ltd.* v. *Gavin and Lloyds* [1901] 2 Ch. 763; *Badische Anilin und Soda Fabrik* v. *Hickson,* 23 R.P.C. 149.

[30] *Ticket Punch Register Co. Ltd.* v. *Colley's Patents Ltd.,* 12 R.P.C. 1 at p. 10.

[31] 21 R.P.C. 403 at p. 412.

[32] See also R.S.C., Ord. 62, r. 2, and *Donald Campbell & Co.* v. *Pollack* [1927] A.C. 732.

[33] *Heginbotham Bros. Ltd.* v. *Burne,* 56 R.P.C. 399 at p. 407.

[34] *Ibid.* And see *Bescol (Electric) Ltd.* v. *Merlin Mouldings Ltd.,* 69 R.P.C. 297.

[35] *Schwank* v. *Radiant Heating Ltd.* [1958] R.P.C. 266.

6. APPEALS TO THE COURT OF APPEAL

995   Appeals to the Court of Appeal are initiated by notice of motion,[36] and, in the case of appeals from final orders made in actions, such notice must be lodged within six weeks of the order " being signed, entered, or otherwise perfected." [37] The procedure on appeal in a patent action is the same as in any other action.[38]

In order that the Court of Appeal may entertain an appeal there must still be a real issue between the parties for determination when the matter comes before that court; otherwise the appeal will be dismissed.[39] Previous to this decision it was not unusual for a patentee who had failed in the court of first instance to make a settlement with the defendant (*e.g.* by granting him a licence on favourable terms) and thereafter to attempt in the Court of Appeal to upset the judgment made against him without having to encounter opposition.[40] This procedure is no longer possible.

The costs of employing an expert to assist counsel in the Court of Appeal will not be allowed save under the most special circumstances.[41]

[The next paragraph is 1001]

---

[36] R.S.C., Ord. 59, r. 3.
[37] R.S.C., Ord. 59, r. 4.
[38] But see R.S.C., Ord. 59, rr. 17, 18.
[39] *Martin* v. *Selsdon Fountain Pen Co. Ltd.*, 66 R.P.C. 294; *Sun Life Assurance Co. of Canada* v. *Jervis* [1944] A.C. 111.
[40] See *Norton and Gregory* v. *Jacobs*, 54 R.P.C. 271; *Manbré and Garton* v. *Albion Sugar Co.*, 54 R.P.C. 243.
[41] *Consolidated Pneumatic Tool Co.* v. *Ingersoll Sergeant Drill Co.*, 25 R.P.C. 574; *Société Anonyme Servo-Frein Dewandre* v. *Citroen Cars Ltd.*, 47 R.P.C. 221 at p. 282.

CHAPTER 15

USE BY THE CROWN, INCOME TAX, STAMPS, ETC.

1. USE BY THE CROWN

1001 History

Prior to the Act of 1883 the Crown was entitled to use patented inventions without the assent of or compensation to the patentee,[1] though it was the practice to reward the patentee *ex gratia*. The exemption of the Crown did not, however, extend to protect contractors who supplied patented articles to the Crown,[2] as distinguished from servants or agents of the Crown, at any rate where such contractors could if they had so wished have supplied instead articles which were not patented.

1002 Present law

Since the Act of 1883, and now under the present law, a patent has the same effect against the Crown as against a subject.[3] This, however, is subject to very wide rights of user by the Crown, as set out below. By section 3 of the Crown Proceedings Act 1947[4] a patentee is able to sue the Crown in civil proceedings for infringement, if the Crown purports to authorise any infringing act otherwise than in accordance with its statutory rights.

1003 Authorisation for services of Crown

Any government department, and any person authorised in writing by a government department, may make, use and exercise any patented invention for the services of the Crown.[5] The requirement that the authorisation must be in writing was first introduced by the Act of 1919. It would seem that such written authorisation need not be directed specifically to the use of the particular patent concerned, and that a written authorisation or requirement of a department that a contractor should supply apparatus of a certain type is sufficient if it is in fact impossible for the contractor to supply such apparatus without infringing the patent.[6]

1004   In *Aktiengesellschaft für Aluminium Schweissung* v. *London Aluminium Co. Ltd. (No. 2)*,[7] Sargant J. said: " The origin of the

---

[1] *Feather* v. *R.*, 6 B. & S. 257.
[2] *Dixon* v. *London Small Arms Co.*, L.R. 10 Q.B. 130; 1 Q.B.D. 384; 1 App.Cas. 632.
[3] s. 21 (2).
[4] See *post*, § 1733.
[5] s. 46 (1).
[6] See *Pyrene Co. Ltd.* v. *Webb Lamp Co. Ltd.*, 37 R.P.C. 57.
[7] 40 R.P.C. 107 at p. 116.

[393]

section, of course, is well known; it is to be found undoubtedly in the decision of the House of Lords in *Dixon* v. *London Small Arms Co. Ltd.*,[8] where it was held that the right of the Crown to use a patented article or process could not extend to contractors who were employed as contractors by the Government. The difficulty that arises is this: In some cases it is clear that the defendants, who were the direct contractors with the Government, were told to use this particular process, and in those cases it is not questioned by counsel for the plaintiffs that no damages can be assessed. The right of the patentees in that case will be under section 29 (now section 46). . . . But there are a number of cases where the facts are nothing like so simple, cases where the company, the defendants, have not been contracting directly with the Government, but have been, for instance, supplying persons who themselves were the direct contractors with the Government; in those cases it is said that the protection of the section does not apply and that the patentees accordingly are entitled to the ordinary remedy against the defendant company. It seems to me really that it is impossible to deal as a whole with the various contracts that are now in question. In my judgment, the section is primarily an agency section; that is to say, protection is afforded to the government department, and to any person or persons, contractors or others, who are acting as agents for, or by the express or implied authority of, a government department. In each case it will have to be ascertained, if the parties think fit to fight out each individual case, whether the acts of the defendant company in that particular case were acts done for the purposes of the Crown, and with the authority or by the direction of the Crown. In that case they will not be liable; but where the acts that they have done have not been done by virtue of some express or implied authority from the Crown, then it seems to me they will be liable. It may be in many cases that, where they are sub-contractors, there will have been such a relation between them and their contractors, such a direction given by the Government to the contractors, or such a direct supervision over the employers by the Government, as will amount to an implied authority sufficient to make the company in that individual case an agent acting by the authority, and for the purposes, of the Crown."

1005   Services of the Crown

Use for the services of the Crown is use by members of such services in the course of their duties. Thus the use of patented drugs in the treatment of National Health Service hospital patients has been held to be use for the services of the Crown.[9]

---

[8] 1 App.Cas. 632.
[9] *Pfizer Corpn.* v. *Minister of Health* [1965] R.P.C. 261; [1965] A.C. 512.

1006 Scope of authority

The right to authorise given by the Act applies to a patented invention or to an alleged invention that is the subject of a patent application.[10] The authority may be given either before or after the patent is granted and either before or after the acts authorised are done.[11] The sale of a patented article to a government department for the services of the Crown is a " use " of the patented invention which may be authorised by that department.[9] The Crown may also sell to anybody patented articles made pursuant to an authority given by a government department when these are no longer required for the purpose for which they were made,[12] and the purchaser of such articles and any person claiming through him may deal with such articles freely, as though the patent were held by the Crown.[13] During a period of emergency very wide powers are conferred on the Crown.[14]

1007 Use for health services

It has now been enacted that the powers exercisable in relation to patented inventions under section 46 of the Patents Act 1949 include power to make, use, exercise and vend patented inventions for the production or supply of drugs and medicines required for the health services, such power to be exercisable under regulations to be made by statutory instrument.[15]

1008 Use for foreign government and authority to sell

The Crown may authorise the use of an invention for the purposes of a foreign government, in pursuance of treaty obligations, if such use is required for the defence of the foreign country [16] and may sell the patented articles to that foreign country.[17]

1009 Compensation for Crown use

If the invention has been recorded by or tried by or on behalf of a government department [18] before the relevant priority date [19] otherwise than in consequence of a communication directly or indirectly from the patentee or a predecessor in title, any use of the invention may be made free of any royalty or other payment. But if the invention has not been so recorded or tried, any use made after the acceptance of the complete specification or in consequence of such a

---

[10] *American Flange and Manufacturing Co. Inc.* v. *Van Leer*, 65 R.P.C. 305 at p. 318.
[11] s. 46 (4).   [12] s. 46 (6) (*b*).
[13] s. 46 (7) and see *ante*, § 1003.
[14] s. 49.
[15] Health Services and Public Health Act 1968, s. 59.
[16] s. 46 (6) and Defence Contracts Act 1958, s. 1, *post*, § 1253.
[17] s. 46 (6) (*a*).
[18] See *Re Carbonit A.G.*, 40 R.P.C. 360.
[19] See *ante*, § 165.

communication of the invention is to be on terms to be agreed between the government department and the patentee with the approval of the Treasury or in default of agreement to be settled by the High Court,[20] which may refer the whole proceedings or any issue of fact to a special or official referee or an arbitrator.[21]

The sum payable by way of compensation under section 46 (3) of the Act is in the nature of remuneration payable to the inventor or his successor in title for the use made by the Crown of his invention pursuant to that concurrent right; he is not entitled to compensation on any other basis, for instance, in his status as a manufacturer for loss of chance to manufacture.[22]

1010 *Date from which compensation runs*

It is to be noted that compensation is payable in respect of use from the date of acceptance of the complete specification or the date of communication of the invention and not from the date of publication of the complete specification as in the case of damages for infringement against a private individual. The reason for this is that the Crown may require the patent to be kept secret,[24] and, if the date of publication were the relevant date, could thereby deprive the patentee of compensation altogether.

The court may order interest to be paid to the patentee on the compensation sum.[23]

1011 **Information as to use to be given**

Where the use of an invention is authorised by a government department the latter must notify the patentee as soon as practicable after the use has begun and give information from time to time as to the extent of the use, unless it would be contrary to the public interest to do so.[25]

1012 **Terms of any licence etc. to be inoperative**

A government department may authorise a licensee of the patentee to make, use or exercise the invention and in such a case the terms of any licence or agreement (other than one made with a government department) are inoperative as regards such user.[26] Similarly, the patentee may be authorised to use or supply the patented invention

---

[20] ss. 46 (3), 48 (1). As to inventions made by enemies during the last war see Enemy Property Act 1953, s. 8.
[21] s. 48 (5).
[22] *Patchett's Patent* [1967] R.P.C. 237 at pp. 246, 251, 257.
[23] *Patchett's Patent* [1967] R.P.C. 237.
[24] See *ante*, § 142.
[25] s. 46 (5).
[26] s. 47 (1). See *No-Nail Cases Proprietary Ltd.* v. *No-Nail Boxes Ltd.*, 61 R.P.C. 94.

for the services of the Crown, notwithstanding the terms of any assignment or agreement which purport to debar him from so doing.[27] And any provisions which restrict or regulate the use of the invention or of any model, document, or information relating to the invention are inoperative.[28] Furthermore, the reproduction or publication of any model or document in connection with such use is not to be deemed an infringement of copyright.[28]

1013 *Compensation to licensee or assignor*

An exclusive licensee[29] whose licence was granted for a consideration other than a royalty assessed by reference to use can claim compensation for Crown user,[30] including user by the patentee for the services of the Crown.[31] Similarly, where a patent or the right to apply for a patent has been assigned in consideration of the payment of royalties the assignor can claim compensation and any sum payable is to be divided between assignor and patentee as may be agreed or be settled by reference to the court.[32] An exclusive licensee whose licence was granted in consideration of the payment of royalties can recover such proportion of any payment made to the patentee as may be agreed or determined by the court.[33]

Where co-owners of a patent have previously agreed on the proportions in which they will divide any royalties or other proceeds from exploitation of the patent, the court will apportion in those proportions any compensation awarded under section 46 (3) in respect of Crown use of the patent.[34]

1014 Procedure

The procedure on reference to the High Court is by way of originating notice of motion assigned to Group A of the Chancery Division.[35] On the first hearing of the motion the usual practice is to order pleadings and give other directions, such as discovery.[36]

1015 Validity may be challenged

In proceedings for the assessment of compensation for Crown user, if the patentee is a party the government department may apply

[27] s. 47 (1), overruling *Foster Wheeler Ltd.* v. *E. Green & Son Ltd.*, 63 R.P.C. 10.
[28] s. 47 (1).
[29] See *ante*, § 609.
[30] s. 47 (3) (*b*).
[31] s. 47 (2).
[32] s. 47 (3).
[33] s. 47 (4).
[34] *Patchett's Patent* [1967] R.P.C. 237.
[35] R.S.C., Ord. 103, r. 28.
[36] See *e.g. Re Carbonit*, 41 R.P.C. 203 at p. 209 and *Sageb's Claim*, 68 R.P.C. 73 at p. 77.

for revocation of the patent and in any case may put validity in issue without applying for revocation.[37]

Where the Crown puts validity in issue and there is also concurrently an action for infringement of the patent against a third party who has also put validity in issue, the Crown proceedings and the action may be ordered to be heard together so far as they raise common issues.[38]

1016 Confidential disclosure

If any question arises as to whether or not an invention has been recorded or tried by a government department and any disclosure would be contrary to the public interest, such disclosure may be made confidentially to counsel or to an independent expert mutually agreed on.[39]

1017 Any benefit received to be taken into account

Any benefit or compensation that the claimant or his predecessor in title may have received or be entitled to receive directly or indirectly from any government department in respect of the invention is to be taken into account in assessing compensation.[40] If, during the course of proceedings for the assessment of compensation for Crown user, amendment of the patent specification is sought and allowed, the court may consider limitation of the period of compensation as a term of allowing the amendment.[41]

1018 Costs in proceedings against the Crown

In any civil proceedings, or arbitration, to which the Crown (or a government department) is a party, the court, or arbitrator, may make " *an order for the payment of costs by or to the Crown.*" [42]

1019 Articles forfeited under customs law

Section 102 (2) says: " *Nothing in this Act shall affect the right of the Crown or of any person deriving title directly or indirectly from the Crown to sell or use articles forfeited under the laws relating to customs or excise.*"

This subsection does not confer any rights upon the Crown or persons deriving title from the Crown, but merely states that existing rights are not affected. It is a matter of doubt whether purchasers from the Crown of articles manufactured in infringement of a patent

---

[37] s. 48 (2).
[38] *Anxionnaz* v. *Ministry of Aviation* [1966] R.P.C. 510.
[39] s. 48 (3).   [40] s. 48 (4).
[41] *Electric and Musical Industries' Patent* [1963] R.P.C. 241.
[42] See Administration of Justice (Miscellaneous Provisions) Act 1933, s. 7 (1) (2); and see *Patchett's Patent* [1967] R.P.C. 237 at p. 259.

and forfeited under the laws relating to the customs or excise are entitled to use them without the licence of the patentee.[43]

2. STAMP DUTY

1020 The question of the stamping of documents is of considerable importance in view of the provisions of section 74 (6) of the Act whereby patentees, licensees, and others who fail to register the documents under which they derive their title are placed under certain disabilities. The Comptroller is liable to a penalty of £10 if he registers a document which is not duly stamped,[44] and he may, therefore, refuse to register a document where he is not satisfied that the true consideration is stated on the face of the document.[45] The proper mode of questioning the legality of his refusal is to obtain the opinion of the Commissioners of Inland Revenue.[46] An appeal from their decision lies to the High Court.

An assignment of a patent requires to be stamped as a conveyance or transfer on sale on the *ad valorem* scale imposed by section 55 (1) of and Part I of Schedule 11 to the Finance Act 1963 as amended by section 27 (1) of the Finance Act 1967. The scale is arranged in stepped stages, and must be consulted.

An irrevocable licence to use and vend is also liable to conveyance duty on sums reserved by way of fixed royalties during the life of the patent, but if the licence contains a power of revocation no conveyance duty is payable in practice though covenant duty may be payable.

1021 For the purposes of conveyance duty it is immaterial whether a conveyance is under hand or under seal, and subject to the exemption from duty of any instrument in respect of a sale where the amount or value of the consideration is £5,500 or under,[47] a deed must always bear a 50p stamp unless the *ad valorem* duty exceeds this amount. Licences which are not liable to conveyance duty because they are revocable may be liable to covenant duty, which is an *ad valorem* duty of $\frac{1}{8}$ per cent., in so far as they contain a covenant to pay fixed royalties, and the duty will be calculated on the amount to be received for the whole life of the patent or period of the licence. However, section 35 (1) of the Finance Act 1958 exempts from covenant duty any agreement or covenant to pay sums for or in relation to the sale or hire of any goods. The words " in relation to " have been given a liberal construction [48] and it is submitted that the

[43] See *British Mutoscope and Biograph Co. Ltd.* v. *Homer*, 18 R.P.C. 177.
[44] Stamp Act 1891, s. 17.
[45] *Maynard* v. *Consolidated Kent Collieries*, 19 T.L.R. 448.
[46] *R.* v. *Registrar of Joint Stock Companies*, 21 Q.B.D. 131.
[47] Finance Act 1967, s. 27 (1).   [48] *Warrington* v. *Furbor* (1807) 8 East 242.

periodic payment of sums for the sale of goods made by a patented process would fall within this exemption.   In any event no duty is payable on the royalty per article, apart from any minimum, as it is indeterminate, and no *ad valorem* duty is payable in respect of a lump sum of money paid in consideration of the grant of a revocable licence.

By section 59, subsection (4), of the Stamp Act 1891 the *ad valorem* stamp is not required for the mere purpose of enforcing specific performance or recovering damages for the breach of a contract or agreement for a licence.

It was held in *Smelting Company of Australia* v. *Commissioners of Inland Revenue* [49] that a share in a patent and sole licence to use the patented invention are " property " within section 59, subsection (1) of the Stamp Act 1891; and this part of the decision does not appear to be affected by the decision in *English, Scottish and Australian Bank* v. *Inland Revenue Commissioners*.[50]

In view of the decision in the latter case, however, an interest in a foreign or colonial patent is an interest in " property locally situate out of the United Kingdom," and, therefore, an agreement relating to such rights is not liable to " conveyance duty."

The question of the " local situation " of interests in foreign patents is also of importance in connection with estate duty.[51]

3. INCOME TAX AND CORPORATION TAX

1022   There are two basic and quite separate inquiries underlying the taxation of patent rights.   One is to determine what allowances one is entitled to in respect of monies expended on such rights and the other is to determine what monies received in respect of such rights are liable to tax.   However, before either of these questions can be determined it is first of all necessary to decide whether such monies expended or received in respect of patent rights are of an income or capital nature.

1023   Income or capital nature

The distinction between capital and income monies is a question of fact.[52]   As Lord Denning M.R. said in *Murray (Inspector of Taxes)* v. *Imperial Chemical Industries* [53]: " I see no difference in this regard between an assignment of patent rights and the grant of an exclusive licence for the period of the patent.   It is the disposal of a capital

---

[49] [1897] 1 Q.B. 175 at p. 181.
[50] [1932] A.C. 238.
[51] Finance Act 1894, s. 2 (2).
[52] *Inland Revenue Commissioners* v. *British Salmson Aero Engines Ltd.* [1938] 2 K.B. 482; 22 T.C. 29.
[53] [1967] Ch. 1038 at p. 1052; [1967] R.P.C. 216.

asset. But this does not determine the quality of the money received. A man may dispose of a capital asset outright for a lump sum which is then a capital receipt. Or he may dispose of it in return for an annuity, in which case the annual payments are revenue receipts. Or he may dispose of it in part for one and in part for the other. Each case must depend on its own circumstances. But it seems to me fairly clear that if, and in so far as, a man disposes of patent rights outright (for example by an assignment of his patent, or by the grant of an exclusive licence) and receives in return *royalties* calculated by reference to the actual user, the royalties are clearly revenue receipts. If, and in so far as, he disposes of them for *annual payments* over the period, which can fairly be regarded as compensation for the user during the period, then those also are revenue receipts. If, and in so far as, he disposes of the patent rights outright for a *lump sum,* which is arrived at by reference to some anticipated quantum of user, it will normally be income in the hands of the recipient (see the judgment of Lord Greene M.R. in *Withers* v. *Nethersole* [54] approved by Lord Simon in the House of Lords [55]). But if, and in so far as, he disposes of them outright for a lump sum which has no reference to anticipated user, it will normally be capital. It is different when a man does not dispose of his patent rights, but retains them and grants a non-exclusive licence. He does not then dispose of a capital asset. He retains the asset and he uses it to bring in money for him. A lump sum may in those cases be a revenue receipt: see *Rustproof Metal Window Co. Ltd.* v. *Inland Revenue Commissioners.*" [56]

Capital expenditure and capital sums do not include sums which are treated as revenue expenditure or receipts nor do they include sums on which a deduction of tax falls or may fall to be made by the payer other than a capital sum in respect of a United Kingdom patent paid to a person not resident in the United Kingdom.[57]

1024   Who entitled to allowances and liable to tax

Persons entitled to allowances in respect of expenditure on patent rights and liable to tax on sums received in respect of such rights are as follows:

(1) Any person residing in the United Kingdom in respect of any patent rights (whether situate in the United Kingdom or elsewhere).

---

[54] [1946] 1 All E.R. 711 at p. 716; 28 T.C. 501.
[55] [1948] 1 All E.R. 400 (H.L.).
[56] [1947] 2 All E.R. 454 at p. 459; 29 T.C. 243; see also *Constantinesco* v. *R.,* 11 T.C. 730; *Mills* v. *Jones,* 14 T.C. 769; affirmed 14 T.C. 785 (H.L.) and *International Combustion Ltd.* v. *Inland Revenue Commissioners,* 16 T.C. 532 royalties in respect of foreign patent.
[57] s. 82 (1), (3), Capital Allowances Act 1968 and s. 387, Income and Corporation Taxes Act 1970 (referred to hereafter as the I.C.T.A. 1970). See *post,* § 1736 *et seq.*

(2) Any person residing in the United Kingdom carrying on a business or trade,[58] in respect of patent rights used or acquired for that person's trade (whether the business or trade is carried on in the United Kingdom or elsewhere).

(3) Any person whether a British subject or not, not resident in the United Kingdom, in respect of United Kingdom patent rights or of any trade or business carried on in the United Kingdom in respect of patent rights used or acquired for that trade.[59]

1025   A. *Allowances*

Expenditure in respect of which allowances may be claimed may be divided as follows:

(1) Expenses incurred in devising an invention and patenting it.

(2) Expenditure on purchase of patent rights.

Patent rights used for the purposes of a trade.

In the case of a trader (company, firm or person) whose profits or gains are chargeable to tax under Case I of Schedule D and where the patent rights are to be used for the purposes of a trade, allowances are to be deducted in computing the trading income for corporation tax or in assessing the profits or gains of the trade to income tax.[60] If the allowance is more than the assessment for the year in which an allowance becomes due then any balance may be carried forward to the following year and so on for succeeding years (without limit).

Patent rights held by non-trader

In the case of a non-trader allowances are to be made by way of discharge or repayment of tax and are available against income from patents.[61] Where the allowance is more than the patent income for the year in which an allowance becomes due then any balance may be carried forward and is available against income from patents in succeeding years.[61]

Income from patents is defined as (1) any royalty or other sum paid in respect of the user of a patent, and (2) any amount on which tax is payable for any accounting period of a company or any year of assessment by virtue of section 379 (3), section 380 or section 381 of the Income and Corporation Taxes Act 1970 [62] and, therefore, is

---

[58] See *Inland Revenue Commissioners* v. *Marine Steam Turbine Co.* [1920] 1 K.B. 193; 12 T.C. 174; a company sold its business for a royalty for a term of years was held not to be carrying on a business.

[59] ss. 108 (1), 129 (1), I.C.T.A. 1970.

[60] s. 385 (1), I.C.T.A. 1970.

[61] s. 385 (2), (3), I.C.T.A. 1970.

[62] s. 388 (1), I.C.T.A. 1970.

deemed to include both royalties and other sums payable in respect of the user of a patent and capital sums received for the sale of patent rights chargeable to tax by reason of the above sections.

1026 **(1) Expenses incurred in devising an invention, patenting and maintaining the patent**

Where a patent is granted, the actual devisor of the invention may claim an allowance equal to the net amount of any expenses incurred by him (whether he was the sole or joint inventor) [63] except where an allowance falls to be made under some other provision of the Income and Corporation Taxes Act 1970.

All fees paid by a trader (whether Patent Office fees, renewal fees for Letters Patent or Patent Agents' charges) or expenses incurred in obtaining for the purposes of the trade the grant of a patent or an extension of the term of a patent may be deducted in the computation of trade profits or in maintaining a patent including litigation expenses for purpose of protecting and enforcing patentees rights. [64]

Similarly fees paid or expenses incurred in connection with any application for a patent which is rejected or abandoned shall be allowable as if the patent had been granted. [64] In the case of a non-trader such fees or expenses may be allowed against income. [65]

1027 **(2) Expenditure on purchase of patent rights**

Where a person incurs capital expenditure (after April 6, 1946) on the purchase of patent rights, there shall be made to him writing-down allowances in respect of that expenditure for the writing-down period. [66]

Expenditure incurred after July 9, 1952, in obtaining a right to acquire in the future patent rights in any invention in respect of which the patent has not yet been granted is deemed to be expenditure on the purchase of patent rights. [67]

Writing-down allowances are calculated by dividing the capital expenditure into the writing-down period. [68] The writing-down period is seventeen years from the accounting period of the company (or year of assessment) in which the capital expenditure is incurred or where the rights purchased are for a lesser period or if the remaining life of the patent is less, that lesser period. [66]

Where a person who has purchased patent rights before the end of the writing-down period either sells the patent rights or part of

[63] s. 382 (2), I.C.T.A. 1970.
[64] s. 132, I.C.T.A. 1970.
[65] s. 382 (1), I.C.T.A. 1970.
[66] s. 378, I.C.T.A. 1970.
[67] s. 388 (4), (5), I.C.T.A. 1970.
[68] s. 75 (2), Capital Allowances Act 1968.

them (for a sum equal to or greater than the amount of capital expenditure remaining unallowed) or the rights come to an end, he will receive no further writing-down allowances.[69]   Where part of the patent rights are sold for less than the amount of capital expenditure remaining unallowed, then the writing-down allowance is adjusted (by dividing the difference between the sale price and the unallowed sum by the number of years of writing-down period left).[70]

Where before the end of such writing-down period such patent rights come to an end or the net proceeds of the sale (so far as they consist of capital sums) are less than the amount of the capital expenditure remaining unallowed, a balancing allowance equal to the amount of capital expenditure remaining unallowed (less the net proceeds of the sale in the case of a sale) shall be made to that person.[71] However, where such net proceeds of the sale exceed the amount of the capital expenditure remaining unallowed (if any) a balancing charge equal to the excess (or where the outstanding unallowed expenditure is nil, to the net proceeds) will be made provided that the total amount on which a balancing charge is made in respect of any expenditure shall not exceed the total writing-down allowances actually made in respect of that expenditure.[72]   In addition to such a balancing charge, there will be a capital gain which is liable to tax (see below).

1028   B. *Taxation of Receipts*

Taxation of sums received in respect of patent rights may be considered as follows:
 (1) Charges on capital sums received for sale of patent rights;
 (2) Charges on royalties received in respect of patent rights;
 (3) Miscellaneous.

1029   **(1) Sale of patent rights**
Capital sums received for the sale of any patent rights [73] when the sale took place after April 6, 1946, or capital sums received after July 9, 1952, for the sale of part of any patent right (which includes any assignment or licence) or any sum received for a right to acquire, in the future, patent rights as respects any invention in respect of which the patent has not yet been granted,[73] are chargeable to tax as follows:

[69] s. 379 (1), I.C.T.A. 1970.
[70] s. 379 (4), I.C.T.A. 1970.
[71] s. 379 (2), I.C.T.A. 1970.
[72] s. 379 (3), (6), I.C.T.A. 1970.
[73] s. 388, I.C.T.A. 1970.

1030   (a) *Vendor resident in U.K.*

Where the vendor is resident in the United Kingdom he will normally be charged to tax under Case VI of Schedule D on one-sixth of the sum liable to tax for the accounting period or year of assessment in which such capital sum is received and for each of the succeeding five years. However, the vendor may elect to be charged upon the whole sum for the accounting period or year of assessment in which it is received, in which case he must give notice in writing to the Inspector of Taxes not later than two years after the end of the chargeable period in which the capital sum was received.[74]

Where the patent rights to be sold were acquired by the vendor by payment of a capital sum, the vendor will be charged on the net capital gain. The net proceeds of sale when the vendor sells the patent rights are reduced by the amount the vendor paid for the patent rights for the purposes of assessment for tax.[75] Patent rights and rights to be acquired in the future in respect of an invention for which patent is not yet granted are not chargeable assets for the purposes of Case VII and therefore not subject to short-term capital gains.[76]

1031   *Deaths, windings up and partnership changes* [77]

If the vendor dies or the trade of a partnership is discontinued or being a body corporate is wound up before the beginning of the last six years, no sums will be charged for any year subsequent to the year in which the death or discontinuance takes place or the winding up commences, but the amount to be charged for the year or accounting period in which the death or discontinuance takes place or winding up commences will be the total amount which but for the death or discontinuance or winding up would be charged for subsequent years.

In the case of a death, the personal representatives are entitled to have the income tax payable out of the deceased's estate reduced so as not to exceed the total amount of income tax which would have been payable by the deceased if the charge had been spread over the period of years from when the capital sum was received until the year of death.

In the case of the discontinuance of a partnership, the additional amount on which tax is chargeable is to be apportioned among the members of the partnership according to their respective shares in the partnership profits, immediately before the discontinuance. Each partner (or, if dead, his personal representatives) has the same right to reduction of income tax payable as in the case of a death.

[74] s. 380 (1), I.C.T.A. 1970.   [75] s. 380 (4), I.C.T.A. 1970.
[76] s. 161 (5), I.C.T.A. 1970.   [77] s. 381, I.C.T.A. 1970.

1032 (b) Vendor non-resident

Where the vendor is not resident in the United Kingdom and sells United Kingdom patent rights, the vendor is assessable under Case VI of Schedule D and provision is made for deduction of tax by the person by or through whom any payment of capital sum is made at the standard rate in force at the time of payment and for paying over the tax to the Inland Revenue.[78]

The non-resident vendor may elect (by notice in writing to the Commissioners of Inland Revenue to be given not later than two years after the end of the accounting period or years of assessment) to spread the capital sum over six years, in which case repayment will then be made on a year-by-year assessment.[78] Further, the non-resident vendor may apply for repayment of part of the tax on account of the cost of acquiring the patent rights.

1033 **Sale of patent rights not at arm's length**

If the vendor or purchaser has control over the other (e.g. purchase or sale by majority shareholder in company) or if they are under common control (e.g. subsidiary companies controlled by parent company) then the value of the patent rights in open market may be substituted for the actual sale price.[79] These provisions, however, do not apply to the sale of know-how.

1034 **(2) Charges on royalties**

A manufacturer is not allowed to make any deduction from his profits for purposes of income tax in respect of royalties which he has paid,[80] but is entitled, where he pays royalties out of profits or gains in respect of which he has paid income tax, to deduct from his payments to the patentee a sum representing the tax at the standard rate for the year in which the royalties are payable[81]; or where the royalty is paid out of profits on which income tax has not wholly been paid the person through whom the royalty is paid *must* deduct income tax and account for the sum deducted to the Commissioners of Inland Revenue.[82]

As Lord Greene M.R. said in *Inland Revenue Commissioners* v. *British Salmson Aero Engines Limited* [83]: " . . . where a business is

---

[78] s. 380 (2), (3), I.C.T.A. 1970.
[79] s. 78, Sched. 7, Capital Allowances Act 1968.
[80] s. 130 (n), I.C.T.A. 1970; see *Paterson Engineering Co. Ltd.* v. *Dutt*, 25 T.C. 43, royalty relating to use of secret processes, advice and use of trade marks held to be deductible but royalty relating to use of patents not deductible.
[81] s. 52 (2) (a), I.C.T.A. 1970; see *Desoutter Brothers Ltd.* v. *Hanger & Co. Ltd. and Artificial Limb Makers Ltd.* [1936] 1 All E.R. 535, instalment of lump sum paid in advance for anticipated user held to be capital sum— income tax therefore not deductible.
[82] s. 53 (1) (b), I.C.T.A. 1970.   [83] [1938] 2 K.B. 482 at p. 496; 22 T.C. 29.

being carried on with the use of patents in respect of which royalties or other sums fall to be paid, the person carrying on the business, in computing his profits, cannot deduct the sums in question. On the other hand, he is entitled under rule 19 (now section 52 (2)) and bound under rule 21 (now section 53) when he comes to make the payment, to deduct the tax."

Deduction of income tax on royalties at the source secures the collection of the tax on the profits derived from the working of patents in the United Kingdom payable to patentees who reside abroad and have no agent resident in this country; an agreement to pay the full amount of a royalty without any deduction is void.[84]

In cases of failure to deduct the tax there is no prohibition against making a direct assessment on the recipient of such royalties.[85]

Where a person receives a royalty or other non-capital payment in respect of the past user of a patent which extended over six or more years, that person may require that the income tax (including surtax) or corporation tax payable shall be reduced so as not to exceed the total amount of income or corporation tax which would have been payable if the payment had been made in six equal instalments at yearly intervals, the last of which being made on the date on which the payment was in fact made.[86] If such payment is in respect of at least two years but less than six years' user the patentee may claim an adjustment so that his liability is spread over the number of complete years in the period of user.[87]

1035   (3) Miscellaneous

Invention income

An individual's income derived from an invention actually devised and patented by him whether alone or jointly is treated as earned income for the purposes of earned income relief.[88]

Double taxation agreements [89]

Sums on the sale of patent rights and patent royalties arising in one country and payable to a resident of another country may be exempt from tax.

[The next paragraph is 1131]

---

[84] s. 106 (2), Taxes Management Act 1970.
[85] *Wild* v. *Ionides*, 9 T.C. 392.
[86] s. 384 (1), (4), I.C.T.A. 1970.
[87] s. 384 (2), I.C.T.A. 1970.
[88] s. 383, I.C.T.A. 1970.
[89] Pt. XVIII, I.C.T.A. 1970.

APPENDIX

TABLE OF CONTENTS

PART 1

PART 2

PART 3

PART 4

PART 1

Patents Act 1949

ARRANGEMENT OF SECTIONS

Appendix—Part 1

[412]

PATENTS ACT 1949

An Act to consolidate certain enactments relating to patents.

[16th December, 1949.]

Application, Investigation, Opposition, Etc.

1131   Persons entitled to make application

1.—(1) An application for a patent for an invention may be made by any of the following persons, that is to say:

(*a*) by any person claiming to be the true and first inventor of the invention;

(*b*) by any person being the assignee of the person claiming to be the true and first inventor in respect of the right to make such an application;

and may be made by that person either alone or jointly with any other person.

(2) Without prejudice to the foregoing provisions of this section, an application for a patent for an invention in respect of which protection has been applied for in a convention country may be made by the person by whom the application for protection was made or by the assignee of that person:

Provided that no application shall be made by virtue of this subsection after the expiration of twelve months from the date of the application for protection in a convention country or, where more than one such application for protection has been made, from the date of the first application.

(3) An application for a patent may be made under subsection (1) or subsection (2) of this section by the personal representative of any deceased person who, immediately before his death, was entitled to make such an application.

(4) An application for a patent made by virtue of subsection (2) of this section is in this Act referred to as a convention application.

1132   Application

2.—(1) Every application for a patent shall be made in the prescribed form and shall be filed at the Patent Office in the prescribed manner.

(2) If the application (not being a convention application) is made by virtue of an assignment of the right to apply for a patent for the invention, there shall be furnished with the application or within such period as may be prescribed after the filing of the application a declaration, signed by the person claiming to be the true and first inventor or his personal representative, stating that he assents to the making of the application.

(3) Every application (other than a convention application) shall state that the applicant is in possession of the invention and shall name the person claiming to be the true and first inventor; and where the person so claiming is not the applicant or one of the applicants, the application shall contain a declaration that the applicant believes him to be the true and first inventor.

(4) Every convention application shall specify the date on which and the convention country in which the application for protection,

or the first such application, was made, and shall state that no application for protection in respect of the invention had been made in a convention country before that date by the applicant or any person from whom he derives title.

(5) Where applications for protection have been made in one or more convention countries in respect of two or more inventions which are cognate or of which one is a modification of another, a single convention application may, subject to the provisions of section four of this Act, be made in respect of those inventions at any time within twelve months from the date of the earliest of the said applications for protection:

Provided that the fee payable on the making of any such application shall be the same as if separate applications had been made in respect of each of the said inventions; and the requirements of the last foregoing subsection shall in the case of any such application apply separately to the applications for protection in respect of each of the said inventions.

1133 Complete and provisional specifications

3.—(1) Every application for a patent (other than a convention application) shall be accompanied by either a complete specification or a provisional specification; and every convention application shall be accompanied by a complete specification.

(2) Where an application for a patent is accompanied by a provisional specification, a complete specification shall be filed within twelve months from the date of filing of the application and if the complete specification is not so filed the application shall be deemed to be abandoned:

Provided that the complete specification may be filed at any time after twelve months but within fifteen months from the date aforesaid if a request to that effect is made to the comptroller and the prescribed fee paid on or before the date on which the specification is filed.

(3) Where two or more applications accompanied by provisional specifications have been filed in respect of inventions which are cognate or of which one is a modification of another, a single complete specification may, subject to the provisions of this and the next following section, be filed in pursuance of those applications, or, if more than one complete specification has been filed, may with the leave of the comptroller be proceeded with in respect of those applications.

(4) Where an application for a patent (not being a convention application) is accompanied by a specification purporting to be a complete specification, the comptroller may, if the applicant so requests at any time before the acceptance of the specification, direct that it shall be treated for the purposes of this Act as a provisional specification, and proceed with the application accordingly.

(5) Where a complete specification has been filed in pursuance of an application for a patent accompanied by a provisional specification or by a specification treated by virtue of a direction under the last foregoing subsection as a provisional specification, the comptroller may, if the applicant so requests at any time before the acceptance

of the complete specification, cancel the provisional specification and post-date the application to the date of filing of the complete specification.

1134   Contents of specification

4.—(1) Every specification, whether complete or provisional, shall describe the invention, and shall begin with a title indicating the subject to which the invention relates.

(2) Subject to any rules made by the Board of Trade under this Act, drawings may, and shall if the comptroller so requires, be supplied for the purposes of any specification, whether complete or provisional; and any drawing so supplied shall, unless the comptroller otherwise directs, be deemed to form part of the specification, and references in this Act to a specification shall be construed accordingly.

(3) Every complete specification—

     (a) shall particularly describe the invention and the method by which it is to be performed;

     (b) shall disclose the best method of performing the invention which is known to the applicant and for which he is entitled to claim protection; and

     (c) shall end with a claim or claims defining the scope of the invention claimed.

(4) The claim or claims of a complete specification must relate to a single invention, must be clear and succinct, and must be fairly based on the matter disclosed in the specification.

(5) Rules made by the Board of Trade under this Act may require that in such cases as may be prescribed by the rules, a declaration as to the inventorship of the invention, in such form as may be so prescribed, shall be furnished with the complete specification or within such period as may be so prescribed after the filing of that specification.

(6) Subject to the foregoing provisions of this section, a complete specification filed after a provisional specification, or filed with a convention application, may include claims in respect of developments of or additions to the invention which was described in the provisional specification or, as the case may be, the invention in respect of which the application for protection was made in a convention country, being developments or additions in respect of which the applicant would be entitled under the provisions of section one of this Act to make a separate application for a patent.

(7) Where a complete specification claims a new substance, the claim shall be construed as not extending to that substance when found in nature.

1135   Priority date of claims of complete specification

5.—(1) Every claim of a complete specification shall have effect from the date prescribed by this section in relation to that claim (in this Act referred to as the priority date); and a patent shall not be invalidated by reason only of the publication or use of the invention, so far as claimed in any claim of the complete specification, on or after the priority date of that claim, or by the grant of another patent upon a specification claiming the same invention in a claim of the same or later priority date.

(2) Where the complete specification is filed in pursuance of a single application accompanied by a provisional specification or by a specification which is treated by virtue of a direction under subsection (4) of section three of this Act as a provisional specification, and the claim is fairly based on the matter disclosed in that specification, the priority date of that claim shall be the date of filing of the application.

(3) Where the complete specification is filed or proceeded with in pursuance of two or more applications accompanied by such specifications as are mentioned in the last foregoing subsection, and the claim is fairly based on the matter disclosed in one of those specifications, the priority date of that claim shall be the date of filing of the application accompanied by that specification.

(4) Where the complete specification is filed in pursuance of a convention application and the claim is fairly based on the matter disclosed in the application for protection in a convention country or, where the convention application is founded upon more than one such application for protection, in one of those applications, the priority date of that claim shall be the date of the relevant application for protection.

(5) Where, under the foregoing provisions of this section, any claim of a complete specification would, but for this provision, have two or more priority dates, the priority date of that claim shall be the earlier or earliest of those dates.

(6) In any case to which subsections (2) to (5) of this section do not apply, the priority date of a claim shall be the date of filing of the complete specification.

1136 Examination of application

6.—(1) When the complete specification has been filed in respect of an application for a patent, the application and specification or specifications shall be referred by the comptroller to an examiner.

(2) If the examiner reports that the application or any specification filed in pursuance thereof does not comply with the requirements of this Act or of any rules made by the Board of Trade thereunder, or that there is lawful ground of objection to the grant of a patent in pursuance of the application, the comptroller may either—

(a) refuse to proceed with the application; or

(b) require the application or any such specification as aforesaid to be amended before he proceeds with the application.

(3) At any time after an application has been filed under this Act and before acceptance of the complete specification, the comptroller may, at the request of the applicant and upon payment of the prescribed fee, direct that the application shall be post-dated to such date as may be specified in the request:

Provided that—

(a) no application shall be post-dated under this subsection to a date later than six months from the date on which it was actually made or would, but for this subsection, be deemed to have been made; and

[417]

(*b*) a convention application shall not be post-dated under this subsection to a date later than the last date on which, under the foregoing provisions of this Act, the application could have been made.

(4) Where an application or specification filed under this Act is amended before acceptance of the complete specification, the comptroller may direct that the application or specification shall be post-dated to the date on which it is amended or, if it has been returned to the applicant, to the date on which it is refiled.

(5) Rules made by the Board of Trade under this Act may make provision for securing that where, at any time after an application or specification has been filed under this Act and before acceptance of the complete specification, a fresh application or specification is filed in respect of any part of the subject matter of the first-mentioned application or specification, the comptroller may direct that the fresh application or specification shall be ante-dated to a date not earlier than the date of filing of the first-mentioned application or specification.

(6) An appeal shall lie from any decision of the comptroller under subsection (2) or subsection (4) of this section.

1137 **Search for anticipation by previous publication**

7.—(1) Subject to the provisions of the last foregoing section, the examiner to whom an application for a patent is referred under this Act shall make investigation for the purpose of ascertaining whether the invention, so far as claimed in any claim of the complete specification, has been published before the date of filing of the applicant's complete specification in any specification filed in pursuance of an application for a patent made in the United Kingdom and dated within fifty years next before that date.

(2) The examiner shall, in addition, make such investigation as the comptroller may direct for the purpose of ascertaining whether the invention, so far as claimed in any claim of the complete specification, has been published in the United Kingdom before the date of filing of the applicant's complete specification in any other document (not being a document of any class described in subsection (1) of section fifty of this Act).

(3) If it appears to the comptroller that the invention, so far as claimed in any claim of the complete specification, has been published as aforesaid, he may refuse to accept the specification unless the applicant either—

(*a*) shows to the satisfaction of the comptroller that the priority date of the claim of his complete specification is not later than the date on which the relevant document was published; or

(*b*) amends his complete specification to the satisfaction of the comptroller.

(4) An appeal shall lie from any decision of the comptroller under this section.

1138 Search for anticipation by prior claim

8.—(1) In addition to the investigation required by the last foregoing section, the examiner shall make investigation for the purpose of ascertaining whether the invention, so far as claimed in any claim of the complete specification, is claimed in any claim of any other complete specification published on or after the date of filing of the applicant's complete specification, being a specification filed—

(a) in pursuance of an application for a patent made in the United Kingdom and dated before that date; or

(b) in pursuance of a convention application founded upon an application for protection made in a convention country before that date.

(2) If it appears to the comptroller that the said invention is claimed in a claim of any such other specification as aforesaid, he may, subject to the provisions of this section, direct that a reference to that other specification shall be inserted by way of notice to the public in the applicant's complete specification unless within such time as may be prescribed either—

(a) the applicant shows to the satisfaction of the comptroller that the priority date of his claim is not later than the priority date of the claim of the said other specification; or

(b) the complete specification is amended to the satisfaction of the comptroller.

(3) If in consequence of the investigation under section seven of this Act or otherwise it appears to the comptroller—

(a) that the invention, so far as claimed in any claim of the applicant's complete specification, has been claimed in any such specification as is mentioned in subsection (1) of that section; and

(b) that the other specification was published on or after the priority date of the applicant's claim,

then unless it has been shown to the satisfaction of the comptroller under that section that the priority date of the applicant's claim is not later than the priority date of the claim of that other specification, the provisions of subsection (2) of this section shall apply as they apply in relation to a specification published on or after the date of filing of the applicant's complete specification.

(4) The powers of the comptroller under this section to direct the insertion of a reference to another specification may be exercised either before or after a patent has been granted for the invention claimed in that other specification, but any direction given before the grant of such a patent shall be of no effect unless and until such a patent is granted.

(5) An appeal shall lie from any direction of the comptroller under this section.

1139 Reference in case of potential infringement

9.—(1) If, in consequence of the investigations required by the foregoing provisions of this Act or of proceedings under section fourteen or section thirty-three of this Act, it appears to the comptroller that an invention in respect of which application for a patent has been made cannot be performed without substantial risk of infringement of a claim of any other patent, he may direct that a reference to that other patent shall be inserted in the applicant's complete specification by way of notice to the public unless within such time as may be prescribed either—

(a) the applicant shows to the satisfaction of the comptroller that there are reasonable grounds for contesting the validity of the said claim of the other patent; or

(b) the complete specification is amended to the satisfaction of the comptroller.

(2) Where, after a reference to another patent has been inserted in a complete specification in pursuance of a direction under the foregoing subsection,—

(a) that other patent is revoked or otherwise ceases to be in force; or

(b) the specification of that other patent is amended by the deletion of the relevant claim; or

(c) it is found, in proceedings before the court or the comptroller, that the relevant claim of that other patent is invalid or is not infringed by any working of the applicant's invention,

the comptroller may, on the application of the applicant, delete the reference to that other patent.

(3) An appeal shall lie from any decision or direction of the comptroller under this section.

1140 Refusal of application in certain cases

10.—(1) If it appears to the comptroller in the case of any application for a patent—

(a) that it is frivolous on the ground that it claims as an invention anything obviously contrary to well-established natural laws; or

(b) that the use of the invention in respect of which the application is made would be contrary to law or morality; or

(c) that it claims as an invention a substance capable of being used as food or medicine which is a mixture of known ingredients possessing only the aggregate of the known properties of the ingredients, or that it claims as an invention a process producing such a substance by mere admixture,

he may refuse the application.

(2) If it appears to the comptroller that any invention in respect of which an application for a patent is made might be used in any manner contrary to law, he may refuse the application unless the specification is amended by the insertion of such disclaimer in respect of that use of the invention, or such other reference to the illegality thereof, as the comptroller thinks fit.

(3) An appeal shall lie from any decision of the comptroller under this section.

1141 Supplementary provisions as to searches, etc.

11.—(1) The powers of the comptroller under section eight or section nine of this Act may be exercised either before or after the complete specification has been accepted or a patent granted to the applicant, and references in those sections to the applicant shall accordingly be construed as including references to the patentee.

(2) Where a complete specification is amended under the foregoing provisions of this Act before it has been accepted, the amended specification shall be examined and investigated in like manner as the original specification.

(3) The examination and investigations required by the foregoing provisions of this Act shall not be deemed to warrant the validity of any patent, and no liability shall be incurred by the Board of Trade or any officer thereof by reason of or in connection with any such examination or investigation or any report or other proceedings consequent thereon.

1142 Time for putting application in order for acceptance

12.—(1) An application for a patent shall be void unless within *twelve months from the date of filing of the complete specification* [such period, beginning with the date of filing of the complete specification, as may be prescribed [1]], or within such longer period as may be allowed under the following provisions of this section, the applicant has complied with all requirements imposed on him by or under this Act, whether in connection with the complete specification or otherwise in relation to the application; and where the application or any specification or, in the case of a convention application, any document filed as part of the application, has been returned to the applicant by the comptroller in the course of the proceedings, the applicant shall not be deemed to have complied with the said requirements unless and until he has refiled it.

(1A) [2] The period prescribed for the purposes of the foregoing subsection shall not be shorter than twelve months or longer than four years.

(2) The period allowed by subsection (1) of this section shall be extended to such period, *not exceeding fifteen months from the date of filing of the complete specification* [ending not later than three months after the date on which the period allowed under that subsection (apart from any extension thereof) would otherwise have expired,[1]] as may be specified in a notice given by the applicant to the comptroller, if the notice is given and the prescribed fee paid before the expiration of the period so specified.

(3) If at the expiration of the period allowed under the foregoing provisions of this section an appeal to the Appeal Tribunal is pending under any of the provisions of this Act in respect of the application (or, in the case of an application for a patent of addition, either in respect of that application or in respect of the application for the patent for the main invention) or the time within which such an appeal could be brought in accordance with the rules of that Tribunal (apart from any future extension of time thereunder) has not expired, then—

[1] The words in square brackets were substituted for the original wording (printed in italics) by the Patents Act 1957, *post*, § 1250 *et seq.*
[2] Subs. (1A) was inserted by the Patents Act 1957, *post*, § 1250.

(*a*) where such an appeal is pending, or is brought within the time aforesaid or before the expiration of any extension of that time granted (in the case of a first extension) on an application made within that time or (in the case of a subsequent extension) on an application made before the expiration of the last previous extension, the said period shall be extended until such date as the Appeal Tribunal may determine;

(*b*) where no such appeal is pending or is so brought, the said period shall continue until the end of the time aforesaid, or, if any extension of that time is granted as aforesaid, until the expiration of the extension or last extension so granted.

1143   Acceptance and publication of complete specification

13.—(1) Subject to the provisions of the last foregoing section, the complete specification filed in pursuance of an application for a patent may be accepted by the comptroller at any time after the applicant has complied with the requirements mentioned in subsection (1) of that section, and if not so accepted within the period allowed under that section for compliance with those requirements, shall be accepted as soon as may be thereafter:

Provided that the applicant may give notice to the comptroller requesting him to postpone acceptance until such date, not being later than fifteen months from the date of filing of the complete specification, as may be specified in the notice; and if such notice is given and, where the notice requests a postponement to a date later than twelve months from the date aforesaid, the prescribed fee is paid, the comptroller may postpone acceptance accordingly.

(2) On the acceptance of a complete specification the comptroller shall give notice to the applicant, and shall advertise in the Journal the fact that the specification has been accepted and the date on which the application and the specification or specifications filed in pursuance thereof will be open to public inspection.

(3) Any reference in this Act to the date of publication of a complete specification shall be construed as a reference to the date advertised as aforesaid.

(4) After the date of the publication of a complete specification and until the sealing of a patent in respect thereof, the applicant shall have the like privileges and rights as if a patent for the invention had been sealed on the date of the publication of the complete specification:

Provided that an applicant shall not be entitled to institute any proceedings for infringement until the patent has been sealed.

1144   Opposition to grant of patent

14.—(1) At any time within three months from the date of the publication of a complete specification under this Act, any person interested may give notice to the comptroller of opposition to the grant of the patent on any of the following grounds:

(*a*) that the applicant for the patent, or the person described in the application as the true and first inventor, obtained the invention or any part thereof from him, or from a person of whom he is the personal representative;

(b) that the invention, so far as claimed in any claim of the complete specification, has been published in the United Kingdom, before the priority date of the claim—

    (i) in any specification filed in pursuance of an application for a patent made in the United Kingdom and dated within fifty years next before the date of filing of the applicant's complete specification;

    (ii) in any other document (not being a document of any class described in subsection (1) of section fifty of this Act);

(c) that the invention, so far as claimed in any claim of the complete specification, is claimed in any claim of a complete specification published on or after the priority date of the applicant's claim and filed in pursuance of an application for a patent in the United Kingdom, being a claim of which the priority date is earlier than that of the applicant's claim;

(d) that the invention, so far as claimed in any claim of the complete specification, was used in the United Kingdom before the priority date of that claim;

(e) that the invention, so far as claimed in any claim of the complete specification, is obvious and clearly does not involve any inventive step having regard to matter published as mentioned in paragraph (b) of this subsection, or having regard to what was used in the United Kingdom before the priority date of the applicant's claim;

(f) that the subject of any claim of the complete specification is not an invention within the meaning of this Act;

(g) that the complete specification does not sufficiently and fairly describe the invention or the method by which it is to be performed;

(h) that, in the case of a convention application, the application was not made within twelve months from the date of the first application for protection for the invention made in a convention country by the applicant or a person from whom he derives title,

but on no other ground.

(2) Where any such notice is given, the comptroller shall give notice of the opposition to the applicant, and shall give to the applicant and the opponent an opportunity to be heard before he decides on the case.

(3) The grant of a patent shall not be refused on the ground specified in paragraph (c) of subsection (1) of this section if no patent has been granted in pursuance of the application mentioned in that paragraph; and for the purposes of paragraph (d) or paragraph (e) of the said subsection (1) no account shall be taken of any secret use.

(4) An appeal shall lie from any decision of the comptroller under this section.

1145 Refusal of patent without opposition

15.—(1) If at any time after the acceptance of the complete specification filed in pursuance of an application for a patent and before
the grant of a patent thereon it comes to the notice of the comptroller,
otherwise than in consequence of proceedings in opposition to the
grant under the last foregoing section, that the invention, so far as
claimed in any claim of the complete specification, has been published
in the United Kingdom before the priority date of the claim—

(*a*) in any specification filed in pursuance of an application for a
patent made in the United Kingdom and dated within fifty
years next before the date of filing of the applicant's complete
specification; or

(*b*) in any other document (not being a document of any class
described in subsection (1) of section fifty of this Act),

the comptroller may refuse to grant the patent unless within such
time as may be prescribed the complete specification is amended to
his satisfaction.

(2) An appeal shall lie from any decision of the comptroller under
this section.

1146 Mention of inventor as such in patent

16.—(1) If the comptroller is satisfied, upon a request or claim
made in accordance with the provisions of this section—

(*a*) that the person in respect of or by whom the request or claim
is made is the inventor of an invention in respect of which
application for a patent has been made, or of a substantial
part of that invention; and

(*b*) that the application for the patent is a direct consequence of
his being the inventor,

the comptroller shall, subject to the provisions of this section, cause
him to be mentioned as inventor in any patent granted in pursuance
of the application, in the complete specification, and in the register
of patents:

Provided that the mention of any person as inventor under this
section shall not confer or derogate from any rights under the patent.

(2) For the purposes of this section the actual deviser of an
invention or a part of an invention shall be deemed to be the inventor,
notwithstanding that any other person is for any of the other purposes
of this Act treated as the true and first inventor; and no person
shall be deemed to be the inventor of an invention or a part of an
invention by reason only that it was imported by him into the United
Kingdom.

(3) A request that any person shall be mentioned as aforesaid may
be made in the prescribed manner by the applicant for the patent or
(where the person alleged to be the inventor is not the applicant or
one of the applicants) by the applicant and that person.

(4) If any person (other than a person in respect of whom a
request in relation to the application in question has been made under
the last foregoing subsection) desires to be mentioned as aforesaid,
he may make a claim in the prescribed manner in that behalf.

(5) A request or claim under the foregoing provisions of this

section must be made not later than two months after the date of the publication of the complete specification, or within such further period (not exceeding one month) as the comptroller may, on an application made to him in that behalf before the expiration of the said period of two months and subject to payment of the prescribed fee, allow.

(6) No request or claim under the foregoing provisions of this section shall be entertained if it appears to the comptroller that the request or claim is based upon facts which, if proved in the case of an opposition under the provisions of paragraph (a) of subsection (1) of section fourteen of this Act by the person in respect of or by whom the request or claim is made, would have entitled him to relief under that section.

(7) Subject to the provisions of the last foregoing subsection, where a claim is made under subsection (4) of this section, the comptroller shall give notice of the claim to every applicant for the patent (not being the claimant) and to any other person whom the comptroller may consider to be interested; and before deciding upon any request or claim made under subsection (3) or subsection (4) of this section, the comptroller shall, if required, hear the person in respect of or by whom the request or claim is made, and, in the case of a claim under the said subsection (4), any person to whom notice of the claim has been given as aforesaid.

(8) Where any person has been mentioned as inventor in pursuance of this section, any other person who alleges that he ought not to have been so mentioned may at any time apply to the comptroller for a certificate to that effect, and the comptroller may, after hearing, if required, any person whom he may consider to be interested, issue such a certificate, and if he does so, he shall rectify the specification and the register accordingly.

(9) An appeal shall lie from any decision of the comptroller under this section.

1147   Substitution of applicants, etc.

17.—(1) If the comptroller is satisfied, on a claim made in the prescribed manner at any time before a patent has been granted, that by virtue of any assignment or agreement made by the applicant or one of the applicants for the patent, or by operation of law, the claimant would, if the patent were then granted, be entitled thereto or to the interest of the applicant therein, or to an undivided share of the patent or of that interest, the comptroller may, subject to the provisions of this section, direct that the application shall proceed in the name of the claimant or in the names of the claimant and the applicant or the other joint applicant or applicants, according as the case may require.

(2) No such direction as aforesaid shall be given by virtue of any assignment or agreement made by one of two or more joint applicants for a patent except with the consent of the other joint applicant or applicants.

(3) No such direction as aforesaid shall be given by virtue of any assignment or agreement for the assignment of the benefit of an invention unless either—

(*a*) the invention is identified therein by reference to the number of the application for the patent; or

(*b*) there is produced to the comptroller an acknowledgment by the person by whom the assignment or agreement was made that the assignment or agreement relates to the invention in respect of which that application is made; or

(*c*) the rights of the claimant in respect of the invention have been finally established by a decision of any court or by a determination of the comptroller or the Appeal Tribunal under the following provisions of this Act.

(4) Where one of two or more joint applicants for a patent dies at any time before the patent has been granted, the comptroller may, upon a request in that behalf made by the survivor or survivors, and with the consent of the personal representative of the deceased, direct that the application shall proceed in the name of the survivor or survivors alone.

(5) If any dispute arises between joint applicants for a patent whether or in what manner the application should be proceeded with, the comptroller may, upon application made to him in the prescribed manner by any of the parties, and after giving to all parties concerned an opportunity to be heard, give such directions as he thinks fit for enabling the application to proceed in the name of one or more of the parties alone or for regulating the manner in which it shall be proceeded with, or for both those purposes, according as the case may require.

(6) An appeal shall lie from any decision of the comptroller under this section.

1148 **Provisions for secrecy of certain inventions**

18.—(1) Where, either before or after the commencement of this Act, an application for a patent has been made in respect of an invention, and it appears to the comptroller that the invention is one of a class notified to him by a competent authority as relevant for defence purposes, he may give directions for prohibiting or restricting the publication of information with respect to the invention, or the communication of such information to any person or class of persons specified in the directions; and while such directions are in force the application may, subject to the directions, proceed up to the acceptance of the complete specification, but the acceptance shall not be advertised nor the specification published, and no patent shall be granted in pursuance of the application.

(2) Where the comptroller gives any such directions as aforesaid, he shall give notice of the application and of the directions to a competent authority, and thereupon the following provisions shall have effect, that is to say:

(*a*) the competent authority shall, upon receipt of such notice, consider whether the publication of the invention would be prejudicial to the defence of the realm and unless a notice under paragraph (*c*) of this subsection has previously been given by that authority to the comptroller, shall reconsider that question before the expiration of nine months from the date of filing of the application for the patent and at least once in every subsequent year;

(*b*) for the purpose aforesaid, the competent authority may, at any time after the complete specification has been accepted or, with the consent of the applicant, at any time before the complete specification has been accepted, inspect the application and any documents furnished to the comptroller in connection therewith;

(*c*) if upon consideration of the invention at any time it appears to the competent authority that the publication of the invention would not, or would no longer, be prejudicial to the defence of the realm, that authority shall give notice to the comptroller to that effect;

(*d*) on the receipt of any such notice the comptroller shall revoke the directions and may, subject to such conditions, if any, as he thinks fit, extend the time for doing anything required or authorised to be done by or under this Act in connection with the application, whether or not that time has previously expired.

1149 (3) Where a complete specification filed in pursuance of an application for a patent for an invention in respect of which directions have been given under this section or under section twelve of the Atomic Energy Act, 1946, is accepted during the continuance in force of the directions, then—

(*a*) if any use of the invention is made during the continuance in force of the directions by or on behalf of or to the order of a Government department, the provisions of sections forty-six to forty-nine of this Act shall apply in relation to that use as if the patent had been granted for the invention; and

(*b*) if it appears to a competent authority that the applicant for the patent has suffered hardship by reason of the continuance in force of the directions, that authority may, with the consent of the Treasury, make to him such payment (if any) by way of compensation as appears to them to be reasonable having regard to the novelty and utility of the invention and the purpose for which it is designed, and to any other relevant circumstances.

(4) Where a patent is granted in pursuance of an application in respect of which directions have been given under this section or under section twelve of the Atomic Energy Act, 1946, no renewal fees shall be payable in respect of any period during which those directions were in force.

(5) No person resident in the United Kingdom shall, except under the authority of a written permit granted by or on behalf of the comptroller, make or cause to be made any application outside the United Kingdom for the grant of a patent for an invention unless—

(*a*) an application for a patent for the same invention has been made in the United Kingdom not less than six weeks before the application outside the United Kingdom; and

(*b*) either no directions have been given under subsection (1) of this section or under section twelve of the Atomic Energy Act,

1946, in relation to the application in the United Kingdom, or all such directions have been revoked:

Provided that this subsection shall not apply in relation to an invention for which an application for protection has first been filed in a country outside the United Kingdom by a person resident outside the United Kingdom.

(6) If any person fails to comply with any direction given under this section or makes or causes to be made an application for the grant of a patent in contravention of this section, he shall be guilty of an offence and liable—

(a) on summary conviction, to imprisonment for a term not exceeding three months or to a fine not exceeding one hundred pounds, or to both such imprisonment and such fine, or

(b) on conviction on indictment, to imprisonment for a term not exceeding two years or to a fine not exceeding five hundred pounds, or to both such imprisonment and such fine.

(7) In this section the expression "competent authority" means a Secretary of State, the Admiralty or the Minister of Supply.[2a]

Grant, Effect and Term of Patent

1150   Grant and sealing of patent

19.—(1) Subject to the provisions of this Act with respect to opposition, and to any other power of the comptroller to refuse the grant, a patent sealed with the seal of the Patent Office shall, if the prescribed request is made within the time allowed under this section, be granted to the applicant or applicants within that time or as soon as may be thereafter; and the date on which the patent is sealed shall be entered in the register of patents.

(2) Subject to the following provisions of this Act with respect to patents of addition, a request under this section for the sealing of a patent shall be made not later than the expiration of four months from the date of the publication of the complete specification:

Provided that—

(a) where at the expiration of the said four months any proceeding in relation to the application for the patent is pending in any court or before the comptroller or the Appeal Tribunal, the request may be made within the prescribed period after the final determination of that proceeding;

(b) where the applicant or one of the applicants has died before the expiration of the time within which under the provisions of this subsection the request could otherwise be made, the said request may be made at any time within twelve months after the date of the death or at such later time as the comptroller may allow.

(3) The period within which under the last foregoing subsection a request for the sealing of a patent may be made may from time to time be extended by the comptroller to such longer period as may be specified in an application made to him in that behalf, if the application is made and the prescribed fee paid within that longer period:

2a See S.I. 1971 No. 719.

Provided that the first-mentioned period shall not be extended under this subsection by more than six months or such shorter period as may be prescribed.

(4) Where in any case the longest period for making a request for the sealing of a patent allowable in that case by or under the foregoing provisions of this section has been allowed, and it is proved to the satisfaction of the comptroller that hardship would arise in connection with the prosecution by an applicant of an application for a patent in any country outside the United Kingdom unless that period is extended, that period may be extended from time to time to such longer period as appears to the comptroller to be necessary in order to prevent that hardship arising if an application in that behalf is made to him, and the prescribed fee is paid, within the first-mentioned period, or in the case of a second or subsequent application under this subsection, within the period to which that period was extended on the last preceding application thereunder.

(5) For the purposes of this section a proceeding shall be deemed to be pending so long as the time for any appeal therein (apart from any future extension of that time) has not expired, and a proceeding shall be deemed to be finally determined when the time for any appeal therein (apart from any such extension) has expired without the appeal being brought.

1151 Amendment of patent granted to deceased applicant

20.—Where at any time after a patent has been sealed in pursuance of an application under this Act, the comptroller is satisfied that the person to whom the patent was granted had died, or (in the case of a body corporate) had ceased to exist, before the patent was sealed, he may amend the patent by substituting for the name of that person the name of the person to whom the patent ought to have been granted; and the patent shall have effect, and shall be deemed always to have had effect, accordingly.

1152 Extent, effect and form of patent

21.—(1) A patent sealed with the seal of the Patent Office shall have the same effect as if it were sealed with the Great Seal of the United Kingdom, and shall have effect throughout the United Kingdom and the Isle of Man:

Provided that a patent may be assigned for any place in or part of the United Kingdom or Isle of Man as effectually as if it were granted so as to extend to that place or part only.

(2) Subject to the provisions of this Act and of subsection (3) of section three of the Crown Proceedings Act, 1947, a patent shall have the same effect against the Crown as it has against a subject.

(3) A patent shall be in such form as may be authorised by rules made by the Board of Trade under this Act.

(4) A patent shall be granted for one invention only; but it shall not be competent for any person in an action or other proceeding to take any objection to a patent on the ground that it has been granted for more than one invention.

[429]

1153 Date and term of patent

22.—(1) Every patent shall be dated with the date of filing of the complete specification:

Provided that no proceeding shall be taken in respect of an infringement committed before the date of the publication of the complete specification.

(2) The date of every patent shall be entered in the register of patents.

(3) Except as otherwise expressly provided by this Act, the term of every patent shall be sixteen years from the date of the patent.

(4) A patent shall cease to have effect, notwithstanding anything therein or in this Act, on the expiration of the period prescribed for the payment of any renewal fee if that fee is not paid within the prescribed period or within that period as extended under this section.

(5) The period prescribed for the payment of any renewal fee shall be extended to such period, not being more than [six [3]] months longer than the prescribed period, as may be specified in a request made to the comptroller if the request is made and the renewal fee and the prescribed additional fee paid before the expiration of the period so specified.

1154 Extension on ground of inadequate remuneration

23.[4]—(1) If upon application made by a patentee in accordance with this section the court is satisfied that the patentee has not been adequately remunerated by the patent, the court may by order extend the term of the patent, subject to such restrictions, conditions and provisions, if any, as may be specified in the order, for such period (not exceeding five years or, in an exceptional case, ten years) as may be so specified; and any such order may be made notwithstanding that the term of the patent has previously expired.

(2) An application for an order under this section shall be made by petition after such advertisement as may be prescribed by rules of court, and shall be made not more than twelve nor less than six months before the expiration of the term of the patent or at such later time (not being later than the expiration of the said term) as the court may allow.

(3) Any person desiring to oppose the making of an order under this section, or to claim the inclusion therein of any restrictions, conditions or provisions, may within such period as may be prescribed by rules of court give notice of opposition to the court.

(4) On the hearing of any application under this section the applicant and any person by whom notice of opposition has been duly given shall be made parties to the proceeding; and the comptroller shall be entitled to appear and be heard, and shall appear if so directed by the court.

(5) In considering any application under this section the court shall have regard to the nature and merits of the invention in relation to the public, to the profits made by the patentee as such, and to all the circumstances of the case.

[3] Substituted by Patents and Designs (Renewals, Extensions and Fees) Act 1961.

[4] ss. 23, 24 amended as relates to N.I. by Northern Ireland Act 1962.

(6) Not more than one order shall be made under this section in respect of the same patent, but an order may be made under this section in respect of a patent in respect of which one or more orders have been made under the next following section.

1155 Extension on ground of war loss

24.[4]—(1) If upon application made by a patentee in accordance with this section the court or the comptroller is satisfied that the patentee as such has suffered loss or damage (including loss of opportunity of dealing in or developing the invention) by reason of hostilities between His Majesty and any foreign state, the court or comptroller may by order extend the term of the patent subject to such restrictions, conditions and provisions, if any, as may be specified in the order, for such period (not exceeding ten years) as may be so specified; and any such order may be made notwithstanding that the term of the patent has previously expired.

(2) An application for an order under this section may be made at the option of the applicant to the court or to the comptroller: but if the comptroller considers that an application made to him raises issues of a kind which would be more fittingly decided by the court, he may if he thinks fit refer the application for decision by the court.

(3) An application under this section shall be made not more than twelve nor less than six months before the expiration of the term of the patent or at such later time as the court or comptroller may allow:

Provided that the court or comptroller shall not allow an application to be made later than the expiration of the said term unless satisfied that the applicant has been prevented from making the application before the expiration of that term by being on active service or by other circumstances arising by reason of any such hostilities as aforesaid.

(4) Where an application under this section is made to the court, it may be made by petition or by originating summons after such advertisement as may be prescribed by rules of court; and where an application under this section is made to the comptroller, it shall be made in such manner as may be prescribed by rules made by the Board of Trade under this Act.

(5) Any person desiring to oppose the making of an order under this section, or to claim the inclusion therein of any restrictions, conditions or provisions, may give notice of opposition to the court or, as the case may be, the comptroller—

    (*a*) in the case of an application to the court, within such period as may be prescribed by rules of court; and

    (*b*) in the case of an application to the comptroller, within such period as may be prescribed by rules made by the Board of Trade under this Act.

(6) On the hearing of any application under this section the applicant and any person by whom notice of opposition has been duly given shall be made parties to the proceeding; and in the case of an application to the court, the comptroller shall be entitled to appear and be heard, and shall appear if so directed by the court.

(7) Two or more orders may be made under this section in respect of the same patent, and an order may be made under this section in

respect of a patent in respect of which an order has been made under the last foregoing section: but the aggregate term of any extensions granted in pursuance of orders made under this section shall not exceed ten years.

(8) No order shall be made under this section on the application of—

    (*a*) a person who is a subject of such a foreign state as is mentioned in subsection (1) of this section; or

    (*b*) a company the business of which is managed or controlled by such persons or is carried on wholly or mainly for the benefit of or on behalf of such persons, notwithstanding that the company may be registered within His Majesty's dominions;

and for the purpose of this section no account shall be taken of any loss or damage suffered by any person during any period during which he was such a subject as aforesaid, or by any company during any period during which its business was managed or controlled or carried on as aforesaid.

(9) An appeal shall lie from any decision of the comptroller under this section.

1156   Extension on ground of war loss of licensee

25. Subject to the provisions of the last foregoing section, an order for the extension of the term of a patent may be made under that section on the application of a person holding a licence from the patentee giving to the licensee, or to the licensee and persons authorised by him, to the exclusion of all other persons, permission to make, use, exercise and vend the invention, if the court or comptroller is satisfied that the licensee as such has suffered any such loss or damage as is mentioned in subsection (1) of that section.

1157   Patents of addition

26.—(1) Subject to the provisions of this section, where application is made for a patent in respect of any improvement in or modification of an invention (in this Act referred to as " the main invention ") and the applicant also applies or has applied for a patent for that invention or is the patentee in respect thereof, the comptroller may, if the applicant so requests, grant the patent for the improvement or modification as a patent of addition.

(2) Subject to the provisions of this section, where an invention, being an improvement in or modification of another invention, is the subject of an independent patent and the patentee in respect of that patent is also the patentee in respect of the patent for the main invention, the comptroller may, if the patentee so requests, by order revoke the patent for the improvement or modification and grant to the patentee a patent of addition in respect thereof, bearing the same date as the date of the patent so revoked.

(3) A patent shall not be granted as a patent of addition unless the date of filing of the complete specification was the same as or later than the date of filing of the complete specification in respect of the main invention.

(4) A patent of addition shall not be sealed before the sealing of the patent for the main invention; and if the period within which, but

for this provision, a request for the sealing of a patent of addition could be made under section nineteen of this Act expires before the period within which a request for the sealing of the patent for the main invention may be so made, the request for the sealing of the patent of addition may be made at any time within the last-mentioned period.

1158

(5) A patent of addition shall be granted for a term equal to that of the patent for the main invention, or so much thereof as is unexpired, and shall remain in force during that term or until the previous cesser of the patent for the main invention and no longer:
Provided that—

(a) if the term of the patent for the main invention is extended under the foregoing provisions of this Act, the term of the patent of addition may also be extended accordingly; and

(b) if the patent for the main invention is revoked under this Act, the court or comptroller, as the case may be, may order that the patent of addition shall become an independent patent for the remainder of the term of the patent for the main invention, and thereupon the patent shall continue in force as an independent patent accordingly.

(6) No renewal fees shall be payable in respect of a patent of addition; but, if any such patent becomes an independent patent by virtue of an order under the last foregoing subsection, the same fees shall thereafter be payable, upon the same dates, as if the patent had been originally granted as an independent patent.

(7) The grant of a patent of addition shall not be refused, and a patent granted as a patent of addition shall not be revoked or invalidated, on the ground only that the invention claimed in the complete specification does not involve any inventive step having regard to any publication or use of—

(a) the main invention described in the complete specification relating thereto; or

(b) any improvement in or modification of the main invention described in the complete specification of a patent of addition to the patent for the main invention or of an application for such a patent of addition;

and the validity of a patent of addition shall not be questioned on the ground that the invention ought to have been the subject of an independent patent.

(8) An appeal shall lie from any decision of the comptroller under this section.

Restoration of Lapsed Patents and Patent Applications

1159 Restoration of lapsed patents

27.—(1) Where a patent has ceased to have effect by reason of a failure to pay any renewal fee within the prescribed period or within that period as extended under section twenty-two of this Act, and the comptroller is satisfied, upon application made within three years from the date on which the patent ceased to have effect, that the failure was unintentional and that no undue delay has occurred in the making or prosecution of the application, he shall by order restore the patent and any patent of addition specified in the application which has ceased to have effect on the cesser of that patent.

(2) An application under this section may be made by the person who was the patentee or by his personal representative; and where the patent was held by two or more persons jointly, the application may, with the leave of the comptroller, be made by one or more of them without joining the others.

(3) An application under this section shall contain a statement (to be verified in such manner as may be prescribed) fully setting out the circumstances which led to the failure to pay the renewal fee; and the comptroller may require from the applicant such further evidence as he may think necessary.

1160   (4) If after hearing the applicant (if the applicant so requires or the comptroller thinks fit) the comptroller is satisfied that a prima facie case has been made out for an order under this section, he shall advertise the application in the Journal; and within the prescribed period any person may give notice to the comptroller of opposition thereto on either or both of the following grounds; that is to say—

(*a*) that the failure to pay the renewal fee was not unintentional; or

(*b*) that there has been undue delay in the making of the application.

(5) If notice of opposition is given within the period aforesaid, the comptroller shall notify the applicant, and shall give to him and to the opponent an opportunity to be heard before he decides the case.

(6) If no notice of opposition is given within the period aforesaid or if, in the case of opposition, the decision of the comptroller is in favour of the applicant, the comptroller shall, upon payment of any unpaid renewal fee and such additional fee as may be prescribed, make the order in accordance with the application.

(7) An order under this section for the restoration of a patent—

(*a*) may be made subject to such conditions as the comptroller thinks fit, including in particular a condition requiring the registration in the register of patents of any matter in respect of which the provisions of this Act as to entries in that register have not been complied with; and

(*b*) shall contain such provision as may be prescribed for the protection of persons who may have begun to avail themselves of the patented invention between the date when the patent ceased to have effect and the date of the application under this section;

and if any condition of an order under this section is not complied with by the patentee, the comptroller may, after giving to the patentee an opportunity to be heard, revoke the order and give such directions consequential on the revocation as he thinks fit.

(8) An appeal shall lie from any decision of the comptroller under this section.

1161   **Restoration of lapsed applications for patents**

28.—(1) Where a patent has not been sealed by reason only that the prescribed request was not made within the time allowed for that purpose by or under section nineteen of this Act, then if the comptroller is satisfied, upon application made within six months after the expiration of that time by the applicant for the patent, that the failure to make the request was unintentional, he may order the patent to be sealed notwithstanding that the prescribed request was not made as aforesaid.

(2) An application under this section shall contain a statement (to be verified in such manner as may be prescribed) fully setting out the circumstances which led to the failure to make the prescribed request; and the comptroller may require from the applicant such further evidence as he may think necessary.

(3) If after hearing the applicant (if the applicant so requires or the comptroller thinks fit) the comptroller is satisfied that a prima facie case has been made out for an order under this section, he shall advertise the application in the Journal; and within the prescribed period any person may give notice to the comptroller of opposition thereto on the ground that the failure to make the prescribed request was not unintentional.

(4) If notice of opposition is given within the period aforesaid, the comptroller shall notify the applicant and shall give to him and to the opponent an opportunity to be heard before he decides the case.

(5) If no notice of opposition is given within the period aforesaid, or if in the case of opposition the decision of the comptroller is in favour of the applicant, the comptroller shall, upon payment of the fee prescribed in respect of the making of the request for sealing and of such additional fee as may be prescribed, make the order in accordance with the application.

(6) An order under this section for the sealing of a patent shall contain such provision as may be prescribed for the protection of persons who may have begun to avail themselves of the invention between the date when the time allowed by or under section nineteen of this Act for making the prescribed request expired and the date of the application under this section.

(7) An appeal shall lie from any decision of the comptroller under this section.

Amendment of Specifications

1162 Amendment of specification with leave of comptroller

29.—(1) Subject to the provisions of section thirty-one of this Act, the comptroller may, upon application made under this section by a patentee, or by an applicant for a patent at any time after the acceptance of the complete specification, allow the complete specification to be amended subject to such conditions, if any, as the comptroller thinks fit:

Provided that the comptroller shall not allow a specification to be amended under this section upon an application made while any action before the court for infringement of the patent or any proceeding before the court for the revocation of the patent is pending.

(2) Every application for leave to amend a specification under this section shall state the nature of the proposed amendment and shall give full particulars of the reasons for which the application is made.

(3) Any application for leave to amend a specification under this section, and the nature of the proposed amendment, shall be advertised in the prescribed manner:

Provided that where the application is made before the publication of the complete specification, the comptroller may, if he thinks fit, dispense with advertisement under this subsection or direct that advertisement shall be postponed until the complete specification is published.

(4) Within the prescribed period after the advertisement of an application under this section, any person may give notice to the comptroller of opposition thereto; and where such a notice is given within the period aforesaid, the comptroller shall notify the person by whom the application under this section is made and shall give to that person and to the opponent an opportunity to be heard before he decides the case.

(5) An appeal shall lie from any decision of the comptroller under this section.

(6) This section shall not apply in relation to any amendment of a specification effected in proceedings in opposition to the grant of a patent or on a reference to the comptroller of a dispute as to the infringement or validity of a claim, or effected in pursuance of any provision of this Act authorising the comptroller to direct a reference to another specification or patent to be inserted, or to refuse to grant a patent, or to revoke a patent, unless the specification is amended to his satisfaction.

1163 Amendment of specification with leave of the court

30.—(1) In any action for infringement of a patent or any proceeding before the court for the revocation of a patent, the court may, subject to the provisions of the next following section, by order allow the patentee to amend his complete specification in such manner, and subject to such terms as to costs, advertisements or otherwise, as the court may think fit; and if in any such proceedings for revocation the court decides that the patent is invalid, the court may allow the specification to be amended under this section instead of revoking the patent.

(2) Where an application for an order under this section is made to the court, the applicant shall give notice of the application to the comptroller, and the comptroller shall be entitled to appear and be heard, and shall appear if so directed by the court.

1164 Supplementary provisions as to amendment of specification

31.—(1) After the acceptance of a complete specification, no amendment thereof shall be effected except by way of disclaimer, correction or explanation, and no amendment thereof shall be allowed, except for the purpose of correcting an obvious mistake, the effect of which would be that the specification as amended would claim or describe matter not in substance disclosed in the specification before the amendment, or that any claim of the specification as amended would not fall wholly within the scope of a claim of the specification before the amendment.

(2) Where, after the date of the publication of a complete specification, any amendment of the specification is allowed or approved by the comptroller, the court or the Appeal Tribunal under this Act, the right of the patentee or applicant to make the amendment shall not be called in question except on the ground of fraud; and the amendment shall in all courts and for all purposes be deemed to form part of the specification:

Provided that in construing the specification as amended reference may be made to the specification as originally published.

(3) Where, after the date of the publication of a complete specification, any amendment of the specification is allowed or approved as aforesaid, the fact that the specification has been amended shall be advertised in the Journal.

Revocation and Surrender of Patents

1165 Revocation of patent by court

32.—(1) Subject to the provisions of this Act, a patent may, on the petition of any person interested, be revoked by the court on any of the following grounds, that is to say,—

(a) that the invention, so far as claimed in any claim of the complete specification, was claimed in a valid claim of earlier priority date contained in the complete specification of another patent granted in the United Kingdom;

(b) that the patent was granted on the application of a person not entitled under the provisions of this Act to apply therefor;

(c) that the patent was obtained in contravention of the rights of the petitioner or any person under or through whom he claims;

(d) that the subject of any claim of the complete specification is not an invention within the meaning of this Act;

(e) that the invention, so far as claimed in any claim of the complete specification, is not new having regard to what was known or used, before the priority date of the claim, in the United Kingdom;

(f) that the invention, so far as claimed in any claim of the complete specification, is obvious and does not involve any inventive step having regard to what was known or used, before the priority date of the claim, in the United Kingdom;

(g) that the invention, so far as claimed in any claim of the complete specification, is not useful;

(h) that the complete specification does not sufficiently and fairly describe the invention and the method by which it is to be performed, or does not disclose the best method of performing it which was known to the applicant for the patent and for which he was entitled to claim protection;

(i) that the scope of any claim of the complete specification is not sufficiently and clearly defined or that any claim of the complete specification is not fairly based on the matter disclosed in the specification;

(j) that the patent was obtained on a false suggestion or representation;

(*k*) that the primary or intended use or exercise of the invention is contrary to law;

(*l*) that the invention, so far as claimed in any claim of the complete specification, was secretly used in the United Kingdom, otherwise than as mentioned in subsection (2) of this section, before the priority date of that claim.

1166   (2) For the purposes of paragraph (*l*) of subsection (1) of this section, no account shall be taken of any use of the invention—

(*a*) for the purpose of reasonable trial or experiment only; or

(*b*) by a Government department or any person authorised by a Government department, in consequence of the applicant for the patent or any person from whom he derives title having communicated or disclosed the invention directly or indirectly to a Government department or person authorised as aforesaid; or

(*c*) by any other person, in consequence of the applicant for the patent or any person from whom he derives title having communicated or disclosed the invention, and without the consent or acquiescence of the applicant or of any person from whom he derives title;

and for the purposes of paragraph (*e*) or paragraph (*f*) of the said subsection (1) no account shall be taken of any secret use.

(3) Without prejudice to the provisions of subsection (1) of this section, a patent may be revoked by the court on the petition of a Government department, if the court is satisfied that the patentee has without reasonable cause failed to comply with a request of the department to make, use or exercise the patented invention for the services of the Crown upon reasonable terms.

(4) Every ground on which a patent may be revoked shall be available as a ground of defence in any proceeding for the infringement of the patent.

1167   Revocation of patent by comptroller

33.—(1) At any time within twelve months after the sealing of a patent, any person interested who did not oppose the grant of the patent may apply to the comptroller for an order revoking the patent on any one or more of the grounds upon which the grant of the patent could have been opposed:

Provided that when an action for infringement, or proceedings for the revocation, of a patent are pending in any court, an application to the comptroller under this section shall not be made except with the leave of the court.

(2) Where an application is made under this section, the comptroller shall notify the patentee and shall give to the applicant and the patentee an opportunity to be heard before deciding the case.

(3) If on an application under this section the comptroller is satisfied that any of the grounds aforesaid are established, he may by order direct that the patent shall be revoked either unconditionally or unless within such time as may be specified in the order the complete specification is amended to his satisfaction:

Provided that the comptroller shall not make an order for the unconditional revocation of a patent under this section unless the circumstances are such as would have justified him in refusing to grant the patent in proceedings under section fourteen of this Act.

(4) An appeal shall lie from any decision of the comptroller under this section.

1168 Surrender of patent

34.—(1) A patentee may at any time by notice given to the comptroller offer to surrender his patent.

(2) Where such an offer is made the comptroller shall advertise the offer in the prescribed manner; and within the prescribed period after such advertisement any person interested may give notice to the comptroller of opposition to the surrender.

(3) Where any such notice of opposition is duly given the comptroller shall notify the patentee.

(4) If the comptroller is satisfied, after hearing the patentee and any opponent, if desirous of being heard, that the patent may properly be surrendered, he may accept the offer and by order revoke the patent.

(5) An appeal shall lie from any decision of the comptroller under this section.

Voluntary Endorsement of Patent

1169 Endorsement of patent " licences of right "

35.—(1) At any time after the sealing of a patent the patentee may apply to the comptroller for the patent to be endorsed with the words " licences of right "; and where such an application is made, the comptroller shall notify the application to any person entered on the register as entitled to an interest in the patent, and if satisfied, after giving any such person an opportunity to be heard, that the patentee is not precluded by contract from granting licences under the patent, cause the patent to be endorsed accordingly.

(2) Where a patent is endorsed under this section—

    (*a*) any person shall, at any time thereafter, be entitled as of right to a licence under the patent upon such terms as may, in default of agreement, be settled by the comptroller on the application of the patentee or the person requiring the licence;

    (*b*) the comptroller may, on the application of the holder of any licence granted under the patent before the endorsement, order the licence to be exchanged for a licence to be granted by virtue of the endorsement upon terms to be settled as aforesaid;

    (*c*) if in proceedings for infringement of the patent (otherwise than by the importation of goods) the defendant undertakes to take a licence upon terms to be settled by the comptroller as aforesaid, no injunction shall be granted against him, and the amount (if any) recoverable against him by way of damages shall not exceed double the amount which would have been payable by him as licensee if such a licence had been granted before the earliest infringement;

(*d*) the renewal fees payable in respect of the patent after the date of the endorsement shall be one half of the renewal fees which would be payable if the patent were not so endorsed.

1170   (3) The licensee under any licence granted by virtue of the endorsement of a patent under this section shall (unless, in the case of a licence the terms of which are settled by agreement, the licence otherwise expressly provides) be entitled to call upon the patentee to take proceedings to prevent any infringement of the patent; and if the patentee refuses or neglects to do so within two months after being so called upon, the licensee may institute proceedings for the infringement in his own name as if he were patentee, making the patentee a defendant:

Provided that a patentee so added as defendant shall not be liable for any costs unless he enters an appearance and takes part in the proceedings.

(4) An application for the endorsement of a patent under this section shall contain a statement (to be verified in such manner as may be prescribed) that the patentee is not precluded by contract from granting licences under the patent; and the comptroller may require from the applicant such further evidence as he may think necessary.

(5) An application made under this section for the endorsement of a patent of addition shall be treated as an application for the endorsement of the patent for the main invention also, and an application made under this section for the endorsement of a patent in respect of which a patent of addition is in force shall be treated as an application for the endorsement of the patent of addition also; and where a patent of addition is granted in respect of a patent already endorsed under this section, the patent of addition shall also be so endorsed.

(6) All endorsements of patents under this section shall be entered in the register of patents and shall be published in the Journal and in such other manner as the comptroller thinks desirable for bringing the endorsement to the notice of manufacturers.

(7) An appeal shall lie from any decision of the comptroller under this section.

1171   Cancellation of endorsement under section 35

36.—(1) At any time after a patent has been endorsed under the last foregoing section, the patentee may apply to the comptroller for cancellation of the endorsement; and where such an application is made and the balance paid of all renewal fees which would have been payable if the patent had not been endorsed, the comptroller may, if satisfied that there is no existing licence under the patent or that all licensees under the patent consent to the application, cancel the endorsement accordingly.

(2) Within the prescribed period after a patent has been endorsed as aforesaid, any person who claims that the patentee is, and was at the time of the endorsement, precluded by a contract in which the claimant is interested from granting licences under the patent may apply to the comptroller for cancellation of the endorsement.

(3) Where the comptroller is satisfied, on application made under the last foregoing subsection, that the patentee is and was precluded as aforesaid, he shall cancel the endorsement; and thereupon the patentee shall be liable to pay, within such period as may be prescribed, a sum equal to the balance of all renewal fees which would have been payable if the patent had not been endorsed, and if that sum is not paid within that period the patent shall cease to have effect at the expiration of that period.

(4) Where the endorsement of a patent is cancelled under this section, the rights and liabilities of the patentee shall thereafter be the same as if the endorsement had not been made.

(5) The comptroller shall advertise in the prescribed manner any application made to him under this section; and within the prescribed period after such advertisement—

(a) in the case of an application under subsection (1) of this section, any person interested; and

(b) in the case of an application under subsection (2) of this section, the patentee,

may give notice to the comptroller of opposition to the cancellation.

(6) Where any such notice of opposition is given, the comptroller shall notify the applicant, and shall give to the applicant and the opponent an opportunity to be heard before deciding the case.

(7) An application made under this section for the cancellation of the endorsement of a patent of addition shall be treated as an application for the cancellation of the endorsement of the patent for the main invention also, and an application made under this section for the cancellation of the endorsement of a patent in respect of which a patent of addition is in force shall be treated as an application for the cancellation of the endorsement of the patent of addition also.

(8) An appeal shall lie from any decision of the comptroller under this section.

Compulsory Licences, Etc.

1172 Compulsory endorsement

37.—(1) At any time after the expiration of three years from the date of the sealing of a patent, any person interested may apply to the comptroller upon any one or more of the grounds specified in the next following subsection for a licence under the patent or for the endorsement of the patent with the words " licences of right."

(2) The grounds upon which application may be made for an order under this section are as follows, that is to say:

(a) that the patented invention, being capable of being commercially worked in the United Kingdom, is not being commercially worked therein or is not being so worked to the fullest extent that is reasonably practicable;

(b) that a demand for the patented article in the United Kingdom is not being met on reasonable terms, or is being met to a substantial extent by importation;

(c) that the commercial working of the invention in the United Kingdom is being prevented or hindered by the importation of the patented article;

(d) that by reason of the refusal of the patentee to grant a licence or licences on reasonable terms—

    (i) a market for the export of the patented article manufactured in the United Kingdom is not being supplied; or

    (ii) the working or efficient working in the United Kingdom of any other patented invention which makes a substantial contribution to the art is prevented or hindered; or

    (iii) the establishment or development of commercial or industrial activities in the United Kingdom is unfairly prejudiced;

(e) that by reason of conditions imposed by the patentee upon the grant of licences under the patent, or upon the purchase, hire or use of the patented article or process, the manufacture, use or sale of materials not protected by the patent, or the establishment or development of commercial or industrial activities in the United Kingdom is unfairly prejudiced.

1173 (3) Subject as hereinafter provided, the comptroller may, if satisfied that any of the grounds aforesaid are established, make an order in accordance with the application; and where the order is for the grant of a licence, it may require the licence to be granted upon such terms as the comptroller thinks fit:

Provided that—

(a) where the application is made on the ground that the patented invention is not being commercially worked in the United Kingdom or is not being worked to the fullest extent that is reasonably practicable, and it appears to the comptroller that the time which has elapsed since the sealing of the patent has for any reason been insufficient to enable it to be so worked, he may by order adjourn the application for such period as will in his opinion give sufficient time for the invention to be so worked;

(b) an order shall not be made under this section for the endorsement of a patent on the ground that a market for the export of the patented article is not being supplied, and any licence granted under this section on that ground shall contain such provisions as appear to the comptroller to be expedient for restricting the countries in which the patented article may be sold or used by the licensee;

(c) no order shall be made under this section in respect of a patent on the ground that the working or efficient working in the United Kingdom of another patented invention is prevented or hindered unless the comptroller is satisfied that the patentee in respect of that other invention is able and willing to grant to the patentee and his licensees a licence in respect of that other invention on reasonable terms.

(4) An application under this section may be made by any person notwithstanding that he is already the holder of a licence under the patent; and no person shall be estopped from alleging any of the matters specified in subsection (2) of this section by reason of any

admission made by him, whether in such a licence or otherwise, or by reason of his having accepted such a licence.

(5) In this section the expression " patented article " includes any article made by a patented process.

1174 Provisions as to licences under section 37

38.—(1) Where the comptroller is satisfied, on application made under the last foregoing section, that the manufacture, use or sale of materials not protected by the patent is unfairly prejudiced by reason of conditions imposed by the patentee upon the grant of licences under the patent, or upon the purchase, hire or use of the patented article or process, he may, subject to the provisions of that section, order the grant of licences under the patent to such customers of the applicant as he thinks fit as well as to the applicant.

(2) Where an application under the last foregoing section is made by a person being the holder of a licence under the patent, the comptroller may, if he makes an order for the grant of a licence to the applicant, order the existing licence to be cancelled, or may, if he thinks fit, instead of making an order for the grant of a licence to the applicant, order the existing licence to be amended.

(3) Where on an application under the last foregoing section the comptroller orders the grant of a licence, he may direct that the licence shall operate—

(*a*) to deprive the patentee of any right which he may have as patentee to make, use, exercise or vend the invention or to grant licences under the patent;

(*b*) to revoke all existing licences in respect of the invention.

(4) Subsection (3) of section thirty-five of this Act shall apply to any licence granted in pursuance of an order under the last foregoing section as it applies to a licence granted by virtue of the said section thirty-five.

1175 Exercise of powers on applications under section 37

39.—(1) The powers of the comptroller upon an application under section thirty-seven of this Act shall be exercised with a view to securing the following general purposes, that is to say:

(*a*) that inventions which can be worked on a commercial scale in the United Kingdom and which should in the public interest be so worked shall be worked therein without undue delay and to the fullest extent that is reasonably practicable;

(*b*) that the inventor or other person beneficially entitled to a patent shall receive reasonable remuneration having regard to the nature of the invention;

(*c*) that the interests of any person for the time being working or developing an invention in the United Kingdom under the protection of a patent shall not be unfairly prejudiced.

(2) Subject to the foregoing subsection, the comptroller shall, in determining whether to make an order in pursuance of any such application, take account of the following matters, that is to say:

(*a*) the nature of the invention, the time which has elapsed since the sealing of the patent and the measures already taken by the patentee or any licensee to make full use of the invention;

(b) the ability of any person to whom a licence would be granted under the order to work the invention to the public advantage; and

(c) the risks to be undertaken by that person in providing capital and working the invention if the application is granted;

but shall not be required to take account of matters subsequent to the making of the application.

1176   Endorsement, etc., on application of Crown

40.—(1) At any time after the expiration of three years from the date of the sealing of a patent, any Government department may apply to the comptroller upon any one or more of the grounds specified in section thirty-seven of this Act for the endorsement of the patent with the words " licences of right " or for the grant to any person specified in the application of a licence under the patent; and the comptroller may, if satisfied that any of those grounds are established, make an order in accordance with the application.

(2) Subsections (3) and (5) of section thirty-seven of this Act and sections thirty-eight and thirty-nine of this Act shall, so far as applicable, apply in relation to an application and an order under the last foregoing subsection as they apply in relation to an application and an order under the said section thirty-seven.

1177   (3) Where according to a report of the Monopolies and Restrictive Practices Commission as laid before Parliament under section nine of the Monopolies and Restrictive Practices (Inquiry and Control) Act, 1948, conditions to which that Act applies prevail in respect of the supply of goods of any description which consist of or include patented articles, or in respect of exports of such goods, or in respect of the application to goods of any description of any process which consists of or includes a patented process, and, not earlier than three months from the date on which the report was laid before the Commons House of Parliament, a resolution has been passed by that House declaring that those conditions or any things which, according to the report as laid before Parliament, are done by the parties concerned, as a result of or for the purpose of preserving those conditions, operate or may be expected to operate against the public interest, [the Secretary of State [5]] may apply to the comptroller for an order under the next following subsection in respect of the patent.

(4) If upon an application under the last foregoing subsection it appears to the comptroller that the matters which, according to the resolution mentioned in that subsection, operate or may be expected to operate against the public interest include—

(a) any conditions in a licence or licences granted by the patentee under the patent restricting the use of the invention by the licensee or the right of the patentee to grant other licences under the patent; or

(b) a refusal by the patentee to grant licences under the patent on reasonable terms,

he may by order cancel or modify any such condition as aforesaid or may, if he thinks fit, instead of making such an order or in addition

[5] Substituted by S.I. 1969 No. 1534.

to making such an order, order the patent to be endorsed with the words " licences of right."

1178 Inventions relating to food or medicine, etc.

41.—(1) Without prejudice to the foregoing provisions of this Act, where a patent is in force in respect of—

(a) a substance capable of being used as food or medicine or in the production of food or medicine; or

(b) a process for producing such a substance as aforesaid; or

(c) any invention capable of being used as or as part of a surgical or curative device,

the comptroller shall, on application made to him by any person interested, order the grant to the applicant of a licence under the patent on such terms as he thinks fit, unless it appears to him that there are good reasons for refusing the application.

(2) In settling the terms of licences under this section the comptroller shall endeavour to secure that food, medicines, and surgical and curative devices shall be available to the public at the lowest prices consistent with the patentees' deriving a reasonable advantage from their patent rights.

(3) A licence granted under this section shall entitle the licensee to make, use, exercise and vend the invention as a food or medicine, or for the purposes of the production of food or medicine or as or as part of a surgical or curative device, but for no other purposes.

1179 Revocation of patent

42.—(1) Where an order for the grant of a licence under a patent has been made in pursuance of an application under section thirty-seven of this Act, any person interested may, at any time after the expiration of two years from the date of that order, apply to the comptroller for the revocation of the patent upon any of the grounds specified in subsection (2) of the said section thirty-seven; and if upon any such application the comptroller is satisfied—

(a) that any of the said grounds are established; and

(b) that the purposes for which an order may be made in pursuance of an application under the said section thirty-seven could not be achieved by the making of any such order as is authorised to be made in pursuance of such an application,

he may order the patent to be revoked.

(2) An order for the revocation of a patent under this section may be made so as to take effect either unconditionally or in the event of failure to comply, within such reasonable period as may be specified in the order, with such conditions as may be imposed by the order with a view to achieving the purposes aforesaid; and the comptroller may, on reasonable cause shown in any case, by subsequent order extend any period so specified.

1180 Procedure on application under sections 37 to 42

43.—(1) Every application under sections thirty-seven to forty-two of this Act shall specify the nature of the order sought by the applicant and shall contain a statement (to be verified in such manner as may be prescribed) setting out the nature of the applicant's interest (if any) and the facts upon which the application is based.

(2) Where the comptroller is satisfied, upon consideration of any such application, that a prima facie case has been made out for the making of an order, he shall direct the applicant to serve copies of the application upon the patentee and any other persons appearing from the register of patents to be interested in the patent in respect of which the application is made, and shall advertise the application in the Journal.

(3) The patentee or any other person desiring to oppose the application may, within such time as may be prescribed or within such further time as the comptroller may on application (made either before or after the expiration of the prescribed time) allow, give to the comptroller notice of opposition.

(4) Any such notice of opposition shall contain a statement (to be verified in such manner as may be prescribed) setting out the grounds on which the application is opposed.

(5) Where any such notice of opposition is duly given, the comptroller shall notify the applicant, and shall, subject to the provisions of the next following section with respect to arbitration, give to the applicant and the opponent an opportunity to be heard before deciding the case.

(6) In any proceedings on an application made in relation to a patent under sections thirty-seven to forty-two of this Act, any statement with respect to the making, using, exercising or vending of the patented invention, or with respect to the grant or refusal of licences under the patent, contained in a report of the Monopolies and Restrictive Practices Commission as laid before Parliament under section nine of the Monopolies and Restrictive Practices (Inquiry and Control) Act, 1948, shall be prima facie evidence of the matters stated.

1181   **Appeal and references to arbitrator**

44.—(1) An appeal shall lie from any order made by the comptroller in pursuance of an application under sections thirty-seven to forty-two of this Act.

(2) On any appeal under this section the Attorney General or such other counsel as he may appoint shall be entitled to appear and be heard.

(3) Where any such application is opposed in accordance with the last foregoing section, and either—

(a) the parties consent; or

(b) the proceedings require a prolonged examination of documents or any scientific or local investigation which cannot in the opinion of the comptroller conveniently be made before him;

the comptroller may at any time order the whole proceedings, or any question or issue of fact arising therein, to be referred to an arbitrator agreed on by the parties, or, in default of agreement, appointed by the comptroller.

(4) Where the whole proceedings are referred as aforesaid, section nine of the Arbitration Act, 1934 (which relates to the statement of cases by arbitrators) shall not apply to the arbitration; but unless the

parties otherwise agree before the award of the arbitrator is made, an appeal shall lie from the award to the Appeal Tribunal.

(5) Where a question or issue of fact is referred as aforesaid, the arbitrator shall report his findings to the comptroller.

1182 Supplementary provisions

45.—(1) Any order under this Act for the grant of a licence shall, without prejudice to any other method of enforcement, have effect as if it were a deed, executed by the patentee and all other necessary parties, granting a licence in accordance with the order.

(2) An order may be made on an application under sections thirty-seven to forty of this Act for the endorsement of a patent with the words "licences of right" notwithstanding any contract which would have precluded the endorsement of the patent on the application of the patentee under section thirty-five of this Act; and any such order shall for all purposes have the same effect as an endorsement made in pursuance of an application under the said section thirty-five.

(3) No order shall be made in pursuance of any application under sections thirty-seven to forty-two of this Act which would be at variance with any treaty, convention, arrangement or engagement applying to the United Kingdom and any convention country.

Use of Patented Inventions for Services of the Crown

1183 Use of patented inventions for services of the Crown

46.—(1) Notwithstanding anything in this Act, any Government department, and any person authorised in writing by a Government department, may make, use and exercise any patented invention for the services of the Crown in accordance with the following provisions of this section.

(2) If and so far as the invention has before the priority date of the relevant claim of the complete specification been duly recorded by or tried by or on behalf of a Government department [or the United Kingdom Atomic Energy Authority [6]] otherwise than in consequence of the communication thereof directly or indirectly by the patentee or any person from whom he derives title, any use of the invention by virtue of this section may be made free of any royalty or other payment to the patentee.

(3) If and so far as the invention has not been so recorded or tried as aforesaid, any use of the invention made by virtue of this section at any time after the acceptance of the complete specification in respect of the patent, or in consequence of any such communication as aforesaid, shall be made upon such terms as may be agreed upon, either before or after the use, between the Government department and the patentee with the approval of the Treasury, or as may in default of agreement be determined by the court on a reference under section forty-eight of this Act.

(4) The authority of a Government department in respect of an invention may be given under this section either before or after the patent is granted and either before or after the acts in respect of which

---

[6] Amended by Atomic Energy Authority Act 1954.

the authority is given are done, and may be given to any person whether or not he is authorised directly or indirectly by the patentee to make, use, exercise or vend the invention.

(5) Where any use of an invention is made by or with the authority of a Government department under this section, then, unless it appears to the department that it would be contrary to the public interest so to do, the department shall notify the patentee as soon as practicable after the use is begun, and furnish him with such information as to the extent of the use as he may from time to time require.

1184   (6) For the purposes of this and the next following section " the services of the Crown " shall be deemed to include—

(*a*) the supply to the government of any country outside the United Kingdom, in pursuance of an agreement or arrangement between Her Majesty's Government in the United Kingdom and the government of that country, of articles required—

(i) for the defence of that country; or

(ii) for the defence of any other country whose government is party to any agreement or arrangement with Her Majesty's said Government in respect of defence matters;

(*b*) the supply to the United Nations, or to the government of any country belonging to that organisation, in pursuance of an agreement or arrangement between Her Majesty's Government and that organisation or government, of articles required for any armed forces operating in pursuance of a resolution of that organisation or any organ of that organisation;

and the power of a Government department or a person authorised by a Government department under this section to make, use and exercise an invention shall include power to sell to any such government or to the said organisation any articles the supply of which is authorised by this subsection, and to sell to any person any articles made in the exercise of the powers conferred by this section which are no longer required for the purpose for which they were made.[7]

(7) The purchaser of any articles sold in the exercise of powers conferred by this section, and any person claiming through him, shall have power to deal with them in the same manner as if the patent were held on behalf of His Majesty.

1185   **Rights of third parties in respect of Crown use**

47.—(1) In relation to any use of a patented invention, or an invention in respect of which an application for a patent is pending, made for the services of the Crown—

(*a*) by a Government department or a person authorised by a Government department under the last foregoing section; or

(*b*) by the patentee or applicant for the patent to the order of a Government department,

the provisions of any licence, assignment or agreement made, whether

---

[7] Subs. (6) was substituted for the original by the Defence Contracts Act 1958. See *post*, § 1253.

before or after the commencement of this Act, between the patentee or applicant for the patent, or any person who derives title from him or from whom he derives title, and any person other than a Government department shall be of no effect so far as those provisions restrict or regulate the use of the invention, or any model, document or information relating thereto, or provide for the making of payments in respect of any such use, or calculated by reference thereto; and the reproduction or publication of any model or document in connection with the said use shall not be deemed to be an infringement of any copyright subsisting in the model or document.

(2) Where an exclusive licence granted otherwise than for royalties or other benefits determined by reference to the use of the invention is in force under the patent, then—

(*a*) in relation to any use of the invention which, but for the provisions of this and the last foregoing section, would constitute an infringement of the rights of the licensee, subsection (3) of the last foregoing section shall have effect as if for the reference to the patentee there were substituted a reference to the licensee; and

(*b*) in relation to any use of the invention by the licensee by virtue of an authority given under the last foregoing section, that section shall have effect as if the said subsection (3) were omitted.

(3) Subject to the provisions of the last foregoing subsection, where the patent, or the right to apply for or obtain the patent, has been assigned to the patentee in consideration of royalties or other benefits determined by reference to the use of the invention, then—

(*a*) in relation to any use of the invention by virtue of section forty-six of this Act, subsection (3) of that section shall have effect as if the reference to the patentee included a reference to the assignor, and any sum payable by virtue of that subsection shall be divided between the patentee and the assignor in such proportion as may be agreed upon between them or as may in default of agreement be determined by the court on a reference under the next following section; and

(*b*) in relation to any use of the invention made for the services of the Crown by the patentee to the order of a Government department, subsection (3) of section forty-six of this Act shall have effect as if that use were made by virtue of an authority given under that section.

1186 (4) Where, under subsection (3) of section forty-six of this Act, payments are required to be made by a Government department to a patentee in respect of any use of an invention, any person, being the holder of an exclusive licence under the patent (not being such a licence as is mentioned in subsection (2) of this section) authorising him to make that use of the invention, shall be entitled to recover from the patentee such part (if any) of those payments as may be agreed upon between that person and the patentee, or as may in default of agreement be determined by the court under the next following section to be just having regard to any expenditure incurred by that person—

[449]

(*a*) in developing the said invention; or

(*b*) in making payments to the patentee, other than royalties or other payments determined by reference to the use of the invention, in consideration of the licence;

and if, at any time before the amount of any such payment has been agreed upon between the Government department and the patentee, that person gives notice in writing of his interest to the department, any agreement as to the amount of that payment shall be of no effect unless it is made with his consent.

1187　**Reference of disputes as to Crown use**

48.[8]—(1) Any dispute as to the exercise by a Government department or a person authorised by a Government department of the powers conferred by section forty-six of this Act, or as to terms for the use of an invention for the services of the Crown thereunder, or as to the right of any person to receive any part of a payment made in pursuance of subsection (3) of that section, may be referred to the court by either party to the dispute in such manner as may be prescribed by rules of court.

(2) In any proceedings under this section to which a Government department are a party, the department may—

(*a*) if the patentee is a party to the proceedings, apply for revocation of the patent upon any ground upon which a patent may be revoked under section thirty-two of this Act;

(*b*) in any case, put in issue the validity of the patent without applying for its revocation.

(3) If in such proceedings as aforesaid any question arises whether an invention has been recorded or tried as mentioned in section forty-six of this Act, and the disclosure of any document recording the invention, or of any evidence of the trial thereof, would in the opinion of the department be prejudicial to the public interest, the disclosure may be made confidentially to counsel for the other party or to an independent expert mutually agreed upon.

(4) In determining under this section any dispute between a Government department and any person as to terms for the use of an invention for the services of the Crown, the court shall have regard to any benefit or compensation which that person or any person from whom he derives title may have received, or may be entitled to receive, directly or indirectly from any Government department in respect of the invention in question.

(5) In any proceedings under this section the court may at any time order the whole proceedings or any question or issue of fact arising therein to be referred to a special or official referee or an arbitrator on such terms as the court may direct; and references to the court in the foregoing provisions of this section shall be construed accordingly.

[8] s. 48 amended as relates to N.I. by the Northern Ireland Act 1962.

1188 Special provisions as to Crown use during emergency

49.—(1) During any period of emergency within the meaning of this section, the powers exercisable in relation to an invention by a Government department, or a person authorised by a Government department under section forty-six of this Act, shall include power to make, use, exercise and vend the invention for any purpose which appears to the department necessary or expedient—

(a) for the efficient prosecution of any war in which His Majesty may be engaged;

(b) for the maintenance of supplies and services essential to the life of the community;

(c) for securing a sufficiency of supplies and services essential to the well-being of the community;

(d) for promoting the productivity of industry, commerce and agriculture;

(e) for fostering and directing exports and reducing imports, or imports of any classes, from all or any countries and for redressing the balance of trade;

(f) generally for ensuring that the whole resources of the community are available for use, and are used, in a manner best calculated to serve the interests of the community; or

(g) for assisting the relief of suffering and the restoration and distribution of essential supplies and services in any part of His Majesty's dominions or any foreign countries that are in grave distress as the result of war;

and any reference in that section or in section forty-seven or section forty-eight of this Act to the services of the Crown shall be construed as including a reference to the purposes aforesaid.

(2) In this section the expression " period of emergency " means the period ending with the tenth day of December, nineteen hundred and fifty, or such later date as may be prescribed by Order in Council, and any other period beginning on such date as may be declared by Order in Council to be the commencement, and ending on such date as may be so declared to be the termination, of a period of emergency for the purposes of this section.

(3) A draft of any Order in Council under this section shall be laid before Parliament; and the draft shall not be submitted to His Majesty except in pursuance of an Address presented by each House of Parliament praying that the Order be made.

Anticipation, Etc.

1189 Previous publication

50.—(1) An invention claimed in a complete specification shall not be deemed to have been anticipated by reason only that the invention was published in the United Kingdom—

(a) in a specification filed in pursuance of an application for a patent made in the United Kingdom and dated more than fifty years before the date of filing of the first-mentioned specification;

(b) in a specification describing the invention for the purposes of an application for protection in any country outside the United Kingdom made more than fifty years before that date; or

(c) in any abridgment of or extract from any such specification published under the authority of the comptroller or of the government of any country outside the United Kingdom.

(2) Subject as hereinafter provided, an invention claimed in a complete specification shall not be deemed to have been anticipated by reason only that the invention was published before the priority date of the relevant claim of the specification, if the patentee or applicant for the patent proves—

(a) that the matter published was obtained from him or (where he is not himself the true and first inventor) from any person from whom he derives title, and was published without his consent or the consent of any such person; and

(b) where the patentee or applicant for the patent or any person from whom he derives title learned of the publication before the date of the application for the patent or (in the case of a convention application) before the date of the application for protection in a convention country, that the application or the application in a convention country, as the case may be, was made as soon as reasonably practicable thereafter:

Provided that this subsection shall not apply if the invention was before the priority date of the claim commercially worked in the United Kingdom, otherwise than for the purpose of reasonable trial, either by the patentee or applicant for the patent or any person from whom he derives title or by any other person with the consent of the patentee or applicant for the patent or any person from whom he derives title.

(3) Where a complete specification is filed in pursuance of an application for a patent made by a person being the true and first inventor or deriving title from him, an invention claimed in that specification shall not be deemed to have been anticipated by reason only of any other application for a patent in respect of the same invention, made in contravention of the rights of that person, or by reason only that after the date of filing of that other application the invention was used or published, without the consent of that person, by the applicant in respect of that other application, or by any other person in consequence of any disclosure of the invention by that applicant.

(4) Notwithstanding anything in this Act, the comptroller shall not refuse to accept a complete specification or to grant a patent, and a patent shall not be revoked or invalidated, by reason only of any circumstances which, by virtue of this section, do not constitute an anticipation of the invention claimed in the specification.

1190 **Previous communication, display or working**

51.—(1) An invention claimed in a complete specification shall not be deemed to have been anticipated by reason only of the communication of the invention to a Government department or to any person authorised by a Government department to investigate the invention or its merits, or of anything done, in consequence of such a communication, for the purpose of the investigation.

(2) An invention claimed in a complete specification shall not be deemed to have been anticipated by reason only of—

(a) the display of the invention with the consent of the true and first inventor at an exhibition certified by the Board of Trade for the purposes of this section, or the use thereof with his consent for the purposes of such an exhibition in the place where it is held;

(b) the publication of any description of the invention in consequence of the display or use of the invention at any such exhibition as aforesaid;

(c) the use of the invention, after it has been displayed or used at any such exhibition as aforesaid and during the period of the exhibition, by any person without the consent of the true and first inventor; or

(d) the description of the invention in a paper read by the true and first inventor before a learned society or published with his consent in the transactions of such a society,

if the application for the patent is made by the true and first inventor or a person deriving title from him not later than six months after the opening of the exhibition or the reading or publication of the paper as the case may be.

(3) An invention claimed in a complete specification shall not be deemed to have been anticipated by reason only that, at any time within one year before the priority date of the relevant claim of the specification, the invention was publicly worked in the United Kingdom—

(a) by the patentee or applicant for the patent or any person from whom he derives title; or

(b) by any other person with the consent of the patentee or applicant for the patent or any person from whom he derives title,

if the working was effected for the purpose of reasonable trial only and if it was reasonably necessary, having regard to the nature of the invention, that the working for that purpose should be effected in public.

(4) Notwithstanding anything in this Act, the comptroller shall not refuse to accept a complete specification or to grant a patent, and a patent shall not be revoked or invalidated, by reason only of any circumstances which, by virtue of this section, do not constitute an anticipation of the invention claimed in the specification.

1191 Use and publication after provisional specification or foreign application

    52.—(1) Where a complete specification is filed or proceeded with in pursuance of an application which was accompanied by a provisional specification or by a specification treated by virtue of a direction under subsection (4) of section three of this Act as a provisional specification, then, notwithstanding anything in this Act, the comptroller shall not refuse to grant the patent, and the patent shall not be revoked or invalidated by reason only that any matter described in the provisional specification or in the specification treated as aforesaid as a provisional specification was used or published at any time after the date of filing of that specification.

    (2) Where a complete specification is filed in pursuance of a convention application, then, notwithstanding anything in this Act, the comptroller shall not refuse to grant the patent, and the patent shall not be revoked or invalidated by reason only that any matter disclosed in any application for protection in a convention country upon which the convention application is founded was used or published at any time after the date of that application for protection.

1192 Priority date in case of obtaining

    53. Where an application is made for a patent for an invention which has been claimed in a complete specification filed in pursuance of any other such application, then if—

        (*a*) the comptroller has refused to grant a patent in pursuance of that other application on the ground specified in paragraph (*a*) of subsection (1) of section fourteen of this Act;

        (*b*) a patent granted in pursuance of that other application has been revoked by the court or the comptroller on the ground specified in paragraph (*a*) of subsection (1) of section fourteen or paragraph (*c*) of subsection (1) of section thirty-two of this Act; or

        (*c*) the complete specification filed in pursuance of the said other application has, in proceedings under section fourteen or section thirty-three of this Act, been amended by the exclusion of the claim relating to the said invention in consequence of a finding by the comptroller that the invention was obtained by the applicant or patentee from any other person,

the comptroller may direct that the first-mentioned application and any specification filed in pursuance thereof shall be deemed, for the purposes of the provisions of this Act relating to the priority date of claims of complete specifications, to have been filed on the date on which the corresponding document was or was deemed to have been filed in the proceedings upon the said other application.

Miscellaneous Provisions as to the Rights in Inventions

1193 Co-ownership of patents

    54.—(1) Where after the commencement of this Act, a patent is granted to two or more persons, each of those persons shall, unless an agreement to the contrary is in force, be entitled to an equal undivided share in the patent.

(2) Subject to the provisions of this and the next following section, where two or more persons are registered as grantee or proprietor of a patent, then, unless an agreement to the contrary is in force, each of those persons shall be entitled, by himself or his agents, to make, use, exercise and vend the patented invention for his own benefit without accounting to the other or others.

(3) Subject to the provisions of the next following section, and to any agreement for the time being in force, a licence under a patent shall not be granted, and a share in a patent shall not be assigned, except with the consent of all persons, other than the licensor or assignor, who are registered as grantee or proprietor of the patent.

(4) Where an article is sold by one of two or more persons registered as grantee or proprietor of a patent, the purchaser and any person claiming through him shall be entitled to deal with it in the same manner as if the article had been sold by a sole patentee.

(5) Subject to the provisions of this section, the rules of law applicable to the ownership and devolution of personal property generally shall apply in relation to patents as they apply in relation to other choses in action; and nothing in subsection (1) or subsection (2) of this section shall affect the mutual rights or obligations of trustees or of the personal representatives of a deceased person, or their rights or obligations as such.

1194 Power of comptroller to give directions to co-owners

55.—(1) Where two or more persons are registered as grantee or proprietor of a patent, the comptroller may, upon application made to him in the prescribed manner by any of those persons, give such directions in accordance with the application as to the sale or lease of the patent or any interest therein, the grant of licences under the patent, or the exercise of any right under the last foregoing section in relation thereto, as he thinks fit.

(2) If any person registered as grantee or proprietor of the patent fails to execute any instrument or to do any other thing required for the carrying out of any direction given under this section within fourteen days after being requested in writing so to do by any of the other persons so registered, the comptroller may, upon application made to him in the prescribed manner by any such other person, give directions empowering any person to execute that instrument or to do that thing in the name and on behalf of the person in default.

(3) Before giving directions in pursuance of an application under this section, the comptroller shall give an opportunity to be heard—

(a) in the case of an application under subsection (1) of this section, to the other person or persons registered as grantee or proprietor of the patent;

(b) in the case of an application under subsection (2) of this section, to the person in default.

(4) An appeal shall lie from any decision or direction of the comptroller under this section.

(5) No directions shall be given under this section so as to affect the mutual rights or obligations of trustees or of the personal representatives of a deceased person, or their rights or obligations as such.

1195   Disputes as to inventions made by employees

56.—(1) Where a dispute arises between an employer and a person who is or was at the material time his employee as to the rights of the parties in respect of an invention made by the employee either alone or jointly with other employees or in respect of any patent granted or to be granted in respect thereof, the comptroller may, upon application made to him in the prescribed manner by either of the parties, and after giving to each of them an opportunity to be heard, determine the matter in dispute, and may make such orders for giving effect to his decision as he considers expedient:

Provided that if it appears to the comptroller upon any application under this section that the matter in dispute involves questions which would more properly be determined by the court, he may decline to deal therewith.

(2) In proceedings before the court between an employer and a person who is or was at the material time his employee, or upon an application made to the comptroller under subsection (1) of this section, the court or comptroller may, unless satisfied that one or other of the parties is entitled, to the exclusion of the other, to the benefit of an invention made by the employee, by order provide for the apportionment between them of the benefit of the invention, and of any patent granted or to be granted in respect thereof, in such manner as the court or comptroller considers just.

(3) A decision of the comptroller under this section shall have the same effect as between the parties and persons claiming under them as a decision of the court.

(4) An appeal shall lie from any decision of the comptroller under this section.

1196   Avoidance of certain restrictive conditions

57.—(1) Subject to the provisions of this section, any condition of a contract for the sale or lease of a patented article or of an article made by a patented process or for licence to use or work a patented article or process, or relating to any such sale, lease or licence, shall be void in so far as it purports—

(a) to require the purchaser, lessee or licensee to acquire from the vendor, lessor or licensor, or his nominees, or prohibit him from acquiring from any specified person, or from acquiring except from the vendor, lessor or licensor, or his nominees, any articles other than the patented article or an article made by the patented process;

(b) to prohibit the purchaser, lessee or licensee from using articles (whether patented or not) which are not supplied by, or any patented process which does not belong to, the vendor, lessor or licensor, or his nominees, or to restrict the right of the purchaser, lessee or licensee to use any such articles or process.

(2) In proceedings against any person for infringement of a patent, it shall be a defence to prove that at the time of the infringement there was in force a contract relating to the patent made by or with the consent of the plaintiff and containing a condition void by virtue of this section.

(3) A condition of a contract shall not be void by virtue of this section if—

    (*a*) at the time of the making of the contract the vendor, lessor or licensor was willing to sell or lease the article, or grant a licence to use or work the article or process, as the case may be, to the purchaser, lessee or licensee, on reasonable terms specified in the contract and without any such condition as is mentioned in subsection (1) of this section; and

    (*b*) the purchaser, lessee or licensee is entitled under the contract to relieve himself of his liability to observe the condition upon giving to the other party three months' notice in writing and subject to payment to him of such compensation (being, in the case of a purchase a lump sum, and in the case of a lease or licence a rent or royalty for the residue of the term of the contract) as may be determined by an arbitrator appointed by the Board of Trade.

(4) If in any proceeding it is alleged that any condition of a contract is void by virtue of this section, it shall lie on the vendor, lessor or licensor to prove the matters set out in paragraph (*a*) of the last foregoing subsection.

(5) A condition of a contract shall not be void by virtue of this section by reason only that it prohibits any person from selling goods other than those supplied by a specified person, or, in the case of a contract for the lease of or licence to use a patented article, that it reserves to the lessor or licensor or his nominees the right to supply such new parts of the patented article as may be required to put or keep it in repair.

¶197 Determination of certain contracts

58.—(1) Any contract for the sale or lease of a patented article or for licence to manufacture, use or work a patented article or process, or relating to any such sale, lease or licence, whether made before or after the commencement of this Act, may at any time after the patent or all the patents by which the article or process was protected at the time of the making of the contract has or have ceased to be in force, and notwithstanding anything to the contrary in the contract or in any other contract, be determined by either party on giving three months notice in writing to the other party.

(2) Where notice is given under this section to determine a contract made before the twenty-eighth day of August, nineteen hundred and seven, the party by whom the notice is given shall be liable to pay to the other party such compensation as may, in default of agreement, be determined by an arbitrator appointed by the Board of Trade.

(3) The provisions of this section shall be without prejudice to any right of determining a contract exercisable apart from this section.

Proceedings for Infringement, Etc.

¶198 Restrictions on recovery of damages for infringement

59.—(1) In proceedings for the infringement of a patent damages shall not be awarded against a defendant who proves that at the date of the infringement he was not aware, and had no reasonable ground for supposing, that the patent existed; and a person shall not be deemed to have been aware or to have had reasonable grounds for supposing as aforesaid by reason only of the application to an article of the word " patent," " patented," or any word or words expressing or implying that a patent has been obtained for the article, unless the number of the patent accompanied the word or words in question.

(2) In any proceeding for infringement of a patent the court may, if it thinks fit, refuse to award any damages in respect of any infringement committed after a failure to pay any renewal fee within the prescribed period and before any extension of that period.

(3) Where an amendment of a specification by way of disclaimer, correction or explanation has been allowed under this Act after the publication of the specification, no damages shall be awarded in any proceeding in respect of the use of the invention before the date of the decision allowing the amendment, unless the court is satisfied that the specification as originally published was framed in good faith and with reasonable skill and knowledge.

(4) Nothing in this section shall affect the power of the court to grant an injunction in any proceedings for infringement of a patent.

1199 Order for account in action for infringement

60. In an action for infringement of a patent the plaintiff shall be entitled, at his option, to an account of profits in lieu of damages.

1200 Counterclaim for revocation in action for infringement

61.[9] A defendant in an action for infringement of a patent may, without presenting a petition, apply in accordance with rules of court by way of counterclaim in the action for revocation of the patent.

1201 Relief for infringement of partially valid specification

62.—(1) If in proceedings for infringement of a patent it is found that any claim of the specification, being a claim in respect of which infringement is alleged, is valid, but that any other claim is invalid, the court may grant relief in respect of any valid claim which is infringed:

Provided that the court shall not grant relief by way of damages or costs except in the circumstances mentioned in the next following subsection.

(2) Where the patent is dated before the first day of November, nineteen hundred and thirty-two, or the plaintiff proves that the invalid claim was framed in good faith and with reasonable skill and knowledge, the court shall grant relief in respect of any valid claim which is infringed subject to the discretion of the court as to costs and as to the date from which damages should be reckoned.

(3) As a condition of relief under subsection (1) or subsection (2) of this section the court may direct that the specification shall be amended to its satisfaction upon an application made for that purpose under section thirty of this Act, and such an application may be made accordingly whether or not all other issues in the proceedings have been determined.

9 s. 61 amended as relates to N.I. by the Northern Ireland Act 1962.

(4) In relation to a patent which is dated before the first day of November, nineteen hundred and thirty-two, the provisions of this section shall have effect notwithstanding anything in subsection (3) of section fifty-nine of this Act.

1202 Proceedings for infringement by exclusive licensee

63.—(1) Subject to the provisions of this section, the holder of an exclusive licence under a patent shall have the like right as the patentee to take proceedings in respect of any infringement of the patent committed after the date of the licence, and in awarding damages or granting any other relief in any such proceedings, the court shall take into consideration any loss suffered or likely to be suffered by the exclusive licensee as such or, as the case may be, the profits earned by means of the infringement so far as it constitutes an infringement of the rights of the exclusive licensee as such.

(2) In any proceedings taken by the holder of an exclusive licence by virtue of this section, the patentee shall, unless he is joined as plaintiff in the proceedings, be added as defendant:

Provided that a patentee so added as defendant shall not be liable for any costs unless he enters an appearance and takes part in the proceedings.

1203 Certificate of contested validity of specification

64.—(1) If in any proceedings before the court the validity of any claim of a specification is contested, and that claim is found by the court to be valid, the court may certify that the validity of that claim was contested in those proceedings.

(2) Where any such certificate has been granted, then if in any subsequent proceedings before the court for infringement of the patent or for revocation of the patent, a final order or judgment is made or given in favour of the party relying on the validity of the patent, that party shall, unless the court otherwise directs, be entitled to his costs as between solicitor and client so far as concerns the claim in respect of which the certificate was granted:

Provided that this subsection shall not apply to the costs of any appeal in any such proceedings as aforesaid.

1204 Remedy for groundless threats of infringement proceedings

65.—(1) Where any person (whether entitled to or interested in a patent or an application for a patent or not) by circulars, advertisements or otherwise threatens any other person with proceedings for infringement of a patent, any person aggrieved thereby may bring an action against him for any such relief as is mentioned in the next following subsection.

(2) Unless in any action brought by virtue of this section the defendant proves that the acts in respect of which proceedings were threatened constitute or, if done, would constitute, an infringement of a patent or of rights arising from the publication of a complete specification in respect of a claim of the specification not shown by the plaintiff to be invalid, the plaintiff shall be entitled to the following relief, that is to say:

(*a*) a declaration to the effect that the threats are unjustifiable;
(*b*) an injunction against the continuance of the threats; and
(*c*) such damages, if any, as he has sustained thereby.

(3) For the avoidance of doubt it is hereby declared that a mere notification of the existence of a patent does not constitute a threat of proceedings within the meaning of this section.

1205 Power of court to make declaration as to non-infringement

66.—(1) A declaration that the use by any person of any process, or the making or use or sale by any person of any article, does not or would not constitute an infringement of a claim of a patent may be made by the court in proceedings between that person and the patentee or the holder of an exclusive licence under the patent, notwithstanding that no assertion to the contrary has been made by the patentee or licensee, if it is shown—

(*a*) that the plaintiff has applied in writing to the patentee or licensee for a written acknowledgment to the effect of the declaration claimed, and has furnished him with full particulars in writing of the process or article in question; and

(*b*) that the patentee or licensee has refused or neglected to give such an acknowledgment.

(2) The costs of all parties in proceedings for a declaration brought by virtue of this section shall, unless for special reasons the court thinks fit to order otherwise, be paid by the plaintiff.

(3) The validity of a claim of the specification of a patent shall not be called in question in proceedings for a declaration brought by virtue of this section, and accordingly the making or refusal of such a declaration in the case of a patent shall not be deemed to imply that the patent is valid.

(4) Proceedings for a declaration may be brought by virtue of this section at any time after the date of the publication of the complete specification in pursuance of an application for a patent, and references in this section to the patentee shall be construed accordingly.

1206 Reference to comptroller of disputes as to infringement

67.—(1) Any dispute between a patentee or an exclusive licensee and any other person—

(*a*) whether any claim of the specification of a patent is infringed by anything done by that other person; or

(*b*) whether any such claim which is alleged to be so infringed is valid,

may, by agreement between the parties, be referred to the comptroller for determination in accordance with such procedure as may be prescribed by rules made by the Board of Trade under this Act:

Provided that if it appears to the comptroller that any dispute referred to him under this section involves questions which would more properly be determined by the court, he may decline to deal therewith.

(2) If on a reference under this section the comptroller finds that any claim of the specification of the patent is valid and is infringed,

he may, subject to the provisions of this section and of section fifty-nine of this Act, grant relief by way of damages; but the damages awarded in the proceedings shall not (unless otherwise agreed between the parties) exceed one thousand pounds.

(3) Subsection (1) of section thirty and section sixty-two of this Act shall apply to proceedings before the comptroller on a reference under this section as they apply to proceedings for infringement of a patent before the court.

(4) The Arbitration Acts, 1889 and 1934, shall not apply to proceedings before the comptroller on a reference under this section.

(5) The decision of the comptroller on a reference under this section shall not be binding upon any party thereto in any subsequent proceedings before the court for infringement of the patent or for revocation of the patent; but a patentee or licensee shall not be entitled, in any such subsequent proceedings for infringement, to any relief in respect of an alleged infringement which was in issue in proceedings under this section.

International Agreements, Etc.

1207 Orders in Council as to convention countries

68.—(1) His Majesty may, with a view to the fulfilment of a treaty, convention, arrangement or engagement, by Order in Council declare that any country specified in the Order is a convention country for the purposes of this Act:

Provided that a declaration may be made as aforesaid for the purposes either of all or of some only of the provisions of this Act, and a country in the case of which a declaration made for the purposes of some only of the provisions of this Act is in force shall be deemed to be a convention country for the purposes of those provisions only.

(2) His Majesty may by Order in Council direct that any of the Channel Islands, any colony, any British protectorate or protected State, or any territory administered by His Majesty's Government in the United Kingdom under the trusteeship system of the United Nations, shall be deemed to be a convention country for the purposes of all or any of the provisions of this Act; and an Order made under this subsection may direct that any such provisions shall have effect, in relation to the territory in question, subject to such conditions or limitations, if any, as may be specified in the Order.

(3) For the purposes of subsection (1) of this section, every colony, protectorate, territory subject to the authority or under the suzerainty of another country, and territory administered by another country in accordance with a mandate from the League of Nations or under the trusteeship system of the United Nations, shall be deemed to be a country in the case of which a declaration may be made under that subsection.

1208 Supplementary provisions as to convention applications

69.—(1) Where a person has applied for protection for an invention by an application which—

(*a*) in accordance with the terms of a treaty subsisting between any two or more convention countries, is equivalent to an application duly made in any one of those convention countries, or

(*b*) in accordance with the law of any convention country, is equivalent to an application duly made in that convention country,

he shall be deemed for the purposes of this Act to have applied in that convention country.

(2) For the purpose of this Act, matter shall be deemed to have been disclosed in an application for protection in a convention country if it was claimed or disclosed (otherwise than by way of disclaimer or acknowledgment of prior art) in that application or in documents submitted by the applicant for protection in support of and at the same time as that application; but no account shall be taken of any disclosure effected by any such document unless a copy of the document is filed at the Patent Office with the convention application or within such period as may be prescribed after the filing of that application.

1209 Special provisions as to vessels, aircraft and land vehicles

70.—(1) Where a vessel or aircraft registered in a convention country, or a land vehicle owned by a person ordinarily resident in such a country, comes into the United Kingdom or the Isle of Man (including the territorial waters thereof) temporarily or accidentally only, the rights conferred by a patent for an invention shall not be deemed to be infringed by the use of the invention—

(*a*) in the body of the vessel or in the machinery, tackle, apparatus or other accessories thereof, so far as the invention is used on board the vessel and for its actual needs only; or

(*b*) in the construction or working of the aircraft or land vehicle or of the accessories thereof,

as the case may be.

(2) This section shall not affect the provisions of section fifty-three of the Civil Aviation Act, 1949 (which exempts certain aircraft from seizure on patent claims).

1210 Extension of time for certain convention applications

71.—(1) If the Board of Trade are satisfied that provision substantially equivalent to the provision to be made by or under this section has been or will be made under the law of any convention country, they may make rules empowering the comptroller to extend the time for making application under subsection (2) of section one of this Act for a patent for an invention in respect of which protection has been applied for in that country in any case where the period specified in the proviso to that subsection expires during a period prescribed by the rules.

(2) Rules made under this section—

(*a*) may, where any agreement or arrangement has been made between His Majesty's Government in the United Kingdom and the government of the convention country for the supply or mutual exchange of information or articles, provide, either generally or in any class of case specified in the rules, that an extension of time shall not be granted under the section unless the invention has been communicated in accordance with the agreement or arrangement;

(b) may, either generally or in any class of case specified in the rules, fix the maximum extension which may be granted under this section and provide for reducing the term of any patent granted on an application made by virtue of this section, and (notwithstanding anything in section ninety-nine of, or the First Schedule to, this Act) vary, with the approval of the Treasury, the time for the payment of renewal fees in respect of such a patent and the amount of such fees;

(c) may prescribe or allow any special procedure in connection with applications made by virtue of this section;

(d) may empower the comptroller to extend, in relation to an application made by virtue of this section, the time limited by or under the foregoing provisions of this Act for doing any act, subject to such conditions, if any, as may be imposed by or under the rules;

(e) may provide for securing that the rights conferred by a patent granted on an application made by virtue of this section shall be subject to such restrictions or conditions as may be specified by or under the rules and in particular to restrictions and conditions for the protection of persons (including persons acting on behalf of His Majesty) who, otherwise than as the result of a communication made in accordance with such an agreement or arrangement as is mentioned in paragraph (a) of this subsection, and before the date of the application in question or such later date as may be allowed by the rules, may have made, used, exercised or vended the invention or may have applied for a patent in respect thereof.

1211 Protection of inventions communicated under international agreements

72.—(1) Subject to the provisions of this section, the Board of Trade may make rules for securing that, where an invention has been communicated in accordance with an agreement or arrangement made between His Majesty's Government in the United Kingdom and the government of any other country for the supply or mutual exchange of information or articles,—

(a) an application for a patent made by the person from whom the invention was communicated or his personal representative or assignee shall not be prejudiced, and a patent granted on such an application shall not be invalidated, by reason only that the invention has been communicated as aforesaid or that in consequence thereof—

(i) the invention has been published, made, used, exercised or vended, or

         (ii) an application for a patent has been made by any other person, or a patent has been granted on such an application;

   (*b*) any application for a patent made in consequence of such a communication as aforesaid may be refused and any patent granted on such an application may be revoked.

(2) Rules made under subsection (1) of this section may provide that the publication, making, use, exercise or vending of an invention, or the making of any application for a patent in respect thereof shall, in such circumstances and subject to such conditions or exceptions as may be prescribed by the rules, be presumed to have been in consequence of such a communication as is mentioned in that subsection.

(3) The powers of the Board of Trade under this section, so far as they are exercisable for the benefit of persons from whom inventions have been communicated to His Majesty's Government in the United Kingdom by the government of any other country, shall only be exercised if and to the extent that the Board are satisfied that substantially equivalent provision has been or will be made under the law of that country for the benefit of persons from whom inventions have been communicated by His Majesty's Government in the United Kingdom to the government of that country.

(4) References in the last foregoing subsection to the communication of an invention to or by His Majesty's Government or the government of any other country shall be construed as including references to the communication of the invention by or to any person authorised in that behalf by the government in question.

Register of Patents, Etc.

1212   Register of patents

   73.—(1) There shall be kept at the Patent Office a register of patents, in which there shall be entered particulars of patents in force, of assignments and transmissions of patents and of licences under patents, and notice of all matters which are required by or under this Act to be entered in the register and of such other matters affecting the validity or proprietorship of patents as the comptroller thinks fit.

(2) Subject to the provisions of this Act and to rules made by the Board of Trade thereunder, the register of patents shall, at all convenient times, be open to inspection by the public; and certified copies, sealed with the seal of the Patent Office, of any entry in the register shall be given to any person requiring them on payment of a prescribed fee.

(3) The register of patents shall be prima facie evidence of any matters required or authorised by or under this Act to be entered therein.

(4) No notice of any trust, whether expressed, implied or constructive, shall be entered in the register of patents, and the comptroller shall not be affected by any such notice.

1213 Registration of assignments, etc.

74.—(1) Where any person becomes entitled by assignment, transmission or operation of law to a patent or to a share in a patent, or becomes entitled as mortgagee, licensee or otherwise to any other interest in a patent, he shall apply to the comptroller in the prescribed manner for the registration of his title as proprietor or co-proprietor, or, as the case may be, of notice of his interest, in the register of patents.

(2) Without prejudice to the provisions of the foregoing subsection, an application for the registration of the title of any person becoming entitled by assignment to a patent or a share in a patent, or becoming entitled by virtue of a mortgage, licence or other instrument to any other interest in a patent, may be made in the prescribed manner by the assignor, mortgagor, licensor or other party to that instrument, as the case may be.

(3) Where application is made under this section for the registration of the title of any person, the comptroller shall, upon proof of title to his satisfaction—

(a) where that person is entitled to a patent or a share in a patent, register him in the register of patents as proprietor or co-proprietor of the patent, and enter in that register particulars of the instrument or event by which he derives title; or

(b) where that person is entitled to any other interest in the patent, enter in that register notice of his interest, with particulars of the instrument (if any) creating it.

(4) Subject to the provisions of this Act relating to co-ownership of patents, and subject also to any rights vested in any other person of which notice is entered in the register of patents, the person or persons registered as grantee or proprietor of a patent shall have power to assign, grant licences under, or otherwise deal with the patent, and to give effectual receipts for any consideration for any such assignment, licence or dealing:

Provided that any equities in respect of the patent may be enforced in like manner as in respect of any other personal property.

(5) Rules made by the Board of Trade under this Act may require the supply to the comptroller for filing at the Patent Office of copies of such deeds, licences and other documents as may be prescribed by the rules.

(6) Except for the purposes of an application to rectify the register under the following provisions of this Act, a document in respect of which no entry has been made in the register of patents under subsection (3) of this section shall not be admitted in any court as evidence of the title of any person to a patent or share of or interest in a patent unless the court otherwise directs.

1214 Rectification of register

75.—(1) The court may, on the application of any person aggrieved, order the register of patents to be rectified by the making of any entry therein or the variation or deletion of any entry therein.

(2) In proceedings under this section the court may determine

any question which it may be necessary or expedient to decide in connection with the rectification of the register.

(3) Notice of any application to the court under this section shall be given in the prescribed manner to the comptroller, who shall be entitled to appear and be heard on the application, and shall appear if so directed by the court.

(4) Any order made by the court under this section shall direct that notice of the order shall be served on the comptroller in the prescribed manner; and the comptroller shall, on the receipt of the notice, rectify the register accordingly.

1215   Power to correct clerical errors, etc.

76.—(1) The comptroller may, in accordance with the provisions of this section, correct any clerical error in any patent, any application for a patent or any document filed in pursuance of such an application, or any error in the register of patents.

(2) A correction may be made in pursuance of this section either upon a request in writing made by any person interested and accompanied by the prescribed fee, or without such a request.

(3) Where the comptroller proposes to make any such correction as aforesaid otherwise than in pursuance of a request made under this section, he shall give notice of the proposal to the patentee or the applicant for the patent, as the case may be, and to any other person who appears to him to be concerned, and shall give them an opportunity to be heard before making the correction.

(4) Where a request is made under this section for the correction of any error in a patent or application for a patent or any document filed in pursuance of such an application, and it appears to the comptroller that the correction would materially alter the meaning or scope of the document to which the request relates, and ought not to be made without notice to persons affected thereby, he shall require notice of the nature of the proposed correction to be advertised in the prescribed manner.

(5) Within the prescribed time after any such advertisement as aforesaid any person interested may give notice to the comptroller of opposition to the request, and where such notice of opposition is given the comptroller shall give notice thereof to the person by whom the request was made, and shall give to him and to the opponent an opportunity to be heard before he decides the case.

1216   Evidence of entries, documents, etc.

77.—(1) A certificate purporting to be signed by the comptroller and certifying that any entry which he is authorised by or under this Act to make has or has not been made, or that any other thing which he is so authorised to do has or has not been done, shall be prima facie evidence of the matters so certified.

(2) A copy of any entry in any register or of any document kept in the Patent Office or of any patent, or an extract from any such register or document, purporting to be certified by the comptroller and to be sealed with the seal of the Patent Office, shall be admitted

in evidence without further proof and without production of the original.

1217 Requests for information as to patent or patent application

78. The comptroller shall, on request made to him in the prescribed manner by any person and on payment of the prescribed fee, furnish the person making the request with such information relating to any patent or application for a patent as may be specified in the request, being information in respect of any such matters as may be prescribed.

1218 Restriction upon publication of specifications, etc.

79.—(1) An application for a patent, and any specification filed in pursuance thereof, shall not, except with the consent of the applicant, be published by the comptroller or be open to public inspection at any time before the date advertised in the Journal in pursuance of subsection (2) of section thirteen of this Act.

(2) The reports of examiners made under this Act shall not be open to public inspection or be published by the comptroller; and such reports shall not be liable to production or inspection in any legal proceeding unless the court or officer having power to order discovery in the proceeding certifies that the production or inspection is desirable in the interests of justice, and ought to be allowed:

Provided that the comptroller may, on application made in the prescribed manner by any person, disclose the result of any search made under section seven or section eight of this Act in respect of any application for a patent where the complete specification has been published.

1219 Loss or destruction of patent

80. Where the comptroller is satisfied that a patent has been lost or destroyed or cannot be produced, he may at any time cause a duplicate thereof to be sealed.

Proceedings before Comptroller

1220 Exercise of discretionary powers of comptroller

81. Without prejudice to any provisions of this Act requiring the comptroller to hear any party to proceedings thereunder, or to give to any such party an opportunity to be heard, the comptroller shall give to any applicant for a patent, or for amendment of a specification, an opportunity to be heard before exercising adversely to the applicant any discretion vested in the comptroller by or under this Act.

1221 Costs and security for costs

82.—(1) The comptroller may, in any proceedings before him under this Act, by order award to any party such costs as he may consider reasonable, and direct how and by what parties they are to be paid; and any such order may be made a rule of court.

(2) If any party by whom notice of any opposition is given under this Act or by whom application is made to the comptroller for the revocation of a patent or for the grant of a licence under a patent or for the determination of a dispute as to an invention under section fifty-six of this Act, or by whom notice of appeal is given from any decision of the comptroller under this Act, neither resides nor carries on business in the United Kingdom or the Isle of Man, the comptroller, or in the case of appeal, the Appeal Tribunal, may require him to give security for the costs of the proceedings or appeal, and in default of such security being given may treat the opposition, application or appeal as abandoned.

1222 Evidence before comptroller

83.—(1) Subject to rules made by the Board of Trade under this Act the evidence to be given in any proceedings before the comptroller under this Act may be given by affidavit or statutory declaration; but the comptroller may if he thinks fit in any particular case take oral evidence in lieu of or in addition to such evidence as aforesaid, and may allow any witness to be cross-examined on his affidavit or declaration.

(2) Subject to any such rules as aforesaid, the comptroller shall, in respect of the examination of witnesses on oath and the discovery and production of documents, have all the powers of an official referee of the Supreme Court, and the rules applicable to the attendance of witnesses in proceedings before such a referee shall apply to the attendance of witnesses in proceedings before the comptroller.

The Court and the Appeal Tribunal

1223 The Court

84.[10]—(1) Subject to the provisions of this Act relating to Scotland, Northern Ireland and the Isle of Man, any petition under section twenty-three or section twenty-four of this Act and any reference or application to the court under this Act shall, subject to rules of court, be dealt with by such judge of the High Court as the Lord Chancellor may select for the purpose.

(2) Rules of court shall make provision for the appointment of scientific advisers to assist the court in proceedings for infringement of patents and in proceedings under this Act, and for regulating the functions of such advisers.

(3) The remuneration of any adviser appointed in pursuance of rules made in accordance with this section shall be defrayed out of moneys provided by Parliament.

(4) Any action for infringement of a patent shall be tried without a jury unless the court otherwise directs.

1224 The Appeal Tribunal

85.—(1) Subject to the provisions of this Act with respect to Scottish appeals, any appeal from the comptroller under this Act shall lie to the Appeal Tribunal.

[10] s. 84 amended as relates to N.I. by the Northern Ireland Act 1962.

(2)[11] The Appeal Tribunal shall consist of one or more judges of the High Court nominated for the purpose by the Lord Chancellor.

(2A)[12] At any time when it consists of two or more judges, the jurisdiction of the Appeal Tribunal—

(a) where in the case of any particular appeal the senior of those judges so directs, shall be exercised in relation to that appeal by both of the judges, or (if there are more than two) by two of them, sitting together, and

(b) in relation to any appeal in respect of which no such direction is given, may be exercised by any one of the judges;

and, in the exercise of that jurisdiction, different appeals may be heard at the same time by different judges.

(3) The expenses of the Appeal Tribunal shall be defrayed and the fees to be taken therein may be fixed as if the Tribunal were a court of the High Court.

(4) The Appeal Tribunal may examine witnesses on oath and administer oaths for that purpose.

(5) Upon any appeal under this Act the Appeal Tribunal may by order award to any party such costs as the Tribunal may consider reasonable and direct how and by what parties the costs are to be paid; and any such order may be made a rule of court.

(6) [Subsection (6) was repealed by the Administration of Justice Act 1970.]

(7) Upon any appeal under this Act the Appeal Tribunal may exercise any power which could have been exercised by the comptroller in the proceeding from which the appeal is brought.

(8) Subject to the foregoing provisions of this section, the Appeal Tribunal may make rules for regulating all matters relating to proceedings before it under this Act.

(8A)[13] At any time when the Appeal Tribunal consists of two or more judges, the power to make rules under sub-section (8) of this section shall be exercisable by the senior of those judges:

Provided that another of those judges may exercise that power if it appears to him that it is necessary for rules to be made and that the judge (or, if more than one, each of the judges) senior to him is for the time being prevented by illness, absence or otherwise from making them.

(9) Rules made under this section shall provide for the appointment of scientific advisers to assist the Appeal Tribunal upon appeals under this Act and for regulating the functions of such advisers; and the remuneration of a scientific adviser appointed in accordance with such rules shall be defrayed out of moneys provided by Parliament.

(10) An appeal to the Appeal Tribunal under this Act shall not be deemed to be a proceeding in the High Court.

(11)[14] For the purposes of this section the seniority of judges shall

---

[11] Subs. (2) was substituted for the original by the Administration of Justice Act 1969.

[12] Subs. (2A) was inserted by the Administration of Justice Act 1969.

[13] Subs. (8A) was inserted by the Administration of Justice Act 1969.

[14] Subs. (11) was inserted by the Administration of Justice Act 1969.

be reckoned by reference to the dates on which they were appointed judges of the High Court respectively.

1225   Appeals from decisions of the comptroller in Scottish cases

86.—(1) Where, in accordance with rules made by the Board of Trade under this Act, the comptroller has directed that any hearing for the purpose of proceedings under section fifty-five or section fifty-six of this Act shall be held in Scotland, any appeal from the comptroller in those proceedings shall lie to the Scottish Appeal Tribunal constituted in accordance with the provisions of this section.

(2) The Scottish Appeal Tribunal shall consist of a judge of the Court of Session nominated for the purpose by the Lord President of that Court.

(3) The Courts of Law Fees (Scotland) Act, 1895 (which confers power on the Court of Session to regulate fees), shall apply to the Scottish Appeal Tribunal as if the Tribunal were a court the fees payable in which would be regulated by the Lords of Council and Session under section two of that Act.

(4) The Scottish Appeal Tribunal may examine witnesses on oath and administer oaths for that purpose.

(5) Upon any appeal under this section, the Scottish Appeal Tribunal may by order award to any party such expenses as the Tribunal may consider reasonable and direct how and by what party the expenses are to be paid; and any such order may be recorded for execution in the books of council and session and shall be enforceable accordingly.

(6) Upon any appeal under this section, the Scottish Appeal Tribunal may exercise any power which could have been exercised by the comptroller in the proceeding from which the appeal is brought.

(7) Subject to the foregoing provisions of this section, rules may be made by Act of Sederunt for regulating all matters relating to proceedings before the Scottish Appeal Tribunal under this section.

(8) Rules made under this section shall provide for the appointment of scientific advisers to assist the Scottish Appeal Tribunal upon appeals under this Act and for regulating the functions of such advisers; and the remuneration of a scientific adviser appointed in accordance with such rules shall be defrayed out of moneys provided by Parliament.

(9) An appeal to the Scottish Appeal Tribunal under this section shall not be deemed to be a proceeding in the Court of Session.

1226   Appeals to Court of Appeal and Court of Session

87.—(1) An appeal shall lie to the Court of Appeal—

    (*a*) from any decision of the Appeal Tribunal on an appeal under section thirty-three or section forty-two of this Act where the effect of the decision is the revocation of a patent;

    (*b*) from any decision of the Appeal Tribunal under section fifty-five of this Act;

    (*c*) with the leave of the Tribunal, from any decision of the Tribunal under section fourteen of this Act, where the effect of the decision is the refusal of the grant of a patent on the ground specified in paragraph (*d*) or paragraph (*e*) of subsection (1) of that section.

(2) No appeal shall lie from any decision of the court under section twenty-three or section twenty-four of this Act.

(3) An appeal shall lie to the Court of Session from any decision of the Scottish Appeal Tribunal under section fifty-five of this Act.

Patent Agents

1227 **Restrictions on practice as patent agent**

88.—(1) An individual shall not, either alone or in partnership with any other person, practise, describe himself or hold himself out as a patent agent, or permit himself to be so described or held out, unless he is registered as a patent agent in the register of patent agents or, as the case may be, unless he and all his partners are so registered; and a company shall not practise, describe itself or hold itself out or permit itself to be described or held out as aforesaid unless—

(*a*) in the case of a company which began to carry on business as a patent agent before the seventeenth day of November, nineteen hundred and seventeen, a director or the manager of the company is registered as aforesaid and the name of that director or manager is mentioned as being so registered in all professional advertisements, circulars or letters issued by or with the consent of the company in which the name of the company appears;

(*b*) in any other case, every director of the company and, if the company has a manager who is not a director, that manager, is registered as aforesaid.

(2) Any person who contravenes the provisions of this section shall be liable on summary conviction to a fine not exceeding, in the case of a first offence, twenty pounds, and in the case of a second or subsequent offence, fifty pounds.

(3) Notwithstanding anything in any enactment prescribing the time within which proceedings may be brought before a court of summary jurisdiction, proceedings for an offence under this section may be begun at any time within twelve months from the date of the offence.

(4) Nothing in this section shall be construed as prohibiting solicitors from taking such part in proceedings under this Act as has heretofore been taken by solicitors.

(5) A patent agent shall not be guilty of an offence under section forty-seven of the Solicitors Act, 1932, or section thirty-nine of the Solicitors (Scotland) Act, 1933 (which prohibits the preparation for reward of certain instruments by persons not legally qualified) by reason only of the preparation by him for use in proceedings under this Act before the comptroller or the Appeal Tribunal of any document other than a deed.

(6) No person who was not registered in the register of patent agents before the fifteenth day of July, nineteen hundred and nineteen, shall be so registered unless he is a British subject or a citizen of the Republic of Ireland.

1228   Power of comptroller to refuse to deal with certain agents

89.—(1) Rules made by the Board of Trade under this Act may authorise the comptroller to refuse to recognise as agent in respect of any business under this Act—

(*a*) any individual whose name has been erased from, and not restored to, the register of patent agents, or who is for the time being suspended from acting as a patent agent;

(*b*) any person who has been convicted of an offence under the last foregoing section;

(*c*) any person who is found by the Board of Trade (after being given an opportunity to be heard) to have been convicted of any offence or to have been guilty of any such misconduct as, in the case of an individual registered in the register of patent agents, would render him liable to have his name erased therefrom;

(*d*) any person, not being registered as a patent agent, who in the opinion of the comptroller is engaged wholly or mainly in acting as agent in applying for patents in the United Kingdom or elsewhere in the name or for the benefit of a person by whom he is employed;

(*e*) any company or firm, if any person whom the comptroller could refuse to recognise as agent in respect of any business under this Act is acting as a director or manager of the company or is a partner in the firm.

(2) The comptroller shall refuse to recognise as agent in respect of any business under this Act any person who neither resides nor has a place of business in the United Kingdom or the Isle of Man.

Offences

1229   Falsification of register, etc.

90. If any person makes or causes to be made a false entry in any register kept under this Act, or a writing falsely purporting to be a copy of an entry in any such register, or produces or tenders or causes to be produced or tendered in evidence any such writing, knowing the entry or writing to be false, he shall be guilty of a misdemeanour.

1230   Unauthorised claim of patent rights

91.—(1) If any person falsely represents that any article sold by him is a patented article, he shall be liable on summary conviction to a fine not exceeding [fifty pounds [15]] and for the purposes of this provision a person who sells an article having stamped, engraved or impressed thereon or otherwise applied thereto the word " patent " or " patented," or any other word expressing or implying that the article is patented, shall be deemed to represent that the article is a patented article.

(2) If any person uses on his place of business, or on any document issued by him, or otherwise, the words " Patent Office " or any other words suggesting that his place of business is, or is officially connected with, the Patent Office, he shall be liable on summary conviction to a fine not exceeding twenty pounds.

[15] Substituted by the Criminal Justice Act 1967.

1231 Unauthorised assumption of Royal Arms

92.—(1) The grant of a patent under this Act shall not be deemed to authorise the patentee to use the Royal Arms or to place the Royal Arms on any patented article.

(2) If any person, without the authority of His Majesty, uses in connection with any business, trade, calling or profession the Royal Arms (or Arms so nearly resembling them as to be calculated to deceive) in such manner as to be calculated to lead to the belief that he is duly authorised to use the Royal Arms, then, without prejudice to any proceedings which may be taken against him under section sixty-one of the Trade Marks Act, 1938, he shall be liable on summary conviction to a fine not exceeding twenty pounds:

Provided that this section shall not affect the right, if any, of the proprietor of a trade mark containing such Arms to continue to use that trade mark.

1232 Offences by companies

93. Where an offence under section eighteen or section eighty-eight of this Act is committed by a body corporate, every person who at the time of the commission of the offence is a director, general manager, secretary or other similar officer of the body corporate, or is purporting to act in any such capacity, shall be deemed to be guilty of that offence unless he proves that the offence was committed without his consent or connivance and that he exercised all such diligence to prevent the commission of the offence as he ought to have exercised having regard to the nature of his functions in that capacity and to all the circumstances.

Rules, Etc.

1233 General power of Board of Trade to make rules, etc.

94.—(1) Subject to the provisions of this Act, the Board of Trade may make such rules as they think expedient for regulating the business of the Patent Office in relation to patents and for regulating all matters by this Act placed under the direction or control of the comptroller or the Board, and in particular, but without prejudice to the generality of the foregoing provision—

(a) for prescribing the form of applications for patents and of any specifications, drawings or other documents which may be filed at the Patent Office, and for requiring copies to be furnished of any such documents;

(b) for regulating the procedure to be followed in connection with any application or request to the comptroller or in connection with any proceeding before the comptroller and for authorising the rectification of irregularities of procedure;

(c) for regulating the keeping of the register of patents and the registration of patent agents, and for authorising, in such cases as may be prescribed by the rules, the erasure from the register of patent agents of the name of any person registered therein or the suspension of the right of any such person to act as a patent agent;

    (*d*) for authorising the publication and sale of copies of specifications, drawings and other documents in the Patent Office, and of indexes to and abridgements of such documents;

    (*e*) for prescribing anything authorised or required by this Act to be prescribed by rules made by the Board.

    (2) Rules made under this section shall provide for the publication by the comptroller—

    (*a*) of a journal (in this Act referred to as " the Journal ") containing particulars of applications for patents and other proceedings under this Act; and

    (*b*) of reports of cases relating to patents, trade marks and registered designs decided by the comptroller, the Appeal Tribunal or any court.

1234   Provisions as to rules and orders

    95.—(1) Any rules made by the Board of Trade under this Act shall be advertised twice in the Journal.

    (1A) [16] Where the Board of Trade have made rules prescribing a period for the purposes of subsection (1) of section twelve of this Act, and subsequently make rules prescribing a different period for those purposes, the subsequent rules may provide that the different period so prescribed shall apply only to applications made on or after a date specified in those rules and that the period previously prescribed shall continue to apply to applications made before that date.

    (2) Any rules made by the Board of Trade in pursuance of section seventy-one or section seventy-two of this Act, and any order made, direction given, or other action taken under the rules by the comptroller, may be made, given or taken so as to have effect as respects things done or omitted to be done on or after such date, whether before or after the coming into operation of the rules or of this Act, as may be specified in the rules.

    (3) Any power to make rules conferred by this Act on the Board of Trade or on the Appeal Tribunal shall be exercisable by statutory instrument; and the Statutory Instruments Act, 1946, shall apply to a statutory instrument containing rules made by the Appeal Tribunal in like manner as if the rules had been made by a Minister of the Crown.

    (4) Any statutory instrument containing rules made by the Board of Trade under this Act shall be subject to annulment in pursuance of a resolution of either House of Parliament.

    (5) Any Order in Council made under this Act may be revoked or varied by a subsequent Order in Council.

1235   Proceedings of Board of Trade

    96.—(1) [*Subsection* (1) *was repealed by the Industrial Expansion Act* 1968.]

    (2) All documents purporting to be orders made by the Board of Trade and to be sealed with the seal of the Board, or to be signed by a secretary, under-secretary or assistant secretary of the Board, or by

---

[16] Subs. (1A) was inserted by the Patents Act 1957, *post*, § 1250.

any person authorised in that behalf by the President of the Board, shall be received in evidence, and shall be deemed to be such orders without further proof, unless the contrary is shown.

(3) A certificate, signed by the President of the Board of Trade, that any order made or act done is the order or act of the Board, shall be conclusive evidence of the fact so certified.

Supplemental

1236 Service of notices, etc., by post

97. Any notice required or authorised to be given by or under this Act, and any application or other document so authorised or required to be made or filed, may be given, made or filed by post.

1237 Hours of business and excluded days

98.—(1) Rules made by the Board of Trade under this Act may specify the hour at which the Patent Office shall be deemed to be closed on any day for purposes of the transaction by the public of business under this Act or of any class of such business, and may specify days as excluded days for any such purposes.

(2) Any business done under this Act on any day after the hour specified as aforesaid in relation to business of that class, or on a day which is an excluded day in relation to business of that class, shall be deemed to have been done on the next following day not being an excluded day; and where the time for doing anything under this Act expires on an excluded day, that time shall be extended to the next following day not being an excluded day.

1238 Fees

99. Subject to the provisions of this Act, there shall be paid in respect of the grant of patents and applications therefor, and in respect of other matters relating to patents arising under this Act, such fees as may be prescribed by rules made by the Board of Trade with the consent of the Treasury:

Provided that the fees so prescribed in respect of the instruments and matters specified in the First Schedule to this Act shall not exceed the amounts specified in that Schedule.

1239 Annual report of comptroller

100. Before the first day of June in every year the comptroller shall cause to be laid before both Houses of Parliament a report with respect to the execution of this Act, and every such report shall include an account of all fees, salaries and allowances, and other money received and paid under this Act during the previous year.

1240 Interpretation

101.—(1) In this Act, except where the context otherwise requires, the following expressions have the meanings hereby respectively assigned to them, that is to say—

[" Appeal Tribunal " means the Appeal Tribunal constituted and

[475]

acting in accordance with section 85 of this Act as amended by the Administration of Justice Act, 1969 [17];]

" applicant " includes a person in whose favour a direction has been given under section seventeen of this Act, and the personal representative of a deceased applicant;

" article " includes any substance or material, and any plant, machinery or apparatus, whether affixed to land or not;

" assignee " includes the personal representative of a deceased assignee, and references to the assignee of any person include references to the assignee of the personal representative or assignee of that person;

" comptroller " means the Comptroller-General of Patents, Designs and Trade Marks;

" convention application " has the meaning assigned to it by subsection (4) of section one of this Act;

" court " means the High Court;

" date of filing ", in relation to any document filed under this Act, means the date on which the document is filed or, where it is deemed by virtue of any provision of this Act or of rules made thereunder, to have been filed on any different date, means the date on which it is deemed to be filed;

" exclusive licence " means a licence from a patentee which confers on the licensee, or on the licensee and persons authorised by him, to the exclusion of all other persons (including the patentee), any right in respect of the patented invention, and " exclusive licensee " shall be construed accordingly;

" invention " means any manner of new manufacture the subject of letters patent and grant of privilege within section six of the Statute of Monopolies and any new method or process of testing applicable to the improvement or control of manufacture, and includes an alleged invention;

" Journal " has the meaning assigned to it by subsection (2) of section ninety-four of this Act;

" patent " means Letters Patent for an invention;

" patent agent " means a person carrying on for gain in the United Kingdom the business of acting as agent for other persons for the purpose of applying for or obtaining patents in the United Kingdom or elsewhere;

" patent of addition " means a patent granted in accordance with section twenty-six of this Act;

" patentee " means the person or persons for the time being entered on the register of patents as grantee or proprietor of the patent;

" prescribed " means prescribed by rules made by the Board of Trade under this Act;

" priority date " has the meaning assigned to it by section five of this Act;

" published ", except in relation to a complete specification, means made available to the public; and without prejudice to the

---

[17] The words in square brackets were substituted for the original wording by the Administration of Justice Act 1969.

generality of the foregoing provision a document shall be deemed for the purposes of this Act to be published if it can be inspected as of right at any place in the United Kingdom by members of the public, whether upon payment of a fee or otherwise;

" the Statute of Monopolies " means the Act of the twenty-first year of the reign of King James the First, chapter three, intituled " An Act concerning monopolies and dispensations with penal laws and the forfeiture thereof ".

(2) For the purposes of subsection (3) of section one, so far as it relates to a convention application, and for the purposes of section seventy-two of this Act, the expression " personal representative ", in relation to a deceased person, includes the legal representative of the deceased appointed in any country outside the United Kingdom.

1241 Saving for Royal prerogative, etc.

102.—(1) Nothing in this Act shall take away, abridge or pre-judicially affect the prerogative of the Crown in relation to the granting of letters patent or to the withholding of a grant thereof.

(2) Nothing in this Act shall affect the right of the Crown or of any person deriving title directly or indirectly from the Crown to sell or use articles forfeited under the laws relating to customs or excise.

1242 Application to Scotland

103. In the application of this Act to Scotland—

(1) In any action for infringement of a patent in Scotland the action shall be tried without a jury unless the court otherwise direct, but otherwise nothing shall affect the jurisdiction and forms of process of the courts in Scotland in such an action or in any action or proceeding respecting a patent hitherto competent to those courts:

(2) Proceedings for revocation of a patent shall be in the form of an action of reduction, and service of all writs and summonses in that action shall be made according to the forms and practice existing immediately before the commencement of the Patents and Designs Act, 1907:

(3) The provisions of this Act conferring a special jurisdiction on the court as defined by this Act shall not, except so far as the jurisdiction extends, affect the jurisdiction of any court in Scotland in any proceedings relating to patents; and with reference to any such proceedings, the term " the Court " shall mean the Court of Session:

(4) Notwithstanding anything in this Act, the expression " the Court " shall in reference to proceedings in Scotland for the extension of the term of a patent mean the Court of Session:

(5) If any rectification of a register under this Act is required in pursuance of any proceeding in a court, a copy of the order, decree, or other authority for the rectification shall be served on the comptroller, and he shall rectify the register accordingly:

(6) The expression "injunction" means "interdict"; the expression "chose in action" means a right of action or an incorporeal moveable; the expression "an account of profits" means "an accounting and payment of profits"; the expression "arbitrator" means "arbiter"; the expression "plaintiff" means "pursuer"; the expression "defendant" means "defender".

1243   Application to Northern Ireland

104. In the application of this Act to Northern Ireland—

(1) All parties shall, notwithstanding anything in this Act, have in Northern Ireland their remedies under or in respect of a patent as if the same had been granted to extend to Northern Ireland only:

(2) The provisions of this Act conferring a special jurisdiction on the court, as defined by this Act, shall not, except so far as the jurisdiction extends, affect the jurisdiction of any court in Northern Ireland in any proceedings relating to patents; and with reference to any such proceedings the term "the Court" means the High Court in Northern Ireland:

(3) If any rectification of a register under this Act is required in pursuance of any proceeding in a court, a copy of the order, decree, or other authority for the rectification shall be served on the comptroller, and he shall rectify the register accordingly.

(4) References to enactments of the Parliament of the United Kingdom shall be construed as references to those enactments as they apply in Northern Ireland:

(5) References to a Government department shall be construed as including references to a department of the Government of Northern Ireland:

(6) [*Subsection (6) was repealed by the Northern Ireland Act 1962.*]

1244   Isle of Man

105. This Act shall extend to the Isle of Man, subject to the following modifications:

(1) Nothing in this Act shall affect the jurisdiction of the courts in the Isle of Man in proceedings for infringement, or in any action or proceeding respecting a patent competent to those courts;

(2) The punishment for a misdemeanour under this Act in the Isle of Man shall be imprisonment for any term not exceeding two years, with or without hard labour, and with or without a fine not exceeding one hundred pounds, at the discretion of the court:

(3) Any offence under this Act committed in the Isle of Man which would in England be punishable on summary conviction may be prosecuted, and any fine in respect thereof recovered, at the instance of any person aggrieved, in the

manner in which offences punishable on summary conviction may for the time being be prosecuted.

1245 Repeals, transitional provisions and amendment

106.—(1) Subject to the provisions of this section, the enactments specified in the Second Schedule to this Act are hereby repealed to the extent specified in the third column of that Schedule.

(2) Without prejudice to the provisions of the Interpretation Act, 1889, with respect to repeals, the transitional provisions set out in the Third Schedule to this Act shall have effect for the purposes of the transition to the provisions of this Act from the law in force before the commencement of the Patents and Designs Act, 1949.

(3) For subsection (8) of section twelve of the Atomic Energy Act, 1946, there shall be substituted the following subsection:

" (8) The power of the Minister of Supply and persons authorised by the Minister of Supply under section forty-six of the Patents Act, 1949, shall include power to make, use, exercise or vend an invention for such purposes relating to the production or use of atomic energy or research into matters connected therewith as the Minister thinks necessary or expedient, and any reference in that section or in sections forty-seven and forty-eight of that Act to the services of the Crown shall be construed as including a reference to those purposes."

1246 Short title and commencement

107.—(1) This Act may be cited as the Patents Act, 1949.

(2) This Act shall come into operation on the first day of January, nineteen hundred and fifty, immediately after the coming into operation of the Patents and Designs Act, 1949.

SCHEDULES

1247 Section 99   FIRST SCHEDULE

MAXIMUM FEES [18]

	£
On application for patent	1
On filing of complete specification	30
On sealing of patent	10
Renewal fees in respect of—	
Fifth year of patent	20
Sixth year of patent	21
Seventh year of patent	23
Eighth year of patent	25
Ninth year of patent	28
Tenth year of patent	31
Eleventh year of patent	34
Twelfth year of patent	38
Thirteenth year of patent	42
Fourteenth year of patent	46
Fifteenth year of patent	50
Sixteenth year of patent	54

[18] As substituted by S.I. 1961 No. 1499. Maximum fees may be varied by Order in Council: Patents and Designs (Renewals, Extensions and Fees) Act 1961.

1248   Section 106   SECOND SCHEDULE [19]

ENACTMENTS REPEALED

Session and Chapter	Short title	Extent of Repeal
7 Edw. 7. c. 29.	The Patents and Designs Act, 1907	The whole Act, except section forty-seven, subsections (1), (2) and (3) of section sixty-two, sections sixty-three and sixty-four, and except sections eighty-two, ninety-one and ninety-one A in their application to trade marks and except section eighty-eight in its application to any Order in Council made under section ninety-one A.

[Spent (repeals)]

1249   Section 106   THIRD SCHEDULE

Transitional Provisions

1. Subject to the provisions of this Schedule, any Order in Council, rule, order, requirement, certificate, notice, decision, direction, authorisation, consent, application, request or thing made, issued, given or done under any enactment repealed by this Act shall, if in force at the commencement of this Act, and so far as it could have been made, issued, given or done under this Act, continue in force and have effect as if made, issued, given or done under the corresponding enactment of this Act.

2. Section five of this Act shall apply in relation to a complete specification filed before the commencement of this Act as it applies to a complete specification filed after the commencement of this Act:

Provided that for the purposes of the said section five a claim of any such specification filed after a provisional specification shall be deemed to be fairly based on the matter disclosed in the provisional specification unless the claim is for a further or different invention to that contained in the provisional specification.

3. Notwithstanding anything in subsection (2) of section three of this Act, a complete specification shall not be filed in pursuance of an application which, by virtue of section five of the Patents and Designs Act, 1907, was deemed to be abandoned at any time before the commencement of this Act:

Provided that nothing in this paragraph shall affect any power of the comptroller under section six of the Patents, Designs, Copyright and Trade Marks (Emergency) Act, 1939, to extend the time for filing a complete specification.

4. Where a complete specification has been filed before the commencement of this Act but has not been accepted, then, in relation to matters arising before the acceptance or refusal of acceptance of the complete specification, the provisions of this Act shall not apply, but the provisions of the Patents and Designs Act, 1907, shall continue to apply notwithstanding the repeal of that Act.

5. The provisions of sections fourteen and thirty-three of this Act relating to the grounds on which the grant of a patent may be opposed or on which a patent may be revoked by the comptroller shall not apply in any case where the complete specification was accepted before the commencement of this Act,

[19] Printed as repealed in part by S.L.R. 1953, and amended by S.I. 1970 No. 1953.

but the provisions of the Patents and Designs Act, 1907, relating to those matters shall continue to apply in any such case notwithstanding the repeal of that Act.

6. The power of the comptroller under section fifteen of this Act to refuse the grant of a patent unless the complete specification is amended to his satisfaction shall not be exercisable in relation to any complete specification which was accepted before the commencement of this Act.

7. The provisions of section fifty-three of this Act shall apply in relation to any application for a patent made before the commencement of this Act as they apply in relation to such an application made after the commencement of this Act.

8. Notwithstanding anything in this Act, a patent sealed before the commencement of this Act, and bearing a date within the period beginning with the third day of September, nineteen hundred and thirty-nine and ending with the commencement of this Act, may be revoked by the Court on the ground specified in paragraph (oo) of subsection (2) of section twenty-five of the Patents and Designs Act, 1907.

9. Where, in relation to any invention, the time for giving notice to the comptroller under section forty-five of the Patents and Designs Act, 1907, expired before the commencement of this Act and the notice was not given, subsections (2) and (4) of section fifty-one of this Act shall not apply in relation to that invention or any patent for that invention.

10. In relation to a complete specification which was accepted before the commencement of this Act, this Act shall have effect as if for the words " the date of the publication ", wherever those words occur, there were substituted the words " the date of the acceptance ".

11. Where a specification filed before the commencement of this Act has become open to public inspection, it shall continue to be open to public inspection notwithstanding anything in section seventy-nine of this Act.

12. Where a specification which, before the commencement of this Act, has become open to public inspection under subsection (4) of section ninety-one of the Patents and Designs Act, 1907, has been amended before acceptance, nothing in subsection (2) of section thirty-one of this Act shall be construed as authorising reference to be made, in construing the specification, to the specification as it subsisted before acceptance.

13. Where two or more persons are registered as grantee or proprietor in respect of a patent which was granted or for which application was made before the commencement of this Act, the right of each of those persons to assign the whole or part of his interest in the patent shall not be restricted by reason only of the provisions of section fifty-four of this Act.

14. A condition of any contract in force immediately before the commencement of this Act shall not be invalidated by reason only of the provisions of section fifty-seven of this Act.

15. The provisions of section thirty of the Patents and Designs Act, 1907, and of any rules made by virtue of that section shall continue to apply in relation to any patent granted before the commencement of this Act in pursuance of that section notwithstanding the repeal of that Act.

16. Notwithstanding the repeal of the Patents and Designs Act, 1907, subsection (2) of section thirty-eight A of that Act shall continue to apply in any case where the complete specification was filed before the commencement of this Act.

17. Subsections (1) and (3) of section twenty-two of this Act shall not apply to any patent granted before the commencement of this Act.

18. Subsection (1) of section twenty-six of this Act shall apply in relation to any application made before the commencement of this Act as it applies in relation to an application made after the commencement of this Act.

19. Section twenty-seven of this Act shall have effect, in relation to a patent which has ceased to have effect before the commencement of this Act,

as if for the reference to section twenty-two of this Act there were substituted a reference to section seventeen of the Patents and Designs Act, 1907.

20. Where the time allowed under section twelve of the Patents and Designs Act, 1907, for the sealing of a patent has expired before the commencement of this Act and the patent has not been sealed, section twenty-eight of this Act shall have effect in relation to the application for the patent as if for the reference to section nineteen of this Act there was substituted a reference to section twelve of the Patents and Designs Act, 1907.

21. In relation to any proceedings pending at the commencement of this Act the provisions of sections thirty and sixty-two of this Act shall not apply but the provisions of sections twenty-two and thirty-two A of the Patents and Designs Act, 1907, shall continue to apply notwithstanding the repeal of that Act.

22. Section sixty-three of this Act shall not apply in relation to any infringement of a patent committed before the commencement of this Act.

23. Any register kept under the Patents and Designs Act, 1907, shall be deemed to form part of the corresponding register under this Act.

24. Nothing in this Act shall affect the term of any patent granted before the commencement of the Patents, etc. (International Conventions) Act, 1938.

25. Nothing in this Act shall affect the operation of section four of the Patents and Designs Act, 1946.

26. Any document referring to any enactment repealed by this Act shall be construed as referring to the corresponding enactment of this Act.

27. Any reference in this Schedule to the Patents and Designs Act, 1907, shall be construed as a reference to that Act as amended by any subsequent enactment other than the Patents and Designs Act, 1949.

Table of Statutes referred to in this Act

Short Title	Session and Chapter
Statute of Monopolies	21 Jac. 1. c. 3.
Petty Sessions (Ireland) Act, 1851	14 & 15 Vict. c. 93.
Interpretation Act, 1889	52 & 53 Vict. c. 63.
Courts of Land Fees (Scotland) Act, 1895 ...	58 & 59 Vict. c. 14.
Patents and Designs Act, 1907	7 Edw. 7. c. 29.
Solicitors Act, 1932	22 & 23 Geo. 5. c. 37.
Solicitors (Scotland) Act, 1933	23 & 24 Geo. 5. c. 21.
Arbitration Act, 1934	24 & 25 Geo. 5. c. 14.
Trade Marks Act, 1938	1 & 2 Geo. 6. c. 22.
Patents, etc. (International Conventions) Act, 1938	1 & 2 Geo. 6. c. 29.
Patents, Designs, Copyright and Trade Marks (Emergency) Act, 1939	2 & 3 Geo. 6. c. 107.
Statutory Instruments Act, 1946	9 & 10 Geo. 6. c. 36.
Patents and Designs Act, 1946	9 & 10 Geo. 6. c. 44.
Atomic Energy Act, 1946	9 & 10 Geo. 6. c. 80.
Crown Proceedings Act, 1947	10 & 11 Geo. 6. c. 44.
Monopolies and Restrictive Practices (Inquiry and Control) Act, 1948	11 & 12 Geo. 6. c. 66.
Patents and Designs Act, 1949	12, 13 & 14 Geo. 6. c. 62.
Civil Aviation Act, 1949	12, 13 & 14 Geo. 6. c. 67.

Patents Act, 1957

An Act to provide for extending time limits for certain purposes relating to applications for patents; to validate extensions of time under section six of the Patents, Designs, Copyright and Trade Marks (Emergency) Act, 1939, in connection with such applications in so far as any such extensions may have been invalid; and for purposes connected with the matters aforesaid.

[March 21, 1957]

1250 Time limits under ss. 12 and 13 of Patents Act, 1949

1.—(1) Section twelve of the Patents Act, 1949 (whereby an application for a patent is required to be put in order for acceptance within twelve months from the date of filing of the complete specification, subject to a right for the applicant, on payment of a fee, to have the period extended for a further three months), shall have effect subject to the following amendments, that is to say,—

(a) in subsection (1) of the section, for the words " twelve months from the date of filing of the complete specification " there shall be substituted the words " such period, beginning with the date of filing of the complete specification, as may be prescribed ";

(b) after subsection (1) of the section there shall be inserted the following subsection:
" (1A) The period prescribed for the purposes of the foregoing subsection shall not be shorter than twelve months or longer than four years ";

(c) in subsection (2) of the section, for the words " not exceeding fifteen months from the date of filing of the complete specification " there shall be substituted the words " ending not later than three months after the date on which the period allowed under that subsection (apart from any extension thereof) would otherwise have expired ".

(2) In section ninety-five of the Patents Act, 1949 (which relates to rules made for the purposes of that Act), the following subsection shall be inserted after subsection (1):
" (1A) Where the Board of Trade have made rules prescribing a period for the purposes of subsection (1) of section twelve of this Act, and subsequently make rules prescribing a different period for those purposes, the subsequent rules may provide that the different period so prescribed shall apply only to applications made on or after a date specified in those rules and that the period previously prescribed shall continue to apply to applications made before that date."

1251 Provisions as to pending applications

2.—(1) In this section—
" the original period ", in relation to an application for a patent, means the period allowed under subsection (1) of

[483]

section twelve of the Patents Act, 1949, apart from any extension thereof, and apart from the preceding section;

" the revised period ", in relation to such an application, means the period allowed under subsection (1) of the said section twelve, as amended by the preceding section, but apart from any extension of that period;

" the first year of this Act " means the period of twelve months beginning with the date of the commencement of this Act;

" prescribed " means prescribed by rules made by the Board of Trade under this section.

(2) Subject to the following provisions of this section, the amendments made by the preceding section shall apply in relation to applications for patents made before the commencement of this Act, including such applications in the case of which extensions of time have been granted under section six of the Patents, Designs, Copyright and Trade Marks (Emergency) Act, 1939 (which empowered the comptroller to extend time limits having regard to war circumstances), as they apply in relation to applications made after the commencement of this Act:

Provided that nothing in the preceding section shall be construed as reducing the duration of any extension of time granted under section six of the said Act of 1939.

(3) Where before the commencement of this Act the original period has, in the case of an application, been extended, by virtue of section six of the said Act of 1939, so as to expire on a date (in this subsection referred to as " the present date of expiry ")—

(a) after the commencement of this Act, and

(b) not less than three months after the end of the revised period, but

(c) not later than the end of the first year of this Act,

the revised period shall, in the case of that application, be extended so as to expire on such date (not being more than three months after the present date of expiry nor later than the end of the first year of this Act) as may be specified in a notice given by the applicant to the comptroller, if that notice is given and the prescribed fee paid before the date specified in the notice.

(4) Where the revised period, in the case of an application made before the commencement of this Act,—

(a) is after the commencement of this Act extended under subsection (2) of section twelve of the Patents Act, 1949 (as amended by the preceding section), or under the last preceding subsection, but

(b) as so extended, would (if not further extended) expire before the end of the first year of this Act,

the comptroller may, if he thinks fit, further extend that period until such date, not being later than the end of the first year of this Act, as he may consider reasonable in the circumstances:

Provided that the revised period shall not be extended by virtue of this subsection to a date more than three months after the date on which apart from this subsection that period would have expired.

(5) Subsection (3) of section twelve of the Patents Act, 1949 (which provides for an extension of time where an appeal is pending

or the time for appealing has not expired), shall apply in relation to the revised period as extended by virtue of the preceding provisions of this section as it applies in relation to the period referred to in that subsection.

(6) The Board of Trade may make rules prescribing anything authorised or required to be prescribed by rules under this section; and subsections (1), (3) and (4) of section ninety-five of the Patents Act, 1949, shall apply in relation to rules made under this section as they apply in relation to rules under that Act.

(7) Section ninety-six of the Patents Act, 1949 (which relates to the performance of functions thereunder by the Board of Trade), and section ninety-seven of that Act (which relates to notices), shall apply for the purposes of this section as they apply for the purposes of that Act.

1252 Extension of time under s. 6 of Patents, Designs, Copyright and Trade Marks (Emergency) Act, 1939

3. Every extension of the time limited by or under the Patents Act, 1949, or the enactments repealed by that Act, for the doing of anything in connection with an application for a patent, being an extension which the comptroller has before the commencement of this Act granted, or purported to grant, by virtue of section six of the said Act of 1939, shall be deemed to have been validly granted by virtue of that section, if apart from this section it was not validly granted by virtue of that section.

Interpretation

4.—(1) In this Act " the comptroller " means the Comptroller-General of Patents, Designs and Trade Marks.

(2) Except in so far as the context otherwise requires, any reference in this Act to an enactment shall be construed as a reference to that enactment as amended or extended by or under any other enactment.

Short title, citation, extent and commencement

5.—(1) This Act may be cited as the Patents Act, 1957; and the Patents Act, 1949, and this Act may be cited together as the Patents Acts, 1949 and 1957.

(2) This Act shall extend to the Isle of Man.

(3) It is hereby declared that this Act extends to Northern Ireland.

(4) This Act shall come into operation at the end of the period of one month beginning with the day on which it is passed.

Defence Contracts Act, 1958

ARRANGEMENT OF SECTIONS

An Act to amend the enactments authorising the use of patented
inventions and registered designs for the services of the Crown
in respect of articles required for defence and similar purposes
by the Governments of allied or associated countries or the United
Nations; to make permanent provision with respect to the use for
defence and similar purposes of other technical information
protected by contractual arrangements; to repeal certain emergency provisions relating to inventions and designs; and for
purposes connected with the matters aforesaid.

[July 7, 1958]

**1253 Amendments of statutory provisions for use of patented inventions
and registered designs for services of the Crown**

1.—(1) The following shall be substituted for subsection (6) of
section forty-six of the Patents Act, 1949 (which section relates to the
use of patented inventions for the services of the Crown):

" (6) For the purposes of this and the next following section
' the services of the Crown ' shall be deemed to include—

    (a) the supply to the government of any country outside the
United Kingdom, in pursuance of an agreement or arrangement between Her Majesty's Government in the United
Kingdom and the government of that country, of articles
required—

        (i) for the defence of that country; or

        (ii) for the defence of any other country whose govern-
ment is party to any agreement or arrangement
with Her Majesty's said Government in respect of
defence matters;

    (b) the supply to the United Nations, or to the government of
any country belonging to that organisation, in pursuance

of an agreement or arrangement between Her Majesty's Government and that organisation or government, of articles required for any armed forces operating in pursuance of a resolution of that organisation or any organ of that organisation;

and the power of a Government department or a person authorised by a Government department under this section to make, use and exercise an invention shall include power to sell to any such government or to the said organisation any articles the supply of which is authorised by this subsection, and to sell to any person any articles made in the exercise of the powers conferred by this section which are no longer required for the purpose for which they were made."

1254   (2) Where any models, documents or information relating to an invention are used in connection with any such use of the invention as is described in subsection (1) of section forty-seven of the Patents Act, 1949, subsection (3) of section forty-six of that Act (which regulates in certain cases the terms on which inventions may be used for the services of the Crown under that section) shall, whether or not it applies to the use of the invention, apply to the use of the models, documents or information as if for the reference therein to the patentee there were substituted a reference to the person entitled to the benefit of any provision of an agreement which is rendered inoperative by the said section forty-seven in relation to that use; and in section forty-eight of that Act (which provides for the determination of disputes) the references to terms for the use of an invention shall be construed accordingly.

(3) Nothing in section forty-seven of the Patents Act, 1949, shall be construed as authorising the disclosure to a Government department or any other person of any model, document or information to the use of which that section applies in contravention of any such licence, assignment or agreement as is therein mentioned.

(4) The foregoing provisions of this section shall apply in relation to registered designs as they apply in relation to patented inventions, and accordingly—

(a) references to section forty-six of the Patents Act, 1949, to subsections (3) and (6) of that section, to section forty-seven of that Act and to subsection (1) of that section shall include references to paragraph 1 of the First Schedule to the Registered Designs Act, 1949, to sub-paragraphs (3) and (6) of that paragraph, to paragraph 2 of that Schedule and to sub-paragraph (1) of that paragraph, as the case may be; and

(b) in relation to registered designs, subsection (1) of this section shall have effect as if for the words " the next following section " there were substituted the words " the next following paragraph " and for the words " make, use and exercise " there were substituted the word " use."

255   Provision for use of other technical information by Crown contractors for production and supply of defence materials

2.—(1) For the purposes of any contract or order for the production of defence materials, any person authorised in that behalf by a competent authority may make use of any technical information to which this section applies of which he is in possession, and supply articles produced by means of the use of any such information, discharged—

(a) from any restriction imposed by any agreement to which he is party (whether made before or after the commencement of this Act); and

(b) from any obligation to make payments to any other person in pursuance of any such agreement in respect of the use or supply.

(2) Any authorisation given for the purposes of subsection (1) of this section shall be given in writing, and shall—

(a) describe the defence materials in connection with which the authorisation is given; and

(b) identify the restrictions or obligations from which the person to whom the authorisation is given is thereby discharged;

and so much of any agreement (whether made before or after the commencement of this Act) as restricts the disclosure of terms of that or any other agreement shall be of no effect in relation to the disclosure to a competent authority of information required by that authority for the purpose of compliance with paragraph (b) of this subsection.

1256   (3) An authorisation given for the purposes of subsection (1) of this section may apply to things done before as well as after the date on which it is given.

(4) Where any person is discharged by virtue of an authorisation under this section from the obligation to make payments in respect of the use of any technical information or the supply of any articles, so much of any agreement (whether made before or after the commencement of this Act) as provides for the making by any other person of payments in respect of the use of the information or the supply of articles of that description shall be of no effect in relation to any use or supply in respect of which the first-mentioned person is so discharged.

(5) Nothing in this section shall affect any restriction or obligation imposed by an agreement to which any Government department are party.

(6) Nothing in this section or in any authorisation given thereunder shall be construed as authorising the disclosure to a competent authority or any other person of any technical information to which this section applies in contravention of any agreement.

(7) The technical information to which this section applies is any specification or design for articles, and any process or technique used in the production of articles (not being in any case a patented invention or registered design), and any drawing, model, plan, document or other information relating to the application or operation of any such specification, design, process or technique; and references in this Act to the use of technical information include references—

(a) to the production of articles to any such specification or design, or by means of any such process or technique, as aforesaid; and (*b*) to the reproduction of any such drawing, model, plan or document as aforesaid.

1257 Procedure in connection with authorisations under s. 2

3.—(1) Subject to subsection (3) of this section, a competent authority shall, before giving to any person an authorisation under section two of this Act in respect of any restriction or obligation, serve on that person a notice in writing requesting him to treat with the party entitled to enforce that restriction or obligation for such waiver or modification as will enable the technical information to be used or the articles supplied upon terms approved by the competent authority; and the authorisation shall not be given unless either—

(*a*) at the expiration of such period, not being less than three months beginning with the date of the service of the notice, as may be specified therein, no agreement for such waiver or modification as aforesaid has been concluded to the satisfaction of the competent authority; or

(*b*) before the expiration of the said period, the person on whom the notice was served has given notice in writing to the competent authority that no such agreement is likely to be concluded within that period.

(2) Where an authorisation is given under the said section two in respect of any restriction or obligation, the competent authority shall, subject to subsection (3) of this section, give notice to that effect to the person who, apart from the authorisation, would be entitled to enforce that restriction or obligation, and to such other persons (if any) as appear to the authority, after making such enquiries as are reasonably practicable in the circumstances, to be persons whose interests are affected by the authorisation.

(3) An authorisation under the said section two may be given by a competent authority without compliance with subsection (1) of this section in any case where it appears to the authority, and is certified in the authorisation, that the disclosure of the production or supply of the defence materials concerned would be prejudicial to the safety of the State; and in any such case—

(*a*) the competent authority shall not be required to give notice of the authorisation in pursuance of subsection (2) of this section unless and until they are satisfied that the disclosure would no longer be prejudicial as aforesaid; and

(*b*) unless and until the competent authority, being satisfied as aforesaid, otherwise direct, the person to whom the authorisation is given shall be discharged thereby from any obligation to which he would otherwise be subject by virtue of any agreement to give information to any other person in respect of the use of the information or the supply of articles to which the authorisation relates.

258 Payments for use and determination of disputes

4.[20]—(1) A competent authority by whom an authorisation is given under section two of this Act shall pay to the person entitled to the benefit of any restriction or obligation in respect of which the

[20] s. 4 amended as relates to N.I. by Northern Ireland Act 1962.

authorisation is given, or of any such provision of an agreement as is mentioned in subsection (4) of that section (whether or not he would himself be entitled, apart from the authorisation, to enforce the restriction, obligation or provision by legal proceedings) such sum (if any) as may be agreed upon between him and the competent authority with the approval of the Treasury or as may, in default of such agreement, be determined by the court under this section to be just having regard—

> (a) to the extent of the use made in pursuance of the authorisation;
>
> (b) to the value of any services performed by that person in connection with the conception, development, improvement or adaptation of any specification, design, process or technique used in pursuance of the authorisation;
>
> (c) to any benefit or compensation which that person or any person from whom he derives title may have received, or may be entitled to receive, directly or indirectly from any Government department in respect of any technical information so used; and
>
> (d) to any other relevant circumstances.

(2) Any dispute between a competent authority and any other person as to the exercise of powers conferred by section two of this Act, as to the making of a payment under this section, or as to the amount of any such payment, shall be determined by the court upon a reference made by either party to the dispute in such manner as may be prescribed by rules of court.

(3) Without prejudice to any rule of law enabling a court to sit in camera, the court may make such orders for the exclusion of the public from proceedings under this section, and for prohibiting the publication of any technical information to which section two of this Act applies so far as disclosed or recorded in such proceedings, as appear to the court to be necessary or expedient in the public interest or in the interests of any parties to the proceedings.

(4) In this section "the court" has the same meaning as in the Patents Act, 1949; and subsection (1) of section eighty-four of that Act (which provides for the allocation to a selected judge of certain proceedings under that Act) shall apply to references to the court under this section as it applies to references under that Act.

1259 Expenses

5. There shall be defrayed out of moneys provided by Parliament any increase attributable to section one of this Act in the sums required for making payments on behalf of a Government department under section forty-six of the Patents Act, 1949, or under paragraph 1 of the First Schedule to the Registered Designs Act, 1949, and any sums required by a competent authority for making payments under section four of this Act.

1260 Interpretation, etc.

6.—(1) In this Act the following expressions have the meaning hereby respectively assigned to them, that is to say:

> " agreement " includes a licence, assignment or assignation;

"article" includes any substance or material, and any plant, machinery or apparatus, whether affixed to land or not;

"competent authority" means a Secretary of State, *the Admiralty, the Minister of Supply or the Minister of Defence [or the Minister of Aviation* [21]]

"defence materials" means—

(a) articles required for the armed forces of the Crown, or for any such supply to the governments of countries outside the United Kingdom, or to the United Nations, as is authorised by the enactments amended by section one of this Act, being articles designed or adapted for the use of armed forces or components of articles so designed or adapted;

(b) articles required for purposes of civil defence within the meaning of the Civil Defence Act, 1948, being articles designed or adapted for use for those purposes or components of articles so designed or adapted;

(c) articles required by the [*Admiralty or the Minister of Supply*, the Secretary of State for Defence or the Minister of Aviation [21a]] for the production of any such articles as aforesaid;

"production" includes repair, maintenance, testing and development.

(2) This Act shall apply in relation to restrictions subsisting by reason of the existence of copyright in any work as it applies in relation to restrictions imposed by an agreement.

1261 Repeal and transitional provisions

7.—(1) The Defence (Patents, Trade Marks, etc.) Regulations 1941, and any Order in Council in force at the commencement of this Act under subsection (2) of section forty-nine of the Patents Act, 1949, or sub-paragraph (2) of paragraph 4 of the First Schedule to the Registered Designs Act, 1949, are hereby repealed.

(2) Any authorisation given before the commencement of this Act under section forty-six of the Patents Act, 1949, as extended by section forty-nine of that Act, or under paragraph 1 of the First Schedule to the Registered Designs Act, 1949, as extended by paragraph 4 of that Schedule, shall, if in force immediately before the commencement of this Act, and so far as it could be given under the said section forty-six or the said paragraph 1 as amended by section one of this Act, continue in force and have effect as if so given.

(3) Any authorisation in force under paragraph (5) of Regulation 3 of the said Regulations immediately before the commencement of this Act shall, in so far as it relates to the production or supply of defence materials, continue in force and have effect as if duly given under section two of this Act in respect of all such restrictions and obligations as are mentioned in subsection (1) of that section; and that section and section four of this Act shall apply accordingly in relation to anything done after the commencement of this Act in pursuance of such authorisation.

[21] Amended by S.I. 1964 No. 488, S.I. 1971 No. 719.
[21a] Amended by S.I. 1971 No. 719.

1262   Citation, construction, commencement and extent

    8.—(1) This Act may be cited as the Defence Contracts Act, 1958.

    (2) Section one of this Act, so far as it amends the Patents Act, 1949, shall be construed as one with that Act and may be cited together with that Act as the Patents Acts, 1949 and 1958; and so far as it amends the Registered Designs Act, 1949, shall be construed as one with that Act and may be cited together with that Act as the Registered Designs Acts, 1949 and 1958.

    (3) This Act shall come into operation at the expiration of the period of one month beginning with the date on which it is passed.

    (4) This Act shall extend to the Isle of Man; and it is hereby declared that this Act extends to Northern Ireland.

[The next paragraph is 1313.]

Patents Appeal Tribunal Rules, 1950

(S.I. 1950, No. 392/L.8, as amended) [22]

Made - - - -	*20th March*, 1950
Coming into Operation	*1st April*, 1950

I, the Honourable George Harold Lloyd-Jacob, Knight, the Judge of the High Court nominated by the Lord Chancellor to be the Appeal Tribunal constituted under section 85 (2) of the Patents Act, 1949, do, by virtue of section 85 (8) of the Act and all other Powers enabling me in this behalf, hereby make the following Rules: —

1313   **1.**[23]—(1) Any person who desires to appeal to the Appeal Tribunal from a decision of the Comptroller-General of Patents, Designs and Trade Marks (in these Rules referred to as " the Comptroller ") in any case in which a right of appeal is given by the Patents Act 1949 (in these Rules referred to as " the Act ") shall file with the Registrar of the Patents Appeal Tribunal (in these Rules referred to as " the Registrar ") at the Royal Courts of Justice, London, a notice of appeal in the form set out in the schedule to these Rules.

(2) The notice of appeal shall be filed—

    (*a*) in the case of a decision on a matter of procedure, within 14 days after the date of the decision; and

    (*b*) in any other case, within six weeks after the date of the decision.

(3) The Comptroller may determine whether any decision is on a matter of procedure and any such determination shall itself be a decision on a matter of procedure.

1314   **2.** The notice shall state the nature of the decision appealed against, and whether the appeal is from the whole, or part only, and if so, what part of the decision.

1315   **3.**[23] The appellant shall, within two days of filing the notice of appeal, send a copy thereof to the Comptroller and to any person who appeared or gave notice of opposition on the proceedings before the Comptroller.

1316   **4.** On receiving the notice of appeal the Comptroller shall forthwith transmit to the Registrar all the papers relating to the matter which is the subject of the appeal.

1317   **5.**[23] Except by leave of the Appeal Tribunal, no appeal shall be entertained unless notice of appeal has been given within the period specified in rule 1 (2) or within such further time as the Comptroller may allow upon request made to him prior to the expiry of that period.

1318   **5A.**[24] Where a respondent desires to contend on the appeal that the decision appealed against should be affirmed on grounds other

---

[22] The Patents Appeal Tribunal Rules 1950 are printed as amended by the Patents Appeal Tribunal (Amendment) Rules 1961 and 1970.

[23] Rules 1, 3 and 5 are printed as amended by the Patents Appeal Tribunal (Amendment) Rules 1970.

[24] Rule 5A was inserted by the Patents Appeal Tribunal (Amendment) Rules 1961.

than those set out in the decision, he shall, within seven days, after receipt by him of the notice of appeal, [or such further time as the Appeal Tribunal may direct,[25]] send to the appellant and the Comptroller notice of his desire, specifying the grounds of his contention, and shall, within two days after doing so, furnish the Registrar with two copies of the notice.

1319   **6.** The Registrar shall give to the appellant and the Comptroller and to any opposing party not less than seven days' notice of the time and place appointed for the hearing of the appeal, unless the Appeal Tribunal expressly directs that shorter notice may be given.

1320   **6A.**[26]—(1) A party to an appeal before the Appeal Tribunal may appear and be heard either in person or by a patent agent, a solicitor, or counsel.

(2) In this Rule "counsel" means a member of the Bar of England and Wales or of Northern Ireland or a member of the Faculty of Advocates in Scotland.

1321   **7.** The evidence used on appeal to the Appeal Tribunal shall be the same as that used before the Comptroller and no further evidence shall be given, except with the leave of the Appeal Tribunal given upon application made for that purpose.

1322   **8.** The regulations applicable to the filing of documentary evidence on proceedings before the Comptroller shall apply to documentary evidence filed on an appeal to the Appeal Tribunal.

1323   **9.** The Appeal Tribunal may, at the request of any party, order the attendance at the hearing for the purpose of cross-examination of any person who has made a declaration in the matter to which the appeal relates.

1324   **10.** Any person requiring the attendance of a witness for cross-examination shall tender to the witness whose attendance is required a reasonable sum for conduct money.

1325   **11.** On any appeal the Appeal Tribunal may, at any time, either of its own motion or on the application of any party, appoint an independent scientific adviser to assist the Appeal Tribunal or to enquire and report upon any question of fact or of opinion not involving questions of law or construction.

1326   **12.** Any report, so far as it is not accepted by all parties, shall be treated as information furnished to the Appeal Tribunal, and shall be given such weight as the Appeal Tribunal may think fit.

1327   **13.** All reports shall be made in writing to the Appeal Tribunal, together with such copies as the Appeal Tribunal may require, and copies of the report shall be forwarded by the Registrar to the parties or their Agents.

1328   **14.** Any party may, within fourteen days after receiving a copy of the report, or within such other time as the Appeal Tribunal may direct, apply for leave to cross-examine the scientific adviser on his

[25] The words in square brackets were inserted by the Patents Appeal Tribunal (Amendment) Rules 1969.
[26] Rule 6A was inserted by the Patents Appeal Tribunal (Amendment) Rules 1970.

report, and the Appeal Tribunal may on such application make an order for the cross-examination of the scientific adviser at the hearing of the appeal. The Appeal Tribunal shall at the hearing direct at what stage the scientific adviser is to be called.

1329 **15.** If the scientific adviser considers that any experiment or test (other than one of a trifling character) is necessary to enable him to report in a satisfactory manner he shall inform the parties or their Agents and shall endeavour to agree with them as to the expenses involved and as to the persons to attend the experiment or test. In default of agreement between the parties, all such matters shall be determined by the Appeal Tribunal.

1330 **16.** The Appeal Tribunal may at any time direct the scientific adviser to make a further or supplemental report and the provisions of Rules 12, 13, 14 and 15 shall apply to such report as they apply to an original report.

1331 **17.** The remuneration of the scientific adviser shall be fixed by the Appeal Tribunal, and shall include the costs of making a report and a proper daily fee for any day on which the scientific adviser is required to attend before the Appeal Tribunal.

1332 **18.** The Appeal Tribunal may, in awarding costs, either fix the amount thereof or direct by whom and in what manner the amount of the costs is to be ascertained.

1333 **19.** If any costs awarded are not paid within fourteen days after the amount thereof has been fixed or ascertained, or within such shorter period as may be directed by the Appeal Tribunal, the party to whom the costs are payable may apply to the Appeal Tribunal for an order for payment under the provisions of section 85 (5) of the Act.

1334 **20.** *Any notice of appeal to the Court of Appeal from a decision of the Appeal Tribunal shall be in the form set out in the Second Schedule hereto.*[27]

1335 **21.** Any notice or other document required to be filed with or sent to the Registrar under these Rules may be sent by prepaid letter through the post.

1336 **22.** The Interpretation Act, 1889, shall apply to the interpretation of these Rules as it applies to the interpretation of an Act of Parliament.

1337 **23.** In these Rules the expression " scientific adviser " includes persons with scientific qualifications, medical practitioners, engineers, architects, surveyors, accountants, actuaries, and any other specially skilled persons whose opinion in relation to any matter arising on an appeal may be of assistance to the Appeal Tribunal.

1338 **24.** The Patents Appeal Tribunal Rules, 1932, are hereby revoked,

[27] r. 20 of the Patents Appeal Tribunal Rules 1950 and Sched. II thereto were revoked by the Patents Appeal Tribunal (Amendment) Rules 1956 (S I. 1956 No. 470). The form of notice of appeal from the Appeal Tribunal to the Court of Appeal is now regulated by R.S.C., Ord. 59, *post,* § 1618 *et seq.*

without prejudice to any appeal or other matter pending thereunder at the date on which these Rules come into force.

1339   25. These Rules may be cited as the Patents Appeal Tribunal Rules, 1950, and shall come into force on the first day of April, 1950. Dated the 20th day of March, 1950.

G. H. Lloyd-Jacob.

1340   SCHEDULE [28]

Notice of Appeal to Appeal Tribunal

(a) Here insert the nature of the application or proceedings, the name of the applicant and the number of the application for Letters Patent.

IN THE MATTER OF AN APPLICATION (a)

and

(b) Here insert the name(s) of the opponent(s) if the application is opposed.

IN THE MATTER OF AN OPPOSITION THERETO BY (b)

(c) Here insert name(s) and full address(es) of appellant(s).

I/We (c)

of

(d) Here insert "The decision" or "that part of the decision" as the case may be.

hereby give notice of appeal to the Appeal Tribunal (d)

(e) Here insert "Comptroller-General" or "Officer acting for Comptroller-General" as the case may be.

of the (e)

dated the   day of   19

(f) Here insert "refused (or allowed) application for Letters Patent" or "refused (or allowed) application for leave to amend specification" or otherwise as the case may be.

whereby he (f)

(g) To be signed by the appellant personally or by his duly authorised representative.

Signature (g) ....

Address ....

....

Date ....

NOTE:—This notice must be sent to the Registrar of the Patents Appeal Tribunal, Royal Courts of Justice, London, WC2A 2LL and must bear an impressed judicature fee stamp for £6. An unstamped copy of the notice must be sent to the Comptroller-General at the Patent Office, 25 Southampton Buildings, London, W.C.2, and to any person who appeared or gave notice of opposition on the proceedings from which the appeal is brought, within the period prescribed by the Patents Appeal Tribunal Rules.[29]

[28] Heading amended by Patents Appeal Tribunal (Amendment) Rules 1970.
[29] Note printed as amended by Patents Appeal Tribunal (Amendment) Rules 1970.

[496]

Patents Appeal Tribunal Rules 1959

(S.I. 1959 No. 278)

Made -   -   -   -   -   *17th February,* 1959
Coming into Operation   *1st March,* 1959

I, the Honourable George Harold Lloyd-Jacob, the Judge of the High Court nominated by the Lord Chancellor to be the Appeal Tribunal constituted under section 85 (2) of the Patents Act, 1949, do, by virtue of section 85 (8) of the Act and all other powers enabling me in this behalf, hereby make the following Rules:

1341   **1.** The Appeal Tribunal may, either of its own motion or on the application of any party, direct that the appeal be heard in public or, as the case may be, that the decision of the Tribunal on the appeal shall be given in public.

1342   **2.**—(1) These Rules may be cited as the Patents Appeal Tribunal Rules, 1959, and shall be construed as one with the Patents Appeal Tribunal Rules, 1950.

(2) These Rules shall come into force on the first day of March, 1959.

Dated the 17th day of February, 1959.

G. H. *Lloyd-Jacob.*

[The next paragraph is 1349.]

Patents Rules 1968

(S.I. 1968 No. 1389, as amended) [30]

Made - - - - -	*27th August,* 1968
Laid before Parliament	*12th September,* 1968
Coming into Operation	*1st November,* 1968

The Board of Trade, in pursuance of the powers conferred upon them by sections 94, 95 and 99 of the Patents Act, 1949, as amended by the Patents Act, 1957, and Patents and Designs (Renewals, Extensions and Fees) Act, 1961, and the Patents (Fees Amendment) Order, 1961, and of all other powers enabling them in that behalf, after consultation with the Council on Tribunals, and, as regards Rule 3 hereof, with the consent of the Treasury hereby make the following Rules:

Citation, Commencement and Interpretation

1349   **1.** These Rules may be cited as the Patents Rules, 1968, and shall come into operation on the 1st day of November, 1968.

1350   **2.**—(1) In these Rules, unless the context otherwise requires:
" the Act " means the Patents Act, 1949, as amended by the Patents Act, 1957, and the Patents and Designs (Renewals, Extensions and Fees) Act, 1961, and, save where otherwise indicated, any reference to a section is a reference to that section of the Act.
" Journal " means the Official Journal (Patents) published in accordance with Rule 143;
" Office " means the Patent Office;
" register " means the register of patents kept under the provisions of Section 73;
" United Kingdom " includes the Isle of Man.

(2) The Interpretation Act, 1889, shall apply to the interpretation of these Rules as it applies to the interpretation of an Act of Parliament, and as if these Rules and the Rules hereby revoked were Acts of Parliament.

Fees and Forms

1351   **3.** The fees to be paid in respect of any matters arising under the Act shall be those specified in Schedule 1 to these Rules and in any case where a form specified in that Schedule as the corresponding form in relation to any matter is required to be used that form shall be accompanied by the fee specified in respect of that matter.

1352   **4.** The forms mentioned in these Rules are those set out in Schedule 2 to these Rules and such forms shall be used in all cases in which they are applicable and may be modified as directed by the Comptroller.

[30] The Patents Rules 1968 are printed as amended by the Patents (Amendment) Rules 1968 (S.I. 1968 No. 1702).

Documents

1353   5.—(1) All documents and copies of documents, except drawings, filed at the Office shall, unless the Comptroller otherwise directs, be written, typewritten, lithographed or printed in the English language

(a) [31] upon strong white paper of a size 330 mm by 200 to 210 mm (13 inches by 8 inches to 8¼ inches) or of A4 size (297 mm by 210 mm: 11¾ inches by 8¼ inches);

(b) in legible characters with a dark indelible ink;

(c) with the lines widely spaced;

(d) except in the case of statutory declarations and affidavits, on one side only;

(e) [31] leaving a margin of at least 25 mm (1 inch) on the left-hand part thereof; and

(f) [31] in the case of each of the forms set out in Schedule 2 hereto, leaving a space of about 80 mm (3 inches) blank at the top of the form.

(2) Duplicate documents required under these Rules may be carbon copies of the original documents provided that they are on paper of good quality and the typing is black and distinct.

1354   6. Any notice, application, or other document sent to the Office by post shall be deemed to have been given, made or filed at the time when the letter containing the document would be delivered in the ordinary course of post.

1355   7. Every person concerned in any proceedings to which these Rules relate, and every patentee, shall furnish to the Comptroller an address for service in the United Kingdom and that address may be treated for all purposes connected with such proceedings or patent as the address of the person concerned in the proceedings or the patentee.

Agency

1356   8.—(1) With the exception of documents mentioned in sub-rule (2) and unless the Comptroller otherwise directs in any particular case, all notices, applications or other documents filed under the Act may be signed by, and all attendances upon the Comptroller may be made by or through, an agent duly authorised to the satisfaction of the Comptroller.

(2) The following documents are excepted from sub-rule (1):—the authorisation of an agent; an application for a patent, for the grant of a patent of addition in lieu of an independent patent, or for a complete specification to be treated as a provisional specification; a notice of opposition; and an application, request, notice, claim or declaration on any of the following forms, namely Patents Forms numbers 4, 6, 14, 15, 17 to 19, 27, 29, 32, 35, 38 to 40, 42 to 45, 47 to 50, 53 to 57, and 68.

(3) The Comptroller may refuse to recognise as such agent in respect of any business under the Act

(a) any individual whose name has been erased from, and not

[31] Rule 5 (1) (a), (e), (f) are printed as amended by the Patents (Amendment) Rules 1970.

restored to, the register of patent agents, or who is for the time being suspended from acting as a patent agent;

(b) any person who has been convicted of an offence under Section 88;

(c) any person who is found by the Board of Trade (after being given an opportunity to be heard) to have been convicted of any such offence, or to have been guilty of any such misconduct, as, in the case of an individual registered in the register of patent agents, would render him liable to have his name erased therefrom;

(d) any person, not being registered as a patent agent, who in the opinion of the Comptroller is engaged wholly or mainly in acting as agent in applying for patents in the United Kingdom or elsewhere in the name or for the benefit of a person by whom he is employed;

(e) any company or firm, if any person whom the Comptroller could refuse to recognise as agent in respect of any business under the Act is acting as a director or manager of the company or is a partner in the firm.

Applications for the grant of patents

1357 9.—(1) An application, other than a Convention application, shall be made on Patents Form No. 1 or, provided the application is made and signed by the applicant personally and not by a nominee, on the form reproduced at 1A in Schedule 3 hereto (being the form adopted for the purpose by the European Convention relating to the Formalities required for Patent Applications done at Paris on 11th December, 1953).

(2) In the case of an application by the assignee of the person claiming to be the true and first inventor there shall be furnished at the time of filing such application, or within a period of three months thereafter, the declaration required by Section 2 (2).

(3) A Convention application shall be made on Patents Form No. 1 Con. or, provided the application is made and signed by the applicant personally and not by a nominee, on the form reproduced at 1B in Schedule 3 hereto (being the form adopted for the purpose by the said European Convention).

(4) An application for the grant of a patent of addition in lieu of an independent patent shall be made on Patents Form No. 1 Add.

1358 10. In the case of an application, other than a Convention application, by the personal representative of a deceased person who, immediately before his death, was entitled to make such an application, the probate of the will of the deceased, or the letters of administration of his estate, or an official copy of the probate or letters of administration, shall be produced at the Office in proof of the applicant's title to act as personal representative.

1359 11.—(1) Except in the case of an application (other than a Convention application) which is accompanied by a complete specification, Patents Form No. 4, including a declaration as to the inventorship of the invention disclosed in the complete specification, shall be filed with the complete specification, or subsequently at any time before the expiration of the period allowed by or under Section 12 for putting the application in order.

(2) When so requested by the applicant the Comptroller may, if he sees fit, dispense with the said declaration.

1360 12. Where, in pursuance of Section 3 (3), the Comptroller allows a single complete specification to be proceeded with in respect of two or more applications in respect of which two or more complete specifications have been filed, the single complete specification may include any matter disclosed in any of the said specifications and shall be deemed to have been filed on such date, not earlier than the earliest date on which all the matter disclosed in the said single complete specification has been disclosed to the Office in or in connection with the applications, as the Comptroller may direct.

1361 13.—(1) Where an applicant has made an application for a patent and, before the acceptance of the complete specification, makes a fresh application for a patent for matter included in the first mentioned application or in any specification filed in pursuance thereof, the Comptroller may direct that the fresh application or any specification filed in pursuance thereof shall be ante-dated to a date not earlier than the date of filing of the first mentioned application or specification if the applicant includes in the fresh application a request to that effect.

(2) Where an applicant having made an application for a patent subsequently discloses to the Office additional matter in connection therewith, and before the acceptance of the complete specification makes a fresh application for a patent in respect of the additional matter, the Comptroller may direct that the fresh application or any specification filed in pursuance thereof shall be ante-dated to a date not earlier than the date on which the matter was first disclosed to the Office if the applicant includes in the fresh application a request to that effect.

(3) The Comptroller may require such amendment of the complete specification filed in pursuance of either of the said applications as may be necessary to ensure that neither of the said complete specifications includes a claim for matter claimed in the other.

1362 14. Where a complete specification has been filed pursuant to two or more applications accompanied by provisional specifications for inventions which the applicant believes to be cognate or modifications one of another and the Comptroller is of opinion that such inventions are not cognate or modifications one of another, the Comptroller may allow the complete specification to be divided into such number of complete specifications as may be necessary to enable the applications to be proceeded with as two or more separate applications for patents.

1363 15.—(1) In addition to the specification filed with every Convention application, there shall be filed with the application, or within three months thereafter, a copy of the specification and drawings or documents filed in respect of the relevant application for protection in a Convention country or of each such application, duly certified by the official chief or head of the Patent Office of the Convention country, or otherwise verified to the satisfaction of the Comptroller.

(2) If any specification or other document relating to the application is in a foreign language, it shall be accompanied by a translation thereof verified by statutory declaration or otherwise to the satisfaction of the Comptroller.

1364   **16.** Where a single Convention application has been made in respect of all or part of the inventions in respect of which two or more applications for protection have been made in one or more Convention countries, and the Examiner reports that the claims of the specification filed with the said Convention application relate to more than one invention, the Comptroller may allow one or more further applications to be filed and the specification to be divided into such number of specifications as may be necessary to enable two or more separate Convention applications to be proceeded with and may direct that the said applications be deemed to have been filed on the date of filing of the original application.

Drawings

1365   **17.** Drawings, when supplied, shall be furnished in duplicate and shall accompany the provisional or complete specification to which they refer, except in the case provided for by Rule 24.

1366   **18.**—(1) Drawings shall be hand-made or reproduced on white, hot-pressed, rolled or calendered strong drawing paper of smooth surface, good quality, and medium thickness, without washes or colours, in such a way as to admit of being clearly reproduced on a reduced scale by photography, or, without any intermediary steps, on a stereotype.

(2) Mounted drawings may not be used.

1367   **19.**[32]—(1) Subject to the provisions of this Rule drawings shall be on sheets of a size 330 mm by 200 to 210 mm (13 inches by 8 to $8\frac{1}{4}$ inches) or of A4 size (297 mm by 210 mm: $11\frac{3}{4}$ inches by $8\frac{1}{4}$ inches) and a clear margin of 13 mm ($\frac{1}{2}$ an inch) shall be left at the edges of each sheet.

(2) If a figure or figures cannot be shown satisfactorily on one sheet of either of these dimensions it or they may be continued on subsequent sheets of the same dimensions.

(3) If it can be shown to the satisfaction of the Comptroller that a large figure cannot be shown satisfactorily, even on a reduced scale, on a sheet or sheets of the above mentioned dimensions, a sheet or sheets each of a size 330 mm by 400 to 420 mm (13 inches by 16 to $16\frac{1}{2}$ inches) may be used and a clear margin of 13 mm ($\frac{1}{2}$ an inch) shall be left at the edges of each sheet.

(4) In a case falling within sub-rule (3) of this Rule one or more of the smaller sheets shall additionally be used only when it is not possible to show all the figures comprising the drawings on the sheet or sheets used by virtue of that sub-rule.

(5) No more sheets shall be employed than are necessary.

(6) The figures shall be numbered consecutively without regard to the number of sheets, and shall as far as possible be arranged in numerical order, separated by a sufficient space to keep them distinct.

[32] Rule 19 is printed as amended by Patents (Amendments) Rules 1970.

(7) Where figures on a number of sheets form in effect a single complete figure, they shall be so arranged that the complete figure can be assembled without concealing any part of another figure.

1368 **20.** Drawings shall be prepared in accordance with the following requirements:

(a) they shall be executed in durable, very dark markings;

(b) each line shall be firmly and evenly drawn, sharply defined, and of the same strength throughout;

(c) section lines, lines for effect, and shading lines shall be as few as possible, and shall not be closely drawn;

(d) shading lines shall not contrast excessively in thickness with the general lines of the drawing;

(e) sections and shading shall not be represented by solid black or washes;

(f) they shall be on a scale sufficiently large to show the invention clearly, and only so much of the apparatus, machine, or article may appear as effects this purpose;

(g) if the scale is given, it shall be drawn, and not denoted by words, and no dimensions may be marked on the drawings;

(h) reference letters and numerals, and index letters and numerals used in conjunction therewith, shall be bold, distinct and not less than one-eighth of an inch [32 mm [33]] in height; the same letters or numerals shall be used in different views of the same parts, and where the reference letters or numerals are shown outside the parts referred to they shall be connected with the said parts by fine lines.

1369 **21.**—(1) Drawings shall bear:

(a) in the left-hand top corner the name of the applicant and, in the case of drawings filed with a complete specification after one or more provisional specifications, the numbers and years of the applications;

(b) in the right-hand top corner the number of sheets of drawings sent and the consecutive number of each sheet, and the words " original " or " duplicate " as the case may require;

(c) in the right-hand bottom corner the signature of the applicant or his agent.

(2) The title of the invention shall not appear on the drawings.

1370 **22.**—(1) No descriptive matter shall appear on constructional drawings, but drawings in the nature of flow sheets may bear descriptive matter to show the materials used and the chemical or other reactions or treatments effected in carrying out the invention.

(2) Drawings showing a number of instruments or units of apparatus and their interconnections, either mechanical or electrical, where each such instrument or unit is shown only symbolically, may bear such descriptive matter as is necessary to identify the instruments or units or their interconnections.

(3) No drawing or sketch, other than a graphic chemical formula or a mathematical formula, symbol, or equation, shall appear in the

[33] Added by the Patents (Amendment) Rules 1970.

verbal part of the specification and if such a formula, symbol or equation is used therein a copy thereof, prepared in the same manner as drawings, shall be furnished if the Comptroller so directs.

1371   **23.** Drawings shall be delivered at the Office free from folds, breaks or creases which would render them unsuitable for reproduction by photography.

1372   **24.** If an applicant desires to adopt the drawings filed with his provisional specification as the drawings or part of the drawings for his complete specification, he shall refer to them in the complete specification as those filed with the provisional specification.

Extension of the period for filing complete specification

1373   **25.** A request for an extension of the period for filing a complete specification up to a period not exceeding fifteen months from the date of filing of the application shall be made on Patents Form No. 5.

Request for post-dating an application

1374   **26.** Where an applicant for a patent desires that his application shall be post-dated in pursuance of the provisions of Section 6 (3), he shall make a request on Patents Form No. 6.

Procedure under Sections 7, 8 and 9

1375   **27.**—(1) When the Examiner, in making the investigation under Section 7, reports that the invention so far as claimed in any claim of the complete specification has been published in any specification or other document falling within Section 7 (1) or 7 (2), the applicant shall be so informed and shall be afforded an opportunity of amending his specification.

(2) If the Examiner finds that substantially the whole of the invention claimed has been published in one or more such specifications or documents he may, without continuing the investigation, make a provisional report to that effect.

(3) If the applicant re-files his specification and the Examiner is not satisfied either that the invention so far as claimed in any claim has not been published in any specification or other document cited by the Examiner or that the priority date of the claim is not later than the date on which the relevant document was published, the applicant shall be given an opportunity to be heard in the matter if he so requests.

(4) Whether or not the applicant has re-filed his specification, the Comptroller may appoint a hearing if he considers it desirable to do so, having regard to the time remaining for putting the application in order or other circumstances of the case.

(5) When a hearing is appointed, the applicant shall be given at least ten days' notice of the appointment or such shorter notice as appears to the Comptroller to be reasonable in the circumstances and shall as soon as possible notify the Comptroller whether he will attend the hearing.

(6) After hearing the applicant, or without a hearing if the applicant has not attended or has notified that he does not desire to be

heard, the Comptroller may prescribe or permit such amendment of the specification as will be to his satisfaction and may refuse to accept the specification unless the amendment is made within such period as he may fix.

1376   **28.**—(1) When the Examiner reports that the invention so far as claimed in any claim of the complete specification is claimed in any claim of any other complete specification falling within Section 8 (1) or 8 (3), the applicant shall be so informed and shall be afforded an opportunity of amending, or submitting amendments of, his specification.

(2) If, when the applicant's specification is otherwise in order for acceptance, an objection under Section 8 is outstanding, the Comptroller may accept the specification and allow a period of two months from the date of its publication for removing the objection.

(3) If an objection under Section 8 is communicated to the applicant after acceptance of the specification, a period of two months from the date of the communication shall be allowed for removing the objection.

1377   **29.**—(1) If the applicant so requests at any time, or if the Examiner is not satisfied that the objection has been met within the period prescribed by Rule 28, including any extension thereof which the Comptroller may allow, a time for hearing the applicant shall be appointed and the applicant shall be given at least ten days' notice of the appointment and shall, as soon as possible, notify the Comptroller whether he will attend the hearing.

(2) After hearing the applicant, or without a hearing if the applicant has not attended or has notified that he does not desire to be heard, the Comptroller may prescribe or permit such amendment of the specification as will be to his satisfaction and may direct that a reference to such other specification as he shall mention shall be inserted in the applicant's specification unless the amendment is made or agreed to within such period as he may fix.

1378   **30.** The periods mentioned in Rules 28 and 29 may be extended if a request for such extension is made on Patents Form No. 7 at any time within the extended period specified in the request, provided that the total extension of either period allowed under this provision shall not exceed six months.

1379   **31.** When, in pursuance of Rule 29, the Comptroller directs that reference to another specification shall be inserted in the applicant's complete specification, the reference shall be inserted after the claims and shall be in the following form:

" Reference has been directed, in pursuance of Section 8 of the Patents Act, 1949, to specification No.   ."

1380   **32.** An application under the proviso to Section 79 (2), for disclosure of the result of a search made under Sections 7 and 8, shall be made on Patents Form No. 8.

1381   **33.** When in making the investigations under Sections 7 and 8 it appears to the Examiner that the applicant's invention cannot be performed without substantial risk of infringement of a claim of another patent, the applicant shall be so informed and the procedure provided in Rules 28 to 30 shall apply.

1382   **34.** When, pursuant to such procedure, the Comptroller directs that reference to a patent shall be inserted in the applicant's complete specification, the reference shall be inserted after the claims and shall be in the following form:

"Reference has been directed in pursuance of Section 9, subsection (1) of the Patents Act, 1949, to patent No.   ."

1383   **35.** An application under Section 9 (2) for the deletion of a reference inserted pursuant to a direction under Section 9 (1) shall be made on Patents Form No. 9, and shall state fully the facts relied upon in support of the application.

1384   **36.** In the application of Rules 28 to 31, 33 and 34 to proceedings subsequent to the grant of the patent, references to the patentee shall be substituted for references to the applicant.

Putting Applications in order and acceptance of complete specifications (Sections 12 and 13)

1385   **37.**—(1) There is hereby prescribed for the purposes of Section 12 (1) as the period within which an application for the grant of a patent is to be put in order for acceptance—

     (*a*) in the case of an application for the grant of a patent filed before 1st January 1962, a period of three years and six months;

     (*b*) in the case of an application for the grant of a patent filed on or after that date but before 1st January 1964, a period of three years;

     (*c*) in the case of an application for the grant of a patent filed on or after 1st January 1964, a period of two years and six months.

(2) Where an application for the grant of a patent is post-dated under any of the provisions of the Act, it shall nevertheless be treated for the purpose of determining the relevant period prescribed for the purposes of Section 12 (1) as if it had not been so post-dated.

(3) A notice under Section 12 (2) requesting an extension of the period allowable under Section 12 (1) for putting an application in order shall be given on Patents Form No. 10.

(4) A notice under the proviso to Section 13 (1) requesting postponement of the acceptance of a complete specification to a date later than twelve months from the date of its filing, shall be given on Patents Form No. 11.

1386   **38.**—(1) After the date of the publication of a complete specification the application and specification as accepted together with the drawings and documents (if any) filed in pursuance of Rule 15 may be inspected at the Office upon payment of a fee prescribed by these Rules.

(2) The documents (if any) filed in pursuance of Rule 15 or photographic copies thereof may be made available for inspection without fee.

Opposition to grant of patent (Section 14)

1387   **39.**—(1) A notice of opposition to the grant of a patent—

(*a*) shall be given on Patents Form No. 12,

(*b*) shall state the ground or grounds on which the opponent intends to oppose the grant, and

(*c*) shall be accompanied by a copy thereof and shall be supported by a statement (in duplicate) setting out fully the nature of the opponent's interest, the facts upon which he relies and the relief which he seeks.

(2) A copy of the notice and of the statement shall be sent by the Comptroller to the applicant.

1388   **40.** If the applicant desires to proceed with his application, he shall, within three months of the receipt of such copies, file a counter-statement setting out fully the grounds upon which the opposition is contested and deliver to the opponent a copy thereof.

1389   **41.** The opponent may within three months from the receipt of the copy of the counterstatement file evidence in support of his case and shall deliver to the applicant a copy of the evidence.

1390   **42.** Within three months from the receipt of the copy of the opponent's evidence or, if the opponent does not file any evidence, within three months from the expiration of the time within which the opponent's evidence might have been filed, the applicant may file evidence in support of his case and shall deliver to the opponent a copy of the evidence; and within three months from the receipt of the copy of the applicant's evidence the opponent may file evidence confined to matters strictly in reply and shall deliver to the applicant a copy of the evidence.

1391   **43.** No further evidence shall be filed by either party except by leave or direction of the Comptroller.

1392   **44.**—(1) Copies of all documents, other than printed United Kingdom specifications, referred to in the notice of opposition or in any statement or evidence filed in connection with the opposition, authenticated to the satisfaction of the Comptroller, shall be furnished (in duplicate) for the Comptroller's use unless he otherwise directs. Such copies shall accompany the notice, statement or evidence in which they are referred to.

(2) Where a specification or other document in a foreign language is referred to, a translation thereof, verified by statutory declaration or otherwise to the satisfaction of the Comptroller, and one additional copy of the translation, shall also be furnished.

1393   **45.**—(1) On completion of the evidence (if any), or at such other time as he may see fit, the Comptroller shall appoint a time for the hearing of the case, and shall give the parties at least fourteen days' notice of the appointment.

(2) If either party desires to be heard he shall notify the Comptroller on Patents Form No. 13 and the Comptroller may refuse to hear either party who has not filed the said form prior to the date of hearing.

(3) If either party intends to refer at the hearing to any publication not already mentioned in the proceedings, he shall give to the

other party and to the Comptroller at least ten days' notice of his intention, together with details of each publication to which he intends to refer.

(4) After hearing the party or parties desiring to be heard or, if neither party desires to be heard, then without a hearing, the Comptroller shall decide the case and notify his decision to the parties giving reasons for his decision if so required by any party.

1394   **46.** If in consequence of the proceedings the Comptroller directs that a reference to another patent shall be inserted in the applicant's specification under Section 9 (1), the reference shall be as prescribed by Rule 34.

1395   **47.** If the applicant notifies the Comptroller that he does not desire to proceed with the application, the Comptroller, in deciding whether costs should be awarded to the opponent, shall consider whether proceedings might have been avoided if the opponent had given reasonable notice to the applicant before the opposition was filed.

Procedure under Section 15

1396   **48.** If at any time after the acceptance of a complete specification and before the grant of the patent it comes to the notice of the Comptroller, otherwise than in consequence of proceedings in opposition to the grant, that the invention so far as claimed in any claim of the complete specification has been published in any specification or other document falling within Section 15 (1), the applicant shall be so informed and shall be allowed a period of two months within which to submit such amendment of his specification as will be to the Comptroller's satisfaction.

1397   **49.**—(1) If the specification has not been amended to the Comptroller's satisfaction within the period allowed under Rule 48, including any extension thereof which the Comptroller may allow, a time for hearing the applicant shall be appointed, and the applicant shall be given at least ten days' notice of the appointment, and shall, as soon as possible, notify the Comptroller whether he will attend the hearing.

(2) After hearing the applicant, or without a hearing if the applicant has not attended or has notified that he does not desire to be heard, the Comptroller may prescribe or permit such amendment of the specification as will be to his satisfaction and may refuse to grant a patent unless the amendment is made or agreed to within such period as he may fix.

1398   **50.** The period mentioned in Rules 48 and 49 may be extended if a request for such extension is made on Patents Form No. 7 at any time within the extended period specified in the request, provided that the total extension of either period allowed under this provision shall not exceed six months.

Mention of inventor as such (Section 16)

1399   **51.** A request by the applicant for a patent, or, if the actual deviser of the invention or of a substantial part thereof is not the applicant or one of the applicants, by the applicant and the said deviser, under Section 16 (3) shall be made on Patents Form No. 14 and shall be accompanied by a statement setting out fully the facts relied upon.

1400 52.—(1) A claim under Section 16 (4) shall be made on Patents Form No. 15 and shall be accompanied by a statement setting out fully the facts relied upon.

(2) A copy of the claim and of the statement shall be sent by the Comptroller to every applicant for the patent (not being the claimant) and to any other person whom the Comptroller may consider to be interested and the applicant shall supply a sufficient number of copies for that purpose.

(3) The Comptroller may give such directions (if any) as he may think fit with regard to the subsequent procedure.

1401 53. An application under Section 16 (5) for an extension of the period for making a request or claim shall be made on Patents Form No. 16.

1402 54.—(1) An application under Section 16 (8) for a certificate shall be made on Patents Form No. 17 and shall be accompanied by a statement setting out fully the facts relied upon.

(2) A copy of the application and of the statement shall be sent by the Comptroller to each patentee (not being the applicant), to the person mentioned as the actual deviser, and to any other person whom the Comptroller may consider to be interested and the applicant shall supply a sufficient number of copies for that purpose.

(3) The Comptroller may give such directions (if any) as he may think fit with regard to the subsequent procedure.

1403 55. Any mention of an actual deviser as inventor under Section 16 (1) may be made in the patent after the name of the Comptroller, and on the complete specification at the head of Patents Form No. 3, and may be in the form " The inventor of this invention in the sense of being the actual deviser thereof within the meaning of Section 16 of the Patents Act, 1949, is   of   ", or " The inventor of a substantial part of this invention in the sense of being the actual deviser thereof within the meaning of Section 16 of the Patents Act, 1949, is   of   ", as the case may require.

Procedure under Section 17

1404 56.—(1) A claim under Section 17 (1) that an application for a patent shall proceed in the name of the claimant or in the names of the claimant and the applicant or the other joint applicant or applicants shall be made on Patents Form No. 18 and shall be accompanied by a certified copy of any assignment or agreement upon which the claim is based.

(2) The original assignment or agreement shall also be produced for the Comptroller's inspection, and the Comptroller may call for such other proof of title or written consent as he may require.

1405 57.—(1) An application under Section 17 (5) by a joint applicant for the directions of the Comptroller as to the names or manner in which an application for a patent shall be proceeded with shall be made on Patents Form No. 19 and shall be accompanied by a statement setting out fully the facts upon which the applicant relies and the directions which he seeks.

(2) A copy of the application and statement shall be sent by the Comptroller to each other joint applicant and the person making the application under Section 17 (5) shall supply a sufficient number of copies for that purpose.

(3) The Comptroller may give such directions as he may think fit with regard to the subsequent procedure.

Sealing and form of patent

1406　　**58.** A request for the sealing of a patent on an application shall be made on Patents Form No. 20.

1407　　**59.** The period within which a request for the sealing of a patent may be made under proviso (a) to Section 19 (2) shall be two months from the final determination of the proceedings.

1408　　**60.**—(1) An application under Section 19 (3) for the extension of the period for making a request for the sealing of a patent shall be made on Patents Form No. 21.

(2) Such extension shall not be more than three months.

1409　　**61.**—(1) An application under Section 19 (4) for extension of the period for making a request for the sealing of a patent shall be made on Patents Form No. 22.

(2) Such extension shall not be more than six months on any one application under the subsection.

1410　　**62.** A patent shall be in the Form A or Form B (whichever is applicable) set out in Schedule 4 to these Rules, or such modification of either of these forms as the Comptroller directs.

Amendment of patent (Section 20)

1411　　**63.** An application under Section 20 for the amendment of a patent shall be made on Patents Form No. 23 and shall be accompanied by evidence verifying the statements therein and by the Letters Patent.

Renewal fees (Section 22)

1412　　**64.** If it is desired, at the expiration of the fourth year from the date of a patent or of any succeeding year during the term of the patent, to keep the patent in force, Patents Form No. 24 accompanied by the prescribed renewal fee shall be filed before the expiration of that year; Provided that, where a patent is sealed after the expiration of the fourth or any succeeding year, except in cases mentioned in Rule 69, Patents Form No. 24 in respect of the fifth and any succeeding year, may be filed at any time before the expiration of three months from the date of sealing the patent.

65. All or any of the prescribed annual renewal fees may be paid in advance.

1413　　**66.** A request for extension of the period for payment of any renewal fee shall be made on Patents Form No. 25.

67. On due compliance with the terms of Rule 64 the Comptroller shall issue a Certificate on Patents Form No. 26 that the prescribed fee has been duly paid.

1414 **68.** At any time not less than one month before the date when any renewal fee will become due in respect of any patent, the Comptroller shall send to the patentee or patentees at his or their address or addresses for service, and to the address of the person or persons who paid the last renewal fee, a notice reminding him or them of the date when such fee will become due, and of the consequences of the non-payment thereof.

1415 **69.** Where directions given by the Comptroller under Section 18 (1) of the Act or under Section 12 of the Atomic Energy Act, 1946, prohibiting the publication of information with respect to an invention forming the subject of an application for a patent have been revoked and a patent is granted on the application, no renewal fees shall be payable in respect of any year which commenced in the period during which the directions were in force.

Extension of term of patent (Sections 24 and 25)

1416 **70.**—(1) An application to the Comptroller under Section 24 or 25 for an Order extending the term of a patent shall be made on Patents Form No. 27.

(2) The application shall state the period of the extension which is sought and shall be supported by evidence setting out fully the facts relied upon, such evidence being filed either with the application or at any time within one month from the date thereof.

1417 **71.** When an application is formally in order the Comptroller shall advertise it in two issues of the Journal and the applicant shall notify registered licensees and, in the case of an application under Section 25, the patentee, of the advertisement.

1418 **72.**—(1) At any time within two months from the date of the first advertisement of the application in the Journal any person may give notice of opposition.

(2) Such notice shall be on Patents Form 28, shall be accompanied by a copy thereof and shall be supported by a statement (in duplicate) setting out fully the nature of the opponent's interest, the grounds of opposition, and the relief which he seeks and evidence (in duplicate) of the facts upon which he relies.

(3) A copy of the notice, the statement and the evidence shall be sent by the Comptroller to the applicant, who, within three months from the receipt thereof, may file evidence confined to matters strictly in reply and shall deliver to the opponent a copy of the evidence.

1419 **73.**—(1) An opponent shall be entitled on request made to the applicant within one month of the giving of the notice of opposition, to be supplied, at his own expense, by the applicant with a copy of the application and of the evidence filed in support.

(2) Within three months of the receipt of the copy of the evidence filed in support of the application the opponent may file additional

evidence and shall deliver to the applicant a copy of such evidence and, within three months of the receipt of the copy of the opponent's additional evidence, the applicant may file further evidence confined to matters strictly in reply and shall deliver to the opponent a copy of such evidence.

1420　　**74.** No further evidence shall be filed by either party except by leave or direction of the Comptroller.

1421　　**75.**—(1) On completion of the evidence or at such other time as he may see fit, the Comptroller shall appoint a time for the hearing of the case, and shall give the parties at least fourteen days' notice of the appointment.

(2) If either party desires to be heard he shall notify the Comptroller on Patents Form No. 13 and the Comptroller may refuse to hear either party who has not filed the said form prior to the date of the hearing.

(3) After hearing the party or parties desiring to be heard or, if neither party desires to be heard, then without a hearing, the Comptroller shall decide the case and notify his decision to the parties.

1422　　**76.** If no notice of opposition to the application is given the Comptroller shall, on the expiration of the period prescribed by Rule 72 (1), after hearing the applicant if desiring to be heard, decide the case and notify his decision to the applicant.

1423　　**77.** If at any stage of the application the Comptroller decides to refer the application for decision by the court he shall notify the applicant and any opponent accordingly.

Restoration of lapsed patents and lapsed applications for patents (Sections 27 and 28)

1424　　**78.** An application under Section 27 for restoration of a patent shall be made on Patents Form No. 29 and shall be accompanied by evidence in support of the statements made in the application.

1425　　**79.**—(1) If, upon consideration of the evidence, the Comptroller is not satisfied that a prima facie case for an order under Section 27 has been made out, he shall notify the applicant accordingly and, unless within one month the applicant requests to be heard in the matter, the Comptroller shall refuse the application.

(2) If the applicant requests a hearing within the time allowed, the Comptroller after giving the applicant an opportunity of being heard shall determine whether the application may proceed to advertisement or whether it shall be refused.

1426　　**80.**—(1) At any time within two months of the advertisement of the application under Section 27 (4), any person may give notice of opposition thereto on Patents Form No. 30.

(2) Such notice shall be accompanied by a copy thereof and shall be supported by a statement (in duplicate), setting out fully the nature of the opponent's interest and the facts upon which he relies.

(3) A copy of the notice and of the statement shall be sent by the Comptroller to the applicant.

1427   **81.** Upon notice of opposition being given the provisions of Rules 40 to 45 shall apply.

1428   **82.** If the Comptroller decides in favour of the applicant, he shall notify him accordingly, and require him to file Patents Form No. 31 together with Patents Form No. 24 accompanied by fees to the amount of the unpaid renewal fees.

1429   **83.** In every order of the Comptroller restoring a patent the following provision shall be inserted for the protection of persons who have begun to avail themselves of the patented invention between the date when the patent ceased to have effect and the date of the application:

" (1) No action or other proceeding shall be commenced or prosecuted nor any damage recovered in respect of any manufacture, use, or sale of the invention the subject of the patent in the interim period as hereinafter defined by any person not being a licensee under the patent at the date when it ceased to have effect, the   , who after such date and before the   , the date of the application has made, used, exercised or sold the invention the subject of the patent or has manufactured or installed any plant, machinery or apparatus claimed in the specification of the patent or for carrying out a method or process so claimed. Any such person shall be deemed to have so acted with the licence of the patentee and shall thereafter be entitled to continue to make, use, exercise or sell the invention without infringement of the patent to the extent hereinafter specified that is to say:

(a) In so far as the complete specification of the patent claims an article (other than plant, machinery or apparatus or part thereof as specified under head (b) hereof) and any article so claimed has been manufactured by him during the said interim period, that particular article may at all times be used or sold.

(b) In so far as the complete specification claims any plant, machinery or apparatus or part thereof for the production of an article, then any particular plant, machinery or apparatus or part thereof so claimed, which has been manufactured or installed by him during the said interim period, and the products thereof, may at all times be used or sold and so that in the event of any such plant, machinery, apparatus or part thereof being impaired by wear or tear or accidentally destroyed, a like licence shall extend to any replacement thereof and to the products of such replacement.

(c) In so far as the complete specification claims any process for the making or treating of any article or any method or process of testing, any particular plant, machinery or apparatus which during the said interim period has been manufactured or installed by him or exclusively or mainly used by him for carrying

[513]

on such method or process may at all times be so used or continued to be so used and the products thereof may at all times be used or sold and so that in the event of any such plant, machinery or apparatus being impaired by wear or tear or accidentally destroyed a like licence shall extend to such method or process when carried on in any replacement of such plant, machinery or apparatus and to the products of the process so carried on.

" (2) In the foregoing paragraph, ' article ' has the same meaning as in Section 101 of the Patents Act, 1949, and ' the interim period ' means the period between the date when the patent ceased to have effect and the date of this Order."

1430   **84.** An application under Section 28 for the sealing of a patent shall be made on Patents Form No. 32 and shall be accompanied by evidence in support of the statements made in the application.

1431   **85.**—(1) If, upon consideration of the evidence, the Comptroller is not satisfied that a prima facie case for an order under Section 28 has been made out he shall notify the applicant accordingly and unless within one month from that notification the applicant requests to be heard in the matter, the Comptroller shall refuse the application.

(2) If the applicant requests a hearing within the time allowed, the Comptroller, after giving the applicant an opportunity of being heard, shall determine whether the application may proceed to advertisement or whether it shall be refused.

1432   **86.**—(1) At any time within two months of the advertisement of an application under Section 28 (3) any person may give notice of opposition thereto on Patents Form No. 33.

(2) Such notice shall be accompanied by a copy thereof and shall be supported by a statement (in duplicate), setting out fully the nature of the opponent's interest and the facts upon which he relies.

(3) A copy of the notice and statement shall be sent by the Comptroller to the applicant.

1433   **87.** Upon notice of opposition being given the provisions of Rules 40 to 45 shall apply.

1434   **88.** If the Comptroller decides in favour of the applicant, he shall notify the applicant accordingly and require him to file Patents Form No. 34 together with Patents Form No. 20.

1435   **89.** In every order of the Comptroller under Section 28 for the sealing of a patent the same provision shall be inserted for the protection of persons who have begun to avail themselves of the invention between the date when the time allowed by or under Section 19 for making the prescribed request for sealing expired, and the date of the application for an order for sealing, as are specified in Rule 83 for the protection of persons who have begun to avail themselves of a patented invention between the date when the patent ceased to have effect and the date of the application for restoration, there being substituted for references to the date when the patent ceased to have effect references to the date when the time allowed by or under Section 19 for making the request for sealing expired.

Amendment of specification or application for patent

1436   **90.** An application to the Comptroller for leave to amend an accepted complete specification under Section 29 shall be made on Patents Form No. 35, and, subject to the proviso to Section 29 (3), shall be advertised by publication of the application and the nature of the proposed amendment in the Journal, and in such other manner, if any, as the Comptroller may in each case direct.

1437   **91.**—(1) Any person wishing to oppose the application shall, within one month from the date of the advertisement in the Journal, or such further period not exceeding three months from the said date as the Comptroller may in special cases allow, give notice to the Comptroller on Patents Form No. 36.

(2) Such notice shall be accompanied by a copy thereof and shall be supported by a statement (in duplicate) setting out fully the nature of the opponent's interest, the facts upon which he relies and the relief which he seeks. A copy of the notice and of the statement shall be sent by the Comptroller to the applicant.

1438   **92.** Upon such notice of opposition being given and a copy thereof sent to the applicant the provisions of Rules 40 to 45 shall apply.

1439   **93.** Unless the Comptroller otherwise directs, an application or proposal for amendment of an accepted complete specification shall be accompanied by a copy of the printed specification and drawings clearly showing in red ink the amendment sought.

1440   **94.**—(1) An application for leave to amend a complete specification which has not been accepted, except when the amendment is made to meet an objection contained in an Examiner's report, shall be made on Patents Form No. 37.

(2) An application for leave to convert an application for a patent to a Convention application may be made at any time within twelve months from the date of the first application for protection in a Convention country and shall be made on Patents Form No. 38 Con.

(3) Any other application for leave to amend an application for a patent shall be made on Patents Form No. 38.

441   **95.** Where leave to amend a specification is given the applicant shall, if the Comptroller so requires, and within a time to be fixed by him, file a new specification and drawings as amended, which shall be prepared in accordance with Rules 5 and 18 to 23.

Application for the revocation of a patent

442   **96.**—(1) An application for the revocation of a patent shall:
(a) be made on Patents Form No. 39,
(b) state the ground or grounds for the application, and
(c) be accompanied by a copy thereof and shall be supported by a statement (in duplicate) setting out fully the nature of the applicant's interests, the facts upon which he relies, and the relief which he seeks.

(2) A copy of the application and of the statement shall be sent by the Comptroller to the patentee.

443   **97.** Upon such application being made and a copy thereof sent to the patentee the provisions of Rules 40 to 46 shall apply with such consequential adaptations as the case requires and in particular with the substitution of references to the patentee for references to the applicant and of references to the applicant for references to the opponent.

1444   **98.** If the patentee offers under Section 34 to surrender his patent the Comptroller, in deciding whether costs should be awarded to the applicant for revocation, shall consider whether proceedings might have been avoided if the applicant had given reasonable notice to the patentee before the application was filed.

1445   **99.** A notice of an offer by a patentee under Section 34 to surrender his patent shall be given on Patents Form No. 40, and shall be advertised by the Comptroller in the Journal.

1446   **100.**—(1) At any time within one month from the advertisement any person may give notice of opposition to the Comptroller on Patents Form No. 41, which shall be accompanied by a copy thereof and shall be supported by a statement (in duplicate) setting out fully the nature of the opponent's interest, the facts upon which he relies, and the relief which he seeks.

(2) A copy of the notice and of the statement shall be sent by the Comptroller to the patentee.

1447   **101.** Upon such notice of opposition being given and a copy thereof sent to the patentee, the provisions of Rules 40 to 45 shall apply with the substitution of references to the patentee for references to the applicant.

Voluntary endorsement of patents " Licences of Right " (Sections 35 and 36)

1448   **102.** An application under Section 35 (1) for endorsement of a patent " Licences of Right " shall be made on Patents Form No. 42, and shall be accompanied by evidence verifying the statement in the application, and by the Letters Patent.

1449   **103.**—(1) An application under Section 35 (2) (*a*) or Section 35 (2) (*b*) for settlement of the terms of a licence under a patent endorsed " Licences of Right " shall be made on Patents Form No. 43, and shall be accompanied by a copy thereof and a statement (in duplicate) setting out fully the facts upon which the applicant relies, and the terms of the licence which he is prepared to accept or grant.

(2) A copy of the application and statement shall be sent by the Comptroller to the patentee or the person requiring a licence, as the case may be, who, if he does not agree to the terms set out in the statement, shall, within six weeks of the receipt of such copies, file a counterstatement setting out fully the grounds of his objection and send a copy thereof to the applicant.

(3) The Comptroller shall give such directions as he may think fit with regard to the filing of evidence and the hearing of the parties.

1450   **104.** An application under Section 36 (1) for the cancellation of an endorsement shall be made on Patents Form No. 44, and shall be accompanied by evidence verifying the statement in the application, and by Patents Form No. 24 accompanied by fees to the amount of the balance of all renewal fees which would have been payable if the patent had not been endorsed.

1451   105. An application under Section 36 (2) for the cancellation of an endorsement shall be made on Patents Form No. 45 within two months after the patent has been endorsed and shall be accompanied by a copy and a statement (in duplicate) setting out fully the nature of the applicant's interest, and the facts upon which he relies.

1452   106.—(1) Every application under Section 36 (1) or 36 (2) shall be advertised in the Journal, and the period within which notice of opposition to the cancellation of an endorsement may be given under Section 36 (5) shall be one month after the advertisement.

(2) Such notice shall be given on Patents Form No. 46 and shall be accompanied by a copy thereof, and shall be supported by a statement (in duplicate) setting out fully the facts upon which the opponent relies and, in the case of opposition to an application under Section 36 (1), the nature of his interest.

1453   107.—(1) A copy of the notice and of the statement shall be sent by the Comptroller to the applicant for cancellation of the endorsement and thereafter Rules 40 to 45 shall apply.

(2) Where the Comptroller cancels the endorsement pursuant to Section 36 (3), the patentee shall, within one month from the cancellation of the endorsement, file Patents Form No. 24 accompanied by fees to the amount of the balance of all renewal fees which would have been payable if the patent had not been endorsed.

Compulsory licence, compulsory endorsement of patent " Licences of Right " and revocation (Sections 37 to 45)

1454   108. An application under Section 37 for a licence under a patent or for endorsement of a patent " Licences of Right " shall be made on Patents Form No. 47.

1455   109. An application under Section 40 (1) for the endorsement of a patent " Licences of Right " or for the grant of a licence under a patent to a specified person shall be made on Patents Form No. 48.

1456   110. An application under Section 40 (3) for an Order of the Comptroller under Section 40 (4) shall be made on Patents Form No. 49.

1457   111. An application under Section 42 for the revocation of a patent shall be made on Patents Form No. 50.

1458   112. An application under Section 37, Section 40 or Section 42 shall be accompanied by evidence verifying the statements in the application.

1459   113.—(1) If upon consideration of the evidence the Comptroller is not satisfied that a prima facie case has been made out for the making of an order, he shall notify the applicant accordingly, and unless within one month the applicant requests to be heard in the matter the Comptroller shall refuse the application.

(2) If the applicant requests a hearing within the time allowed,

the Comptroller, after giving the applicant an opportunity of being heard, shall determine whether the application may proceed to advertisement or whether it shall be refused.

1460   114.—(1) If the Comptroller allows the application to proceed to advertisement, he shall direct the applicant to serve copies of the application and of the evidence filed in support thereof upon the patentee and any other persons appearing from the register to be interested in the patent and upon any other person on whom, in his opinion, copies should be so served.

(2) The time within which notice of opposition under Section 43 (3) may be given shall be two months after the advertisement of the application under Section 43 (2).

(3) Such notice shall be given on Patents Form No. 51, accompanied by a copy thereof, and shall be supported by evidence (in duplicate) verifying the statements made therein.

(4) The Comptroller shall send a copy of the notice and the evidence to the applicant and thereafter the provisions of Rule 42 (so far as they are applicable) and of Rules 43 to 45 shall apply.

1461   115.—(1) An application under Section 41 for a licence under a patent shall be made on Patents Form No. 52.

(2) The procedure to be followed in connection with such application shall be the same as that prescribed in Rules 112 to 114 for an application under Section 37.

Directions to co-owners (Section 55)

1462   116.—(1) An application for directions under Section 55 (1) by a co-grantee or co-proprietor of a patent shall be made on Patents Form No. 53 and shall be accompanied by a statement setting out fully the facts upon which the applicant relies and the directions which he seeks.

(2) A copy of the application and of the statement shall be sent by the Comptroller to each other person registered as grantee or proprietor of the patent and the applicant shall supply a sufficient number of copies for that purpose.

(3) Thereafter the Comptroller may give such directions as he may think fit with regard to the subsequent procedure.

1463   117.—(1) An application for directions under Section 55 (2) by a co-grantee or co-proprietor of a patent shall be made on Patents Form No. 54, and shall be accompanied by a copy thereof, and a statement (in duplicate) setting out fully the facts upon which the applicant relies and the directions which he seeks.

(2) A copy of the application and of the statement shall be sent by the Comptroller to the person in default.

(3) Thereafter the Comptroller may give such directions as he may think fit with regard to the subsequent procedure.

Disputes as to inventions made by employees (Section 56)

1464   118.—(1) An application under Section 56 (1) to determine a dispute as to rights in an invention shall be made on Patents Form No. 55 and shall be accompanied by a copy thereof, together with a statement (in duplicate) setting out fully the facts of the dispute and the relief which is sought.

(2) A copy of the application and of the statement shall be sent by the Comptroller to the other party to the dispute, who, within three months after receipt thereof, shall file a counterstatement (in duplicate) setting out fully the grounds on which he disputes the right of the applicant to the relief sought.

(3) The Comptroller shall send a copy of this counterstatement to the applicant and thereafter, subject to such directions as the Comptroller may think fit to give, the provisions of Rules 41 to 45 shall apply with the substitution of references to the applicant for references to the opponent and references to the other party for references to the applicant.

Reference to Comptroller of disputes as to infringement (Section 67)

1465   **119.** Where the parties to a dispute of the kind specified in Section 67 (1) agree to refer the dispute to the Comptroller they shall give notice to him on Patents Form No. 56 giving full particulars of the matters which are in dispute, and of the matters on which the parties are in agreement.

1466   **120.**—(1) The procedure set out in this Rule shall apply unless the only matter stated in the notice to be in dispute is the validity of any claim of the specification of the patent alleged to be infringed.

(2) The patentee or exclusive licensee (referred to in this and the next following Rule as the plaintiff), shall with such notice or within one month thereafter, file a statement (in duplicate) giving full particulars of his case on the matters in dispute.

(3) A copy of the plaintiff's statement shall be sent by the Comptroller to the other party to the dispute (referred to in this and the next following Rule as the defendant), who shall, within one month after receipt thereof, file a counterstatement setting out fully the grounds on which he contests the plaintiff's case and shall deliver to the plaintiff a copy thereof.

(4) If the defendant alleges in his counterstatement that any claim of the specification alleged by the plaintiff to have been infringed is not valid, the plaintiff, within one month after receipt of the copy of the counterstatement, shall file a further statement setting out fully the grounds on which he contests the defendant's allegation, and shall deliver to the defendant a copy thereof.

(5) The Comptroller may at any time require the statements to be amplified or amended to his satisfaction.

(6) Subject to such directions as the Comptroller may think fit to give the plaintiff may, within six weeks of filing his further statement, file evidence in support of his case, and shall deliver to the defendant a copy thereof, and thereafter the provisions of Rules 42 to 45 shall apply with the substitution of references to the plaintiff for references to the opponent and references to the defendant for references to the applicant.

1467   **121.**—(1) The procedure set out in this Rule shall apply if the only matter stated in the notice to be in dispute is the validity of any claim of the specification alleged to be infringed.

(2) The defendant shall, with the notice, or within one month thereafter, file a statement (in duplicate) giving full particulars of the ground on which he alleges that the claim is invalid.

(3) A copy of the defendant's statement shall be sent by the Comptroller to the plaintiff, who shall, within one month after the receipt thereof, file a counterstatement giving full particulars of the grounds on which he contests the defendant's allegations, and shall deliver to the defendant a copy thereof.

1468   (4) The Comptroller may at any time require the statements to be amplified or amended to his satisfaction.

(5) Subject to such directions as the Comptroller may think fit to give the defendant may within six weeks after the receipt of the copy of the plaintiff's counterstatement, file evidence in support of his case, and shall deliver to the plaintiff a copy thereof, and thereafter the provisions of Rules 42 to 45 shall apply with the substitution of references to the defendant for references to the opponent and references to the plaintiff for references to the applicant.

1469   122. If the Comptroller decides that relief shall be granted, he may require the parties to supply him with such information or evidence as he considers to be necessary to assist him in assessing the amount of the damages.

Register of Patents (Sections 73 and 74)

1470   123.—(1) Upon the sealing of a patent the Comptroller shall cause to be entered in the register the name, address, and nationality of the grantee as the patentee thereof, the title of the invention, the date of the patent, and the date of the sealing thereof, together with the address for service.

(2) The Comptroller may at any time enter in the register such other particulars as he may deem necessary.

1471   124.—(1) A request by a patentee for the alteration of a name, nationality or address or address for service entered in the register in respect of his patent shall be made on Patents Form No. 57.

(2) Before acting on a request to alter a name or nationality, the Comptroller may require such proof of the alteration as he may think fit.

(3) If the Comptroller is satisfied that the request may be allowed, he shall cause the register to be altered accordingly.

1472   125.—(1) An application for the registration of the title of any person becoming entitled by assignment, transmission or operation of law to a patent or to a share in a patent, or becoming entitled by virtue of a mortgage, licence or other instrument to any other interest in a patent, shall be made

    (*a*) in the case of an application under Section 74 (1), by the person becoming so entitled on Patents Form No. 58 or Patents Form No. 59, and

    (*b*) in the case of an application under Section 74 (2), by the assignor, mortgagor, licensor, or other party conferring the interest, on Patents Form No. 60 or Patents Form No. 61, as the case may be.

(2) Application may be made on Patents Form No. 62 for entry in the register of notification of any other document purporting to affect the proprietorship of a patent.

1473 **126.**—(1) An official or certified copy of a document which is referred to in an application under Rule 125 and is a matter of record in the United Kingdom shall be produced to the Comptroller with the application.

(2) Unless the Comptroller otherwise directs, the original of any other documents so referred to shall be produced to him with the application and a certified copy of any such document shall be filed.

1474 **127.** Upon the issue of a certificate of payment under Rule 67, the Comptroller shall enter in the register the fact that the fee has been paid, and the date of payment as stated on the certificate.

1475 **128.** Where an Order for the extension of the term of a patent under Section 23 or 24 or 25 contains a provision that persons claiming to be deemed to have acted with the licence of the patentee or exclusive licensee shall make application for entry of their claim upon the register, the application shall be made on Patents Form No. 63.

Correction of clerical errors (Section 76)

1476 **129.** A request for the correction of a clerical error in an application for a patent or in any document filed in pursuance of such an application or in any patent or in the register, shall be made on Patents Form No. 64.

1477 **130.** Where the Comptroller requires notice of the nature of the proposed correction to be advertised, the advertisement shall be made by publication of the request and the nature of the proposed correction in the Journal, and in such other manner (if any) as the Comptroller may direct.

1478 **131.**—(1) Any person may, at any time within one month from the date of the advertisement in the Journal, give notice to the Comptroller of opposition to the proposed correction on Patents Form No. 65.

(2) Such notice shall be accompanied by a copy thereof and shall be supported by a statement (in duplicate) setting out fully the nature of the opponent's interest, the facts on which he relies, and the relief which he seeks.

(3) A copy of the notice and of the statement shall be sent by the Comptroller to the person making the request, and thereafter the provisions of Rules 40 to 45 shall apply.

1479 **132.** Where, in accordance with Section 76 (3), a hearing is appointed, at least fourteen days' notice of the appointment shall be given to the patentee or the applicant for a patent and to any other person to whom notice of the proposed correction has been given by the Comptroller.

Certificates and information

480 **133.** A request for a certificate of the Comptroller for the purposes of Section 77 (1) shall be made on Patents Form No. 66.

1481　　　**134**. Certified copies of an entry in the register, or certified copies of, or extracts from, patents, specifications, and other public documents in the Office, or of or from registers and other records kept there, may be furnished by the Comptroller on payment of the fees prescribed in Schedule 1 to these Rules.

1482　　　**135**.—(1) A request under Section 78 for information relating to any patent or application for a patent may be made

　　(*a*) as to when a complete specification following a provisional specification has been filed or when a period of fifteen months from the date of the application has expired and a complete specification has not been filed,

　　(*b*) as to when a complete specification is or will be published, or when an application for a patent has become void,

　　(*c*) as to when a patent has been sealed or when the time for requesting sealing has expired,

　　(*d*) as to when a renewal fee has been paid,

　　(*e*) as to when a patent has expired,

　　(*f*) as to when an entry has been made in the register or application has been made for the making of such entry, or

　　(*g*) as to when any application is made or action taken involving an entry in the register or advertisement in the Journal, if the nature of the application or action is specified in the request,

　　(*h*) as to when any document filed in proceedings after acceptance of the complete specification may be inspected in accordance with the provisions of Rule 146.

(2) Any such request shall be made on Patents Form No. 67 and a separate form shall be used in respect of each item of information required.

Duplicate patent

1483　　　**136**. An application under Section 80 for a duplicate of a patent shall be made on Patents Form No. 68 and shall be accompanied by evidence setting out fully and verifying the circumstances in which the patent was lost or destroyed, or cannot be produced.

Evidence before Comptroller

1484　　　**137**. Where under these Rules evidence is required to be filed it shall be by statutory declaration or affidavit unless otherwise expressly provided in these Rules.

1485　　　**138**.—(1) The statutory declarations and affidavits required by these Rules, or used in any proceedings thereunder, shall be headed in the matter or matters to which they relate, and shall be divided into paragraphs consecutively numbered, and each paragraph shall so far as possible be confined to one subject.

(2) Every statutory declaration or affidavit shall state the description and true place of abode of the person making the same, and shall be written, typed, lithographed or printed.

1486　　　**139**. The statutory declarations and affidavits shall be made and subscribed as follows:

　　(*a*) In the United Kingdom, before any justice of the peace, or any commissioner or other officer authorised by law in any part of the United Kingdom to administer an oath for the purpose of any legal proceedings;

(*b*) In any other part of Her Majesty's dominions, or in any British protectorate or protected state or in any mandated territory as defined in the British Nationality Act 1948, or in any trust territory as so defined or in the Republic of Ireland, before any court, judge, justice of the peace, or any officer authorised by law to administer an oath there for the purpose of any legal proceedings; and

(*c*) Elsewhere, before a British Minister, or person exercising the functions of a British Minister, or a Consul, Vice-Consul, or other person exercising the functions of a British Consul, or before a notary public, or before a judge or magistrate.

1487   **140.** Any document purporting to have affixed, impressed or subscribed thereto or thereon the seal or signature of any person authorised by the last foregoing Rule to take a declaration, in testimony that the declaration was made and subscribed before him, may be admitted by the Comptroller without proof of the genuineness of the seal or signature or of the official character of the person or his authority to take the declaration.

1488   **141.** At any stage of any proceedings before the Comptroller he may direct that such documents, information or evidence as he may require shall be furnished within such period as he may fix.

Hearing in Scottish cases (Section 86)

1489   **142.**—(1) Any party or parties to proceedings under Sections 55 (1), 55 (2) or 56 (1) of the Act may request the Comptroller to direct that any hearing in such proceedings shall be held in Scotland.

(2) A request made under sub-rule (1) shall—

(*a*) be in writing;

(*b*) be accompanied by a statement of facts setting out the grounds upon which the request is made; and

(*c*) be lodged with the Comptroller at any time before the Comptroller issues notification to the parties that a hearing has been appointed, or, with the leave of the Comptroller, within fourteen days thereafter.

(3) The Comptroller, upon a request being made under sub-rule (1) of this rule, shall forthwith intimate such request by sending a copy thereof together with the relevant statement of facts to any party to the proceedings who has not signed the request as a consenter thereto, and for the purpose of such intimation sufficient copies of the request and statement shall be lodged with the Comptroller by the party or parties making the request.

(4) Any party or parties to the proceedings having objection to a request intimated under sub-rule (3) may, within one month of such intimation, lodge with the Comptroller a counterstatement setting out the grounds upon which objection is taken, and the Comptroller shall forthwith intimate the objection by sending a copy of the counterstatement to any party who is not a signatory, and for the purpose of such intimation sufficient copies of the counterstatement shall be

lodged with the Comptroller by the party or parties making the objection.

(5) Subject to the foregoing provisions the Comptroller may give such directions as he thinks fit with regard to the procedure to be followed in dealing with a request made under sub-rule (1) including any hearing thereon which may appear to him to be necessary.

(6) Where the Comptroller, after consideration of a request made under sub-rule (1), is satisfied, having regard to the balance of convenience in all the circumstances of the case, that any hearing thereon should be held in Scotland, he shall grant the request and issue such directions as shall seem to him appropriate.

(7) Any decision of the Comptroller under this rule shall be final.

The Journal, Reports of Cases, and publication of documents

1490   **143.**—(1) The Comptroller shall publish a journal containing particulars of applications for patents and other proceedings under the Act and any other information that he may deem to be generally useful or important.

(2) The journal shall be entitled " The Official Journal (Patents)."

(3) Unless the Comptroller otherwise directs, the journal shall be published weekly.

1491   **144.** The Comptroller shall publish from time to time reports of such cases relating to patents, trade marks and registered designs as he may deem to be generally useful or important.

145. The Comptroller may arrange for the publication and sale of copies of specifications, drawings and other documents in the Office, and of indexes to and abridgments of such documents.

1492   **146.**[34]—(1) In addition to the documents open to public inspection by virtue of section 13 (2) and Rule 38 (1), and subject to the provisions of this Rule, every Patents Form filed in pursuance of an application for a patent or in relation to a patent shall be open to public inspection after the date of publication of the complete specification and every document filed with or sent to the Office after the said date for the purposes of any proceedings relating to a patent or an application for a patent shall be open to public inspection after the expiry of the period of 14 days from its being filed or sent.

(2) Sub-rule (1) of this Rule shall not apply to—

(a) Patents Forms Nos. 1, 1 Con., 2, 3, 8, 37, 66 and 67;

(b) any document sent to the Office, at its request or otherwise, for inspection and subsequent return to the sender.

(3) (a) Where a document other than a Patents Form is filed or sent after the date of the publication of the complete specification and the person filing or sending it or any other party to the proceedings to which the document relates so requests, giving his reasons, within 14 days of the filing or sending of the document, the Comptroller may direct it to be treated as confidential; and the document shall not be open to public inspection while the matter is being determined by the Comptroller.

[34] Rule 146 is printed as amended by Patents (Amendment) Rules 1970.

(*b*) Where such a direction has been given and not withdrawn, nothing in this Rule shall be taken to authorise or require any person to be allowed to inspect the document to which the direction relates except by leave of the Comptroller.

(*c*) The Comptroller shall not withdraw any direction given under this sub-rule nor shall he give leave for any person to inspect any document to which a direction which has not been withdrawn relates without prior consultation with the person at whose request the direction was given, unless the Comptroller is satisfied that such prior consultation is not reasonably practicable.

(*d*) Where such a direction is given or withdrawn a record of the fact shall be filed with the document to which it relates.

(*e*) Where the time prescribed in paragraph (*a*) of this sub-rule is extended under Rule 154, the relevant document shall not be, or if the time is extended after the time has expired shall cease to be, open to public inspection until the expiry of the extended time, and if a request for a direction is made the document shall not be open to public inspection while the matter is being determined by the Comptroller.

(4) Nothing in this Rule shall be construed as imposing upon the Comptroller the duty of making available for public inspection any documents filed with or sent to the office before 1st November 1968.

Hours of business and excluded days (Section 98)

1493   **147.**—(1) The following shall be excluded days for purposes of the transaction by the public of business of all classes under the Act:

Christmas Day, Good Friday, the Saturday following Good Friday and all Sundays.

(2) Days which may, from time to time, be notified by a notice posted in a conspicuous place in the Office shall be excluded days for purposes of the transaction of business of all classes or such class or classes as may be specified in the notice.

(3) All Saturdays, other than those falling within sub-rule (1) or (2), shall be excluded days for purposes of the transaction of all classes of business other than the filing of new applications for patents which are not Convention applications.

1494   **148.** The Office shall be deemed to be closed at the following hours for the transaction of business of the classes specified:

    (*a*) On weekdays other than Saturdays, at six o'clock for the filing of applications, forms and other documents, and at four o'clock for all other business;

    (*b*) On Saturdays, at one o'clock for the filing of new applications for patents which are not Convention applications.

Applications to and Orders of Court

1495   **149.** Where an application to the Court under Section 75 for rectification of the register has been made, the applicant shall forthwith serve an office copy of the application on the Comptroller, who shall enter a notice of the application on the register.

1496   **150.** Where any Order has been made by the Court under the Act revoking a patent or extending the term of a patent, or allowing a patentee to amend his specification, or affecting the validity or proprietorship of a patent or any rights thereunder, the person in whose favour such order has been made shall file Patents Form No. 69 accompanied by an office copy of such order, and thereupon the specification shall be amended or the register rectified or altered as the case may be.

General

1497 **151.** Except as otherwise provided in these Rules, before exercising any discretionary power given to him by the Act or these Rules adversely to an applicant for a patent or for amendment of a specification, the Comptroller shall give at least ten days' notice to the applicant of the time when he may be heard.

1498 **152.** Any document filed in any proceedings before the Comptroller may, if he thinks fit, be amended, and any irregularity in procedure may be rectified, on such terms as he may direct.

1499 **153.**—(1) Where by virtue of any of the Rules mentioned in sub-rule (2) of this Rule any notice of opposition or application for the revocation of a patent is required to be supported by a statement or evidence, such statement or evidence shall be filed on, or within 14 days after, the date on which the notice is given or the application is made.

(2) The Rules referred to in sub-rule (1) are Rules 39 (1), 72 (2), 80 (2), 86 (2), 91 (2), 96 (1), 100 (1), 106 (2), 114 (3) and 131 (2).

1500 **154.** The times prescribed by these Rules for doing any act, or taking any proceeding thereunder, other than the times prescribed by Rules 37, 59, 72 (1), 80, 86, 100 and 106, may be extended by the Comptroller if he thinks fit, upon such notice to the parties and upon such terms, as he may direct, and such extension may be granted although the time has expired for doing such act or taking such proceeding.

1501 **155.** Where, under these Rules, any person is required to do any act or thing, or any document or evidence is required to be produced or filed, and it is shown to the satisfaction of the Comptroller that from any reasonable cause that person is unable to do that act or thing, or that that document or evidence cannot be produced or filed, the Comptroller may, upon the production of such evidence and subject to such terms as he thinks fit, dispense with the doing of any such act or thing, or the production or filing of such document or evidence.

1502 **156.** Where the hearing before the Comptroller of any dispute between two or more parties relating to any matter in connection with a patent or an application for a patent takes place after the date of the publication of the complete specification, the hearing of the dispute shall be in public unless the Comptroller, after consultation with those parties to the dispute who appear in person or are represented at the hearing, otherwise directs.

Revocation of existing Rules

1503 **157.** The Patents Rules 1958, the Patents (Amendment) Rules 1964, the Patents (Amendment No. 2) Rules 1964, the Patents

(Amendment) Rules 1966, the Patents (Amendment) Rules 1967 and the Patents (Amendment No. 2) Rules 1967, are hereby revoked:

Provided that the Patents Rules 1939, as amended by the Patents (Amendment) Rules 1942, and the Patents (Amendment) Rules 1946, shall continue to apply in relation to any matter to which by virtue of Schedule 3 to the Act the provisions of the Patents and Designs Acts 1907 to 1946, continue to apply.

27th August 1968.

Edmund Dell.
Minister of State,
Board of Trade.

We consent to the making of Rule 3 of these Rules.
26th August 1968.

B. K. O'Malley,
Joseph Harper,
Two of the Lords Commissioners
of Her Majesty's Treasury.

1504 Rules 3 and 134 SCHEDULE 1 [35]

LIST OF FEES PAYABLE

	£ s. d.	Corresponding Form
1. On application for a patient ...	1 0 0*	Patents Form No. 1 or Schedule 3 Form 1A.
2. On Convention application for a patent: In respect of each application for protection in a Convention country	1 0 0*	Patents Form No. 1 Con. or Schedule 3 Form 1B.
3. On filing specification: Provisional	—	Patents Form No. 2.
Complete	15 0 0	Patents Form No. 3.
4. On application for grant of patent of addition in lieu of an independent patent ...	6 0 0*	Patents Form No. 1 Add.
5. Declaration of inventorship of invention disclosed in complete specification	—	Patents Form No. 4.

[35] Schedule 1 printed as amended by the Patents (Amendment) Rules 1969 (S.I. No. 482):
The decimalised figures have been inserted, where appropriate, inside square brackets, under the original sterling figure for the fees payable; the Decimal Currency Act 1969, s. 3 (1) provides that on or after the appointed day, February 15, 1971, any reference to an amount of money including shillings or pence shall be read as referring to the corresponding amount in the new currency. Schedule 1 to that Act gives a conversion table to decimal currency. With the exceptions indicated by the asterisks, the fees payable under the Rules are increased.

	£ s. d.	Corresponding Form
6. For extension of the period for filing complete specification ...	3 10 0* [£3·50]	Patents Form No. 5.
7. On request for the post-dating of an application under Section 6 (3)	3 10 0* [£3·50]	Patents Form No. 6.
8. For extension of time under Rule 30 or 33 or 50:		
Not exceeding one month ...	1 5 0* [£1·25]	Patents Form No. 7.
Each succeeding month ...	1 5 0* [£1·25]	„ „ „
9. On application for result of search made under Sections 7 and 8	1 0* [£0·05]	Patents Form No. 8.
10. On application under Section 9 (2) for deletion of reference ...	1 5 0* [£1·25]	Patents Form No. 9.
11. For extension of the period for putting an application in order:		
Up to one month after the period allowed by Section 12 (1)	3 0 0	Patents Form No. 10.
Up to two months	6 0 0	„ „ „
Up to three months ...	9 0 0	„ „ „
12. For postponement of acceptance of complete specification:		
Up to 13 months from date of filing of complete specification	3 0 0	Patents Form No. 11.
From 13 months to 14 months	3 0 0	„ „ „
From 14 months to 15 months	3 0 0	„ „ „
13. On notice of opposition to grant of patent. By opponent ...	2 10 0* [£2·50]	Patents Form No. 12.
14. On hearing by Comptroller. By each party	3 0 0	Patents Form No. 13.
15. On a request under Section 16 (3)	1 5 0* [£1·25]	Patents Form No. 14.
16. On a claim under Section 16 (4)	1 5 0* [£1·25]	Patents Form No. 15.
17. On an application for extension of the period under Section 16 (5)	1 5 0* [£1·25]	Patents Form No. 16.
18. On an application for a certificate under Section 16 (8) ...	2 10 0* [£2·50]	Patents Form No. 17.
19. On a claim under Section 17 (1) for application to proceed in name of claimants	2 10 0* [£2·50]	Patents Form No. 18.
20. On application for directions under Section 17 (5)	7 10 0 [£7·50]	Patents Form No. 19.
21. On a request for sealing of a patent	6 0 0	Patents Form No. 20.

		Corresponding Form
	£ s. d.	
22. On application for extension of the period for requesting the sealing of a patent under Section 19 (3):		
Not exceeding one month ...	3 0 0	Patents Form No. 21.
,, ,, two months ..	6 0 0	,, ,, ,,
,, ,, three months .	9 10 0 [£9·50]	,, ,, ,,
23. On application for extension of the period for requesting the sealing of a patent under Section 19 (4):		
Not exceeding one month ...	1 10 0 [£1·50]	Patents Form No. 22.
Each succeeding month ...	15 0 [£0·75]	,, ,, ,,
24. On application under Section 20 for amendment of a patent ...	6 0 0*	Patents Form No. 23.
25. †On application for certificate of payment of renewal fee:		
Before the expiration of the 4th year from the date of the patent and in respect of the 5th year	11 0 0	Patents Form No. 24.
Before the expiration of the 5th year from the date of the patent and in respect of the 6th year	12 0 0	,, ,, ,,
Before the expiration of the 6th year from the date of the patent and in respect of the 7th year	13 0 0	,, ,, ,,
Before the expiration of the 7th year from the date of the patent and in respect of the 8th year	14 0 0	,, ,, ,,
Before the expiration of the 8th year from the date of the patent and in respect of the 9th year	16 0 0	,, ,, ,,
Before the expiration of the 9th year from the date of the patent and in respect of the 10th year	18 0 0	,, ,, ,,
Before the expiration of the 10th year from the date of the patent and in respect of the 11th year	20 0 0*	,, ,, ,,
Before the expiration of the 11th year from the date of the patent and in respect of the 12th year	22 0 0*	,, ,, ,,

† One-half only of these fees payable on patents endorsed " Licences of Right "

	£ s. d.	Corresponding Form
25.—*cont.*		
Before the expiration of the 12th year from the date of the patent and in respect of the 13th year	24 0 0*	,, ,, ,,
Before the expiration of the 13th year from the date of the patent and in respect of the 14th year	26 0 0*	,, ,, ,,
Before the expiration of the 14th year from the date of the patent and in respect of the 15th year	28 0 0*	,, ,, ,,
Before the expiration of the 15th year from the date of the patent and in respect of the remainder of the term of the patent ...	30 0 0*	,, ,, ,,
26. On extension of the period for payment of renewal fees:		
Not exceeding one month ...	3 0 0	Patents Form No. 25
,, ,, two months ..	6 0 0	,, ,, ,,
,, ,, three months .	9 0 0	,, ,, ,,
,, ,, four months ..	12 0 0	,, ,, ,,
,, ,, five months ..	15 0 0	,, ,, ,,
,, ,, six months ...	18 0 0	,, ,, ,,
27. Certificate of payment of renewal fee	—	Patents Form No. 26.
28. On application under Section 24 or 25 for extension of term of patent	6 0 0*	Patents Form No. 27.
29. On opposition to application for extension of term of patent ...	2 10 0* [£2·50]	Patents Form No. 28.
30. On application for restoration of a patent	4 10 0 [£4·50]	Patents Form No. 29.
31. On notice of opposition to application for restoration of patent	2 10 0* [£2·50]	Patents Form No. 30.
32. Additional fee on restoration of patent	15 0 0	Patents Form No. 31.
33. On application under Section 28 for sealing of patent	4 10 0 [£4·50]	Patents Form No. 32.
34. On opposition to application under Section 28	2 10 0* [£2·50]	Patents Form No. 33.
35. Additional fee for sealing under Section 28	15 0 0	Patents Form No. 34.
36. On application to amend specification after acceptance:		
Up to sealing. By applicant	3 10 0* [£3·50]	Patents Form No. 35.
After sealing. By patentee	6 0 0*	,, ,, ,,
37. On notice of opposition to amendment. By opponent ...	2 10 0* [£2·50]	Patents Form No. 36.
38. On application to amend specification not yet accepted ...	2 10 0* [£2·50]	Patents Form No. 37.
39. On application to amend an application for a patent ...	2 10 0* [£2·50]	Patents Form No. 38.

	£ s. d.	Corresponding Form
39a. Application for the conversion of an application for a patent to a Convention application under Rule 94 (2)	—	Patents Form No. 38. Con.
40. On application for revocation of a patent under Section 33 ...	3 10 0* [£3·50]	Patents Form No. 39.
41. On offer to surrender a patent under Section 34	—	Patents Form No. 40.
42. On notice of opposition to surrender of a patent	2 10 0* [£2·50]	Patents Form No. 41.
43. On application for endorsement of patent " Licences of Right "	1 10 0 [£1·50]	Patents Form No. 42.
44. On application for settlement of terms of licence under patent endorsed " Licences of Right "	7 10 0 [£7·50]	Patents Form No. 43.
45. On application by patentee for cancellation of endorsement of patent " Licences of Right " ...	3 0 0	Patents Form No. 44.
46. On application for cancellation of endorsement " Licences of Right "	3 10 0 [£3·50]	Patents Form No. 45.
47. On notice of opposition to cancellation of endorsement of patent " Licences of Right " ...	3 10 0 [£3·50]	Patents Form No. 46.
48. On application under Section 37 for grant of compulsory licence or endorsement of a patent " Licences of Right "	7 10 0 [£7·50]	Patents Form No. 47.
49. On application under Section 40 (1) for endorsement of patent " Licences of Right " or grant of licence	7 10 0 [£7·50]	Patents Form No. 48.
50. On application under Section 40 (3) for Order of Comptroller	7 10 0 [£7·50]	Patents Form No. 49.
51. On application under Section 42 for revocation	7 10 0 [£7·50]	Patents Form No. 50.
52. On opposition to application under Section 37, 40, 41 or 42	3 0 0	Patents Form No. 51.
53. On application for licence under Section 41	7 10 0 [£7·50]	Patents Form No. 52.
54. On application under Section 55 (1) for directions of Comptroller	7 10 0 [£7·50]	Patents Form No. 53.
55. On application under Section 55 (2) for directions of Comptroller	7 10 0 [£7·50]	Patents Form No. 54.
56. On application under Section 56 (1) to determine dispute ...	7 10 0 [£7·50]	Patents Form No. 55.
57. On reference of dispute to Comptroller under Section 67 (1)	7 10 0 [£7·50]	Patents Form No. 56.
58. For altering name or nationality or address or address for service in register, for each patent	8 0 [£0·40]	Patents Form No. 57.

		Corresponding Form
	£ s. d.	
59. On application for entry of name of subsequent proprietor in the register if made within six months from date of acquisition of proprietorship:	1 10 0 [£1·50]	Patents Form No. 58 or 60.
If made after the expiration of six months but within twelve months from the date of acquisition of proprietorship	3 15 0 [£3·75]	,, ,, ,,
If made after expiration of twelve months from date of acquisition of proprietorship	4 10 0 [£4·50]	,, ,, ,,
On each application covering more than one patent, the devolution of title being the same as in the first patent. For each additional patent	4 0 [£0·20]	Patents Form No. 58 or 60.
60. On application for entry of notice of a mortgage or licence in the register, if made within six months from date of acquisition of interest or the sealing of the patent (whichever is the later)	1 10 0 [£1·50]	Patents Form No. 59 or 61.
If made after expiration of six months but within twelve months from date of acquisition of interest or the sealing of the patent (whichever is the later)	3 15 0 [£3·75]	,, ,, ,,
If made after expiration of twelve months from date of acquisition of interest or the sealing of the patent (whichever is the later)	4 10 0 [£4·50]	,, ,, ,,
On each application covering more than one patent, the devolution of title being the same as in the first patent. For each additional patent	4 0 [£0·20]	,, ,, ,,
61. On application for entry of notification of a document in the register, if made within six months from date of document or the sealing of the patent (whichever is the later):	1 10 0 [£1·50]	Patents Form No. 62.
If made after expiration of six months but within twelve months from date of document or the seal-		

	£ s. d.	Corresponding Form
61—cont.		
ing of the patent (which-ever is the later)	3 15 0 [£3·75]	Patents Forms No. 62
If made after expiration of twelve months from date of document or the seal-ing of the patent (which-ever is the later)	4 10 0 [£4·50]	„ „ „
On each application cover-ing more than one patent, for each additional patent referred to in the same document as the first patent	4 0 [£0·20]	„ „ „
62. On application for entry in the register of claim to a licence under a patent extended under Section 23, 24 or 25	1 10 0 [£1·50]	Patents Form No. 63.
63. On request to Comptroller to correct a clerical error: Up to sealing	15 0 [£0·75]	Patents Form No. 64.
After sealing	1 10 0 [£1·50]	„ „ „
64. On notice of opposition to the correction of a clerical error	1 10 0 [£1·50]	Patents Form No. 65.
65. For certificate of Comptroller under Section 77 (1) ...	15 0 [£0·75]	Patents Form No. 66.
66. On request for information as to a matter affecting a patent or an application therefor ...	1 5 0* [£1·25]	Patents Form No. 67.
67. For duplicate of patent	3 10 0* [£3·50]	Patents Form No. 68.
68. On notice of Order of Court ...	15 0 [£0·75]	Patents Form No. 69.
69. On inspection of register or supply of an extract from register, or on inspection of original documents (other than provisional specifications), samples or specimens	2 6* [£0·12½]	
70. For typewritten office copies (every 100 words) (but never less than two shillings) ...	1 0* [£0·05]	
71. For photographic office copies and office copies of drawings	Cost accor-ding to agreement	
72. For office copy of patent ...	6 0 [£0·30]	
73. For certifying office copies, MSS., printed or photographic ... ... each	4 0 [£0·20]	
74. On written enquiry as to whether a patent or patents is or are in force; for each patent	1 0* [£0·05]	

1505

SCHEDULE 2

PATENTS FORM No. 1   GENERAL FORMS   Rules 4 and 5 (1) (*f*)
PATENTS ACT, 1949

APPLICATION FOR PATENT

(*To be accompanied by two copies of Patents Form No. 2 or of Patents Form No. 3*)

NOTE.—This is a comprehensive form and parts inappropriate to a particular application should be cancelled. In the case of an application by the inventor, only sections 1, 4 and 6 of this form are appropriate, and section 5 if a Patent of Addition is applied for.

(*a*) Insert (in full) name, address and nationality of applicant(s).

1. I/We (*a*) ....
....
....
....

am/are in possession of an invention which is described in the accompanying

(*b*) Delete the words which are not applicable.
(*c*) Insert title of invention.

(*b*) $\dfrac{\text{provisional}}{\text{complete}}$ specification under the title (*c*) ....
....

(*b*) { I / We / The said (*d*) ....

(*d*) Insert name of inventor *if included at* (*a*).

claim . . . to be the true and first inventor . . . of the invention.

or

(*e*) Insert (in full) name, address and nationality of inventor(s) *if not included at* (*a*).

2. I/We believe (*e*) ....
....
....

to be the true and first inventor of the invention and

(*b*) { I / we / the said ....

(*b*) { is / am / are } the (*b*) { assignee . . . of the said inventor . . . in respect of the right to make this application personal representative . . . of the said inventor . . .

3. The invention or a part of the invention was communicated to

(*b*) { me / us / the said ....

(*f*) Insert (in full) name, address and nationality of communicator.

....
by (*f*) ....
....
....

Use of the invention in the United Kingdom before the date of the application for a patent is a lawful ground of objection.

4. I/We declare that to the best of my/our knowledge and belief the statements made above are correct and there is no lawful ground of objection to the grant of a patent to me/us on this application and I/we pray that a patent may be granted to me/us for the said invention;

[534]

5. And I/we request that the patent may be granted as a patent of addition to (*b*) { the patent to be granted on application No...................... patent No......................

6. And I/we request that all notices, requisitions, and communications relating to this application may be sent to..............
at (*g*) ....
....
(*h*) who is/are hereby appointed to act for me/us.
(*i*)..................................
....

(*g*) The address must be within the United Kingdom.
(*h*) Delete if not applicable.
(*i*) To be signed by applicant(s).

Declaration to be signed by any person named as inventor who is not an applicant
....

I/We claim to be the true and first inventor(s) and assent to the making of this application
....
....
....

To the Comptroller,
    The Patent Office,
        25, Southampton Buildings,
            Chancery Lane, London, W.C.2.

PATENTS FORM NO. 1 CON.

PATENTS ACT, 1949

1506   **CONVENTION APPLICATION FOR A PATENT**
(*To be accompanied by two copies of Patents Form No. 3*)

NOTE:—This is a comprehensive form, and parts inappropriate to a particular application should be cancelled.
    1. I/We (*a*) ....
....
....
....
hereby declare that an application or applications for protection for an invention or inventions has or have been made in the following country or countries and on the following official date or dates, namely:
in (*b*) .... on (*c*) ....
by (*d*) ....
....
in (*b*) .... on (*c*) ....
by (*d*) ....
....
in (*b*) .... on (*c*) ....
by (*d*) ....
....
and that the said application or each of the said applications was the first application in a Convention country in respect of the relevant invention by me/us or by any person from whom I/we derive title.
    2. I am/We are (*e*) the assignee . . . of the said (*d*) ....
.... by virtue of (*f*) ....

(*a*) Insert (in full) name, address and nationality of applicant(s).

(*b*) Insert the name of the Convention country in which the *first* application was made.
(*c*) Insert the official date of the *first* application in a Convention country.
(*d*) Insert name of applicant and (if not included at (*a*)) address and nationality. Particulars of any further applications

[535]

should be given
on the back of
this form or on
a separate
sheet.
(*e*) Delete
whichever does
not apply.
(*f*) Give
particulars of
the assignment.

....

or (*e*) the personal representative . . . of the said (*d*) ....

    3. I/We declare that to the best of my/our knowledge and belief there is no lawful ground of objection to the grant of a patent to me/us on this application, and pursuant to subsection (2) (and subsection (3)) of Section 1 of the Act I/we pray that a patent may be granted to me/us with priority founded on the above-mentioned application . . . in a Convention country or countries as provided by subsection (4) of Section 5, for the invention described in the accompanying complete specification under the title ....

....

    4. And I/we request that the patent may be granted as a patent

of addition to (*e*) $\begin{cases} \text{patent No. ....} \\ \text{the patent to be granted on} \\ \text{application No. ....} \end{cases}$

    5. And I/we request that all notices, requisitions, and communications relating to this application may be sent to ....

(*g*) The address
must be
within the
United
Kingdom.
(*h*) Delete if
not applicable.
(*i*) To be signed
by applicant(s).

at (*g*) ....

....

(*h*) who is/are hereby appointed to act for me/us.

                   (*i*)...................................

                   ....

                   ....

To the Comptroller,
    The Patent Office,
        25, Southampton Buildings,
            Chancery Lane, London, W.C.2.

PATENTS FORM NO. 1 ADD.

PATENTS ACT, 1949

1507

APPLICATION FOR THE GRANT OF A PATENT OF ADDITION IN LIEU OF AN INDEPENDENT PATENT

(*a*) State full
name, address
and nationality
of patentee or
patentees.

(*a*) I/We ....

....

....

hereby request that patent No. .... of which I am/we are the patentee . . . be revoked and that in lieu thereof a patent of addition to patent No. .... of which I am/we are also the patentee be granted to me/us, such patent of addition to bear the same date as the patent so revoked.

(*b*) To be signed
by patentee.

                   (*b*)...................................

                   ....

                   ....

To the Comptroller,
    The Patent Office,
        25, Southampton Buildings,
            Chancery Lane, London, W.C.2.

PATENTS FORM NO. 2

PATENTS ACT, 1949

1508

PROVISIONAL SPECIFICATION
(*To be furnished in duplicate*)

(*a*) ....
....
....
....

(*b*) I/We ....
....
....
....
....
....

do hereby declare this invention to be described in the following
statement :—

(*c*) ....
....
....
....
....
....
....
....
....
....
....
....
....
....
....
....
....
....

(*a*) Insert title verbally agreeing with that in the application form.

(*b*) State (in full) name, address and nationality of applicant or applicants as in application form.

(*c*) Here begin description of the invention. The continuation of the specification should be on one side only of paper of the same size as this form with the lines well spaced and with a margin of one inch and a half on the left-hand part of the paper. The specification and the duplicate thereof must be signed at the end.

PATENTS FORM NO. 3

1509   **PATENTS ACT, 1949**

COMPLETE SPECIFICATION
(*To be furnished in duplicate—one unstamped*)

Where priority as provided by subsection (2) or (3) of Section 5 is desired in respect of one or more provisional specifications, quote No. or Nos. and date or dates.

No. ....

Date ....

(*a*) ....
....
....

(*b*) I/We ....
....
....
....

do hereby declare the invention for which I/we pray that a patent
may be granted to me/us, and the method by which it is to be

(*a*) Insert title of invention.

(*b*) State (in full) name, address and nationality of applicant or applicants as in application form.

performed, to be particularly described in and by the following statement:—

(c) ....

....

....

....

....

....

....

....

NOTE.—The claims must relate to a single invention, must be clear and succinct and must be fairly based on the matter disclosed in the specification. They should form in brief a clear statement of that which constitutes the invention. Applicants should be careful that their claims include neither more or less than they desire to protect by their patent. Any unnecessary multiplicity of claims or prolixity of language should be avoided. Claims should not be made for the efficiency or advantages of the invention.

(c) Here begin full description of invention. The continuation of the specification should be upon paper of the same size as this form, on one side only, with the lines well spaced and with a margin of one inch and a half on the left-hand part of the paper. The completion of the description should be followed by the words " What I (or we) claim is " after which should be written the claim or claims numbered consecutively (see note below). The specification and the duplicate thereof must be signed at the end.

PATENTS FORM No. 4

PATENTS ACT, 1949

————

1510   **DECLARATION AS TO INVENTORSHIP (SECTION 4 (5))**

————

I/We (a) ....
do hereby declare that the true and first inventor . . . of the invention disclosed in the complete specification filed in pursuance of my/our application . . . numbered................. and dated the .... day of ....19...... is/are:

(a) Insert name(s) of applicant(s).

(b) ....

....

....

....

and that my/our right to apply for a patent for the invention as follows

(b) State name, address and nationality of inventor or of each inventor.

(c) ....

....

....

....

....

....

....

(d)..................................

....

Except in the case of a Convention Application, if any person named as inventor at (b) above is not so named in the application or in any of the applications, he must sign the following statement:

(c) This need not be filled in if the inventor(s) named at (b) is or are an applicant, or applicants, or if the right to apply is as stated on the application form.
(d) To be signed by applicant(s).

I assent to the invention referred to in the above declaration, being included in the complete specification filed in pursuance of the stated application(s).

....

To the Comptroller,
    The Patent Office,
        25, Southampton Buildings,
            Chancery Lane, London, W.C.2.

PATENTS FORM No. 5

PATENTS ACT, 1949

1511 APPLICATION FOR EXTENSION OF THE PERIOD FOR FILING A COMPLETE SPECIFICATION

I/We hereby, in respect of application No. .... dated ...., request an extension of the period in which to file a complete specification to a period not exceeding fifteen months from the date of the application.

(a).....................................   (a) To be signed by
....   applicant or
....   applicants, or
                                          his or their
To the Comptroller,   agent.
    The Patent Office,
        25, Southampton Buildings,
            Chancery Lane, London, W.C.2.

PATENTS FORM No. 6

PATENTS ACT, 1949

1512 REQUEST FOR THE POST-DATING OF AN APPLICATION UNDER SECTION 6 (3)

I/We hereby request that application No......................filed on the .... of ....19...... be deemed to have been made on the following date, namely, the................. of ....19......

(a).....................................   (a) To be
....   signed by
....   applicant(s).
....

To the Comptroller,
    The Patent Office,
        25, Southampton Buildings,
            Chancery Lane, London, W.C.2.

PATENTS FORM NO. 7

PATENTS ACT, 1949

1513

APPLICATION FOR EXTENSION OF TIME UNDER RULE 30 OR 33 OR 50

Application No..................... dated.........................
I/We hereby apply for....................month...... extension of
time within which

(a), (b), (c) and
(d) Delete the
words which
are not
applicable.

     (*a*) to remove an objection under Section 8 (Rule 28),
     (*b*) agreement to the amendment of the specification or to the
         insertion of a reference under Rule 29 or 33 may be
         notified,
     (*c*) to submit an amendment under Section 15 (Rule 48),
     (*d*) agreement to the amendment of the specification under
         Rule 49 may be notified.

(e) To be signed
by applicant
or applicants,
or his or their
agent.

                 (*e*)...................................
                                            ....
                                            ....

To the Comptroller,
     The Patent Office,
         25, Southampton Buildings,
         Chancery Lane, London, W.C.2.

PATENTS FORM NO. 8

PATENTS ACT, 1949

1514

APPLICATION UNDER SECTION 79 (2) FOR THE RESULT OF A SEARCH MADE UNDER SECTIONS 7 AND 8

I/We hereby request that I/we may be informed of the result
of the search made under Sections 7 and 8 in connection with
Application for Patent No.............................

(a) Insert name
and full address
to which
information is
to be sent.

(*a*) ....
....

To the Comptroller,
     The Patent Office,
         25, Southampton Buildings,
         Chancery Lane, London, W.C.2.

(This part to be filled in at the Patent Office.)

Result of the search made under Sections 7 and 8 of the
Patents Act, 1949, in connection with Application for Patent
No......................................

Specifications or other publications cited as the result of the search made under Section 7	Specifications cited as the result of the search made under Section 8

NOTE.—Citations may be made during the examination of the specifications which are not relevant to the specification as accepted. Citations under Section 7 are completed before acceptance of the specification, but citations under Section 8 may be made subsequently.

PATENTS FORM NO. 9

PATENTS ACT, 1949

1515 APPLICATION UNDER SECTION 9 (2) FOR DELETION OF REFERENCE

I/We (a) ....

....

hereby apply for deletion of the reference to patent No.............
which has been inserted in the complete specification of my/our
(b) (application for a) patent No................... in pursuance of a
direction under Section 9 (1).

The facts relied upon in support of this application are (c) ......

....

....

....

....

Communications should be sent to ....

....

at (d) ....

....

(e) who is/are hereby appointed to act for me/us.

(f)..................................

....

....

To the Comptroller,
    The Patent Office,
        25, Southampton Buildings,
            Chancery Lane, London, W.C.2.

(a) State, in full, name and address of applicant(s).

(b) Delete the words in brackets if a patent has been granted.
(c) The facts must be stated fully.

(d) The address must be within the United Kingdom.
(e) Delete if not applicable.
(f) To be signed by applicant(s) or his or their authorised agent.

PATENTS FORM NO. 10

PATENTS ACT, 1949

1516 NOTICE OF DESIRE FOR EXTENSION OF THE PERIOD FOR PUTTING AN APPLICATION IN ORDER

I/We hereby give notice that I/we desire the period for putting
in order Application No. .... dated ....
to be extended to .... months from the date
of filing of the complete specification.

(a)..................................

....

....

To the Comptroller,
    The Patent Office,
        25, Southampton Buildings,
            Chancery Lane, London, W.C.2.

(a) To be signed by applicant or applicants or his or their agent.

[541]

PATENTS FORM NO. 11

PATENTS ACT, 1949

1517

REQUEST FOR POSTPONEMENT OF ACCEPTANCE OF COMPLETE SPECIFICATION

I/We hereby request a postponement of the acceptance of the complete specification of Application No. .... dated .... to a date not later than the expiration of .... months from the date of filing of the complete specification.

(a) To be signed by applicant or applicants or his or their agent.

(a).....................................
....
....

To the Comptroller,
    The Patent Office,
        25, Southampton Buildings,
            Chancery Lane, London, W.C.2.

1518

PATENTS FORM NO. 12

PATENTS ACT, 1949

NOTICE OF OPPOSITION TO GRANT OF PATENT (SECTION 14)

(To be accompanied by a copy, and a statement of case in duplicate)

(a) State full name and address.

(a) I/We ....
....
....

hereby give notice of opposition to the grant of a patent upon Application No. .... applied for by ....
....

(b) State upon which of the grounds of opposition permitted by Section 14 of the Act the grant is opposed, and identify all specifications and other publications relied upon.

upon the ground *(b)* ....
....
....
....
....
....
....
....
....

Communications should be sent to: ....
....

(c) The address must be within the United Kingdom.
(d) Delete if not applicable.
(e) To be signed by opponent(s).

at *(c)* ....
....

(d) who is/are hereby appointed to act for me/us.

(e).....................................
....

To the Comptroller,
    The Patent Office,
        25, Southampton Buildings,
            Chancery Lane, London, W.C.2.

PATENTS FORM NO. 13

PATENTS ACT, 1949

1519 NOTICE THAT HEARING BEFORE THE COMPTROLLER WILL BE ATTENDED

(a) I/We ....

....

hereby give notice that the Hearing fixed for the (b) ....

in reference to (c) ....

....

.... will be attended by myself/ourselves

or by some person on my/our behalf.

(d)......................................

....

....

(a) State name and address.
(b) Insert date of Hearing.
(c) Give particulars (i.e., number of application or patent, names of parties and nature of proceedings).
(d) Signature.

To the Comptroller,
    The Patent Office,
        25, Southampton Buildings,
            Chancery Lane, London, W.C.2.

PATENTS FORM NO. 14

PATENTS ACT, 1949

1520 REQUEST UNDER SECTION 16 (3)

(a) I/We ....

....

....

who made Application No. .... on the ....

..............................19........ for the grant of a

patent for an invention the title of which is (b) ....

....

and (c) I/we ....

...., hereby

declare that the said (d) ....

is/are the inventor . . . in the sense of being the actual deviser . . .

of (a substantial part of) the invention, and that the Application

for the patent is a direct consequence of his/their being such

inventor . . ., and we hereby request that the said (d) ....

....

be mentioned as such inventor . . . in accordance with Section 16.

A statement setting out the circumstances upon which we rely
to justify this request is attached.

Communications should be sent to ....

.... at (e) ....

....

(f) who is/are hereby appointed to act for us.

(g)......................................

....

....

(a) State (in full) name, address and nationality of applicant or applicants for the patent.
(b) Insert title of invention.
(c) State the name, address and nationality of the deviser or devisers if not included at (a).
(d) Insert name of deviser or devisers.

(e) The address must be within the United Kingdom.
(f) Delete if not applicable.
(g) To be signed by all the persons making the request.

To the Comptroller,
    The Patent Office,
        25, Southampton Buildings,
            Chancery Lane, London, W.C.2.

[543]

PATENTS FORM NO. 15

PATENTS ACT, 1949

1521

CLAIM UNDER SECTION 16 (4)

(To be accompanied by a copy or copies as required by Rule 52)

(a) State (in full) name, address and nationality of the claimant.
(b) Insert title of invention.

(a) I ....
....
hereby declare that I am the inventor in the sense of being the actual deviser of (a substantial part of) the invention entitled (b)

(c) Insert name and address of applicant or applicants for the patent.

....
in respect of which Application No. .... for patent was made by (c) ....
....
on the ....19......, and that the application for the patent is a direct consequence of my being such inventor, and I hereby claim to be mentioned as such inventor in accordance with Section 16 (4).

A statement setting out the circumstances upon which I rely to justify this claim is attached together with a copy/copies thereof as required by Rule 52.

Communications should be sent to ....

(d) The address must be within the United Kingdom.
(e) Delete if not applicable.
(f) To be signed by the claimant.

....
at (d) ....
....
(e) who is/are hereby appointed to act for me.
(f)..

To the Comptroller,
   The Patent Office,
     25, Southampton Buildings,
      Chancery Lane, London, W.C.2.

PATENTS FORM NO. 16

PATENTS ACT, 1949

1522

APPLICATION UNDER SECTION 16 (5)

(a) State (in full) name, address and nationality of the person or persons making this application.
(b) Insert name, address and nationality of applicant or applicants for the patent.
(c) Insert title of invention.

(a) I/We ....
....
hereby apply for an extension of time (not exceeding one month) for making a request under Section 16 (3) (or a claim under Section 16 (4)) in respect of Application No. .... for a patent made by (b) ....
....
....
on the ....19......, in respect of an invention the title of which is (c) ....
....
Communications should be sent to ....
....
....

[544]

at (d) .... (d) The address
.... must be within
(e).. the United
Kingdom.
.... (e) To be signed
by the person
.... or all the
To the Comptroller, persons making
The Patent Office, the application
25, Southampton Buildings, or by his or
Chancery Lane, London, W.C.2. their duly
authorised
agent.

PATENTS FORM No. 17

PATENTS ACT, 1949

1523

APPLICATION UNDER SECTION 16 (8)

(To be accompanied by unstamped copies as required by Rule 54)

(a) I/We .... (a) State (in
full) name,
.... address and
hereby declare that (b) .... nationality of
the person
.... or persons
ought not to have been mentioned under Section 16 as the inventor making this
application.
in the sense of being the actual deviser of (a substantial part of) (b) Insert the
the invention covered by Application No. .... dated the name of the
person
.................................19......, and entitled (c) .... mentioned
as the actual
and I/we hereby apply for a certificate to that effect. deviser.
(c) Insert title
A statement setting out the circumstances upon which I/we of invention.
rely to justify this Application is attached together with copies
thereof as required by Rule 54.

Communications should be sent to ....
....
at (d) .... (d) The address
must be within
.... the United
(e) who is/are hereby appointed to act for me/us. Kingdom.
(e) Delete if
(f)............................... not applicable.
(f) To be signed
.... by all the
.... persons making
To the Comptroller, the application.
The Patent Office,
25, Southampton Buildings,
Chancery Lane, London, W.C.2.

PATENTS FORM No. 18

PATENTS ACT, 1949

1524

CLAIM UNDER SECTION 17 (1) TO PROCEED
AS AN APPLICANT OR CO-APPLICANT

I/We (a) .... (a) State name
of claimant(s).
.... (b) State the
number and
hereby request that the Patent Application No. (b) .... date of the
application
.... dated .... for patent.

T.P.—18

(c) State name
of the
applicant or
applicants
for patent.

(d) Insert
(in full) name,
address and
nationality of
the person or
persons in
whose name(s)
it is requested
that the
application
shall proceed.

(e) Give the
particulars of
such document,
giving its date
and the parties
to the same,
and showing
how the claim
here made is
substantiated.

(f) State the
nature of the
document.
The certified
copy should
be written,
type-written
or printed on
foolscap paper.

(g) The address
must be within
the United
Kingdom.

(h) Delete if not
applicable.

(i) To be signed
by claimant(s).

(j) To be signed
by the
applicant(s).

made by (c) ....

....

may proceed in the name(s) of (d) ....

....

....

....

I/We claim to be entitled to proceed as applicant(s) for the patent
by virtue of (e) ....

........................,..

....

....

....

....

....

And in proof whereof I/we transmit the accompanying (f) ......

....

Communications should be sent to ....

at (g) ....

(h) who is/are hereby appointed to act for me/us.

(i)....................................

....

(j) I/We ....
consent to the above request.

....

To the Comptroller,
    The Patent Office,
        25, Southampton Buildings,
          Chancery Lane, London, W.C.2.

PATENTS FORM No. 19

PATENTS ACT, 1949

1525

APPLICATION FOR DIRECTIONS UNDER SECTION 17 (5) AS TO PROCEEDING WITH AN APPLICATION FOR A PATENT IN CASE OF DISPUTE BETWEEN JOINT APPLICANTS

(To be accompanied by a statement of case and by copies of the application and statement as required by Rule 57)

(a) State name
and address.

(b) State name
and address
of other
applicant(s).

(a) I ....

....

....

being a joint applicant with (b)..

....

....

in the application for a patent numbered ....
hereby declare that a dispute has arisen between us and request
that an order of the Comptroller be made giving directions for
enabling the application to proceed.

Particulars of the matters in dispute are given in the annexed
statement setting out the facts upon which I rely, and the relief
which I seek.

Communications should be sent to ....

.... at (c) .... (c) The address must be within the United Kingdom.

....

....

(d) who is hereby appointed to act for me. (d) Delete if not applicable.

(e)............................... (e) Signature.

To the Comptroller,
    The Patent Office,
        25, Southampton Buildings,
            Chancery Lane, London, W.C.2.

PATENTS FORM NO. 20

PATENTS ACT, 1949

1526   REQUEST FOR THE SEALING OF A PATENT

I/We (a) .... (a) State name of applicant
.... request or applicants.
that a patent may be sealed on my/our
(b) Application No. .... and that the following may be (b) Both these numbers to be inserted.
    Acceptance No. ....
entered on the Register as my/our address for service:—
(c) .... (c) The address must be within the United Kingdom.
....
....
....
(d) .... (d) Signature.

To the Comptroller,
    The Patent Office,
        25, Southampton Buildings,
            Chancery Lane, London, W.C.2.

PATENTS FORM NO. 21

PATENTS ACT, 1949

527   APPLICATION UNDER SECTION 19 (3) FOR EXTENSION
       OF THE PERIOD FOR MAKING A REQUEST FOR
       SEALING OF A PATENT

I/We hereby apply for .... month ....
extension of the period for making a request for the sealing of a
patent upon Application No. ....
(a)................................ (a) Signature
....
....

To the Comptroller,
    The Patent Office,
        25, Southampton Buildings,
            Chancery Lane, London, W.C.2.

[547]

PATENTS FORM No. 22

PATENTS ACT, 1949

1528

**APPLICATION UNDER SECTION 19 (4) FOR AN
EXTENSION OF THE PERIOD FOR MAKING A
REQUEST FOR THE SEALING OF A PATENT**

(a) Not more than six months' extension may be applied for at one time.

I/We hereby apply for (a) .... month .... extension of the period for making a request for the sealing of a patent upon Application No. ....

(b) The circumstances and grounds must be stated in detail.

The circumstances in and grounds upon which this extension is applied for are as follows (b):—

....
....

....

I/We hereby declare that

(c) and (d) Delete the words which are not applicable.

(c) An extension of time of three months for making a request for sealing has been allowed under Section 19 (3) and has not yet expired.

(d) An extension of time of .... months for making a request for sealing has been allowed under Section 19 (4) and has not yet expired.

(e) Signature.

(e)....................................

....

To the Comptroller,
    The Patent Office,
        25, Southampton Buildings,
            Chancery Lane, London, W.C.2.

PATENTS FORM No. 23

PATENTS ACT, 1949

1529

**APPLICATION UNDER SECTION 20 FOR AMENDMENT
OF LETTERS PATENT**

(To be accompanied by evidence verifying the statements made in this application)

(a) State name and address.

I/We (a) ....

....

hereby request that Letters Patent No. .... granted to

....

(b) State name, address and nationality of person to whom patent should have been granted.

may be amended by substituting the name of (b) ....

............,...

....

for the name of the grantee.

My/Our address for service in the United Kingdom is.........

....

(c) Signature.

(c)....................................

To the Comptroller,
    The Patent Office,
        25, Southampton Buildings,
            Chancery Lane, London, W.C.2.

PATENTS FORM No. 24

[When stamped this Form must be at once sent to or left at the Patent Office]

PATENTS ACT, 1949

1530

PAYMENT OF RENEWAL FEE

I/We (a) ....
....
hereby transmit the fee prescribed for the continuation in force of
(b) ....
Patent No. .... for a further period of .... and
request that the Certificate of Payment may be sent to me/us at (c)
....
....

(a) State name of person tendering the fee.

(b) Here insert name of patentee(s).

(c) Here insert full address.

NOTE.—If the address given above is not that entered in the Register of Patents as the Patentee's Address for Service and it is desired to amend the entry in the Register, application therefor must be made on Patents Form No. 57.

To the Comptroller,
    The Patent Office,
        25, Southampton Buildings,
            Chancery Lane, London, W.C.2.

PATENTS FORM No. 25

PATENTS ACT, 1949

1531

REQUEST FOR EXTENSION OF THE PERIOD FOR PAYMENT OF RENEWAL FEE

I/We hereby apply for an extension of .... month(s) of the period prescribed for payment of the renewal fee of ....
upon my/our Patent No. ....
(a) ....
....
....

(a) State name and full address to which receipt is to be sent.

To the Comptroller,
    The Patent Office,
        25, Southampton Buildings,
            Chancery Lane, London, W.C.2.

PATENTS FORM No. 26

PATENTS ACT, 1949

1532

CERTIFICATE OF PAYMENT OF RENEWAL FEE

Letters Patent No. ....
This is to certify that ....
did this .... day of ....19......, make

the prescribed payment of £............ in respect of a period of
.... from ....
The Patent Office,
London.

PATENTS FORM NO. 27

PATENTS ACT, 1949

1533

APPLICATION UNDER SECTION 24 OR 25 FOR EXTENSION OF TERM OF PATENT

(*To be accompanied by evidence in support of the application*)

(a) State (in full) name, address and nationality of applicant or applicants.

I/We (a) ....
....
....

hereby apply for extension of the term of Patent No. ....

(b) Insert period for which extension is sought.

for (b)......................................

Communications should be sent to ....

(c) The address must be within the United Kingdom.

.... at (c) ....
....
....

(d) Delete if not applicable.

(d) who is/are hereby appointed to act for me/us.

(e) To be signed by the applicant or applicants.

(e)................................
....
....

To the Comptroller,
    The Patent Office,
        25, Southampton Buildings,
            Chancery Lane, London, W.C.2.

PATENTS FORM NO. 28

PATENTS ACT, 1949

1534

NOTICE OF OPPOSITION TO APPLICANT FOR EXTENSION OF TERM OF PATENT

(*To be accompanied by a copy, and evidence (in duplicate) in support of the opposition*)

(a) State (in full) name, address and nationality of opponent or opponents.

I/We (a) ....
....
....

hereby give notice of opposition to the application for extension of the term of Patent No. ....

Communications should be sent to ....

(b) The address must be within the United Kingdom.

.... at (b) ....
....

(c) Delete if not applicable.

(c) who is/are hereby appointed to act for me/us.

(d) To be signed by the opponent or opponents.

(d)................................
....

To the Comptroller,
    The Patent Office,
        25, Southampton Buildings,
            Chancery Lane, London, W.C.2.

PATENTS FORM No. 29

PATENTS ACT, 1949

1535 ## APPLICATION UNDER SECTION 27 FOR THE RESTORATION OF A PATENT

(To be accompanied by evidence verifying the statements made in this application)

I/We (a) ....   (a) State name and address.

....

....

hereby apply for an order for the restoration of Patent No. ....

The circumstances which led to the failure to pay the renewal fee of (b) .... on or before the (c) .... are as follows   (b) State amount of fee.
(d) ....   (c) State date when fee was due.

....   (d) The circumstances must be stated in detail.

....

....

....

....

Communications should be sent to ....

....

at (e) ....   (e) The address must be within the United Kingdom.
(f) who is/are hereby appointed to act for me/us.

(g)...   (f) Delete if not applicable.

....   (g) To be signed by applicant.

....

To the Comptroller,
    The Patent Office,
        25, Southampton Buildings,
            Chancery Lane, London, W.C.2.

PATENTS FORM No. 30

PATENTS ACT, 1949

1536 ## NOTICE OF OPPOSITION TO AN APPLICATION UNDER SECTION 27 FOR THE RESTORATION OF A PATENT

(To be accompanied by a copy, and a statement of case in duplicate)

I/We (a) ....   (a) State name and address.

....

....

hereby give notice of opposition to the application for restoration of Patent No. .... for the following reason: ....

....

....

....

....

....

[551]

Communications should be sent to ....
....

(b) The address
must be within
the United
Kingdom.

at *(b)* ....
(c) who is/are hereby appointed to act for me/us.

(c) Delete if
not applicable.

(d) Signature
of opponent.

                               (d)...................

To the Comptroller,
    The Patent Office,
        25, Southampton Buildings,
            Chancery Lane, London, W.C.2.

PATENTS FORM NO. 31

PATENTS ACT, 1949

1537

ADDITIONAL FEE ON AN APPLICATION UNDER SECTION 27 FOR RESTORATION OF A PATENT

(a) State name
and address.

I/We *(a)* ....
....
....
....

the applicant(s) for the restoration of Patent No. ....
hereby transmit the prescribed additional fee, together with Patents
Form No. 24 in respect of the unpaid renewal fee(s).

(b) Signature
of applicant(s).

                             (b)...................................

To the Comptroller,
    The Patent Office
        25, Southampton Buildings,
            Chancery Lane, London, W.C.2.

PATENTS FORM NO. 32

PATENTS ACT, 1949

1538

APPLICATION UNDER SECTION 28 FOR THE SEALING OF A PATENT

(To be accompanied by evidence verifying the statements made in this application)

(a) State name
and address.

I/We *(a)* ....
....
....

the applicant(s) for a patent numbered .... hereby
apply for an order for a patent to be sealed thereon.

    The circumstances which led to the failure to make the

(b) State date
when request
was due.

(c) The
circumstances
must be stated
in detail.

prescribed request for sealing on or before the *(b)* ....
are as follows *(c)* ....
....
....
....
....
....
....
....

Communications should be sent to ....

.... at (d) .... *(d) The address must be within the United Kingdom.*

....

(e) who is/are hereby appointed to act for me/us. *(e) Delete if not applicable.*

(f)................................... *(f) Signature.*

To the Comptroller,
The Patent Office,
25, Southampton Buildings,
Chancery Lane, London, W.C.2.

PATENTS FORM NO. 33

PATENTS ACT, 1949

1539 **NOTICE OF OPPOSITION TO AN APPLICATION UNDER SECTION 28 FOR THE SEALING OF A PATENT**

(To be accompanied by a copy, and a statement of case in duplicate)

I/We (a) .... *(a) State name and address.*

....

....

hereby give notice of opposition to the application for the sealing of a patent on Application No. .... for the following reasons:— ....

....

....

....

....

....

....

Communications should be sent to ....

.... at (b) .... *(b) The address must be within the United Kingdom.*

....

(c) who is/are hereby appointed to act for me/us. *(c) Delete if not applicable.*

(d).................................. *(d) Signature.*

To the Comptroller,
The Patent Office,
25, Southampton Buildings,
Chancery Lane, London, W.C.2.

PATENTS FORM NO. 34

PATENTS ACT, 1949

1540 **ADDITIONAL FEE ON AN APPLICATION UNDER SECTION 28 FOR THE SEALING OF A PATENT**

I/We (a) .... *(a) State name and address.*

....

....

....

the applicant(s) for the sealing of a patent on Application No. .... hereby transmit the prescribed additional fee,

[553]

together with Patents Form No. 20 bearing the fee prescribed in respect of the making of the request for sealing.

(*b*) Signature of applicants for sealing.

(*b*)...............................

To the Comptroller,
　　The Patent Office,
　　　　25, Southampton Buildings,
　　　　　　Chancery Lane, London, W.C.2.

PATENTS FORM NO. 35

PATENTS ACT, 1949

1541

APPLICATION UNDER SECTION 29 FOR AMENDMENT OF A COMPLETE SPECIFICATION AFTER ACCEPTANCE

(*a*) State full name and address of applicant or patentee.

(*a*) I/We ....

....

....

....

seek leave to amend the complete specification No. ....
as shown in red ink in the copy of the printed specification hereunto annexed.

(*b*) These words are to be struck out when a patent has not been sealed.

(*b*) I/We declare that no action for infringement or proceeding before the Court for revocation of the Patent is pending.

My/Our reasons for making this amendment are in detail as follows : —

(*c*) State full particulars of the reasons for seeking amendment. If this space is not sufficient the particulars may be continued on a separate sheet.

(*c*) ....

....

....

....

Communications should be sent to ....

(*d*) The address must be within the United Kingdom.

at (*d*) ....

....

(*e*) Delete if not applicable.

(*e*) who is/are hereby appointed to act for me/us.

(*f*) To be signed by applicant or patentee.

(*f*)..................................

....

To the Comptroller,
　　The Patent Office,
　　　　25, Southampton Buildings,
　　　　　　Chancery Lane, London, W.C.2.

PATENTS FORM NO. 36

PATENTS ACT, 1949

1542

NOTICE OF OPPOSITION TO AMENDMENT OF SPECIFICATION UNDER SECTION 29

(To be accompanied by a copy, and a statement of case in duplicate)

(*a*) State full name and address.

(*a*) I/We ....

....

....

hereby give notice of opposition to the proposed amendment of specification No. .... for the following reason:

....
....
....
....
....
....
....
....
....
....
....
....
....
....
....
....
....

Communications should be sent to ....
....
at (b) ....
(c) who is/are hereby appointed to act for me/us.
                                                        (d)..................................

To the Comptroller,
    The Patent Office,
        25, Southampton Buildings,
            Chancery Lane, London, W.C.2.

(b) The address must be within the United Kingdom.

(c) Delete if not applicable.

(d) To be signed by the opponent.

PATENTS FORM NO. 37

PATENTS ACT, 1949

1543   **APPLICATION FOR AMENDMENT OF A COMPLETE SPECIFICATION NOT YET ACCEPTED**

I/We (a) ....
....
....
....
seek leave to amend the specification of application No. ....
of .... as shown in red ink in the copy of the original specification hereunto annexed.

My/Our reasons for making this amendment are as follows (b)
....
....
....
....
....
....
....
                                                        (c).................................

To the Comptroller,
    The Patent Office,
        25, Southampton Buildings,
            Chancery Lane, London, W.C.2.

(a) State (in full) name and address of applicant or applicants.

(b) State reasons for seeking amendment.

(c) To be signed by applicant or applicants, or his or their agent.

PATENTS FORM No. 38

PATENTS ACT, 1949

1544

APPLICATION FOR AMENDMENT OF AN APPLICATION FOR A PATENT

(a) State full
name and
address of
applicant or
applicants.

(a) I/We ....

....

....

....

seek leave to amend my/our Application No. ....
of .... as shown in red ink in the copy of
the original Application hereunto annexed.

(b) State
reasons for
seeking
amendment.

My/Our reasons for making this amendment are as follows (b)

....

....

....

....

....

....

....

(c) To be
signed by
applicant or
applicants.

(c).....................................

....

....

To the Comptroller,
　　The Patent Office,
　　　　25, Southampton Buildings,
　　　　　　Chancery Lane, London, W.C.2.

PATENTS FORM No. 38 CON.

PATENTS ACT, 1949

1545

APPLICATION FOR THE CONVERSION OF AN APPLICATION FOR A PATENT TO A CONVENTION APPLICATION UNDER RULE 94 (2)

(a) State full
name and
address of
applicant or
applicants.

I/We (a) ....

....

....

....

....

seek leave to amend my/our Application No. .... of
.... so as to convert it to a Convention
application as shown in red ink in the copy of the original
Application hereunto annexed.

(b) To be
signed by
applicant or
applicants.

(b).....................................

....

....

To the Comptroller,
　　The Patent Office,
　　　　25, Southampton Buildings,
　　　　　　Chancery Lane, London, W.C.2.

PATENTS FORM No. 39

PATENTS ACT, 1949

1546 APPLICATION UNDER SECTION 33 FOR THE REVOCATION OF A PATENT

(To be accompanied by a copy, and a statement of case in duplicate)

(a) I/We ....
....
....

(a) State full name and address.

hereby apply for an Order for the revocation of Patent No. .... on the following grounds:

(b) ....
....
....
....
....
....

*(b) State upon which of the grounds the application is based and identify all specifications and other publications relied upon.**

(c) I/We declare that no action for infringement or proceeding in any Court for the revocation of the patent is pending.

Communications should be sent to ....
.... at (d) ....
....

(e) who is/are hereby appointed to act for me/us.

(f)....................................

To the Comptroller,
The Patent Office,
25, Southampton Buildings,
Chancery Lane, London, W.C.2.

Note: Such ground or grounds can only be one or more of the grounds on which the grant of a patent could have been opposed under Section 14.

(c) If such action or proceeding is pending in any Court the application cannot be made without the leave of the Court.

(d) The address must be within the United Kingdom.

(e) Delete if not applicable.

(f) To be signed by applicant.

PATENTS FORM No. 40

PATENTS ACT, 1949

547 OFFER UNDER SECTION 34 TO SURRENDER A PATENT

(a) I/We ....
....
....
....

(a) State full name and address.

hereby offer to surrender Patent No. ....

(b) I/We declare that no action for infringement or proceeding in any Court for the revocation of the patent is pending.

My/Our reasons for making this offer are as follows: ....
....
....

(b) Delete if any action or proceeding is pending, and furnish full particulars of such action or proceeding.

[557]

Communications should be sent to ....
.... at (c) ....
....

(c) The address must be within the United Kingdom.

(d) who is/are hereby appointed to act for me/us.

(d) Delete if not applicable.

(e)...................................

(e) To be signed by the patentee.

To the Comptroller,
The Patent Office,
25, Southampton Buildings,
Chancery Lane, London, W.C.2.

PATENTS FORM No. 41

PATENTS ACT, 1949

1548

NOTICE OF OPPOSITION UNDER SECTION 34 TO OFFER TO SURRENDER A PATENT

(To be accompanied by a copy, and a statement of case in duplicate)

(a) State full name and address.

(a) I/We ....
....
....

hereby give notice of opposition to the offer to surrender Patent No. .... for the following reason:.......................
....
....
....
....
....

Communications should be sent to ....
....

(b) The address must be within the United Kingdom.

at (b) ....
....

(c) Delete if not applicable.

(c) who is/are hereby appointed to act for me/us.

(d) To be signed by the opponent.

(d)...................................

To the Comptroller,
The Patent Office,
25, Southampton Buildings,
Chancery Lane, London, W.C.2.

PATENTS FORM No. 42

PATENTS ACT, 1949

1549

VOLUNTARY APPLICATION FOR ENDORSEMENT OF PATENT "LICENCES OF RIGHT"

(To be accompanied by evidence verifying the statement in the application and by the Letters Patent)

(a) State name and address.

I/We (a) ....
....

hereby request that Patent No. .... may be endorsed "Licences of Right."

I am/We are not precluded by contract from granting licences under the patent.

[558]

Communications should be sent to ....
.... at (b) .... (b) The address
(c) who is/are hereby appointed to act for me/us. must be within
the United
(d)............................... Kingdom.
.... (c) Delete if
not applicable.
To the Comptroller, (d) To be
The Patent Office, signed by the
25, Southampton Buildings, patentee.
Chancery Lane, London, W.C.2.

PATENTS FORM NO. 43

PATENTS ACT, 1949

1550 **APPLICATION UNDER SECTION 35 (2) FOR SETTLEMENT OF TERMS OF LICENCE UNDER PATENT ENDORSED "LICENCES OF RIGHT"**

(To be accompanied by a copy, and a statement of case in duplicate)

I/We (a) .... (a) State name
.... and address.
....

hereby apply for settlement of the terms of a licence to be granted
under Patent No. ....
I am/We are the
(b) patentee(s) (b) (c) (d)
(c) person(s) requiring a licence Delete the two
categories not
(d) holder(s) of a licence under the Patent granted before applicable.
endorsement.
I/We (e) request that an Order may be made entitling me/us (e) Delete if
to exchange my/our existing licence for a licence to be granted the applicant
is not the
upon the terms as settled. holder of
Communications should be sent to .... a licence.
.... at (f) .... (f) The address
must be within
.... the United
(g) who is/are hereby appointed to act for me/us. Kingdom.
(h)................................ (g) Delete if
not applicable.
To the Comptroller, (h) Signature
The Patent Office, of applicant.
25, Southampton Buildings,
Chancery Lane, London, W.C.2.

PATENTS FORM NO. 44

PATENTS ACT, 1949

551 **APPLICATION UNDER SECTION 36 (1) BY PATENTEE FOR CANCELLATION OF ENDORSEMENT OF A PATENT "LICENCES OF RIGHT"**

(To be accompanied by evidence in support of the application)

I/We (a) .... (a) State name
.... and address.
hereby request that the endorsement of Patent No. ....

[559]

" Licences of Right " may be cancelled, and I/we enclose Patents Form No. 24 accompanied by the balance of all renewal fees which would have been payable if the patent had not been endorsed.

(b) (c) Delete whichever is not applicable.

I/We declare (b) that there is no existing licence under the Patent, or (c) all the licensees consent to this application.

(d) The address must be within the United Kingdom.

Communications should be sent to ....
.... at (d) ....
....

(e) Delete if not applicable.

(e) who is/are hereby appointed to act for me/us.

(f) To be signed by the patentee.

(f)....................................
....

To the Comptroller,
    The Patent Office,
        25, Southampton Buildings,
            Chancery Lane, London, W.C.2.

PATENTS FORM No. 45

PATENTS ACT, 1949

1552

APPLICATION UNDER SECTION 36 (2) BY ANY PERSON INTERESTED FOR CANCELLATION OF ENDORSEMENT OF PATENT " LICENCES OF RIGHT "

(To be accompanied by a copy, and a statement of case in duplicate)

(a) State name and address.

I/We (a) ....
....
hereby claim that the endorsement of Patent No. ....
" Licences of Right " is and was at the time of the endorsement contrary to a contract in which I am/we are interested and I/we request that such endorsement may be cancelled.

Communications should be sent to ....

(b) The address must be within the United Kingdom.

.... at (b) ....
....

(c) Delete if not applicable.

(c) who is/are hereby appointed to act for me/us.

(d) To be signed by the applicant(s).

(d)....................................
....

To the Comptroller,
    The Patent Office,
        25, Southampton Buildings,
            Chancery Lane, London, W.C.2.

PATENTS FORM No. 46

PATENTS ACT, 1949

1553

NOTICE OF OPPOSITION BY PATENTEE OR BY ANY PERSON INTERESTED TO CANCELLATION OF ENDORSEMENT OF A PATENT " LICENCES OF RIGHT "

(To be accompanied by a copy, and a statement of case in duplicate)

(a) State name and address.

I/We (a) ....
....
....

hereby give notice of opposition to the application for the cancellation of the endorsement "Licences of Right" in respect of Patent No. ....

Communications should be sent to..................................
.... at (b) .... *(b) The address must be within the United Kingdom.*
....
(c) who is/are hereby appointed to act for me/us. *(c) Delete if not applicable.*
(d).................................
.... *(d) To be signed by the opponent.*

To the Comptroller,
The Patent Office,
25, Southampton Buildings,
Chancery Lane, London, W.C.2.

PATENTS FORM No. 47

PATENTS ACT, 1949

1554 **APPLICATION FOR COMPULSORY LICENCE OR FOR COMPULSORY ENDORSEMENT "LICENCES OF RIGHT"**

I/We (a) .... *(a) State name and address.*
....................,...

hereby apply for an Order of the Comptroller in respect of Patent No. ....
    (b) for a licence under the patent to be granted to me/us; *(b) (c) Delete whichever is not applicable.*
    or
    (c) for the endorsement of the patent "Licences of Right",
for the following reasons:—(d)... *(d) State the nature of the applicant's interest, the facts upon which he relies, and the grounds upon which the application is made.*
....
....
....
....
....
....
....
....

Communications should be sent to ....
.... at (e) .... *(e) The address must be within the United Kingdom.*
....
(f) who is/are hereby appointed to act for me/us. *(f) Delete if not applicable.*
(g)................................. *(g) To be signed by the applicant(s).*
To the Comptroller,
The Patent Office,
25, Southampton Buildings,
Chancery Lane, London, W.C.2.

PATENTS FORM No. 48

PATENTS ACT, 1949

1555 **APPLICATION BY GOVERNMENT DEPARTMENT UNDER SECTION 40 (1)**

I/We (a) .... *(a) State name and address of Department.*
....................,...
....

hereby apply for an Order of the Comptroller in respect of Patent
No. ....

(b) (c) Delete
whichever is
not applicable.

      (b) for the endorsement of the patent "Licences of Right"
        or

(d) Insert
name, address
and nation-
ality of person
to whom
licence is to
be granted.

      (c) for the grant of a licence under the patent to (d) ....
....

for the following reasons:—(e)..

....

(e) State the
facts and
grounds on
which the case
is based.

....

....

....

....

My/Our address for service in the United Kingdom is ....

....

....

(f) Signature
of applicant.

                               (f)..................................

To the Comptroller,
    The Patent Office,
        25, Southampton Buildings,
           Chancery Lane, London, W.C.2.

PATENTS FORM NO. 49

PATENTS ACT, 1949

1556

**APPLICATION UNDER SECTION 40 (3) BY A COMPETENT
AUTHORITY FOR AN ORDER UNDER SECTION 40 (4)**

(a) State name
and address of
competent
authority.

I/We (a) ....

....

....

....

hereby apply for an Order of the Comptroller in respect of Patent

(b) (c) Delete
whichever is
not applicable.

No. .... (b) for the cancellation or modification of
conditions in a licence or licences granted by the patentee under
date .... to ....

.... ;

or (c) for the endorsement of the patent "Licences of Right" for
the following reasons:—

(d) State the
facts and
grounds upon
which the
application
is based.

(d) ....

....

....

....

....

....

....

My/Our address for service in the United Kingdom is:—......

....

(e) Signature
of applicant.

                               (e)..................................

To the Comptroller,
    The Patent Office,
        25, Southampton Buildings,
           Chancery Lane, London, W.C.2.

PATENTS FORM No. 50

PATENTS ACT, 1949

1557   **APPLICATION UNDER SECTION 42 FOR REVOCATION OF A PATENT**

I/We (a) ....   (a) State name and address.

....

....

hereby apply for the revocation of Patent No. ....
for the following reasons:—

(b) ....   (b) State the nature of applicant's interest, the facts upon which he relies and the grounds upon which the application is made.

....

....

....

Communications should be sent to ....

.... at (c) ....

....   (c) The address must be within the United Kingdom.

....
(d) who is/are hereby appointed to act for me/us.   (d) Delete if not applicable

(e)...................................   (e) Signature.

To the Comptroller,
    The Patent Office,
        25, Southampton Buildings,
        Chancery Lane, London, W.C.2.

PATENTS FORM No. 51

PATENTS ACT, 1949

1558   **NOTICE OF OPPOSITION UNDER SECTION 43 TO AN APPLICATION FOR AN ORDER UNDER SECTION 37, 40, 41 OR 42**

(To be accompanied by evidence verifying the statement at (f) below)

I/We (a) ....   (a) State name and address.

....

hereby give notice of opposition to the application made in respect
of Patent No. .... by ....

....

....

   (b) for a licence under the patent   (b) to (e) Delete whichever is not applicable.
   (c) for the endorsement of the patent " Licences of Right "
   (d) for the grant of a licence to the person specified in the
       application
   (e) for the revocation of the patent under Section 42.

My/Our grounds for opposing are (f) ....   (f) Insert statement of grounds on which application is opposed.

....

....

....

....

....

[563]

Communications should be sent to ....

(g) The address must be within the United Kingdom.

.... at *(g)* ....

....

....

(h) Delete if not applicable.

(h) who is/are hereby appointed to act for me/us.

(i) Signature.

(i)....................................

To the Comptroller,
    The Patent Office,
        25, Southampton Buildings,
            Chancery Lane, London, W.C.2.

PATENTS FORM No. 52

PATENTS ACT, 1949

1559

APPLICATION UNDER SECTION 41 FOR LICENCE

(a) State name and address.

I/We *(a)* ....

....

....

hereby apply for a licence under Patent No. .... for the making, using, exercising and vending the invention

(b) *(c)* *(d)* Delete whichever is not applicable.

    (b) as food or medicine;

    (c) for the purposes of the production of food or medicine; or

    (d) as or as part of a surgical or curative device

(e) State nature of applicant's interest, and the facts relied upon.

for the following reasons :—*(e)*...

....

....

....

....

(f) The address must be within the United Kingdom.

Communications should be sent to ....

.... at *(f)* ....

....

(g) Delete if not applicable.

(g) who is/are hereby appointed to act for me/us.

(h) Signature of applicant.

(h)....................................

To the Comptroller,
    The Patent Office,
        25, Southampton Buildings,
            Chancery Lane, London, W.C.2.

PATENTS FORM No. 53

PATENTS ACT, 1949

1560

APPLICATION FOR DIRECTIONS UNDER SECTION 55 (1)

(To be accompanied by a statement of case and by copies of the application and statement as required by Rule 116)

(a) State name and address.

I/We *(a)* ....

....

hereby apply for the following directions in respect of Patent No. ....

(b) ....   (b) State the
.... directions
.... sought.
....

Communications should be sent to ....
.... at (c) .... (c) The address
.... must be within
(d) who is/are hereby appointed to act for me/us.   the United
                                                                        Kingdom.
                              (e)...................................
                                                                        (d) Delete if
To the Comptroller,   not applicable.
     The Patent Office,   (e) To be signed
          25, Southampton Buildings,   by the patentee
               Chancery Lane, London, W.C.2.   seeking
                                                                        directions.

PATENTS FORM NO. 54

PATENTS ACT, 1949

1561   APPLICATION FOR DIRECTIONS UNDER SECTION 55 (2)

(To be accompanied by a copy, and a statement of case
in duplicate)

I/We (a) ....   (a) State name
                                                                        and address of
.... patentee or
.... joint patentees.
hereby apply for directions in respect of the failure of (b) ....   (b) State name
                                                                        of person
.... in default.
to comply with the directions of the Comptroller given under
Section 55 (1) on the .... in the following matter: (c)......   (c) State the
                                                                        directions
.... sought.
....

Communications should be sent to ....
....

at (d) ....   (d) The address
                                                                        must be within
(e) who is/are hereby appointed to act for me/us.   the United
                                                                        Kingdom.
                              (f)...................................
                                                                        (e) Delete if
                              ....   not applicable.
To the Comptroller,   (f) To be signed
     The Patent Office,   by the
          25, Southampton Buildings,   patentee.
               Chancery Lane, London, W.C.2.

PATENTS FORM NO. 55

PATENTS ACT, 1949

562   APPLICATION UNDER SECTION 56 TO DETERMINE A DISPUTE BETWEEN EMPLOYER AND EMPLOYEE AS TO RIGHTS IN AN INVENTION

(To be accompanied by a copy and a statement in duplicate
setting out the facts of the dispute and the relief sought)

I/We (a) ....   (a) State name
                                                                        and address.
....

hereby declare that in respect of the rights in the invention for
which an application for a patent was made by ....
....
....

(b) Delete if a
patent has not
been granted.

(c) State name
and address of
other party
to dispute.

and numbered .... (b) and upon which a patent has
been granted, a dispute has arisen between me/us and (c) ....
....
....

and I/we hereby apply to the Comptroller to determine the
dispute.

The facts of the dispute, and the relief which I/we seek are
set out fully in the accompanying statement.

Communications should be sent to ....

(d) The address
must be within
the United
Kingdom.

(e) Delete if
not applicable.

(f) Signature.

at (d) ....
....
(e) who is/are hereby appointed to act for me/us.

                                                    (f)...............................
                                                    ....

To the Comptroller,
    The Patent Office,
        25, Southampton Buildings,
            Chancery Lane, London, W.C.2.

PATENTS FORM NO. 56

PATENTS ACT, 1949

1563

**REFERENCE TO THE COMPTROLLER OF A DISPUTE AS
TO INFRINGEMENT (SECTION 67)**

(a) Insert, in
full, name and
address of
patentee or
exclusive
licensee.

(b) Insert, in
full, name and
address of the
other party to
the dispute.

(c) Insert
name as
at (a).

(d) Delete
whichever does
not apply.

(e) Insert
name as
at (b).

(f) State full
particulars of
these matters.
They may be
given or con-
tinued on a
separate sheet
or sheets.

(g) The address
must be within
the United
Kingdom.

(h) Delete if
not applicable.

We (a) ....
....
and (b) ....
....
hereby refer to the Comptroller for determination of a dispute
whether any claim of the specification of Patent No. ....
of which the said (c) ....
is/are the (d) (patentee) (exclusive licensee) has been infringed by
anything done by the said (e) ....
.... or whether any such claim alleged to be
infringed is valid.

The matters in dispute are (f) ....
....
....

The matters on which we are in agreement are (f) ....
....
....

(To be signed by the patentee or exclusive licensee)

Communications should be sent to ....
....
at (g) ....
....
(h) who is/are hereby appointed to act for me/us.
                                                    ....

(To be signed by the other party to the dispute)

Communications should be sent to ....

....

at (g) ....

(h) who is/are hereby appointed to act for me/us.

....

To the Comptroller,
    The Patent Office,
        25, Southampton Buildings,
            Chancery Lane, London, W.C.2.

PATENTS FORM NO. 57

PATENTS ACT, 1949

───────

1564   **REQUEST FOR ALTERATION OF A NAME OR
NATIONALITY OR AN ADDRESS OR AN ADDRESS
FOR SERVICE IN THE REGISTER OF PATENTS**

───────

In the matter of Patent No. ....

I/We (a) ....   (a) State (in
full) name and
....   address of
applicant or
....   applicants.

hereby request that the (b) name   (b) Strike out
                          (b) nationality   words not
                                                                             applicable.
                          (b) address
                          (b) address for service
now upon the Register of Patents may be altered to (c) ....   (c) Insert name,
                                                                             nationality, or
....   address or
                                                                             address for
                                (d).................................   service, as the
                                                                             case may be.
    NOTE.—Where the request is for alteration in a name or   (d) Signature
nationality, evidence of the alteration must be furnished.   of applicant
                                                                             or applicants.
To the Comptroller,
    The Patent Office,
        25, Southampton Buildings,
            Chancery Lane, London, W.C.2.

PATENTS FORM NO. 58

PATENTS ACT, 1949

───────

1565   **APPLICATION FOR ENTRY OF NAME OF PROPRIETOR
OR CO-PROPRIETOR IN THE REGISTER OF PATENTS**

───────

I/We (a) ....   (a) Insert (in
full) name,
....   address and
                                                                             nationality.
....
hereby apply that you will enter my/our name in the Register of
Patents as proprietor .... (or co-proprietor.........) of Patent   (b) Give name
No. .... at present registered in the name of (b)*............   of registered
                                                                             proprietor.
....   (c) Specify the
                                                                             particulars of
    I/We claim to be so entitled by virtue of (c)   such document
                                                                             giving its date,
....   and the parties
                                                                             to the same,
....   and showing
                                                                             how the claim
....   here made is
....   substantiated.
....

[567]

(d) Insert the nature of the document. The certified copy should be written, typewritten or printed on foolscap paper on one side only.

And in proof whereof I/we transmit the accompanying (d)......

.... with a certified copy thereof.

My/Our address for service in the United Kingdom is........

....

(e)....................................

(f)....................................

*If the application is in respect of more than one patent, the numbers thereof, as well as the particulars required at (b) above, should be given in a separate schedule which should be attached to this Form.

(e) Signature.

(f) State in what capacity the signatory is acting.

To the Comptroller,

   The Patent Office,

      25, Southampton Buildings,

         Chancery Lane, London, W.C.2.

PATENTS FORM NO. 59

PATENTS ACT, 1949

1566

APPLICATION FOR ENTRY OF NOTICE OF A MORTGAGE OR LICENCE IN THE REGISTER OF PATENTS

(a) Insert (in full) name, address and nationality.

I/We (a) ....

....

....

hereby apply that you will enter in the Register of Patents a notice of the following interest in a patent:—

(b) Insert the nature of the claim, whether by way of mortgage or licence.

I/We claim to be entitled (b) ....

.... to an interest in

Patent No. ....* at present registered in the

name of (c) ....

(c) Give name of registered proprietor.

by virtue of (d) ....

(d) Specify the particulars of such document, giving its date, and the parties to the same.

....

....

....

....

....

....

(e) Insert the nature of the document. The certified copy should be written, typewritten or printed on foolscap paper on one side only.

And in proof whereof I/we transmit the accompanying (e) ...

.... with a certified copy thereof.

My/Our address for service in the United Kingdom is ....

....

....

(f)....................................

(g)....................................

(f) Signature.

(g) State in what capacity the signatory is acting.

*If the application is in respect of more than one patent, the numbers thereof, as well as the particulars required at (c) and (d) above, should be given in a separate schedule which should be attached to this Form.

To the Comptroller,

   The Patent Office,

      25, Southampton Buildings,

         Chancery Lane, London, W.C.2.

PATENTS FORM NO. 60

PATENTS ACT, 1949

1567 APPLICATION UNDER SECTION 74 (2) BY ASSIGNOR FOR ENTRY OF NAME OF PROPRIETOR OR CO-PROPRIETOR IN THE REGISTER OF PATENTS

I/We (a) ....
....
....

(a) Insert (in full) name and address.

hereby apply that you will enter the name(s) of (b) ....
....
....

(b) Insert name address and nationality of person(s) to be registered.

in the Register of Patents as proprietor (or part proprietor) of Patent No. ....* of which I am/we are the registered proprietor(s).

He is/they are entitled to the said patent or to a share therein by virtue of (c) ....
....
....
....
....

(c) Specify the particulars of such document, giving its date, and the parties to the same, and showing how the claim is substantiated.

And in proof whereof I/we transmit the accompanying (d) .... with a certified copy thereof.

My/Our address for service in the United Kingdom is ....
....

(d) Insert the nature of the document. The certified copy should be written, typewritten or printed on foolscap paper on one side only.

The address for service in the United Kingdom of the person(s) to be registered as proprietor or co-proprietor is:—.................
....

(e)...............................
(f)................................

(e) Signature.

(f) State in what capacity the signatory is acting.

* If the application is in respect of more than one patent, the numbers thereof, as well as the particulars required at (b) and (c) above, should be given in a separate schedule which should be attached to this Form.

To the Comptroller,
The Patent Office,
25, Southampton Buildings,
Chancery Lane, London, W.C.2.

PATENTS FORM NO. 61

PATENTS ACT, 1949

1568 APPLICATION UNDER SECTION 74 (2) BY MORTGAGOR OR LICENSOR FOR ENTRY OF NOTICE OF A MORTGAGE OR LICENCE IN THE REGISTER OF PATENTS

I/We (a) ....
....

(a) Insert (in full) name and address.

hereby apply that you will enter in the Register of Patents a notice of the following interest in a patent:—(b) ....
....

(b) Insert name, address and nationality of mortgagee or licensee.

(c) Insert the nature of the claim, whether by way of Mortgage or Licence.

(d) Specify the particulars of such document, giving its date, and the parties to the same.

He is/They are entitled (c) ....
.... to an interest in Patent
No. ....*, of which I am/we are the registered
proprietor(s), by virtue of (d) ....
....
....
....
....
....

(e) Insert the nature of the document. The certified copy should be written, typewritten or printed on *foolscap paper on one side only.*

And in proof whereof I/we transmit the accompanying (e) ...
.... with a certified copy thereof.
My/Our address for service in the United Kingdom is ....
....

The address for service in the United Kingdom of the person(s)
to be registered as mortgagee or licensee is:—......................
....

(f) Signature.

(g) State in what capacity the signatory is acting.

(f).................................
(g).................................

* If the application is in respect of more than one patent, the numbers thereof, as well as the particulars required at (c) and (d) above, should be given in a separate schedule which should be attached to this Form.

To the Comptroller,
    The Patent Office,
        25, Southampton Buildings,
            Chancery Lane, London, W.C.2.

PATENTS FORM No. 62

PATENTS ACT, 1949

1569

APPLICATION FOR ENTRY OF NOTIFICATION OF DOCUMENT IN REGISTER OF PATENTS

(a) Insert (in full) name, address and nationality of the party benefiting under the document.

(b) Specify the particulars of the document, giving its nature, date, and the parties to the same.

I/We (a) ....
....
transmit the accompanying (b) ....
....
....

(together with a certified copy thereof) (c) affecting the proprietorship of Patent No. ....* at present registered in the name of (d) ....

(c) The certified copy should be written, typewritten or printed on *foolscap paper on one side only.*

and request that a notification thereof may be entered in the Register of Patents.

(d) State name of registered proprietor.

(e).................................
(f).................................

(e) Signature.

(f) State in what capacity the signatory is acting.

* If the application is in respect of more than one patent the numbers and particulars thereof should be given in a separate schedule which should be attached to this Form.

To the Comptroller,
    The Patent Office,
        25, Southampton Buildings,
            Chancery Lane, London, W.C.2.

PATENTS FORM NO. 63

PATENTS ACT, 1949

1570 APPLICATION FOR ENTRY OF A CLAIM TO BE DEEMED A LICENSEE IN THE REGISTER OF PATENTS

I/We (a) .... (a) State name,
.... address and
.... nationality.

hereby apply that you will enter my/our claim to be deemed to have acted with the licence of the patentee (exclusive licensee) in accordance with the conditions in the Order dated ....
.... extending the term of Patent No. ....

Evidence in support of my/our claim accompanies this application.

My/Our address for service in the United Kingdom is ....

....
....
....
....

(b)................................... (b) Signature.

To the Comptroller,
    The Patent Office,
        25, Southampton Buildings,
        Chancery Lane, London, W.C.2.

PATENTS FORM NO. 64

PATENTS ACT, 1949

1571 REQUEST FOR CORRECTION OF CLERICAL ERROR (SECTION 76)

I/We (a) .... (a) State full
.... name and
.... address.

hereby request that the clerical error(s) in the (b) .... (b) State
relating to application/Patent No. .... indicated in red whether in
ink in the annexed copy of the said (b) .... application,
or shown as follows:—   specification,
                                                                     entry in
.... register,
.... patent, or
.... the particular
.... relevant
.... document.

may be corrected.

Communications should be sent to .... (c) The address
.... at (c) .... must be within
(d) who is/are hereby appointed to act for me/us.   the United
                                                                     Kingdom.
(e)...................................   (d) Delete if
To the Comptroller,   not applicable.
    The Patent Office,   (e) To be
        25, Southampton Buildings,   signed by
        Chancery Lane, London, W.C.2.   applicant or
                                                                     his authorised
                                                                     agent.

PATENTS FORM No. 65

PATENTS ACT, 1949

1572

NOTICE OF OPPOSITION TO THE CORRECTION OF A CLERICAL ERROR

(To be accompanied by a copy, and a statement of case in duplicate)

(a) State (in full) name and address.

I/We (a) ....

....

....

hereby give notice of opposition to the correction of an alleged clerical error in ....

....

which said correction has been applied for by ....

....

The grounds upon which the said correction is opposed are as follows:—

....

....

....

....

(b) The address must be within the United Kingdom.

(c) Delete if not applicable.

(d) To be signed by opponents.

Communications should be sent to ....

at (b) ....

(c) who is/are hereby appointed to act for me/us.

                                     (d)................................

To the Comptroller,
    The Patent Office,
        25, Southampton Buildings,
            Chancery Lane, London, W.C.2.

PATENTS FORM No. 66

PATENTS ACT, 1949

1573

REQUEST FOR CERTIFICATE OF COMPTROLLER

(a) Here set out the particulars which the Comptroller is requested to certify, and of any copies of documents which are to be annexed to the Certificate, stating also the purpose for which the copies are required.

(b) Name and full address to which Certificate is to be sent.

Patent (or Application) No. .... of 19......

....

    I/We ....

of ....

hereby request you to furnish me/us with your Certificate to the effect that (a) ....

....

....

....

....

....

(b) ....

To the Comptroller,
    The Patent Office,
        25, Southampton Buildings,
            Chancery Lane, London, W.C.2.

PATENTS FORM NO. 67

PATENTS ACT, 1949

1574 **REQUEST FOR INFORMATION AS TO A MATTER AFFECTING A PATENT OR AN APPLICATION THEREFOR**

Patent (or Application) No. .... of 19......

I/We ....

of ....

hereby request you to furnish me/us with the following information affecting the patent (or application) aforesaid:—

(a) ....

....

....

(b)..

To the Comptroller,

The Patent Office,

25, Southampton Buildings,

Chancery Lane, London, W.C.2.

(a) Here set out particulars as to the matter in respect of which information is sought.

(b) To be signed by the person or persons seeking information, or by their agent.

PATENTS FORM NO. 68

PATENTS ACT, 1949

1575 **APPLICATION FOR A DUPLICATE OF LETTERS PATENT**

I/We have to inform you that the Letters Patent dated (a) .... No. .... granted to .... for an invention the title of which is (b) ....

....

has been lost or destroyed, or cannot be produced in the following circumstances:— (c) ....

....

....

I/We accordingly apply for the issue of a duplicate of such Letters Patent. (d)

(e)..

To the Comptroller,

The Patent Office,

25, Southampton Buildings,

Chancery Lane, London, W.C.2.

(a) State date, number, and full name and address of grantee or grantees.

(b) Insert title of invention.

(c) State, in full, the circumstances of the case, *which must be verified by evidence.*

(d) State interest possessed by applicant or applicants in the Patent.

(e) Signature of patentee or patentees and full address to which the duplicate is to be sent.

PATENTS FORM NO. 69

PATENTS ACT, 1949

1576 **APPLICATION FOR ENTRY OF ORDER OF COURT IN THE REGISTER**

I/We (a) ....

....

....

....

(a) State (in full) name and address of applicant or applicants.

[573]

hereby transmit an office copy of an Order of the Court with
reference to (b) ....
....
....
• • • ....

(c)................................

SCHEDULE 3

FORMS ADOPTED BY THE EUROPEAN CONVENTION RELATING TO THE
FORMALITIES REQUIRED FOR PATENT APPLICATIONS DONE AT
PARIS ON 11TH DECEMBER, 1953 (Cmd. 9095).

1A   (*Form reproduced from Annex I of the Convention*)

1577

APPLICATION FOR PATENT

I/We the undersigned (1) ....
*acting { in my/our own name ....
{ on behalf of (2) ....

Hereby make application for a patent for the invention described
in the accompanying specification (and drawings) and entitled......
....

I/We, the applicant {
claim(s) to be the true (and first) inventor(s) of the
invention
claim(s) the following of us (them), namely
    to be the true and first inventor(s)

(*or*)
believe(s) .... to be the
true and first inventor(s)

(*and*)
claim(s) to be the { Assignee(s)
                    Personal   } of the inventor
                    Representative(s) }

by virtue of (3) ....

I/We request that the patent may be granted as a (4) ....
....
....
....

to Patent (5) { No. ....
              { Application No. .... dated ....
(6) ....
....

Dated this .... day of ....19......
................................(Signature)

List of documents accompanying this application:
....
....
....

N.B.—Delete where not applicable or required.

[574]

INSTRUCTIONS

(1) Give the following particulars:

(a) When this form is signed by the applicant(s), here insert his/their first names, surname(s), full address(es) and nationality(ies) or the name and full address where the applicant is not a physical person;

(b) When the form is signed by a nominee of the applicant(s) here insert the first names, surname and full address of the nominee.

(2) In the case (1) (b), insert here the particulars at (1) (a).

Note: Nominees cannot apply in certain countries.*

(3) Here insert particulars of the assignment or other document.

(4) Here indicate the nature of the protection applied for, *e.g.*, independent patent, patent of importation, patent for an improvement, patent or certificate of addition.

(5) In the case of a divisional application or where otherwise applicable, insert here the number of the related patent, or, where the related patent application is still pending, the number and date of such application.

(6) Insert here, where necessary, any other relevant particulars such as the authorisation of an agent in the country in which the application is made, or, if no such agent is appointed an address for service in that country.

* *Nominee applications are not accepted in the United Kingdom.*

1B   (*Form reproduced from Annex II of the Convention*)

1578   **CONVENTION APPLICATION FOR PATENT**

I/We the undersigned (1) ....

*acting { in my/our own name ....

on behalf of (2) ....

Hereby declare that (an) application(s) for protection for an invention or inventions has(ve) been made in the following country(ies) on the following date(s), namely:—

in .... on ....
by ....
in .... on ....
by ....

and that the said application or each of the said applications was the first application in a Convention country.

I am/We are the assignee(s) of the said ....
or the personal representative(s) of the said ....
by virtue of (3) ....

I/We request that a patent may be granted with priority founded on the above-mentioned application(s) in (a) Convention country(ies) for the invention described in the accompanying specification (and drawings) and entitled

....
....

I/We request that the patent may be granted as a (4) ....

....
....

to Patent (5) $\left\{\begin{array}{l}\text{No. } \text{...} \\ \text{Application No. } \text{...............} \text{ dated } \text{...................}\end{array}\right.$

(6) ....

....

Dated this .... day of ....19......

....(Signature)

List of documents accompanying this application:

....

....

N.B.—Delete where not applicable or required.

INSTRUCTIONS

(1) Give the following particulars:

(a) When this form is signed by the applicant(s), here insert his/their first names, surname(s), full address(es) and nationality(ies) or the name and full address where the applicant is not a physical person;

(b) When the form is signed by a nominee of the applicant(s) here insert the first names, surname and full address of the nominee.

Note: Nominees cannot apply in certain countries.*

(2) In the case (1) (b), insert here the particulars at 1 (a).

(3) Here insert particulars of the assignment or other document.

(4) Here indicate the nature of the protection applied for, e.g., independent patent, patent of importation, patent for an improvement, patent or certificate of addition.

(5) In the case of a divisional application or where otherwise applicable insert here the number of the related patent, or, where the related patent application is still pending, the number and date of such application.

(6) Insert here, where necessary, any other relevant particulars such as the authorisation of an agent in the country in which the application is made, or if no such agent is appointed, an address for service in that country.

* Nominee applications are not accepted in the United Kingdom.

1579

SCHEDULE 4

FORM OF PATENT

Form A

ELIZABETH the Second by the Grace of God of the United Kingdom of Great Britain and Northern Ireland and of Her other Realms and Territories, Queen, Head of the Commonwealth, Defender of the Faith: To all to whom these presents shall come greeting:

WHEREAS a request for the grant of a patent has been made by
for the sole use and advantage of an invention for

AND WHEREAS We, being willing to encourage all inventions which may be for the public good, are graciously pleased to condescend to the request:

1580   KNOW YE, THEREFORE, that We, of our especial grace, certain knowledge, and mere motion do by these presents, for Us, our heirs and successors, give and grant unto the person(s) above named and any successor(s), executor(s), administrator(s) and assign(s) (each and any of whom are hereinafter referred to as the patentee) our especial licence, full power, sole privilege, and authority, that the patentee or any agent or licensee of the patentee and no others, may subject to the conditions and provisions prescribed by any statute or order for the time being in force at all times hereafter during the term of years herein mentioned, make, use, exercise and vend the said invention within our United Kingdom of Great Britain and Northern Ireland, and the Isle of Man, and that the patentee shall have and enjoy the whole profit and advantage from time to time accruing by reason of the said invention, during the term of sixteen years from the date hereunder written of these presents: AND to the end that the patentee may have and enjoy the sole use and exercise and the full benefit of the said invention, We do by these presents for Us, our heirs and successors, strictly command all our subjects whatsoever within our United Kingdom of Great Britain and Northern Ireland, and the Isle of Man, that they do not at any time during the continuance of the said term either directly or indirectly make use of or put in practice the said invention, nor in anywise imitate the same, without the written consent, licence or agreement of the patentee on pain of incurring such penalties as may be justly inflicted on such offenders for their contempt of this our Royal command, and of being answerable to the patentee according to law for his damages thereby occasioned:

PROVIDED ALWAYS that these letters patent shall be revocable on any of the grounds from time to time by law prescribed as grounds for revoking letters patent granted by Us, and the same may be revoked and made void accordingly: PROVIDED ALSO that nothing herein contained shall prevent the granting of licences in such manner and for such considerations as they may by law be granted: AND lastly, We do by these presents for Us, our heirs and successors, grant unto the patentee that these our letters patent shall be construed in the most beneficial sense for the advantage of the patentee.

IN WITNESS whereof We have caused these our letters to be made patent as of the   day of   one thousand nine hundred and   and to be sealed.

Comptroller-General of Patents,
Designs, and Trade Marks.

Seal of
Patent Office.

1581   FORM OF PATENT OF ADDITION
Form B

ELIZABETH the Second by the Grace of God of the United Kingdom of Great Britain and Northern Ireland and of Her other Realms and Territories, Queen, Head of the Commonwealth,

[577]

Defender of the Faith: To all to whom these presents shall come greeting:

WHEREAS a request for the grant of a patent has been made by

for the sole use and advantage of an invention for

and it has been further requested that the patent may be granted as a patent of addition to Patent No.   dated the
day of   19   (hereinafter referred to as the main patent):

AND WHEREAS We, being willing to encourage all inventions which may be for the public good, are graciously pleased to condescend to the request:

KNOW YE, THEREFORE, that We, of our especial grace, certain knowledge, and mere motion do by these presents, for Us, our heirs and successors, give and grant unto the person(s) above named and any successor(s), executor(s), administrator(s) and assign(s) (each and any of whom are hereinafter referred to as the patentee) our especial licence, full power, sole privilege, and authority, that the patentee or any agent, or licensee of a patentee and no others, may subject to the conditions and provisions prescribed by any statute or order for the time being in force at all times hereafter during the term of years herein mentioned, make, use, exercise and vend the said invention within our United Kingdom of Great Britain and Northern Ireland, and the Isle of Man, and that the patentee shall have and enjoy the whole profit and advantage from time to time accruing by reason of the said invention during a term beginning on the date hereunder written of these presents and ending at the expiration of sixteen years from the   day of   one thousand nine hundred and   , the date of said main patent: AND to the end that the patentee may have and enjoy the sole use and exercise and the full benefit of the said invention, We do by these presents for Us, our heirs and successors, strictly command all our subjects whatsoever within our United Kingdom of Great Britain and Northern Ireland, and the Isle of Man, that they do not at any time during the continuance of the said term either directly or indirectly make use of or put in practice the said invention, nor in anywise imitate the same, without the written consent, licence or agreement of the patentee on pain of incurring such penalties as may be justly inflicted on such offenders for their contempt of this our Royal command, and of being answerable to the patentee according to law for damages thereby occasioned:

PROVIDED ALWAYS that these letters patent shall be revocable on any of the grounds from time to time by law prescribed as grounds for revoking letters patent granted by Us, and the same may be revoked and made void accordingly: PROVIDED ALSO that nothing herein contained shall prevent the granting of licences in such manner and for such considerations as they may by law be granted: AND lastly, We do by these presents for Us, our heirs and successors, grant unto the said patentee that these our letters patent shall be construed in the most beneficial sense for the advantage of the said patentee.

[578]

IN WITNESS whereof We have caused these our letters to be made patent as of the   day of   one thousand nine hundred and   and to be sealed.

Comptroller-General of Patents, Designs, and Trade Marks.

Seal of Patent Office.

EXPLANATORY NOTE

(This Note is not part of the Rules.)

These Rules consolidate and amend the Patents Rules 1958, the Patents (Amendment) Rules 1964, the Patents (Amendment No. 2) Rules 1964, the Patents (Amendment) Rules 1966, the Patents (Amendment) Rules 1967 and the Patents (Amendment No. 2) Rules 1967. The principal amendments are—

(1) a new Rule (Rule 146) makes provision for the documents therein described to be open to public inspection;

(2) the Forms of Patents and Patents of Addition (Schedule 4) are modified.

Patents and Registered Designs Appeal Tribunal Fees Order 1970

(1970, No. 529 (L.13))

Made -   -   -   -   *26th March* 1970
Coming into Operation   *20th April* 1970

1582 The Lord Chancellor, in exercise of the powers conferred on him by section 85 (3) of the Patents Act 1949, section 28 (3) of the Registered Designs Act 1949, section 213 of the Supreme Court of Judicature (Consolidation) Act 1925, and sections 2 and 3 of the Public Offices Fees Act 1879, with the advice and consent of the Judges of the Supreme Court and with the concurrence of the Treasury, hereby makes the following Order: —

1583 **1.** This Order may be cited as the Patents and Registered Designs Appeal Tribunal Fees Order 1970 and shall come into operation on 20th April 1970.

1584 **2.** A fee of £6 shall be taken upon the filing of every notice of appeal to the Appeal Tribunal constituted under section 85 of the Patents Act 1949 and section 28 of the Registered Designs Act 1949.

1585 **3.** The fee referred to in paragraph 2 shall be taken by a judicature fee stamp impressed on the notice of appeal.

1586 **4.** Where it appears to the Lord Chancellor that the payment of the fee referred to in paragraph 2 would, owing to the exceptional circumstances of the particular case, involve hardship, the Lord

Chancellor may, with the concurrence of the Treasury, reduce or remit the fee in that particular case.

1587   **5.** The Patents and Registered Designs Appeal Tribunal Fees Order 1950 is hereby revoked.

R.S.C., Order 103

THE PATENTS ACTS 1949 TO 1961; THE REGISTERED DESIGNS ACTS 1949 TO 1961; THE DEFENCE CONTRACTS ACT 1958

Definitions

1588   **1.** In this Order—
" the Act " means the Patents Act 1949;
" the Comptroller " means the Comptroller-General of Patents, Designs and Trade Marks;
" the Journal " means the Official Journal (Patents).

Assignment of proceedings

1589   **2.** Subject to any order or direction made or given by the Lord Chancellor, all proceedings in the High Court under the Patents Acts 1949 to 1961, the Registered Designs Acts 1949 to 1961 and the Defence Contracts Act 1958 shall be assigned to the Chancery Division.

Advertisement of petition for extension of patent under s. 23 of the Act

1590   **3.**—(1) A person intending to apply for an order under section 23 of the Act extending the term of a patent must insert an advertisement giving notice of his intention once in an appropriate trade paper, once in a newspaper circulating throughout the United Kingdom and once in the London Gazette.

(2) When the applicant sends the advertisement to an appropriate trade paper for insertion therein, he must send a copy of the advertisement to the Comptroller who shall thereupon cause the advertisement to be inserted in the two next following issues of the Journal.

(3) The advertisement must state—
(a) the object of the petition;
(b) the day, being a day fixed for the purpose and not earlier than 8 weeks after the publication of the advertisement for the second time in the Journal, on which the applicant intends to apply to the Court for directions fixing the date of hearing of the petition and other directions;
(c) that notices of opposition to the petition must be lodged at the Chancery Registrars' Office not less than 14 days before the day on which the applicant intends to apply to the Court as aforesaid;
(d) the applicant's address for service within the United Kingdom.

(4) In this rule " appropriate trade paper " means a newspaper or other periodical published in the United Kingdom which is appropriate to the art to which the patent in question relates.

Presentation of petition, etc.

1591   **4.**—(1) A petition under section 23 of the Act must be presented within one week after the publication in the Journal for the second time of the advertisement required by rule 3, and a copy of the petition must at the same time be served on the solicitor to the Board of Trade.

(2) Order 9, rule 3 (1), shall not apply in relation to such a petition.

(3) The Comptroller shall be made respondent to the petition.

(4) The petition shall be assigned to Group A and made returnable for the day stated in the advertisement as that on which the petitioner intends to apply to the Court for directions.

(5) The petition must be accompanied by an affidavit or affidavits proving compliance with rule 3.

(6) Not less than 4 weeks before the day referred to in paragraph (4), the petitioner must lodge in the Chancery Registrars' Office two printed copies of the specification of the patent.

(7) A petition under section 23 of the Act may be presented in the Long Vacation without the leave of the Court.

Notice of intention to oppose petition under s. 23

1592   **5.**—(1) Any person who intends to oppose the making of an order under section 23 of the Act, or to claim the inclusion therein of any restrictions, conditions or provisions, must lodge notice of his intention in the Chancery Registrars' Office not less than 14 days before the day named in the petitioner's advertisements as that on which he intends to apply to the Court for directions and at the same time serve a copy of the notice on the petitioner and the solicitor to the Board of Trade.

The notice must state an address for service within the United Kingdom of the person giving the notice.

(2) A petitioner on whom a notice under paragraph (1) is served must forthwith serve a copy of the petition on the person by whom the notice was served.

(3) A person who has under paragraph (1) served notice of his intention to oppose a petition under the said section 23 shall be entitled to be heard on the petitioner's application for directions.

Directions by Court in proceedings by petition under s. 23

1593   **6.**—(1) On the hearing, on the date fixed for the purpose, of the petitioner's application for directions in proceedings for an order under section 23 of the Act, or a subsequent hearing, the Court shall give such directions for the conduct of the proceedings as it thinks necessary or expedient and, without prejudice to the generality of the foregoing provision, it shall—

    (*a*) specify the period within which the petitioner must lodge in the Chancery Registrars' Office two copies of the accounts of expenditure and receipts relating to his petition, being the accounts which are to be proved at the hearing of the petition;

    (*b*) specify the period within which each person by whom notice has been served under rule 5 (1) must lodge in the said Office two copies of particulars of the objections on which he intends to rely;

    (*c*) give directions as to the manner in which the evidence shall be given at the hearing of the petition and, if the evidence is to be given by affidavit specify the period within which the affidavit must be filed;

(d) fix the date of hearing of the petition.

(2) Where the petition includes an application for extension of the time allowed by subsection (2) of the said section 23, the Court may, on the application of the petitioner made on the hearing of his application for directions under this rule, and on such terms as to costs or otherwise as it thinks just, give directions for the determination before the hearing of the petition of the application for such leave, and where it does so, it shall give directions as to the manner in which the evidence shall be given at the hearing of the application and fix the date of the hearing.

Lodging of accounts, particulars of objections, etc.

1594   **7.**—(1) At the time when the petitioner for an order under section 23 of the Act lodges copies of the accounts referred to in rule 6 (1) (a) in compliance with directions given under that rule he must send two copies of those accounts to the solicitor to the Board of Trade, and, on receiving notice in that behalf, the petitioner must give to the said solicitor or a person deputed by him for that purpose reasonable facilities for inspecting and taking extracts from the books of account by which the petitioner proposes to verify those accounts or from which those accounts have been derived.

(2) At the time when any person opposing a petition for an order under the said section 23 lodges copies of particulars of objections in compliance with directions given under rule 6 (1) (b) he must serve one copy of those particulars on the petitioner and three copies on the solicitor to the Board of Trade.

(3) Subject to rule 14, a person who fails to comply with paragraph (2) or the directions referred to therein shall be deemed to have abandoned his opposition to the petition.

(4) A person opposing a petition under the said section 23 shall not be entitled on the hearing of the petition to rely on any ground of objection not specified in his particulars of objection.

(5) A person who served particulars of objection on the petitioner shall be entitled, at his own expense, to obtain from the petitioner a copy of the accounts lodged by the petitioner in compliance with directions under rule 6 (1) (a).

Setting down petition under s. 23

1595   **8.**—(1) A petition under section 23 of the Act shall be set down for hearing not less than 14 days before the date fixed for the hearing but before it is set down a certificate signed by the petitioner or his solicitor certifying that copies of the petition and notice of the said date have been served on every person opposing the petition and on the solicitor to the Board of Trade must be lodged in the Chancery Registrars' Office.

(2) Unless the Court otherwise directs, the petition shall be set down in the same manner as a witness action and shall be set down in the patents list.

Application by petition for extension of patent under s. 24 of the Act

1596   **9.**—(1) Rules 3 to 8 shall, with the necessary modifications, apply in relation to an application to the High Court by petition for an order under section 24 of the Act extending the term of a patent and to such an application made by virtue of section 25 of the Act.

(2) If any person wishes to apply both for an order under section 23 of the Act and for an order under section 24 thereof, he may apply for both orders by the same petition, and rules 3 to 8 shall, with the necessary modifications, apply in relation to the application.

Application by summons for extension of patent under s. 24

1597   **10.**—(1) Where an application to the High Court for an order under section 24 of the Act extending the term of a patent, or such an application made by virtue of section 25 of the Act, is made by originating summons, the Comptroller shall be made defendant to the summons and the summons must be served on the solicitor to the Board of Trade.

The summons shall be assigned to Group A.

(2) Not less than 7 days before the day fixed under Order 28, rule 2, for the hearing of the summons the plaintiff must file and serve on the solicitor to the Board of Trade an affidavit of the facts on which the plaintiff relies.

Advertisement of application for extension of patent under s. 24

1598   **11.**—(1) On the first or any adjourned hearing of an originating summons for extension of the term of a patent, the Court shall give directions for advertisement of the application for extension and shall adjourn the hearing to a specified day (in this rule and rules 12 and 13 referred to as " the appointed day ") fixed in accordance with paragraph (5).

(2) The advertisement required by this rule shall, unless the Court otherwise directs, be inserted at least twice in the Journal, and before insertion its contents shall be approved by the Court.

(3) Subject to any directions given by the Court, the advertisement must state—

(*a*) the object of the originating summons;

(*b*) the appointed day;

(*c*) that notices of objections to the summons must be lodged in the judge's chambers not less than 7 days before the appointed day;

(*d*) the plaintiff's address for service within the United Kingdom.

(4) Within 3 days after the advertisement has been approved by the Court, the plaintiff must serve a copy thereof on the Comptroller, and, subject to any directions of the Court under paragraph (2), the Comptroller shall thereupon cause the advertisement to be inserted in the two next following issues of the Journal.

(5) The appointed day shall be a day not less than 4 weeks after the estimated date of publication of the advertisement for the first time in the Journal.

(6) Except with the leave of the Court, no affidavit shall be filed by the plaintiff between the publication of the advertisement for the first time in the Journal and the appointed day.

Opposition to summons under s. 24

1599   **12.**—(1) Any person who intends to oppose the making (on application by originating summons) of an order under section 24 of the Act, or to claim the inclusion therein of any restrictions, conditions or provisions, must not less than 7 days before the appointed day lodge notice of his intention in the judge's chambers and at the same time serve a copy of the notice on the plaintiff and the solicitor to the Board of Trade.

The notice must state an address for service within the United Kingdom of the person giving the notice.

(2) A plaintiff on whom a notice under paragraph (1) is served must forthwith serve a copy of the originating summons and of any supporting affidavit filed by him on the person by whom the notice was served.

Directions by Court

1600   **13.** On the hearing on the appointed day or a subsequent hearing the Court shall give directions for the service of particulars of objections by any person who has lodged a notice under rule 12 (1) and for the filing of any affidavits and as to the further conduct of the proceedings.

Power to dispense with procedural requirements

1601   **14.** The Court may, on sufficient reason being shown for doing so, excuse an applicant for an order under section 23 or 24 of the Act and any person opposing the application from compliance with any obligation imposed on him by rule 3, 4, 5, 7, 8, 10, 11 or 12.

Provisions where Comptroller appears on hearing

1602   **15.** Where the Comptroller elects, or is required by the Court, to appear on the hearing of an application under section 23 or 24 of the Act, he shall not be required to give notice of the grounds of any objection he may think fit to take or of any evidence he may think fit to submit to the Court, but he may give the applicant written notice before the hearing of any observations on the applicant's petition or originating summons, as the case may be, and on the applicant's evidence and accounts which he may think fit to make at the hearing.

Reference to Court of application to Comptroller under s. 24

1603   **16.**—(1) Where an application for an order under section 24 of the Act, or an application for such an order made by virtue of section 25 thereof, is made to the Comptroller and the Comptroller decides to refer the application for decision by the Court, he shall give notice of his decision to the applicant and to any person opposing the making of the order or claiming the inclusion therein of any restrictions, conditions or provisions.

(2) Within 28 days after receipt of such notice the applicant may apply by originating motion for an order under the said section 24 and notice of the motion must be served on the solicitor to the Board of Trade and on any such person as is referred to in paragraph (1).

The applicant must also serve on the said solicitor two copies of any evidence filed in support of or in opposition to the application.

(3) Unless the Court for some special reason otherwise orders, the

motion shall be heard by the judge selected by the Lord Chancellor under section 84 of the Act.

(4) An applicant who fails to serve notice of the motion in accordance with paragraph (2) shall be deemed to have abandoned his application.

(5) Within 14 days after service of notice of the motion on the solicitor to the Board of Trade the Comptroller shall send his file of the proceedings on the matter to the chief registrar of the Chancery Division together with a statement to the Court of his reasons for referring the application to the Court.

(6) Subject to any directions given by the Court, the procedure on an application for an order under the said section 24 referred to the Court by the Comptroller shall be the same as on an application for such an order made to the Court by originating summons and rules 11 to 15 shall, so far as applicable, apply with the necessary adaptations.

Application for leave to amend specification under s. 30 of the Act

1604   **17.**—(1) A patentee intending to apply under section 30 of the Act for leave to amend his specification must give notice of his intention to the Comptroller accompanied by a copy of an advertisement—

(*a*) identifying the proceedings pending before the Court in which it is intended to apply for such leave,

(*b*) giving particulars of the amendment sought,

(*c*) stating the applicant's address for service within the United Kingdom, and

(*d*) stating that any person intending to oppose the amendment who is not a party to the proceedings must within 14 days after the appearance of the advertisement give written notice of his intention to the applicant;

and the Comptroller shall insert the advertisement once in the Journal.

A person who gives notice in accordance with the advertisement shall be entitled to be heard on the application subject to any direction of the Court as to costs.

(2) As soon as may be after the expiration of 21 days from the appearance of the advertisement the applicant must make his application under the said section 30 by motion in the proceedings pending before the Court; and notice of the motion, together with a copy of the specification certified by the Comptroller and showing in coloured ink the amendment sought, must be served on the Comptroller, the parties to the proceedings and any person who has given notice of his intention to oppose the amendment.

(3) On the hearing of the motion the Court shall give such directions for the further conduct of the proceedings on the motion as it thinks necessary or expedient and, in particular, directions—

(*a*) requiring the applicant and any party or person opposing the amendment sought to exchange statements of the grounds for allowing the amendment and of objections to the amendment;

(*b*) determining whether the motion shall be heard with the other proceedings relating to the patent in question or separately and, if separately, fixing the date of hearing thereof;

[585]

(c) as to the manner in which the evidence shall be given and, if the evidence is to be given by affidavit, fixing the times within which the affidavits must be filed.

(4) Where the Court allows a specification to be amended, the applicant must forthwith lodge with the Comptroller an office copy of the order made by the Court and, if so required by the Court or Comptroller, leave at the Patent Office a new specification and drawings as amended prepared in compliance with the Act and rules made thereunder.

The Comptroller shall cause a copy of the order to be inserted once at least in the Journal.

Revocation of patent under s. 32 of the Act

1605   **18.**—(1) Any person presenting a petition under section 32 of the Act for the revocation of a patent must serve with his petition particulars of the objections to the validity of the patent on which he intends to rely.

(2) The respondent to such a petition must serve an answer on the petitioner within 21 days after service of the petition on him.

(3) On the hearing of such petition the respondent shall be entitled to begin and to adduce evidence in support of the patent; and if the petitioner adduces evidence impeaching the validity of the patent, the respondent shall be entitled to reply.

Actions for infringement : particulars of pleading

1606   **19.**—(1) The plaintiff in an action for infringement of a patent must serve with his statement of claim particulars of the infringements relied on.

(2) If a defendant in such an action disputes the validity of the patent, he must serve with his defence particulars of the objections to the validity of the patent on which he relies in support of the allegation of invalidity.

(3) If a defendant in such an action alleges, as a defence to the action, that at the time of the infringement there was in force a contract or contracts relating to the patent made by or with the consent of the plaintiff and containing a condition void by virtue of section 57 of the Act, he must serve on the plaintiff particulars of the date of, and parties to, each such contract and particulars of each such condition.

(4) A defendant to such an action who in pursuance of section 61 of the Act applies by counterclaim in the action for revocation of the patent must, with his counterclaim, serve particulars of the objections to the validity of the patent on which he relies in support of his counterclaim.

Particulars of infringements

1607   **20.** Particulars of infringements of a patent must specify which of the claims in the specification of the patent are alleged to be infringed and must give at least one instance of each type of infringement alleged.

Particulars of objections

1608   **21.**—(1) Particulars of objections to the validity of a patent must state every ground on which the validity of the patent is disputed and must include such particulars as will clearly define every issue which it is intended to raise.

(2) If the grounds stated in the particulars of objections include want of novelty or want of any inventive step, the particulars must state the manner, time and place of every prior publication or user relied upon and, if prior user is alleged, must—

(*a*)   specify the name of every person alleged to have made such user,

(*b*)   state whether such user is alleged to have continued until the priority date of the claim in question of the complete specification and, if not, the earliest and latest date on which such user is alleged to have taken place,

(*c*)   contain a description, accompanied by drawings, if necessary, sufficient to identify such user, and

(*d*)   if such user relates to machinery or apparatus, state whether the machinery or apparatus is in existence and where it can be inspected.

(3) If—

(*a*)   one of the grounds stated in the particulars of objection is that the invention, so far as claimed in any claim of the complete specification, is not useful, and

(*b*)   it is intended, in connection with that ground, to rely on the fact that an example of the invention which is the subject of any such claim cannot be made to work, either at all or as described in the specification,

the particulars must state that fact and identify each such claim and must include particulars of each such example, specifying the respects in which it is alleged that it does not work or does not work as described.

Amendment of particulars

1609   **22.** Without prejudice to Order 20, rule 5, the Court may at any stage of the proceedings allow a party to amend any particulars served by him under the foregoing provisions of this Order on such terms as to costs or otherwise as may be just.

Further particulars

1610   **23.** The Court may at any stage of the proceedings order a party to serve on any other party further or better particulars of infringements or of objections.

Restrictions on admission of evidence

1611   **24.**—(1) Except with the leave of the judge hearing any action or other proceeding relating to a patent, no evidence shall be admissible in proof of any alleged infringement, or of any objection to the validity, of the patent, if the infringement or objection was not raised in the particulars of infringements or objections, as the case may be.

(2) In any action or other proceeding relating to a patent, evidence which is not in accordance with a statement contained in particulars

of objections to the validity of the patent shall not be admissible in support of such an objection unless the judge hearing the proceeding allows the evidence to be admitted.

(3) If any machinery or apparatus alleged to have been used before the date first mentioned in rule 21 (2) (*b*) is in existence at the date of service of the particulars of objections, no evidence of its user before that date shall be admissible unless it is proved that the party relying on such user offered, where the machinery or apparatus is in his possession, inspection of it to the other parties to the proceedings, or, where it is not, did his best to obtain inspection of it for those parties.

Proceedings for infringement or revocation: admissions must be requested

1612   **25.**—(1) In an action for infringement of a patent (whether or not any other relief is claimed) and in proceedings by petition for the revocation of a patent, each party must, within 14 days after service of a reply or answer or after the expiration of the period fixed for service thereof, write to each other party from whom he requires an admission for the purpose of the action or proceedings requesting him to make the admission, and the party receiving the request must within 14 days after the receipt thereof reply in writing making the admission or stating that he refuses to make it.

(2) No order shall be made authorising a party to any such action or proceedings to serve any interrogatory on any other party unless the first-mentioned party requested that other party in accordance with paragraph (1) to admit the facts sought to be proved by the answer to the interrogatory and the other party refused or failed to comply with the request.

Proceedings for infringement or revocation: summons for directions

1613   **26.**—(1) In such an action, and in such proceedings, as are referred to in rule 25 (1), the plaintiff or petitioner must—

(*a*) within one month after the date on which the last reply to a request made under rule 25 (1) is received or after the date on which the period fixed for making such a reply expires, whichever first occurs, or

(*b*) if no request for an admission is made by any party to the action or proceedings, within one month after service of a reply or answer or after the expiration of the period fixed for service thereof,

take out a summons for directions as to the place and mode of trial returnable in not less than 21 days, and if the plaintiff or petitioner does not take out such a summons in accordance with this paragraph, the defendant or respondent, as the case may be, may do so.

The summons may be heard in chambers or in court as the Court thinks fit.

(2) The Court hearing a summons under this rule may give such directions—

(*a*) for the service of further pleading or particulars,
(*b*) for the discovery of documents,
(*c*) (subject to rule 25 (2)) for the service of interrogatories and of answers thereto,

(*d*) for the taking by affidavit of evidence relating to matters requiring expert knowledge, and for the filing of such affidavits and the service of copies thereof on the other parties,

(*e*) for the service on the other parties, by any party desiring to submit experimental proof, of full and precise particulars of the experiments proposed and of the facts which he claims to be able to establish thereby,

(*f*) for the making of experiments, tests, inspections or reports,

(*g*) for the hearing, as a preliminary issue, of any question that may arise (including any question as to the construction of the specification or other documents),

and otherwise as the Court thinks necessary or expedient for the purpose of defining and limiting the issues to be tried, restricting the number of witnesses to be called at the trial of any particular issue and otherwise securing that the case shall be disposed of, consistently with adequate hearing, in the most expeditious manner.

Where evidence is directed to be given by affidavit, the deponents must attend at the trial for cross-examination unless, with the concurrence of the Court, the parties otherwise agree.

(3) Order 24, rules 1 and 2, shall not apply in an action for infringement of a patent.

(4) No action for infringement of a patent or petition for the revocation of a patent shall be set down for trial unless and until a summons under this rule in the action or proceedings has been taken out and the directions given on the summons have been carried out or the time fixed by the Court for carrying them out has expired.

(5) A petition for the revocation of a patent shall not be tried sooner than 21 days after the petition has been set down for trial.

Appointment of scientific adviser

1614 **27.**—(1) In an action for infringement of a patent and in any proceedings under the Act, the Court may at any time, and on or without the application of any party, appoint an independent scientific adviser to assist the Court or to inquire and report on any question of fact or of opinion not involving questions of law or construction.

(2) The Court may nominate the scientific adviser and shall settle the question or instructions to be submitted or given to him.

(3) The remuneration of any adviser appointed under this rule shall be fixed by the Court and shall include the costs of making any report and a proper daily fee for any day on which he is required to attend before the Court.

(4) Order 40, rules 2, 3, 4 and 6, shall apply in relation to an adviser appointed under this rule and any report made by him as they apply in relation to a Court expert and a report made by him.

Proceedings for determination of certain disputes

1615 **28.**—(1) Proceedings for the determination of any dispute referred to the Court under—

(*a*) section 48 of the Act,

(*b*) paragraph 3 of Schedule 1 to the Registered Designs Act 1949, or

(*c*) section 4 of the Defence Contracts Act 1958,

must be begun by originating motion assigned to Group A.

(2) Unless the Court for some special reason otherwise orders, the motion shall be heard by the judge selected by the Lord Chancellor under section 84 of the Act or section 27 of the Registered Designs Act 1949, as the circumstances of the case require.

(3) There must be at least 10 clear days between the service of notice of a motion under this rule and the day named in the notice for hearing the motion.

(4) On the hearing of a motion under this rule the Court shall give such directions for the further conduct of the proceedings as it thinks necessary or expedient and, in particular, directions for the service of particulars and as to the manner in which the evidence shall be given and as to the date of the hearing.

Application for rectification of register of patents or designs

1616   29. An application to the Court for an order that the register of patents or the register of designs be rectified must be made by originating motion, except where it is made in a petition for the revocation of a patent or by way of counterclaim in proceedings for infringement or by originating summons in proceedings for an order under section 51 of the Trustee Act 1925.

1617   *Counterclaim for rectification of register of designs*

30.—(1) Where in any proceedings a claim is made for relief for infringement of the copyright in a registered design, the party against whom the claim is made may in his defence put in issue the validity of the registration of that design or may counterclaim for an order that the register of designs be rectified by cancelling or varying the registration or may do both those things.

(2) A party to any such proceedings who in his pleading (whether a defence or counterclaim) disputes the validity of the registration of a registered design must serve with the pleading particulars of the objections to the validity of the registration on which he relies in support of the allegation of invalidity.

(3) A party to any such proceedings who counterclaims for an order that the register of designs be rectified must serve on the Comptroller a copy of the counterclaim together with a copy of the particulars mentioned in paragraph (2); and the Comptroller shall be entitled to take such part in the proceedings as he thinks fit but need not serve a defence or other pleading unless ordered to do so by the Court.

R.S.C., Order 59

APPEALS TO THE COURT OF APPEAL

*   *   *   *   *

Appeal against order for revocation of patent

1618   17.—(1) The following provisions of this rule shall apply to any appeal to the Court of Appeal from an order for the revocation of a patent made on a petition under section 32 of the Patents Act, 1949, or on a counterclaim under section 61 of that Act.

(2) The notice of appeal must be served on the Comptroller-General of Patents, Designs and Trade Marks (in this rule referred to as " the Comptroller ") as well as on the party or parties required to be served under rule 3.

(3) If, at any time before the appeal comes on for hearing, the respondent decides not to appear on the appeal or not to oppose it, he must forthwith serve notice of his decision upon the Comptroller and the appellant, and any such notice served on the Comptroller must be accompanied by a copy of the petition or of the pleadings in the action and the affidavits filed therein.

(4) The Comptroller must, within 14 days after receiving notice of the respondents' decision, serve on the appellant a notice stating whether or not he intends to appear on the appeal.

(5) The Comptroller may appear and be heard in opposition to the appeal—

(a) in any case where he has given notice under paragraph (4) of his intention to appear, and

(b) in any other case (including, in particular, a case where the respondent withdraws his opposition to the appeal during the hearing) if the Court of Appeal so directs or allows.

(6) The Court of Appeal may make such orders for the postponement or adjournment of the hearing of the appeal as may appear to the Court necessary for the purpose of giving effect to the foregoing provisions of this rule.

Appeal from Patents Appeal Tribunal [36]

1619   18.—(1) The following provisions of this rule shall apply to any appeal to the Court of Appeal from a decision of the Appeal Tribunal constituted under section 85 of the Patents Act, 1949 (in this rule referred to as " the Tribunal ").

(2) The notice of appeal must be served within 14 days from the date of the decision or within such further time as the Tribunal may allow, and must be served upon the Comptroller-General of Patents, Designs and Trade Marks as well as on the party or parties required to be served under rule 3; and the appellant must, within that period, file two copies of the notice with the registrar of the Tribunal.

(3) Rule 5 shall not apply to the appeal, but the registrar of the Tribunal shall make arrangements with the proper officer as defined by that rule to set down the appeal in the Patents Tribunal appeals list and shall give to the appellant, and to all parties served with the notice of appeal, at least 7 days' notice of the earliest date on which the appeal can come on to be heard.

(4) On receiving the notice given by the registrar under paragraph (3), the appellant must lodge with the registrar, for the use of the Court of Appeal, a signed copy of the decision of the Tribunal and two additional unsigned copies, together with three copies of the notice of appeal and of all the evidence used before the Tribunal.

(5) Any respondent to the appeal may apply to the Tribunal for an order requiring the appellant to give security for the costs of and occasioned by the appeal.

[36] The cases in which an appeal lies from the Patents Appeal Tribunal to the Court of Appeal are set out in s. 87 of the Patents Act 1949, *ante*, § 1226.

R.S.C., Order 62

COSTS

Application

1620   2.—(4) The powers and discretion of the Court as to costs under section 50 of the Act (which provides that the costs of and incidental to proceedings in the Supreme Court shall be in the discretion of the Court and that the Court shall have full power to determine by whom and to what extent the costs are to be paid), and under the enactments relating to the costs of criminal proceedings to which this Order applies, shall be exercised subject to and in accordance with this Order.

Restriction of discretion to order costs

6.—(1) (*e*) except in special circumstances, no order shall be made giving more than one set of costs among all the opponents of a petition or originating summons for extension of the term of a patent under section 23, 24 or 25 of the Patents Act, 1949, if the Court refuses the prayer of the petition or the relief sought by the summons.

APPENDIX 2

PART X

GENERAL

1621   4.—(3) If any action or counterclaim for the infringement of a patent or any petition for revocation of a patent under section 32 of the Patents Act, 1949, or any counterclaim for the revocation of a patent under section 61 of that Act, proceeds to trial, no costs shall be allowed to the parties serving any particulars of breaches or particulars of objection in respect of any issues raised in those particulars and relating to that patent except in so far as those issues or particulars have been certified by the Court to have been proven or to have been reasonable and proper.

[The next paragraph is 1722]

THIS Part sets out certain unrepealed provisions of enactments referred to in the Second Schedule of the Patents Act, 1949, and certain other enactments relating to patents.

Patents and Designs Act, 1907

* * * * *

1722 Patent Museum

47.—(1) The control and management of the Patent Museum and its contents shall remain vested in the Board of Education, subject to such directions as His Majesty in Council may think fit to give.

(2) The Board of Education may at any time require a patentee to furnish them with a model of his invention on payment to the patentee of the cost of the manufacture of the model, the amount to be settled, in case of dispute, by the Board of Trade.

* * * * *

1723 Patent Office

62.—(1) The Treasury may continue to provide for the purposes of this Act and the Trade Marks Act, 1905, an office with all requisite buildings and conveniences, which shall be called, and is in this Act referred to as, the Patent Office.

(2) The Patent Office shall be under the immediate control of the comptroller, who shall act under the superintendence and direction of the Board of Trade.

(3) Any act or thing directed to be done by or to the comptroller may be done by or to any officer authorised by the Board of Trade.

1724 Officers and Clerks

63.—(1) There shall continue to be a comptroller-general of patents, designs, and trade marks, and the Board of Trade may, subject to the approval of the Treasury, appoint the comptroller, and so many examiners and other officers and clerks, with such designations and duties as the Board of Trade think fit, and may remove any of those officers and clerks.

* * * * *

1725 Seal of Patent Office

64. Impressions of the seal of the Patent Office shall be judicially noticed and admitted in evidence.

Patents and Designs (Limits of Time) Act, 1939

1726 Provisions as to failure to comply with certain time limits of the principal Act

4.—(1) No patent granted, and no extension of the period of copyright in a registered design made, before the commencement of this Act shall be treated as invalid by reason only of an act done before the commencement of this Act by an applicant, the comptroller or any other person, not having been done within the time limited for the doing thereof by the Patents and Designs Act, 1907, or that Act as amended at the time the said act was done, or by rules made thereunder.

(2) In the case of an application for a patent made before the commencement of this Act which has not up to that time been treated by the comptroller otherwise than as a subsisting application, but which under the provisions of the Patents and Designs Act, 1907, as for the time being amended, is deemed to have been abandoned, or has become void, at any time before the commencement of this Act, by reason only of the failure of the applicant, or of the comptroller or of any other person, to comply with any requirement as to time limits of that Act as so amended or of rules made thereunder, the comptroller may, if it appears to him that there would have been no substantial non-compliance with the provisions of the principal Act, as amended by this Act, if this Act had been in force at the date of the failure, permit the application to proceed, and thereupon the application shall be treated as not having been abandoned, or as not having become void, as the case may be.

Patents and Designs Act, 1946

1727 Inventions and designs made in Germany or Japan

4.—(1) An application for a patent or for the registration of a design may be refused by the comptroller at any stage of the proceedings on the ground that the invention or design was, during the period beginning with the third day of September, nineteen hundred and thirty-eight, and ending with the thirty-first day of December, nineteen hundred and forty-five, invented or designed in Germany or Japan or invented or designed by a German or Japanese national in any territory which was then enemy territory.

(2) The ground mentioned in subsection (1) of this section shall be an additional ground for opposing under section eleven of the principal Act an application for a patent, or for revoking a patent under section twenty-five or section twenty-six of the principal Act or for cancelling the registration of a design under section fifty-eight of the principal Act or (by way of rectification of the register) under section seventy-two of the principal Act, and shall also, on infringement proceedings, be an additional ground of defence or for a counterclaim for the revocation of a patent or the cancellation of the registration of a design.

(3) The foregoing provisions of this section shall not apply in any case where—

(a) the applicant, patentee, or proprietor of a registered design, as the case may be, proves that the invention or design was invented or designed in Germany before the third day of September, nineteen hundred and thirty-nine, or was invented or designed in Japan before the seventh day of December, nineteen hundred and forty-one, and has at no time since the said third day of September or, as the case may be, the said seventh day of December, been beneficially owned in whole or in part by a German or Japanese national or a German or Japanese company; or

(b) the application for the patent or for the registration of the design was made before the first day of February, nineteen hundred and forty-six, and the applicant, patentee, or proprietor of the design, as the case may be, proves that the invention or design was independently invented or designed outside Germany and Japan by a person, other than a German or Japanese national, being either the applicant, patentee or proprietor or a person through whom he claims; or

(c) the invention or design was invented or designed by a prisoner of war in German or Japanese hands, unless it is shown that it was subsequently obtained from him by any German or Japanese national before the first day of January, nineteen hundred and forty-six.

(4) An appeal shall lie from any decision of the comptroller under this section to the Appeal Tribunal, and the provisions of the principal Act relating to appeals to the Appeal Tribunal shall apply to appeals under this section.

(5) The Board of Trade may make rules under section eighty-six of the principal Act for carrying this section into effect and in particular for requiring applicants for a patent or for the registration of a design to furnish information as to matters arising under this section.

*   *   *   *   *

1728 Interpretation [1]

7.—(1) In this Act the following expressions have the meanings hereby respectively assigned to them, that is to say:

" company " means any body of persons, corporate or unincorporate, and, in relation to a country, means any such body having its principal place of business in that country or controlled by the government of that country or by a national thereof or by any such body having its principal place of business in that country; and the expressions " British company ", " German company " and " Japanese company " shall be construed accordingly;

" enemy territory " means—

(a) any area which was enemy territory as defined by subsection (1) of section fifteen of the Trading with the Enemy Act, 1939;

(b) any area in relation to which the provisions of the said Act applied by virtue of an order made under subsection (1A) of the said section fifteen (as amended by the Defence (Trading with the Enemy) Regulations, 1940), as they applied in relation to enemy territory as so defined; and

(c) any area which, by virtue of Regulation six or Regulation seven of the said Regulations or any order made thereunder, was treated for any of the purposes of the said Act

---

[1] Printed as amended by Patents Act 1949 (c. 87), s. 106, Sched. 2 and Registered Designs Act 1949 (c. 88), s. 48, Sched. 2.

as enemy territory as so defined or as such territory as is referred to in the last foregoing paragraph;

" Germany " means territory comprised in the German State on the first day of March, nineteen hundred and thirty-eight;

" German national " does not include any person who at the relevant time was a German national by reason only of the incorporation of any territory in the German State after the first day of March, nineteen hundred and thirty-eight, or was not an enemy for any of the purposes of the Trading with the Enemy Act, 1939;

" principal Act " means the Patents and Designs Act, 1907, as amended by the amending Acts;

" the amending Acts " means the Patents and Designs Act, 1914, the Patents and Designs Act, 1919, the Patents and Designs (Convention) Act, 1928, the Patents and Designs Act, 1932, the Patents, etc. (International Conventions) Act, 1938, the Patents and Designs (Limits of Time) Act, 1939, and sub-section (1) of section one and sections two and three of the Patents and Designs Act, 1942;

and other expressions have the same meanings as in the principal Act.

1729 Short title, citation, extent and printing [1]

8.—(1) This Act may be cited as the Patents and Designs Act, 1946; and the Patents and Designs Acts, 1907 to 1942, and this Act may be cited together as the Patents and Designs Acts, 1907 to 1946.

(2) It is hereby declared that this Act extends to Northern Ireland.

(3) This Act shall extend to the Isle of Man.

Atomic Energy Act, 1946

Special provisions as to inventions

1730 Special provisions as to inventions [2]

12.—(1) Where an application has been made to the Comptroller General of Patents, Designs and Trade Marks (hereafter in this section referred to as the " Comptroller General ") for the grant of a patent, and it appears to the Comptroller General that the invention which is the subject matter of the application relates to the production or use of atomic energy or research into matters connected therewith, he shall serve a notice in writing on the Minister to that effect, and may, notwithstanding anything in any Act, omit or delay the doing of anything which he would otherwise be required to do in relation to the application, and give directions for prohibiting or restricting the publication of information with respect to the subject matter of the application, or the communication of such information to particular persons or classes of persons; and any person who contravenes any such direction shall be guilty of an offence under this Act.

(2) Where the Minister is notified as aforesaid, he shall forthwith consider whether the invention which is the subject matter of the

---

[2] See also Patents Act 1949, s. 18 (3) (4) (5).

application in question is of importance for purposes of defence and may inspect [or authorise the United Kingdom Atomic Energy Authority to inspect ³] all documents and information furnished to the Comptroller General in connection with the application and if he is satisfied either then or subsequently that the invention is not of importance for purposes of defence, he shall serve a notice in writing on the Comptroller General to that effect, and thereupon the Comptroller General shall cease to exercise his powers under the last foregoing subsection in relation to that application and shall forthwith revoke any directions given under those powers in relation thereto.

(3) Where any notice is given by or to the Comptroller General under the foregoing provisions of this section in relation to any application, he shall serve a copy of the notice on the applicant.

(4) Where on an application to the Comptroller General for the grant of a patent a notice has been served under subsection (1) of this section and six months have elapsed from the date of the service of that notice without the service of a notice under subsection (2) of this section in relation to that application, any person who has, before the date of the application, incurred expense or done work in connection with the discovery or development of the invention concerned, shall be entitled to be paid such compensation in respect of that expense or work as the Minister may with the approval of the Treasury determine, and the compensation shall not in any case be less than the amount of the expense reasonably so incurred, such amount (in case of dispute) to be settled by arbitration:

Provided that, if a notice is subsequently served by the Minister under subsection (2) of this section in relation to the said application, there shall be recoverable by the Minister as a debt due to the Crown such part of the compensation paid to any person under this subsection in connection with the invention concerned as may be reasonable, having regard to the length of the period during which powers were exercised under subsection (1) of this section in relation to the said application and all the other circumstances of the case; and the amount to be so recovered shall, in default of agreement between the Minister and the said person, be settled by arbitration.

[*Subs.* (5) (*restricting the making of applications outside the United Kingdom for patents for inventions relating to atomic energy*), *repealed; Patents and Designs Act 1949, s. 32* (1).]

1731   (6) Where the Comptroller General in the exercise of powers under subsection (1) of this section, omits or delays the doing of anything or gives directions for prohibiting or restricting the publication or communication of information, he may, subject to such conditions, if any, as he thinks fit to impose, extend the time limited by or under the Patents and Designs Acts, 1907 to 1946, for doing any act, where he is satisfied that such extension ought to be granted by reason of the exercise of the powers aforesaid.

(7) The right of a person to apply for, or obtain, a patent in respect of an invention shall not be prejudiced by reason only of the fact that the invention has previously been communicated to the

---

³ The words in square brackets were added by the Atomic Energy Authority Act 1954.

Minister [or the United Kingdom Atomic Energy Authority [4]] under this section or under section 4 of this Act, and a patent in respect of an invention shall not be held to be invalid by reason only that the invention has been communicated as aforesaid.

[(8) The power of the Minister of Supply and persons authorised by the Minister of Supply under section forty-six of the Patents Act, 1949, shall include power to make, use, exercise or vend an invention for such purposes relating to the production or use of atomic energy or research into matters connected therewith as the Minister thinks necessary or expedient, and any reference in that section or in sections forty-seven and forty-eight of that Act to the services of the Crown shall be construed as including a reference to those purposes.[5]]

* * * * *

1732 Offences and penalties

14.—(1) Any person guilty of an offence under this Act shall be liable—

(a) on summary conviction, to imprisonment for a term not exceeding three months or to a fine not exceeding £100, or to both such imprisonment and such fine; or

(b) on conviction on indictment, to [imprisonment [6]] for a term not exceeding five years or to a fine not exceeding £500, or to both such [imprisonment [6]] and such fine.

(2) Where a person convicted on indictment of an offence under this Act is a body corporate, the provision of the foregoing sub-section limiting the amount of the fine which may be imposed shall not apply and the body corporate shall be liable to a fine of such amount as the court thinks just.

(3) Where any offence under this Act has been committed by a body corporate, every person who at the time of the commission of the offence was a director, general manager, secretary or other similar officer of the body corporate, or was purporting to act in any such capacity, shall be deemed to be guilty of that offence, unless he proves that the offence was committed without his consent or connivance and that he exercised all such diligence to prevent the commission of the offence as he ought to have exercised having regard to the nature of his functions in that capacity and to all the circumstances.

[*Subs.* (4) (*proceedings in respect of an offence under s.* 11), *omitted.*]

Crown Proceedings Act, 1947

1733 Provisions as to industrial property

3.—(1) Where after the commencement of this Act any servant or agent of the Crown infringes a patent, or infringes a registered trade mark, or infringes any copyright (including any copyright in a design subsisting under the Patents and Designs Acts, 1907 to 1946), and

---

[4] The words in square brackets were added by the Atomic Energy Authority Act 1954.

[5] Substituted for original subs. (8) by the Patents Act 1949, s. 106 (3).

[6] Substituted by Criminal Justice Act 1948, s. 1 (1).

the infringement is committed with the authority of the Crown, then, subject to the provisions of this Act, civil proceedings in respect of the infringement shall lie against the Crown.

(2) Nothing in the preceding subsection or in any other provision of this Act shall affect the rights of any Government Department under section twenty-nine or section fifty-eight of the Patents and Designs Act, 1907,[6a] or the rights of the Minister of Supply under section twelve of the Atomic Energy Act, 1946.

(3) Save as expressly provided by this section, no proceedings shall lie against the Crown by virtue of this Act in respect of the infringement of a patent, in respect of the infringement of a registered trade mark, or in respect of the infringement of any such copyright as is mentioned in subsection (1) of this section.

*   *   *   *   *

1734 Nature of relief

21.—(1) In any civil proceedings by or against the Crown the court shall, subject to the provisions of this Act, have power to make all such orders as it has power to make in proceedings between subjects, and otherwise to give such appropriate relief as the case may require:

Provided that:

(a) where in any proceedings against the Crown any such relief is sought as might in proceedings between subjects be granted by way of injunction or specific performance, the court shall not grant an injunction or make an order for specific performance, but may in lieu thereof make an order declaratory of the rights of the parties; and

(b) in any proceedings against the Crown for the recovery of land or other property the court shall not make an order for the recovery of the land or the delivery of the property, but may in lieu thereof make an order declaring that the plaintiff is entitled as against the Crown to the land or property or to the possession thereof.

(2) The court shall not in any civil proceedings grant any injunction or make any order against an officer of the Crown if the effect of granting the injunction or making the order would be to give any relief against the Crown which could not have been obtained in proceedings against the Crown.

Civil Aviation Act, 1949

1735 Exemption of aircraft and parts thereof from seizure on patent claims

53.—(1) Any lawful entry into the United Kingdom or any lawful transit across the United Kingdom, with or without landings, of an aircraft to which this section applies shall not entail any seizure or detention of the aircraft or any proceedings being brought against the owner or operator thereof or any other interference therewith by or on behalf of any person in the United Kingdom, on the ground that the construction, mechanism, parts, accessories or operation of the aircraft is or are an infringement of any patent, design or model.

[6a] See Patents Act 1949, ss. 46–49.

(2) The importation into, and storage in, the United Kingdom of spare parts and spare equipment for an aircraft to which this section applies and the use and installation thereof in the repair of such an aircraft shall not entail any seizure or detention of the aircraft or of the spare parts or spare equipment or any proceedings being brought against the owner or operator of the aircraft or the owner of the spare parts or spare equipment or any other interference with the aircraft by or on behalf of any person in the United Kingdom on the ground that the spare parts or spare equipment or their installation are or is an infringement of any patent, design or model:

Provided that this subsection shall not apply in relation to any spare parts or spare equipment which are sold or distributed in the United Kingdom or are exported from the United Kingdom for sale or distribution.

(3) This section applies—

(a) to an aircraft, other than an aircraft used in military, customs or police services, registered in any country or territory in the case of which there is for the time being in force a declaration made by His Majesty by Order in Council, with a view to the fulfilment of the provisions of the Chicago Convention to which this section relates, that the benefits of those provisions apply to that country or territory, and

(b) to such other aircraft as His Majesty may by order in Council specify.[7]

(4) The provisions of the Eighth Schedule to this Act shall have effect with reference to the detention on patent claims in respect of foreign aircraft other than aircraft to which this section applies.[8]

(5) Part VI of this Act applies to this section.[9]

Income and Corporation Taxes Act 1970

PART II

ANNUAL PAYMENTS AND INTEREST

Deduction of income tax at standard rate

1736   **Payments out of profits or gains brought into charge to income tax**

52.—(2) Where—

(a) any royalty or other sum paid in respect of the user of a patent,

is paid wholly out of profits or gains brought into charge to income tax, the person making the payment shall be entitled on making the payment to deduct and retain out of it a sum representing the amount

---

[7] See Appendix, Part 3, *post.*

[8] Schedule 8 provides that a foreign aircraft is not to be detained or its passage otherwise interfered with on the ground that it infringes a patent if the owner of the aircraft deposits or secures a sum in respect of the alleged infringement.

[9] Part VI contains supplemental provisions as to Orders in Council (s. 57), detention of aircraft (s. 58), extraterritorial effect (s. 59), offences (s. 60) and savings (s. 61).

of the income tax thereon at the standard rate for the year in which the amount payable becomes due.

1737   Payments not out of profits or gains brought into charge to income tax

53.—(1) Where—

    (*b*) any royalty or other sum paid in respect of the user of a patent,

is not payable, or not wholly payable, out of profits or gains brought into charge to income tax, the person by or through whom any payment thereof is made shall, on making the payment, deduct out of it a sum representing the amount of income tax thereon at the standard rate in force at the time of the payment.

(2) Where any such payment as is mentioned in subsection (1) above is made by or through any person, that person shall forthwith deliver to the inspector an account of the payment, and shall be assessable and chargeable with income tax at the standard rate on the payment, or on so much thereof as is not made out of profits or gains brought into charge to income tax.

(3) All the provisions of the Income Tax Acts relating to persons who are to be chargeable with income tax, to income tax assessments, and to the collection and recovery of income tax, shall, so far as they are applicable, apply to the charge, assessment, collection and recovery of income tax under this section.

(4) Subsections (2) and (3) above have effect subject to the provisions of Schedule 9 to this Act with respect to the time and manner in which companies resident in the United Kingdom are to account for and pay income tax in respect of payments from which tax is deductible.

PART VI

SCHEDULE D

CHAPTER I

THE CHARGE

1738   **108.** The Schedule referred to as Schedule D is as follows:—

SCHEDULE D

1. Tax under this Schedule shall be charged in respect of—

    (*a*) the annual profits or gains arising or accruing—

        (i) to any person residing in the United Kingdom from any kind of property whatever, whether situated in the United Kingdom or elsewhere, and

        (ii) to any person residing in the United Kingdom from any trade, profession or vocation, whether carried on in the United Kingdom or elsewhere, and

        (iii) to any person, whether a British subject or not, although not resident in the United Kingdom, from any property whatever in the United Kingdom, or from any trade, profession or vocation exercised within the United Kingdom, and

CHAPTER III

CASES I TO VI: CORPORATION TAX:

BASIS OF ASSESSMENT ETC.

1739 Basis of assessment, apportionments, single assessments, and miscellaneous special provisions

129.—(1) In accordance with Part XI of this Act (company taxation), for the purposes of corporation tax for any accounting period, income shall be computed under Cases I to VI of Schedule D on the full amount of the profits or gains or income arising in the period (whether or not received in or transmitted to the United Kingdom), without any other deduction than is authorised by the Corporation Tax Acts.

1740 General rules as to deductions not allowable

130. Subject to the provisions of the Tax Acts, in computing the amount of the profits or gains to be charged under Case I or Case II of Schedule D, no sum shall be deducted in respect of—

(*n*) any royalty or other sum paid in respect of the user of a patent, or

1741 Deduction of patent etc. fees and expenses

132. Notwithstanding anything in section 130 above, in computing the profits or gains of a trade, there may be deducted as expenses any fees paid or expenses incurred—

(*a*) in obtaining, for the purposes of the trade, the grant of a patent, an extension of the term of a patent, the registration of a design or trade mark, the extension of the period of copyright in a design, or the renewal of registration of a trade mark, or

(*b*) in connection with a rejected or abandoned application for a patent made for the purposes of the trade.

CHAPTER VIII

CASE VII: INCOME TAX ON SHORT TERM CAPITAL GAINS

1742 Chargeable assets

161.—(5) Patent rights (that is to say, the right to do or authorise the doing of anything which would, but for that right, be an infringement of a patent) shall not be chargeable assets, nor shall rights to acquire in the future patent rights as respects any invention in respect of which the patent has not yet been granted.

PART XIV

MISCELLANEOUS SPECIAL PROVISIONS

CHAPTER I

PATENTS AND KNOW-HOW

Patents

1743 Writing-down allowances for capital expenditure on purchase of patent rights

378.—(1) Where a person incurs capital expenditure on the purchase of patent rights, there shall, subject to and in accordance with the following provisions of this Chapter, be made to him writing-down allowances in respect of that expenditure during the writing-down period as hereinafter defined:

Provided that no writing-down allowance shall be made to a person in respect of any expenditure unless—

(a) the allowance falls in accordance with section 385 (1) of this Act to be made to him in taxing his trade; or

(b) any income receivable by him in respect of the rights would be liable to tax.

(2) The writing-down period shall be the seventeen years beginning with the chargeable period related to the expenditure:

Provided that—

(a) where the rights are purchased for a specified period, the preceding provisions of this subsection shall have effect with the substitution for the reference to seventeen years of a reference to seventeen years or the number of years comprised within that period, whichever is the less; and

(b) where the rights purchased begin one complete year or more after the commencement of the patent and paragraph (a) of this proviso does not apply, the said provisions shall have effect with the substitution for the reference to seventeen years of a reference to seventeen years less the number of complete years which, when the rights begin, have elapsed since the commencement of the patent, or, if seventeen complete years have elapsed as aforesaid, of a reference to one year; and

(c) any expenditure incurred for the purposes of a trade by a person about to carry it on shall be treated for the purposes of this subsection as if it had been incurred by that person on the first day on which he does carry it on, unless, before the said first day, he has sold all the rights on the purchase of which the expenditure was incurred.

(3) Subsections (2) and (3) of section 75 of the Capital Allowances Act 1968 (effect of providing for writing-down allowances during a writing-down period of a specified length) shall apply to this section as they apply to the provisions specified in subsection (1) of the said section 75.

1744 Effect of lapses of patent rights, sales, etc.

379.—(1) Where a person incurs capital expenditure on the purchase of patent rights and, before the end of the writing-down period under section 378 above, any of the following events occurs, that is to say—

(a) the rights come to an end without being subsequently revived, or

(b) he sells all those rights or so much thereof as he still owns, or

(c) he sells part of those rights and the net proceeds of the sale (so far as they consist of capital sums) are not less than the amount of the capital expenditure remaining unallowed,

no writing-down allowance shall be made to that person for the chargeable period related to the event or for any subsequent chargeable period.

(2) Where a person incurs capital expenditure on the purchase of patent rights and, before the end of the writing-down period under section 378 above, either of the following events occurs, that is to say—

> (*a*) the rights come to an end without being subsequently revived, or
>
> (*b*) he sells all those rights, or so much thereof as he still owns, and the net proceeds of the sale (so far as they consist of capital sums) are less than the amount of the capital expenditure remaining unallowed,

there shall, subject to and in accordance with the following provisions of this Chapter, be made to him for the chargeable period related to the event an allowance (in this Chapter referred to as " a balancing allowance") equal, if the event is the rights coming to an end, to the amount of the capital expenditure remaining unallowed, and, if the event is a sale, to the amount of the capital expenditure remaining unallowed less the net proceeds of the sale.

1745 (3) Where a person who has incurred capital expenditure on the purchase of patent rights sells all or any part of those rights and the net proceeds of the sale (so far as they consist of capital sums) exceed the amount of the capital expenditure remaining unallowed, if any, there shall, subject to and in accordance with the following provisions of this Chapter, be made on him for the chargeable period related to the sale a charge (in this Chapter referred to as " a balancing charge ") on an amount equal to the excess or, where the amount of the capital expenditure remaining unallowed is nil, to the said net proceeds.

(4) Where a person who has incurred capital expenditure on the purchase of patent rights sells a part of those rights and subsection (3) of this section does not apply, the amount of any writing-down allowance made in respect of that expenditure for the chargeable period related to the sale or any subsequent chargeable period shall be the amount arrived at by—

> (*a*) subtracting the net proceeds of the sale (so far as they consist of capital sums) from the amount of the expenditure remaining unallowed at the time of the sale, and
>
> (*b*) dividing the result by the number of complete years of the writing-down period which remained at the beginning of the chargeable period related to the sale,

and so on for any subsequent sales.

(5) References in the preceding provisions of this section to the amount of any capital expenditure remaining unallowed shall, in relation to any event, be construed as references to the amount of that expenditure less any writing-down allowances made in respect thereof for chargeable periods before that related to the event, and less also the net proceeds of any previous sale by the person who incurred the expenditure of any part of the rights acquired by the expenditure, so far as those proceeds consist of capital sums.

(6) Notwithstanding anything in the preceding provisions of this

section, no balancing allowance shall be made in respect of any expenditure unless a writing-down allowance has been, or, but for the happening of the event giving rise to the balancing allowance, could have been, made in respect of that expenditure, and the total amount on which a balancing charge is made in respect of any expenditure shall not exceed the total writing-down allowances actually made in respect of that expenditure, less, if a balancing charge has previously been made in respect of that expenditure, the amount on which that charge was made.

1746   Taxation as income of capital sums received for sale of patent rights
380.—(1) Where a person resident in the United Kingdom sells all or any part of any patent rights and the net proceeds of the sale consist wholly or partly of a capital sum, he shall, subject to the provisions of this Chapter, be charged to tax under Case VI of Schedule D, for the chargeable period in which the sum is received by him and successive chargeable periods, being charged in each period on the same fraction of the sum as the period is of six years (or such less fraction as has not already been charged):

Provided that if that person, by notice in writing served on the inspector not later than two years after the end of the chargeable period in which the said amount was received, elects that the whole of the said sum shall be charged to tax for the said chargeable period, it shall be charged to tax accordingly. References in this subsection to tax for a chargeable period shall be construed, in relation to corporation tax, as referring to the tax for any financial year which is charged in respect of that period.

(2) Where a person not resident in the United Kingdom sells all or any part of any patent rights and the net proceeds of the sale consist wholly or partly of a capital sum, and the patent is a United Kingdom patent, then, subject to the provisions of this Chapter—

    (a) he shall be chargeable to tax in respect of that sum under Case VI of Schedule D; and

    (b) section 53 of this Act (deduction of income tax at source) shall apply to that sum as if it was an annual sum payable otherwise than out of profits or gains charged to income tax; and

    (c) all the other provisions of the Tax Acts shall, save as therein otherwise provided, have effect accordingly:

Provided that if, not later than two years after the end of the year of assessment in which the sum is paid, the person to whom it is paid, by notice in writing to the Board, elects that the said sum shall be treated for the purpose of income tax for that year and each of the five succeeding years as if one-sixth thereof, and no more, were included in his income chargeable to tax for all those years respectively, it shall be so treated, and all such repayments and assessments of tax for each of those years shall be made as are necessary to give effect to the election, so, however, that—

    (i) the election shall not affect the amount of tax which is to be deducted and assessed under the said section 53; and

    (ii) where any sum is deducted under the said section 53, any adjustments necessary to give effect to the election shall be made by way of repayment of tax; and

(iii) the said adjustments shall be made year by year and as if one-sixth of the sum deducted had been deducted in respect of tax for each year, and no repayment of, or of any part of, that portion of the tax deducted which is to be treated as deducted in respect of tax for any year shall be made unless and until it is ascertained that the tax (other than surtax) ultimately falling to be paid for that year is less than the amount of tax (other than surtax) paid for that year.

1747   (3) In subsection (2) above the word " tax " shall mean income tax, unless the seller of the patent rights, being a company, would be within the charge to corporation tax in respect of any proceeds of the sale not consisting of a capital sum; and where the subsection applies to charge a company to corporation tax in respect of a sum paid to it, the proviso shall not apply, but the company may, by notice in writing given to the Board not later than two years after the end of the accounting period in which the sum is paid, elect that the sum shall be treated as arising rateably in the accounting periods ending not later than six years from the beginning of that in which the sum is paid (being accounting periods during which the company remains within the charge to corporation tax as aforesaid), and there shall be made all such repayments of tax and assessments to tax as are necessary to give effect to any such election.

(4) Where the person selling all or any part of any patent rights acquired the rights sold, or the rights out of which they were granted, by purchase and the price paid by him consisted wholly or partly of a capital sum, the preceding provisions of this section shall apply as if any capital sum received by him when he sells the rights were reduced by the amount of that sum:

Provided that—

    (*a*) where between the said purchase and the said sale he has sold part of the rights acquired by him and the net proceeds of that sale consist wholly or partly of a capital sum, the amount of the reduction falling to be made under this subsection in respect of the subsequent sale shall be itself reduced by the amount of that sum;

    (*b*) nothing in this subsection shall affect the amount of income tax which is to be deducted and assessed under section 53 of this Act by virtue of subsection (2) of this section, and, where any sum is deducted under that section, any adjustment necessary to give effect to the provisions of this subsection shall be made by way of repayment of tax.

(5) A claim for relief under this section shall be made to the Board.

1748   **Capital sums: death, winding up or partnership change**

381.—(1) Where a person on whom, by reason of the receipt of a capital sum, a charge falls or would otherwise fall to be made under section 380 above dies or, being a body corporate, commences to be wound up—

    (*a*) no sums shall be charged under the said section on that person for any chargeable period subsequent to that in which the death takes place or the winding up commences; and (*b*) the amount falling to be charged for the chargeable period in which the death occurs or the winding up commences shall be increased by the total amounts which, but for the death or winding up, would have fallen to be charged for subsequent chargeable periods;

provided that, in the case of a death the personal representatives may, by notice in writing served on the inspector not later than thirty days after notice has been served on them of the charge falling to be made by virtue of this subsection require that the income tax (including surtax) payable out of the estate of the deceased by reason of the increase provided for by this subsection shall be reduced so as not to exceed the total amount of income tax (including surtax) which would have been payable by him out of his estate by reason of the operation of section 380 above in relation to that sum, if, instead of the amount falling to be charged for the year in which the death occurs being increased by the whole amount of the sums charged for subsequent years, the several amounts falling to be charged for the years beginning with that in which the capital sum was received and ending with that in which the death occurred had each been increased by the said whole amount divided by the number of those years.

(2) Where, under section 79 of the Capital Allowances Act 1968 as applied by section 387 below, a charge under section 380 above falls to be made on two or more persons jointly as being the persons for the time being carrying on a trade, and that trade is discontinued, subsection (1) above shall have effect in relation to the discontinuance as it has effect where a body corporate commences to be wound up:

Provided that—

(*a*) the additional sum which, under subsection (1) above, falls to be charged for the chargeable period in which the discontinuance occurs shall be apportioned among the members of the partnership immediately before the discontinuance, according to their respective interests in the partnership profits before the discontinuance, and each partner (or, if he is dead, his personal representatives) shall be charged separately for his proportion; and

(*b*) each partner, or, if he is dead, his personal representatives, shall have the same right to require a reduction of the total income tax (including surtax) payable by him or out of his estate by reason of the increase as would have been exercisable by the personal representatives under subsection (1) above in the case of a death, and the proviso to that subsection shall have effect accordingly, but as if references to the amount of income tax (including surtax) which would have been payable by the deceased or out of his estate in the event therein mentioned were a reference to the amount of income tax (including surtax) which would in that event have fallen to be paid or borne by the partner in question or out of his estate.

(3) In this section, any references to the income tax (including surtax) paid or borne or payable or falling to be paid or borne by a person include, in cases where the income of a wife is deemed to be income of the husband, references to the income tax (including surtax)

paid or borne, or payable or falling to be paid or borne, by his wife or her husband, as the case may be.

1749 Relief for expenses

    382.—(1) Where—

        (*a*) a person, otherwise than for the purposes of a trade carried on by him, pays any fees or incurs any expenses in connection with the grant or maintenance of a patent, or the obtaining of an extension of a term of a patent, or a rejected or abandoned application for a patent, and

        (*b*) those fees or expenses would, if they had been paid or incurred for the purposes of a trade, have been allowable as a deduction in estimating the profits or gains thereof,

there shall be made to him, for the chargeable period in which those expenses were paid or incurred, an allowance equal to the amount thereof.

    (2) Where a patent is granted in respect of any invention, an allowance equal to so much of the net amount of any expenses incurred by an individual who, whether alone or in conjunction with any other person, actually devised the invention as is properly ascribable to the devising thereof (not being expenses in respect of which, or of assets representing which, an allowance falls to be made under any other provision of the Income Tax Acts) shall be made to that individual for the year of assessment in which the expenses were incurred.

1750 Patent income to be earned income in certain cases

    383. Any income from patent rights arising to an individual where the patent was granted for an invention actually devised by him, whether alone or jointly with any other person, shall be treated for all purposes as earned income:

    Provided that where any part of the rights in question or of any rights out of which they were granted has at any time belonged to any other person, so much only of the said income shall be treated as earned income as is not properly attributable to the rights which have belonged to that other person.

1751 Spreading of patent royalties over several years

    384.—(1) Where a royalty or other sum to which section 52 or 53 of this Act (deduction of income tax at standard rate) applies is paid in respect of the user of a patent, and that user extended over a period of six complete years or more, the person receiving the payment may on the making of a claim require that the income tax (including surtax) or corporation tax payable by him by reason of the receipt of that sum shall be reduced so as not to exceed the total amount of income tax (including surtax) or corporation tax which would have been payable by him if that royalty or sum had been paid in six equal instalments at yearly intervals, the last of which was paid on the date on which the payment was in fact made.

    (2) Subsection (1) of this section shall apply in relation to a royalty or other sum where the period of the user is two complete years or more but less than six complete years as it applies to the royalties and sums mentioned in that subsection, but with the substitution for

the reference to six equal instalments of a reference to so many equal instalments as there are complete years comprised in that period.

(3) In this section, any reference to the income tax (including surtax) payable by a person includes, in cases where the income of a wife is deemed to be the income of the husband, references to the income tax (including surtax) payable by his wife or her husband, as the case may be.

(4) Nothing in this section shall apply to any sum to which section 53 of this Act applies by virtue of section 380 (2) (b) above.

1752   Manner of making allowances and charges

385.—(1) An allowance or charge under section 378 or section 379 of this Act shall be made to or on a person in taxing his trade if—

    (a) he is carrying on a trade the profits or gains of which are, or, if there were any, would be, chargeable to tax under Case I of Schedule D for the chargeable period for which the allowance or charge is made, and

    (b) at any time in that chargeable period or its basis period the patent rights in question, or other rights out of which they were granted, were or were to be used for the purposes of that trade.

(2) Where an allowance falls to be made to a person for any year of assessment under section 378, 379 or 382 of this Act as those provisions apply for the purposes of income tax, and the allowance is not to be made in taxing a trade—

    (a) the amount of the allowance shall be deducted from or set off against his income from patents for that year of assessment, and

    (b) if the amount to be allowed is greater than the amount of his income from patents for that year of assessment, the balance shall be deducted from or set off against his income from patents for the next year of assessment, and so on for subsequent years of assessment, and tax shall be discharged or repaid accordingly.

Relief shall be given under this subsection on the making of a claim.

(3) Where an allowance falls to be made to a company for any accounting period under section 378, 379 or 382 of this Act as those provisions apply for the purposes of corporation tax, and is not to be made in taxing a trade—

    (a) the allowance shall, as far as may be, be given effect by deducting the amount of the allowance from the company's income from patents of the accounting period,

    (b) where the allowance cannot be given full effect under paragraph (a) above in that period by reason of a want or deficiency of income from patents, then (so long as the company remains within the charge to corporation tax) the amount unallowed shall be carried forward to the succeeding accounting period, and shall be treated for the purposes of paragraph (a) above, and of any further application of this paragraph, as the amount of a corresponding allowance for that period.

[609]

(4) Effect shall be given to any balancing charge under section 379 of this Act which is not to be made in taxing a trade—
  (a) if a charge to income tax, by making the charge under Case VI of Schedule D,
  (b) if a charge to corporation tax, by treating the amount on which the charge is to be made as income from patents.

1753   Application of Capital Allowances Act 1968

387.—(1) The Tax Acts shall have effect as if this Chapter were contained in Part I of the Capital Allowances Act 1968, and any reference in the Tax Acts to any capital allowance to be given " by way of discharge or repayment of tax and to be available or available primarily against a specified class of income " shall include a reference to any capital allowance given in accordance with subsection (2) or subsection (3) of section 385 above.

(2) In the said Part I as so applied to patent rights, the sum referred to in pargraph 4 (1) (a) of Schedule 7 to the said Act (special provisions as to controlled sales) is the amount of any capital expenditure on the acquisition of the patent rights remaining unallowed, computed in accordance with the provisions of section 379 of this Act.

(3) The reference in section 82 (1) of the Capital Allowances Act 1968 (certain payments not to be treated as capital expenditure) to any expenditure or sum in the case of which a deduction of income tax falls or may fall to be made under Part II of this Act does not include a sum in the case of which such a deduction falls or may fall to be so made by virtue of section 380 (2) (b) above.

(4) In Part I of the Capital Allowances Act 1968 as so applied to know-how—
  (a) references in that Part to property and its purchase or sale include references to know-how and its acquisition or disposal,
  (b) section 78, with Schedule 7 to the Act (special provisions as to controlled sales), shall be omitted.

1754   Interpretation of provisions about patents

388.—(1) In this Chapter—
  " income from patents " means—
      (a) any royalty or other sum paid in respect of the user of a patent; and
      (b) any amount on which tax is payable for any chargeable period by virtue of section 379 (3), section 380 or section 381 of this Act;
  " the commencement of the patent " means, in relation to a patent, the date as from which the patent rights become effective;
  " patent rights " means the right to do or authorise the doing of anything which would, but for that right, be an infringement of a patent;
  " United Kingdom patent " means a patent granted under the laws of the United Kingdom.

(2) In this Chapter, any reference to the sale of part of patent

rights includes a reference to the grant of a licence in respect of the patent in question, and any reference to the purchase of patent rights includes a reference to the acquisition of a licence in respect of a patent:

Provided that if a licence granted by a person entitled to any patent rights is a licence to exercise those rights to the exclusion of the grantor and all other persons for the whole of the remainder of the term for which the rights subsist, the grantor shall be treated for the purposes of this Chapter as thereby selling the whole of the rights.

(3) Where, under sections 46 to 49 of the Patents Act 1949 or any corresponding provisions of the law of any country outside the United Kingdom, an invention which is the subject of a patent is made, used, or exercised or vended by or for the service of the Crown or the government of the country concerned, the provisions of this Chapter shall have effect as if the making, user, exercise or vending of the invention had taken place in pursuance of a licence, and any sums paid in respect thereof shall be treated accordingly.

(4) Expenditure incurred on or after 9th July 1952 (the commencement of the Finance Act 1952) in obtaining a right to acquire in the future patent rights as respects any invention in respect of which the patent has not yet been granted shall be deemed for all the purposes of this Chapter to be expenditure on the purchase of patent rights, and if the patent rights are subsequently acquired the expenditure shall be deemed for those purposes to have been expenditure on the purchase of those rights.

(5) Any sum received from a person which by virtue of subsection (4) above is deemed to be expenditure incurred by him on the purchase of patent rights shall be deemed to be proceeds of a sale of patent rights.

[The next paragraph is 1854]

PART 3

1854 **International Convention for the Protection of Industrial Property**

THE International Convention for the Protection of Industrial Property was signed at Paris on March 20, 1883, and revised at Brussels on December 14, 1900, at Washington on June 2, 1911, at The Hague on November 6, 1925, at London on June 2, 1934, and lastly at Lisbon on October 31, 1958.

The text reproduced below indicates the amendments made in the London text by the recent Lisbon Conference. Deletions are shown in brackets in italic type and additions in heavy type. Some explanatory notes by the United Kingdom delegates to the Lisbon Conference have been added.

The text of the Convention is in the French language. The translation used here, though largely agreed at Lisbon by a number of delegates from the English-speaking countries, is not the official translation referred to in Article 19, which has yet to be established.

ARTICLE 1

1855 (1) The countries to which the present Convention applies constitute themselves into a Union for the protection of industrial property.

(2) The protection of industrial property is concerned with patents, utility models, industrial designs, trademarks, **service marks,** trade names, and indications of source or appellations of origin, and the repression of unfair competition.

(3) Industrial property shall be understood in the broadest sense and shall apply not only to industry and commerce proper, but likewise to agricultural and extractive industries and to all manufactured or natural products; for example, wines, grain, tobacco leaf, fruit, cattle, minerals, mineral waters, beer, flowers, and flour.

(4) The term " patents " shall include the various kinds of industrial patents recognised by the laws of the countries of the Union, such as patents of importation, patents of improvement, patents and certificates of addition, etc.

ARTICLE 2

1856 (1) Nationals of each of the countries of the Union shall, as regards the protection of industrial property, enjoy in all the other countries of the Union the advantages that their respective laws now grant, or may hereafter grant, to their own nationals, without prejudice to the rights specially provided by the present Convention. Consequently, they shall have the same protection as the latter, and the same legal remedy against any infringement of their rights, provided they observe the conditions and formalities imposed upon nationals.

(2) However, no condition as to the possession of a domicile or establishment in the country where protection is claimed may be required of persons entitled to the benefits of the Union for the enjoyment of any industrial property rights.

(3) The provisions of the laws of each of the countries of the

Union relating to judicial and administrative procedure and competence, and to the choice of domicile or the designation of an agent, which may be required by the laws on industrial property, are expressly reserved.

ARTICLE 3

1857   Nationals of countries not forming part of the Union, who are domiciled or who have real and effective industrial or commercial establishments in the territory of one of the countries of the Union, are treated in the same manner as nationals of the countries of the Union.

ARTICLE 4

1858   A.—(1) A person who has duly filed an application for a patent, or for the registration of a utility model, or of an industrial design, or of a trademark, in one of the countries of the Union, or his successors in title, shall enjoy, for the purpose of filing in other countries, a right of priority during the periods hereinafter stated.

(2) Every filing that is equivalent to a regular national filing under the domestic law of any country of the Union or under *international* **bilateral or multilateral** treaties concluded between several countries of the Union shall be recognised as giving rise to a right of priority.

(3) **By a regular national filing is meant any filing that is adequate to establish the date on which the application was filed in the country concerned, whatever may be the outcome of the application.**

B. Consequently, the subsequent filing in any of the other countries of the Union before the expiration of those periods shall not be invalidated through any acts accomplished in the interval, as, for instance, by another filing, by publication or exploitation of the invention, by the putting on sale of copies of the design or model, or by use of the mark, and these acts cannot give rise to any right of third parties, or of any personal possession. Rights acquired by third parties before the date of the first application which serves as the basis for the right of priority are reserved under the domestic legislation of each country of the Union.

C.—(1) The above-mentioned periods of priority shall be twelve months for patents and utility models, and six months for industrial designs and for trademarks.

(2) These periods shall start from the date of filing of the first application; the day of filing shall not be included in the period.

(3) If the last day of the period is an official holiday, or a day when the Office is not open for the filing of applications in the country where protection is claimed, the period shall be extended until the first following working day.

(4) **A subsequent application for the same subject as a previous application filed in the same country of the Union shall be considered as a first application within the meaning of paragraph (2), the filing date of which shall be the starting-point of the period of priority, provided that, at the time of filing the subsequent application, the previous application has been withdrawn, abandoned or refused, without being open to public inspection and without leaving any rights**

outstanding, and has not served as a basis for claiming **a right of priority. The previous application may not thereafter serve as a basis for claiming a right of priority.**

1859   D.—(1) Any person desiring to take advantage of the priority of a previous filing shall be required to make a declaration indicating the date of such filing and the country in which it was made. Each country will determine the latest permissible date for making such declaration.

(2) These particulars shall be mentioned in the publications issued by the competent authority, and in particular in the patents and the specifications relating thereto.

(3) The countries of the Union may require any person making a declaration of priority to produce a copy of the application (specification, drawings, etc.) previously filed. The copy, certified as correct by the authority which received the application, shall not require any authentication, and may in any case be filed, without fee, at any time within three months of the filing of the subsequent application. They may require it to be accompanied by a certificate from the same authority showing the date of filing, and by a translation.

(4) No other formalities may be required for the declaration of priority at the time of filing the application. Each of the countries of the Union shall decide what consequences shall follow the omission of the formalities prescribed by the present Article, but such consequences shall in no case go beyond the loss of the right of priority.

(5) Subsequently, further proof may be required.

A person who avails himself of the priority of a previously filed application shall be required to specify the number of that application, which shall be published under the conditions provided for by paragraph (2) above.

E.—(1) Where an industrial design is filed in a country by virtue of a right of priority based on the filing of a utility model, the period of priority shall be only that fixed for industrial designs.

(2) Furthermore, it is permissible to file a utility model in a country by virtue of a right of priority based on the filing of a patent application, and vice versa.

F. No country of the Union may refuse **a priority or** an application for a patent on the ground that *it contains multiple priority claims* **the applicant claims multiple priorities, even originating in different countries, or on the ground that an application claiming one or more priorities contains one or more elements that were not included in the original application or applications whose priority is claimed,** provided that, **in both cases,** there is unity of invention within the meaning of the law of the country.

With respect to the elements not included in the original application or applications whose priority is claimed, the filing of the later application shall give rise to a right of priority under the usual conditions.

1860   G.—(1) If examination reveals that an application for a patent contains more than one invention, the applicant may divide the application into a certain number of divisional applications and preserve as the date of each the date of the initial application, and the benefit of the right of priority, if any.

(2) The applicant may also, on his own initiative, divide a patent application while preserving as the date of each divisional application the date of the initial application and the benefit of the right of priority, if any. Each country of the Union shall have the right to determine the conditions under which such division shall be authorised.

H. Priority may not be refused on the ground that certain elements of the invention for which priority is claimed do not appear among the claims formulated in the application in the country of origin, provided that the application documents as a whole specifically disclose such elements.

[The change in para. A (2) is of little, if any, importance in the United Kingdom.

Para. A (3) makes it clear that a claim to Convention priority may be based on a first application which has been refused provided that when filed it was adequate to establish a filing date.

Para. C (4) allows priority to be based on a second application but only in the conditions set out.

Para. D (5) will make it easier to trace the various countries in which protection for any given invention is sought or granted.

Para. F sets out more clearly what was the intention of the London text and gives to inventors rights in relation to " partial " as well as " multiple " priorities.

Para. G (2) increases the inventor's rights with regard to dividing his patent application on his own initiative.

All these changes except that at D (5) accord with existing United Kingdom law and practice. The change in D (5) will involve a change in the Patents Rules, 1958.]

ARTICLE 4*bis*

1861
(1) Patents applied for in the various countries of the Union by persons entitled to the benefits of the Union shall be independent of patents obtained for the same invention in other countries, whether members of the Union or not.

(2) This provision is not to be understood in a restricted sense; in particular, it is to be understood to mean that patents applied for during the period of priority are independent, both as regards the grounds for invalidation and for revocation and as regards their normal duration.

(3) The provision shall apply to all patents existing at the time when it comes into effect.

(4) Similarly, it shall apply, in the case of the accession of new countries, to patents in existence on either side at the time of accession.

(5) Patents obtained with the benefit of priority shall have in the various countries of the Union a duration equal to that which they would have had if they had been applied for or granted without the benefit of priority.

ARTICLE 4*ter*

1862
The inventor shall have the right to be mentioned as such in the patent.

Article 4quater

1863   **The grant of a patent shall not be refused and a patent shall not be invalidated on the ground that the sale of the patented product or of a product obtained by means of the patented process is subject to restrictions or limitations resulting from the domestic law.**

[This obliges the member countries to grant patents notwithstanding that the domestic law imposes limitations or restrictions on the sale of the patented articles, *e.g.*, when the state has a monopoly in the articles in question.]

ARTICLE 5

1864   A.—(1) The importation by the patentee into the country where the patent has been granted of articles manufactured in any of the countries of the Union shall not entail revocation of the patent.

(2) [*Nevertheless,*] Each country of the Union shall have the right to take [*the necessary*] legislative measures **providing for the granting of compulsory licences** to prevent the abuses which might result from the exercise of the exclusive rights conferred by the patent, for example, failure to work.

(3) [*These measures shall not provide for the revocation of the patent unless the grant of compulsory licences is insufficient*] **Revocation of the patent shall not be provided for except in cases where the granting of compulsory licences would not have been sufficient to prevent such abuses. No proceeding for the cancellation or revocation of a patent may be instituted before the expiration of two years from the granting of the first compulsory licence.**

(4) [*In any case*] An application for a compulsory licence **on the ground of failure to work or insufficient working** may not be made before the expiration of [*three years from the date of issue of the patent*] **a period of four years from the date of filing of the patent application or three years from the date of the grant of the patent, whichever period last expires; it shall be refused if the patentee justifies his inaction** [*and this licence may be granted only if the patentee fails to justify himself*] by legitimate reasons. [*No proceedings for the revocation of a patent may be instituted before the expiration of two years from the date of the granting of the first compulsory licence.*] **Such a compulsory licence shall be non-exclusive and shall not be transferable, even in the form of the grant of a sub-licence, except with that part of the enterprise or goodwill using such licence.**

(5) The foregoing provisions shall be applicable, mutatis mutandis, to utility models.

B. The protection of industrial designs shall not, under any circumstances, be liable to revocation either by reason of failure to work or by reason of the importation of articles corresponding to those which are protected.

C.—(1) If, in any country, the use of a registered trademark is compulsory, the registration shall not be cancelled until after a reasonable period, and then only if the person concerned cannot justify his inaction.

(2) The use of a trademark by the proprietor in a form differing in features which do not alter the distinctive character of the mark in the form in which it was registered in one of the countries of the

Union, shall not entail invalidation of the registration and shall not diminish the protection granted to the mark.

(3) The concurrent use of the same mark on identical or similar goods by industrial or commercial establishments considered as co-proprietors of the mark according to the provisions of the national law of the country where protection is claimed shall not prevent the registration or diminish in any way the protection granted to the mark in any country of the Union, provided the use does not result in misleading the public and is not contrary to the public interest.

D. No indication or mention of the patent, of the utility model, of the registration of the trademark, or of the deposit of the industrial design shall be required upon the product as a condition of recognition of the right to protection.

[(1) A new time limit (4 years from the date of application) is imposed on the grant of compulsory licences for failure to work a patent.

(2) It is made clear that the time limits imposed relate only to compulsory licences or revocation *on the grounds* of non-working.

(3) These compulsory licences must be non-exclusive and generally non-transferable.

Changes (1) and (3) above will, in practice, make little difference in the United Kingdom.]

ARTICLE 5*bis*

1865   (1) A period of grace of not less than [*three*] **six** months shall be allowed for the payment of the prescribed fees for the maintenance of industrial property rights, subject to the payment of a surcharge, if the domestic law so provides.

(2) [*In the case of patents,*] The countries of the Union [*further undertake, either to increase the above mentioned extension of time to not less than six months or*] **shall have the right** to provide for the restoration of [*a patent*] **patents** which [*has*] **have** lapsed by reason of non-payment of fees. [*Subject to the conditions prescribed by the domestic legislation.*]

[The change in para. (1) will involve legislation to amend section 22 of the Patents Act, 1949.]

ARTICLE 5*ter*

1866   In each of the countries of the Union the following shall not be considered as infringements of the rights of a patentee:

    1. The use on board vessels of other countries of the Union of devices forming the subject of his patent in the body of the vessel, in the machinery, tackle, gear and other accessories, when such vessels temporarily or accidentally enter the waters of a country, provided that such devices are used there exclusively for the needs of the vessel.

    2. The use of devices forming the subject of the patent in the construction or operation of aircraft or land vehicles of other countries of the Union, or of accessories to such aircraft or land vehicles, when those aircraft or land vehicles temporarily or accidentally enter the country.

Article 5quater

1867   **When a product is imported into a country of the Union where there exists a patent protecting a process of manufacture of the said**

[617]

product, the patentee shall have all the rights, with regard to the imported product, as are accorded to him by the domestic law of the country of importation, on the basis of the process patent, with respect to products manufactured in that country.

[This new provision involves no change in United Kingdom law.]

Article 5quinquies

1868   Industrial designs shall be protected in all the countries of the Union.

Article 6

1869   (1) The conditions for the filing and registration of trade marks shall be determined in each country of the Union by its domestic law.

(2) However, an application for the registration of a trademark filed by a national of country of the Union in any country of the Union may not be refused nor may a registration be cancelled on the ground that filing, registration or renewal has not been effected in the country of origin.

(3) A mark duly registered in a country of the Union shall be regarded as independent of marks registered in the other countries of the Union, including the country of origin. [Compare old Art. 6D.]

[This new Article deals with the generality of marks. Most of the provisions of the old Article 6 relating to " telle quelle " marks are now in a new Article 6*quinquies*.]

ARTICLE 6*bis*

1870   (1) The countries of the Union undertake, either administratively if their legislation so permits, or at the request of an interested party, to refuse or to cancel the registration **and to prohibit the use** of a trademark which constitutes a reproduction, imitation or translation liable to create confusion with a mark considered by the competent authority of the country of registration **or use** to be well-known in that country as being already the mark of a person entitled to the benefits of the present Convention and used for identical or similar goods. These provisions shall also apply when the essential part of the mark constitutes a reproduction of any such well-known mark or an imitation liable to create confusion therewith.

(2) A period of at least [*three*] five years from the date of registration shall be allowed for seeking the cancellation of such a mark. **The countries of the Union have the right to provide for a period within which the prohibition of use must be sought.**

(3) No time limit shall be fixed for seeking the cancellation **or the prohibition of the use** of marks registered **or used** in bad faith.

[The amendments give the owner of a " well-known " mark the right to claim prohibition of the use, as well as the cancellation of the registration, of confusingly similar marks. This remedy is available in the United Kingdom by means of a " passing off " action at common law.]

ARTICLE 6*ter*

1871   (1) **(a)** The countries of the Union agree to refuse or to cancel the registration, and to prohibit by appropriate measures the use, without authorisation by the competent authorities, either as trademarks or as elements of trademarks, of armorial bearings, flags and other State emblems of the countries of the Union, official signs and hall-marks indicating control or warranty adopted by them and all imitations thereof from a heraldic point of view.

(b) The provisions of sub-paragraph (a) of this paragraph apply equally to armorial bearings, flags and other emblems, abbreviations or titles of international intergovernmental organisations of which one or more countries of the Union are members, with the exception of armorial bearings, flags and other emblems, abbreviations or titles that are already the subject of existing international agreements intended to ensure their protection.

(c) No country of the Union shall be required to apply the provisions of sub-paragraph (b) of this paragraph to the prejudice of the owners of rights acquired in good faith before the entry into force in that country of the present Convention. The countries of the Union shall not be required to apply the said provisions when the use or registration covered by paragraph (a) is not of such a nature as to suggest to the public that a connection exists between the organisation concerned and the armorial bearings, flags, emblems, abbreviations or titles, or if such use or registration is clearly not of a nature to mislead the public as to the existence of a connection between the user and the organisation.

(2) The prohibition of the use of official signs and hall-marks indicating control or warranty shall apply solely in cases where the marks which contain them are intended to be used on goods of the same or a similar kind.

1872 (3) **(a)** For the application of these provisions the countries of the Union agree to communicate reciprocally, through the International Bureau, the list of State emblems and official signs and hall-marks indicating control or warranty which they desire, or may thereafter desire, to place wholly or within certain limits under the protection of the present Article and all subsequent modifications of this list. Each country of the Union shall in due course make available to the public the lists so communicated.

However, this communication is not compulsory so far as the flags of States are concerned.

(b) The provisions of sub-paragraph (b) of paragraph 1 of this Article shall only apply to armorial bearings, flags and other emblems, abbreviations or titles of international intergovernmental organisations that the latter have communicated to the countries of the Union through the International Bureau.

(4) Any country of the Union may, within a period of twelve months from the receipt of the communication, transmit through the International Bureau its objections, if any, to the country **or international intergovernmental organisation concerned.**

(5) In the case of State [*emblems*] **flags,** [*which are well known,*] the measures prescribed by paragraph 1 shall apply solely to marks registered after November 6, 1925.

(6) In the case of State emblems [*which are not well known*] **other than flags,** and of official signs and hall-marks **of the countries of the Union and in the case of armorial bearings, flags and other emblems, abbreviations or titles of international intergovernmental**

organisations, these provisions shall be applicable only to marks registered more than two months after the receipt of the communication provided for in paragraph 3 above.

(7) In cases of bad faith the countries shall have the right to cancel the registration of marks that contain State emblems, signs or hall-marks even though registered before November 6, 1925.

(8) Nationals of each country who are authorised to make use of State emblems, signs or hall-marks of their country, may use them even though they are similar to those of another country.

(9) The countries of the Union undertake to prohibit the unauthorised use in trade of the State armorial bearings of the other countries of the Union, when the use is of such a nature as to be misleading as to the origin of the goods.

(10) The above provisions shall not prevent the countries from exercising the power given in paragraph (3) of Article 6quinquies B, to refuse or to cancel the registration of marks containing, without authorisation, the armorial bearings, flags, [*decorations*,] and other State emblems or official signs or hall-marks adopted by a country of the Union **as well as the distinctive signs of international inter-governmental organisations mentioned in paragraph (1) of this Article.**

[This Article now allows for the protection of the emblems of international inter-governmental organisations (such as the United Nations) as well as State emblems. " Flags of State " are now protected without the necessity of their being notified through the International Bureau to member countries.]

ARTICLE 6*quater*

1873   (1) When, in accordance with the law of a country of the Union, the assignment of a mark is valid only if it takes place at the same time as the transfer of the business or goodwill to which the mark belongs, it shall suffice for its validity in this respect if the portion of the business or goodwill situated in that country, together with the exclusive right to manufacture or sell in that country the goods bearing the mark assigned, is transferred to the assignee.

(2) This provision does not impose upon the countries of the Union any obligation to regard as valid the assignment of any mark the use of which by the assignee would, in fact, be of such a nature as to mislead the public, particularly as regards the origin, nature or material qualities of the goods to which the mark is applied.

Article 6quinquies

1874   A.—(1) Every trademark duly registered in the country of origin shall be accepted for filing and protected in its original form in the other countries of the Union, subject to the reservations indicated [*below*] **in the present Article.** These countries may, before proceeding to final registration, require production of a certificate of registration in the country of origin, issued by the competent authority. No authentication shall be required for this certificate. [Formerly Article 6A.]

(2) The country of the Union where the applicant has a real and effective industrial or commercial establishment, or, if he has not such an establishment **within the Union,** the Union country where he

has his domicile or, if he has no domicile in the Union, the country of his nationality if he is a national of a Union country, shall be considered his country of origin. [Formerly Article 6C.]

B. [*Registration of the following may be refused or cancelled:*—]

Trademarks under the present Article may not be denied registration or cancelled except in the following cases:

1. [*Marks which*] **When they** are of such a nature as to infringe rights acquired by third parties in the country where protection is claimed;

2. [*Marks which*] **When they** have no distinctive character, or consist exclusively of signs or indications which may serve in trade to designate the kind, quality, quantity, intended purpose, value, place of origin of the goods or time of production, or which have become customary in the current language or in the bona fide and established practices of the trade in the country where protection is sought. [*In arriving at a decision as to the distinctive character of a mark, all the circumstances of the case must be taken into account, including the length of time during which the mark has been in use.*]

3. [*Marks which*] **When they** are contrary to morality or public order and, in particular, of such a nature as to deceive the public. It is understood that a mark may not be considered contrary to public order for the sole reason that it does not conform to a provision of the law relating to trademarks, except where such provision itself relates to public order. [Formerly Article 6B.]

The above is, however, subject to Article 10bis.

1875   C.—**(1)** [*In arriving at a decision as to the distinctive character of a mark.*] **In determining whether a mark is eligible for protection,** all the circumstances of the case must be taken into consideration, particularly the length of time the mark has been in use. [Formerly Article 6B—1 (2).]

(2) Registration of trademarks shall not be refused in the other countries of the Union for the sole reason that they differ from the marks protected in the country of origin only in respect of elements that do not alter their distinctive character and do not affect the identity of the marks in the form in which they are registered in the said country of origin. [Formerly Article 6B—2.]

D. [*When a trademark has been duly registered in the country of origin and then in one or several other countries of the Union, each of these national marks shall be considered, as from the date of its registration, as independent of the mark in the country of origin, provided it conforms to the domestic laws of the country of importation.*] [Formerly Article 6D.]

D. No person may benefit from the provisions of the present Article unless the mark for which he claims protection is and remains registered in the country of origin.

E. **However,** in no case shall the renewal of the registration of a mark in the country of origin involve the obligation to renew the registration in the other Union countries where the mark has been registered. [Formerly Article 6E.]

F. The benefits of priority shall be accorded to applications for the registration of marks filed within the period fixed by Article 4, even when registration in the country of origin does not occur until after the expiration of such period. [Formerly Article 6F.]

[This Article deals with what are known as "telle quelle" marks. It contains most of the provisions of the old Article 6.]

Article 6sexies

1876   **The countries of the Union undertake to protect service marks. They shall not be required to provide for the registration of such marks.**

[The remedies available in the United Kingdom under the common law ensure compliance with this Article.]

Article 6septies

1877   **(1) If the agent or representative of the person who is the proprietor of a mark in one of the countries of the Union applies, without such proprietor's authorisation, for the registration of the mark in his own name in one or more Union countries, the proprietor shall be entitled to oppose the registration applied for or seek cancellation or, if the law of the country so allows, seek assignment in his favour of the said registration, unless such agent or representative justifies his action.**

(2) The proprietor of the mark shall, subject to the reservations of paragraph (1) above, be entitled to oppose the use of the mark by his agent or representative if he has not authorised such use.

(3) Domestic laws may provide an equitable time limit within which the proprietor of a mark must claim the rights provided for in the present Article.

ARTICLE 7

1878   The nature of the goods to which a trademark is to be applied shall in no case form an obstacle to the registration of the mark.

ARTICLE 7*bis*

1879   (1) The countries of the Union undertake to accept for filing and to protect collective marks belonging to associations the existence of which is not contrary to the law of the country of origin, even if such associations do not possess an industrial or commercial establishment.

(2) Each country shall be the judge of the particular conditions under which a collective mark shall be protected and may refuse protection if the mark is contrary to the public interest.

(3) Nevertheless, the protection of these marks shall not be refused to any association the existence of which is not contrary to the law of the country of origin, on the ground that such association is not established in the country where protection is sought or is not constituted according to the law of the latter country.

ARTICLE 8

1880   A trade name shall be protected in all the countries of the Union without the necessity of filing or registration, whether or not it forms part of a trademark.

ARTICLE 9

1881 (1) All goods illegally bearing a trademark or trade name shall be seized on importation into those countries of the Union where such mark or name has a right to legal protection.

(2) Seizure shall likewise be effected in the country where the mark or name was illegally applied or in the country into which the goods bearing it have been imported.

(3) Seizure shall take place at the request either of the public prosecutor or of any other competent authority or of any interested party, whether a natural or a juridical person, in conformity with the domestic law of each country.

(4) The authorities shall not be bound to effect seizure in transit.

(5) If the law of a country does not permit seizure on importation, such seizure shall be replaced by prohibition of importation or by seizure within such country.

(6) If the law of a country permits neither seizure on importation nor prohibition of importation nor seizure within the country, then, until such time as the law is modified accordingly, these measures shall be replaced by the actions and remedies available in such cases to nationals under the law of such country.

ARTICLE 10

1882 (1) The provisions of the preceding Article shall apply [*to all goods which falsely bear as an indication of origin the name of a specified locality or country, when such indication is joined to a trade name of a fictitious character or used with fraudulent intention*] **in cases of direct or indirect use of a false indication of the origin of the product or the identity of the producer, manufacturer or trader.**

(2) Any producer, manufacturer, trader, whether a natural or juridical person, engaged in the production of, or trade in such goods and established either in the locality falsely indicated as the place of origin, in the district where the locality is situated, or in the country falsely indicated, or in the country where the false indication of origin is used, shall in any case be deemed an interested party.

[This considerably strengthens the provisions forbidding the use of false indications of origin.]

ARTICLE 10*bis*

1883 (1) The countries of the Union are bound to assure to persons entitled to the benefits of the Union effective protection against unfair competition.

(2) Any act of competition contrary to honest practices in industrial or commercial matters constitutes an act of unfair competition.

(3) The following in particular shall be prohibited:
1. all acts of such a nature as to create confusion by any means whatever with the establishment, the goods, or the industrial or commercial activities of a competitor;
2. false allegations in the course of trade which are of such a nature as to discredit the establishment, the goods, or the industrial or commercial activities of a competitor.

3. Indications or allegations the use of which in the course of trade is liable to mislead the public as to the nature, the manufacturing process, the characteristics, the suitability for their purpose or the quality of the goods.

[The new sub-para. 3 prohibits a number of the false trade descriptions punishable under the United Kingdom Merchandise Marks Act, 1887–1953.]

ARTICLE 10*ter*

1884   (1) The countries of the Union undertake to provide nationals of the other countries of the Union with appropriate legal remedies to repress effectively all the acts referred to in Articles 9, 10 and 10bis.

(2) They undertake, further, to provide measures to permit syndicates and associations which represent the industrialists, producers or traders concerned and the existence of which is not contrary to the laws of their country, to take action in the Courts or before the administrative authorities, with a view to the repression of the acts referred to in Articles 9, 10 and 10bis, in so far as the law of the country in which protection is claimed allows such action by the syndicates and associations of that country.

ARTICLE 11

1885   (1) The countries of the Union shall in conformity with their domestic law, grant temporary protection to patentable inventions, utility models, industrial designs, and trademarks, in respect of goods exhibited at official, or officially recognised, international exhibitions held in the territory of one of them.

(2) This temporary protection shall not extend the periods provided by Article 4. If later the right of priority is invoked, each country may provide that the period shall start from the date of introduction of the goods into the exhibition.

(3) Each country may require, as proof of the identity of the article exhibited and of the date of its introduction, such evidence as it considers necessary.

ARTICLE 12

1886   (1) Each of the countries of the Union undertakes to establish a special government agency for industrial property and a central office for the communication to the public of patents, utility models, industrial designs, and trademarks.

(2) This agency shall publish an official periodical journal. It shall publish regularly:

> (*a*) the names of the proprietors of patents granted, with a brief description of the inventions patented;
> (*b*) reproductions of trademarks registered.

ARTICLE 13

1887   (1) The international office established [*at Berne*] under the name International Bureau for the Protection of Industrial Property is placed under the high authority of the Government of the Swiss Confederation, which regulates its organisation and supervises its operation.

[2. *The official language of the International Bureau is French.*]

(2) (a) The French and English languages shall be used by the International Bureau in performing the tasks provided for in paragraphs (3) and (5) of this Article.

(b) The conferences and meetings referred to in Article 14 shall be held in the French, English and Spanish languages.

(3) The International Bureau centralises information of every kind relating to the protection of industrial property and compiles and publishes it. It undertakes studies of general utility concerning the Union and edits, with the help of documents supplied to it by the various Administrations, a periodical journal [*in French*] dealing with questions relating to the objects of the Union.

(4) The issues of this journal, as well as all the documents published by the International Bureau, shall be distributed to the Administrations of the countries of the Union in proportion to the number of contributing units mentioned below. Additional copies as may be requested, either by the said Administrations or by companies or private persons, shall be paid for separately.

(5) The International Bureau shall at all times hold itself at the service of the countries of the Union, to supply them with any special information they may need on questions relating to the international industrial property service. The Director of the International Bureau shall make an annual report on its operations, which shall be communicated to all the countries of the Union.

1888 (6) The ordinary expenses of the International Bureau shall be borne by the countries of the Union in common. Until further authorisation is given, they must not exceed the sum of 120,000 Swiss francs per annum. This sum may be increased, when necessary, by a unanimous decision of one of the conferences provided for in Article 14.

(7) Ordinary expenses do not include expenses relating to the work of conferences of plenipotentiaries or administrative conferences or those caused by special work or publications carried out in conformity with the decisions of a conference. Such expenses, the annual total of which may not exceed 20,000 Swiss francs, shall be divided among the countries of the Union in proportion to their contributions towards the operation of the International Bureau in accordance with the provisions of paragraph (8) below.

(8) To determine the contribution of each country to this total, the countries of the Union and those which may afterwards join the Union are divided into six classes, each contributing in the proportion of a certain number of units, namely:

First class	...	...	...	25 Units
Second class	...	...	...	20 „
Third class	...	...	...	15 „
Fourth class	...	...	...	10 „
Fifth class	...	...	...	5 „
Sixth class	...	...	...	3 „

These coefficients are multiplied by the number of countries in each class, and the sum of the products thus obtained gives the number of units by which the total expenditure is to be divided. The quotient gives the amount of the unit of expense.

(9) Each of the countries of the Union shall, at the time it becomes a member, designate the class in which it wishes to be placed. However, any country of the Union may declare later that it desires to be placed in another class.

(10) The Government of the Swiss Confederation will supervise the expenditure and the accounts of the International Bureau and will advance the necessary funds [*and render an annual account, which will be communicated to all the other Administrations.*]

(11) The annual account rendered by the International Bureau shall be communicated to all the other Administrations.

[The changes in paras. (2) and (3) will be of considerable practical benefit in the United Kingdom and elsewhere in the Commonwealth. Those in paras. (10) and (11) are purely administrative.

Lack of unanimity prevented any alteration in the text of paragraphs (6) and (7) relating to the finances of the Union. However, a Resolution was passed unanimously "inviting" the member countries to raise their contributions to bring the funds to the amount of 600,000 Swiss francs annually.]

ARTICLE 14

1889   (1) The present Convention shall be submitted to periodical revision with a view to the introduction of amendments designed to improve the system of the Union.

(2) For this purpose conferences shall be held successively in one of the countries of the Union between the delegates of the said countries.

(3) The Administration of the country in which the conference is to be held shall make preparations for the work of the conference, with the assistance of the International Bureau.

(4) The Director of the International Bureau shall be present at the meetings of the conferences, and take part in the discussions, but without the right of voting.

(5) (a) During the interval between the Diplomatic Conferences of revision, Conferences of representatives of all the countries of the Union shall meet every three years in order to draw up a report on the foreseeable expenditures of the International Bureau for each three-year period to come and to consider questions relating to the protection and development of the Union.

(b) Furthermore, they may modify, by unanimous decision, the maximum annual amount of the expenditures of the International Bureau, provided they meet as a Conference of Plenipotentiaries of all the countries of the Union convened by the Government of the Swiss Confederation.

(c) Moreover, the Conferences provided for in paragraph (a) above may be convened between their three-yearly meetings by either the Director of the International Bureau or the Government of the Swiss Confederation.

ARTICLE 15

1890   It is understood that the countries of the Union reserve the right to make separately between themselves special arrangements for the protection of industrial property, in so far as these arrangements do not contravene the provisions of the present Convention.

ARTICLE 16

1891   (1) Countries which are not parties to the present Convention shall be permitted to accede to it at their request.

(2) Any such accession shall be notified through diplomatic channels to the Government of the Swiss Confederation, and by it to all the other Governments.

(3) Accession shall automatically entail acceptance of all the clauses and admission to all the advantages of the present Convention and shall take effect one month after the dispatch of the notification by the Government of the Swiss Confederation to the other countries of the Union, unless a subsequent date is indicated in the request for accession.

ARTICLE 16*bis*

1892   (1) Any country of the Union may at any time notify in writing the Government of the Swiss Confederation that the present Convention shall be applicable to all or part of its colonies, protectorates, territories under mandate or any other territories subject to its authority, or any territories under its sovereignty, and the Convention shall apply to all the territories named in the notification one month after the dispatch of the communication by the Government of the Swiss Confederation to the other countries of the Union unless a subsequent date is indicated in the notification. Failing such a notification, the Convention shall not apply to such territories.

(2) Any country of the Union may at any time notify in writing the Government of the Swiss Confederation that the present Convention shall cease to apply to all or part of the territories that have formed the subject of a notification under the preceding paragraph, and the Convention shall cease to apply in the territories named in the notification twelve months after the receipt of the notification addressed to the Government of the Swiss Confederation.

(3) All notifications sent to the Government of the Swiss Confederation in accordance with the provisions of paragraphs (1) and (2) of the present Article shall be communicated by that Government to all the countries of the Union.

ARTICLE 17

1893   [*The carrying out of the reciprocal engagements contained in the present Convention is subject, so far as necessary, to the observance of the formalities and rules established by the constitutional laws of those of the countries of the Union which are bound to procure their application, which they engage to do with as little delay as possible.*]

Any country party to this Convention undertakes to adopt, in accordance with its constitution, the measures necessary to ensure the application of this Convention.

It is understood that at the time an instrument of ratification or accession is deposited on behalf of a country such country will be in

a position under its domestic law to give effect to the terms of this Convention.

[The new wording is the same as that in Article X of the Universal Copyright Convention of 1952.]

ARTICLE 17*bis*

1894 (1) The Convention shall remain in force for an indefinite time, until the expiration of one year from the date of its denunciation.

(2) Such denunciation shall be addressed to the Government of the Swiss Confederation. It shall affect only the country in whose name it is made, the Convention remaining in operation as regards the other countries of the Union.

ARTICLE 18

1895 (1) The present Act shall be ratified and the instruments of ratification deposited in [*London*] **Berne** not later than the [*1st July, 1938*] **May 1, 1963.** It shall come into force, between the countries in whose names it has been ratified, one month after that date. However, if before that date it is ratified in the name of at least six countries, it shall come into force between those countries one month after the deposit of the sixth ratification has been notified to them by the Government of the Swiss Confederation, and for countries in whose name it is ratified at a later date, one month after the notification of each of such ratification.

(2) Countries in whose names no instrument of ratification has been deposited within the period referred to in the preceding paragraph shall be permitted to accede under the terms of Article 16.

(3) The present Act shall, as regards the relations between the countries to which it applies, replace the Convention of Paris of 1883 and the subsequent Acts of revision.

(4) As regards the countries to which the present Act does not apply, but to which the Convention of Paris revised at **London in 1934** applies, the latter shall remain in force.

(5) Similarly as regards countries to which neither the present Act nor the Convention of Paris revised at London apply, the Convention of Paris revised at The Hague in 1925 shall remain in force.

(6) Similarly, as regards countries to which neither the present Act **nor the Convention of Paris revised at London,** nor the Convention of Paris revised at The Hague apply, the Convention of Paris revised at Washington in 1911 shall remain in force.

ARTICLE 19

1896 (1) The present Act shall be signed in a single copy **in the French language,** which shall be deposited in the archives of the Government of the [*United Kingdom of Great Britain and Northern Ireland*] **Swiss Confederation.** A certified copy shall be forwarded by the latter to each of the Governments of the countries of the Union.

(2) The present Act shall remain open for signature by the countries of the Union until April 30, 1959.

(3) Official translations of the present Act shall be established in the English, German, Italian, Portuguese and Spanish languages.

In witness whereof the undersigned Plenipotentiaries, after presenting their full powers, have signed the present Act.
Done at Lisbon on October 31, 1958.

Convention Countries

1897   A : The following countries have been declared to be Convention Countries for all purposes.

Australia
Austria
Belgium
Brazil
Cameroon
Canada
Central African Republic
Ceylon
Chad
Congo (Brazzaville)
Cuba
Czechoslovakia
Denmark
Dominican Republic
Finland
France
Gabon
Germany
Greece
Guam
Haiti
Holy See
Hungary
Iceland
Indonesia
Iran
Ireland
Israel
Italy
Ivory Coast
Japan
Kenya
Laos
Lebanon
Liechtenstein
Luxembourg

Malagasy Republic
Mauritania
Mexico
Monaco
Morocco
Netherlands
New Zealand
Niger
Nigeria
Norway
Poland
Portugal
Rumania
San Marino
Senegal
South Africa
Southern Rhodesia
Spain
Sweden
Switzerland
Syria
Tanzania
Trinidad and Tobago
Tunisia
Turkey
Uganda
Union of Soviet Socialist Republics
United Arab Republic
United Kingdom of Great Britain and Northern Ireland
United States of America
Upper Volta
Vietnam
Yugoslavia
Zambia

B: Bulgaria is a Convention Country except for the purposes of section 70.

[The next paragraph is 1998]

PART 4

Forms and Precedents

ACTIONS FOR INFRINGEMENT

1998

Indorsement on Writ

In the High Court of Justice,
    Chancery Division.
      Group A
        Between A B ...   . Plaintiff,
                and
            C D ...   . Defendant.
The plaintiff claims:
(1) An injunction to restrain the defendant from infringing letters patent No.   , by himself his servants or agents.
(2) An inquiry as to damages or at the plaintiff's option an account of profits and payment of the sum found due.
(3) An order for delivery up or destruction upon oath of all articles in the defendant's possession, control or power made in infringement of the said letters patent.
(4) Costs.
(5) Further or other relief.

1999

Notice of Motion for Interlocutory Injunction

Take notice that this honourable Court will be moved on the day of   at 10.30 o'clock in the forenoon or so soon thereafter as counsel can be heard, by counsel for the above-named plaintiff for an injunction restraining the defendant by himself his servants or agents, until judgment in this action or further order from infringing letters patent No.   or for such further or other order as in the premises to the Court may seem meet.

2000

Interlocutory Order to Restrain Infringement of Patent

Upon motion, etc., by counsel for the plaintiff and upon hearing counsel for the defendant [*or* reading and affidavit of service of notice of this motion on the defendant; *or if moved ex parte before the defendant has appeared*, the writ of summons issued in this action on the   day of   ] [*enter affidavits in support and in opposition, if any*], and the plaintiff, by his counsel, undertaking to abide by any order this Court may make as to damages, in case this Court should hereafter be of opinion that the defendant shall have sustained any, by reason of this order, which the plaintiff ought to pay [*if so*, and also undertaking to accept short notice of motion to dissolve the injunction hereby granted], this Court doth order that the defendant be restrained until judgment or further order, from infringing by himself his servants or agents, the plaintiff's letters patent in the said writ mentioned, and that the defendant be restrained until further order from selling or offering for sale, or otherwise parting

[630]

with the custody of any articles, or parts of any articles, which have been manufactured by the defendant in infringement of the said letters patent. Liberty to either party to apply to expedite the hearing and generally.

2001   **Interlocutory Injunction for Infringement refused on Terms**

Upon motion, etc., for injunction to restrain, etc., and the defendant, by his counsel, undertaking to keep an account of all moneys received or to be received by him, by reason of the sale or use of the articles in the writ mentioned, this Court does not think fit to make any order upon the said motion, except that the costs of the said motion be costs in the cause. Liberty to either party to apply to expedite the hearing and generally.

2002   **Statement of Claim**

1. The plaintiff is the registered proprietor of letters patent No.   , in respect of an invention entitled "   ".

2. The said letters patent are valid and subsisting.[1]

3. The defendant has infringed and threatens and intends to infringe the said letters patent in the manner appearing in the particulars of infringements served herewith whereby the plaintiff has suffered and will suffer damage.

The plaintiff claims:

(1) An injunction to restrain the defendant from infringing letters patent No.   , by himself his servants or agents.

(2) An inquiry as to damages or at the plaintiff's option an account of profits and payment of the sum found due.

(3) An order for delivery up or destruction upon oath of all articles in the defendant's possession, control or power made in infringement of the said letters patent.

(4) Costs.

(5) Further or other relief.

Signed
Served.

[Where specification has been amended]

The complete specification of the said letters patent was amended by reason of and in accordance with the decision of the Comptroller-General of patents dated the   day of   [*or* by leave of the Hon. Mr. Justice   granted on the   day of   in an action entitled —— v. ——]. The specification as originally published was framed in good faith and with reasonable skill and knowledge.

---

[1] This plea is usual, though it is probably not strictly necessary: see *Halsey* v. *Brotherhood*, 15 Ch.D. 514 at p. 521; *Amory* v. *Brown*, L.R. 8 Eq. 663 at p. 664.

[Where a certificate of validity has been granted in a previous action]

The plaintiff claims costs as between solicitor and client. In an action No.   entitled —— v. —— [or in a petition for revocation of the said letters patent entitled *etc.*] Mr. Justice certified that the validity of all the claims [or claims   and   *as the case may be*] of the said letters patent were contested in those proceedings.

2003   **Particulars of Infringements**

The following are the particulars of the infringements complained of:

1. Prior to the issue of the writ in this action and subsequent to the publication of the complete specification of the letters patent mentioned in the statement of claim the defendant has infringed the said letters patent by the manufacture, use, sale, offer for sale, and/or supply in this country of machines constructed in accordance with the invention described in the said complete specification and claimed in all the claims [or in claims   and   ] thereof.

2. In particular the plaintiff complains of:

(a) The manufacture by the defendant at his factory at   between the   and   or thereabouts of machines constructed as aforesaid.

(b) The offer for sale by the defendant between the   and   or thereabouts in a catalogue entitled   of machines constructed as aforesaid.

(c) The sale to E F of   by the defendant on or about the   of a machine constructed as aforesaid.

3. The precise number and dates of the defendant's infringements are at present unknown to the plaintiff but the plaintiff will claim to recover damages or an account of profits in respect of all such infringements.

2004   **Defence and Counterclaim**

[N.B.—*One set of Particulars of Objections will serve for Defence and Counterclaim*]

1. The defendant does not admit that the plaintiff is the registered proprietor of the letters patent sued on.

2. If the defendant has manufactured [or sold or used] the articles [or process] as alleged in the particulars of breaches, the same were manufactured (sold or used) by leave and licence of the patentee in the following circumstances: [*set forth particulars*].

3. The defendant has not infringed, nor does he threaten or intend to infringe, the said letters patent as alleged, or at all.

4. The said letters patent are and have at all material times been invalid for the reasons appearing in the particulars of objections served herewith.

5. The defendant will rely as a defence upon the fact that at the time of the alleged infringement there was in force a contract relating to the said letters patent dated the   day of   and

made between   of the one part and   of the other part which contract was made by or with the consent of the plaintiff and contains a condition void by virtue of section 57 of the Patents Act, 1949, in that [set forth particulars].

6. The defendant admits that the complete specification of the said letters patent has been amended but the defendant denies that the complete specification as originally filed was framed in good faith or with reasonable skill or knowledge.

7. As an answer to the plaintiff's claim for damages, the defendant will rely upon the fact that at the date of the alleged infringement he was not aware, and had no reasonable ground for supposing, that the said letters patent existed.

Counterclaim

The defendant repeats paragraph 4 of his defence and counterclaims for revocation of the plaintiff's letters patent.

2005   **Particulars of Objections in an Action for Infringement or Petition for Revocation** [2]

Take notice, that the defendant [or petitioner] will, on the trial of this cause, rely on the following objections to the validity of letters patent No.   :

1. The alleged invention so far as claimed in claims   and of the complete specification was claimed in claim   of the complete specification of letters patent No.   granted to   which last mentioned claim is of earlier priority date than the said claims of the letters patent in suit.

2. The letters patent in suit were granted on the application of   who was not a person entitled under the provisions of the Patents Act, 1949, to apply therefor.

3. The said letters patent were obtained in contravention of the rights of the defendant [or petitioner] [or of X through whom the defendant [or petitioner] claims]. Particulars hereunder are as follows: [set them forth].

4. The alleged invention the subject of claims   and of the complete specification of the said letters patent is not an invention within the meaning of the Patents Act, 1949.

5. The said alleged invention so far as claimed in claims and   of the complete specification was not new at the priority date of the said claims having regard to what was known [and used]. It had been published:

(a) By the public manufacture [or sale or use] of [articles] constructed in accordance with the said invention from the year   to the present day at   by the defendant [or some other, naming him] of   . Articles so manufactured are now in existence and may be inspected by the plaintiff at   .

(b) By the public manufacture [or sale or use] of [articles] constructed in accordance with the said invention from the year   to the   at   by J S of   . The

[2] See s. 32 (1) and Chap. 14.

said articles are no longer in existence. A description and drawings of the said articles are delivered with these particulars.

(c) By the public manufacture [*or* sale *or* use] of [*product*] by means of the patented process at   by   of from the year   until the year   . A description of the said process and drawings of the apparatus used accompanies these particulars. The process is no longer in use, but the apparatus is in possession of   . The defendant will endeavour to obtain inspection of the apparatus by the plaintiff.

(d) By the deposit on the shelves of the Library at the Patent Office of the following specifications of letters patent granted in foreign countries:

Name.	Country. Date and Number.	Parts relied on.	Claims of plaintiff's specification against which relied on.

(e) By the publication of the following specifications of British letters patent—

Name.	Date and Number.	Parts relied on.	Claims of plaintiff's specification against which relied on.

(f) By the deposit in the Library of the British Museum in the year   of a work bearing the title "   " by and in particular by the passage commencing at p.   l. and ending at p.   l.   .

2006   6. The said alleged invention so far as claimed in claims and   of the complete specification was obvious and did not involve any inventive step having regard to what was known and used prior to the priority date of the said claims. The defendant will rely upon all the matters set out in para. 5 above and upon common general knowledge.

7. The said alleged invention so far as claimed in claims and   of the complete specification is not useful. The defendant will rely on [*give the necessary particulars*].

8. The complete specification of the said letters patent does not sufficiently or fairly describe the invention or the method by which it is to be performed. The defendant will rely hereunder on the absence of any, or alternatively any sufficient, directions as to how *etc.*

9. The complete specification of the said letters patent does not disclose the best method of performing the alleged invention which was known to the applicant and for which he was entitled to claim protection, namely [*give the necessary particulars*].

10. The scope of claims   and   of the complete specification is not sufficiently or clearly defined.

11. Claims   and   of the complete specification are not fairly based on the matter disclosed therein.

12. The said letters patent were obtained on the false suggestion [*or* representation] that [*set out the facts alleged to constitute the same*].

13. The primary or intended use of the invention is contrary to law in that [*set out particulars*].

14. The said alleged invention so far as claimed in claims and   was secretly used in the United Kingdom before the priority date of the said claims. The best particulars which the defendant can give of such secret prior user are that *etc.*

[*Where the defendant is a government department.*]

15. The patentee of the said letters patent has without reasonable cause failed to comply with the request of the defendant to make use or exercise the patented invention for the services of the Crown upon reasonable terms in that he [*give the necessary particulars*].

2007   **Order for Liberty to amend Particulars of Objections by adding Fresh Objections upon Terms**

Order that the plaintiff, within six weeks of the date of this order, elect whether he will discontinue this action and withdraw his defence to the counterclaim and consent to an order for the revocation of letters patent No.   and if the plaintiff shall so elect and shall give notice thereof to the defendant within the time aforesaid. It is ordered that letters patent No.   be revoked and that it be referred to the Taxing Master to tax the costs of the defendant of this action up to and including the date of the delivery of the particulars of objections and the counterclaim except in so far as the same have been increased by reason of the failure of the defendant originally to deliver the particulars of objections in their amended form and to tax the costs of the plaintiff of this action subsequent to the date of the delivery of the particulars of objections to the date of this order and of the counterclaim in so far as they have been increased by reason of the failure of the defendant aforesaid And it is ordered that the Taxing Master is to set off the said costs of the defendant and of the plaintiff when so taxed as aforesaid and to certify to which of them the balance after such set-off is due And it is ordered that such balance be paid by the party from whom to the party to whom the same shall be certified to be due and if the plaintiff shall not give notice to the defendant as aforesaid within the time aforesaid It is ordered that the defendant be at liberty to amend his defence and counterclaim and his particulars of objections in the manner indicated in red ink in the copy of the proposed amended defence and counterclaim and particulars of objections already served on the plaintiff and signed by the registrar and that the plaintiff be at liberty to serve within fourteen days an amended reply and defence to counterclaim And it is ordered that the defendant do pay to the plaintiff his costs of and occasioned by the amendments aforesaid including the costs of this application to be taxed by the Taxing Master And the parties are to be at liberty to apply.[3]

---

[3] See *See* v. *Scott Paine*, 50 R.P.C. 56 and see also *Baird* v. *Moule's Earth Closet Co.*, reported in *Edison Telephone Co.* v. *India Rubber Co.*, 17 Ch.D. 137.

2008 **Notice of Motion for Leave to amend Specification where Action for Infringement, or Petition for Revocation Pending** [4]

[Title of action or petition]

Take notice that this Honourable Court will be moved by counsel on behalf of the above named plaintiff that it may be granted leave to amend the complete specification of letters patent No.   by way of (state nature of amendment) as indicated in red ink in the copy of the specification certified by the Comptroller General of Patents, served herewith and that for the purposes of the application for leave to amend directions may be given for the hearing and determination thereof.

2009 **Order allowing Application to amend to Proceed** [5]

The plaintiffs by their counsel undertaking not to proceed with and (if required) to consent to orders staying (pending this application) all proceedings in all other pending actions (if any) for infringement of the said letters patent No.   and not in the meantime to threaten or institute other actions for infringement of the said letters patent. This Court doth order that the applicants be at liberty to proceed with their application for leave to amend the specification of their said letters patent and it is ordered that the application be made on affidavit evidence, all affidavits in opposition to the application by or on behalf of the defendants to be filed within seven weeks after service by the plaintiffs on the defendants of notice of the issue of the advertisement mentioned in Order 103, Rule 17 (1) of the Rules of the Supreme Court and all affidavits in opposition to the application by or on behalf of any other person or persons entitled to be heard upon the hearing of the motion to be filed within four weeks after service on all persons who under paragraph (2) of Order 103, Rule 17 of the Rules of the Supreme Court ought to be served with notice of motion, and all affidavits by or on behalf of the plaintiffs in answer to be filed within three weeks after the expiration of such last mentioned four weeks, or if there is no person who under paragraph (2) of Order 103, Rule 17, ought to be so served then within three weeks after service by the defendants on the plaintiffs of notice of the filing by the defendants of their affidavits in opposition, and all affidavits in reply to be filed within three weeks after service by the plaintiffs on the defendants, and the other persons (if any) filing evidence in opposition of notice of the filing by the plaintiffs of their affidavits in answer, and that no further evidence be filed except by leave of the Judge.

---

[4] See R.S.C., Ord. 103, r. 17.
[5] See *Rheinische Gummi und Celluloid Fabrik* v. *British Xylonite Co., Ltd.*, 29 R.P.C. 672; *N. V. Hollandsche Glas-en-Metaalbank* v. *Rockware Glass Syndicate, Ltd.*, 48 R.P.C. 181; *British Celanese, Ltd.* v. *Courtaulds, Ltd.*, 49 R.P.C. 345.

2010 Final Order allowing Amendment of the Specification on Terms [6]

Upon motion, etc., this Court doth order that plaintiffs be at liberty to amend the complete specification of letters patent No. by making therein the amendments set forth in the schedule hereto. And it is ordered that the plaintiffs be at liberty to use the said complete specification as amended in evidence at the trial of this action. And the plaintiffs are to be at liberty to amend their statement of claim and particulars of breaches so far as the said amendment of the said complete specification may make the same necessary. And that the defendants are to be at liberty to amend their defence and particulars of objections. And it is ordered that the costs of this motion be taxed by the Taxing Master forthwith and paid by the plaintiffs to the defendants. And that the costs of and occasioned by the amendment of the statement of claim, particulars of breaches, defence, and particulars of objections are to be the defendants in any event. And it is ordered that the plaintiffs do forthwith lodge with the Comptroller of Patents an office copy of this order.

2011 Final Judgment in favour of Plaintiff

THIS ACTION coming on for trial before this Court the   day of   , 19   , in the presence of counsel for the plaintiffs and for the defendant, and upon reading the pleadings and the evidence and what was alleged by counsel for the plaintiffs and for the defendant.

THIS COURT did order that this action and counterclaim should stand for judgment, and the same standing this day in the paper accordingly for judgment in the presence of counsel for the plaintiffs and for the defendant.

THIS COURT doth order that the defendant be restrained from infringing by himself his servants or agents the plaintiffs' letters patent No.

AND IT IS ORDERED that an inquiry be made as to what damages have been sustained by the plaintiffs [or, what profits have been made by the plaintiffs] by reason of the said infringement by the defendant of the plaintiffs' said letters patent and that the defendant do pay to the plaintiffs the sum found due.

AND IT IS ORDERED that the defendant do make and file a sufficient affidavit stating what articles were on the date of this judgment in his possession or power made in infringement of the said letters patent and accounting for the same.

AND IT IS ORDERED that the defendant do within 14 days after the filing of the said affidavit deliver up to the plaintiffs [or destroy or render non-infringing] the articles which shall by such affidavit appear to be in his possession or power.

AND THIS COURT certifies that upon the trial of this action the validity of all the claims [or of claims — and —] of the

---

[6] See *Lilley* v. *Artistic Novelties, Ltd.*, 30 R.P.C. 18; as a condition on which leave to amend is granted the patentee may be ordered to discontinue all other actions: *White's Patent* [1958] R.P.C. 287.

specification of the plaintiffs' said letters patent was contested and that the plaintiffs proved the particulars of infringements delivered by them.

AND IT IS ORDERED that the said counterclaim do stand dismissed out of this Court. And that the defendant do pay to the plaintiffs their costs of this action and of the said counterclaim, such costs to be taxed by the Taxing Master [*where so ordered,* as between solicitor and client]. And the costs of the said inquiry are reserved and the parties are to be at liberty to apply.

2012   **Final Judgment in favour of Defendant**

[*Formal parts as before*]

THIS COURT doth order that this action do stand dismissed out of this Court.

AND THIS COURT certifies that paragraphs   and   of the particulars of objections served by the defendant were reasonable and proper.

AND IT IS ORDERED upon the said counterclaim that letters patent No.   be revoked.

And that the plaintiff do pay to the defendant his costs of this action and of the said counterclaim such costs to be taxed.

ACTION TO RESTRAIN THREATS

2013   **Indorsement on Writ**

The plaintiff claims:

1. An injunction restraining the defendant from, by circulars, advertisements, or otherwise, threatening the plaintiff his suppliers and customers with proceedings for infringement of a patent.

2. A declaration that the threats made by the defendant are unjustifiable.

3. An inquiry as to the damages sustained by the plaintiff by reason of the threats made by the defendant.

4. Costs

5. Further or other relief.

2014   **Interlocutory Injunction to restrain Threats**

Upon motion, etc., order that the defendant, his servants and agents, be restrained from threatening any person with proceedings for infringement of a patent in respect of the manufacture, use, sale, or purchase of [*specify the articles*].

2015   **Final Order**

This Court doth order that the defendant be restrained from threatening by himself his servants or agents the plaintiff his suppliers or customers with proceedings for infringement of letters patent No.   .[7]

And doth declare that the threats made by the defendant are unjustifiable.

[7] See *C. & P. Development Co. (London), Ltd.* v. *Sisalero Novelty Co., Ltd.*, 70 R.P.C. 277 at p. 283.

And it is ordered that an inquiry be made as to what damages have been sustained by the plaintiff by reason of the said threats made by the defendant and that the defendant do pay to the plaintiff the sum found due.

2016   DRAFT ADVERTISEMENT

Application For Amendment of Patent

No. —— (*of patent*). A.B. propose to apply in the High Court of Justice in an action entitled " In the High Court of Justice," Chancery Division, Group A,   (No. of action).
BETWEEN

A.B.	*Plaintiffs.*
and	
C.D.	*Defendants*

for leave to amend the Complete Specification of the above-mentioned Letters Patent which is for an invention entitled " Improvements relating to. . . ."

The proposed amendments are as follows, the paging referred to being that of the printed specification : —

(*Set out proposed amendments seriatim*)

Any person desiring to oppose the amendment must within fourteen days of the appearance of this Notice give notice in writing of his desire to oppose to Messrs. X.Y.Z. who are the agents for the Applicants' Solicitors and whose address for service is

Any person giving such notice shall be entitled to be heard upon the application, subject to any direction of the Court as to costs.

2017   PETITION TO THE HIGH COURT FOR REVOCATION

In the High Court of Justice,
    Chancery Division.

Group A.
In the matter of letters patent granted to   , numbered   ,
                                and
In the matter of the Patents Act, 1949.

        To Her Majesty's High Court of Justice.

The humble petition of
SHEWETH as follows:

1. Your petitioner is engaged in the manufacture of   and has a substantial goodwill in the sale of the said articles in the United Kingdom.

2. The respondent claims to have a monopoly in certain articles of the kind marketed by your petitioner by reason of his ownership of the said letters patent and your petitioner's trade and goodwill is seriously hampered by the continued existence of the said letters patent.

3. The said letters patent are wholly invalid by reason of the matters set forth in the particulars of objections accompanying this petition.

Wherefor your petitioner humbly prays that the said letters patent may be revoked.

And your petitioners will ever pray, etc.

[*Particulars of objections similar to those served in an action for infringement must accompany the petition.*]

2018 PETITION FOR EXTENSION OF TERM OF PATENT

(SEE ORDER 103, RULE 3)

Advertisement of Intention to present Petition

In the High Court of Justice,
    Chancery Division.
Group A.
In the matter of the Patents Act 1949,

and

In the matter of letters patent granted to   , of   , and bearing date the   of   , and numbered   .

Notice is hereby given that it is the intention of   to present a petition to the High Court of Justice praying that the term of the said letters patent may be extended. And notice is further given that on the   day of   at   , or so soon thereafter as counsel may be heard, the said   intends to apply to the Court for a day to be fixed before which the petition shall not be in the paper for hearing. Notices of objection must be lodged 14 days before the date above mentioned at the Chancery Registrar's Office. Documents requiring service upon the said   pursuant to the Rules of the Supreme Court, Order 103, Rule 5, may be served at the office of the solicitor to the said   .

Dated this   day of   .

Solicitor to the said   .

Address for service.

2019   **Petition**

In the High Court of Justice,
    Chancery Division.
Group A.
In the matter of the Patents Act 1949,

and

In the matter of letters patent dated the   day of   , numbered   and granted to A B, of   , for the invention of "   ".

To Her Majesty's High Court of Justice

The humble petition of A B, of   , and of C D, of   SHEWETH as follows:

1. On the   day of   letters patent numbered   were granted to your petitioner A B, for an invention entitled   .

2. Your petitioner C D has become entitled to the said letters patent under the circumstances hereinafter appearing.

SET FORTH (a) *The history of the Art with special reference to the invention.*

[640]

(b) *The special utility and advantages of the invention.*
(c) *The circumstances under which the patent was obtained and the rights of C D created.*
(d) *All information relating to foreign patents.*
(e) *The rights of third parties, such as licensees, etc.*
(f) *The difficulties with which the patentee has had to contend in getting his invention taken up.*
(g) *The fact of insufficient remuneration, generally stated without special reference to accounts.*

Your petitioners have given public notice by advertisement caused to be inserted in the " London Gazette " and in a trade paper and a national newspaper pursuant to the rules in such cases made and provided, that it is their intention to apply to this Honourable Court for an extension of the term of the said letters patent.

Your petitioners therefore humbly pray that the said letters patent may be extended for a further term of ten years, or for such other term as to this Honourable Court shall seem fit.

And your petitioners will ever pray, etc.

2020

Affidavit as to Advertisements

[Heading as before]

I,   of   , solicitor, make oath and say as follows:

1. I am acting as solicitor for the petitioners A B and C D in the petition for extension of the above-mentioned letters patent.

2. I caused the advertisement of which a copy is contained in the Schedule hereto to be inserted in the issues of the " London Gazette " of *[date]* and in the issues of *[name papers and give dates]*. Copies of the issues of the said newspapers containing the said advertisements are now produced to me and marked   respectively.

3. I caused a copy of the said advertisement to be sent on the   day of   to the Solicitor to the Department of Trade and Industry and the said advertisement has been inserted in the   issues of the Official Journal (Patents) dated respectively
.

The Schedule above referred to.
[Set forth copy of advertisement]

2021

Notice of Opposition to Petition

[Heading as before]

Notice is hereby given that J. K. & Co., Ltd., of   , intend to oppose the petition for extension of the term of the above-mentioned letters patent.

Dated this   day of   .
(Signed)
Solicitors to the said J. K. & Co., Ltd.
Address for service   .

---

[641]

2022

Notice of Grounds of Objection

[Heading as before]

Notice is hereby given of the particulars of the objections of J. K. & Co., Ltd., of   , to the granting of the prayer of the said petition, that is to say:

1. A judgment was given against the validity of the said letters patent in a certain cause in the High Court of Justice, wherein the petitioner was plaintiff and   defendant.

2. The said letters patent are invalid by reason of the following matters [*set out the grounds relied on in a manner similar to the particulars of objections in an action for infringement*].

3. The alleged invention does not possess sufficient inventive merit and is not of sufficient public utility to justify any prolongation of the term granted by the said letters patent.

4. The petitioner has been sufficiently remunerated and rewarded for all his expenses, labour, and ingenuity respecting the said invention.

5. If the petitioner has failed to obtain a sufficient amount of remuneration or reward he has only failed to do so in consequence of his own negligence.

6. The petitioner has permitted infringements of the said letters patent, and has not taken any proceedings to restrain such infringements.

Dated this   day of   .

(Signed)

Solicitors to the said J. K. & Co., Ltd.

2023

Order for Extension of Lapsed Patent [8]

This Court doth order that the term of the said Letters Patent be extended for a period of   years from the expiry of the said Letters Patent.

Provided that as regards the said Letters Patent any person not being a licensee thereunder at the date of expiry thereof who—

(a) after such date and before the first appearance in the Official Journal (Patents) of the advertisement of the application upon which this order is made has made used exercised or sold the invention the subject of the said patent or has manufactured or installed any apparatus machinery or plant for the purpose of carrying out any process claimed by the complete specification of the said patent and (b) has become qualified as hereinafter mentioned shall be deemed to have so acted with the licence of the patentee under the said patent and shall thereafter be entitled to continue to make use exercise or sell the invention without infringement of the patent to the extent hereinafter specified that is to say—

(1) In so far as the complete specification of the patent claims an article (other than an apparatus machine or plant or part thereof as specified under head 2 hereof) and any article so claimed has been

---

[8] *Pochin's Patent*, 65 R.P.C. 327; *Siemens Brothers & Co., Ltd.'s Patent*, 68 R.P.C. 61. This form of order is known as the "New Gillette" order.

manufactured by him during the interim period as hereinafter defined that particular article may at all times be used or sold.

(2) In so far as the complete specification claims some apparatus machine or plant or part thereof for the production of an article then any particular apparatus machine or plant or part thereof so claimed which has been manufactured or installed by him during the said interim period and the products thereof may at all times be used or sold and so that in the event of any such apparatus machine or plant or part thereof being impaired by wear or tear or accidentally destroyed a like licence shall extend to any replacement thereof and to the products of such replacement.

(3) In so far as the complete specification claims any process for the making or treating of any article any particular apparatus machine or plant which during the said interim period has been manufactured or installed by him or exclusively or mainly used by him for carrying on such process may at all times be so used or continued to be so used and the products thereof may at all times be used or sold and so that in the event of any such apparatus machine or plant being impaired by wear or tear or accidentally destroyed a like licence shall extend to such process when carried on in any replacement of such apparatus machine or plant and to the products of the process so carried on.

And it is declared that in and for the purposes of the foregoing the Register of Patents under Rule 128 of the Patents Rules 1968 of proviso—(a) a person shall become qualified by applying for entry in his claim to be deemed to have acted with the licence of the patentee as aforesaid, if such application is (i) made within eight weeks from the date of advertisement of this order in the Official Journal (Patents) or (ii) made at a later date and the Court is satisfied in any proceeding in which infringement is alleged that such person acted honestly and reasonably and that having regard to all the circumstances of the case he ought to be excused for the failure to make such application within such eight weeks and (iii) supported by a statutory declaration setting out the nature and extent of the manufacture use exercise or sale upon which his claim is based; (b) the word " article " shall be deemed to include any substance material apparatus arrangement machine or plant; and (c) " the interim period " means the period between the date of expiry of the said patent and the date of this order.

LICENCES

Form of Licence

2024 Parties.

THIS LICENCE made the —— day of —— Between —— of —— (hereinafter referred to as " the Patentee ") of the first part and —— of —— (hereinafter referred to as " the Licensees ") of the second part.

Recital.

WHEREAS the Patentee is the registered proprietor of the patents set out in the first part of the Schedule hereto and is entitled to the benefit of the applications for patents set out in the second part of the said Schedule and to any patents which may be granted in pursuance of the said applications.

Grant.

WITNESSETH—

(1) The Patentee hereby grants to the Licensees an exclusive (*or* non-exclusive) licence in respect of all the patents set out in the first part of the said Schedule for the full period of their respective terms including any extension thereof [*or*, for the period of —— years from the date of these presents] in the United Kingdom [*or other agreed territory*] and agrees to grant a licence on the same terms in respect of all patents that may be granted pursuant to the applications set out in the second part of the said Schedule for the full term thereof including any extension thereof [*or*, for the like period].

Improvements.

(2) (a) The Patentee will forthwith disclose to the Licensees any invention which he may devise or otherwise become possessed of relating to any improvement of any of the inventions the subject of the patents or applications set out in the Schedule hereto and shall if so requested by the Licensees but at the expense of the Licensees apply for a patent in respect thereof.

(b) The Patentee if so requested by the Licensees and at the expense of the Licensees will grant a licence on the same terms as the licence hereby granted (except as otherwise provided herein) in respect of any patents hereafter owned or controlled by him relating to any improvement as aforesaid (whether such patent shall have been obtained pursuant to paragraph (a) of this clause or otherwise) for such period as there shall be subsisting a licence pursuant to clause 1 hereof.

Royalties.

(3) The Licensees shall pay to the Patentee or as he shall direct a royalty amounting to —— per cent. upon [*e.g.*, the net amount received by the Licensees in respect of the manufacture sale lease hire or other dealing with any articles constructed in accordance with or by a process of manufacture in accordance with any claim of any subsisting patent in respect of which a licence has been granted to the Licensees pursuant to these presents] PROVIDED that the said royalty per article shall be unaffected by the number of claims or the number of patents concerned.

[*If the licence is exclusive*]

2025 Minimum royalty.

(4) If the royalties payable pursuant to Clause (3) hereof do not amount in any year reckoned from [*e.g.*, the 1st January, 19—] to the sum of £—— the Licensees shall pay in respect of such year such further sum as will amount with the said royalties to a total equal to the said sum of £——.

[*alternatively*]

Exclusive to non-exclusive.

(4) If the royalties payable pursuant to Clause (3) hereof do not amount in any year reckoned from [*e.g.*, the 1st January 19—] to the sum of £—— this licence shall thereupon become non-exclusive PROVIDED that if the Licensees shall with the last royalty payment in respect of such year pay such further sum as will amount to a total for the year equal to the said sum of £—— this licence shall remain exclusive.

Books of Account.

(5) The Licensees shall keep at their usual place of business all proper books of account as may be necessary to enable the royalties payable hereunder to be ascertained and shall produce the same to the Patentee or to his accountants at all reasonable times not exceeding once in every quarter and permit him or them to take copies thereof.

Statements and payment.

(6) The Licensees shall within one month of each of the usual quarter days furnish to the Patentee a statement showing the amount of royalty due pursuant to Clause (3) hereof in respect of the preceding quarter and shall accompany the same with a remittance for the amount shown by such statement to be due.

2026 Infringement.

(7) Each of the parties hereto shall inform the other of any infringement of any patent with which these presents are or may be concerned immediately upon receiving knowledge of the same and if one of the parties hereto desires to take legal proceedings in respect of such infringement and the other does not so wish the latter shall on receiving a fully secured indemnity as to all costs and expenses give to the former party all assistance in his power in relation to such legal proceedings including becoming a party thereto if so requested and in that event any damages profits or other compensation recovered by such legal proceedings shall belong exclusively to such former party.

Marking.

(8) All articles sold leased or hired by the Licensees and constructed in accordance with or by a process of manufacture in accordance with any claim of any subsisting patent in respect of which a licence has been granted to the Licensees pursuant to these presents shall be clearly marked with the number of each such patent preceded by the words " Licensed under Letters Patent Number ——".

Completion of applications and renewal fees.

(9) The Patentee shall use his best endeavours to obtain valid patents pursuant to each of the applications for patents set out in the second part of the Schedule hereto and shall pay all renewal fees in respect of such patents and all patents set out in the first part of the said Schedule as and when the same shall become due PROVIDED that

if the Patentee wishes to abandon any such application or not to maintain any such patent he may give one month's notice in writing to the Licensees of his intention to abandon such application or not to pay the relevant renewal fee as the case may be and unless the Licensees request in writing within such period of one month that such application be not abandoned or that such patent be renewed and provide the funds necessary to proceed with such application or to pay such renewal fee the Patentee may act in accordance with such notice.

Covenant to push.

(10) The Licensees will use their best endeavours to operate in accordance with the patent(s) licensed hereunder to the maximum possible extent.[9]

Breaches.

(11) If the Licensees shall commit any breach of their obligations hereunder the Patentee may serve a notice upon them specifying such breach and stating that unless within 21 days of the receipt of such notice they repair such breach (if the same be repairable) or offer fair compensation therefor (if the same be not repairable) any licence granted pursuant to these presents shall upon the expiry of the said 21 days automatically determine and if the Licensees fail to repair such breach or to offer fair compensation as the case may be within the said period upon the expiry thereof this Licence shall forthwith determine accordingly but without prejudice to any rights obligations or liabilities already accrued prior to such determination.

Liquidation (or bankruptcy).

(12) Should the Licensees go into liquidation (otherwise than for the purpose of amalgamation or reconstruction) [*or*, be adjudicated bankrupt] any licence granted pursuant to these presents shall forthwith automatically determine but without prejudice to any rights obligations or liabilities already accrued prior to such determination.

IN WITNESS WHEREOF, *etc.*

2027   SCHEDULE

PART 1

[Set out particulars of granted patents]

PART 2

[Set out particulars of application for patents]

Form of Formal Licence

(to accompany a separate agreement specifying the
actual terms agreed)

Parties.

THIS LICENCE made the —— day of —— Between —— of —— (hereinafter referred to as " the Patentee ") of the first part and

---

[9] This clause is onerous, see *ante*, § 624.

—— of —— (hereinafter referred to as "the Licensees") of the second part.

Recitals.

WHEREAS (1) the Patentee is the registered proprietor of the patents set out in the Schedule hereto.

(2) The Patentee and the Licensees have entered into an agreement of even date.

Grant.

WITNESSETH—

In pursuance of the said agreement and in consideration of the sum of One Pound now paid by the Licensees to the Patentee (the receipt of which is hereby acknowledged) the Patentee grants to the Licensees an exclusive [*or*, non-exclusive] licence in respect of all the patents set out in the Schedule hereto for the full period of their respective terms including any extension thereof.

IN WITNESS WHEREOF, *etc.*

Schedule
[*Set out particulars of licensed patents*]

INDEX

The references are to paragraph numbers

ABANDONED APPLICATION,
  not published, 127, 271
  when deemed to be, 110

ABANDONED USER, 940

ABRIDGEMENTS OF SPECIFICATIONS,
  fifty-year-old specifications of,
    anticipations, not conclusive as, 271
      but *quaere* whether can be relied on in support of a prior user, 267
    opposition proceedings, not available, to opponent in, 428

ABUSE OF MONOPOLY. *See* COMPULSORY LICENCE.

ACCOUNT,
  assignee of patent may obtain from licensee, 635
  in application for extension of term. *See* EXTENSION OF TERM.
  profits can be claimed, of, 947

ACQUIESCENCE,
  right to injunction, effect on, 941

ACTION FOR INFRINGEMENT,
  account of profits can be claimed in, 947
  appeal, *see* APPEALS.
    obviousness, as to, 883
  appearance,
    default of, practice on, 820
    entry of, 819
      by one co-defendant only, 822
  assessor in, 812. *See also* SCIENTIFIC ADVISER.
  certificates. *See* CERTIFICATES.
  change of parties in, 805
  compromise affecting infant children, 994
  costs in. *See* COSTS.
  counterclaim in, 722, 851. *See also* COUNTERCLAIM.
  damages. *See* DAMAGES.
  defence to, 850
    amendment of, 893–896. *See also* PARTICULARS OF OBJECTIONS.
    damages, as to, 348, 862, 955, 956
    delivery of,
      default in, 866
        by one co-defendant, 822, 866
      time limited for, 850
    infringement, on issue of, 854, 855
      contract against, section 57 . . . 861. *See also* 643–647.
       particulars required, 861
      denial of infringement, 854, 855
      denial of plaintiff's title to patent sued on, 852
       motion to rectify the register is necessary, 852
      ignorance of patent, 346, 862
      infringement not novel, no longer admissible, 344, 865
      invalidity of patent, 345
       particulars required, 867. *See also* PARTICULARS OF OBJECTIONS.
    leave or licence, 853
      particulars required, 853

[649]

ACTION FOR INFRINGEMENT—*continued*
    plaintiff in—*continued*
        licensee,
            exclusive, may sue in own name, 792
            under sections 35 and 37, may sue in own name if patentee
                refuses to sue, 793
            patentee will normally be, 792
            proprietor of part of patent may sue alone as, 795
        pleadings in, 839
            See also " defence," *supra*; " reply "; " statement of claim,"
                infra; PARTICULARS OF INFRINGEMENTS; PARTICULARS OF
                OBJECTIONS.
        amendment of, at trial, 886, 893 *et seq.*
            Court of Appeal, in, 896
    practice,
        application for interlocutory injunction, upon, 828
        general, 813
        Order 103, r. 26, under, 916
        trial, before, 813 *et seq.*
    proof, onus of, in,
        defendant, on,
            where plea is,
                contract, contrary to, section 57 . . . 861
                ignorance of patent as defence to damages, 862
                invalidity, 925
                licence, 853
        plaintiff, on,
            infringement, as to, 854, 922
            validity (if disputed), as to,
                to give prima facie evidence of, 925
                    except on issue of whether patentee not entitled to
                      apply for patent, 925
                where defendant does not appear at the trial, 922
        title of, 924
    relief for infringement of partially valid patent, 969, 970
    remedy in, 933 *et seq. See also* DAMAGES; DELIVERY UP OR DESTRUCTION;
    INJUNCTION.
    reply, 897
    report of expert to court in, 812. *See also* REPORTS.
    scientific adviser. *See also* SCIENTIFIC ADVISER.
    statement of claim in, 840
        allegations necessary in, 840. *See also* PARTICULARS OF INFRINGE-
        MENTS.
        amendment of, 840. *See also* PARTICULARS OF INFRINGEMENTS.
        delivery of, time limited for, 840
    stay of,
        counterclaim not affected by, 722
        pending trial of test action, 918
    step in the action, 917
    summons for directions in,
        Order 95, r. 20, under, 911, 916, 930
            directions to be obtained on, 916
            must be disposed of before action can be set down for trial, 916
    third-party procedure in, 804
    trial of, 918 *et seq.*
        in camera, 921
        limitation of witnesses at, 916. *See also* SCIENTIFIC WITNESSES.
        preliminary issue, 920
        right to begin at, 919
        right to reply, 919
        sequence of issues, 923
        tribunal for 806 *et seq. See also* COUNTY COURT; ISLE OF MAN;
        NORTHERN IRELAND; PALATINE COURT OF LANCASTER; SCOTLAND.
        without jury, 811

AMENDMENT—*continued*
pleadings, of—*continued*
    application for extension of term, in. *See* EXTENSION OF TERM.
    opposition proceedings and revocation proceedings under section 33 in, 453. *See also* OPPOSITION.
specification, of. *See* AMENDMENT OF SPECIFICATION; CLERICAL ERRORS.

AMENDMENT OF SPECIFICATION, 1162–1164. *See also* CLERICAL ERRORS; PROVISIONAL SPECIFICATION.
acceptance, before, 1142
    appeal from order of Comptroller as to, 122
    general powers of Comptroller to require amendments, 119 *et seq.*
    post-dating to date of, 110
applications for extension of term, in, 539
clerical errors, amendment of. *See* CLERICAL ERRORS.
history of law as to, 472 *et seq.*
opposition proceedings, in, 440 *et seq.*
    by insertion of references, 441 *et seq.. See also* REFERENCE.
    general power of, 440
        limited to amendment by way of disclaimer, correction, or explanation, 440
    order for, may be made even if opponent fails, 438
revocation proceedings in,
    petition, by, 734. *See also* "under sections 29 and 30," *infra.*
    application may be made under section 30...734
    court may allow amendment instead of revoking patent, 734
    section 33 (extended opposition), under 451
sections 29 and 30, under,
    advertisement,
        effect of, where amendment differs from that originally proposed, 490
        of application,
            under section 29...490
                effect of error in advertisement, 490
            under section 30...496
    alien enemy respondent to petition for revocation may apply, 797
    ambiguity after amendment an objection, 483
    amendment which leaves patent invalid not allowed, 483
    amendment printed in erased type, 501
    appeals from Comptroller, 490. *See also* APPEALS "to Appeal Tribunal"; APPEALS "to Special Judge."
    application for amendment. *See* "practice," *infra.*
        made to the Comptroller under section 29 if no action pending, 494
            to the court if action pending, 494
        may be made more than once, 484
            but if subsequent to a refusal (not appealed) may not be allowed, 487
    claims may be amended provided amended claims are "fairly based," 476
    conditions may be imposed
        by Comptroller or Appeal Tribunal under section 29...488
            but power rarely exercised, 488
        by the court under section 30...489
        method by which imposed, 492
        nature of, 489
    conditions to be fulfilled, 475
    conduct of person applying taken into account, 486, 487
    correction, meaning of, 478
    costs. *See* COSTS.
    "Covetous" claims may be deleted, not amended, 485, 486
    damages, restriction on recovery of, for act committed prior to amendment, 502, 864
    deleted parts of specification may be referred to in aid of construction, 500
    "disclaimer, correction, or explanation," 477, 478

AMENDMENT OF SPECIFICATION—*continued*
    sections 29 and 30, under—*continued*
        disclaimer
            meaning of, in this connection, 477
            of part of invention faudulently claimed, not allowed, 487
        discretionary powers as to allowance or refusal of amendment, 485
        drawings may be altered to define amendment, 481
        effect of, leave to amend, 499 *et seq.*
            conclusive of right to make amendment, 500
                except in case of fraud, 500
            upon certificate of validity previously granted, 972
            upon enforcement of injunction previously granted, 946
        evidence,
            form of, in proceedings under section 29 . . . 490
            form of, in proceedings under section 30 . . . 496
            of proceedings on application, not admissible subsequently in aid of construction of specification, 500
        explanation, function of, 478
        fact of amendment should be pleaded in action for infringement, 840
        further amendment, may be allowed, 484
        invalid patent, court may allow amendment of specification instead of revoking, 504
        invalidity of patent after amendment, how far considered, 483
        " legal proceedings," meaning of, 494 *et seq.*
            action for infringement ceases to be after judgment, 495
            application for fiat to present petition is not, 495
            instituted after application made do not suspend such application, 495
        nature of permissible amendments, 475 *et seq.*
        novelty (after amendment), whether can be raised by an opponent, 483
        onus on person applying, 503
        opposition to application,
            practice under section 29 . . . 490
            practice under section 30 . . . 496
        partially valid patent, amendment of, 504
        practice,
            under section 29 . . . 490 *et seq.*
            under section 30 . . . 496 *et seq.*
                final order, 489
                notice, applicant must give to Comptroller, 496
                order on leave to proceed, 439, 496
        present law, effect of, 475
        printing of amended specifications, 501
        quantum of invention
            how far considered by Comptroller, 483
        reasons for amendment
            form no part of the amendment, 501
            may be required under section 30 . . . 482
            must be given under section 29 . . . 482
                but need not be conclusively sufficient, 482
            not stated in advertisement, 490
        references may be removed as a result of amendment, 501
            but will then be printed in erased type, 501
        specification after amendment may be used at trial of action, 500
        time at which amendment becomes effective, 490
        vagueness, an objection, 480
        validity of patent after amendment, not affected by adverse decision as to " good faith, etc.," 502
    section 62, under
        court may direct amendment under section 30 as condition of relief under, 504
    section 76, under
        amendment of clerical errors, 474. *And see* CLERICAL ERRORS.
AMERICAN SAMOA,
    convention country, 1897

ANALOGOUS USER,
doctrine of, 317 *et seq.*
    applies only to things in actual use, 319
    limits of, 319

ANTE-DATING,
of application for patent. *See* INTERNATIONAL CONVENTION.

ANTICIPATION, 1137, 1138. *See also* NOVELTY, " prior publication," " prior user."

APPEAL,
obviousness, as to, 883

APPEAL TRIBUNAL, 1123
    appeals from Comptroller to. *See* APPEALS.
    audience, right of, 457
    certiorari, 460
    constitution of, 457
    jurisdiction of, 457
    power of, to obtain assistance of expert, 459
    practice of, 457
    prerogative of Crown exercised by, 15
    proceedings before, not High Court proceedings, 457

APPEALS. *See also* COSTS.
    Appeal Tribunal from Comptroller, to
        application for patent, in proceedings on, 122
        applications to amend specification (under section 29) in, 489
        interim decision, 456
        opposition proceedings, in, 457 *et seq.*
            costs. *See* COSTS.
            cross appeal, 457
            evidence on, 459
            fees on, 457
            further appeal, 461
            is in nature of a re-hearing, 459
            notice of, 457
            time limited for, 457
                extension of, 457
            witnesses, attendance of, may be ordered, 459
        practice, 457 *et seq.*
            appeal is in nature of re-hearing, 459
            costs, 462. *See also* COSTS.
            evidence same as that before Comptroller, 459
                except by leave, 459
            time limited for appeal, 457
        proceedings relating to
            abuse of monopoly under sections 37–42 . . . 713
            amendment of specifications under section 29 after grant, 49
            compulsory endorsement, 1181
            exploitation of patent by co-owners under section 54 . . . 666
            licences for production of food or medicine under section
                41 . . . 710
            licences of right, 660
            revocation under section 33 . . . 451
            Scottish cases, 1181
            surrender of patent under section 34 . . . 465
    court, to, from Commissioner of Inland Revenue, 1020
    Court of Appeal, to
        Appeal Tribunal, from, 1619
            practice on, 995
            Scottish cases, 1225
            time limited, 995
            under section 33 and section 14 . . . 461
            under section 54 . . . 666

APPLICANT. *See also* APPLICATION FOR PATENT; TRUE AND FIRST INVENTOR.
    admissions by in opposition proceedings, 439
    agent, may act by, 115
    convention application by, 72
    good faith of, 229, 230
    substitution of, 1147
    under incapacity, 73
    who may be, 71 *et seq.*

APPLICATION FOR PATENT, 1132
    abandoned, not published, 126
        inspection of, not permitted, 126
            except by order of the court, 127
        when deemed to be, 109
    acceptance of, 126
        notice given to applicant of, 126
    agent may be employed for, 115
        cannot sign application form, 115
        must be authorised, 115
    alien may make, 73
        but *quaere* if an enemy, 73
    amendment of clerical error in, 474
    amendment of, may be required by the Comptroller, 117, 118. *See also*
    AMENDMENT OF SPECIFICATION.
    ante-dating of. *See* INTERNATIONAL CONVENTION.
    " any person " may make, 71
    appeal from Comptroller during proceeding on. *See* APPEALS " to Appeal
    Tribunal."
    applicant must sign, 115
    assignee may make, under International Convention, 72
        or if foreign assignee of foreign inventor, 72, 81
    civil servant making, 74
    cognate. *See* COGNATE INVENTIONS.
    communication as subject-matter of. *See* COMMUNICATION; COMMUNICATION
    FROM ABROAD.
    company may make, as assignee, 75
    concurrent application. *See* CONCURRENT APPLICATIONS.
    corporation making. *See* " company," *supra.*
    date of. *See* PRIORITY DATE.
    declarations made on. *See* DECLARATIONS.
    division of, 113
    examination of, 117, 118
    forms for, 107 *et seq.*
        modification of, by Comptroller, 107
        signature of, by applicant, 115
    fraud of inventor in making, 102, 286
        application after revocation of patent for, 286
            can be ante-dated, 286
    infant making, 73
    information as to, how obtained, 672, 1217, 1218
    International Convention, provisions as to. *See* INTERNATIONAL CONVEN-
    TION.
    joint. *See* JOINT APPLICANTS.
    lapsed, 129, 1161
    legal representative may make, 71
    married woman may make, 73
    mistake in making, 90
    Official Commission or Committee, whether member of may make, 74
    " patent of addition." *See* PATENT OF ADDITION.
    person entitled, 1131
    person under an incapacity may make, 73
    post-dating of. *See* POST-DATING.
    procedure on, 107–143
    reference of, to examiner, 117, 118
    refusal of, 119 *et seq.*, 1140

APPLICATION FOR PATENT—*continued*
    restoration of lapsed, 1161
    rights given on acceptance of. *See* COMPLETE SPECIFICATION; MARKING OF
        GOODS; PROVISIONAL PROTECTION.
    servant may make, 91 *et seq.*
    specification must accompany, 109
    time for putting in order, 123, 1250, 1251, 1252
    who may make, 71 *et seq.*
    wrongful, 286

APPRENTICES,
    provisions in early patents for instruction of, 161

ARBITRATOR,
    costs of Crown in proceedings before, 1018
    reference to,
        by court in disputes between inventors and the Crown, 1009
        in proceedings for abuse of monopoly, 712

ARCHITECTS' PLANS,
    not a manner of manufacture, 46

ASSESSOR. *See* SCIENTIFIC ADVISER.

ASSIGNEE. *See also* ASSIGNMENT; ASSIGNOR; LICENCE.
    account, when may be obtained from licensee by, 635
    application for patent by, discussed, 71, 72, 81
    cannot restrain use of goods sold unconditionally before assignment, 636
    covenants by, effect of, 614
    estoppel against, 615 *et seq. See also* ESTOPPEL.
    extension of term may be obtained by, 520 *et seq. See also* EXTENSION OF
        TERM.
    grant of patent may be made to, 612
    included in term " patentee," 18
    of part of patent holds his share in severalty, 662
    rights of, 608 *et seq.*
        assignee of part only of patent, 662 *et seq.*
        damages, to recover, 957
        infringement, to sue for, 794
    without " notice " of equitable assignment can convey good title, 613

ASSIGNMENT. *See also* LICENCE.
    agreement for,
        made prior to application or grant, 611
            enables grant to be made to assignee, 612
        " notice," rules as to affect, 613 *et seq.*
        proprietorship of patent not affected by, 611
        registration of, effect of, 614
        specific performance of, may be obtained, 611
    " beneficial owner," covenants implied by, in, 625
    co-ownership arising from, 662
    co-patentee, power of, to make, 662
    covenants in, binding on subsequent assignee with notice, 614
        by assignee, effect of, 614
    deed necesary for, 610
    difference between, and licence, 608 *et seq.*
    direction for, by Comptroller, 666
    equitable, may be enforced, 613
    estoppel arising from, 615 *et seq. See also* ESTOPPEL.
        but not executory only, 621
    form of, 610
    implied terms and covenants in, 622 *et seq.*
    improvements, covenants for, in, 638 *et seq. See also* IMPROVEMENT.
    infringment, no warranty against, implied on, 623
    licence. *See* LICENCE.
    limited to part of United Kingdom, 661
    misrepresentation as to validity on, 622 *et seq.*

CERTIFICATES—*continued*
  action to restrain threats, in, 778, 973
  Comptroller, of, admitted in evidence, 671
  Comptroller, of, as to entry in register, 671
  petition for revocation, in, 737

CERTIORARI,
  may lie against Comptroller and Appeal Tribunal, 460

CEYLON,
  convention country, 1897

CHAD,
  convention country, 1897

CHANNEL ISLANDS,
  patent not effective in, 2

CHARGES,
  patents or licences, on, by a company,
    effect of not registering, 603
    registration of, 603

CHEMICAL PROCESS. *See* PROCESS.

CHEMICAL CASES, 323, 324

CIVIL SERVANT,
  application for patent by, 74
  assignment of patent by, to Secretary of State, 74

CLAIM,
  aircraft, 1735
  alloy, for, 223
  ambiguity of, 240. *See also* AMBIGUITY.
  ambit of,
    does not depend on evidence, 180
    duty of patentee to define clearly, 240 *et seq. See also* AMBIGUITY.
    each claim assumed to be different, 195
    may be limited by result to be obtained, 243
    presumed not to cover what is old, 196
  biochemical products as subject-matter of, 42
  broad and indeterminate, 233
  clear and succinct and fairly based on matter disclosed in specification, 177
  combinations as subject-matter of. *See* COMBINATION.
  complete specification, priority date, 165, 1135
  construction of, 179 *et seq.*
  construction for court alone, 180
  disclaimer, effect of, on construction of, 196, 449
  distinction between old and new unnecessary in claim, 239
  duplication of, 195
  "fairly based," must be on matter disclosed in complete specification, 168, 231 *et seq.*
  function of, as compared with description in specification, 183
  history of, 179
  infringement depends solely on construction of, 348. *See also* INFRINGEMENT.
  invalidity of some claims only,
    relief given by section 62 . . . 504
  method, as subject of, 45, 54, 360
  no need to distinguish new from old in claim, 239
  previous construction binding, 197
  "principle" as subject-matter of, 235 *et seq.*
  prior claim. *See* PRIOR CLAIM.
  priority date, every claim has its own, 172
  process, as subject of, 320, 321
  scope of, may be considered in extension application, 568

CLAIM—*continued*
"selection" as subject-matter of, 222. *See also* SELECTION.
statutory requirement for, 177
substances as subject of, 52
"substantially as described," effect of, in claim, 189. *See also* SUB-STANTIALLY AS DESCRIBED.
testing, method of, a subject of, 54
wide claims for new principle, 234 *et seq.*

CLERICAL ERRORS.
amendment of, in application or specification, 474
    in provisional specification, 474
    in Register of Patents, 673
    no appeal from decision of Comptroller as to, 474
    opposition to, 474

COGNATE INVENTIONS,
application for,
    division of, may be required, 112
    one complete specification filed in respect of, 112
single invention, may be regarded as a, 112

CO-GRANTEES. *See* CO-OWNER.

COMBINATION, 326
claim for, infringement of, 392 *et seq. See also* INFRINGEMENT.
integers of, not separately protected by claim for combination, 392
making and selling constituent parts of machine as a collection may be infringement, 359
making and selling elements of, no infringement, 358
patentability of, 326
principles applied in deciding whether obvious, 327

"COMMERCIAL SCALE,"
definition of, 687
working on, in cases where abuse of monopoly alleged, 687 *et seq.*
working discontinued, 692

COMMERCIAL SUCCESS,
as affecting,
    extension of term, 530
    quantum of invention, 313 *et seq.*
    utility, 253

COMMISSIONERS OF INLAND REVENUE,
opinion of, may be taken as to stamp duties, 1020
    with appeal to the court, 1020

COMMON KNOWLEDGE, 300, 881
definition of, 881
documents, statements in, may be, 881
plea of, in action for infringement, 882
prior documents read in light of, 300
proof of, method of, 881
relevant date of, 300

COMMUNICATION. *See also* COMMUNICATION FROM ABROAD.
as subject-matter of application for patent,
    made by foreign subject abroad to foreign applicant, 81, 82
    made in this country,
        agent, by, sent from abroad, 82
        person, by, resident here, 83

COMMUNICATION FROM ABROAD,
application for patent in respect of, 77 *et seq.*
company may apply alone in respect of, 75

COMMUNICATION FROM ABROAD—*continued*
declaration should state if invention is a, 79
disclosure, quantum of, necessary, 80
where part of invention only is communicated. 80

COMPANY. *See also* APPLICATION FOR PATENT; BONA VACANTIA; PARTICULARS
OF INFRINGEMENTS, " directors "; VESTING ORDER.
breach of injunction by, 945
directors of, when liable for infringement, 353
breach of injunction by, 945
dissolution of, 602
interrogatories answered by officer of, 898

COMPENSATION,
cannot be obtained for goods ordered to be delivered up or destroyed, 967
Crown use for,
any benefit to be taken into account, 1017
date from which runs, 1009
to assignor, 1013
to licensee, 1013
to patentee, 1009
where licence terminated under section 58 (1) . . . 1197

COMPLETE SPECIFICATION, 1134–1135. *See also* SPECIFICATION.
acceptance of, 126, 1143
advertised, 126
information as to, how obtained, 672
postponement of, 126
publication on, 126
rights given on, 145
time limited for, 126
extension of, 126
addressee of, 212 *et seq.*
common knowledge assumed to be possessed by, 212
more than one may be necessary, 214
admissions in, 272, 273
advantages of invention need not be stated in, 220
unless of essence of invention, 221. *See also* SELECTION.
ambiguity of, 240 *et seq. See also* AMBIGUITY.
ambit of monopoly must be adequately defined in, 240 *et seq. See also*
AMBIGUITY.
amendment of. *See* AMENDMENT OF SPECIFICATION.
application,
convention, must be accompanied by, 109
non-convention, must be accompanied by provisional or complete
specification, 109
claims of. *See* CLAIM.
construction of,
after amendment, 187
" benevolent," limits of, 181
binding on court in subsequent proceedings, 197, 860
but fresh evidence as to anticipation may be given, 197
court alone must determine. 180
date of, determined by date of publication, 186
evidence inadmissible for, 180
general principles of, 179 *et seq.*
provisional specification, whether may be referred to in aid of, 173
conversion of, into provisional specification, 110
description in,
best method known to applicant must be included in, 226 *et seq.*, 886
on " communication from abroad," 227
quaere here discovered after filing of provisional, 226

[662]

COUNTERCLAIM—*continued*
    defence to, effect of non-delivery of, 851
    defendant may make a, without presenting petition, 722, 851
    discontinuance of action does not affect, 722
    infringement in action for threats, 772. *See also* THREATS OF PROCEEDINGS.
    revocation in action for infringement, 772

COUNTY COURT,
    action for infringement cannot be tried in, 808
        and if commenced in, cannot be removed to High Court by certiorari, 808

COVENANT. *See* ABUSE OF MONOPOLY, "importation"; ASSIGNMENT; LICENSEE; LICENSOR.

COVENANT DUTY. *See* STAMP DUTIES.

CROWN,
    costs of, in legal proceedings, 1018. *See also* COSTS.
    devolution of patent,
        on death of intestate patentee without heirs, 601, 602
        on dissolution of company, 602
    patentee may sue, 1002
    prerogative of. *See* PREROGATIVE OF CROWN.
    proceedings,
        against, costs in, 1018
        Crown Proceedings Act 1947 . . . 1733
    right of, to use invention, 1003 *et seq.*, 1183–1188, 1253–1262
        by authorised agents, 1003 *et seq.*
            authorisation must be in writing, 1003
                quaere if it need refer to patent concerned, 1003
            scope of authority, 1006
        compensation, where exercised, 1009
            benefit received to be taken into account, 1017
            procedure, 1014
            to licensee, 1013
            where patent assigned, 1013
        contract between patentee and third party does not affect, 1012
        date from which compensation runs, 1010
        disputes between patentee and Crown as to,
            to be referred to court, 1009
        for foreign government, 1008
        history of, 1001
        information as to use to be given to patentee, 1011
        present law as to, 1002
        terms on which exercised, how settled, 1009
        validity may be challenged in compensation proceedings, 1015
        where invention previously known to government department, 1009, 1016
    sale of articles not required by, 1019
        or forfeited under excise laws, 1019
    sale of patented articles, right to authorise, 1006

CUBA,
    convention country, 1897

CUSTOM HOUSE AGENTS,
    having custody of goods do not infringe, 378

CUSTOMERS. *See also* PURCHASER.
    names and addresses of,
        must be disclosed on inquiry as to damages, 963
        where prior sale alleged by defendant, 876
        where specific sale alleged by plaintiff, 905

CUSTOMS AND EXCISE,
    sale of articles forfeited under laws relating to, 1019

DEATH,
> inventor, of
>> before application, personal representative may apply, 71
>>> sealing of patent, 129
>> where joint applicant, 128
> patentee, of, devolution of patent on, 599 *et seq.*
>> where deceased is a co-owner, 665

DECLARATIONS,
> applications for patent, on
>> as to ground on which applicant bases claim, 79
>> of assent of inventor where invention assigned, 76
> court, by
>> as to invalidity, action for, may not be brought, 723
>> as to " true and first inventor," 106
>> in action for threats, 777
>> of non-infringement, 343
> proceedings before the Comptroller, in
>> evidence normally given by statutory, 453

DEED, 1081

DEFENCE,
> default of, 820

DELAY,
> in bringing action for infringement does not bar right to final injunction, 94
>> may bar right to amend invalid claim, 486

" DELIVERY UP OR DESTRUCTION,"
> infringing articles, of
>> alteration of articles to avoid necessity for, 967
>> compensation cannot be obtained for, 967
>> discovery in aid of order for, 967
>> order for,
>>> form of, 965
>>> history of, 966
>>> object of, 967
>>> stay of, pending appeal, 968

DENMARK,
> convention country, 1897

DEPARTMENT OF TRADE AND INDUSTRY,
> control of Patent Office by, sections 94, 95, 96 . . . 1233, 1234, 1235
> proceedings of, 1235

DEVOLUTION,
> generally, 599 *et seq.*
> of proprietorship, 600
> on death, 601 *et seq.*

DIRECTORS of limited company. *See* COMPANY; INFRINGEMENT; PARTICULARS OF INFRINGEMENT.

DISCLAIMER. *See also* REFERENCE.
> accurate required, 449
> Comptroller may require, 438, 441
> effect of, 441, 449
> form of, 449
> illegal use of invention, to, 121
> object of, 441

DISCLOSURE. *See* COMPLETE SPECIFICATION, " description "; NOVELTY, " prior publication."

DISCONFORMITY,
> between provisional and complete specification, 166 *et seq.*
>> allegation of, can no longer be relied on against grant or in support of plea of invalidity, 175
>> claims must be; " fairly based " on provisional specification to obtain application date as priority date, 166

[669]

DISCONFORMITY—*continued*
  between provisional and complete specification—*continued*
    effect of, 166
      where application was made under International Convention, 171
    opposition, previous grounds of, based on, have disappeared, 413.
      See also OPPOSITION.
    previous case-law of doubtful assistance, 175
    what is a different invention, 167
  between " title " and specification, former practice as to, 162

DISCONTINUANCE. *See* COSTS; COUNTERCLAIM; ESTOPPEL; PARTICULARS OF
  OBJECTIONS, " amendment."

" DISCOVERY,"
  mere, not proper subject-matter for letters patent, 48

DISCOVERY AND INTERROGATORIES,
  action for infringement, in. *See also* DAMAGES, " injury "; DELIVERY UP OR
    DESTRUCTION.
    application for, 899
    extent of, 899 *et seq.*
    inquiry as to damages, on, 963
    limited to issues defined by particulars, 903
    matter of remedy and not right, 900
    objection to, when taken, 900
    offers of admissions and particulars as affecting order, for, 898
    on issues of
      infringement,
        as to names of defendant's customers, 905
        as to persons supplying defendant with materials, when
          allowed, 906
        form of interrogatories allowed on, 904
        not allowed if construction of specification involved, 903
        only as to infringements specified, 904
      validity, 907 *et seq.*
        documents relevant only to objections not pleaded are
         protected, 904
        interrogatories
          as to " utility," 909
          must not require evidence to be disclosed, 908
          not allowed if involving or relevant only on construction
            of specification, 904
    privilege, claim of, 908, 910
      communications for which claim of, can be made, 910
    time for, 901
    petition for revocation, in, 730
    proceedings before Comptroller, in 455
    proceedings for extension of term, in, 577

DIVISION,
  Comptroller may require complete specification to be divided, 113
  where application divided, no two claims must be co-terminous, 264

DOCUMENTS,
  construction of, for court, 926
  convention applications, in, 111
  posting of, 116

DOMINICAN REPUBLIC,
  convention country, 1897

DRAWINGS,
  ambiguity due to, 245. *See also* AMBIGUITY.
  amendment of, 481
  " anticipation " by, 269 *et seq.*
  form part of specification, 176
  requirement for, in provisional specification, 164, 176
  requirement for, where " prior user " pleaded against validity, 876

[671]

EXAMINATION,
application and complete specification, of, 117, 118

EXAMPLES,
given in specification,
details of. *See* COMPLETE SPECIFICATION, " sufficiency of."

EXECUTORS AND ADMINISTRATORS,
deceased inventor, of, may apply for patent, 71
registered proprietor, of, included in term " patentee," 18
and may take any step required to be taken by patentee, 602
rights and obligations of, not affected by provisions of section 54 . . . 665

EXHIBITIONS,
industrial and scientific, publication at, when protected, 286

EXPERIMENTS,
action for infringement, in, should be performed in presence of both parties, 916, 930
infringement by, 363
publication of invention by experiments in public, 284, 285
sufficiency of specification, necessity for experiment as evidence of lack of, 218

EXPERT. *See* ASSESSOR; SCIENTIFIC WITNESSES. *See also* ORDER 103, r. 27, R.S.C.

" EXTENDED OPPOSITION." *See* REVOCATION UNDER SECTION 33.

EXTENSION OF TERM,
accounts,
applications by petition, in, on ground of inadequate remuneration,
absence of, usually fatal, 524
but may be excused, 524
accuracy and good faith necessary in, 524 *et seq.*
adjournment to amplify only granted for good reason shown, 525
nature of, required, 524 *et seq.*
where several patents involved, 524
applications on ground of " war loss," in, nature of, 569
adjournment, 557
advertisements on application by originating summons, 1597
petition, 551
" alien enemies " may not apply under section 24 (8) . . . 562
unless interest ceased shortly after outbreak of hostilities, 562
" all the circumstances of the case " to be considered, 514
amendment of specification where some claims only extended, 539
appeal,
from decision of Comptroller to Appeal Tribunal, 561
none from decision of court, 561
application for,
Comptroller, to, on grounds of war loss, 561 *et seq.*
may be made as alternative to applying to court, 513, 561
more than one patent may be included in, 573
practice on, 573
originating summons, by, 561
is alternative procedure where " war loss " alleged, 513, 561
except in Scotland, 513
or where other than " war loss " to be considered, 513
practice on, 573
petition on ground of inadequate remuneration, by, 514 *et seq.*
practice on, 549 *et seq.*
" appointed day," for petition, 551
assignee may obtain, 521
unless assignment made shortly before expiry, 523
claim, scope of, may be considered in " war loss " application, 568
commercial success, effect of, 518, 531
Comptroller's duty at hearing, 558
concealment of material facts is fatal, 536

[673]

[675]

FORM AND PROCEEDINGS—*continued*
    action to restrain threats,
        final order, 2015
        indorsement or writ, 2013
        interlocutory injunction, 2014
    licences,
        form of formal licence, 2027
        form of licence, 599
    order for extension of lapsed patent, 2023
    petition for extension of term of patent,
        advertisement of intention to present petition, 2018
        affidavit as to advertisements, 2020
        notice of grounds of objection, 2022
        notice of opposition, 2021
        petition, 2019
        order for liberty to amend particulars of objections, 2007
        particulars of objections, 2005
    petition for revocation, 2017
        notice of motion for leave to amend specification, 2008

FRANCE,
    convention country, 1897

FRAUD,
    application in fraud of person entitled, 102 *et seq.*
    committed abroad, not inquired into in opposition proceedings, 426
    licensee entitled to repudiate licence on ground of, 620
    plea of, in counterclaim or petition for revocation, 721, 871
        not essential in opposition proceedings on ground of " obtaining," 424
        not essential on issue of " true and first inventor," 870
        particulars of, 870
    publication of invention in, protection against, 102 *et seq.*
    refusal of patent applied for in, 421 *et seq. See also* OPPOSITION.
    re-grant of patent after refusal or revocation for, 102. *See also*
        APPLICATION FOR PATENT, " fraud of inventor."
    revocation of patent obtained in. *See* REVOCATION BY PETITION; REVO-
        CATION UNDER SECTION 33, " grounds."

GABON,
    convention country, 1897

GAME,
    cards, of, not patentable, 287

GERMANY,
    1946 Act, 1727
    convention country, 1897

" GILLETTE " DEFENCE, 344, 865

" GILLETTE (NEW) " ORDER, 544, 2023

GOVERNMENT DEPARTMENT,
    opposition to extension of term by, 552
    publication to, when protected, 286
    right of, to use invention. *See* CROWN.
    secret prior user of invention by,
        does not affect validity, 285, 286
        right of patentee to compensation, and, 1009

GRANTEE. *See* ASSIGNEE; CO-OWNER; LETTERS PATENT FOR INVENTION.

GREAT SEAL. *See* SEAL.

INFRINGEMENT—*continued*
    purchase is not of itself, 373 *et seq.*
        but may constitute threat of, 373
    repairing may be, 362
    sale,
        articles, of, to be used for purpose of, 355 *et seq.*
            licensee, by under foreign patent only, is 382
            made by patented process or machine may be, 365
                importation of such articles made abroad may be, 366.
                See also " importation," *supra.*
                onus of proof of manufacture on plaintiff, 367
                    except where articles made abroad and plaintiff unable
                        to fully inspect machinery, 368
                    except where invention is for production of new
                        substance, 368
                    See also " licence," *supra.*
            where contract for
                delivery in this country is, 369 *et seq.*
                export, 372. *See also* " export," *supra.*
                made in this country, 369 *et seq.*
                    for execution abroad is not, 369
        below price fixed by licence. *See* LICENCE, " restrictions in."
        elements of combination, of, 392 *et seq.*
        quaere if sold as a collection, 359
        exposure for sale constitutes, 376
        machine, of,
            capable of being used to infringe " method " claim, is not, 361
                unless not capable of non-infringing use, 360
            containing infringing device is infringement of a " machine "
                claim, 361
    servant liable for, 352, 355
        but actions against not encouraged, 352
    substance of invention, by taking, 387 *et seq.*
    " substantially," where used, 397
    threat of, 373. *See also* " possession," " purchase," *supra*; " transport,"
      infra, and INJUNCTION.
    transhipment by Custom House Agents is not, 378
    transport is not, of itself, 373 *et seq.*
        but may amount to a threat of, 373
        unless involving user, 374
    use of invention is, 350 *et seq.*
        but not for bona fide experiments, 363, 364
        or on British vessel abroad, 377
    warning of, need not be given, 342
    warranty against, not implied in assignments and licences, 623
        but is implied on sale of article, 381
    what amounts to, 386

INJUNCTION,
    action for infringement, in,
        abandoned user, no grounds for, 940
        acquiescence in infringement, bars right to, 941
        against one co-defendant only, 822
        amendment of specification after, effect of, 946
        breach of,
            by limited company, 945
            by person aiding and abetting, 945
            constitutes contempt of court, 945
        consent to, by one co-defendant, 822
        delay does not bar right to final, 941
        duration of, 943
            where patent is subsequently revoked, 945
            where several patents are included, 943
        enforcement of, 945
        ex parte, 825

INJUNCTION—*continued*
    action for infringement in—*continued*
        form of, 943
            against Crown contractors, 944
            where action pending for different type of infringement, 944
            where certain claims only infringed, 943
        " innocent infringement " does not affect right to, 346, 937
        interlocutory, 824 *et seq.*
            delay bars right to, 835
            motion for, 827 *et seq.*
                affidavits, 829
                effect of patent having previously been held valid on, 834
                    and undisturbed possession over long period, 830
                usual order made on, 836
            practice, 828, 836
            principles governing grant of, 824
            refusal of, 832, 833
                even if defendant refuses to keep an account, 833
                in case of new patents, 832
            undertaking as to damages occasioned by grant of, 836
        principles on which granted, 934 *et seq.*
        refusal of, if defendant takes " licence of right," 657, 959
        suspension of, 942
        threat to infringe will justify, 934 *et seq.*
        where patent partially valid, 969
    action for threats, in, 774
    purchase, ownership, possession, transport, may justify, 373, 939

" INNOCENT INFRINGEMENT." *See* DAMAGES; INFRINGEMENT; INJUNCTION.

INQUIRY,
    damages, as to. *See* DAMAGES.

INSPECTION,
    action for infringement, in,
        application for, 911
            practice on, 913–915
            time for, 915
        costs of, 984. *See also* COSTS.
        jurisdiction of court to order, 911
        must be necessary for preparation of party's case, 912
        mutual, may be ordered, 914
        of " prior users " alleged, 876
            but inspection of samples made by a prior " process " will be refused, 875
            must be offered, 875
        of secret process, will be limited to scientific witnesses, 913
        order for, may be obtained on summons under Order 103, r. 26...915
        prima facie case for, must be established, 912
        purpose of, 911
        samples, taking of, on, 913
    petition for revocation, in
        same practice as in action for infringement, 730

INSUFFICIENCY OF SPECIFICATION. *See also* COMPLETE SPECIFICATION.
    ground of opposition, 436 *et seq. See also* OPPOSITION.
    plea of, in counterclaim or petition for revocation, 885

INTERNATIONAL CONVENTION, 1207–1211
    application under, 108 *et seq.*
        may be post-dated, 110
        must be accompanied by complete specification, 109
        must be fairly based on foreign application to have date of that application as priority date, 171
        must be made within twelve months of first foreign application, 108
    cognate inventions, 112. *See also* COGNATE INVENTIONS.

LICENCE OF RIGHT—*continued*
  opposition to,
    application by patentee, 659
    cancellation of endorsement, 660
  patent of addition, effect of endorsement, 659
  rights after endorsement, 657
  terms of, where settled by Comptroller, 656

LICENSEE. *See also* ESTOPPEL; INFRINGEMENT.
  compensation of,
    for Crown user, 1009
    for termination of licence. *See* COMPENSATION.
  estoppel against. *See* ESTOPPEL.
  exclusive, meaning of, 609
    right to damages where plaintiff in infringement action, 955
  " notice," rules as to, affect, 613 *et seq.*
  rights of, 609
    compulsory licence, effect of, on, 707, 709
    exclusive licensee, 609
    exercisable by agents, 635
      but not by independent contractors, 635
    to impose restrictions on articles made under licence, 656
    to oppose application by patentee under section 35 . . . 656
    to sue alone for infringement (under section 35 or 37) . . . 658
    where patent subsequently endorsed " licence of right," 657
  sales by, no bar to restrictions on, 644

LICENSOR. *See also* LICENCE.
  estoppel against, 614 *et seq.*, 616 *et seq.*, 858 *et seq. See also* ESTOPPEL.
  power of, to impose conditions in licence, 616 *et seq.*

LICHTENSTEIN,
  convention country, 1897

LOCUS STANDI. *See* COMPULSORY LICENCE; OPPOSITION; REVOCATION BY
PETITION; REVOCATION UNDER SECTION 33.

" LONG-FELT WANT,"
  evidence of, as affecting quantum of invention, 313, 314, 315

LOSS OF PATENT,
  duplicate may be sealed, 132

" LOSS OR DAMAGE DUE TO HOSTILITIES." *See* EXTENSION OF TERM.

LUNATIC. *See* PERSON UNDER A DISABILITY.

LUXEMBURG,
  convention country, 1897

" MAKE, USE, EXERCISE AND VEND,"
  meaning of, in licences, 634

MALAGASY REPUBLIC,
  convention country, 1897

MANDAMUS,
  may lie against Comptroller, 460

MANNER OF MANUFACTURE,
  apparatus, new methods of operating, 45
  biochemical processes are, 42, 43
  biological processes may be, 44
  consideration of, by Comptroller, 36 *et seq.*, 55
    in opposition and revocation under section 33
      proceedings, 435
    on application for patent, 55

MANNER OF MANUFACTURE—*continued*
    discovery, a mere, not proper subject-matter for letters patent, 48
    food or medicine, 53
    issue of,
        in counterclaim and petition for revocation, 872
        in opposition proceedings, 435
    meaning of, 33 *et seq.*
        decisions of Comptroller as to, 36, 55
    method of testing may be, 54
    new, 32 and *see* NOVELTY.
    non-manufactures, examples of, 46
    " principle " is not, 49. *See also* PRINCIPLE.
    process may be, 34 *et seq. See also* PROCESS.
    subject-matter of patent must be, 32
    test to be applied, 36 *et seq.*

MARKING OF GOODS, 147, 148
    defence to prosecution for false, 147
    penalty for false, 148
    permissible marking,
        after acceptance of application, 147
        after acceptance of complete specification, 147
        after patent has expired, 147
    under licence from patentee, 148

MARRIED WOMAN. *See* APPLICATION FOR PATENT.

MASTER AND SERVANT,
    apportionment of invention, 100
    relative rights of, 91 *et seq.*
        proceedings before Comptroller, 101, 1195
    servant the inventor, 93
    trade secret, right of master to prevent disclosure of, 96

MAURITANIA,
    convention country, 1897

MECHANICAL EQUIVALENTS,
    infringement by, 388 *et seq.*

MEDICINE. *See* LICENCE FOR FOOD OR MEDICINE; SUBSTANCES.

MERGER,
    none where patent vests in Crown *bona vacantia*, 602

METHOD. *See* MANNER OF MANUFACTURE; CLAIM.

MEXICO,
    convention country, 1897

MISREPRESENTATION. *See* ASSIGNMENT; ESTOPPEL; FALSE REPRESEN-
    TATION OR SUGGESTION; LICENCE.

MISTAKE,
    in making application, 90
    licensee may repudiate licence on ground of common, 620

MIXTURE,
    of ingredients may not be proper subject-matter for patent, 53

MONACO,
    convention country, 1897

MONOPOLY SYSTEM, 3

" MONTH,"
    meaning of in assignments and licences, 633

MOROCCO,
    convention country, 1897

MORTGAGE. *See* CHARGES; REGISTER OF PATENTS.

NOVELTY—*continued*
  want of—*continued*
    " prior publication in document " resulting in—*continued*
      " paper anticipation," 301
      photograph,
        construction of, 299
        is sufficient, 299, 304
      plea of, in counterclaim or petition for revocation, 873 *et seq.*
      protection against, statutory provisions for, 286. *See also* FRAUD;
        EXHIBITIONS; LEARNED SOCIETIES; PROVISIONAL PROTECTION;
        GOVERNMENT DEPARTMENT.
      " publication " of document, what is sufficient, 269 *et seq.*
    " prior user " resulting in. *See also* INSPECTION; OPPOSITION.
      in public, 274 *et seq.*
        accidental, not sufficient, 283
        experimental, 276, 284
        inspection of, 876. *See also* INSPECTION.
        opposition proceedings, issue of, may be raised in, 433. *See*
          also OPPOSITION.
        plea of, in counterclaim on petition for revocation, 873 *et seq.*
        " publication " by, what amounts to, 274 *et seq.*
        sale constitutes sufficient, 279
          offer for, is sufficient, 281
        ships, three mile limit for, 278
      samples, manufacture, gift and distribution of sufficient, 282
      secret, 274, 335
        by Government department and section 46 . . . 1009
        can be relied on in infringement action, 890
          but not on a plea of obviousness, 880
        no account taken of in opposition proceedings, 433

OATH,
  power of Comptroller to administer, 455, 1222

OBJECTIONS,
  certificate as to particulars, 978

" OBTAINING,"
  ground for opposition or revocation, 421 *et seq. See also* OPPOSITION.
  plea of, in counterclaim or petition for revocation, 721, 871
  prior date in case of, 1192

" OBVIOUSNESS," 305 *et seq.*
  analogous user, 317–321
  appeal on finding of fact, 883
  automaticity, 322
  chemical process in relation to, 323, 324, 325
  combinations, applied to, 326, 327, 328
  commercial success as a factor determining, 313
  consideration of, in proceedings for extension of term, 516
  defence to action for infringement. See PARTICULARS OF OBJECTIONS.
  effect is to render patent invalid, 305 *et seq. See also* QUANTUM OF
    INVENTION.
  evidence of inventor and experts as to, 330
  how to be judged, 307
  new use of old contrivance, 316
  " novelty " contrasted, 287 *et seq.*
  opposition, as ground of, 434
  plea of, in counterclaim or petition for revocation, 305 *et seq.*
  selection patents, 329
  simplicity no objection, 312
  test of, 307 *et seq.*
  way invention arrived at immaterial . . . 306

OFFENCES, 1229–1232
  marking, false, 147, 148. *See also* MARKING OF GOODS.
  patent agent, false description as, section 88 . . . 1227
  patent office, false description of place of business as, section 91 (2) . . . 675
  register of patents, falsification of, a misdemeanour, 674
" OMNIBUS CLAIM." *See* " SUBSTANTIALLY AS DESCRIBED."

ONUS OF PROOF. *See* AMENDMENT OF SPECIFICATION; ACTION FOR INFRINGE-
    MENT; EXTENSION OF TERM; OPPOSITION; REVOCATION UNDER SECTION 33;
    THREATS OF PROCEEDINGS.

OPPOSITION, 1144
  admissions by applicant, effect of, 439. *See also* " obtaining," *infra.*
  amendment of specification, 440. *See also* AMENDMENT OF SPECIFICATION.
  appeal from Comptroller to Appeal Tribunal, 457, *et seq. See also* APPEALS.
  collusive, 420
  Comptroller, duty of, 439
  costs, 462 *et seq. See also* COSTS.
  counter-statement, 453
  disconformity, previous grounds of opposition based on, have disappeared,
    413
  discovery, power of Comptroller to order, 455
  disputes on technical questions not decided by Comptroller, 439
  documents relied on. *See* " notice," *infra.*
    Comptroller must consider any brought to his notice before decision
      issued, 439
        even if hearing has taken place, 439
    construction of opponent's specification, 446
    " ten-day rule " as to, where not referred previously, 453
  evidence in, 453 *et seq.*
    normally by statutory declaration only, 453
    oral, 455
  grounds of, 411 *et seq.*
    (a) Obtaining, 421–427
      abroad, obtaining, no inquiry into, 426
      admission by one co-applicant, effect of, 425
      " direct " obtaining necessary, 425
      fraud, 424
        committed abroad is not inquired into, 426
        committed in this country, protection under section 53 . . .
          427
        not a necessary part of opponent's case, 424
      joint applicants, 425
      matter not claimed obtained, 424
      " obtained the invention "—refers to identity thereof, 424
      part only of invention obtained, 424, 425
        patent for, may be applied for by successful opponent, 425
        specification may be amended to exclude, 425
      principles on which issue is decided, 421 *et seq.*
      prior publication or prior user deprives opponent of right, 423
      proof, onus of, is on opponent, 427 *et seq.*
        but shifts to applicant where communication prior to
          application is proved, 423
        nature of, 422 *et seq.*
      refusal of grant in clear cases only, 422
      terms giving both parties rights may be imposed, 425
    (b) Prior (documentary) publication, 428–431
      anticipation, ordinary principles as to, apply, 431
      " document," meaning of, 430
      " made available to public by publication," " publication,"
        distinction abolished, 429
      relevant priority dates of claims to be considered, 428
    (c) Prior (concurrent) claim, 432
      principles on which issue decided, 432 *see* 258
      relevant priority dates of claims to be considered, 432
      where no patent granted on earlier application, application not
        refused on this ground, 432

OPPOSITION—*continued*
  right to oppose, not assignable, 419
  statement of case by opponent, 452
  time limited for, 414
  transcripts of proceedings, 464
  withdrawal of,
    grant may be refused notwithstanding, 420
    hearing cannot be obtained after, 454
  witnesses,
    attendance of, how enforced, 455
    cross-examination of, 455

PALATINE COURT OF LANCASTER,
  action for infringement may be tried in, 810

"PAPER ANTICIPATION,"
  meaning of, 301

PARTICULARS. *See* Particulars of Breaches; Particulars of Objections; Threats of Proceedings.

PARTICULARS OF INFRINGEMENTS
  actionable infringement must be alleged, 842
  certificate of, 976, 977. *See also* Certificates.
  claims infringed to be specified in, 843
    but all claims may be relied on subject to costs, 843
  construction of specification, plaintiff not required to place in, 843
  degree of particularity required in, 846, 847
    where action is against vendor, 846
  delivery of, with statement of claim, 841
  difference between, and particulars of objections, 867
  directors of company are defendants, nature of, where, 801
  evidence at trial limited by, 848, 892. *See also* Evidence.
  further and better, order for, 847, 916
    may be postponed until after discovery, 847
  order for in other actions where infringement is an issue, 849
  purpose of, 844
  rules governing, 841
  type of infringement must be specified in, 844
  user, allegation of, in, will not support allegation of manufacture, 849

PARTICULARS OF OBJECTIONS,
  amendment of, 893 *et seq.*
    at trial, 895
    before trial, 894
      effect of order for, 894
      form of order for, 894
        in counterclaim, 894
    Court of Appeal, 896
    discontinuance after, 894
    terms of in discretion of court, 895
      and will not be reviewed by Court of Appeal, 895
  certificate of, 737, 976, 978. *See also* Certificates.
  degree of detail required in, 867
  delivery of with defence or counterclaim, 867
  difference between, and particulars of breaches, 867
  further and better, order for, 916
  grounds relied on, must be separately specified in, 868
    summary of (section 32 (1))
      (a) Prior grant, 869
      (b) Applicant not entitled to apply, 870
      (c) Patent obtained in fraud, 871
      (d) Not an invention, 872

[691]

PATENT OF ADDITION—*continued*
  further patent of addition may be obtained on, 141
  " licence of right," indorsement of, 656
  novel matter, not disclosed in specification of main invention, 138
  power of Comptroller to allow or refuse, 138
  revocation of main patent, effect of, 140
  requirements for, 134
  subject matter of, 138
  subject of litigation in High Court, 138
  term of, 133
  validity of, when not open to attack, 136, 137

PATENT OFFICE, 1723
  hours of business, 1237
  words, false use of, 675

PATENTABILITY. *See* NATURE OF PATENTABLE INVENTIONS.

" PATENTED ARTICLE,"
  meaning of, in section 37 . . . 699
  sale of. *See* INFRINGEMENT; LICENCE, " limited "; WARRANTY.

" PATENTED INVENTION," 689

PATENTEE,
  bankruptcy of. *See* TRUSTEE IN BANKRUPTCY.
  co-patentee. *See* CO-OWNER; LICENCE.
  death of. *See* DEATH.
  definition, 18, 599
  estoppel against, 616 *et seq. See also* ESTOPPEL.
  rights of. *See* ACTION FOR INFRINGEMENT; ASSIGNMENT; CO-OWNER;
    CROWN LICENCE; REGISTERED DESIGN; TRUSTEE IN BANKRUPTCY.
    " locality " of, 607
    nature of, 7, 8, 16, 606, 607
    seizure of, under writ of *fi. fa.* cannot be made, 16, 605
  title of, proof of, in action for infringement, 924

PENALTIES. *See also* MARKING OF GOODS; OFFENCES.
  reference to, in patent, 19

PERPETUAL MOTION MACHINES,
  application for patent for, will be refused, 121

PERSON UNDER A DISABILITY,
  may apply for a patent, 73

PERSONAL REPRESENTATIVE,
  application for patent by, 71, 601, 602, 603
  grant of patent to, 601, 602, 603
  meaning of, 601, 602, 603

PHOTOGRAPHS,
  construction for court on evidence of experts, 926

" PITH AND MARROW,"
  infringement by taking, of invention, 387 *et seq. See also* INFRINGEMENT.

POLAND,
  convention country, 1897

PORTUGAL,
  convention country, 1897

POST-DATING,
  application for patent, of,
    appeal from order for, 122. *See also* APPEALS " to Appeal Tribunal."
    applicant may obtain, 110
    Comptroller may require, 110

[693]

PURCHASER—*continued*
    rights of,
        article purchased without notice of restriction, 381, 382
        article seized and sold under writ of *fi. fa.*, 605
        article sold by Crown,
            on forfeiture under excise laws, 1019
        article sold subject to a condition as to price of resale, 648
        vendor entitled to " make and vend," 634

QUANTUM OF INVENTION. *See also* " OBVIOUSNESS."
    analogous user as affecting, 317 *et seq. See also* ANALOGOUS USER.
    chemical cases, issue of, in, 323. *See also* " selection," *infra.*
    combinations may afford sufficient, 326 *et seq.*
        labour saving devices as special case of, 328
    commercial success as evidence of, 313 *et seq.*
    consideration of,
        Comptroller, by, in opposition proceedings, 434
    distinguished from novelty, 287 *et seq.*
    " long-felt want " as evidence of, 313
    new use,
        of old device may have sufficient, 316 *et seq.*
            but not if analogous to old use, 316 *et seq. See also* ANALOGOUS
                USER.
            but must involve ingenuity, 316
        of old material may afford sufficient, 316
    selection may be sufficient, 329. *See also* SELECTION.
    simplicity no objection, 312
    sufficiency of, principles on which determined, 307 *et seq.*
    utility as evidence of, 313, 314
    verification of prior proposals is not sufficient, 325

" REASONABLE SKILL AND KNOWLEDGE,"
    proof of, when required under section 59 (3)... 502
                  under section 62 (2)... 969, 983

RECEIVER. *See also* TRUSTEE IN BANKRUPTCY.
    cannot be appointed for royalties to satisfy a judgment, 16, 605
    in bankruptcy of registered proprietor included under term " patentee," 18

RECITALS,
    letters patent, in,
        contents of, 13, 14
            basis of grant, 13
            if untrue, patent is invalid, 13
            in early grants, 161
            " suggestions " made by applicant are basis of, 3. *See also* FALSE
                REPRESENTATION OR SUGGESTION.
    specification, in. *See also* DISCLAIMER; REFERENCE.
        prior art are binding on patentee, 449
        must be accurate, 449

RECTIFICATION OF REGISTER. *See* REGISTER OF PATENTS.

REFERENCE. *See also* DISCLAIMER.
    application, insertion of references during progress of, 119, 441 *et seq.*
    general, 442–449
        effect of, 443, 445
    public interest to be considered in insertion of, 445
    specific, 119, 445 *et seq.*
        applicant bound by statement in, 449
            but must not put upon the public what he considers the true
            construction of prior documents, 449

REFERENCE—*continued*
  specific—*continued*
    Comptroller may direct insertion, 119
      in case of prior claiming, 120
      in case of anticipation, 119
      where use of invention likely to infringe another patent, 121
    construction of opponent's patent relevant, 446
    decision as to insertion of, not postponned for result of pending
      proceedings, 448
    effect of, 441 *et seq.*
      may be to introduce ambiguity unless properly worded, 449
    evidence affecting construction of opponent's patent relevant, 447
    expired patent, reference to, not inserted, 448
    form of, 449
      objects of, 441
      order for, may be made to patents other than those requested by
        opponent, 439
      principles on which ordered, 442 *et seq.*
      prior (concurrent) grant, reference to conditional on grant being
        made, 448
      prior patent on same subject, existence of not a ground for
        insertion of, 444
      prior user which would invalidate opponent's patent may now be
        relevant, 447
    removal of, 121
      as result of amendment, 501
      subsequently printed in erased type, 501
    revoked patent,
      reference not inserted to, 448
      reference to may subsequently be removed if misleading, 448
    utility of opponent's inventon not considered, 447

REFUSAL,
  application by Comptroller, of, 119, 120, 121, 1145

REGISTER OF PATENTS,
  assignments entered in, 668
  caveat against entry in, 672
  documents,
    affecting title, not admissible in evidence unless entered in, 600, 668
      except by leave of court, 600
    must be stamped before being entered in, 670
    nature of, permitted to be entered in, 669
  entry in,
    absence of, proof of, 924
    certificate of, 671
      is prima facie evidence, 671
    Comptroller may refuse to make, unless document properly stamped,
      670
    conclusive evidence of right of person registered to sue for infringe-
      ment, 671
    late, will date back, 670
    subject-matter of, 668
    title, nature of, stated in, 669
  errors in. *See* " rectification," *infra.*
  falsification of, 674
  information as to contents of, 672
  licences, entry of in, 613, 668
    limited, registration of, does not constitute notice to purchaser of
      goods, 654
  Order of court, 1495–1496
  penalty,
    for late registration, 668
    on Comptroller where unstamped document entered in, 670
  practice, 1470–1475

REVOCATION BY PETITION—*continued*
  order for revocation—*continued*
    stay of,
      pending appeal, 736
      terms on which granted, 736
  particulars of objections, 727, 737. *See also* PARTICULARS OF OBJECTIONS.
    amendment of, 894, 895, 896
    certificate of proof of, 737
  petition,
    adjournment of, 729
    service of, 727
      out of the jurisdiction, 727
  petitioner, interest required to present petition, 721
  practice before trial, 726–730
  res judicata, 733
  respondent, who should be, 724
  return day, 729
  right to begin at trial, respondent has, 731
  Scotland, form of action in, 725
  summons for directions in, 729
  trial, 731
  tribunal for hearing petition, 725
  validity, certificate of, 737

REVOCATION UNDER SECTION 33. *See also* AMENDMENT OF SPECIFICA-
  TION " in opposition proceedings."
  appeal to Appeal Tribunal in proceedings for, 451. *See also* APPEALS.
  applicant for, who may be, 450
    interest required by, 450
  " belated opposition," 450
  Comptroller, duties of, 451
  costs. *See* COSTS.
  date for application for, 450
  grounds for, 450
  practice, 452 *et seq.*
  proof, onus of, on applicant for, 452
  remedies, 451

ROYALTIES,
  action to recover, may be brought into county court, 808
  damages, quantum of, affected by, 948
  income tax payable on, 1021, 1741. *See also* INCOME TAX.
  minimum, covenants for, 623
  receiver for, not appointed in satisfaction of a judgment, 605
  reasonable, test as to whether, 703

RULES AND ORDERS, 1132–1134, 1163
  (Patents, 1968 and 1969 (Amendment) Rules)
  R.S.C. proceedings under 1949 Act, 1588–1618
  Agency, 1356
  Amendment, 1411, 1436–1441
    forms, 1529, 1541–1544
  Appeal Tribunal 1313 *et seq.*
    fees, 1582 *et seq.*
    form, 1423
    hearing, 1424
  application for patent, 1357 *et seq.*, 1406 *et seq.*, 1424 *et seq.*
    forms, 1505
    notice of hearing, 1497
  certificates, 1480 *et seq.*
    form, 1573
  clerical errors, 1476 *et seq.*
    forms, 1571, 1572

RULES AND ORDERS—*continued*
 Scotland, 1489
 sealing, 1406 *et seq.*
  forms, 1526, 1527, 1528, 1538, 1540
 search, 1380
  form of result of, 1514
 specification, 1385 *et seq.*
  forms for complete, 1509, 1511, 1517
  form for provisional, 1508
 substitution of applicants, 1404 *et seq.*
  forms, 1524, 1525
 surrender,
  forms, 1547, 1548
 term, extension of, 1416 *et seq.*, 1533
 time, extension of, 1500
  forms, 1513

RUMANIA,
 convention country, 1897

SALE. *See* INFRINGEMENT; LICENCE, " ambit of "; PURCHASER.

SALE OF GOODS ACT. *See* WARRANTY. § 384

SAMPLES. *See also* INFRINGEMENT; INSPECTION.
 gift to government official as a private individual, 282
 manufacture and distribution of, constitute publication of invention, 282
 publication of, not made if application abandoned, 127
 secret process, order for taking of, in action concerning, 913

SAN MARINO,
 convention country, 1897

SCIENTIFIC ADVISER,
 to court in action for infringement, 812
  duty of, 812
  reports of, 812
 power of Appeal Tribunal to sit with, 459

SCIENTIFIC WITNESSES,
 evidence of,
  admissibility of, 927
  function of, 928
   in proving common knowledge, 88, 928
  nature of, 927–929
 limitation on number of, called at trial, 916, 931

SCOTLAND,
 action for infringement may be tried in, 809
 appeals from Comptroller, 1225
 application of Act to, 809
 extension of term, application for, is by petition only, 51
 revocation by court, form of action for, in, 725

SEAL,
 Great Seal formerly affixed to patents, 2
 Patent Office, of
  admitted in evidence, section 64 of Patents and Designs Act 1907
   1725
  effect of, the same as that of Great Seal, section 21 (1) . . . 2
  judicially noticed, 2

SPECIFIC REFERENCE, 442 *et seq. See also* REFERENCE.

SPECIFICATION, 1133, 1144
    abridgement. *See* ABRIDGEMENTS OF SPECIFICATIONS.
    complete. *See* COMPLETE SPECIFICATION.
    history of, 161 *et seq.*
    must accompany application, 162
    provisional. *See* PROVISIONAL SPECIFICATION.
    publication of, 1218
    title of, 162

STAMP DUTIES. *See also* COMMISSIONERS OF INLAND REVENUE.
    assignments liable for, 1020
        except of foreign or colonial patents, 1021
    documents must be stamped before registration, 1020. *See also* REGISTER
        OF PATENTS.
    licence, when liable for " conveyance duty," 1020, 1021
        exclusive, and share in patent is " property " for purposes of Stamp
        Act, 1021
    penalty, Comptroller liable to, where unstamped document is registered,
    1020

STATEMENT OF CASE,
    notice of opposition, must accompany, 452

STATUTE OF MONOPOLIES,
    section 6 of, 6, 7, 9, 31

" SUBJECT-MATTER." *See* LETTERS PATENT FOR INVENTION; " OBVIOUS-
NESS " QUANTUM OF INVENTION.

SUB-LICENCE. *See* LICENCE.

SUBSTANCES. *See also* LICENCE FOR FOOD OR MEDICINE.
    chemical process, prepared by, 323. *See also* PROCESS.
    intended for "food or medicine," 53
        meaning of, 53
    natural, not infringement, 52
    patentability of, 32 *et seq.*

" SUBSTANTIALLY AS DESCRIBED,"
    cannot altogether be ignored, 189 *et seq.*
    desirable to include claim with, 194
    effect of, on ambit of claim discussed, 189 *et seq.*
    limitation of ambit of claim may result from presence of, 193
    where claim contains, court decides if infringed, 193

SUBSTITUTION. *See* EQUIVALENTS.

SUFFICIENCY,
    specification, of. *See* COMPLETE SPECIFICATION; OPPOSITION.
        plea of want of, 885–886

SUGGESTIONS. *See also* FALSE REPRESENTATION OR SUGGESTION.
    patent is granted, on which, 13

SURRENDER OF PATENT, 465, 1168

SWEDEN,
    convention country, 1897

SWITZERLAND,
    convention country, 1897

SYRIA,
    convention country, 1897

SYSTEMS,
    indexing, of, not a manufacture, 46
    musical notation, of, not a manufacture, 46

TIME LIMITS,
    extension of, for applications for patents, 1250–1252

TITLE,
    invention, of,
        disconformity between, and specification formerly a ground of invalidity, 162
        function of, now performed by provisional specification, 163
        grant of patent formerly made on lodging of, 162
        patentee, of. *See* PATENTEE.

TRADE SECRET. *See* MASTER AND SERVANT; SECRET PROCESS.

TRINIDAD,
    convention country, 1897

" TRUE AND FIRST INVENTOR,"
    acknowledgment of, 86
    applicant for patent may be, 76
    application, must be named in, 76
    assent of, in writing where applicant is assignee, 89
    assignee of, may be grantee of patent, 76. *See also* " foreign," *infra.*
    communicatee of invention,
        from abroad, is, 81 *et seq. See also* " foreign," *infra.*
        in this country is not, 83
    declaration by court as to, where false claim to be inventor is made, 106
    definition of, 71 *et seq.*
    foreign assignee of foreign inventor may apply as, 81
    foreign communicatee of foreign inventor may apply as, 81
    false claim to be, 106
    fraud not essential to issue of, 870
        except in form raised by section 50 (3) . . . 870
    issue of,
        distinct from, novelty, 84 *et seq.*
    " novelty " distinguished, 81 *et seq.*
    title, chain of, must be derived from, 76
        except in convention applications, 76

TRUST,
    notice of, not registerable, 670

TRUSTEE,
    rights and obligations of, not affected by provisions of section 54 . . . 670

TRUSTEE IN BANKRUPTCY,
    patent,
        after-acquired, may be called for by, 604
            otherwise bona fide sale for value is valid against, 604
        devolves on,
            on bankruptcy of proprietor, 604
            unless held by patentee as a trustee, 604
    royalties, after-acquired, may be called for by, 604
    secret process must be disclosed to, 604

TUNISIA,
    convention country, 1897

TURKEY,
    convention country, 1897

UNDERTAKING,
    action on, 993

UNION OF SOVIET SOCIALISTS REPUBLICS,
    convention country, 1897

UNITED ARAB REPUBLIC,
    convention country, 1897